Cambridge World Atlas

Editor in chief
Guntram H. Herb

Editors
David H. Kaplan, Mark Monmonier

CAMBRIDGE
UNIVERSITY PRESS

CAMBRIDGE UNIVERSITY PRESS
Cambridge, New York, Melbourne, Madrid, Cape Town, Singapore, São Paulo, Delhi

Cambridge University Press
The Edinburgh Building, Cambridge, CB2 8RU, UK

www.cambridge.org
Information on this title: www.cambridge.org/9780521178150

First published 2006.
First Cambridge University Press edition 2009.

Printed and bound in the EU by Firmengruppe APPL, aprinta druck, Wemding, Germany.

A catalogue record for this publication is available from the British Library

ISBN 978-0-521-17815-0 paperback

Cambridge
World Atlas

Acknowledgements

Authors
Prof. Dr. Detlef Busche (world landforms map)
Dr. Jürgen Kempf (Africa ecoregions map)
Willi Stegner (economic maps, ethnic maps)

Cartography
Klett-Perthes, Gotha, Germany
Bernd Creutzberg
Silvia Einsporn
Stephan Frisch
Dr.-Ing. Ulrich Hengelhaupt
Franziska Hohm
Thomas Hönicke
Sylvia Jakuscheit
Anja Krüger
Dr.-Ing. Manfred Reckziegel
Nicole Schramm
Wilfried Schüller
Katrin Stehli
Gerhard Treger

With the assistance of
Ingenieurbüro für Kartographie, Rolf Böhm, Bad Schandau, Germany
Ingenieurbüro für Kartographie, Müller und Richert GbR, Gotha, Germany
KartoGraFix Hengelhaupt, Suhl, Germany

Graphics
Otto Götzl (geotectonic processes)
Horst Peuckert † (ocean floor)

Flags
Jiří Tenora †, Das Flaggenkabinett, Berlin, Germany

Contents

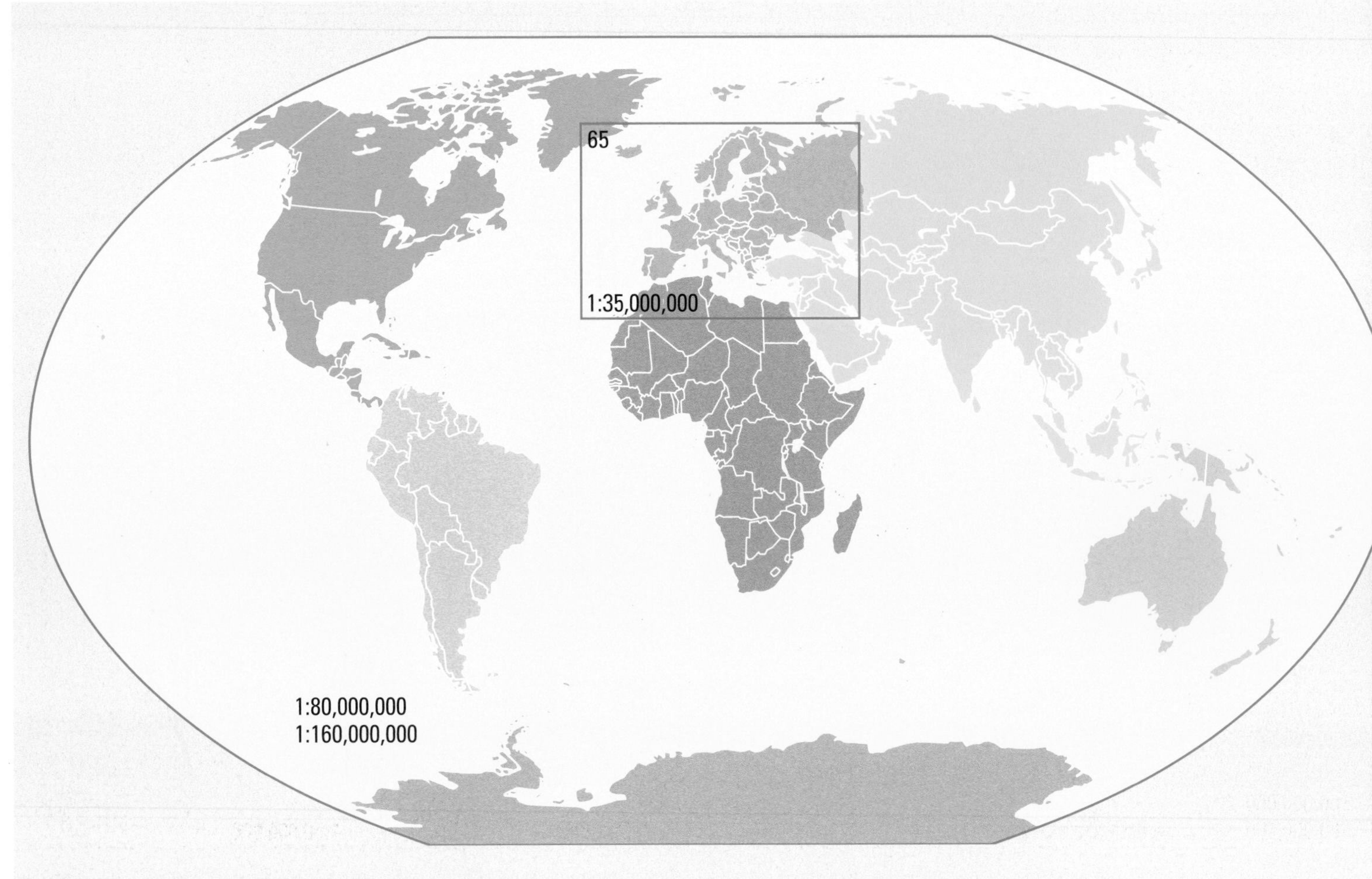

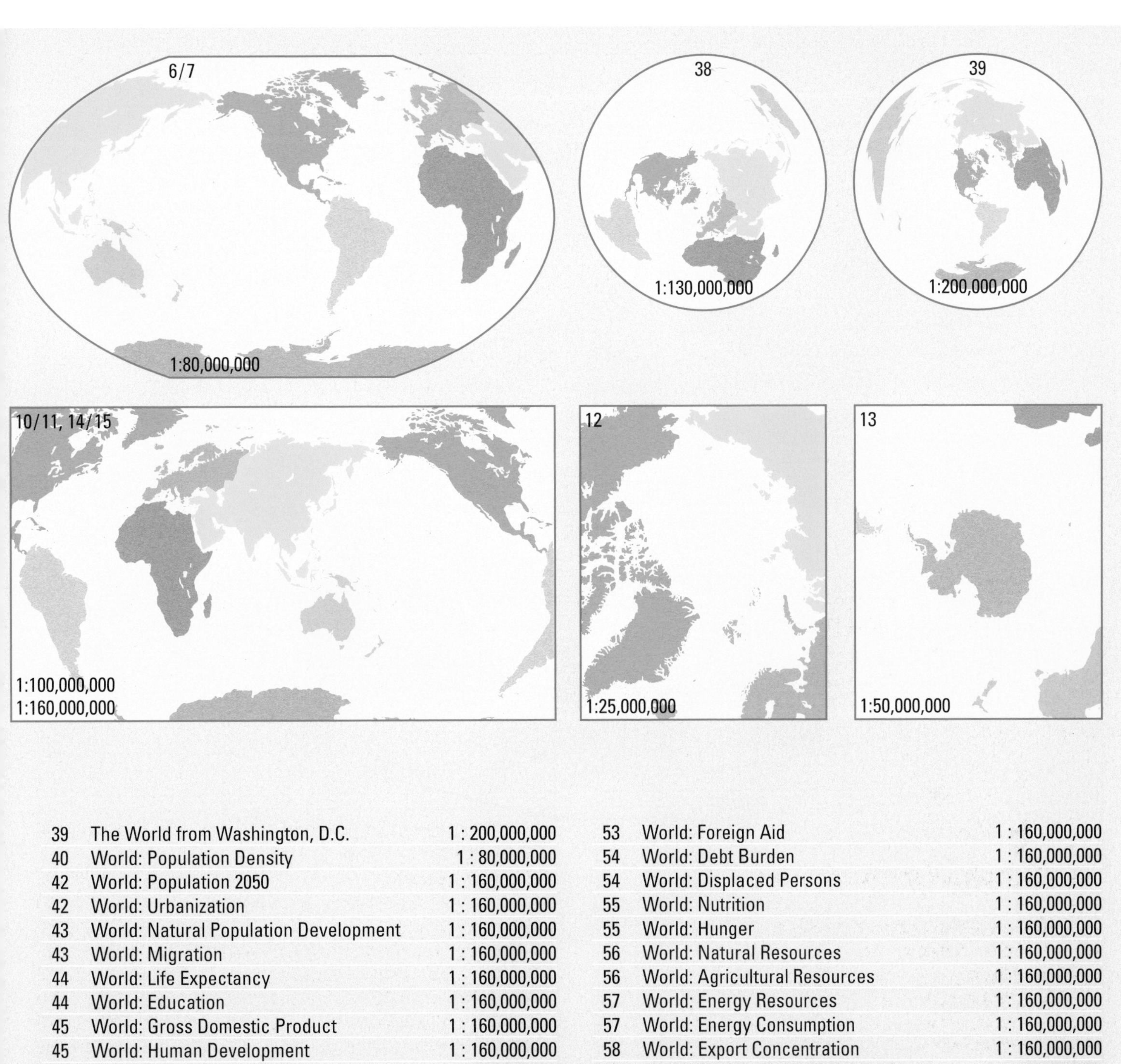
6/7
1:80,000,000
38
1:130,000,000
39
1:200,000,000
10/11, 14/15
1:100,000,000
1:160,000,000
12
1:25,000,000
13
1:50,000,000

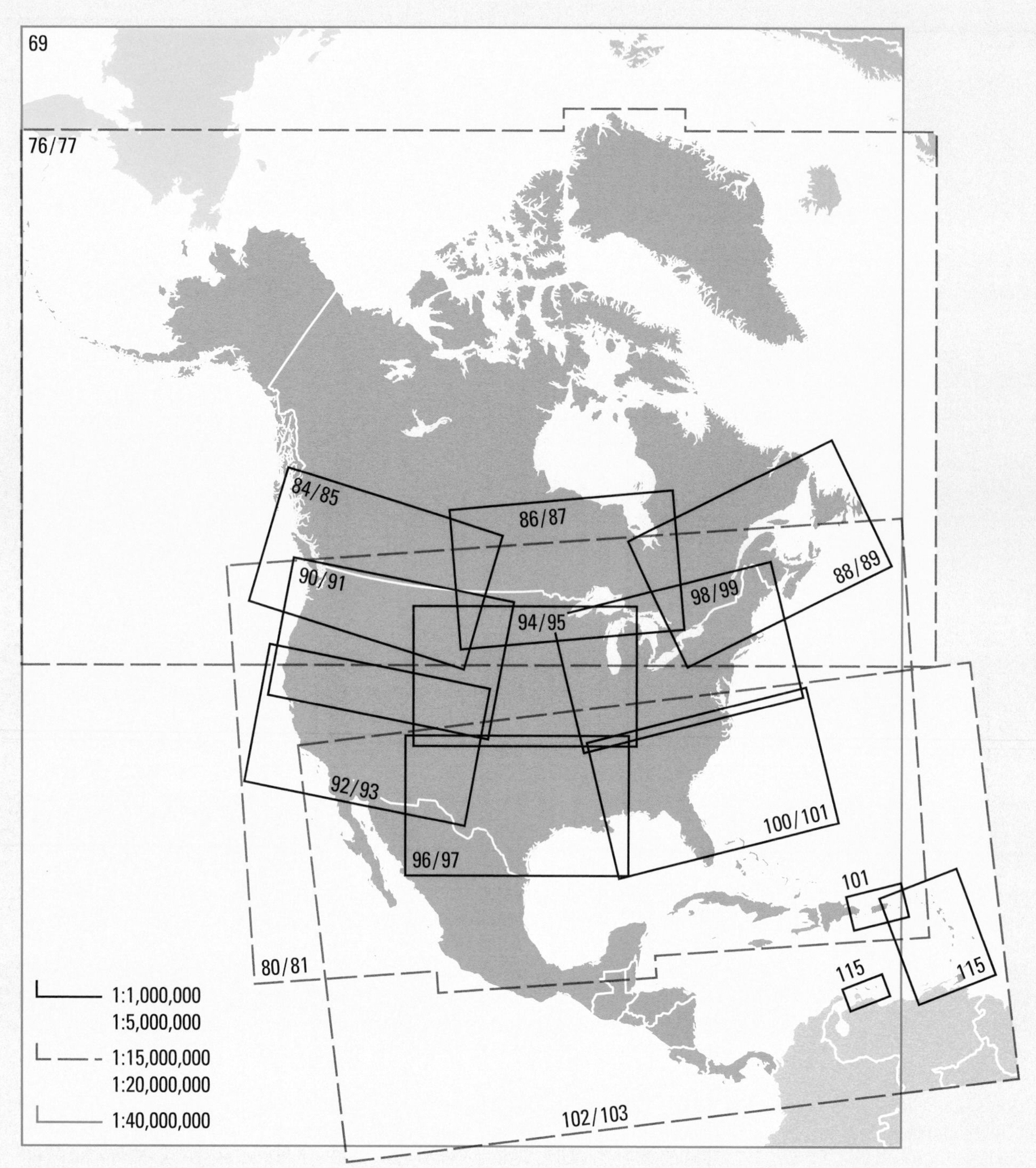
69
76/77
84/85
86/87
88/89
90/91
94/95
98/99
92/93
96/97
100/101
101
115
115
80/81
102/103
1:1,000,000
1:5,000,000
1:15,000,000
1:20,000,000
1:40,000,000

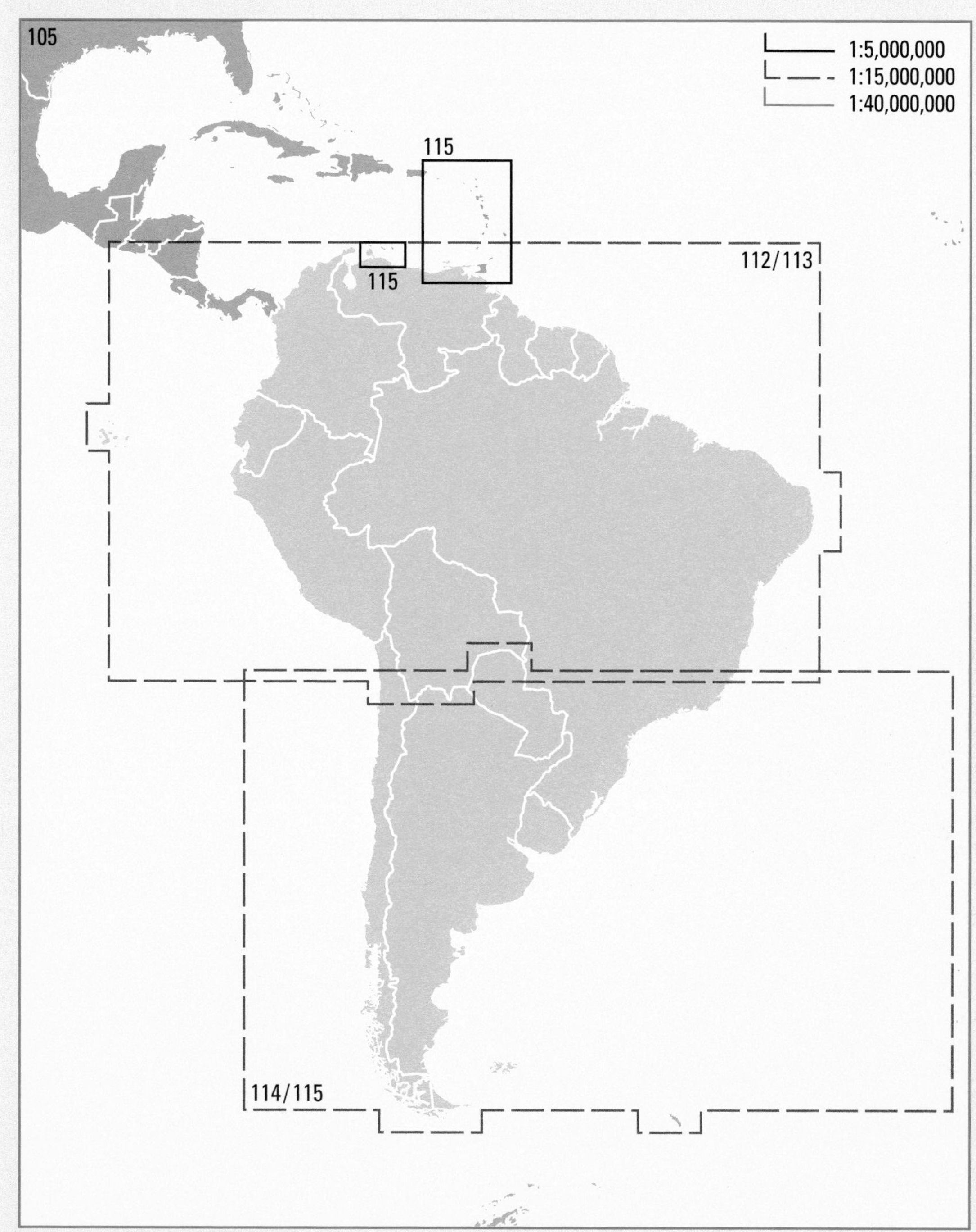
105
1:5,000,000
1:15,000,000
1:40,000,000
115
115
112/113
114/115

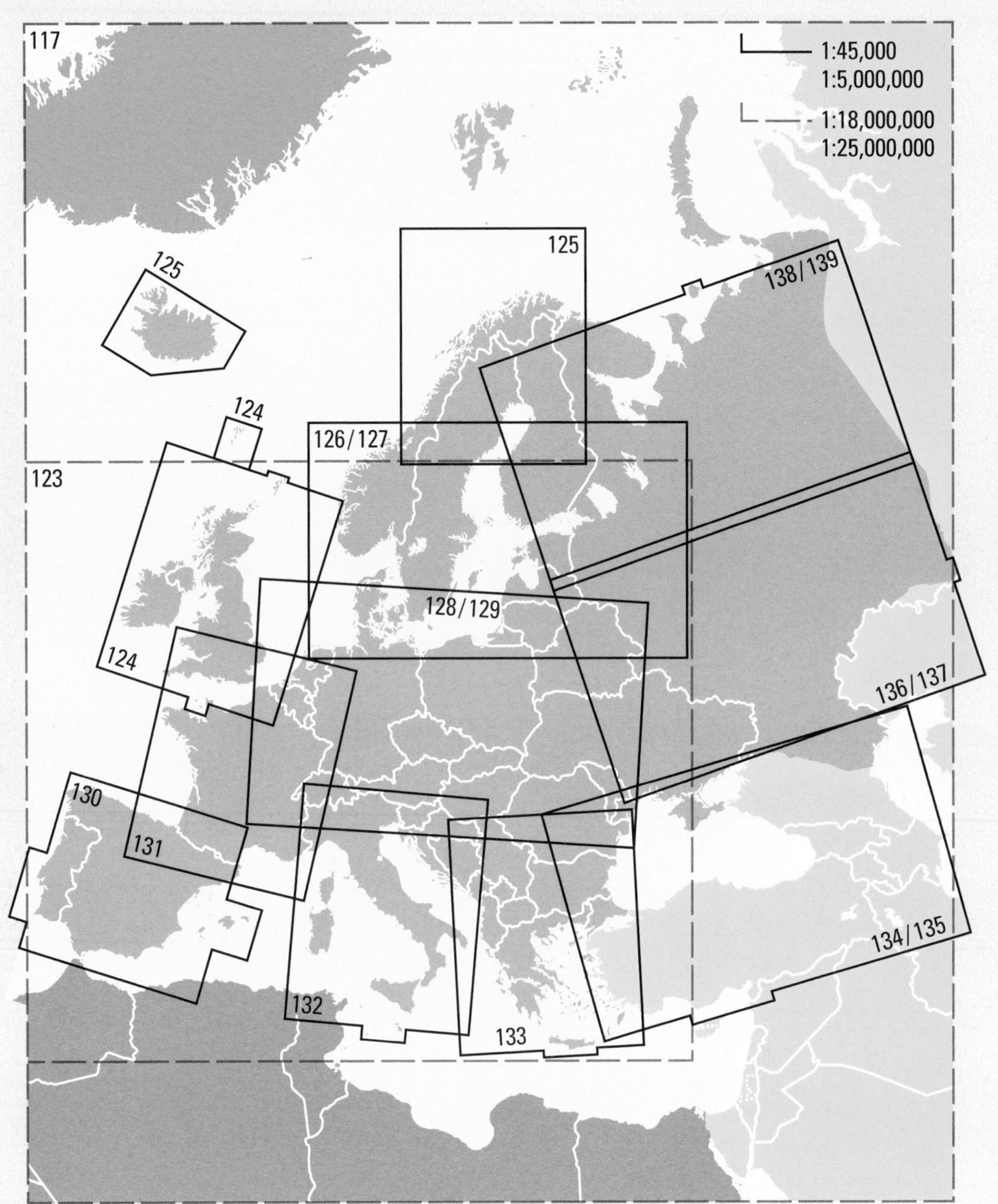
117
1:45,000
1:5,000,000
1:18,000,000
1:25,000,000
125
125
138/139
124
126/127
123
128/129
124
136/137
130
131
134/135
132
133

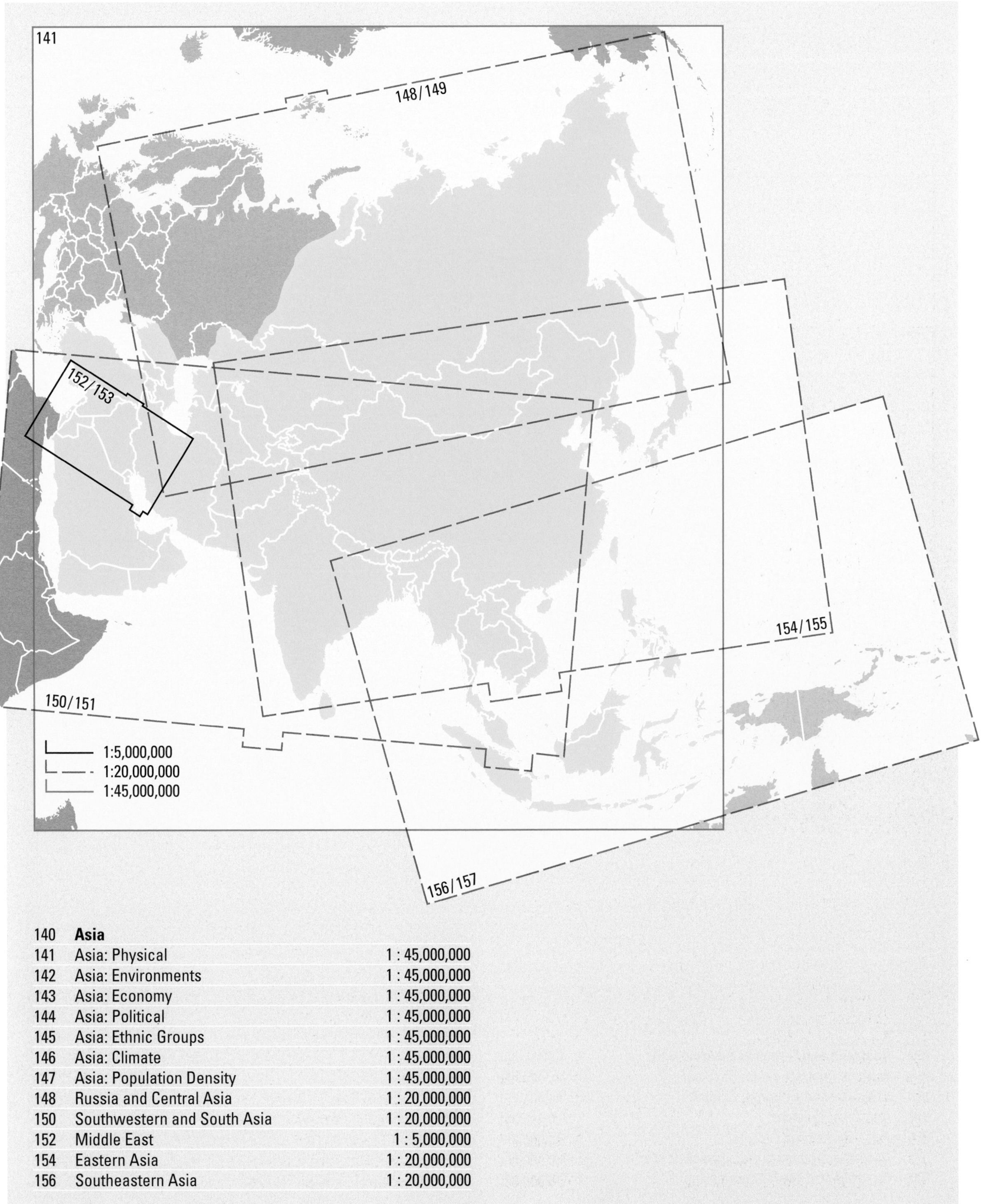

141
148/149
152/153
150/151
154/155
156/157
1:5,000,000
1:20,000,000
1:45,000,000

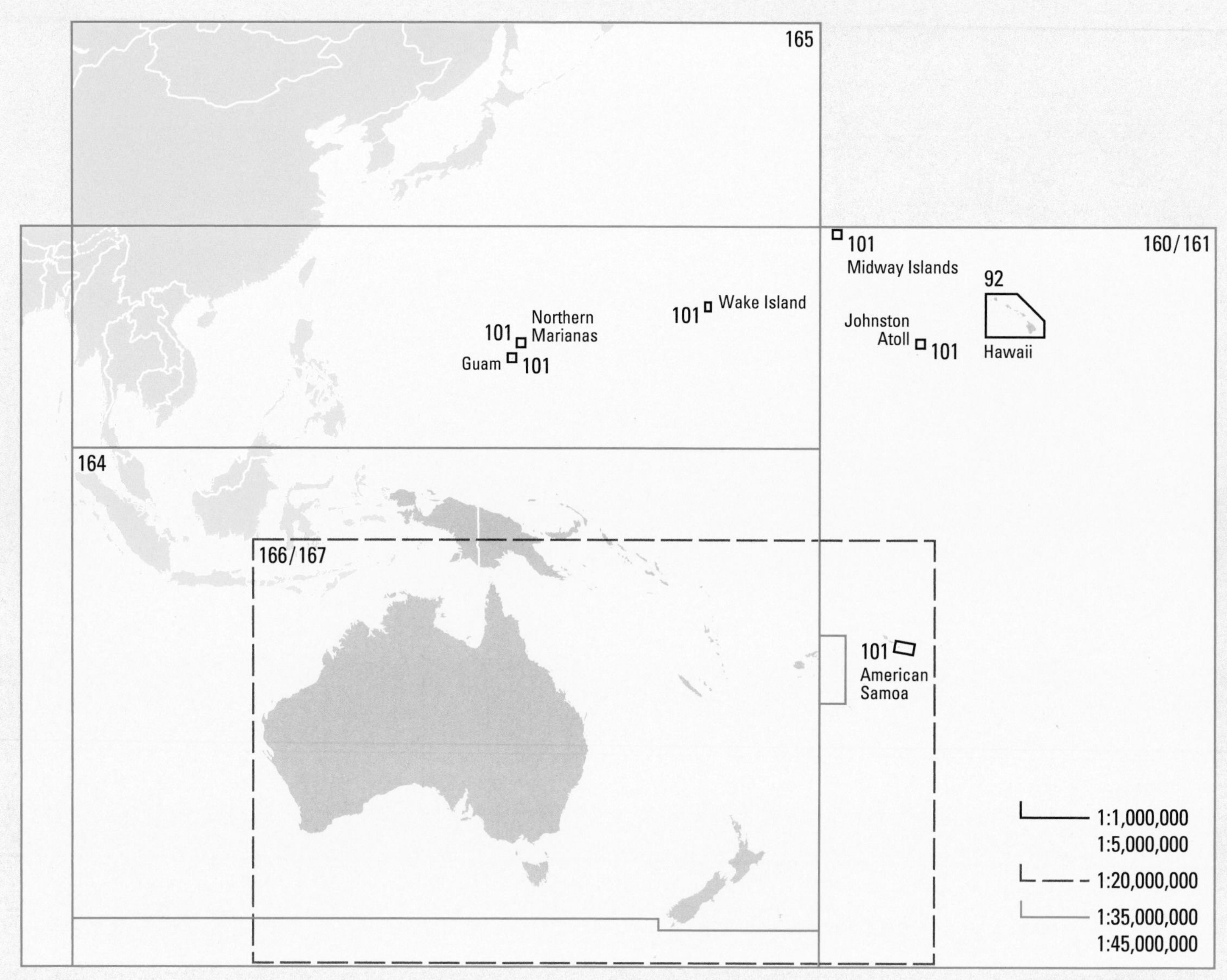
165
101
Midway Islands
160/161
92
101
Wake Island
Northern
Marianas
101
Johnston
Atoll
101
Hawaii
Guam
101
164
166/167
101
American
Samoa
1:1,000,000
1:5,000,000
1:20,000,000
1:35,000,000
1:45,000,000

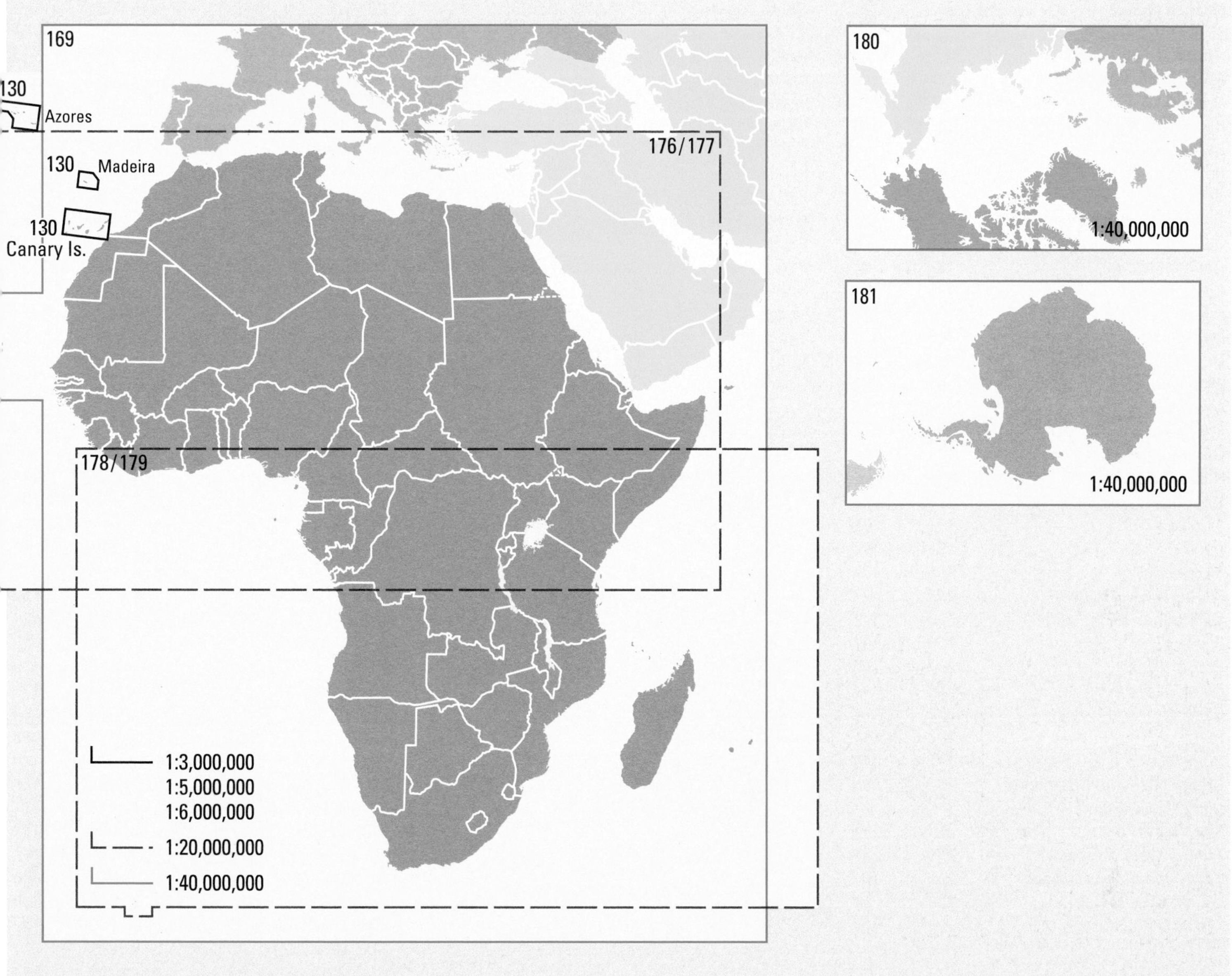

169
130
Azores
130
Madeira
130
Canary Is.
176/177
178/179
1:3,000,000
1:5,000,000
1:6,000,000
1:20,000,000
1:40,000,000
180
1:40,000,000
181
1:40,000,000

Asia	Statistical Gazetteer	Map
Afghanistan	185	150
Akrotiri	*185*	*152*
Armenia	185	134
Azerbaijan	186	134
Bahrain	186	152
Bangladesh	186	150
Bhutan	187	150
Brunei	188	156
Cambodia	188	156
China	189	154
Christmas Island	*189*	*156*
Cocos (Keeling) Islands	*189*	*156*
Cyprus	190	152
Dhelkelia	*190*	*152*
Georgia	192	134
India	194	150
Indonesia	194	156
Iran	194	150
Iraq	194	152
Israel	194	152
Japan	195	154
Jordan	195	152
Kazakhstan	195	148
Korea, North	195	154
Korea, South	195	154
Kuwait	196	152
Kyrgyzstan	196	148
Laos	196	156
Lebanon	196	152
Malaysia	197	156
Maldives	197	150
Mongolia	198	154
Myanmar	198	150
Nepal	199	150
Oman	200	150
Pakistan	200	150
Philippines	200	156
Qatar	201	150
Saudi Arabia	202	150
Singapore	203	156
Sri Lanka	203	150
Syria	204	152
Taiwan	204	154
Tajikistan	204	150
Thailand	204	156
Timor-Leste	204	156
Turkey	205	134
Turkmenistan	205	148
United Arab Emirates	205	150
Uzbekistan	207	148
Vietnam	208	156
Yemen	208	150

Australia and Oceania	Statistical Gazetteer	Map
American Samoa	*185*	*100*
Australia	186	166
Cook Islands	189	160
Fiji	191	166
French Polynesia	*192*	*160*
Guam	*193*	*100*
Johnston Atoll	*195*	*100*
Kiribati	195	160
Marshall Islands	197	160
Micronesia	198	156
Midway Islands	*198*	*100*
Nauru	198	160
New Caledonia	*199*	*166*
New Zealand	199	166
Niue	199	166
Norfolk Island	*199*	*166*
Northern Mariana Islands	*200*	*100*
Palau	200	156
Papua New Guinea	200	156
Pitcairn Islands	*200*	*160*
Samoa	202	166
Solomon Islands	203	166
Tokelau	*205*	*166*
Tonga	205	166
Tuvalu	205	166
Vanuatu	207	166
Wake Island	*208*	*100*
Wallis and Futuna	*208*	*166*

Africa	Statistical Gazetteer	Map
Algeria	185	176
Angola	185	178
Benin	187	176
Botswana	187	178
Burkina Faso	188	176
Burundi	188	178
Cameroon	188	176
Cape Verde	188	176
Central African Republic	188	176
Chad	189	176
Comoros	189	178
Congo, Dem. Rep. of the	189	178
Congo, Republic of the	189	178
Côte d'Ivoire	190	176
Djibouti	190	176
Egypt	191	176
Equatorial Guinea	191	176
Eritrea	191	176
Ethiopia	191	176
Gabon	192	178
Gambia, The	192	176
Ghana	192	176
Guinea	193	176
Guinea-Bissau	193	176
Kenya	195	178
Lesotho	196	178
Liberia	196	176
Lybia	196	176
Madagascar	197	178
Malawi	197	178
Mali	197	*176*
Mauritania	197	176
Mauritius	197	178
Mayotte	*197*	*178*
Morocco	198	176
Mozambique	198	178
Namibia	198	178
Niger	199	176
Nigeria	199	176
Rwanda	201	178
Saint Helena	*202*	*178*
Sao Tome and Principe	202	176
Senegal	202	176
Seychelles	203	178
Sierra Leone	203	176
Somalia	203	176
South Africa	203	178
Sudan, The	204	176
Swaziland	204	178
Tanzania	204	178
Togo	204	176
Tunisia	205	176
Uganda	205	178
Western Sahara	208	176
Zambia	208	178
Zimbabwe	208	178

How to Read and Interpret Maps

Centering Maps

In addition to the choice of projection, where a map is centered (and where Earth's skin is torn) affects how the world looks. A comparison of the Winkel Tripel projection world map on the facing page with the Winkel Tripel projection centered on the Pacific Ocean illustrates the importance of centering.

In general, the place at the center will have less distortion than most other places on the map, especially those near the edge.

Generalization

Like the written word, a map is a language – a form of communication. Look closely at a common map, like a road map, and you will be amazed at the amount of information represented. Think about the difficulty of expressing some of the things easily represented on a map in words alone. Road maps stress transportation and how to get between different places. Other maps express or emphasize other geographic concepts.

Maps cannot possibly convey every aspect of the place they cover. As abstractions that condense Earth's complexity into a small space, they must leave many things out. This process is called *generalization*. All maps have to choose the features they represent and those they omit. Without generalization, maps would be hopelessly cluttered.

Scale

Whenever they create a map, cartographers must specify its *scale*, a term that refers to the ratio between length on the map and the corresponding real-world distance.

A scale of 1:100 means that each inch of map represents 100 inches on the ground. This is called a *representative fraction* because it can be written as 1/100. A scale of 1:100 is useful only for floor plans, gardens, and other small areas. A scale of 1:40,000,000 depicts a large area, like a continent.

Whether a map scale is considered large or small depends on its representative fraction: 1:100 is a huge scale, while 1:100,000,000 is very small. In general, large-scale maps show relatively small areas like a part of a city, while small-scale maps show big areas like the world or the United States.

Examples of Generalization and Scale in the *Perthes World Atlas*

This map of the Eastern Mediterranean, focused on Cyprus, demonstrates how **generalization** works

Some topographic information is represented by shading, but not to the extent of a topographic map. Water depth is not shown.

Only cities of a particular size or importance are represented.

Formation of the coast is smoothed out.

For the most part, only international boundaries are represented. In the case of Cyprus, the internal boundary between Greek and Turkish-dominated regions is considered important enough for inclusion.

This same portion of the world is depicted at three different scales. Note the different levels of generalization in these three maps.

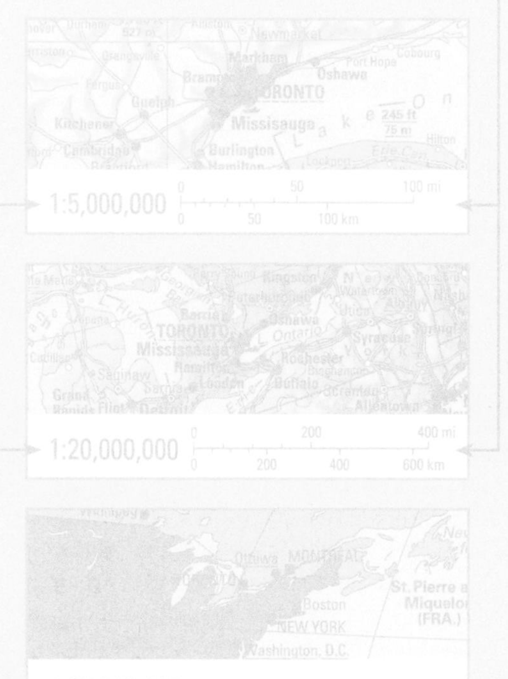

Origin and Meaning of Atlas

Dictionaries define *atlas* as a book of maps, and some attribute the term to Dutch mapmaker Gerard Mercator, who named his monumental 1595 world atlas after the ancient ruler of Mauritania, chronicled in classical mythology as carrying the world on his shoulders as punishment for leading an unsuccessful revolt against the gods. Mercator's *Atlas sive Cosmographiæ Meditationes de Fabrica Mundi et Fabricati Figura* (Atlas, or Cosmographic Meditations on the Fabric of the World and the Figure of the Fabrick'd) had an enormous impact on cartography – translated from Latin into Dutch, French, German, and English, it was reprinted in various versions over the next century and a half. Even so, the title Father of the Modern Atlas more appropriately belongs to Abraham Ortelius, who published his epic atlas *Theatrum Orbis Terrarum* (Theatre of the Whole World) in 1570. Although *Theatrum* was not the first book of maps – bound collections of sailing charts had been around for a century – Ortelius pioneered the coherent structure of standardized content and quality control.

Gerard Mercator (1574)

Ortelius Map of Ireland (1573)

Atlases Today

Modern atlases address diverse themes. Road atlases help us plan cross-country trips, and street atlases locate addresses, landmarks, parks, and other urban sites. Historical atlases narrate the progression of exploration and settlement, wars and diplomacy, development and trade, while school atlases introduce elementary pupils to world and regional geography. Thematic atlases reflect the enormous diversity of map content. As examples, congressional atlases describe the intricacies of election district boundaries, atlases of the Internet portray the locations, linkages, and impacts of cyberspace, and climate atlases depict the spatial patterns of dozens of averaged weather measurements. By contrast, reference atlases like the *Perthes World Atlas* integrate the geographic details of natural regions, political regions, or the entire world. Some atlases have a narrower geographic focus: national atlases offer an integrated overview of a country's evolution and the spatial diversity of its environment, people, and economy, while state atlases offer a similar treatment for a single state.

Like other reference atlases of the world, the *Perthes World Atlas* includes general reference maps, thematic maps, a geographical index, and a statistical gazetteer.

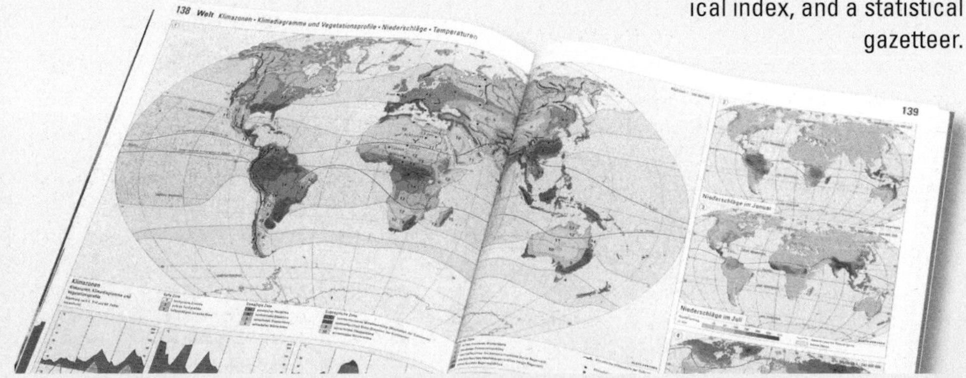

Elements of the *Perthes World Atlas*

Reference maps depict terrain, cities, political boundaries, and rivers at appropriate levels of detail for the whole world or coherent regions of various sizes. Crisscrossed by meridians and parallels to help users find places listed in the index, these maps show a city's larger neighbors, approximate elevation, and relative proximity to the closest ocean, river, or lake.

In this excerpt from the reference map "Asia: Middle East" (p. 152–153) a dotted boundary surrounds the West Bank, a disputed territory controlled by Israel and thus shown in a slightly lighter color.

Thematic maps provide geographic overviews for specific themes like precipitation, birth rate, agricultural production, or dominant religion. This excerpt from the thematic map "World: Life Expectancy" (p. 44) shows huge differences between western Europe and southwest Asia in health care and standard of living. The squares represent a country's population, the colors inside the squares show average life expectancy, and abbreviations identify the larger countries by name.

Iceland (toward the northwest) has a comparatively small population with a relatively long average life span. Germany (GER.) has the largest population in the region but lower longevity than Italy (ITA.). Turkey (TUR.) and Ukraine (UKR.) are populous countries whose residents generally die at an earlier age than residents of Sweden (SWE.).

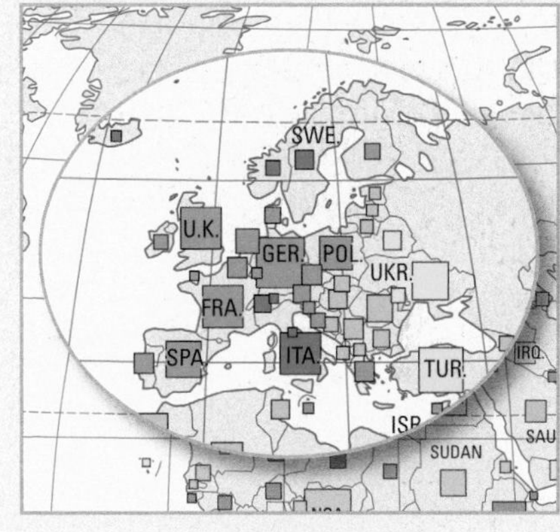

The **geographical index** is an alphabetical inventory of the places and geographic features that are depicted in the maps of the atlas. You can use it to quickly find a place or feature. For example, if you look for "Casablanca" in the index, you will see the entry:

Casablanca (Ad-Dār al-Bayḍā')	**176** F 2

The numbers and letters on the right refer to the page number and points on the reference grid. If you go to the map on page 176 and look for the red letter "F" in the top margin of the map and the red number "2" in the left margin, you will find Casablanca by following a straight line down from "F" and a straight line to the right of "2". Casablanca is a well-known place, but this is not the official name of the city since Moroccans speak Arabic. Therefore, you will find the Arabic transcription next to Casablanca in the index and on the map. The transcription of place names in countries that use different languages and alphabets is rather complicated and even contentious.

Many Arabic places in North Africa are still referred to by their transcriptions into French during the colonial period, even on English language maps. The *Perthes World Atlas* follows the international place name standards set by the United Nations and includes only English transcriptions of Arabic places on its maps. Even so, if you only know a place by its colonial French transcription, you can still find it through the index.

The **statistical gazetteer** lists important information for different countries of the world, such as the size of the territory and population, capital city, administrative organization, languages, religions, currency, and major cities.

As these excerpts from the entry on the United States show, the gazetteer also includes the flag and official name and lists major administrative sub-divisions of countries, such as the 50 American states, and external territories, such as American Samoa or Puerto Rico. All countries are listed by their names in alphabetical order. Inhabited external territories are included under their mother country as well as under their own name, which makes them easier to find.

United States / U.S.A.
United States of America

Area:	9,631,418 km²
Population:	305,826,000 (2007)
Capital:	Washington D.C. (563,000; MSA: 5,090,000)
Administration:	50 states and the District of Columbia
Languages:	English/regionally Spanish
Religions:	Protestant 58%, Roman Catholic 21%, other Christian 6%, Jewish 2%, Muslim 2%
Currency:	1 dollar = 100 cents

Major cities:
New York (8,086,000; MSA: 18,641,000),
Los Angeles (3,820,000; MSA: 12,829,000),
Chicago (2,869,000; MSA: 9,334,000),

Wisconsin	169,643	5,557,000	Madison
Wyoming	253,349	515,000	Cheyenne

* including inland water

Outlying Territories in the Caribbean:

Navassa
claimed by Haiti
Navassa Island

Area/Population:	5 km²/uninhabited

Puerto Rico
Estado Libre Asociado de Puerto Rico/
Commonwealth of Puerto Rico

Area:	9,084 km²
Population:	3,991,000 (2007)
Capital:	San Juan (418,000)
Languages:	Spanish/English
Religions:	Roman Catholic 72%, Protestant 5%

Flat Maps and Coordinates for a Spherical Earth

To understand how map projection works, think of Earth as an orange. Peel off a part of the skin, flatten it out, and the distortion is apparent but minor – much less than for a large section, which cannot be flattened without tearing the skin. Fortunately for geographers and map users, mathematics allows the seamless stretching of the whole globe, or just a portion, into a flat map. To convert the three-dimensional earth into a two-dimensional map, cartographers define locations on the globe with a system of coordinates composed of lines of latitude called *parallels* and lines of longitude called *meridians*. Each intersection of latitude and longitude defines a unique location on the globe.

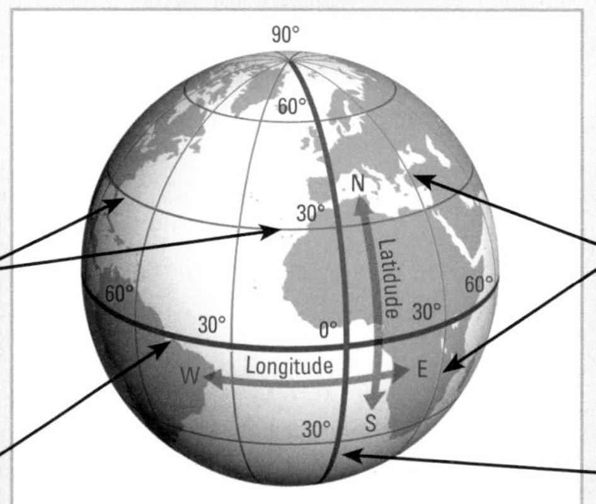

This is a **parallel**, or line of constant **latitude**, which indicates how far north or south a place on that line is from the equator.

This is the **equator**, along which latitude is 0°.

This is a **meridian**, or line of constant **longitude**, which how tells us how far a place is east or west from Greenwich. The greatest longitude from Greenwich in either direction is 180°.

The **prime meridian**, at 0° longitude, passes through Greenwich, England.

Types of Projections

Map projections are created by projecting geographic features from a spherical globe onto one of three simple mathematical surfaces: the **plane**, **cylinder**, and **cone**, which yield projections labeled azimuthal, cylindrical and conic.

The **plane** (azimuthal projection) is generally used for polar maps. Projections for tropical areas are often based on a **cylinder** centered on the equator. Maps for mid-latitude regions like Europe and North America are usually projected onto a **cone** anchored to one or two *standard parallels*, which have the same scale on both map and globe. Conic projections in the *Perthes World Atlas* use two standard parallels because this ensures that the average place can be closer to at least one of the parallels.

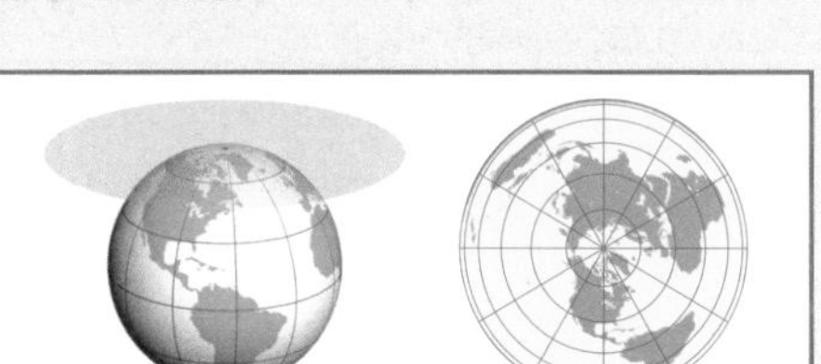

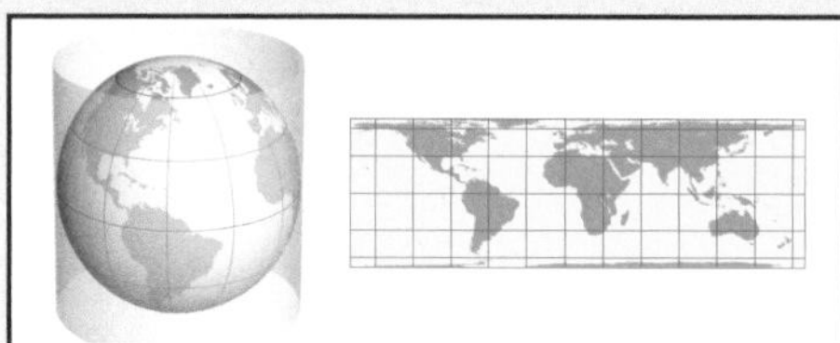

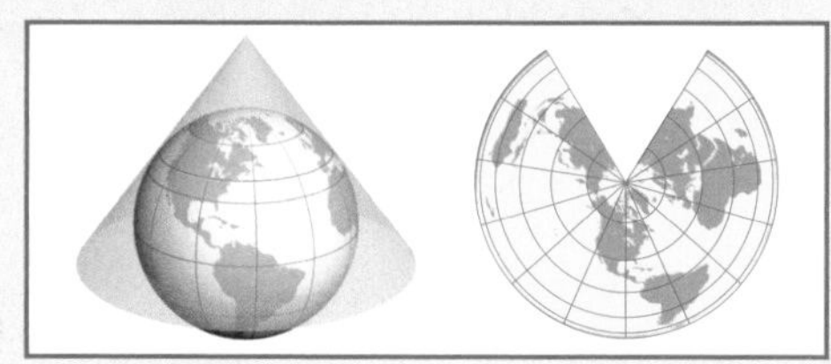

Problems of Distortion

Map projections can distort five geographic properties: area, angles, distance, direction, and gross shapes like the outlines of continents. Although some distortion is unavoidable, angles and relative area can be preserved – but not, unfortunately, in the same projection. Relative area is generally more important than exact angles. Therefore, continental and regional maps in the *Perthes World Atlas* are cast on equal-area projections.

Fitting the whole world onto a single map projection is far trickier than projecting a region or country because of the enormous stretching required. Indeed, distortions of some distances are so extreme that no world map should include a scale bar. Although world projections can preserve relative area exactly, they often incur outrageous distortions of shape, as on the **Peters projection**, which severely stretches continents.

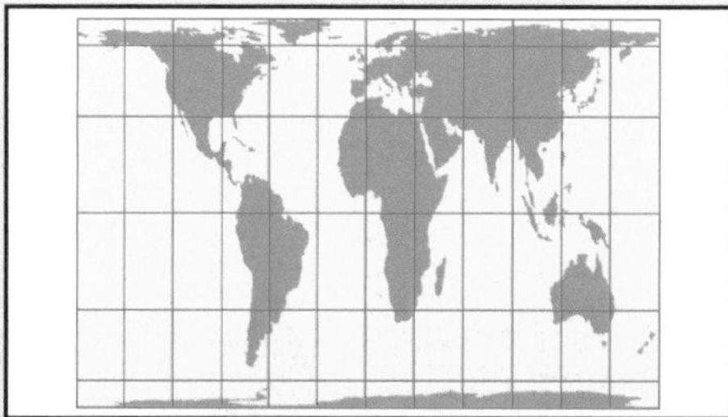

World maps in the *Perthes World Atlas* are cast on the **Winkel Tripel projection**, which offers a balanced treatment of areas and shapes and confines its more severe distortions to the northern and southern polar regions.

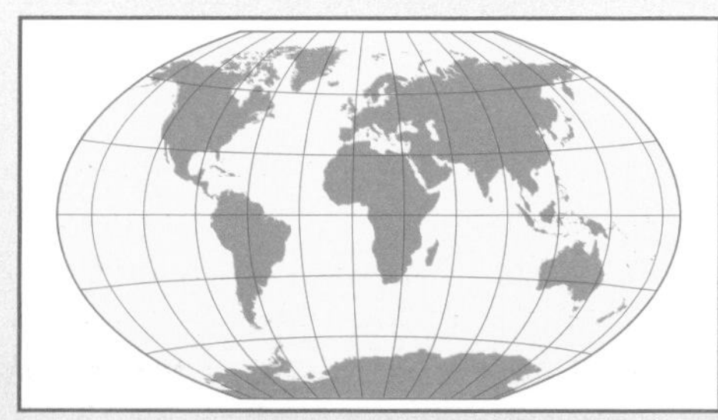

Centering Maps

In addition to the choice of projection, where a map is centered (and where Earth's skin is torn) affects how the world looks. A comparison of the Winkel Tripel projection world map on the facing page with the Winkel Tripel projection centered on the Pacific Ocean illustrates the importance of centering.

In general, the place at the center will have less distortion than most other places on the map, especially those near the edge.

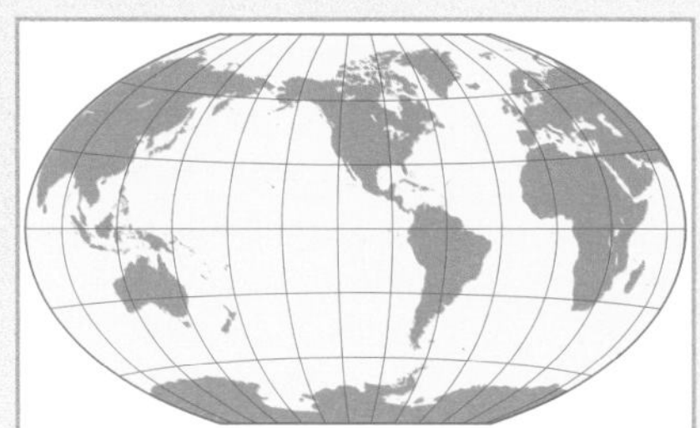

Generalization

Like the written word or mathematics, a map is a language – a form of communication. Look closely at a common map, like a road map, and you will be amazed at the amount of information represented. Think about the difficulty of expressing some of the things easily represented on a map in words alone. Road maps stress transportation and how to get between different places. Other maps express or emphasize other geographic concepts.

Maps cannot possibly convey every aspect of the place they cover. As abstractions that condense Earth's complexity into a small space, they must leave many things out. This process is called *generalization*. All maps have to choose the features they represent and those they omit. Without generalization, maps would be hopelessly cluttered.

Scale

Whenever they make a map, cartographers must specify its *scale*, a term that refers to the ratio between length on the map and the corresponding real-world distance.

A scale of 1:100 means that each inch of map represents 100 inches on the ground. This is called a *representative fraction* because it can be written as 1/100. A scale of 1:100 is useful only for floor plans, gardens, and other small areas. A scale of 1:40,000,000 depicts a large area, like a continent.

Whether a map scale is considered large or small depends on its representative fraction: 1:100 is a huge scale, while 1:100,000,000 is very small. In general, large-scale maps show relatively small areas like a part of a city, while small-scale maps show big areas like the world or the United States.

Examples of Generalization and Scale in the *Perthes World Atlas*

This map of the Eastern Mediterranean, focused on Cyprus, demonstrates how **generalization** works

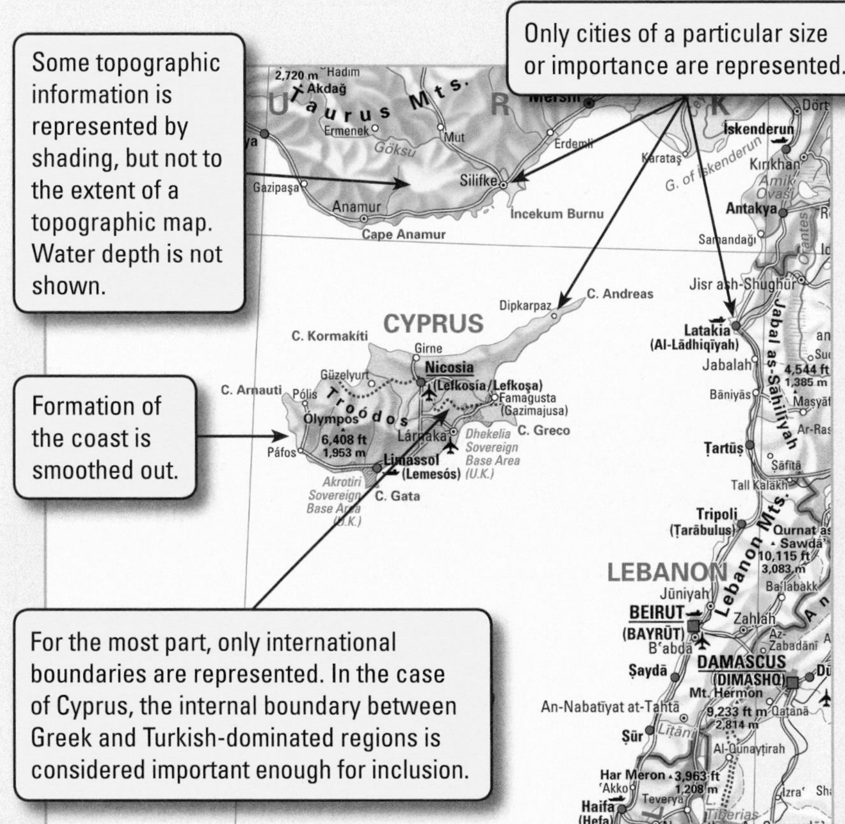

This same portion of the world is depicted at three different scales. Note the different levels of generalization in these three maps.

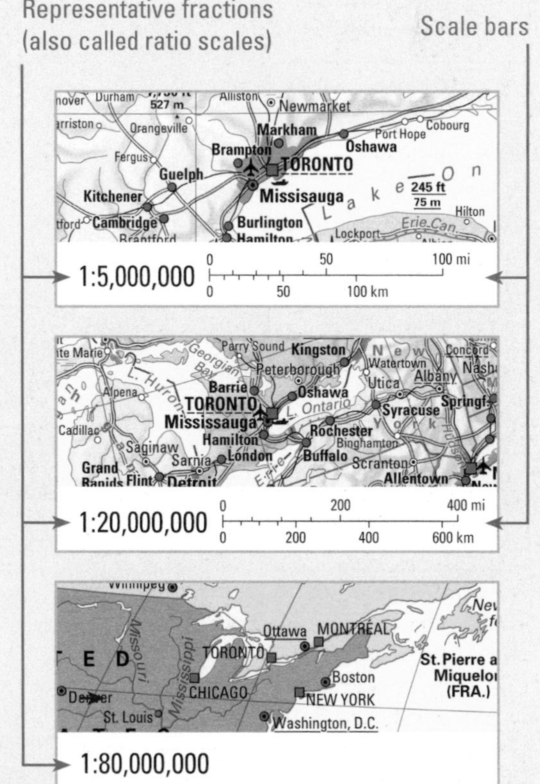

Nuts and Bolts of Maps

Each map is composed of a wide variety of different elements. Knowing what each of these elements means makes it easier for you to find and interpret information on a map. The elements that are depicted depend on the type of map and the scale of the map.

This map of the North Polar Atlantic is a small-scale map in which each unit on the map represents 40,000,000 units on the earth. It is also primarily a physical map that emphasizes physical features like lakes, rivers, coasts, ice, currents, and terrain.

Maps in the atlas include a web of **latitude** and **longitude** lines (**parallels** and **meridians**).

The **scale bar** represents the scale of the map, which indicates how distance on the map corresponds to distance on the earth. The separation of the tics at 0 and 500 represent 500 miles on Earth's surface.

This map uses **color** and **lines** to depict a variety of landforms. Smaller **rivers** are depicted with blue lines, larger **lakes** and seas appear as blue areas bounded by blue lines, and **landforms** are in shades of green and brown.

Maps use boundary lines to represent the **boundaries** between different spatial units. Boundaries between countries are most often depicted, but sometimes internal boundaries are represented as well. On this map, boundaries are shown as red lines. Some boundaries across open water are shown by dashed red lines, like this one, indicating that Spitsbergen belongs to Norway.

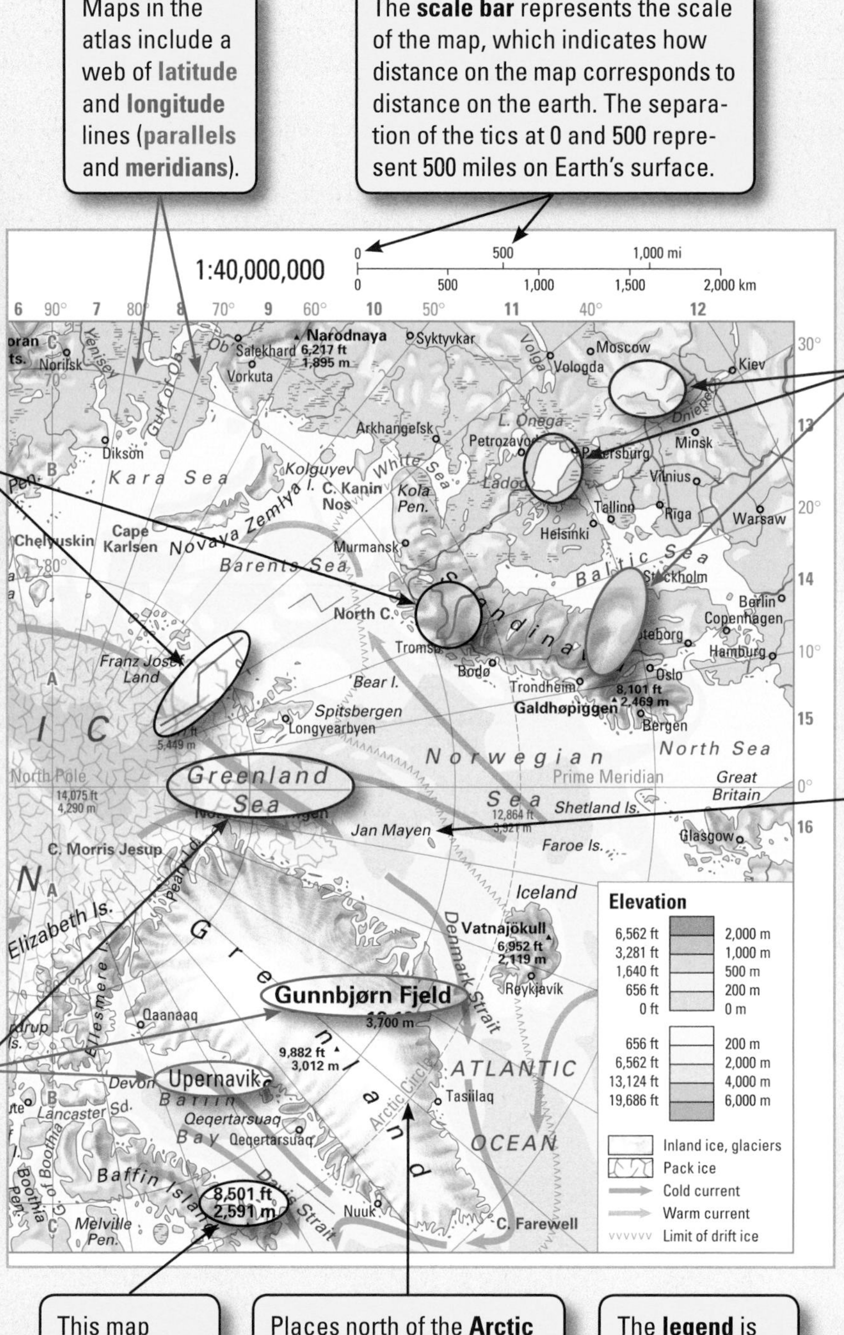

Place names in this atlas are found in the **index**. The index allows you to locate a place by page number and by its position on the map grid. In this case, the index would list "Jan Mayen 180 B 16". The letter indicates a section between two lines of latitude and the number indicates a section between two lines of longitude. Since this is a special projection, the latitude sections are circles and the longitude sections are pie shaped. You can find the island if you follow the red letter "B" along the curve of the latitude lines until you reach the sector with the red number "16".

Names and other **text** are presented using a hierarchical system of fonts, styles, sizes, and colors that provide visual clues to categories of features. For example, **water** features are depicted in blue lettering, while **mountains** and **settlements** are distinguished by different font styles in black lettering.

This map notes significant **elevations**, often high points, in both feet and meters.

Places north of the **Arctic Circle** have at least one period when the sun is above the horizon for more than 24 hours. Everywhere north of the Arctic Circle is in the Polar latitudes.

The **legend** is the part of the map that shows the reader how to interpret various symbols and colors.

Signs and Symbols

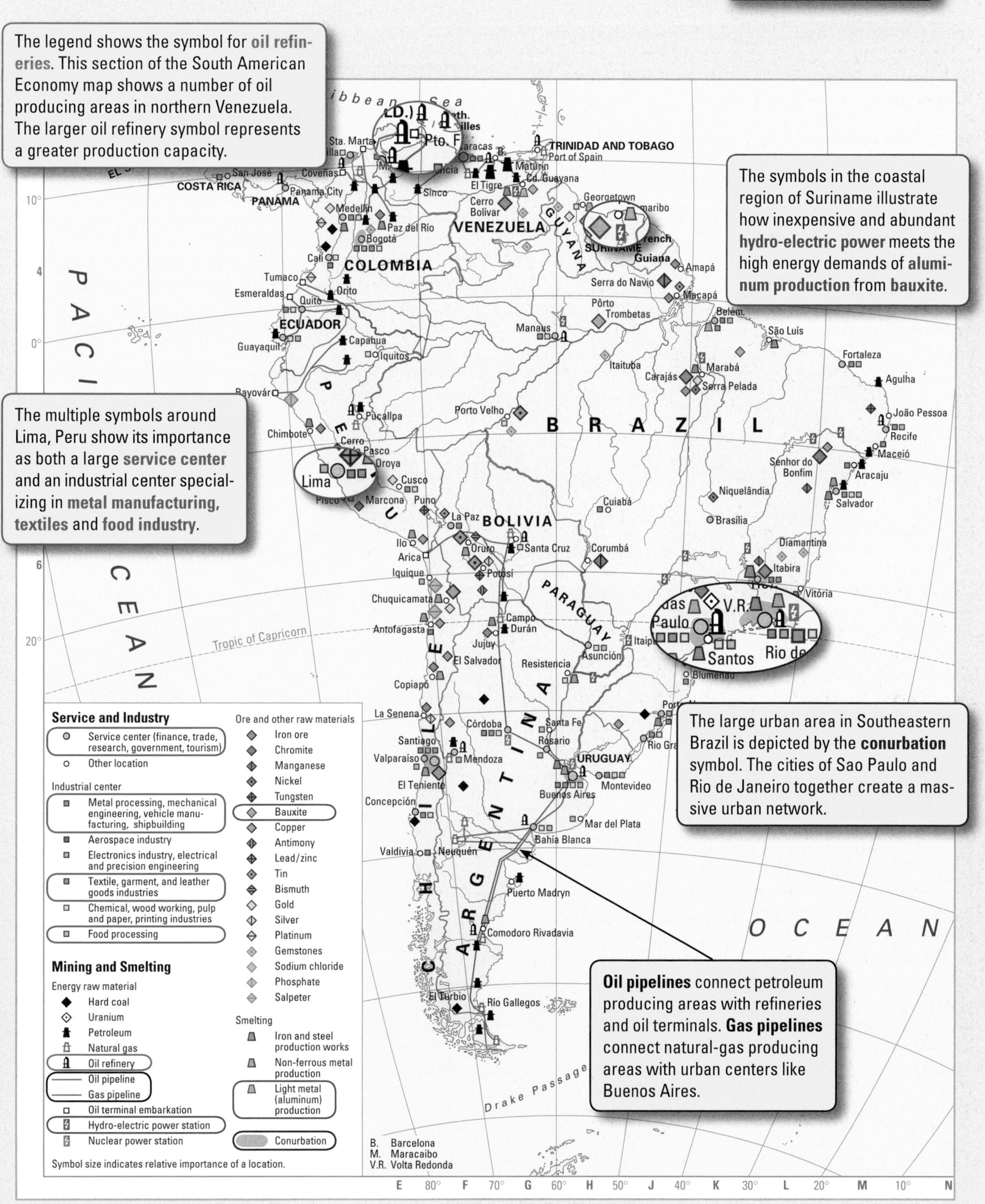

Choropleths and Arrows

Looks complicated? Sure, but a little effort will yield a lot of insight. The maps in this atlas are designed to be easy-to-read as well as informative. As its title and legend indicate, this map shows several things:

(1) the **direction and size of migration flows**;
(2) **average annual rates of net migration**; and
(3) the **percentage of the world's population** living in an area **with a particular migration pattern**.

Countries are shaded in different colors to indicate **average yearly rates of migration**. Countries with yellow or green shades have experienced net in-migration, with more people moving in than moving out, while in countries with an orange or red color, more migrants have moved out than moved in. If you compare the green shades of Canada and the US, you can see that Canada has a higher average annual rate of in-migration than the United States. Maps that show rates or other values by shading areas of varying sizes – in this case countries – are called **choropleth maps**. The term comes from the Greek *choro*, which means place, and *plethos*, which means magnitude.

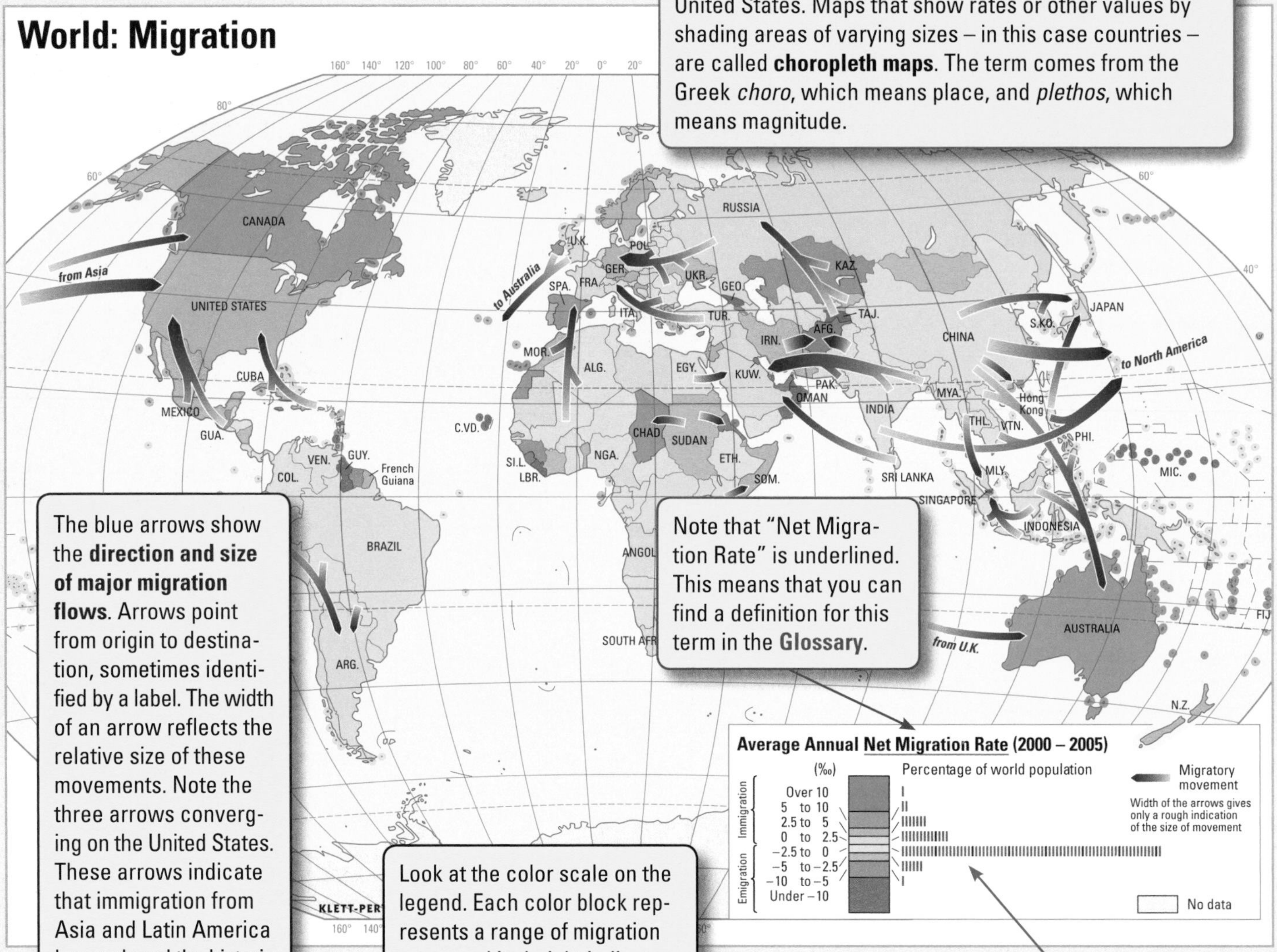

World: Migration

Average Annual Net Migration Rate (2000 – 2005)

(‰) — Percentage of world population

Immigration: Over 10; 5 to 10; 2.5 to 5; 0 to 2.5
Emigration: −2.5 to 0; −5 to −2.5; −10 to −5; Under −10

Migratory movement — Width of the arrows gives only a rough indication of the size of movement

No data

The blue arrows show the **direction and size of major migration flows**. Arrows point from origin to destination, sometimes identified by a label. The width of an arrow reflects the relative size of these movements. Note the three arrows converging on the United States. These arrows indicate that immigration from Asia and Latin America has replaced the historic migrations from Europe.

Note that "Net Migration Rate" is underlined. This means that you can find a definition for this term in the **Glossary**.

Look at the color scale on the legend. Each color block represents a range of migration rates, and its height indicates relative size of the range. For example, the color block for the second darkest shade of green (annual migration rates between 5 % and 10 %) is double the height of the next interval (2.5 % to 5 %). The taller the block, the larger the range of values.

The bars on the right side of the color scale show the **percentage of global population with a given migration rate**. You can see that only about 1 % the world's population lives in countries with the highest rates of net immigration.

Graduated Circles

The map on this page uses graduated circles (circles of different sizes) and a sophisticated legend to present a wealth of information about urban populations in the world. A closer look at the legend indicates that we can read four things from this map:

(1) the change in the size of country's **urban population predicted for 2005 to 2030**;
(2) the **percentage (or share) of a country's population that is urban**;
(3) the **size of a country's population in 2005**; and
(4) **percentage of global population with a given rate of change and a given share of urban population.**

Look at the **different colors of circles** on the map. Note the red circles for the United States and much of Europe and South America and the dark green circles for Niger (NGR.) and Uganda (UGA.). In the United States and other countries with red circles, which are already highly urban, the urban population will grow by no more than 50 %. By contrast, the urban population in Nigeria and other countries with dark green circles will increase between 250 % and 350 %. Note too the purple circles of Russia and much of Eastern Europe, where the share of the urban population is expected to decline over the next 25 years.

World: Urbanization

Look at the legend's vertical axis, which indicates **percentage rate of change in urban population projected for the period 2005 to 2030**. The dark green color at the top left identifies countries whose urban population will grow at a rate between 250 % and 350 % while the three squares with orange and red colors in a row represent countries whose urban populations will increase at rates less than 50 %. By contrast, the purple square highlights countries in which the urban population will shrink.

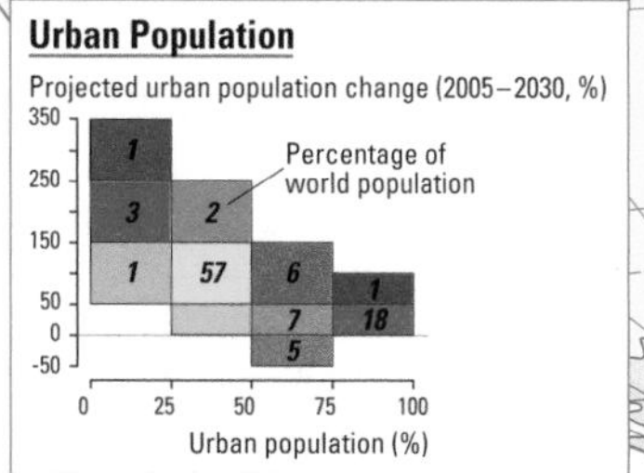

The horizontal axis shows the **share of a country's population that is urban**. The three green squares to the left represent countries in which urban residents account for less than 25 % of the total population. By contrast, the two reddish squares depict highly urbanized countries that are over 75 % urban.

Note the numbers inside the squares, which indicate the **percentage of global population** with a given rate of change and a given share of urban population. More than half (57 %) of the world's population lives in countries with a largely rural population (urban share between 25 % and 50 %) and a projected change between 50 % and 150 %.

Note the **different sizes of circles**, which reflect the size of the population of different countries. The graph below – which is included on all map pages with graduated symbols – helps you determine the **size of the population of different countries in 2005**. India and China stand out as having more than 1 billion people. The color and size of circles on the urbanization map make it easier to notice the categories of relatively small, densely populated countries like Indonesia and Japan, which have significantly larger populations than huge, more sparsely populated nations like Australia and Canada. By contrast, if you look at the choropleth migration map on the facing page, countries with a large land area appear very prominent even if they have small populations.

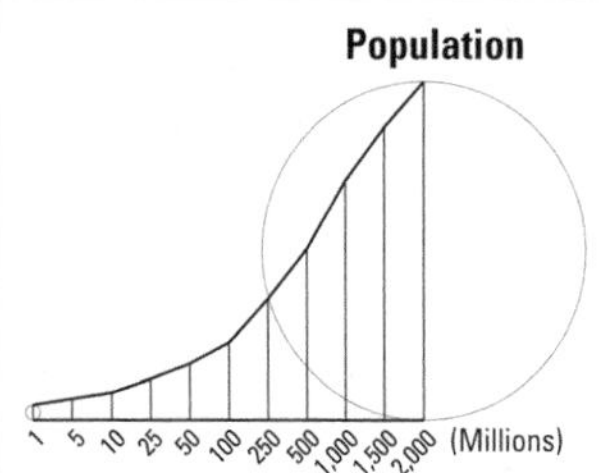

Physical Geographic Issues

An atlas is organized to help you learn more about the world by looking at a variety of maps of the same place or region. When you compare maps of different physical phenomena, such as rainfall and vegetation, with maps of social and economic factors, such as population growth and wealth, you can see new connections and ask new questions. Let's look at some examples in Africa.

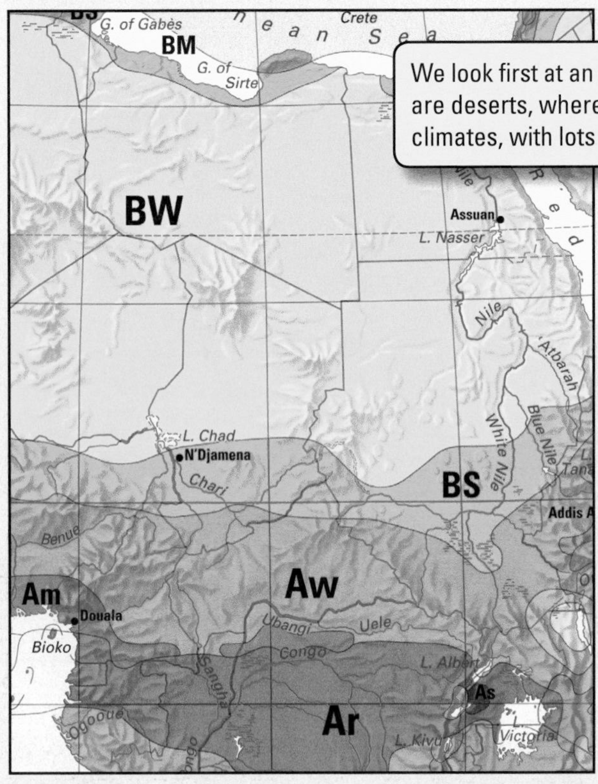

We look first at an excerpt from the "Africa: **Climate**" map (p. 174). The tan areas labeled "BW" are deserts, whereas the "BS" areas are semiarid steppes. Farther south are the tropical "A" climates, with lots of rain, and the "Ar" climates – the wettest and hottest places on Earth.

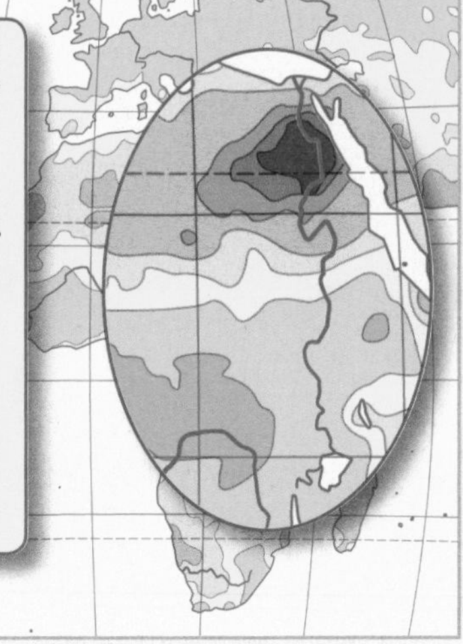

Compare the excerpts for the climate map and the "World: **Precipitation Variability**" map (p. 21). The dark red areas have the highest variation in rainfall from year to year while those in green have the lowest. You can see that in the drier areas, rainfall varies a lot more than in areas where total precipitation is more abundant. Think about agriculture and how difficult it might be to farm in those drier places, where even a little less rain in one year might cost farmers their entire harvest.

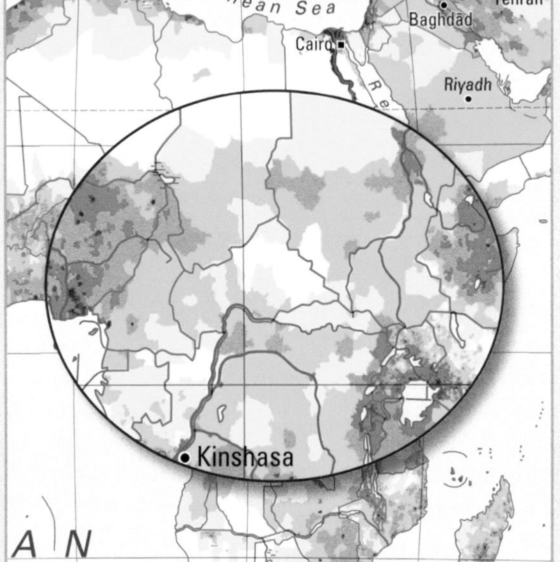

Compare the climate map excerpt to the excerpt of the "Africa: **Environments**" map (p. 170). The pink areas on the environment map are "grasslands," and the dark green areas are "evergreen broadleaf forests," which means tropical rainforests. You can see that tropical rainforests generally coincide with an "Ar" climate and grasslands with a "BS" climate.

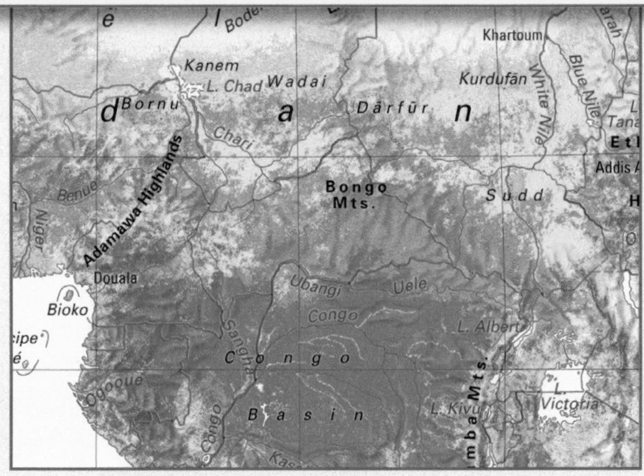

Look at the excerpt from the "World: **Population Density**" map (p. 40–41), on which population density is higher where the shading is darker. Now look at the same area on the **climate** map and note the influence climate on population density, which declines drastically the closer you get to the driest areas, where rainfall becomes so sparse that farming is impossible without irrigation. Now look at the **precipitation variability** map and consider that yearly rainfall becomes less reliable in drier climates. Even so, there is no direct correlation between climate and population density. Look at population densities in the "Aw" climate belt, which includes dense population clusters in the center left part of the map and sparse populations in the center. The **environments** map offers a possible explanation: near its center are the Bongo Mountains, which probably make this area less suitable for agriculture.

Social and Economic Issues

The map comparisons on this page deal with social and economic issues in Africa and Europe.

Let's start with an excerpt from the "World: **Natural Population Development**" map (p. 43). Look at the circles: dark green represents the highest population growth, lighter shades of green show growth rates ranging from high to low, yellow reflects stagnation, and orange indicates decline. You can see that Africa has very high population growth, while most of Europe has stagnation and decline.

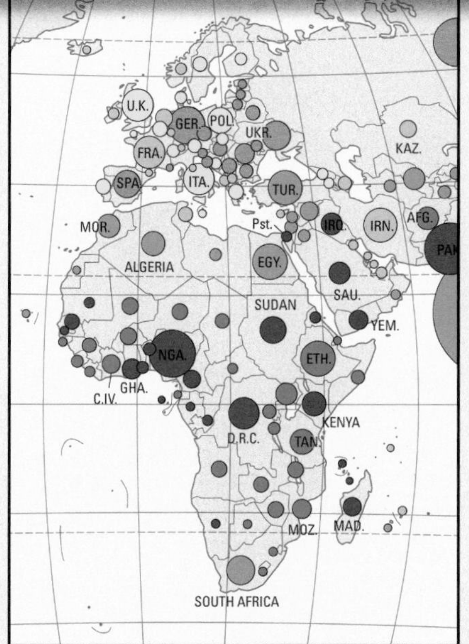

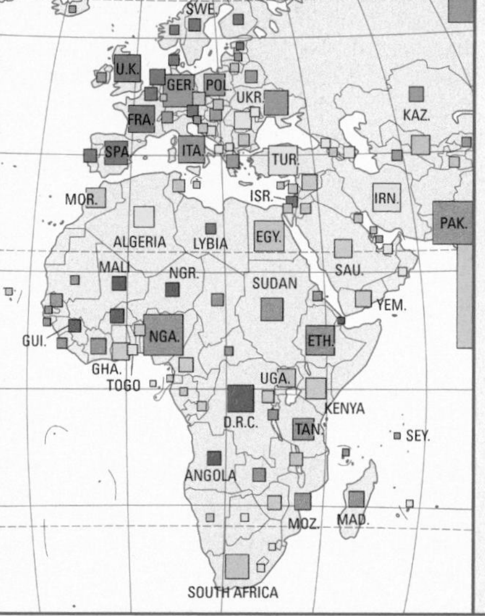

Compare the population growth map excerpt with the "World: **Gross Domestic Product**" map (p. 45) excerpt. Orange and red represents very low yearly per capita GDP (US$ 2,500 or less) while green signifies high yearly per capita GDP's (US$ 20,000 or more). Countries with high population growth have also very low GDP while those with stagnating or declining populations have high GDP. There is clearly a relationship here, but we don't know if one causes the other. Does high population growth put a great strain on the economy, or do poor people have more children to help make ends meet and provide for the parents in their old age? In what kind of economies are children an important source of labor? Map comparison helps you formulate new questions for further inquiry.

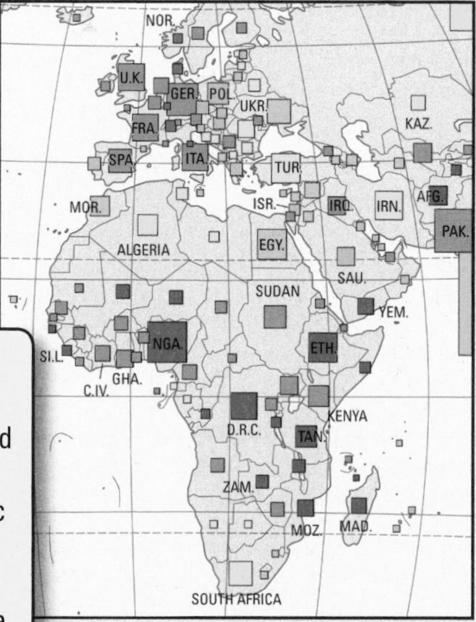

The excerpt from the map "World: **Health**"(p. 47) shows infant mortality rates – the orange and red shades indicate that at least 1 in 10 babies die in their first year of life – and the availability of physicians – the circles with a white background mean there are less than 2 physicians for every 10,000 people. Note how countries with high infant mortality rates and few physicians are also those with low **education**, low **Gross Domestic Product**, and high **population growth**.

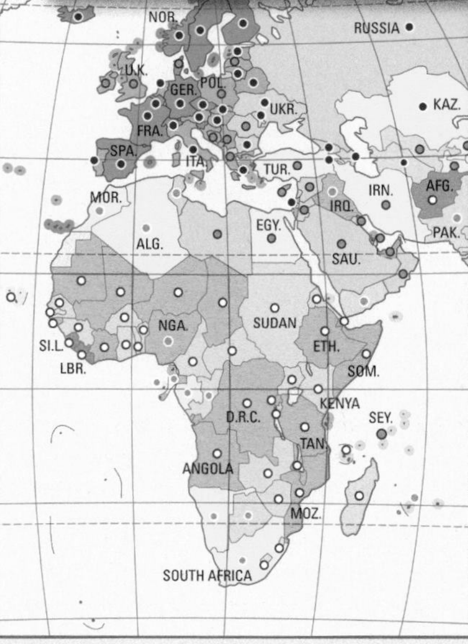

Look at the excerpt from the map "World: **Education**"(p. 44). Green indicates that at least 80 % of the population is enrolled in schools, while red indicates that less than 30 % of the population attends school. Look at the Democratic Republic of the Congo (D.R.C.), which has a very low educational level. The maps of population development and Gross Domestic Product show that the D.R.C. has not only the lowest education level on the continent but also the highest population growth and the lowest GDP. Many countries in Africa have similar socio-economic conditions. Think about the challenges for development. Do low levels of education also mean that people have little knowledge about family planning? What is the link between **education**, **health**, and **population growth**?

We hope that our remarks on the preceding pages have made you eager to explore the wealth of information in the *Perthes World Atlas*.

Guntram H. Herb, David H. Kaplan & Mark Monmonier

Countries

A. & B.	Antigua and Barbuda
AFG.	Afghanistan
AGO.	Angola
ALB.	Albania
ALG.	Algeria
AND.	Andorra
ARG.	Argentina
ARM.	Armenia
AUS.	Australia
AUT.	Austria
AZE.	Azerbaijan
BBD.	Barbados
BDI.	Burundi
BEN.	Benin
B.FS.	Burkina Faso
BGD.	Bangladesh
BGM.	Belgium
B. & H.	Bosnia and Herzegovina
BHM.	Bahamas
BHR.	Bahrain
BHU.	Bhutan
BLR.	Belarus
BLZ.	Belize
BOL.	Bolivia
BOT.	Botswana
BRA.	Brazil
BRU.	Brunei
BUL.	Bulgaria
CAN.	Canada
C.A.R.	Central African Republic
CBD.	Cambodia
CHD.	Chad
CHL.	Chile
CHN.	China
C.IV.	Côte d'Ivoire
CMN.	Cameroon
COL.	Colombia
COM.	Comoros
CON.	Congo
C.RC.	Costa Rica
CRO.	Croatia
CUB.	Cuba
C.VD.	Cape Verde
CYP.	Cyprus
CZ.R.	Czech Republic
DCA.	Dominica
DEN.	Denmark
DJI.	Djibouti
DO.R.	Dominican Republic
D.R.C.	Congo, Democratic Republic of the
ECU.	Ecuador
EGY.	Egypt
EQ.G.	Equatorial Guinea
ERI.	Eritrea
EST.	Estonia
ETH.	Ethiopia
FIN.	Finland
FJI.	Fiji
FRA.	France
GAB.	Gabon
GAM.	Gambia
GCE.	Greece
GEO.	Georgia
GER.	Germany
GHA.	Ghana
GRA.	Grenada
GUA.	Guatemala
GU.B.	Guinea-Bissau
GUI.	Guinea
GUY.	Guyana
HON.	Honduras
HTI.	Haiti
HUN.	Hungary
ICE.	Iceland
IDN.	Indonesia
IND.	India
IRE.	Ireland
IRN.	Iran
IRQ.	Iraq
ISR.	Israel
ITA.	Italy
JAM.	Jamaica
JAP.	Japan
JOR.	Jordan
KAZ.	Kazakhstan
KEN.	Kenya
KIR.	Kiribati
KUW.	Kuwait
KYR.	Kyrgyzstan
LAO.	Laos
LAT.	Latvia
LBR.	Liberia
LBY.	Libya
LEB.	Lebanon
LES.	Lesotho
LIE.	Liechtenstein
LIT.	Lithuania
LUX.	Luxembourg
MAC.	Macedonia, The Former Yugoslav Republic of
MAD.	Madagascar
MA.I.	Marshall Islands
MCO.	Monaco
MDV.	Maldives
MEX.	Mexico
MIC.	Micronesia
MLI.	Mali
MLT.	Malta
MLY.	Malaysia
MNG.	Mongolia
MOL.	Moldova
MOR.	Morocco
MOZ.	Mozambique
MRS.	Mauritius
MRT.	Mauritania
MWI.	Malawi
MYA.	Myanmar
NAM.	Namibia
NAU.	Nauru
NEP.	Nepal
NGA.	Nigeria
NGR.	Niger
NIC.	Nicaragua
N.KO.	Korea, North
NLD.	Netherlands
NOR.	Norway
N.Z.	New Zealand
OMN.	Oman
PAK.	Pakistan
PAL.	Palau
PAN.	Panama
PAR.	Paraguay
PER.	Peru
PHI.	Philippines
P.N.G.	Papua New Guinea
POL.	Poland
POR.	Portugal
Pst.	Palestine
QAT.	Qatar
ROM.	Romania
RUS.	Russia
RWA.	Rwanda
S.AF.	South Africa
SAL.	El Salvador
SAM.	Samoa
SAU.	Saudi Arabia
SEN.	Senegal
SEY.	Seychelles
SGP.	Singapore
SI.L.	Sierra Leone
S.KO.	Korea, South
S. & M.	Serbia and Montenegro
S.MA.	San Marino
SO.I.	Solomon Islands
SOM.	Somalia
SPA.	Spain
SR.L.	Sri Lanka
ST.K.	Saint Kitts and Nevis
ST.L.	Saint Lucia
S.TO.	Sao Tome and Principe
ST.V.	Saint Vincent and the Grenadines
SUD.	Sudan
SUR.	Suriname
SVK.	Slovakia
SVN.	Slovenia
SWA.	Swaziland
SWE.	Sweden
SWI.	Switzerland
SYR.	Syria
TAI.	Taiwan
TAJ.	Tajikistan
TAN.	Tanzania
TGO.	Togo
THL.	Thailand
TI.L.	Timor-Leste
TKM.	Turkmenistan
TON.	Tonga
T. & T.	Trinidad and Tobago
TUN.	Tunisia
TUR.	Turkey
TUV.	Tuvalu
U.A.E.	United Arab Emirates
UGA.	Uganda
U.K.	United Kingdom
UKR.	Ukraine
URU.	Uruguay
U.S.	United States
UZB.	Uzbekistan
VAN.	Vanuatu
VAT.	Vatican City
VEN.	Venezuela
VTN.	Vietnam
W.SA.	Western Sahara
YEM.	Yemen
ZAM.	Zambia
ZIM.	Zimbabwe

Organizations, Institutions, Technical Terms

AETFAT	Association pour l'Etude Taxonomique de la Flore De l'Afrique Tropicale
AIDS	Acquired Immunodeficiency Syndrome
ANZUS	Australia-New Zealand-United States Security Treaty
ASEAN	Association of Southeast Asian Nations
AU	African Union
BGR	Bundesanstalt für Geowissenschaften und Rohstoffe
CIA	Central Intelligence Agency
CIAT	Centro Internacional de Agricultura Tropical
CIESIN	Center for International Earth Science Information Network
CIS	Commonwealth of Independent States
CRED	Center for Research on the Epidemiology of Disasters
DAC	Development Assistance Committee
DAI	Digital Access Index
DWD	Deutscher Wetterdienst
ECOWAS	Economic Community of West African States
EROS	Earth Resources Observation and Science
EU	European Union
FAO	Food and Agriculture Organization of the United Nations
FSC	Forest Stewardship Council
GDP	Gross Domestic Product
GHG	Green House Gasses
GMT	Greenwich Mean Time
GNI	Gross National Income
GWP	Gridded Population of the World
G8	Group of Eight
HDI	Human Development Index
HIIK	Heidelberger Institut für Internationale Konfliktforschung
HIPC	Heavily Indebted Poor Countries
HIV	Human Immunodeficiency Virus
IGBP	International Geosphere-Biosphere Programme
ILO	International Labour Organization
IMF	International Monetary Fund
IPCC	Intergovernmental Panel on Climate Change
ISIC	International Standard Industrial Classification
ITC	Information and Communications Technology
ITU	International Telecommunication Union
IUCN	International Union for Conservation of Nature and Natural Resources
LAS	League of Arab States
MERCOSUR	Mercado Común del Cono Sur
MET	Middle European Standard Time
MEWT	Middle European Winter Time
MHT	Major Habitat Type
MPI	Migration Policy Institute
NAFTA	North American Free Trade Agreement
NATO	North Atlantic Treaty Organization
NRCS	Natural Resources Conservation Service
NZST	New Zealand Standard Time
OA	Official Aid
OAS	Organization of American States
OCHA	United Nations Office for the Coordination of Humanitarian Affairs
ODA	Official Development Assistance
OECD	Organisation for Economic Co-operation and Development
OPEC	Organization of Petroleum Exporting Countries
PIK	Potsdam-Institut für Klimafolgenforschung
PPP	Purchasing Power Parity
PRB	Population Reference Bureau
PRIO	[International] Peace Research Institute, Oslo
SADC	Southern African Development Community
UN	United Nations
UNAIDS	Joint United Nations Programme on HIV/AIDS
UNCTAD	United Nations Conference on Trade and Development
UNDP	United Nations Development Programme
UNEP	United Nations Environment Programme
UNESCO	United Nations Educational, Scientific and Cultural Organization
UNFCCC	United Nations Framework Convention on Climate Change
UNHCR	United Nations High Commissioner for Refugees
UNPD	United Nations Population Division
UNSO	United Nations Sahelian Office
UNWTO	United Nations World Tourism Organization
USDA	United States Department of Agriculture
USGS	United States Geological Survey
UTC	Coordinated Universal Time
WCMC	World Conservation Monitoring Centre
WEC	World Energy Council
WET	Western European Time
WHO	World Health Organization
WMO	World Meteorological Organization
WTO	World Trade Organization
WWF	World Wildlife Fund

Geographical Terms

A.R.	Autonomous Region
Arch.	Archipelago
C.	Cape
C.	City
Cd.	Ciudad
Co.	Cerro
Cr.	Creek
Depr.	Depression
-fj.	-fjorden
G.	Gulf
I.	Island
Is.	Islands
Ind. Res.	Indian Reservation (in U.S.) Indian Reserve (in CAN.)
J.	Jabal
L.	Lake
La.	Laguna
M.	Monte
Mt.	Mont
Mt.	Mount
Mte.	Monte
Mtn.	Mountain
Mts.	Monts
Mts.	Mountains
N.	North
N. P.	National Park
Nat. Mon.	National Monument
Nat. P.	National Park, National Parc
P.	Pico
P.N.	Parque Nacional
Pen.	Peninsula
Pen.	Península
Pk.	Peak
Pt.	Point
Pta.	Punta
R.	Ra's
R.	Rio
R.	Río
R.	River
Ra.	Range
Rep.	Republic
Res.	Reservoir
Rés.	Réservoir
S.	San, Santa, Santo
S.	São
S.	South
Sa.	Serra
Sa.	Sierra
Sd.	Sound
St.	Saint
St	Saint
Sta.	Santa
Str.	Strait

Foreign Geographical Terms

Adrar (Arabic)	Mountain, Mountains
-älv, -en (Swedish)	River
Bahía (Spanish)	Bay
Baía (Portuguese)	Bay
Baie (French)	Bay
Ben (Scottish)	Mountain
Bereg (Russian)	Coast
Bumu (Turkish)	Cape
Cabo (Portuguese, Spanish)	Cape
Cap (French)	Cape
Cerro (Spanish)	Mountain
Ciudad (Spanish)	Town
Cordillera (Spanish)	Cordillera
Costa (Spanish)	Coast
Côte (French)	Coast
Dag (Turkic languages)	Mountain, Mountains
Dağ, -ı (Turkish)	Mountain, Mountains
Dāgh (Turkic languages)	Mountains
Dağlar, -ı (Turkish)	Mountain, Mountains
Dasht (Farsi)	Desert
Détroit (French)	Strait
Erg [ʿIrq] (Arabic)	Desert
Firth (Scottish)	Bay
-fjörður (Icelandic)	Fjord
Gol (Mongolian)	River
Golfo (Spanish, Italian)	Gulf
Guba (Russian)	Bay
Hamadah (Arabic)	Stony desert
He (Chinese)	River
Hu (Chinese)	Lake
Île, -s (French)	Island, -s
Isla, -s (Spanish)	Island, -s
Jabal (Arabic)	Mountain, Mountains
-järv (Estonian)	Lake
-järvi (Finnish)	Lake
Jiang (Chinese)	River
-joki (Finnish)	River
-jökull (Icelandic)	Glacier
Kamen' (Russian)	Mountain
Kūh (Farsi)	Mountain, Mountains
Lac (French)	Lake
Lagoa (Portuguese)	Lagoon
Laguna (Spanish)	Lagoon
Loch (Scottish)	Lake
Lough (Irish)	Lake
-maa (Estonian, Finnish)	Land
Mar (Italian, Portuguese, Spanish)	Sea
-meer (Dutch)	Lake
Mont (French)	Mountain
Monte (Italian, Portuguese, Spanish)	Mountain
Monts (French)	Mountains
Munţii (Romanian)	Mountains
Nahr (Arabic, Urdu)	River, Canal
-nes (Icelandic)	Cape
Nos (Bulgarian, Russian)	Cape
Nosy (Madagascan)	Island
Nur, Nuur (Mongolian)	Lake
Nuruu (Mongolian)	Mountains
-ö (Swedish)	Island
Ostrow, -a (Russian)	Island, -s
-oy, -a (Norwegian)	Island
Ozero (Russian)	Lake
-pan (African)	Salt pan
Parque Nacional (Spanish)	National Park
Pendi (Chinese)	Plain
Pico (Spanish, Portuguese)	Mountain
Pik (Russian)	Mountain
Playa (Spanish)	Beach
Pointe (French)	Cape
Ponta (Portuguese)	Cape
Porto (Italian, Portuguese)	Harbor, Port
Presa (Spanish)	Reservoir
Puerto (Spanish)	Harbor, Port
Punta (Spanish, Italian)	Cape
Puntan (Chamorro)	Cape
Ra's (Arabic)	Cape
Recife (Portuguese, Spanish)	Reef
Réservoire (French)	Reservoir
Rio (Portuguese)	River
Río (Spanish)	River
Rivière (French)	River
Rt (Croatian)	Cape
Sabkhat (Arabic)	Salt flat
Salar (Spanish)	Salt flat
Salina (Spanish)	Salt flat
San (Japanese, Korean)	Mountain
Serra (Portuguese)	Mountain range
Shan (Chinese)	Mountain, Mountains
Sierra (Spanish)	Mountain range
-sjøn (Norwegian)	Lake
-sjön (Swedish)	Lake
Sopka (Russian)	Volcano
Shuţţ (Arabic)	Salt flat
Serranía (Spanish)	Mountain range
Tall (Arabic)	Hill
-tind (Norwegian)	Peak
-van (Swedish)	Lake
-vatn (Icelandic, Norwegian)	Lake
-vesi (Finnish)	Lake
Vila (Portuguese)	Settlement
Villa (Spanish)	Settlement

General Legend

Hydrographic Features

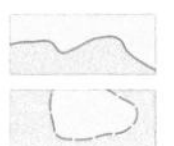
Shoreline
Undefined or fluctuating shorline
River, stream

Seasonal river, intermittent river, wadi

Wadi

Canal
Lake, reservoir

Intermittent lake, reservoir

Dry lake bed
Swamp, marsh
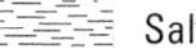
Salt flat

Physical Features

Elevation

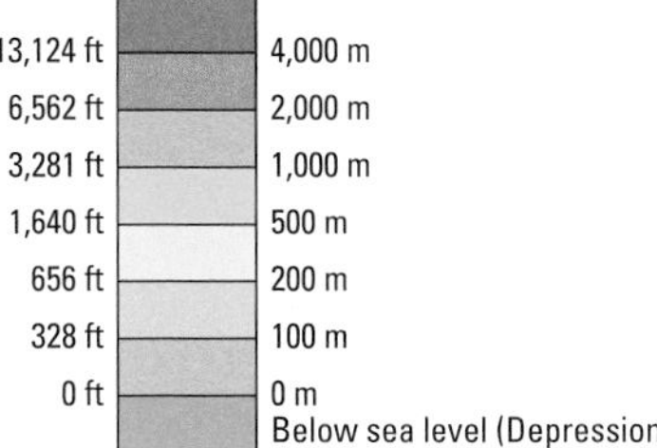

Water Depth

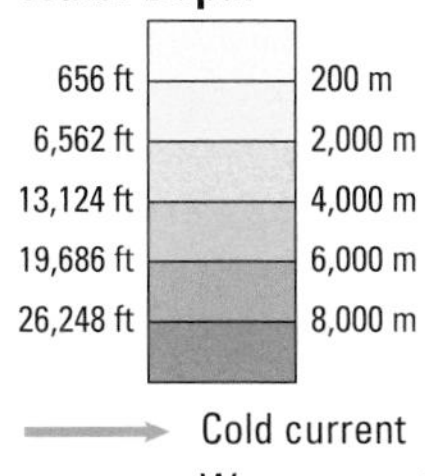

Inland ice, glaciers
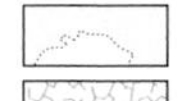
Ice shelf

Pack ice
Limit of drift ice
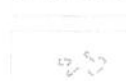
Reef
Elevation above sea level
Elevation below sea level

Political and other Boundaries

Reference Maps

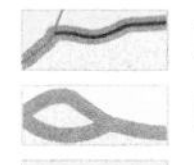
International boundary
Disputed / undefined boundary
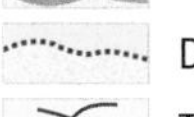
Demarcation line
Territorial limit of a country on water
Internal boundary

Physical and Thematic Maps

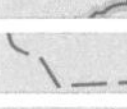
International boundary
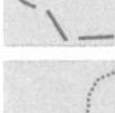
Disputed / undefined boundary
Demarcation line
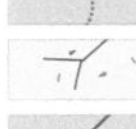
Territorial limit of a country on water
Internal boundary

Boundary of national park
Boundary of indian reservation, indian reserve

Settlements

Political Maps ≥ 1:20,000,000

NEW YORK	more than 1,000,000 inhabitants
Boston	500,000 – 1,000,000 inhabitants
Regina	100,000 – 500,000 inhabitants
Bismarck	50,000 – 100,000 inhabitants
Key West	10,000 – 50,000 inhabitants
Belmopan	fewer than 10,000 inhabitants

Urban agglomeration
(only in maps 1:5,000,000 and 1:15;000,000)

Political Maps ≤ 1:25,000,000

more than 1,000,000 inhabitants
500,000 – 1,000,000 inhabitants
100,000 – 500,000 inhabitants
fewer than 100,000 inhabitants

Archaelogical/historical site

Physical Maps and Thematic Maps

Without classification

Transportation

Expressway, superhighway
Major road
Major railway
Minor railway
Railway tunnel
Ferry

International airport
Major port

Place Names

Regions

MEXICO	Country
Réunion (FRA.)	Dependent territory and mother country
Nevada	Federal state, province
Cocos I. (C.RC.)	Territory and mainland

Settlements

Ottawa	National capital
Cayenne	Capital city of dependent territory or secondary capital
NEW YORK Boston Regina Portland Key West Belmopan	Other Settlements

Physical Features

Andes	Moutains, range
Llano Estacado	Landscape
Sicily	Island
Cape Sable	Cape, headland
Mt. Rainier	Mountain peak, volcano, pass
14,410 ft 4,392 m	Elevation above sea level, mountain height (in feet and meters)
579 ft 176 m	Lake surface elevation (in feet and meters)
14,357 ft 4,376 m	Water depth (in feet and meters)

ATLANTIC OCEAN / Caribbean Sea / Gulf of Maine / Lake Michigan/Seminole Res.	Water bodies
Colorado	River
Lake Eyre	Salt flat

Other Features

Gulf Stream	Current
Yellowstone Nat. Park	National park
North. Cheyenne Ind. Res.	Indian reservation, Indian reserve
Pergamon	Archaeological/histor. site

Measures

Linear, Square, and Cubic Measures

1 inch (in.)	= 25.4 mm	1 mm	= 0.03937 inch
1 foot (ft)	= 0.30479 m	1 m	= 3.28095 feet
1 cubic foot	≈ 0.0283 m^3	1 m^3	≈ 35.3182 cubic feet
1 mile (mi)	≈ 1.6093 km	1 km	≈ 0.6214 mile
1 square mile	≈ 2.5898 km^2	1 km^2	≈ 0.3861 square mile
1 cubic mile	≈ 4.1678 km^3	1 km^3	≈ 0.2399 cubic mile

1,000 m
900 m – 3,000 feet
800 m
700 m – 2,500 feet
600 m – 2,000 feet
500 m
400 m – 1,500 feet
300 m – 1,000 feet
200 m
100 m – 500 feet
0 m – 0 foot

Other Measures

Temperature (T):

$T_{Celsius} = (T_{Fahrenheit} - 32) / 1.8$

$T_{Fahrenheit} = (T_{Celsius} \cdot 1.8) + 32$

Speed:

1 km/h ≈ 0.6214 miles per hour/mph

1 mph ≈ 1.6093 km/h

KLETT-PERTHES

A 160° B 140° C 120° D 100° E 80° F 60° G 40° H 20° J
A R C T I C O
Greenland
70°N
66°30'N
Largest island
836,326 sq mi/2,166,086 km²
A T L A N T I C
36,300,000 sq mi/94,000,000 km²
Mauna Kea
Highest mountain
31,800 ft/9,700 m
(from ocean floor to summit)
P A C I F I C
69,884,100 sq mi/181,000,000 km²
Amazon
River with the largest drainage basin
2,669,000 sq mi/6,915,000 km²
River with the largest volume of water
6,180,000 cu ft/174,900 m³
O C E A N
O C E A N
67°16'W
Total area 197,090,000 sq mi/510,467,000 km²
Land area 57,322,000 sq mi/148,467,000 km²
Water area 139,757,500 sq mi/362,000,000 km²
Population 6,697,312,000
Countries 198

The World

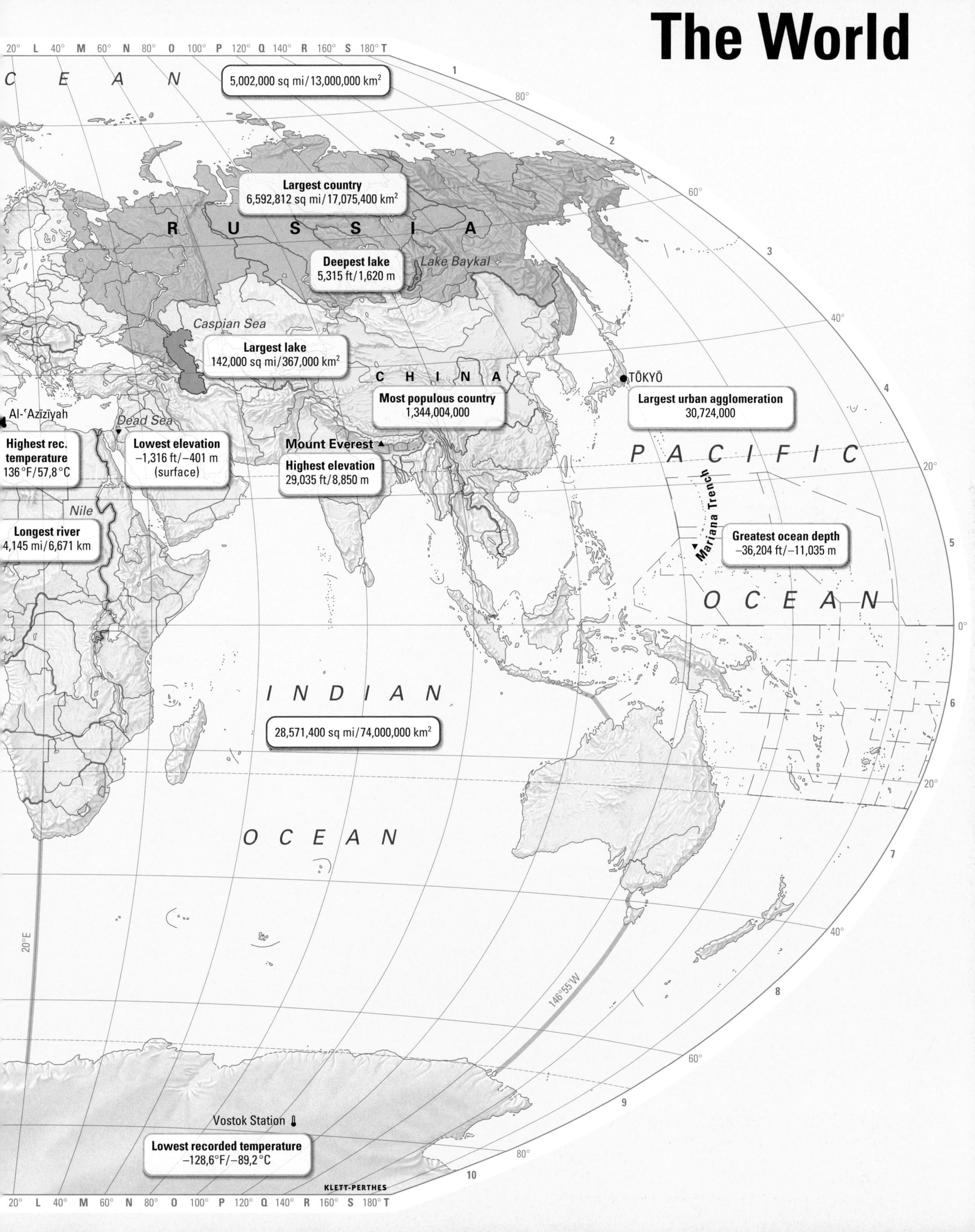
20° L 40° M 60° N 80° O 100° P 120° Q 140° R 160° S 180° T
C E A N
5,002,000 sq mi/13,000,000 km²
80°
1
2
Largest country
6,592,812 sq mi/17,075,400 km²
R U S S I A
60°
Deepest lake
5,315 ft/1,620 m
Lake Baykal
3
Caspian Sea
40°
Largest lake
142,000 sq mi/367,000 km²
C H I N A
TŌKYŌ
4
Most populous country
1,344,004,000
Largest urban agglomeration
30,724,000
Al-ʿAzīzīyah
Dead Sea
Highest rec. temperature
136°F/57,8°C
Lowest elevation
–1,316 ft/–401 m
(surface)
Mount Everest
Highest elevation
29,035 ft/8,850 m
P A C I F I C
20°
Mariana Trench
Nile
Longest river
4,145 mi/6,671 km
Greatest ocean depth
–36,204 ft/–11,035 m
5
O C E A N
0°
I N D I A N
6
28,571,400 sq mi/74,000,000 km²
20°
O C E A N
7
40°
20°E
146°55'W
8
60°
9
Vostok Station
Lowest recorded temperature
–128,6°F/–89,2°C
80°
10
KLETT-PERTHES
20° L 40° M 60° N 80° O 100° P 120° Q 140° R 160° S 180° T

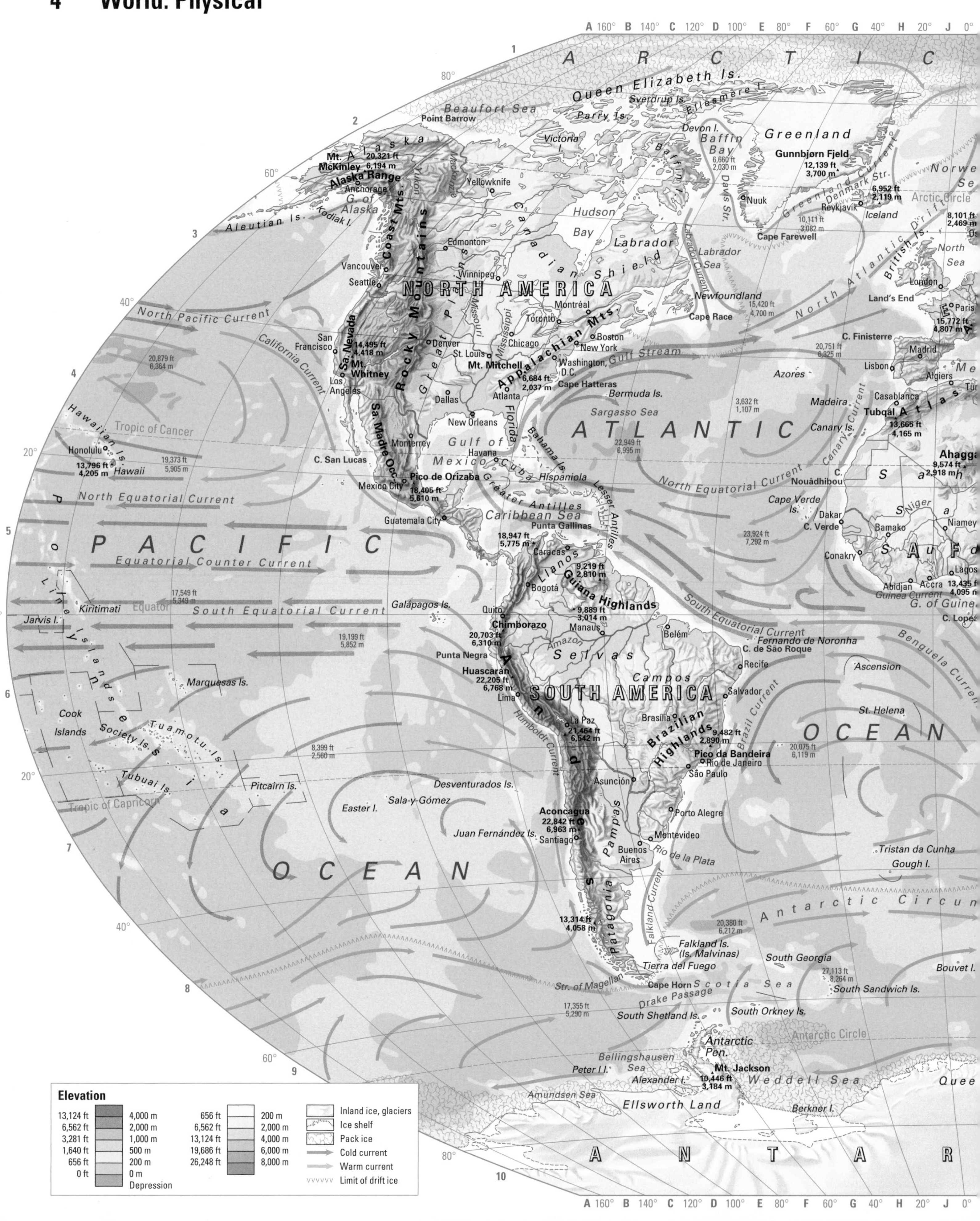
A 160° B 140° C 120° D 100° E 80° F 60° G 40° H 20° J 0°
A R C T I C
Queen Elizabeth Is.
Sverdrup Is.
Ellesmere I.
Parry Is.
Beaufort Sea
Point Barrow
Victoria I.
Devon I.
Baffin Bay
6,660 ft
2,030 m
Baffin I.
Greenland
Gunnbjørn Fjeld
12,139 ft
3,700 m
Alaska
Mt. McKinley
20,321 ft
6,194 m
Alaska Range
Anchorage
G. of Alaska
Kodiak I.
Aleutian Is.
Yukon
Mackenzie
Yellowknife
Coast Mts.
Davis Str.
Nuuk
Greenland Current
Denmark Str.
6,952 ft
2,119 m
Reykjavík
Iceland
Arctic Circle
Norwegian Sea
8,101 ft
2,469 m
Hudson Bay
Canadian Shield
Labrador
Labrador Current
Labrador Sea
Cape Farewell
10,111 ft
3,082 m
Edmonton
Vancouver
Seattle
Winnipeg
Rocky Mountains
Great Plains
NORTH AMERICA
Missouri
Mississippi
Montréal
Toronto
Boston
New York
Chicago
Appalachian Mts.
Newfoundland
Cape Race
15,420 ft
4,700 m
North Atlantic Drift
British Is.
North Sea
London
Land's End
Paris
15,772 ft
4,807 m
North Pacific Current
California Current
San Francisco
Sa. Nevada
14,495 ft
4,418 m
Mt. Whitney
Denver
St. Louis
Mt. Mitchell
6,684 ft
2,037 m
Washington, D.C.
Gulf Stream
Cape Hatteras
Atlanta
C. Finisterre
20,751 ft
6,325 m
Madrid
Lisbon
Algiers
Azores
20,879 ft
6,364 m
Los Angeles
Dallas
Bermuda Is.
3,632 ft
1,107 m
Madeira
Casablanca
Tubqal
13,665 ft
4,165 m
Atlas
Sargasso Sea
New Orleans
Florida
ATLANTIC
Canary Is.
Canary Current
Hawaiian Is.
Tropic of Cancer
Sa. Madre Occ.
Monterrey
Gulf of Mexico
Havana
Cuba
Bahama Is.
22,949 ft
6,995 m
Ahaggar
9,574 ft
2,918 m
Honolulu
13,796 ft
4,205 m
Hawaii
19,373 ft
5,905 m
C. San Lucas
Mexico City
Pico de Orizaba
18,405 ft
5,610 m
Greater Antilles
Hispaniola
Lesser Antilles
North Equatorial Current
C. Nouâdhibou
Cape Verde Is.
Dakar
C. Verde
Niger
Bamako
Niamey
North Equatorial Current
Caribbean Sea
Guatemala City
Punta Gallinas
18,947 ft
5,775 m
23,924 ft
7,292 m
P A C I F I C
Caracas
Llanos
9,219 ft
2,810 m
Conakry
Equatorial Counter Current
Guiana Highlands
Bogotá
Abidjan
Accra
13,435 ft
4,095 m
Lagos
Guinea Current
G. of Guinea
17,549 ft
5,349 m
Kiritimati
Equator
Galápagos Is.
Quito
9,889 ft
3,014 m
South Equatorial Current
Jarvis I.
South Equatorial Current
Chimborazo
20,703 ft
6,310 m
Manaus
Amazon
Belém
C. López
19,199 ft
5,852 m
Fernando de Noronha
C. de São Roque
Benguela Current
Line Islands
Punta Negra
Selvas
Recife
Ascension
Marquesas Is.
Huascarán
22,205 ft
6,768 m
Lima
Campos
SOUTH AMERICA
Salvador
Cook Islands
Society Is.
Tuamotu Is.
Polynesia
La Paz
21,464 ft
6,542 m
Andes
Brasília
Brazilian Highlands
9,482 ft
2,890 m
St. Helena
OCEAN
Humboldt Current
Brazil Current
8,399 ft
2,560 m
Pico da Bandeira
Rio de Janeiro
São Paulo
20,075 ft
6,119 m
Tubuai Is.
Pitcairn Is.
Desventurados Is.
Asunción
Tropic of Capricorn
Easter I.
Sala-y-Gómez
Aconcagua
22,842 ft
6,963 m
Pampas
Porto Alegre
Juan Fernández Is.
Santiago
Montevideo
Buenos Aires
Rio de la Plata
Tristan da Cunha
Gough I.
O C E A N
Patagonia
Falkland Current
Antarctic Circumpolar Current
13,314 ft
4,058 m
20,380 ft
6,212 m
Falkland Is. (Is. Malvinas)
South Georgia
Tierra del Fuego
27,113 ft
8,264 m
Bouvet I.
Str. of Magellan
Cape Horn
Scotia Sea
South Sandwich Is.
Drake Passage
17,355 ft
5,290 m
South Shetland Is.
South Orkney Is.
Antarctic Circle
Antarctic Pen.
Bellingshausen Sea
Peter I I.
Mt. Jackson
10,446 ft
3,184 m
Alexander I.
Weddell Sea
Amundsen Sea
Ellsworth Land
Berkner I.
A N T A R
80°
60°
40°
20°
0°
1
2
3
4
5
6
7
8
9
10
Elevation
13,124 ft
6,562 ft
3,281 ft
1,640 ft
656 ft
0 ft
4,000 m
2,000 m
1,000 m
500 m
200 m
0 m
Depression
656 ft
6,562 ft
13,124 ft
19,686 ft
26,248 ft
200 m
2,000 m
4,000 m
6,000 m
8,000 m
Inland ice, glaciers
Ice shelf
Pack ice
Cold current
Warm current
Limit of drift ice

O C E A N
Franz Josef Land
Severnaya Zemlya
C. Chelyuskin
New Siberian Is.
Laptev Sea
East Siberian Sea
Kara Sea
Novaya Zemlya
Barents Sea
North Cape
Taymyr Pen.
Central Siberian Plateau
Cherskiy Ra.
Norilsk
Yakutia
Yakutsk
West Siberian Plain
Narodnaya
Ural Mts.
St. Petersburg
Stockholm
Moscow
Nizhniy Novgorod
Yekaterinburg
Omsk
Novosibirsk
Sayan
Irkutsk
Baykal
Stanovoy Ra.
Sea of Okhotsk
Sakhalin
Kamchatka
Bering Sea
Klyuchevskaya Sopka
Aleutian Is.
Petropavlovsk-Kamchatskiy
Khabarovsk
Kurile Is.
Warsaw
Kiev
Samara
Volga
Carp. Mts.
Altay Mts.
Ulan Bator
Manchuria
Vladivostok
Hokkaido
North Pacific Current
Aral Sea
Caspian Sea
Ürümqi
Gobi
Shenyang
Sea of Japan
Honshu
Caucasus
Elbrus
Black Sea
Almaty
Tien Shan
Tashkent
Beijing
Korea
Tōkyō
Mt. Fuji
Ōsaka
Rome
Ankara
Anatolia
Elburz Mts.
Altun Shan
Kunlun Shan
Hindu Kush
Tehrān
Kābul
Iranian Plateau
Baghdād
Tibet
Mt. Everest
Himalayas
Lahore
Delhi
Xi'an
Yellow R.
Wuhan
Shanghai
Kyushu
Japan Current (Kuro Shio)
Midway Is.
Athens
Tripoli
Cairo
Libyan Desert
Nile
Red Sea
Arabian Pen.
Riyadh
Jeddah
Karachi
Ra's al-Hadd
Chongqing
Yangtze
Ryukyu Is.
Bonin Is.
PACIFIC
Volcano Is.
Guangzhou
Taiwan
Hong Kong
Hanoi
Kolkata
India
Mumbai
Hainan
Luzon
Wake I.
Mariana Is.
Tibesti
Chad
N'Djamena
Khartoum
Sanaa
Arabian Sea
Socotra
C. Guardafui
Ethiopian Highlands
Addis Ababa
Rangoon
Bay of Bengal
Chennai
Bangkok
South China Sea
Manila
Philippines
Marshall Islands
North Equatorial Current
Caroline Is.
Equatorial Counter Current
Micronesia
Vityaz Depth
Somali Pen.
Cape Comorin
Colombo
Ceylon
Mindanao
Kinabalu
Bangui
Yaoundé
Congo
Congo Basin
Mogadishu
L. Victoria
Nairobi
Kilimanjaro
North Equatorial Current
Maldives
Kuala Lumpur
Singapore
Sumatra
Borneo (Kalimantan)
Celebes (Sulawesi)
Melanesia
OCEAN
South Equatorial Current
Equator
Gilbert Is.
Bismarck Arch.
Phoenix Is.
Kinshasa
Dar es Salaam
Indian Counter Current
Seychelles
Chagos Is.
Greater Sunda Is.
Jakarta
Java
Surabaya
Lesser Sunda Is.
New Guinea
Carstensz Pyramid
Ellice Is.
Luanda
Cabo Delgado
Comoro Is.
INDIAN
Cocos Is.
C. York
Port Moresby
Solomon Is.
Tokelau Is.
Lusaka
Harare
Madagascar
Antananarivo
Mozambique Ch.
Mascarene Is.
South Equatorial Current
Coral Sea
New Hebrides
Wallis Is.
Futuna
Tonga Is.
Fiji Is.
Windhoek
Namib
North West Cape
Great Dividing Range
Johannesburg
Maputo
Drakensberg
AUSTRALIA
Great Victoria Desert
New Caledonia
Brisbane
Cape Town
Cape of Good Hope
Agulhas Current
OCEAN
Perth
Norfolk I.
Kermadec Is.
Amsterdam
Saint-Paul
Cape Leeuwin
Adelaide
Austr. Alps
Sydney
Mt. Kosciusko
Melbourne
Tasman Sea
North Island
Wellington
Polar Current
Crozet Is.
Prince Edward I.
(West Wind Drift)
Kerguelen Is.
Tasmania
South East C.
New Zealand
Mt. Cook
South Island
South West C.
Bounty Is.
Heard
Auckland Is.
Antipodes Is.
Macquarie
Campbell Is.
Maud Land
Wilkes Land
Balleny Is.
Scott I.
Ross Sea
Ross I.
Mt. Erebus
ANTARCTICA
KLETT-PERTHES
5,581 ft 1,701 m
6,217 ft 1,895 m
15,584 ft 4,750 m
35,761 ft 10,900 m
14,783 ft 4,506 m
8,711 ft 2,655 m
18,511 ft 5,642 m
−92 ft −28 m
24,591 ft 7,495 m
25,338 ft 7,723 m
12,388 ft 3,776 m
18,605 ft 5,671 m
33,011 ft 10,062 m
24,790 ft 7,556 m
1,316 ft −401 m
−436 ft −133 m
29,035 ft 8,850 m
12,966 ft 3,952 m
30,039 ft 9,156 m
9,777 ft 2,980 m
11,204 ft 3,415 m
10,076 ft 3,071 m
15,158 ft 4,620 m
12,336 ft 3,760 m
8,842 ft 2,695 m
36,204 ft 11,035 m
34,439 ft 10,497 m
8,281 ft 2,524 m
13,455 ft 4,101 m
19,107 ft 5,824 m
12,467 ft 3,800 m
16,024 ft 4,884 m
19,331 ft 5,892 m
12,060 ft 3,676 m
9,849 ft 3,002 m
9,436 ft 2,876 m
5,023 ft 1,531 m
11,424 ft 3,482 m
20,997 ft 6,400 m
3,319 ft 1,011 m
−39 ft −12 m
7,310 ft 2,228 m
18,605 ft 5,671 m
17,280 ft 5,267 m
9,177 ft 2,797 m
12,349 ft 3,764 m
20,505 ft 6,250 m
13,658 ft 4,163 m
12,447 ft 3,794 m
20° L 40° M 60° N 80° O 100° P 120° Q 140° R 160° S 180° T
80° 60° 40° 20° 0° 20° 40° 60° 80°
1 2 3 4 5 6 7 8 9 10

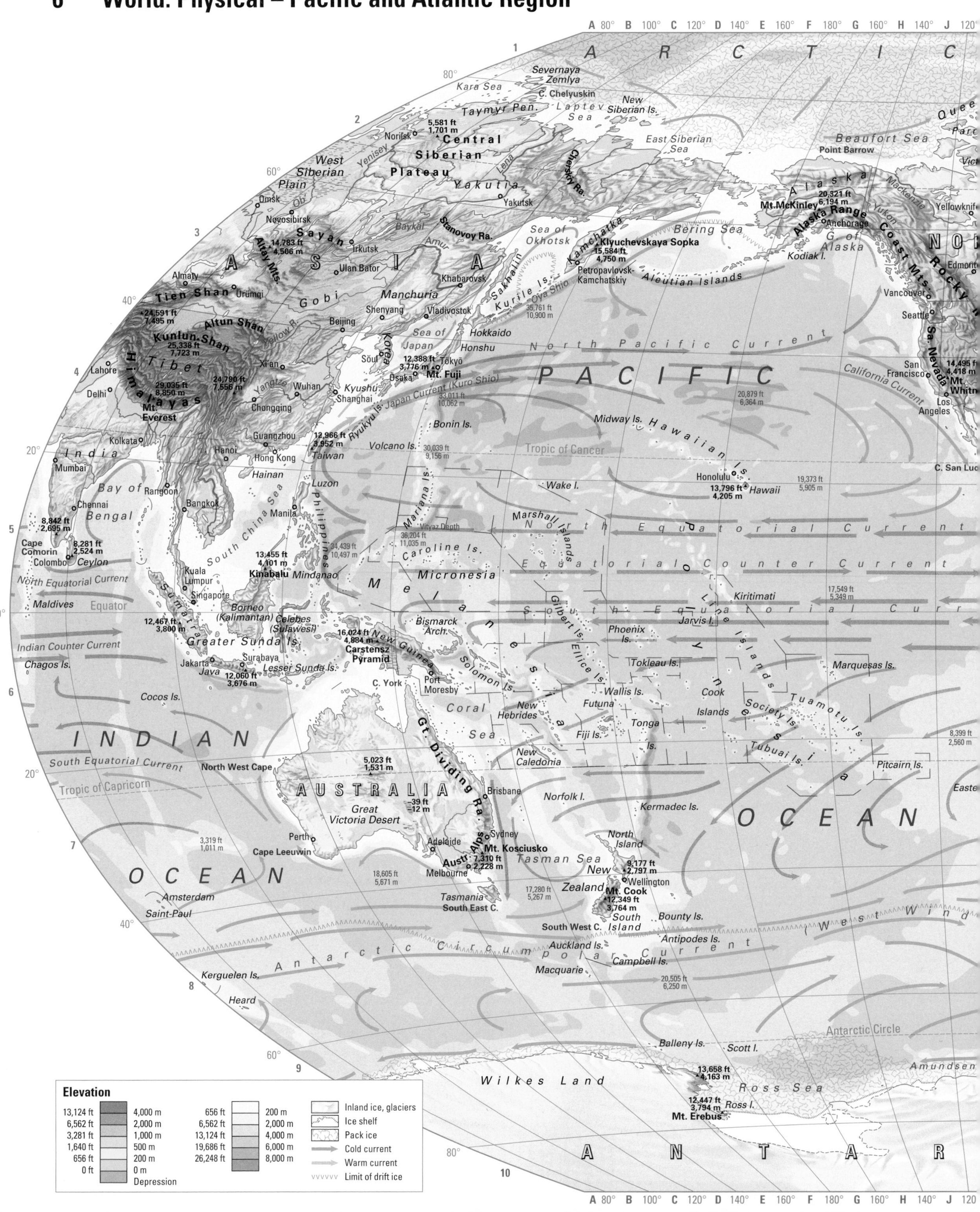
A 80° B 100° C 120° D 140° E 160° F 180° G 160° H 140° J 120°
A R C T I C
Severnaya Zemlya
Kara Sea
C. Chelyuskin
Laptev Sea
New Siberian Is.
Taymyr Pen.
5,581 ft 1,701 m
Noril'sk
Central Siberian Plateau
West Siberian Plain
Yenisey
Lena
East Siberian Sea
Beaufort Sea
Point Barrow
Chersky Ra.
Yakutia
Yakutsk
Omsk
Ob'
Novosibirsk
Sayan
14,783 ft 4,506 m
Altay Mts.
Irkutsk
Baykal
Stanovoy Ra.
Amur
Ulan Bator
Sea of Okhotsk
Kamchatka
Klyuchevskaya Sopka
15,584 ft 4,750 m
Petropavlovsk-Kamchatskiy
Bering Sea
Alaska
Mt.McKinley
20,321 ft 6,194 m
Alaska Range
Anchorage
Gulf of Alaska
Kodiak I.
Aleutian Islands
Mackenzie
Yukon
Yellowknife
Coast Mts.
Rocky
Edmonton
Vancouver
Seattle
A S I A
Almaty
Tien Shan
Ürümqi
Gobi
Khabarovsk
Manchuria
Sakhalin
Kurile Is.
Oya Shio
35,761 ft 10,900 m
Shenyang
Vladivostok
Beijing
24,591 ft 7,495 m
Altun Shan
Kunlun Shan
25,338 ft 7,723 m
Yellow R.
Korea
Sea of Japan
Hokkaido
Honshu
Tibet
Himalayas
Lahore
Delhi
29,035 ft 8,850 m
Mt Everest
24,790 ft 7,556 m
Xi'an
Sŏul
12,388 ft 3,776 m
Tōkyō
Ōsaka
Mt. Fuji
North Pacific Current
PACIFIC
Yangtze
Wuhan
Kyushu
Shanghai
Chongqing
Ryukyu Is.
Japan Current (Kuro Shio)
33,011 ft 10,062 m
20,879 ft 6,364 m
California Current
San Francisco
Sa. Nevada
14,495 ft 4,418 m
Mt. Whitney
Los Angeles
Bonin Is.
Midway Is.
Hawaiian Is.
Guangzhou
Kolkata
12,966 ft 3,952 m
Taiwan
Volcano Is.
30,039 ft 9,156 m
Tropic of Cancer
India
Mumbai
Hanoi
Hong Kong
Hainan
Luzon
Mariana Is.
Wake I.
Honolulu
13,796 ft 4,205 m
Hawaii
19,373 ft 5,905 m
C. San Lucas
Bay of Bengal
Rangoon
Chennai
Bangkok
Manila
South China Sea
Philippines
Marshall Islands
8,842 ft 2,695 m
Cape Comorin
Colombo
8,281 ft 2,524 m
Ceylon
Vityaz Depth
36,204 ft 11,035 m
34,439 ft 10,497 m
North Equatorial Current
Caroline Is.
13,455 ft 4,101 m
Kinabalu
Kuala Lumpur
Mindanao
Equatorial Counter Current
Micronesia
Singapore
Sumatra
Maldives
Equator
Borneo (Kalimantan)
Celebes (Sulawesi)
Melanesia
Polynesia
Line Islands
Kiritimati
17,549 ft 5,349 m
South Equatorial Current
Jarvis I.
Gilbert Is.
Bismarck Arch.
Phoenix Is.
Ellice Is.
12,467 ft 3,800 m
Greater Sunda Is.
16,024 ft 4,884 m
New Guinea
Carstensz Pyramid
Indian Counter Current
Chagos Is.
Jakarta
Surabaya
Java
Lesser Sunda Is.
12,060 ft 3,676 m
Solomon Is.
Tokelau Is.
Marquesas Is.
C. York
Port Moresby
Wallis Is.
Futuna
Cook Islands
Society Is.
Tuamotu Is.
Cocos Is.
Coral Sea
New Hebrides
Fiji Is.
Tonga Is.
8,399 ft 2,560 m
INDIAN
South Equatorial Current
North West Cape
5,023 ft 1,531 m
Gt. Dividing Ra.
New Caledonia
Tubuai Is.
Pitcairn Is.
Tropic of Capricorn
AUSTRALIA
-39 ft -12 m
Brisbane
Norfolk I.
Kermadec Is.
Great Victoria Desert
OCEAN
Perth
Sydney
3,319 ft 1,011 m
Cape Leeuwin
Adelaide
Mt. Kosciusko
Aust. Alps
7,310 ft 2,228 m
Melbourne
North Island
Tasman Sea
9,177 ft 2,797 m
Wellington
New Zealand
Mt. Cook
12,349 ft 3,764 m
OCEAN
18,605 ft 5,671 m
17,280 ft 5,267 m
Amsterdam
Saint-Paul
Tasmania
South East C.
South Island
South West C.
Bounty Is.
Antipodes Is.
Auckland Is.
West Wind Drift
Antarctic Circumpolar Current
Campbell Is.
Macquarie
Kerguelen Is.
20,505 ft 6,250 m
Heard
Antarctic Circle
Balleny Is.
Scott I.
Amundsen
Wilkes Land
13,658 ft 4,163 m
Ross Sea
12,447 ft 3,794 m
Ross I.
Mt. Erebus
ANTAR
Elevation
13,124 ft 4,000 m
6,562 ft 2,000 m
3,281 ft 1,000 m
1,640 ft 500 m
656 ft 200 m
0 ft 0 m
Depression
656 ft 200 m
6,562 ft 2,000 m
13,124 ft 4,000 m
19,686 ft 6,000 m
26,248 ft 8,000 m
Inland ice, glaciers
Ice shelf
Pack ice
Cold current
Warm current
Limit of drift ice

O C E A N
Franz Josef Land
Spitsbergen
5,617 ft
1,712 m
Novaya Zemlya
Kara Sea
Barents Sea
North Cape
Greenland
Gunnbjørn Fjeld
12,139 ft
3,700 m
Baffin Bay
Ellesmere I.
Devon I.
Sverdrup Is.
Elizabeth Is.
Norwegian Sea
Arctic Circle
Denmark Str.
Greenland Current
6,952 ft
2,119 m
Iceland
Reykjavík
Nuuk
Davis Str.
Hudson Bay
Labrador
Labrador Sea
Labrador Current
Cape Farewell
Canadian Shield
Winnipeg
AMERICA
New-foundland
Cape Race
Montréal
Toronto
Boston
New York
Chicago
Denver
St. Louis
Washington
Mt. Mitchell
6,684 ft
2,037 m
Appalachian Mts.
Cape Hatteras
Atlanta
Dallas
New Orleans
Florida
Gulf of Mexico
Monterrey
Havana
Cuba
Mexico City
Pico de Orizaba
18,405 ft
5,610 m
Guatemala City
Bahama Is.
Hispaniola
Greater Antilles
Lesser Antilles
Caribbean Sea
Punta Gallinas
Caracas
18,947 ft
5,775 m
Gulf Stream
Bermuda Is.
Sargasso Sea
ATLANTIC
North Atlantic Drift
North Equatorial Current
British Is.
Azores
Madeira
Canary Is.
Canary Current
Cape Verde Is.
C. Nouâdhibou
Dakar
C. Verde
8,101 ft
2,469 m
Scandinavia
Oslo
Stockholm
St. Petersburg
Moscow
Nizhniy Novgorod
Yekaterinburg
Samara
Ural Mts.
6,217 ft
1,895 m
Narodnaya
Ob
North Sea
London
Land's End
Berlin
Warsaw
Kiev
Paris
EUROPE
Alps
15,772 ft
4,807 m
Carp. Mts.
8,711 ft
2,655 m
Rome
Madrid
Lisbon
C. Finisterre
Algiers
Tunis
Mediterranean Sea
Athens
Ankara
Anatolia
Black Sea
Caucasus
18,511 ft
5,642 m
Elbrus
Volga
Caspian Sea
-92 ft
-28 m
Aral Sea
Tashkent
Elburz Mts.
Tehran
18,605 ft
5,671 m
Kabul
Iranian Plateau
Baghdad
Casablanca
Atlas
Tubqal
13,665 ft
4,165 m
Tripoli
Cairo
-1,316 ft
-401 m
-436 ft
-133 m
Libyan Desert
Nile
Red Sea
Arabian Pen.
Riyadh
Jeddah
Karachi
9,777 ft
2,980 m
Ra's al-Hadd
Arabian Sea
Ahaggar
9,574 ft
2,918 m
Sahara
Tibesti
11,204 ft
3,415 m
Niger
Niamey
Bamako
Conakry
L. Chad
N'Djamena
Khartoum
10,076 ft
3,071 m
Sanaa
12,336 ft
3,760 m
15,158 ft
4,620 m
Ethiopian Highlands
Addis Ababa
Socotra
C. Guardafui
AFRICA
Abidjan
Accra
Lagos
13,435 ft
4,095 m
Yaoundé
Bangui
Guinea Current
G. of Guinea
C. Lopez
Congo
Congo Basin
Kinshasa
L. Victoria
Nairobi
Kilimanjaro
19,331 ft
5,892 m
Somali Pen.
Mogadishu
Equator
INDIAN
Dar es Salaam
Seychelles
Cabo Delgado
Comoro Is.
Luanda
Lusaka
9,849 ft
3,002 m
Harare
Mozambique Ch.
Madagascar
9,436 ft
2,876 m
Antananarivo
Mascarene Is.
Benguela Current
Namib
Windhoek
Johannesburg
Maputo
Drakensberg
11,424 ft
3,482 m
Cape Town
Cape of Good Hope
Agulhas Current
OCEAN
Galápagos Is.
Quito
Bogotá
Llanos
9,219 ft
2,810 m
Guiana Highlands
9,889 ft
3,014 m
Chimborazo
20,703 ft
6,310 m
Amazon
Manaus
Belém
Selvas
Campos
Punta Negra
Huascarán
22,205 ft
6,768 m
Lima
SOUTH AMERICA
C. Fernando de Noronha
de São Roque
Recife
South Equatorial Current
Ascension
Salvador
Brasília
Brazil Current
La Paz
21,464 ft
6,542 m
Humboldt Current
Brazilian Highlands
9,482 ft
2,890 m
Pico da Bandeira
Rio de Janeiro
São Paulo
Asunción
St. Helena
Desventurados Is.
Sala-y-Gómez
Juan Fernández Is.
Aconcagua
22,842 ft
6,963 m
Santiago
Porto Alegre
Montevideo
Pampas
Buenos Aires
Río de la Plata
OCEAN
Tristan da Cunha
Gough I.
13,314 ft
4,058 m
Patagonia
Falkland Current
Andes
Antarctic Circumpolar Current
(West Wind Drift)
Falkland Is.
(Is. Malvinas)
Tierra del Fuego
Str. of Magellan
Cape Horn
South Georgia
Scotia Sea
Drake Passage
South Sandwich Is.
Bouvet I.
Prince Edward I.
Crozet Is.
Kerguelen Is.
South Shetland Is.
South Orkney Is.
Bellingshausen Sea
Peter I I.
Antarctic Pen.
Mt. Jackson
10,446 ft
3,184 m
Alexander I.
Ellsworth Land
Weddell Sea
Berkner I.
Queen Maud Land
ANTARCTICA
KLETT-PERTHES
100° L 80° M 60° N 40° O 20° P 0° Q 20° R 40° S 60° T

A 160° B 140° C 120° D 100° E 80° F 60° G 40° H 20° J 0°
A R C T I C
Queen Elizabeth Is.
Sverdrup Is.
Ellesmere I.
Parry Is.
Beaufort Sea
Victoria I.
Devon I.
Baffin Bay
Greenland
Alaska
Alaska Range
G. of Alaska
Kodiak I.
Aleutian Is.
Coast Mts.
Mackenzie
Yukon
Baffin I.
Davis Str.
Denmark Str.
Iceland
Norwegian Sea
Arctic Circle
Hudson Bay
Labrador
Labrador Sea
Canadian Shield
British Is.
North Sea
Rocky Mountains
Great Plains
NORTH AMERICA
Newfoundland
Appalachian Mts.
Sa. Nevada
Sa. Madre Occ.
Mississippi
Florida
Bermuda Is.
Sargasso Sea
Azores
Madeira
Canary Is.
Atlas
Ahaggar
Sahara
Tropic of Cancer
Hawaiian Is.
Hawaii
Gulf of Mexico
Bahama Is.
Cuba
Hispaniola
Greater Antilles
Lesser Antilles
Caribbean Sea
ATLANTIC
Cape Verde Is.
Niger
P A C I F I C
Polynesia
Line Islands
Kiritimati
Equator
Jarvis I.
Galápagos Is.
Llanos
Guiana Highlands
Amazon
Selvas
G. of Guinea
Fernando de Noronha
Ascension
Marquesas Is.
Campos
SOUTH AMERICA
Andes
Brazilian Highlands
St. Helena
OCEAN
Cook Islands
Society Is.
Tuamotu Is.
Tubuai Is.
Pitcairn Is.
Desventurados Is.
Tropic of Capricorn
Easter I.
Sala-y-Gómez
Juan Fernández Is.
Pampas
Río de la Plata
Tristan da Cunha
Gough I.
O C E A N
Patagonia
Falkland Is. (Is. Malvinas)
Tierra del Fuego
South Georgia
Bouvet I.
Str. of Magellan
Scotia Sea
Drake Passage
South Sandwich Is.
South Shetland Is.
South Orkney Is.
Antarctic Pen.
Antarctic Circle
Bellingshausen Sea
Peter I I.
Alexander I.
Weddell Sea
Queen
Ellsworth Land
Berkner I.
A N T A R C
KLETT-PERTHES
A 160° B 140° C 120° D 100° E 80° F 60° G 40° H 20° J 0°

Landforms
Tertiary planation surfaces and mountains and their Quaternary glacial modification
Dissected Tertiary planation surfaces of mostly medium height and relief cutting across Precambrian metamorphic shield regions
modified by multiple Pleistocene glaciations
Medium-height mountains and uplands of truncated, uplifted and dissected Paleozoic collision zones (Caledonian and Hercynian/Appalachian orogenies) and Mesozoic granitic rocks [G]
modified by multiple Pleistocene glaciations
Dissected plains, plateaus and scarplands of Tertiary planation cutting across gently tilted to horizontal sedimentary rocks of Late Precambrian, Paleozoic and Mesozoic to Tertiary age
blanketed by glacial and fluvioglacial Pleistocene deposits
Planated and dissected plateaus of Mesozoic and Tertiary volcanic rocks, mostly flood basalt, partly modified by Pleistocene glaciations
High-mountain chains of Mesozoic to present collision zones (Alpine orogeny)
modified by multiple Pleistocene valley glaciations
Dissected intermontane plateaus and basins
partly modified by Pleistocene glaciations
with Quaternary, mostly dissected, alluvial fans of arid regions
Extent of last glaciation
Major regions of present glaciation
Southern limit of present continuous permafrost (northern hemisphere)

O C E A N
Franz Josef Land
Severnaya Zemlya
New Siberian Is.
Laptev Sea
East Siberian Sea
Kara Sea
Novaya Zemlya
Taymyr Pen.
Barents Sea
Central Siberian Plateau
Cherskiy Ra.
Bering Sea
Kamchatka
West Siberian Plain
Ural Mts
Yakutia
Lena
Yenisey
Ob
Sea of Okhotsk
Stanovoy Ra.
Baykal
Aleutian Is.
Sakhalin
Kurile Is.
Sayan
Altay Mts
Amur
Manchuria
Hokkaido
Volga
Carp. Mts
Caucasus
Caspian Sea
Aral Sea
Black Sea
Anatolia
Elburz Mts.
Tien Shan
Gobi
Altun Shan
Sea of Japan
Korea
Honshu
Hindu Kush
Kunlun Shan
Tibet
Yellow R.
Kyushu
Midway Is.
Iranian Plateau
Himalayas
Yangtze
Ryukyu Is.
Bonin Is.
PACIFIC
Volcano Is.
Taiwan
Wake I.
Libyan Desert
Nile
Red Sea
Arabian Pen.
India
Mariana Is.
Tibesti
Hainan
Luzon
Philippines
South China Sea
Arabian Sea
Bay of Bengal
Socotra
Marshall Islands
Chad
Ethiopian Highlands
Somali Pen.
Caroline Is.
Ceylon
Mindanao
Micronesia
Maldives
Congo
Congo Basin
L. Victoria
Sumatra
Borneo (Kalimantan)
Celebes (Sulawesi)
Melanesia
OCEAN
Equator
Gilbert Is.
Bismarck Arch.
Phoenix Is.
Seychelles
Chagos Is.
Greater Sunda Is.
New Guinea
Java
Lesser Sunda Is.
Ellice Is.
Comoro Is.
INDIAN
Cocos Is.
Solomon Is.
Tokelau Is.
Wallis Is.
Mozambique Ch.
Madagascar
Mascarene Is.
Coral Sea
New Hebrides
Futuna
Tonga Is.
Fiji Is.
Namib
Drakensberg
AUSTRALIA
Great Victoria Desert
Gt. Dividing Range
New Caledonia
OCEAN
Norfolk I.
Kermadec Is.
Amsterdam
Saint-Paul
Austr. Alps
Tasman Sea
North Island
Crozet Is.
Tasmania
New Zealand
Prince Edward I.
Kerguelen Is.
South Island
Heard
Bounty Is.
Auckland Is.
Antipodes Is.
Macquarie
Campbell Is.
aud Land
TICA
20° L 40° M 60° N 80° O 100° P 120° Q 140° R 160° S 180° T
80° 60° 40° 20° 0° 20° 40°
1 2 3 4 5 6 7 8
Pleistocene and Holocene fluvial, lacustrine, coastal and eolian landforms
Pleistocene and Holocene lowlands with alluvial and lake-alluvial deposits; Pleistocene river terraces, Holocene floodplains, coastral marshes and deltas
Floors of Late Pleistocene ice-dammed glacial meltwater lakes, partly surrounding present lakes
Deposits and shorelines of Mid-Pleistocene to early Holocene pluvial lakes and swamps of arid regions
Quaternary marine terraces [T], near-coastal seafloor raised by glacioisostatic rebound [R] and seafloor of the northern Caspian sea region uplifted by Holocene tectonism [C]
Continental shelf and edge of shelf
Quaternary dune fields (ergs, sand seas)
of hyperarid desert regions, presently active
of semi-arid regions, vegetation-bound
Major Pleistocene loess sheets
Landforms of recent to present volcanism and tectonic deformation, selected mainland and island volcanoes
Eroded and submerged volcanoes topped with coral reefs
Boundary of zone of present-day arid geomorphic processes and resulting surficial features (intermittent runoff, temporary lakes and playas, mostly dissected alluvial fans, desert pavement, eolian sand sheets and sand seas)
20° L 40° M 60° N 80° O 100° P

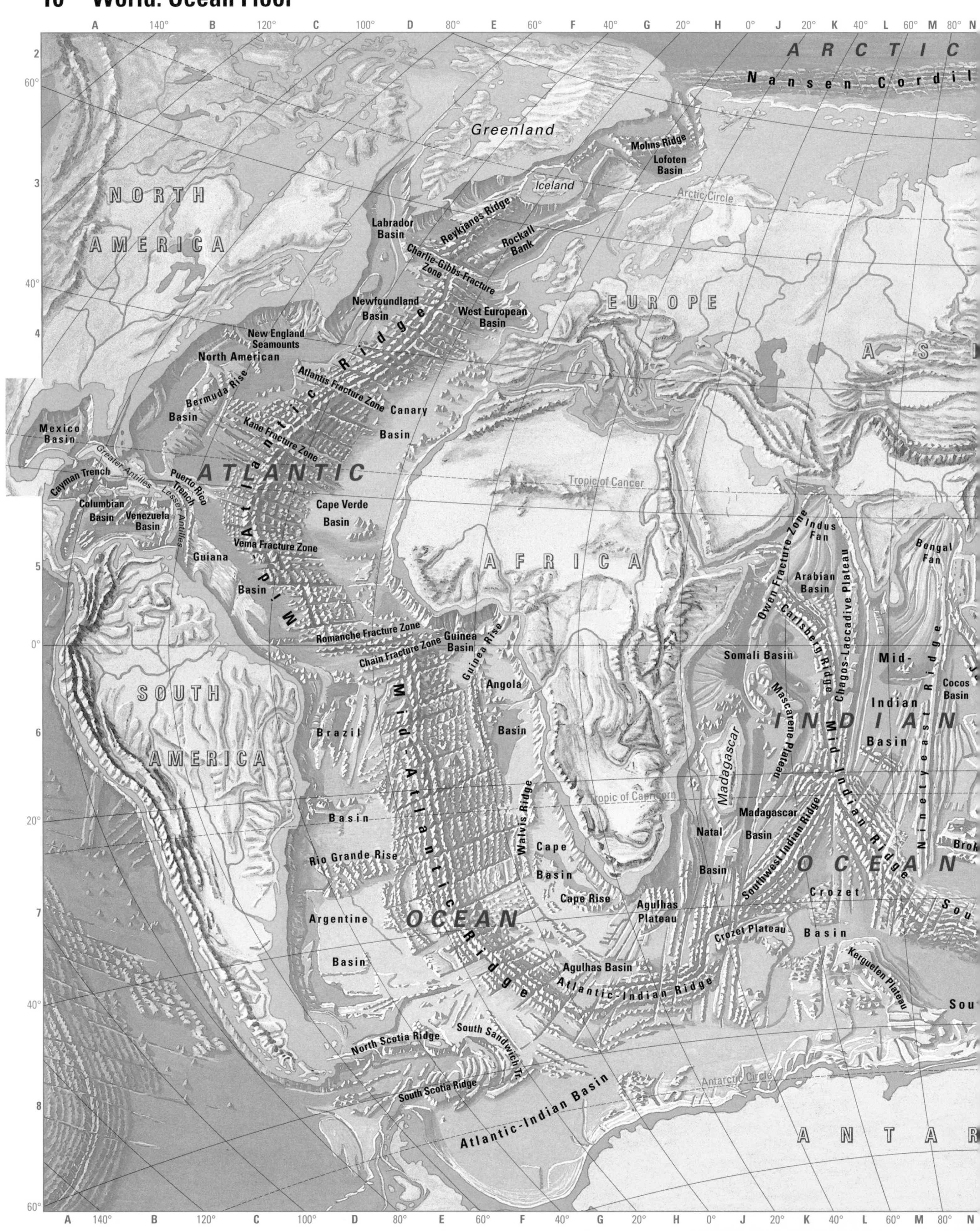
A
140°
B
120°
C
100°
D
80°
E
60°
F
40°
G
20°
H
0°
J
20°
K
40°
L
60°
M
80°
N
2
60°
3
40°
4
5
0°
6
20°
7
40°
8
60°
ARCTIC
Nansen Cordil
Greenland
Mohns Ridge
Lofoten Basin
Iceland
Arctic Circle
NORTH AMERICA
Labrador Basin
Reykjanes Ridge
Rockall Bank
Charlie-Gibbs Fracture Zone
Newfoundland Basin
West European Basin
EUROPE
New England Seamounts
North American
Mid-Atlantic Ridge
Atlantis Fracture Zone
Canary Basin
Bermuda Rise
Basin
Mexico Basin
Kane Fracture Zone
Cayman Trench
Greater Antilles
Puerto Rico Trench
ATLANTIC
Tropic of Cancer
Columbian Basin
Venezuela Basin
Lesser Antilles
Cape Verde Basin
Vema Fracture Zone
Guiana Basin
AFRICA
Indus Fan
Bengal Fan
Owen Fracture Zone
Arabian Basin
Carlsberg Ridge
Chagos-Laccadive Plateau
Romanche Fracture Zone
Guinea Basin
Guinea Rise
Chain Fracture Zone
Somali Basin
Mid-Indian Basin
Ninetyeast Ridge
Cocos Basin
SOUTH AMERICA
Angola Basin
Mascarene Plateau
INDIAN
Brazil Basin
Madagascar
Mid-Indian Ridge
Walvis Ridge
Tropic of Capricorn
Madagascar Basin
Natal Basin
Cape Basin
Rio Grande Rise
Southwest Indian Ridge
OCEAN
Brok
Cape Rise
Agulhas Plateau
Crozet Basin
Argentine Basin
OCEAN
Crozet Plateau
Sou
Kerguelen Plateau
Agulhas Basin
Atlantic-Indian Ridge
Sou
North Scotia Ridge
South Sandwich Tr.
Antarctic Circle
South Scotia Ridge
Atlantic-Indian Basin
ANTAR

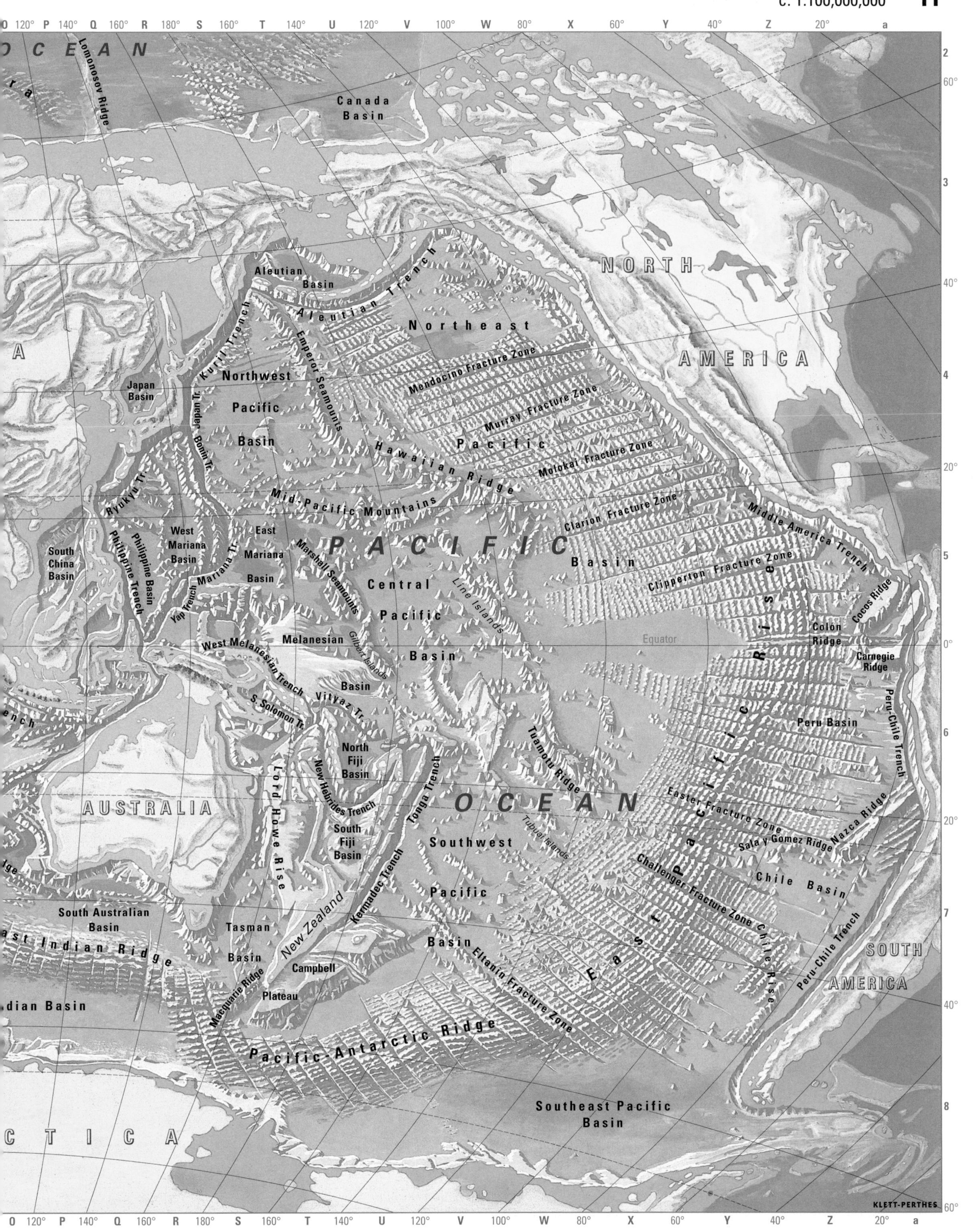
PACIFIC OCEAN
NORTH AMERICA
SOUTH AMERICA
AUSTRALIA
Lomonosov Ridge
Canada Basin
Aleutian Basin
Aleutian Trench
Northeast Pacific Basin
Kuril Trench
Japan Basin
Northwest Pacific Basin
Japan Tr.
Bonin Tr.
Emperor Seamounts
Mendocino Fracture Zone
Murray Fracture Zone
Molokai Fracture Zone
Hawaiian Ridge
Mid-Pacific Mountains
Clarion Fracture Zone
Clipperton Fracture Zone
Middle America Trench
Cocos Ridge
Colon Ridge
Carnegie Ridge
Equator
Ryukyu Tr.
Philippine Trench
Philippine Basin
West Mariana Basin
East Mariana Basin
Mariana Tr.
Yap Trench
South China Basin
Marshall Seamounts
Central Pacific Basin
Line Islands
Melanesian Basin
Gilbert Islands
West Melanesian Trench
Vityaz Tr.
S. Solomon Tr.
North Fiji Basin
New Hebrides Trench
South Fiji Basin
Lord Howe Rise
Tonga Trench
Kermadec Trench
Tuamotu Ridge
Tubuai Islands
Southwest Pacific Basin
East Pacific Rise
Easter Fracture Zone
Sala y Gomez Ridge
Nazca Ridge
Peru Basin
Peru-Chile Trench
Chile Basin
Challenger Fracture Zone
Chile Rise
South Australian Basin
Indian Ridge
Tasman Basin
New Zealand
Campbell Plateau
Macquarie Ridge
Eltanin Fracture Zone
Pacific-Antarctic Ridge
Southeast Pacific Basin
KLETT-PERTHES

North Polar Region: Ocean Floor

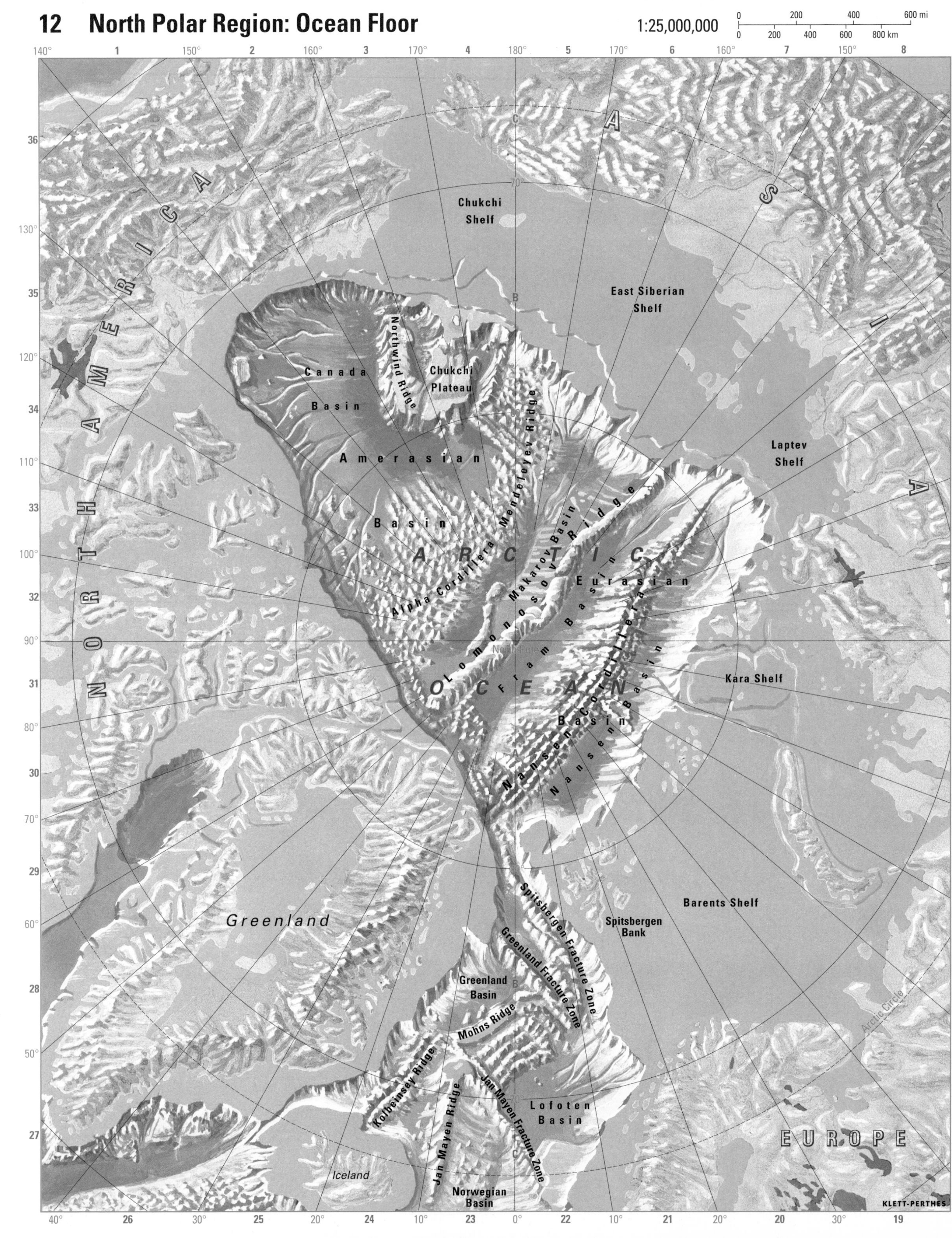

0 500 1,000 mi
0 500 1,000 1,500 2,000 km
ATLANTIC OCEAN
Rio Grande Rise
Mid-Atlantic Ridge
Cape Basin
AFRICA
Cape Rise
Natal Basin
Madagascar
Agulhas Plateau
Agulhas Basin
Argentine Basin
Atlantic-Indian Ridge
Crozet Plateau
Southwest Indian Ridge
South Sandwich Trench
North Scotia Ridge
South Scotia Ridge
Atlantic-Indian Basin
Crozet Basin
INDIAN OCEAN
SOUTH AMERICA
Antarctic Circle
10,420 ft 3,176 m
11,909 ft 3,630 m
Queen Maud Land
Kerguelen Plateau
Antarctandes
West Antarctica
East Antarctica
ANTARCTICA
Maud Subglacial Basin
11,007 ft 3,355 m
Ronne Ice Shelf
Shackleton Range
Prince Charles Mts.
Pensacola Mts.
Southeast Pacific Basin
16,066 ft 4,897 m
Polar S.B.
11,122 ft 3,390 m
Gamburtsev Mts.
Ellsworth Range
South Pole
−8,382 ft −2,555 m
Byrd S.B.
14,855 ft 4,528 m
Wilkes Subglacial Basin
Shmidt S.B.
−4,921 ft −1,500 m
13,717 ft 4,181 m
−4,265 ft −1,300 m
Ross Ice Shelf
14,271 ft 4,350 m
Transantarctic Mountains
South Indian Basin
Southeast Indian Ridge
East Pacific Ridge
Eltanin Fracture Zone
Pacific-Antarctic Ridge
PACIFIC OCEAN
Macquarie Ridge
South Australian Basin
South Tasman Rise
Southwest Pacific Basin
Campbell Plateau
Tasmania
Chatham Rise
New Zealand
Tasman Basin
AUSTRALIA
S.B. Subglacial Basin
KLETT-PERTHES

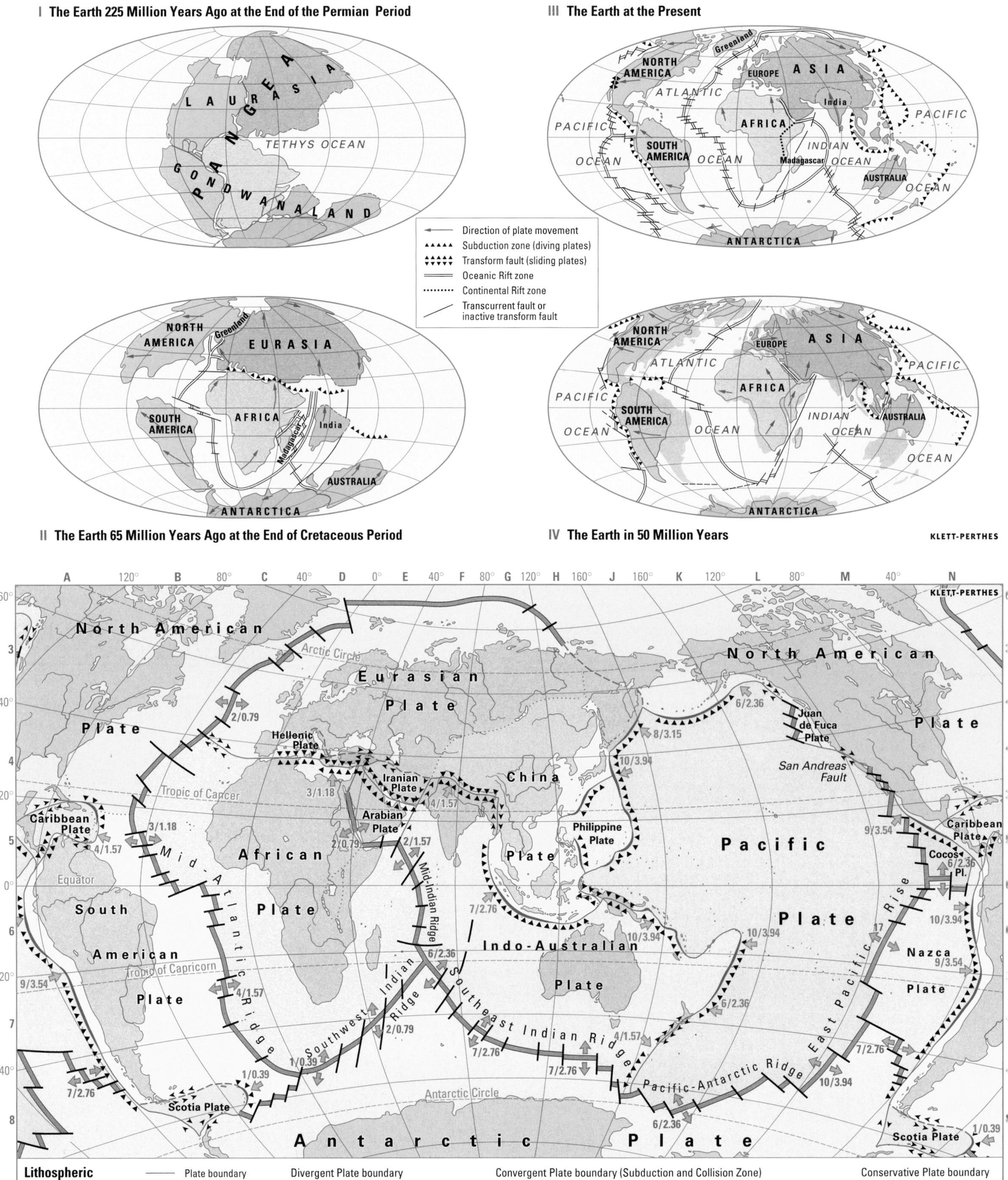
I The Earth 225 Million Years Ago at the End of the Permian Period
PANGEA
LAURASIA
GONDWANALAND
TETHYS OCEAN
II The Earth 65 Million Years Ago at the End of Cretaceous Period
NORTH AMERICA
Greenland
EURASIA
SOUTH AMERICA
AFRICA
Madagascar
India
AUSTRALIA
ANTARCTICA
III The Earth at the Present
NORTH AMERICA
Greenland
EUROPE
ASIA
ATLANTIC
PACIFIC
OCEAN
India
AFRICA
SOUTH AMERICA
OCEAN
INDIAN
Madagascar
OCEAN
PACIFIC
AUSTRALIA
OCEAN
ANTARCTICA
IV The Earth in 50 Million Years
NORTH AMERICA
EUROPE
ASIA
ATLANTIC
PACIFIC
AFRICA
SOUTH AMERICA
OCEAN
OCEAN
INDIAN
OCEAN
AUSTRALIA
OCEAN
ANTARCTICA
Direction of plate movement
Subduction zone (diving plates)
Transform fault (sliding plates)
Oceanic Rift zone
Continental Rift zone
Transcurrent fault or inactive transform fault
KLETT-PERTHES
North American Plate
Eurasian Plate
Hellenic Plate
Iranian Plate
Arabian Plate
China
Philippine Plate
Caribbean Plate
African Plate
South American Plate
Mid-Atlantic Ridge
Mid-Indian Ridge
Southwest Indian Ridge
Southeast Indian Ridge
Indo-Australian Plate
Pacific Plate
Juan de Fuca Plate
San Andreas Fault
Cocos Pl.
Nazca Plate
East Pacific Rise
Pacific-Antarctic Ridge
Scotia Plate
Antarctic Plate
Arctic Circle
Tropic of Cancer
Equator
Tropic of Capricorn
Antarctic Circle
2/0.79
3/1.18
4/1.57
9/3.54
7/2.76
1/0.39
6/2.36
8/3.15
10/3.94
17
Lithospheric Plates
Plate boundary
Uncertain plate boundary
Supposed plate boundary
Divergent Plate boundary
Oceanic rift zone
Direction of plate movement
6/2.36 Speed of movement (cm/in. per year)
Convergent Plate boundary (Subduction and Collision Zone)
Subduction zone (diving plates)
Collision zone (plates colliding to form a mountain range)
Direction of plate subduction
10/3.94 Speed of subduction (cm/in. per year)
Ocean trench
Conservative Plate boundary
Transform fault (sliding plates)
Transcurrent fault or inactive transform fault

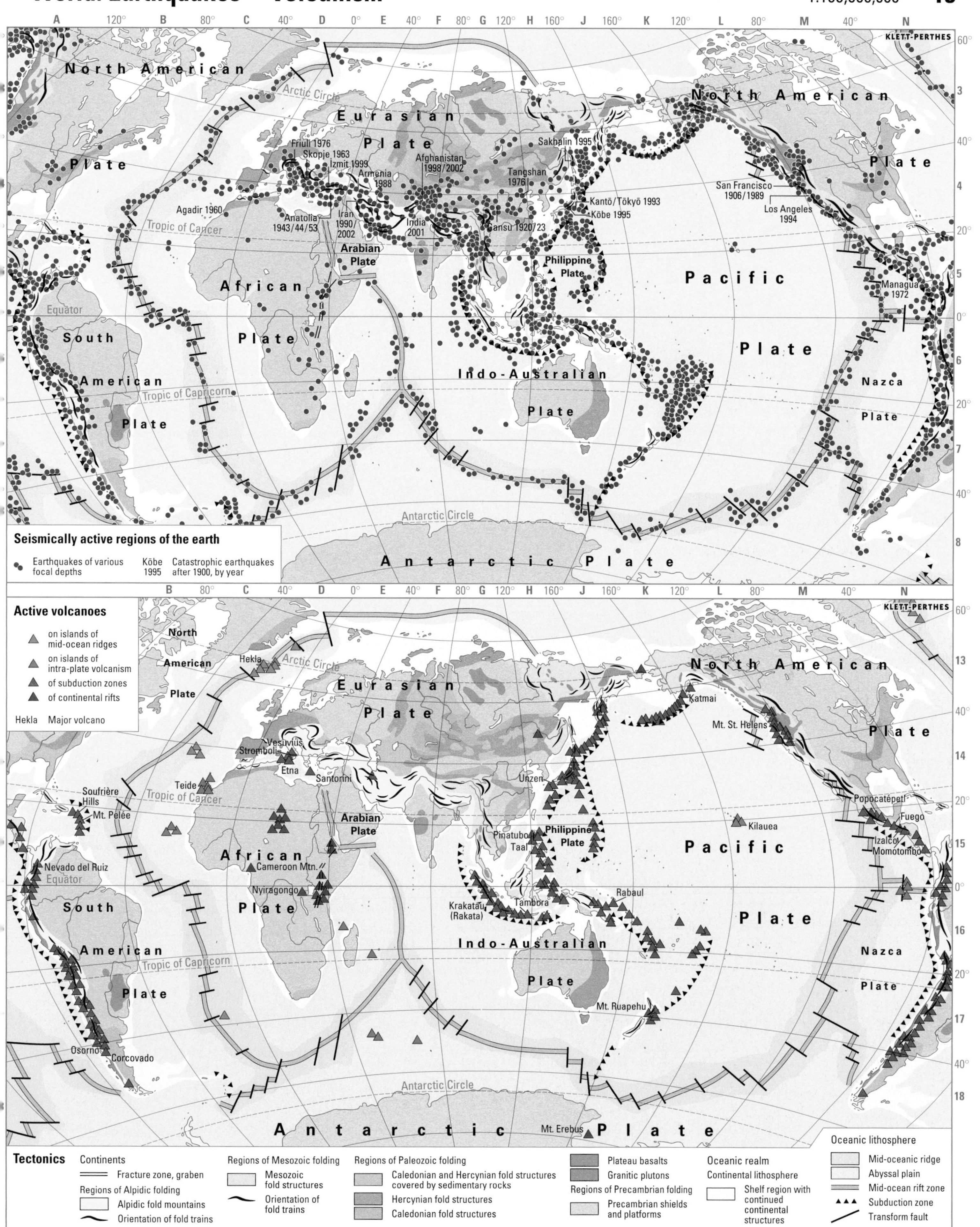
KLETT-PERTHES
North American Plate
Eurasian Plate
African Plate
Arabian Plate
Philippine Plate
Pacific Plate
Indo-Australian Plate
South American Plate
Nazca Plate
Antarctic Plate
Arctic Circle
Tropic of Cancer
Equator
Tropic of Capricorn
Antarctic Circle
Friuli 1976
Skopje 1963
Izmit 1999
Armenia 1988
Afghanistan 1998/2002
Agadir 1960
Anatolia 1943/44/53
Iran 1990/2002
India 2001
Gansu 1920/23
Tangshan 1976
Sakhalin 1995
Kantō/Tōkyō 1993
Kōbe 1995
San Francisco 1906/1989
Los Angeles 1994
Managua 1972
Seismically active regions of the earth
Earthquakes of various focal depths
Kōbe 1995 Catastrophic earthquakes after 1900, by year
Active volcanoes
on islands of mid-ocean ridges
on islands of intra-plate volcanism
of subduction zones
of continental rifts
Hekla Major volcano
Hekla
Vesuvius
Stromboli
Etna
Santorini
Teide
Soufrière Hills
Mt. Pelée
Nevado del Ruiz
Cameroon Mtn.
Nyiragongo
Osorno
Corcovado
Unzen
Pinatubo
Taal
Krakatau (Rakata)
Tambora
Rabaul
Mt. Ruapehu
Mt. Erebus
Katmai
Mt. St. Helens
Kilauea
Popocatépetl
Fuego
Izalco
Momotombo
Tectonics
Continents
Fracture zone, graben
Regions of Alpidic folding
Alpidic fold mountains
Orientation of fold trains
Regions of Mesozoic folding
Mesozoic fold structures
Orientation of fold trains
Regions of Paleozoic folding
Caledonian and Hercynian fold structures covered by sedimentary rocks
Hercynian fold structures
Caledonian fold structures
Plateau basalts
Granitic plutons
Regions of Precambrian folding
Precambrian shields and platforms
Oceanic realm
Continental lithosphere
Shelf region with continued continental structures
Oceanic lithosphere
Mid-oceanic ridge
Abyssal plain
Mid-ocean rift zone
Subduction zone
Transform fault

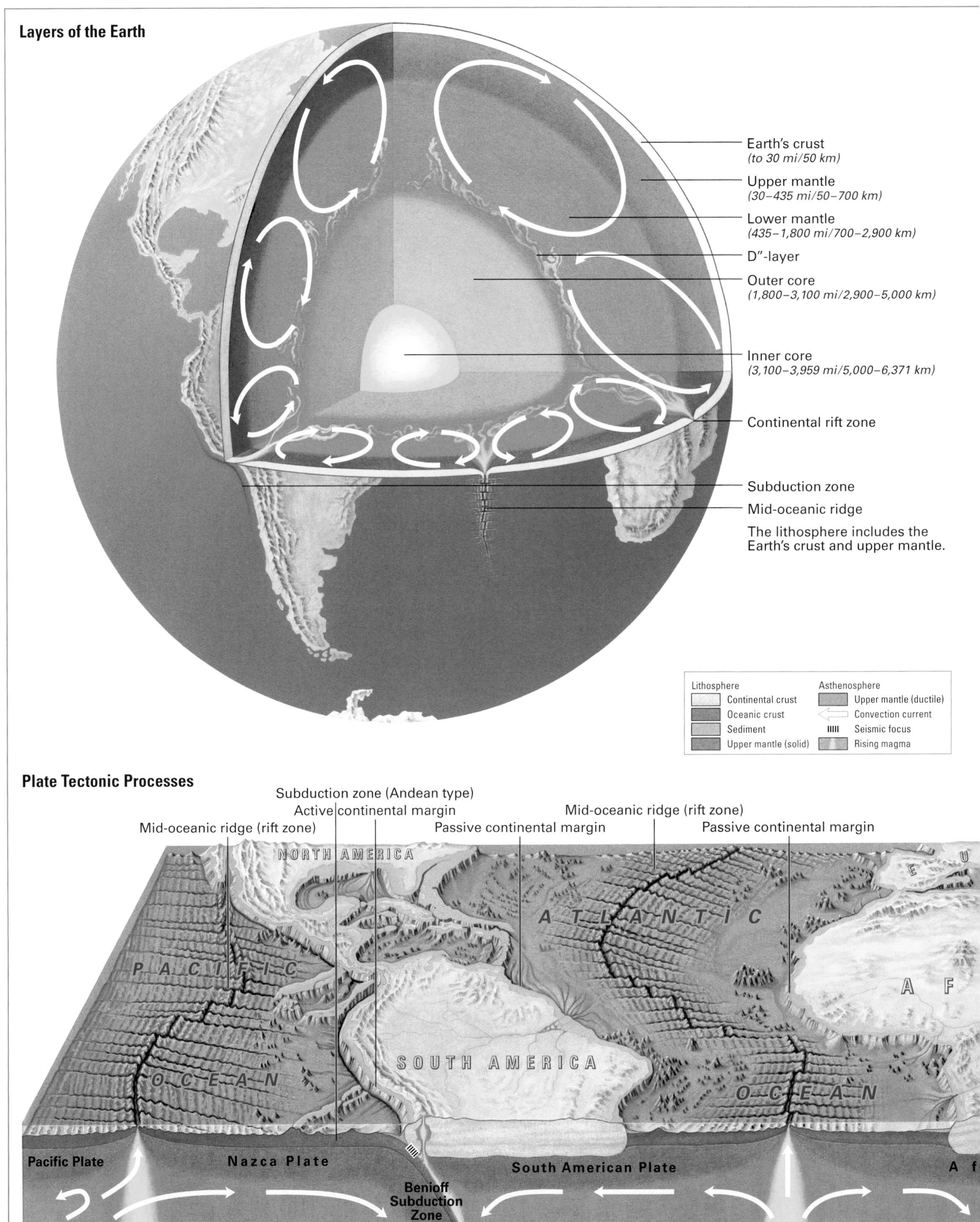
Layers of the Earth
Earth's crust
(to 30 mi/50 km)
Upper mantle
(30–435 mi/50–700 km)
Lower mantle
(435–1,800 mi/700–2,900 km)
D"-layer
Outer core
(1,800–3,100 mi/2,900–5,000 km)
Inner core
(3,100–3,959 mi/5,000–6,371 km)
Continental rift zone
Subduction zone
Mid-oceanic ridge
The lithosphere includes the Earth's crust and upper mantle.
Lithosphere
Continental crust
Oceanic crust
Sediment
Upper mantle (solid)
Asthenosphere
Upper mantle (ductile)
Convection current
Seismic focus
Rising magma
Plate Tectonic Processes
Subduction zone (Andean type)
Active continental margin
Mid-oceanic ridge (rift zone)
Passive continental margin
Mid-oceanic ridge (rift zone)
Passive continental margin
NORTH AMERICA
ATLANTIC
PACIFIC
OCEAN
SOUTH AMERICA
OCEAN
Pacific Plate
Nazca Plate
Benioff Subduction Zone
South American Plate

Subduction

Collision zone
Volcanic activity
Active continental margin
Deep sea trench
Oceanic crust
Continental crust
Subducted oceanic lithosphere
Lithosphere
Benioff Subduction Zone
Asthenosphere
Magma generation
Asthenosphere

Seafloor Spreading

Divergence zone
Passive continental margin
Sediment
Mid-oceanic ridge (rift zone)
Passive continental margin
Sediment
Oceanic crust
Oceanic crust
Lithosphere
Lithosphere
Asthenosphere
Asthenosphere

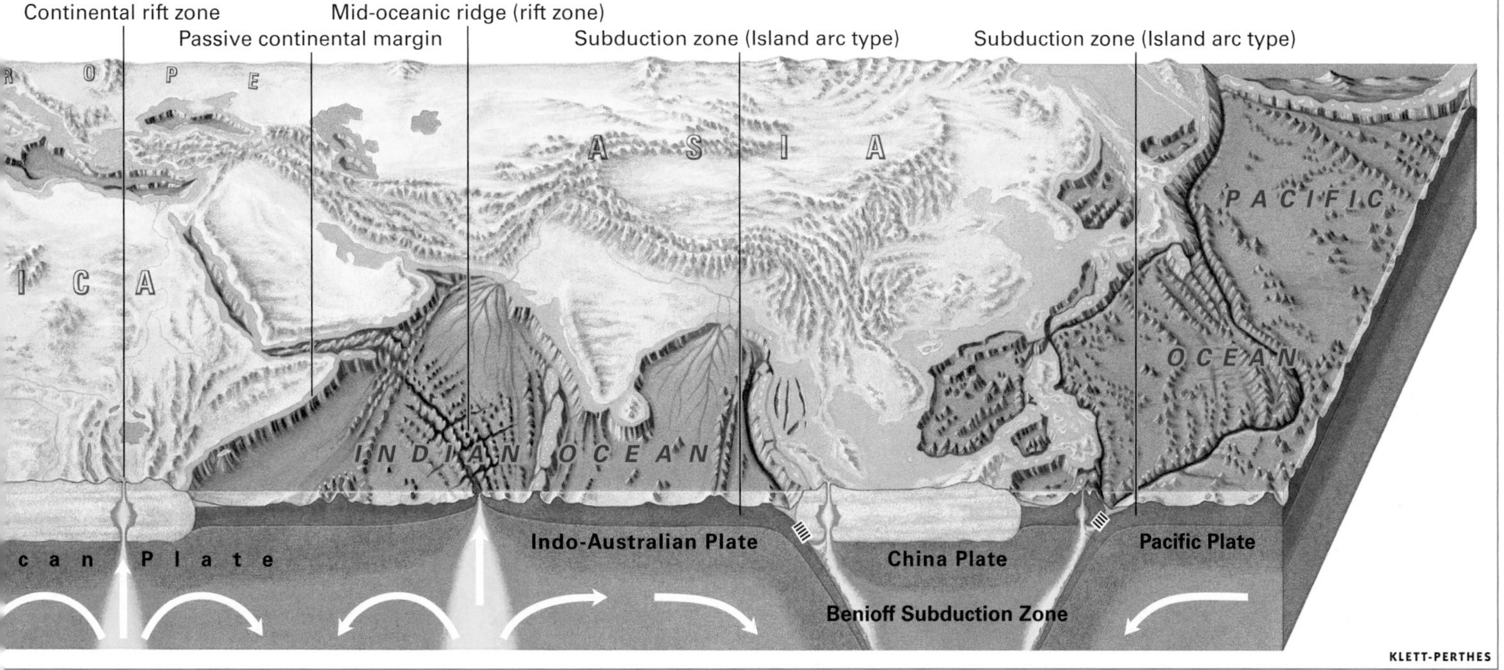

A 160° B 140° C 120° D 100° E 80° F 60° G 40° H 20° J 0°
A R C T I C
FI
Queen Elizabeth Is.
Sverdrup Is.
Ellesmere I.
Qaanaaq/Thule
Beaufort Sea
Parry Is.
FT
Victoria I.
Devon I.
Baffin Bay
Greenland
Eismitte
Mackenzie
Yukon
Baffin I.
Davis Str.
Denmark Str.
Norw S
Arctic Circle
Eo
Yakutat
G. of Alaska
Aleutian Is.
Ec
Churchill
Hudson Bay
Iceland
Labrador Sea
British Is.
North Sea
Do
Winnipeg
NORTH AMERICA
Missouri
Mississippi
Dc
Newfoundland
Paris
A Coruña
Cr
San Francisco
Denver
Washington, D.C.
Cs
BS
Azores
Algiers
Ar
Phoenix
Bermuda Is.
Madeira
Hawaiian Is.
(Ar/As/B/Cr)
Honolulu
Hawaii
Tropic of Cancer
BM
BW
New Orleans
Gulf of Mexico
Sargasso Sea
Miami
Bahama Is.
(Ar/Aw/Am)
ATLANTIC
Canary Is.
(BS/BW/Cs)
Cuba
Sabana de la Mar
Mexico City
Cw
Aw
Greater Antilles
(Ar/Aw/Al)
Lesser Antilles
Caribbean Sea
Cape Verde Is.
(BS/BW)
Niger
Tegucigalpa
Barranquilla
Maracaibo
Am
PACIFIC
Polynesia
Line Islands
Kiritimati
Equator
Jarvis I.
As
Macapá
Lomé
G. of Guinea
Galápagos Is.
(BS/Aw)
Iquitos
Amazon
Fernando de Noronha
Ascension
Marquesas Is.
SOUTH AMERICA
Aracaju
Cook Islands
Society Is.
(Ar/Am)
Tahiti
Tuamotu Is.
Brasilia
St. Helena
(Cr)
Arica
Tubuai Is.
Pitcairn Is.
Desventurados Is.
Salta
Tropic of Capricorn
Sala-y-Gómez
Easter I.
OCEAN
Juan Fernández Is.
Santiago
Buenos Aires
Río de la Plata
Tristan da Cunha
Gough I.
Puerto Montt
Comodoro Rivadavia
Balmaceda
Falkland Is.
(Is. Malvinas)
South Georgia
Bouvet I.
Tierra del Fuego
Ushuaia
Str. of Magellan
Scotia Sea
South Sandwich Is.
Drake Passage
Orcadas
South Shetland Is.
South Orkney Is.
Antarctic Circle
Weddell Sea
Amundsen-Scott
KLETT-PERTHES
Climatic Regions (Modified Koeppen System based on Trewartha)
A Tropical Rainy Climates
Absolutely no frost in the region, average temperature of the coldest month at least 18 °C (64.4 °F) over ocean waters
Ar Tropical (permanently) rainy climate
No more than two months with less than 60 mm (2.4 in.) of monthly rainfall
Am Tropical monsoon rain climate (wet and dry with an extremely wet season)
More than two months with less than 60 mm (2.4 in.) of monthly rainfall, dry season compensated for by high rainfall during the rainy season, if r ≥ 25 (100 – r*)
Aw Tropical summer rain climate (winter-dry)
More than 2 winter months with less than 60 mm (2.4 in.) of monthly rainfall
As Tropical winter rain climate (summer-dry)
More than 2 summer months with less than 60 mm (2.4 in.) of monthly rainfall
B Dry Climates
Boundary condition: r < 20 (t – 10 + 0.3 PS)
BS Steppe climate (semiarid climate)
Boundary condition: r ≥ 10 (t – 10 + 0.3 PS)
BW Desert climate (arid climate)
Boundary condition: r < 10 (t – 10 + 0.3 PS)
BM Marine dry climate
Humid-air dry climate above ocean surfaces with the universally valid boundary condition of r < 20 (t – 10 + 0.3 PS)
C Subtropical Climates
Average temperature of the coldest month less than 18 °C (64.4 °F), 8 to 12 months with an average temperature of at least 10 °C (50.0 °F)
Cr Subtropical (permanently) rainy climate
Lesser precipitation differences between the extreme months than for Cw or Cs climates
Cw Subtropical summer rain climate (winter-dry)
Precipitation sum of the wettest summer month at least 10 times that of the driest winter month
Cs Subtropical winter rain climate (summer-dry)
Precipitation sum of the wettest winter month at least 3 times that of the driest summer month
D Temperate Climates
4 to 7 months with an average temperature of at least 10 °C (50.0 °F)
Do Oceanic temperate climate
Average temperature of the coldest month 0 °C (32.0 °F) or above
Dc Continental temperate climate
Average temperature of the coldest month below 10 °C (50.0 °F)

20° L 40° M 60° N 80° O 100° P 120° Q 140° R 160° S 180° T
O C E A N
FI
Franz Josef Land
Severnaya Zemlya
New Siberian Is.
East Siberian Sea
Laptev Sea
Kara Sea
Novaya Zemlya
Longyearbyen
Barents Sea
Dickson
Verkhoyansk
Lena
Yenisey
Ob'
Arkhangel'sk
Ec
FT
Bering Sea
Sea of Okhotsk
Aleutian Is.
Sakhalin
Kurile Is.
Simushir I.
Eo
Baltic S.
Moscow
Petropavl
Dc
Volga
E U R O P E
Baykal
Amur
Astrakhan'
Aral Sea
Caspian Sea
BS
A S I A
BW
Dalandzadgad
Do
Hokkaido
Sea of Japan
Honshu
Tōkyō
Cr
Cs
Mediterranean Sea
Jerusalem
Tehrān
Bs
Yellow R.
Zhengzhou
Kyushu
Ryukyu Is.
Midway Is.
Yangtze
Cw
Kunming
Bonin Is.
P A C I F I C
Volcano Is.
Nile
Red Sea
Riyadh
Assuan
Taiwan
Mariana Is.
Wake I.
Kolkata
Am
Aw
Hainan
Luzon
Ar
Philippines
South China Sea
Chad
N'Djamena
Arabian Sea
Bay of Bengal
Socotra
Dawei
Agaña
Marshall Islands
A F R I C A
Addis Ababa
BM
Ceylon (Aw/Ar/As/Am)
Hambantota
Caroline Is.
Micronesia
Mindanao
Congo
Maldives
Singapore
Borneo (Kalimantan)
Celebes (Sulawesi)
Sumatra
M e l a n e s i a
O C E A N
Gilbert Is.
Equator
Phoenix Is.
As
L. Victoria
Malindi
Bismarck Arch.
Madang
New Guinea
Seychelles
Chagos Is.
Greater Sunda Is.
Lesser Sunda Is.
Java
Solomon Is.
Ellice Is.
Tokleau Is.
Dar es Salaam
Comoro Is.
(Ar/Aw)
I N D I A N
Cocos Is.
Darwin
Kabwe
Toamasina
Mascarene Is.
(Ar/Cr)
Mozambique Ch.
Madagascar
Coral Sea
New Hebrides
Wallis Is.
Futuna
Tonga Is.
Fiji Is.
Bulawayo
Mackay
New Caledonia
A U S T R A L I A
Oodnadatta
Durban
Kalgoorlie
Perth
Cs Cape Town
O C E A N
Norfolk I.
Kermadec Is.
Amsterdam
Saint-Paul
Sydney
North Island
Tasman Sea
New Zealand
Tasmania
Crozet Is.
Prince Edward I.
Kerguelen Is.
Mt. Cook
Christchurch
South Island
Bounty Is.
Heard
Auckland Is.
Macquarie
Campbell Is.
A N T A R C T I C A
1 2 3 4 5 6 7 8
80° 60° 40° 20° 0° 20° 40°
Meteorological station with climate diagram in the continental maps
Limits of the Regions of Dry Climates
r = 20 (t – 10 + 0.3 PS)
r = 10 (t – 10 + 0.3 PS)
r total annual precipitation [mm]
r* total precipitation of the driest month [mm]
t average annual temperature [°C]
PS percentage of summer precipitation April–September [%]:
PS = 30 with rainfall concentration in winter
PS = 50 with rainfall evenly distributed
PS = 67 with rainfall concentration in summer
t [°C]
°F
PS = 33 50 67 33 50 67
arid
semiarid
BW
BS
A, C, D
humid
0 100 200 300 400 500 600 700 800 900 r [mm]
0 5 10 15 20 25 30 35 in.
E Boreal Climates
1 to 3 months with an average temperature of at least 10 °C (50.0 °F)
Eo Oceanic boreal climate
Average temperature of the coldest month –10 °C (14.0 °F) or above
Ec Continental boreal climate
Average temperature of the coldest month below –10 °C (14.0 °F)
F Polar Climates
Average temperature of the warmest month below 10 °C (50.0 °F)
FT Tundra climate
Average temperature of the warmest month above 0 °C (32.0 °F)
FI Perpetual frost climate
Average temperature of the warmest month no more than 0 °C (32.0 °F)

World: Precipitation in January and July

1:160,000,000

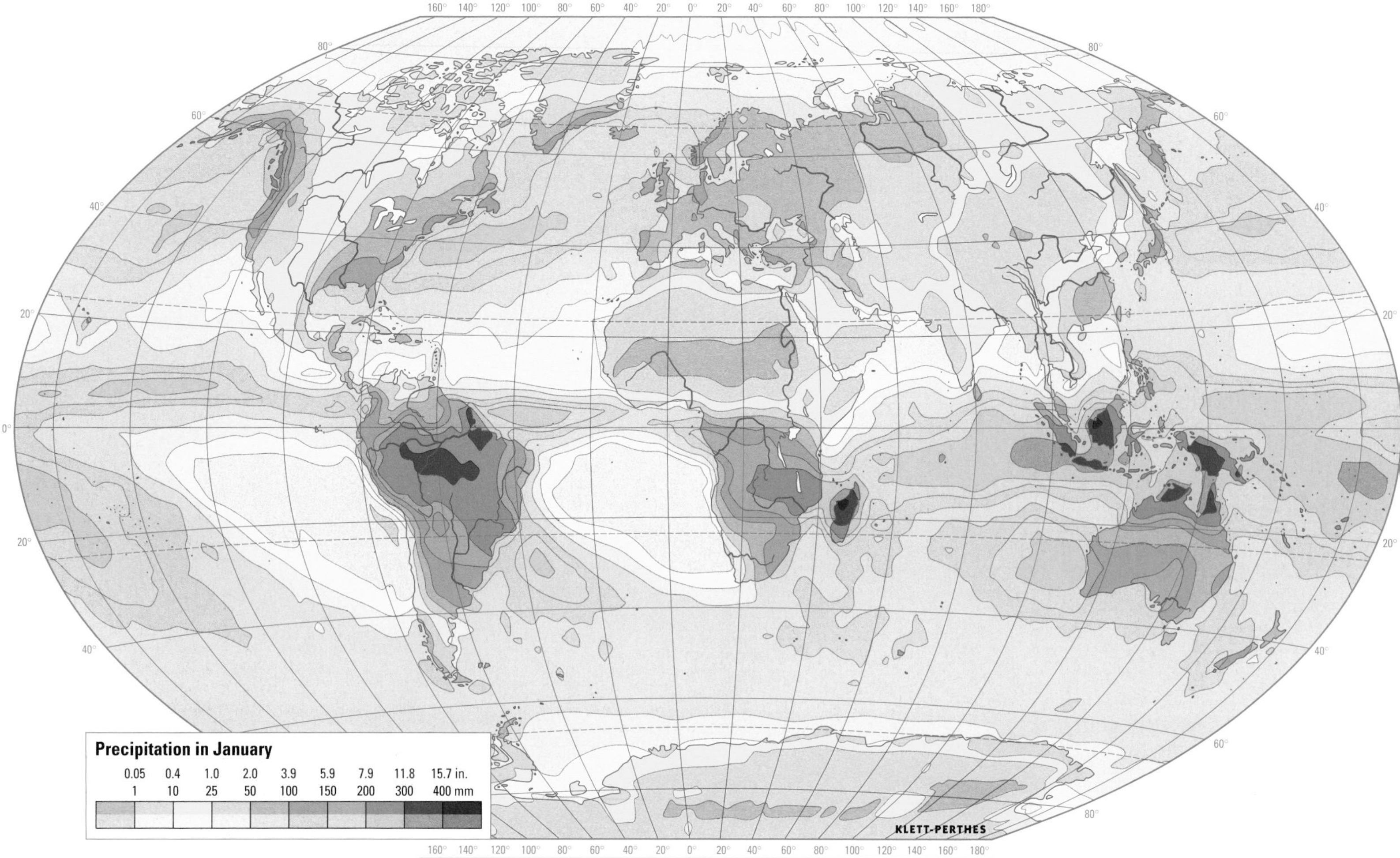

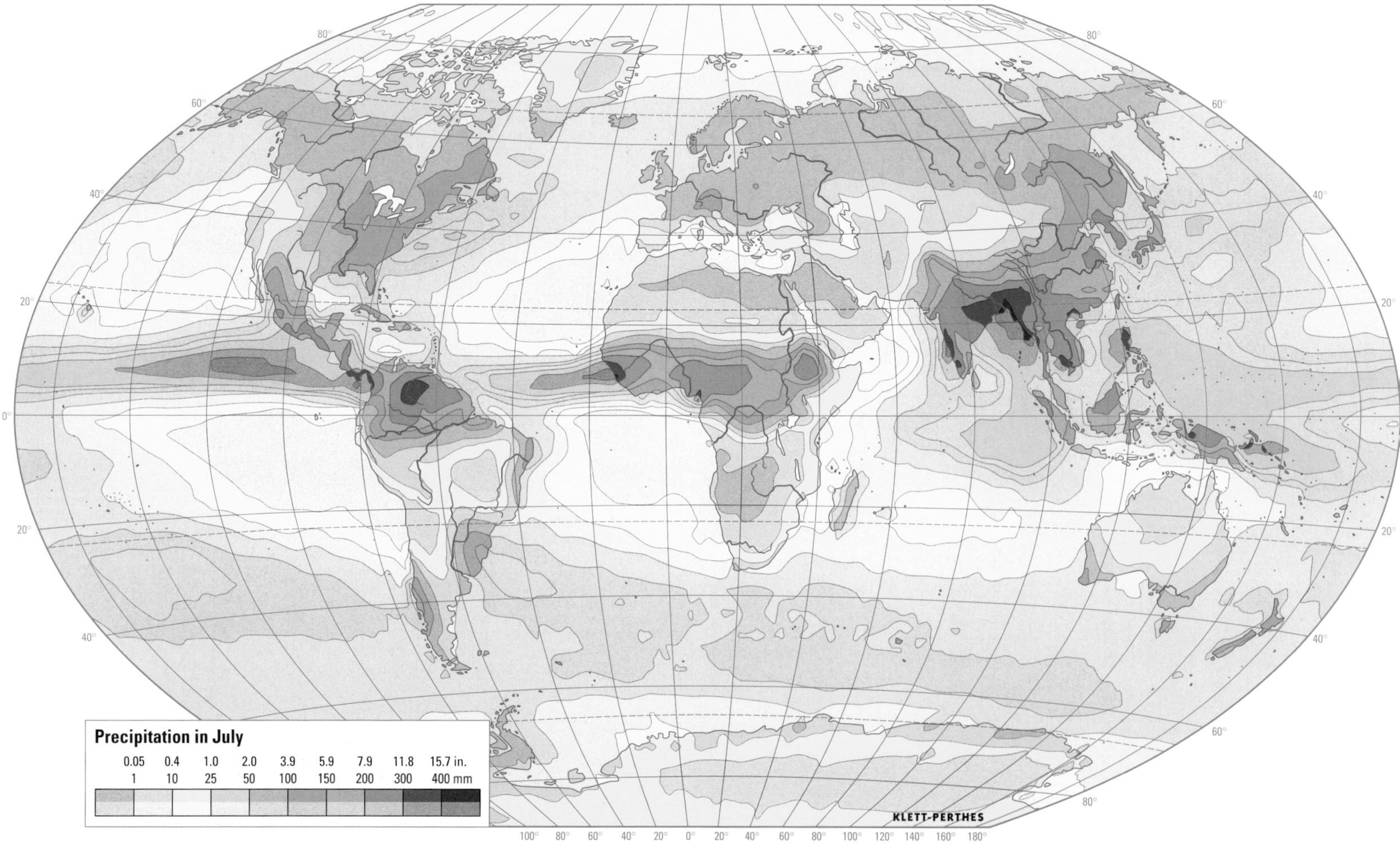

Precipitation in January

0.05	0.4	1.0	2.0	3.9	5.9	7.9	11.8	15.7 in.
1	10	25	50	100	150	200	300	400 mm

KLETT-PERTHES

Precipitation in July

0.05	0.4	1.0	2.0	3.9	5.9	7.9	11.8	15.7 in.
1	10	25	50	100	150	200	300	400 mm

KLETT-PERTHES

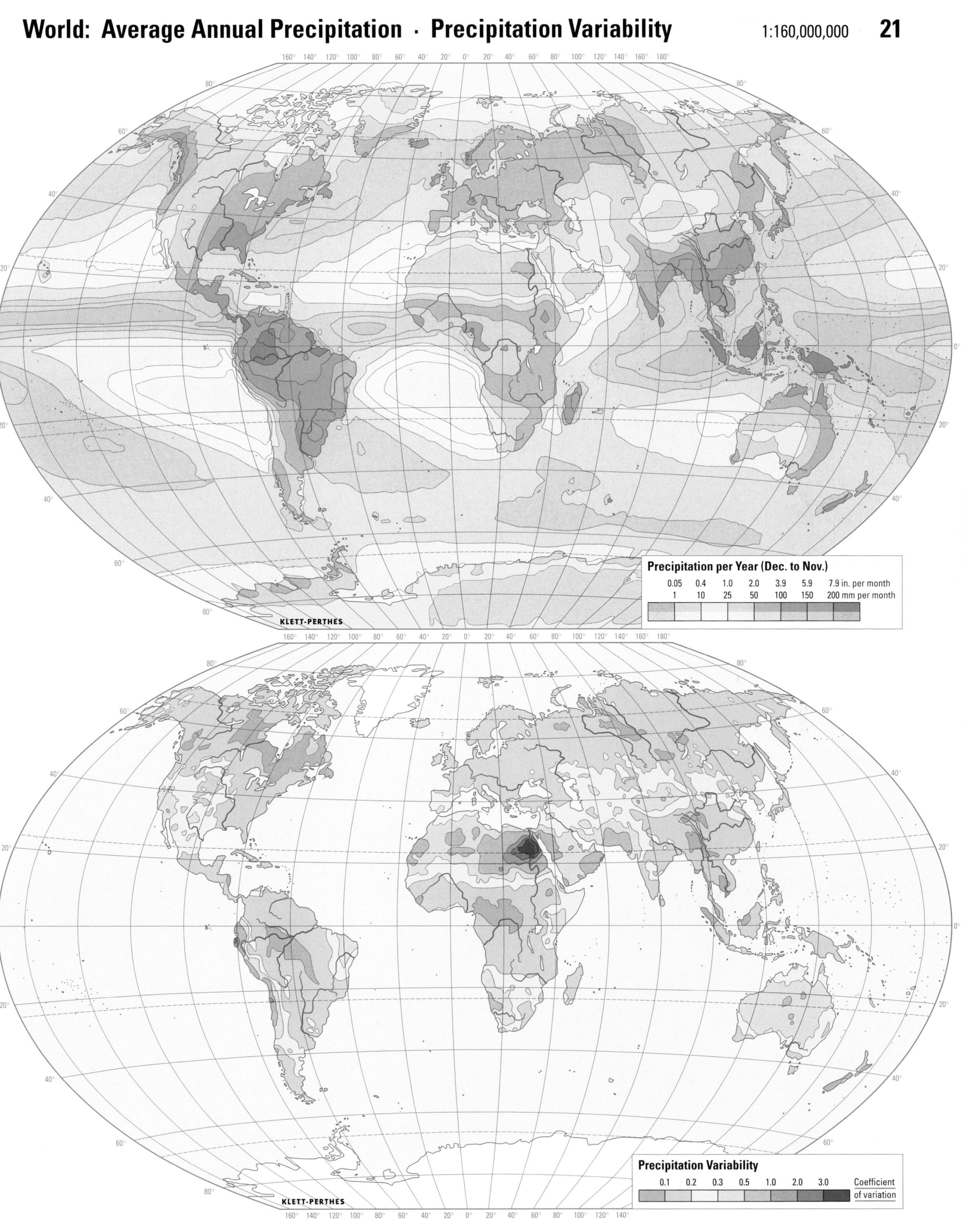
Precipitation per Year (Dec. to Nov.)
0.05 0.4 1.0 2.0 3.9 5.9 7.9 in. per month
1 10 25 50 100 150 200 mm per month
KLETT-PERTHES
Precipitation Variability
0.1 0.2 0.3 0.5 1.0 2.0 3.0 Coefficient of variation
KLETT-PERTHES

1:160,000,000

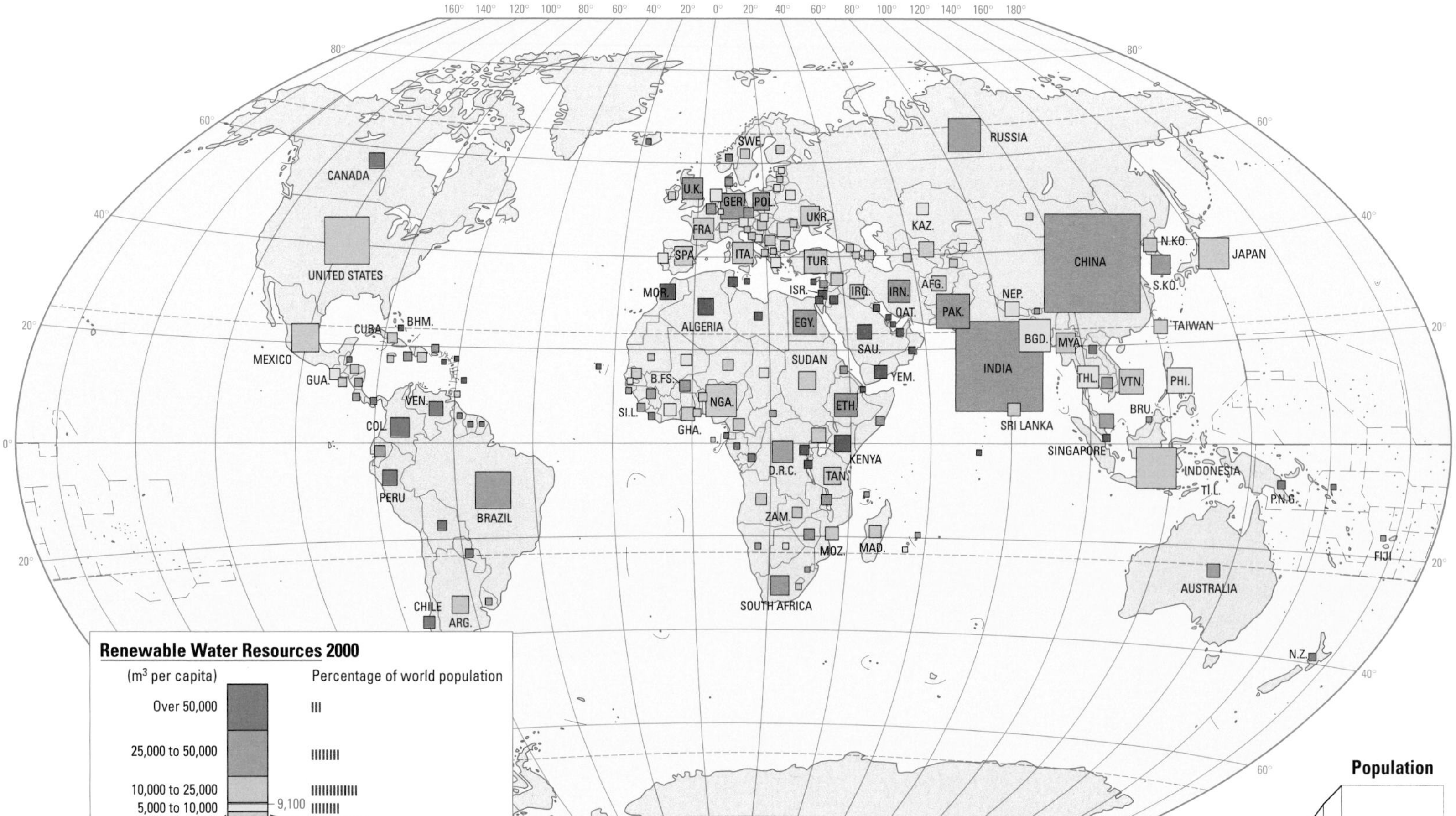

Water Resources 2000

Renewable Water Resources 2000

(m³ per capita)	Percentage of world population
Over 50,000	III
25,000 to 50,000	IIIIIII
10,000 to 25,000	IIIIIIIIIII
5,000 to 10,000	IIIIIII
2,500 to 5,000	IIIIIIIIIIIIIII
1,000 to 2,500	IIIIIIIIIIIIIIIIIIIIIIIIIIIIIIIIIIIIIIIIIIIIIIIII
Scarcity: under 1,000	III

9,100

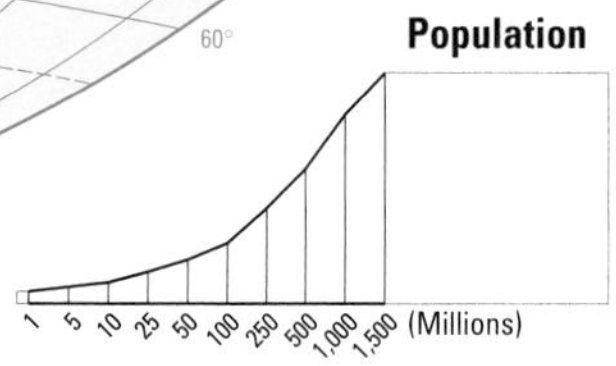

Population

1 5 10 25 50 100 250 500 1,000 1,500 (Millions)

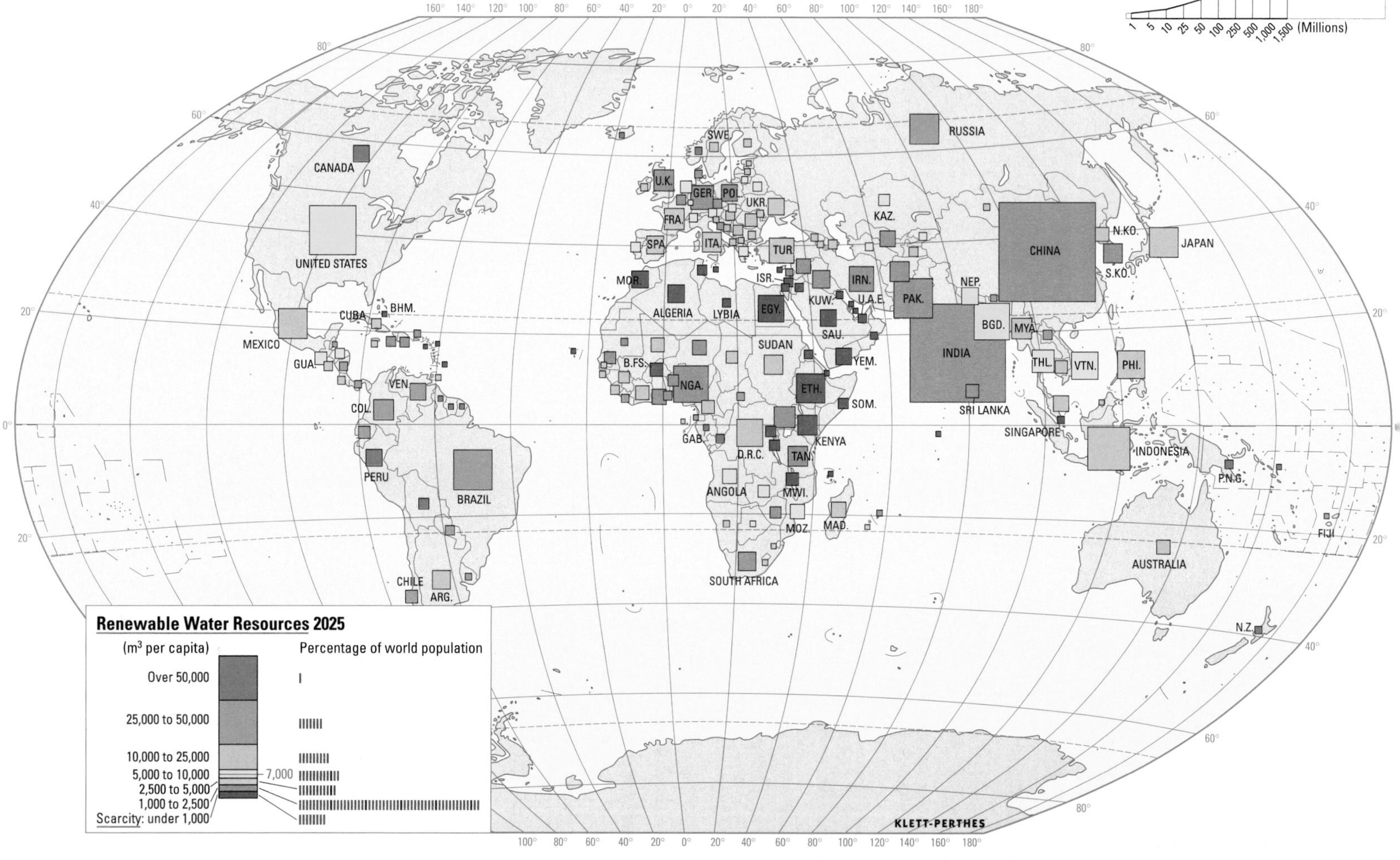

Water Resources 2025

Renewable Water Resources 2025

(m³ per capita)	Percentage of world population
Over 50,000	I
25,000 to 50,000	IIIIIII
10,000 to 25,000	IIIIIIIII
5,000 to 10,000	IIIIIIIIIIII
2,500 to 5,000	IIIIIIIIIII
1,000 to 2,500	IIIIIIIIIIIIIIIIIIIIIIIIIIIIIIIIIIIIIIIIIIIIIIIIIIIIIIII
Scarcity: under 1,000	IIIIIIII

7,000

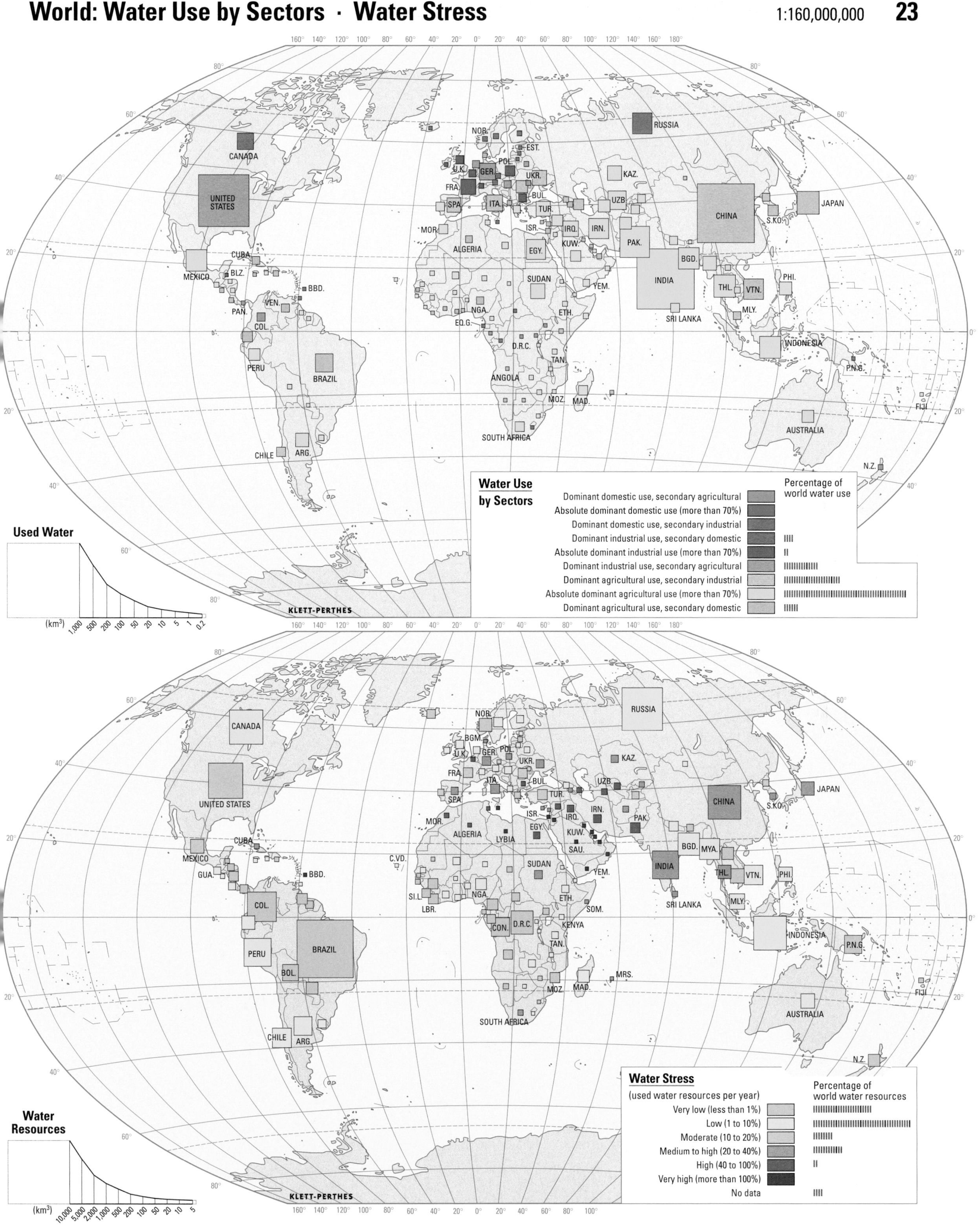
Water Use
by Sectors
Percentage of world water use
Dominant domestic use, secondary agricultural
Absolute dominant domestic use (more than 70%)
Dominant domestic use, secondary industrial
Dominant industrial use, secondary domestic
Absolute dominant industrial use (more than 70%)
Dominant industrial use, secondary agricultural
Dominant agricultural use, secondary industrial
Absolute dominant agricultural use (more than 70%)
Dominant agricultural use, secondary domestic
Used Water
(km³)
1,000 500 200 100 50 20 10 5 1 0.2
RUSSIA
CANADA
UNITED STATES
MEXICO
CHINA
INDIA
JAPAN
BRAZIL
AUSTRALIA
INDONESIA
SOUTH AFRICA
KLETT-PERTHES
Water Stress
(used water resources per year)
Percentage of world water resources
Very low (less than 1%)
Low (1 to 10%)
Moderate (10 to 20%)
Medium to high (20 to 40%)
High (40 to 100%)
Very high (more than 100%)
No data
Water
Resources
(km³)
10,000 5,000 2,000 1,000 500 200 100 50 20 10 5

World: Temperatures in January and July

1:160,000,000

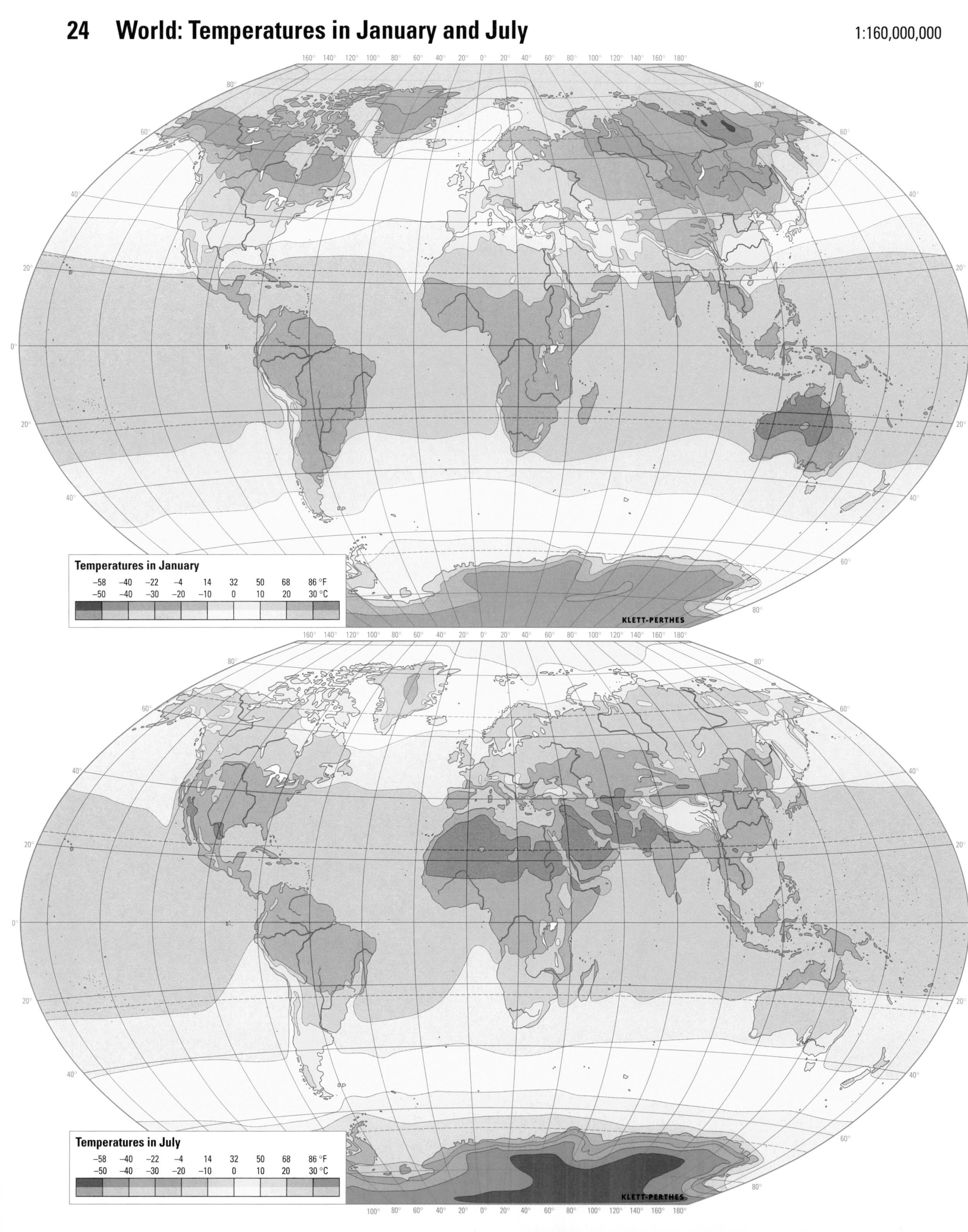

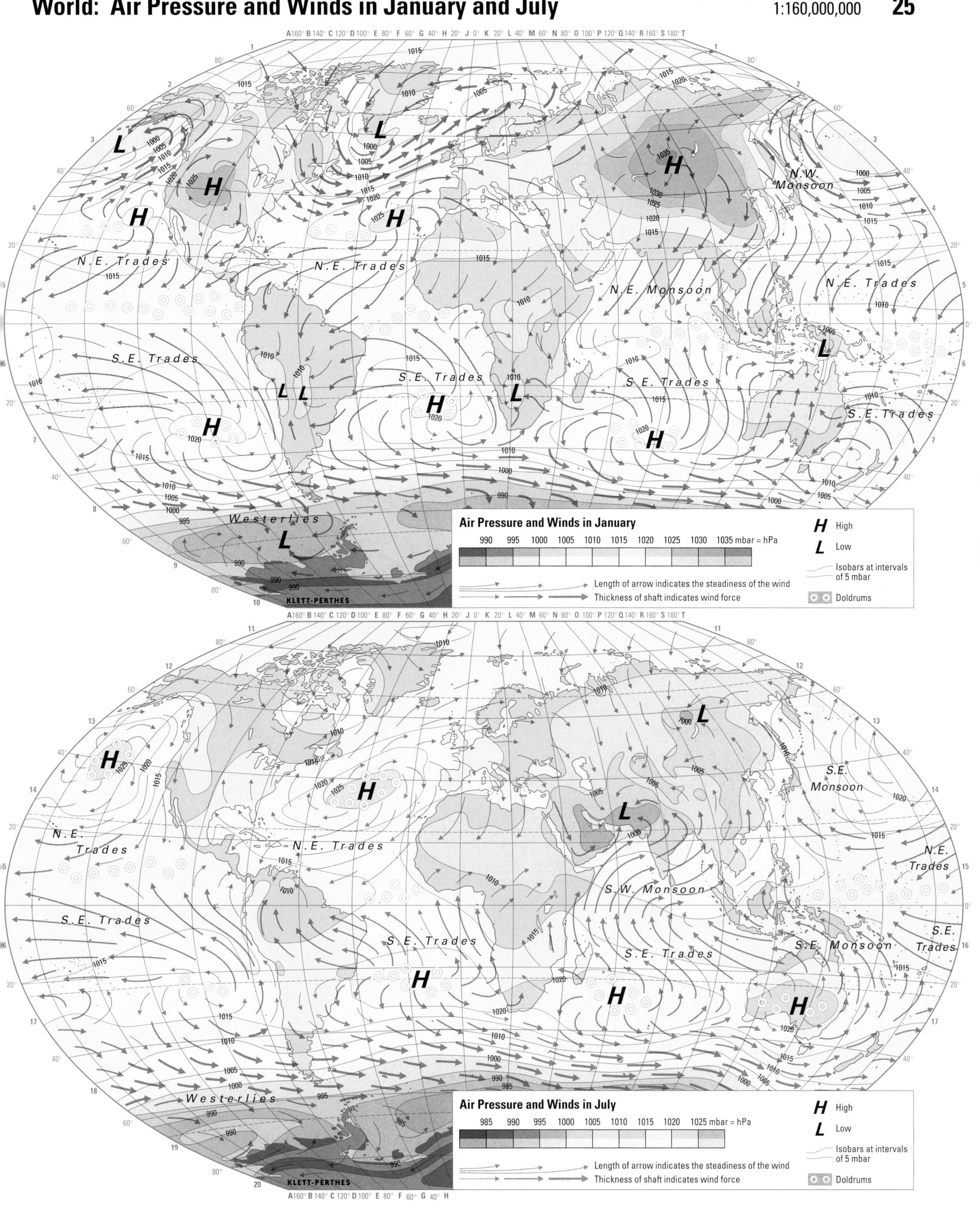
Air Pressure and Winds in January
990 995 1000 1005 1010 1015 1020 1025 1030 1035 mbar = hPa
H High
L Low
Isobars at intervals of 5 mbar
Length of arrow indicates the steadiness of the wind
Thickness of shaft indicates wind force
Doldrums
N.E. Trades
S.E. Trades
N.E. Monsoon
N.W. Monsoon
Westerlies
KLETT-PERTHES
Air Pressure and Winds in July
985 990 995 1000 1005 1010 1015 1020 1025 mbar = hPa
H High
L Low
Isobars at intervals of 5 mbar
Length of arrow indicates the steadiness of the wind
Thickness of shaft indicates wind force
Doldrums
S.E. Monsoon
S.W. Monsoon
KLETT-PERTHES

A 160° B 140° C 120° D 100° E 80° F 60° G 40° H 20° J 0
A R C T I C
Queen Elizabeth Is.
Sverdrup Is.
Ellesmere I.
Beaufort Sea
Parry Is.
Devon I.
Victoria I.
Baffin Bay
Greenland
Baffin I.
Davis Str.
Denmark Str.
Arctic Circle
Iceland
Mackenzie
Yukon
G. of Alaska
Kodiak I.
Aleutian Is.
Hudson Bay
NEARCTIC
Labrador Sea
British Is.
North Sea
Newfoundland
Missouri
Mississippi
Azores
Bermuda Is.
Madeira
ATLANTIC
Canary Is.
Hawaiian Is.
Hawaii
Tropic of Cancer
Gulf of Mexico
Bahama Is.
Cuba
Hispaniola
Greater Antilles
Lesser Antilles
Caribbean Sea
Cape Verde Is.
Niger
PACIFIC
Line Islands
Kiritimati
Equator
Jarvis I.
Galápagos Is.
Amazon
NEOTROPIC
Fernando de Noronha
Ascension
Marquesas Is.
OCEANIA
Cook Islands
Society Is.
Tuamotu Is.
OCEAN
St. Helena
Tropic of Capricorn
Tubuai Is.
Pitcairn Is.
Desventurados Is.
Juan Fernández Is.
Río de la Plata
Tristan da Cunha
Gough I.
Falkland Is. (Is. Malvinas)
Tierra del Fuego
South Georgia
Bouvet I.
Str. of Magellan
Scotia Sea
South Sandwich Is.
Drake Passage
South Shetland Is.
South Orkney Is.
Antarctic Circle
ANT
1
2
3
4
5
6
80°
60°
40°
20°
0°
20°
13
10
8

O C E A N
Franz Josef Land
Severnaya Zemlya
New Siberian Is.
Laptev Sea
East Siberian Sea
Kara Sea
Novaya Zemlya
Barents Sea
Bering Sea
Sea of Okhotsk
Aleutian Is.
Sakhalin
Kurile Is.
Baykal
Amur
Lena
Yenisey
Ob'
Volga
Baltic S.
P A L E A R C T I C
Aral Sea
Caspian Sea
Black Sea
Hokkaido
Sea of Japan
Honshu
Kyushu
Yellow R.
Yangtze
Midway Is.
Bonin Is.
Ryukyu Is.
P A C I F I C
Volcano Is.
Taiwan
Mariana Is.
Wake I.
Hainan
Luzon
Philippines
O C E A N I A
Marshall Islands
Nile
Red Sea
Arabian Sea
Bay of Bengal
South China Sea
L. Chad
Socotra
I N D O - M A L A Y
Ceylon
Caroline Is.
Micronesia
Mindanao
O C E A N
Melanesia
Congo
L. Victoria
Maldives
Sumatra
Borneo (Kalimantan)
Celebes (Sulawesi)
Bismarck Arch.
New Guinea
Gilbert Is.
Phoenix Is.
Equator
Seychelles
Chagos Is.
Greater Sunda Is.
Lesser Sunda Is.
Java
Solomon Is.
Ellice Is.
Tokleau Is.
Wallis Is.
Futuna
Comoro Is.
I N D I A N
Cocos Is.
Coral Sea
New Hebrides
Tonga Is.
Fiji Is.
Mozambique Ch.
Madagascar
Mascarene Is.
New Caledonia
A U S T R A L A S I A
Norfolk I.
Kermadec Is.
O C E A N
Amsterdam
Tasman Sea
North Island
Tasmania
New Zealand
South Island
Bounty Is.
Auckland Is.
Antipodes Is.
Macquarie
Campbell Is.
Biomes
1 Tundra
2 Boreal forests/Taiga
3 Temperate conifer forests
4 Temperate broadleaf and mixed forests
5 Temperate grasslands, savannas and shrublands
6 Mediterranean forests, woodlands and shrub
7 Deserts and xeric shrublands
8 Tropical and subtropical coniferous forests
9 Tropical and subtropical moist broadleaf forests
10 Tropical and subtropical dry broadleaf forests
11 Tropical and subtropical grasslands, savannas and shrublands
12 Flooded grasslands and savannas
13 Mangroves
14 Montane grasslands and shrublands
Biogeographic Realms
N E A R C T I C
Rock and ice
KLETT-PERTHES
10
11
12
13
14

A 160° B 140° C 120° D 100° E 80° F 60° G 40° H 20° J
1
2
3
4
5
6
10
80°
60°
40°
20°
0°
20°
80°
A R C T I C
Queen Elizabeth Is.
Sverdrup Is.
Ellesmere I.
Parry Is.
Beaufort Sea
Victoria I.
Devon I.
Baffin Bay
Baffin I.
Greenland
Davis Str.
Denmark Str.
Iceland
Arctic Circle
Norw
Mackenzie
Yukon
G. of Alaska
Kodiak I.
Aleutian Is.
Hudson Bay
Labrador Sea
British Is.
North Sea
NORTH AMERICA
Missouri
Mississippi
Newfoundland
Azores
Madeira
Canary Is.
Bermuda Is.
Sargasso Sea
Hawaiian Is.
Hawaii
Tropic of Cancer
Gulf of Mexico
Bahama Is.
Cuba
Hispaniola
Greater Antilles
Lesser Antilles
Caribbean Sea
ATLANTIC
Cape Verde Is.
Niger
PACIFIC
Equator
Kiritimati
Galápagos Is.
G. of Guinea
OCEAN
Amazon
Fernando de Noronha
Ascension
Marquesas Is.
SOUTH AMERICA
St. Helena
Tropic of Capricorn
Desventurados Is.
OCEAN
Juan Fernández Is.
Rio de la Plata
Tristan da Cunha
Gough I.
Falkland Is. (Is. Malvinas)
Tierra del Fuego
South Georgia
Bouvet I.
Str. of Magellan
Scotia Sea
South Sandwich Is.
Drake Passage
South Shetland Is.
South Orkney Is.
Antarctic Circle
Bellingshausen Sea
Peter I I.
Alexander I.
Weddell Sea
Amundsen Sea
Berkner I.
A N T A R
A 160° B 140° C 120° D 100° E 80° F 60° G 40° H 20° J 0°
Soil Orders
Gelisols
Soils of very cold climates with permafrost within 2 meters of the surface; limited to high-latitude polar regions and most high mountains.
Histosols
Soils composed of mainly organic matter; low bulk densities, temporarily good agricultural soils after drainage of swamplands in warm environments, but rapid oxidizing disintegration.
Spodosols
Acidic soils characterized by an ashy grey near-surface horizon above a horizon stained with humus, iron and aluminium oxides leached from above; typical soil of the coniferous Boreal forests; generally marginal for agriculture.
Andisols
Formed in volcanic ash or other volcanic ejecta; dominated by glass and poorly crystalline colloidal materials.
Oxisols
Intensively weathered tropical and subtropical soils of low natural fertility; low base saturation; generally ill suited for intensive agricultural production.
Vertisols
Clay-rich tropical and subtropical soils that shrink and swell with changes in moisture content; shrink/swell action creates serious engineering problems; generally fertile and well suited to crop production.
Aridisols
Frequently CaCO3-containing soils of arid regions, largely paleosoils of more humid phases of the past, with at least some subsurface horizon development; low organic-matter content; dry most of the year; made productive for agriculture by irrigation.
Ultisols
Strongly leached, acid forest soils with relatively low native fertility; found primarily in humid temperate and tropical areas; with a subsurface horizon to which clays have been washed down; base saturation less than 35%; often marginal for agriculture.
Mollisols
Soils of grassland ecosystems; characterized by a thick, dark, humus-rich surface horizon; high base saturation; very productive for grain crops.
Alfisols
Moderately leached forest soils of relatively high native fertility; well developed, with a subsurface horizon in which clays have accumulated from above; base saturation of 35% or greater; mostly found in temperate humid and subhumid regions.
Inceptisols
Humid-region soils that exhibit minimal horizon development; relatively youthful in age.
Entisols
Soils of recent origin, with little or no soil-morphological development, lacking pedogenic horizons; characterized by great diversity in environmental setting, fertility and land use.
Rock land
Shifting sand
Ice/glacier

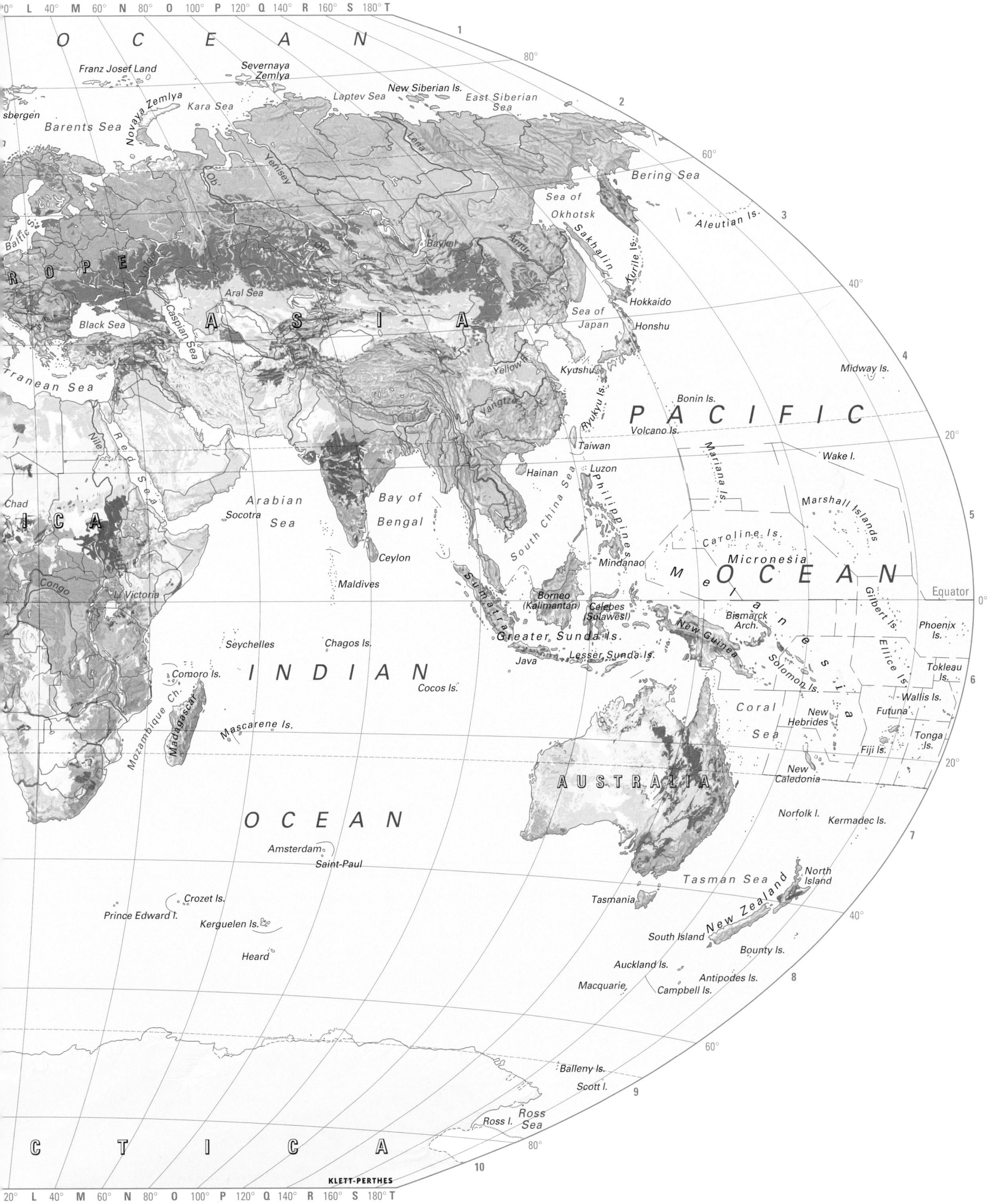

O C E A N
Franz Josef Land
Severnaya Zemlya
New Siberian Is.
Laptev Sea
East Siberian Sea
Kara Sea
Novaya Zemlya
Barents Sea
Lena
Yenisey
Ob'
Bering Sea
Sea of Okhotsk
Aleutian Is.
Sakhalin
Kurile Is.
Amur
L. Baykal
Baltic S.
ROPE
Volga
Aral Sea
Caspian Sea
Black Sea
A S I A
Hokkaido
Sea of Japan
Honshu
Kyushu
Yellow R.
Midway Is.
Yangtze
Bonin Is.
Ryukyu Is.
P A C I F I C
Volcano Is.
Taiwan
Wake I.
Mariana Is.
Hainan
Luzon
Philippines
Nile
Red Sea
Chad
Arabian Sea
Socotra
Bay of Bengal
South China Sea
Marshall Islands
Caroline Is.
Micronesia
ICA
Ceylon
Mindanao
M e l a n e s i a
O C E A N
Maldives
Congo
L. Victoria
Sumatra
Borneo (Kalimantan)
Celebes (Sulawesi)
Gilbert Is.
Equator
Bismarck Arch.
New Guinea
Phoenix Is.
Seychelles
Chagos Is.
Greater Sunda Is.
Java
Lesser Sunda Is.
Solomon Is.
Ellice Is.
Tokleau Is.
Comoro Is.
I N D I A N
Cocos Is.
Wallis Is.
Coral Sea
Futuna
New Hebrides
Mozambique Ch.
Madagascar
Mascarene Is.
Tonga Is.
Fiji Is.
New Caledonia
A U S T R A L I A
Norfolk I.
Kermadec Is.
O C E A N
Amsterdam
Saint-Paul
Tasman Sea
North Island
Tasmania
New Zealand
Crozet Is.
Prince Edward I.
Kerguelen Is.
South Island
Heard
Bounty Is.
Auckland Is.
Antipodes Is.
Macquarie
Campbell Is.
Balleny Is.
Scott I.
Ross Sea
Ross I.
C T I C A

KLETT-PERTHES

1:160,000,000

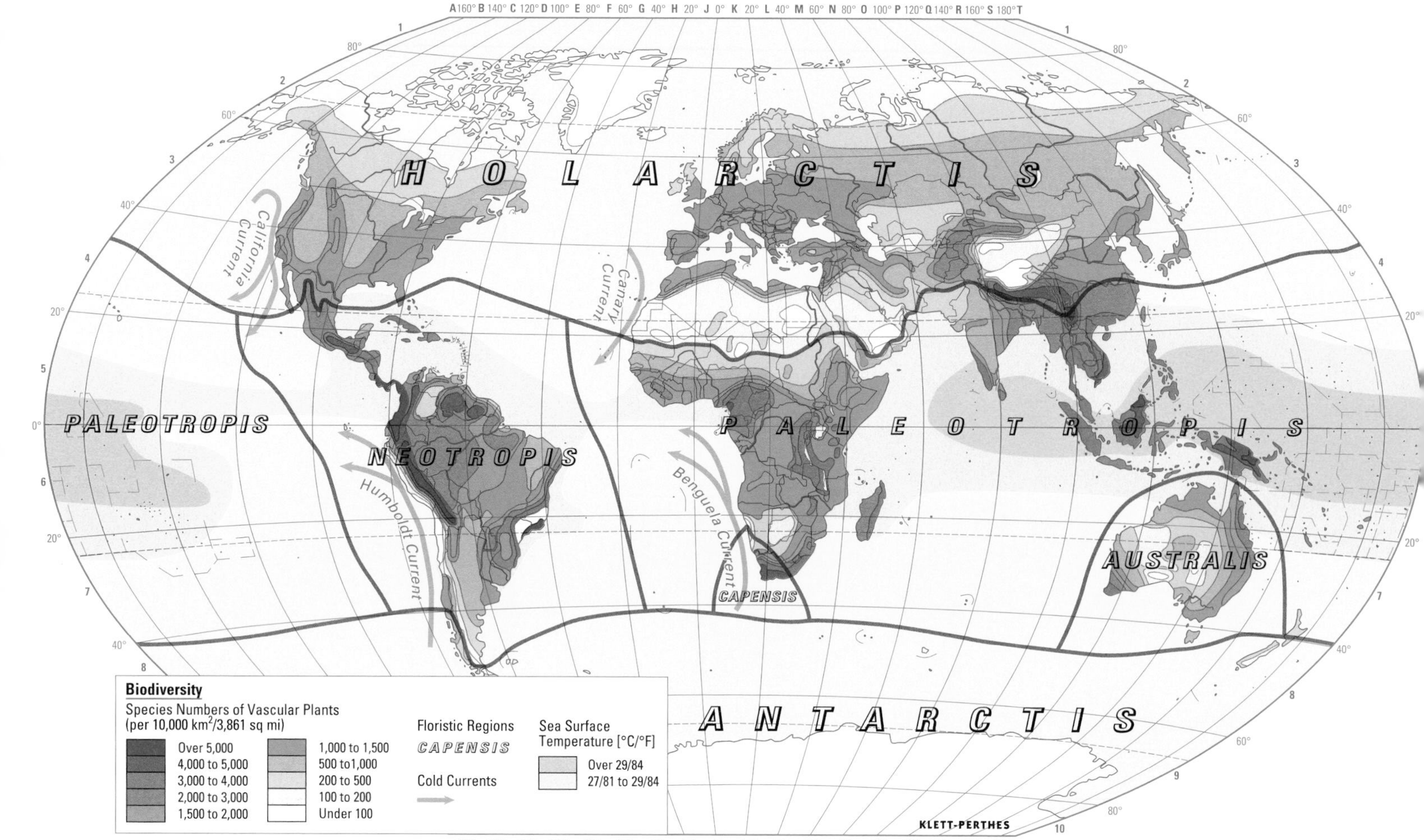

Biodiversity

Species Numbers of Vascular Plants (per 10,000 km²/3,861 sq mi)

- Over 5,000
- 4,000 to 5,000
- 3,000 to 4,000
- 2,000 to 3,000
- 1,500 to 2,000
- 1,000 to 1,500
- 500 to1,000
- 200 to 500
- 100 to 200
- Under 100

Floristic Regions
CAPENSIS

Cold Currents

Sea Surface Temperature [°C/°F]

- Over 29/84
- 27/81 to 29/84

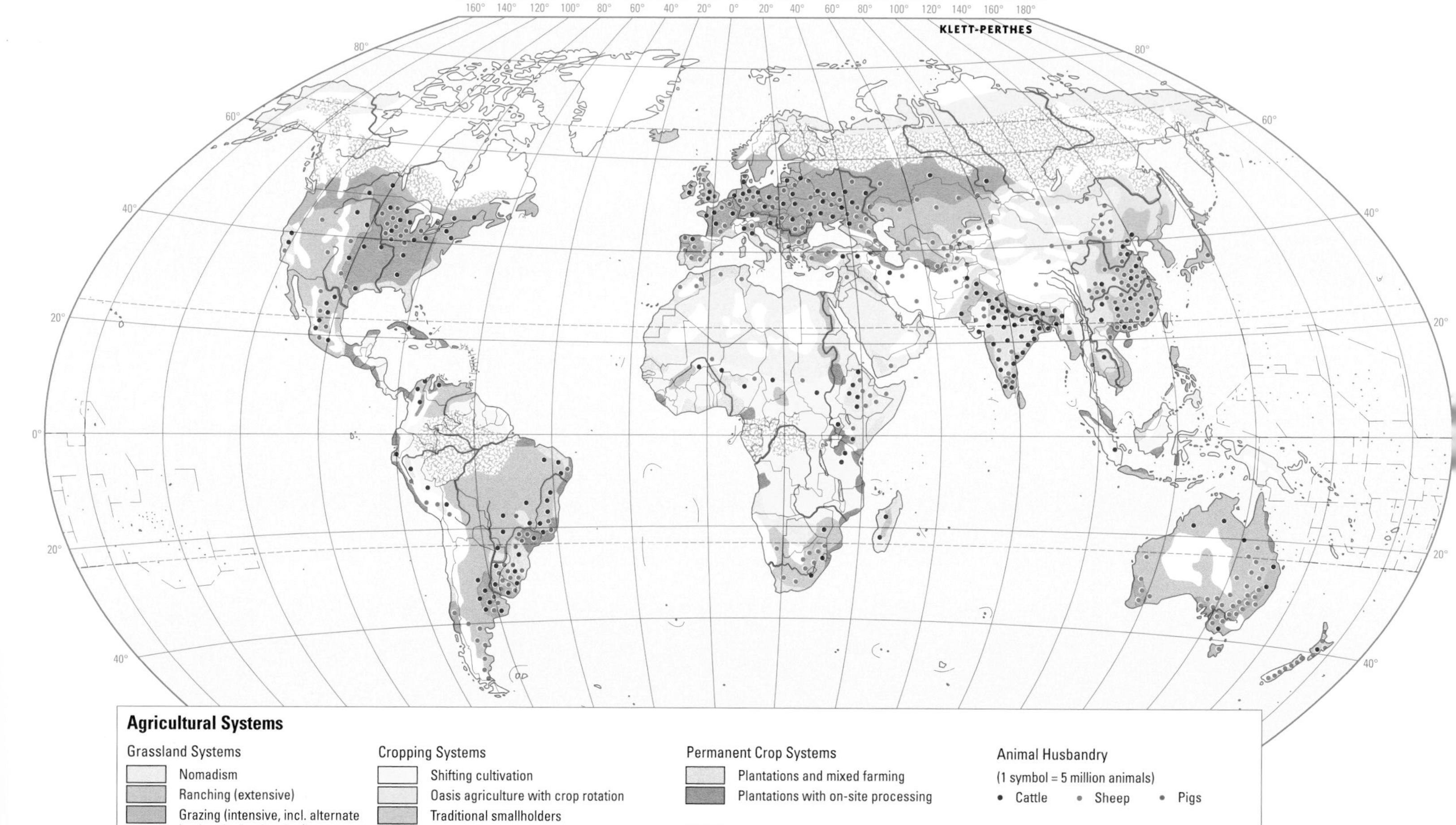

Agricultural Systems

Grassland Systems

- Nomadism
- Ranching (extensive)
- Grazing (intensive, incl. alternate husbandry/ley farming)

Cropping Systems

- Shifting cultivation
- Oasis agriculture with crop rotation
- Traditional smallholders
- Mechanized medium-size and large farms

Permanent Crop Systems

- Plantations and mixed farming
- Plantations with on-site processing

Animal Husbandry
(1 symbol = 5 million animals)

- Cattle
- Sheep
- Pigs

Forests with marginal economic activity (agriculture, animal husbandry, logging, hunting etc.)

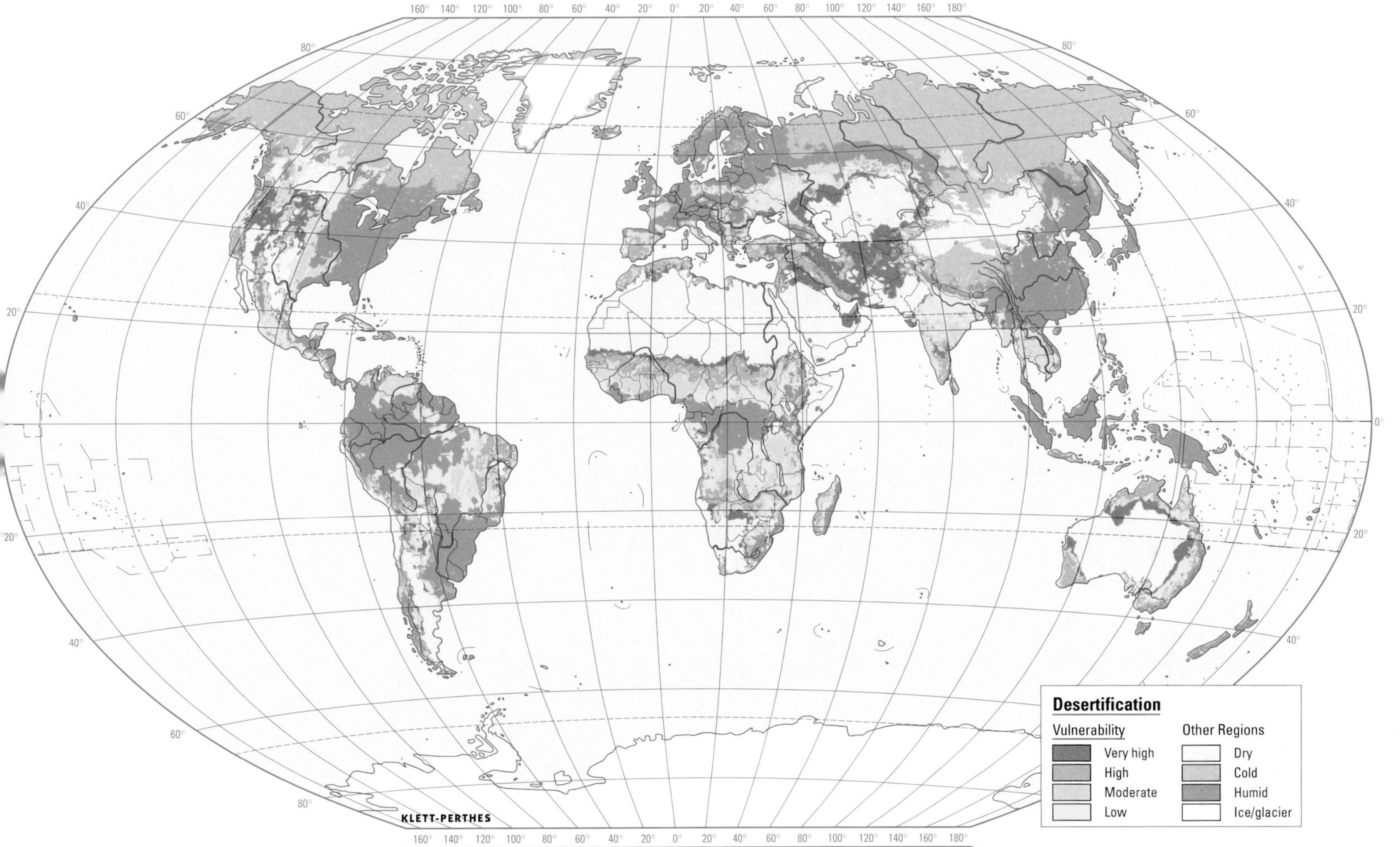

Desertification
Vulnerability
Very high
High
Moderate
Low
Other Regions
Dry
Cold
Humid
Ice/glacier
KLETT-PERTHES

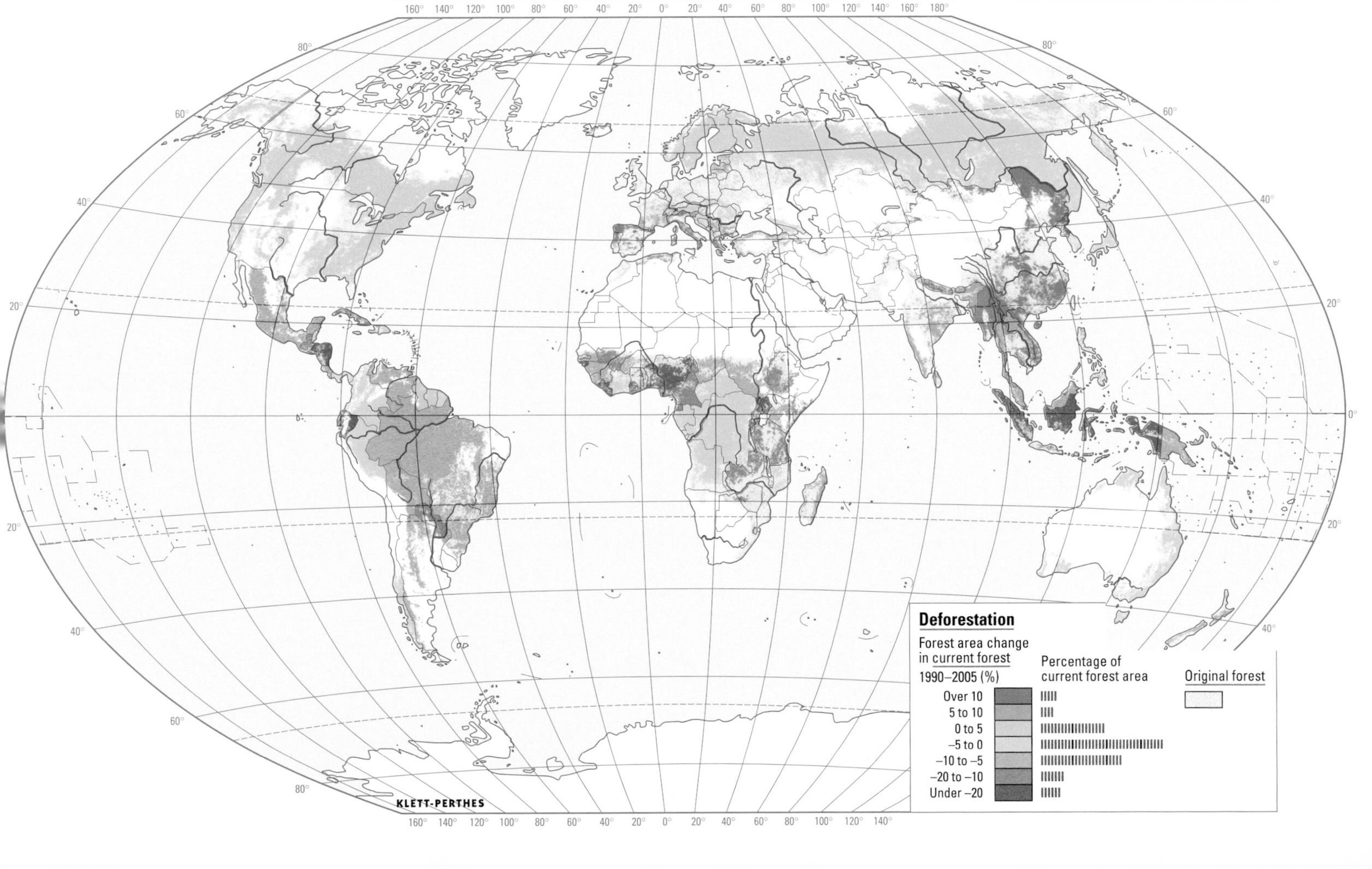

Deforestation
Forest area change in current forest 1990–2005 (%)
Over 10
5 to 10
0 to 5
–5 to 0
–10 to –5
–20 to –10
Under –20
Percentage of current forest area
Original forest
KLETT-PERTHES

Land Cover
Natural Vegetation
Evergreen needleleaf forests
Lands dominated by woody vegetation with a percent cover >60% and height exceeding 2 meters. Almost all trees remain green all year. Canopy is never without green foliage.
Evergreen broadleaf forests
Lands dominated by woody vegetation with a percent cover >60% and height exceeding 2 meters. Almost all trees and shrubs remain green year round. Canopy is never without green foliage.
Deciduous needleleaf forests
Lands dominated by woody vegetation with a percent cover >60% and height exceeding 2 meters. Consists of seasonal needleleaf tree communities with an annual cycle of leaf-on and leaf-off periods.
Deciduous broadleaf forests
Lands dominated by woody vegetation with a percent cover >60% and height exceeding 2 meters. Consists of broadleaf tree communities with an annual cycle of leaf-on and leaf-off periods.
Mixed forests
Lands dominated by trees with a percent cover >60% and height exceeding 2 meters. Consists of tree communities with interspersed mixtures or mosaics of the other four forest types. None of the forest types exceeds 60% of landscape.
Closed shrublands
Lands with woody vegetation less than 2 meters tall and with shrub canopy cover >60%. The shrub foliage can be either evergreen or deciduous.
Open shrublands
Lands with woody vegetation less than 2 meters tall and with shrub canopy cover between 10-60%. The shrub foliage can be either evergreen or deciduous.
Woody savannas
Lands with herbaceous and other understory systems, and with forest canopy cover between 30-60%. The forest cover height exceeds 2 meters.
Savannas
Lands with herbaceous and other understory systems, and with forest canopy cover between 10-30%. The forest cover height exceeds 2 meters.
Grasslands
Lands with herbaceous types of cover. Tree and shrub cover is less than 10%.
Permanent wetlands
Lands with a permanent mixture of water and herbaceous or woody vegetation. The vegetation can be present in either salt, brackish, or fresh water.
Developed and Mosaic Lands
Croplands
Lands covered with temporary crops followed by harvest and a bare soil period (e.g., single and multiple cropping systems). Note that perennial woody crops will be classified as the appropriate forest or shrub land cover type.
Cropland/natural vegetation mosaic
Lands with a mosaic of croplands, forests, shrubland, and grasslands in which no one component comprises more than 60% of the landscape.
Urban and built-up lands
Land covered by buildings and other man-made structures.
Non-Vegetated Lands
Snow and ice
Lands under snow/ice cover throughout the year.
Barren or sparsely vegetated
Lands with exposed soil, sand, rocks, or snow and never has more than 10% vegetated cover during any time of the year.
Water bodies
Oceans, seas, lakes, reservoirs, and rivers. Can be either fresh or salt-water bodies.
No data
A 160° B 140° C 120° D 100° E 80° F 60° G 40° H 20° J
ARCTIC
Queen Elizabeth Is.
Sverdrup Is.
Ellesmere I.
Parry Is.
Beaufort Sea
Victoria I.
Devon I.
Baffin Bay
Baffin I.
Greenland
Davis Str.
Denmark Str.
Iceland
Arctic Circle
Alaska
Alaska Range
G. of Alaska
Kodiak I.
Aleutian Is.
Yukon
Mackenzie
Hudson Bay
Canadian Shield
Labrador
Labrador Sea
British Is.
North Sea
London
Newfoundland
NORTH AMERICA
Rocky Mountains
Great Plains
Missouri
Mississippi
Denver
Chicago
Appalachian Mts.
Boston
New York
Washington, D.C.
Atlanta
Los Angeles
Houston
PACIFIC
OCEAN
Hawaiian Is.
Hawaii
Tropic of Cancer
Bermuda Is.
Sargasso Sea
Azores
Madeira
Canary Is.
Atlas
ATLANTIC
Gulf of Mexico
Bahama Is.
Cuba
Hispaniola
Greater Antilles
Lesser Antilles
Caribbean Sea
Mexico City
Cape Verde Is.
Niger
G. of Guinea
Equator
Llanos
Guiana Highlands
Galápagos Is.
Amazon
Selvas
Campos
SOUTH AMERICA
Andes
Brazilian Highlands
Fernando de Noronha
Ascension
St. Helena
Tropic of Capricorn
Rio De Janeiro
São Paulo
Desventurados Is.
Juan Fernández Is.
Santiago
Pampas
Buenos Aires
Río de la Plata
Tristan da Cunha
Gough I.
Patagonia
Falkland Is. (Is. Malvinas)
Tierra del Fuego
Str. of Magellan
South Georgia
Bouvet I.
Scotia Sea
South Sandwich Is.
Drake Passage
South Shetland Is.
South Orkney Is.
Antarctic Circle
Antarctic Pen.
Bellingshausen Sea
Peter I I.
Alexander I.
Amundsen Sea
Weddell Sea
Ellsworth Land
Berkner I.
ANTAR

O C E A N
Franz Josef Land
Severnaya Zemlya
New Siberian Is.
Laptev Sea
East Siberian Sea
Kara Sea
Taymyr Pen.
Novaya Zemlya
Barents Sea
Central Siberian Plateau
Yakutia
Lena
Yenisey
West Siberian Plain
Ural Mts.
Ob
Bering Sea
Kamchatka
Sea of Okhotsk
Sakhalin
Aleutian Is.
Kurile Is.
Amur
Baykal
Moscow
Volga
Baltic S.
Altay Mts.
Aral Sea
Caspian Sea
Black Sea
Tashkent
Tien Shan
Gobi
Manchuria
Beijing
Hokkaido
Sea of Japan
Honshu
Korea
Tōkyō
Anatolia
Tehrān
Baghdad
Iranian Plateau
Kunlun Shan
Tibet
Himalayas
Yellow R.
Kyushu
Shanghai
Midway Is.
Cairo
Libyan Desert
Nile
Red Sea
Arabian Pen.
Delhi
Yangtze
Ryukyu Is.
Bonin Is.
PACIFIC
Volcano Is.
Taiwan
Kolkata
India
Mariana Is.
Wake I.
Hainan
Luzon
Philippines
Chad
Arabian Sea
Bay of Bengal
Bangkok
South China Sea
Marshall Islands
Socotra
Ethiopian Highlands
Somali Pen.
Caroline Is.
Micronesia
Ceylon
Mindanao
Maldives
Congo
Congo Basin
Victoria
Sumatra
Borneo (Kalimantan)
Celebes (Sulawesi)
OCEAN
Melanesia
Gilbert Is.
Equator
Phoenix Is.
Bismarck Arch.
New Guinea
Greater Sunda Is.
Jakarta
Java
Lesser Sunda Is.
Seychelles
Chagos Is.
Ellice Is.
Tokleau Is.
Solomon Is.
Comoro Is.
INDIAN
Cocos Is.
Wallis Is.
Futuna
Coral Sea
New Hebrides
Tonga Is.
Fiji Is.
Mozambique Ch.
Madagascar
Mascarene Is.
Namib
Johannesburg
AUSTRALIA
Great Dividing Range
Great Victoria Desert
New Caledonia
Cape Town
OCEAN
Perth
Norfolk I.
Kermadec Is.
Amsterdam
Saint-Paul
Austr. Alps
Sydney
Melbourne
Tasman Sea
North Island
Tasmania
Crozet Is.
Prince Edward I.
Kerguelen Is.
New Zealand
South Island
Heard
Bounty Is.
Auckland Is.
Antipodes Is.
Macquarie
Campbell Is.
aud Land
Wilkes Land
Balleny Is.
Scott I.
Ross I.
Ross Sea
C T I C A
KLETT-PERTHES

World: Natural Hazards

O C E A N
Franz Josef Land
Severnaya Zemlya
New Siberian Is.
Laptev Sea
East Siberian Sea
Kara Sea
Barents Sea
Novaya Zemlya
Norilsk
Lena
Yenisey
Ob'
Yakutsk
Bering Sea
R U S S I A
FINLAND
Sea of Okhotsk
Aleutian Is.
Petropavlovsk-Kamchatskiy
Sakhalin
Kurile Is.
ST. PETERSBURG
NIZHNIY NOVGOROD
YEKATERINBURG
OMSK
NOVOSIBIRSK
Irkutsk
L. Baykal
Amur
Khabarovsk
MOSCOW
SAMARA
WARSAW
POLAND
KIEV
UKRAINE
KAZAKHSTAN
Ulan Bator
MONGOLIA
SHENYANG
Vladivostok
Hokkaido
HUN.
ROM.
BUL.
Black Sea
GEO.
Caspian Sea
UZB.
Bishkek
ALMATY
KYR.
ÜRÜMQI
BEIJING
NORTH KOREA
Sea of Japan
Honshu
GCE.
Athens
TURKEY
ANKARA
BAKU
TASHKENT
TAJ.
C H I N A
SÖUL
SOUTH
TŌKYŌ
OSAKA
JAPAN
Midway Is. (U.S.)
Mediterranean Sea
TEHRAN
IRAQ
BAGHDAD
IRAN
KABUL
AFG.
Islamabad
LAHORE
XI'AN
Yellow R.
SHANGHAI
Kyushu
Ryukyu Is.
Bonin Is.
LIBYA
CAIRO
EGYPT
Kuwait
PAKISTAN
NEPAL
Kathmandu
DELHI
CHONGQING
Yangtze
WUHAN
P A C I F I C
SAUDI ARABIA
RIYADH
Nile
Red Sea
Abu Dhabi
KARACHI
BGD.
GUANGZHOU
Volcano Is.
Wake I. (U.S.)
JEDDAH
KOLKATA
INDIA
MYANMAR
HANOI
HONG KONG
TAIWAN
Luzon
Hainan
Northern Mariana Is. (U.S.)
CHAD
Chad
SANAA
ERI.
MUMBAI
Arabian Sea
Bay of Bengal
RANGOON
THAILAND
South China Sea
MANILA
PHILIPPINES
Guam (U.S.)
Marshall Islands
KHARTOUM
SUDAN
YEMEN
Socotra (YEM.)
DJI.
N'Djamena
ADDIS ABABA
CHENNAI
BANGKOK
VIETNAM
Caroline Is.
Palikir
Uliga
C.A.R.
Bangui
ETHIOPIA
SOMALIA
Colombo
SRI LANKA
KUALA LUMPUR
MICRONESIA
Mindanao
Congo
DEM. REP. OF THE CONGO
UGA.
KENYA
MOGADISHU
Male
MALDIVES
Sumatra
MALAYSIA
SINGAPORE
Melanesia
OCEAN
KINSHASA
BDI.
NAIROBI
Victoria
Borneo (Kalimantan)
Celebes (Sulawesi)
Bairiki
Equator
KIRIBATI
TANZANIA
Victoria
INDIAN
Brit. Indian Ocean Terr. (U.K.)
JAKARTA
INDONESIA
New Guinea
Bismarck Arch.
PAPUA NEW GUINEA
LUANDA
ANGOLA
DAR ES SALAAM
SEYCHELLES
COMOROS
Java
SURABAYA
Christmas I. (AUS.)
Port Moresby
Solomon Is.
Ellice Is.
Tokelau (N.Z.)
ZAMBIA
LUSAKA
HARARE
ZIM.
MOZAMBIQUE
ANTANANARIVO
Cocos Is. (AUS.)
Coral Sea
Coral Sea Is. (AUS.)
VANUATU
Port Vila
Wallis and Futuna (FRA.)
SAMOA
Apia
NAMIBIA
Windhoek
MADAGASCAR
Réunion (FRA.)
Suva
FIJI
TONGA
JOHANNESBURG
SOUTH AFRICA
MAPUTO
CAPE TOWN
AUSTRALIA
New Caledonia (FRA.)
BRISBANE
OCEAN
PERTH
Kermadec Is. (N.Z.)
Norfolk I. (AUS.)
ADELAIDE
SYDNEY
Canberra
Amsterdam
Saint-Paul
MELBOURNE
Tasman Sea
North Island
Prince Edward and Marion Is. (S.AF.)
French Southern Terr.
Crozet Is.
Tasmania
NEW ZEALAND
Wellington
Kerguelen Is.
Chatham Is.
South Island
Bounty Is.
(N.Z.)
Heard and the McDonald Is. (AUS.)
Auckland Is. (N.Z.)
Antipodes Is.
Macquarie (AUS.)
Campbell Is. (N.Z.)
Balleny Is.
Scott I.
A N T A R C T I C A
KLETT-PERTHES
Natural Disaster (2004, 2005)
Type of Disaster
Slide
Wind storm
Drought
Earthquake
Extreme temperature
Flood
Wave, surge
Epidemic
Disaster Victims
50 to 100 killed
100 to 1,000 killed
1,000 to 10,000 killed
10,000 to 100,000 killed
More than 100,000 killed
Extratropical Storms, Winter Storms
High extratropical storm hazard, mainly in winter
Principal tracks of extratropical storms
Other Natural Hazards
Limit of drift ice
Pack ice (winter maximum)
High seas with wave heights over 5 metres

AFG.	AFGHANISTAN	B.FS.	BURKINA FASO	BLR.	BELARUS	C.IV.	CÔTE D'IVOIRE	DJI.	DJIBOUTI	GAB.	GABON
ALB.	ALBANIA	BDI.	BURUNDI	BLZ.	BELIZE	C.RC.	COSTA RICA	DEN.	DENMARK	GAM.	GAMBIA
ARM.	ARMENIA	BEN.	BENIN	BOT.	BOTSWANA	CBD.	CAMBODIA	DO.R.	DOMINICAN REP.	GCE.	GREECE
AUT.	AUSTRIA	BGD.	BANGLADESH	BRU.	BRUNEI	CMN.	CAMEROON	ERI.	ERITREA	GEO.	GEORGIA
AZE.	AZERBAIJAN	BGM.	BELGIUM	BUL.	BULGARIA	CRO.	CROATIA	EST.	ESTONIA	GHA.	GHANA
B. & H.	BOSNIA AND HERZEGOVINA	BHR.	BAHRAIN	C.A.R.	CENTRAL AFRICAN REPUBLIC	CYP.	CYPRUS	EQ.G.	EQUATORIAL GUINEA	GUA.	GUATEMALA
		BHU.	BHUTAN			CZ.R.	CZECH REPUBLIC				

B.	GUINEA-BISSAU	K.	KOSOVO	LUX.	LUXEMBOURG	PAN.	PANAMA	SUR.	SURINAME	TKM.	TURKMENISTAN
N.	HONDURAS	KUW.	KUWAIT	M.	MONTENEGRO	QAT.	QATAR	SVK.	SLOVAKIA	TUN.	TUNISIA
N.	HUNGARY	KYR.	KYRGYZSTAN	MAC.	MACEDONIA	ROM.	ROMANIA	SVN.	SLOVENIA	U.A.E.	UNITED ARAB EMIRATES
.	HAITI	LAT.	LATVIA	MOL.	MOLDOVA	RWA.	RWANDA	SWA.	SWAZILAND		
	ISRAEL	LEB.	LEBANON	MWI.	MALAWI	SAL.	EL SALVADOR	SWI.	SWITZERLAND	UGA.	UGANDA
M.	JAMAICA	LES.	LESOTHO	NLD.	NETHERLANDS	SEN.	SENEGAL	TAJ.	TAJIKISTAN	UZB.	UZBEKISTAN
R.	JORDAN	LIT.	LITHUANIA	NIC.	NICARAGUA	SGP.	SINGAPORE	TGO.	TOGO	ZIM.	ZIMBABWE

1:130,000,000

180°
24
12:00 p.m. (±12)
1
165°
1:00 a.m. (−11)
11:00 p.m. (+11)
23
2
International Date Line East IDLE/[3]
Intern. Date Line West IDLW
12:45 a.m.
Wellington
150°
2:00 a.m. (−10)
Aleutian Standard Time AST
10:00 p.m. (+10)
Guam Standard Time GST
22
(+13)
Suva
11:30 p.m.
Port Vila
3
Hawaii Standard Time HST
Sydney
East Australian Standard Time EAST
135°
3:00 a.m. (−9)
Alaska Standard Time AKST
(+13)
Nauru
9:00 p.m. (+9)
Papeete
(+14)
Adelaide
Japan Standard Time JST
21
Sunday
Monday
9:30 p.m.
4
2:30 a.m.
Hawaiian Is.
AUSTRALIA
120°
4:00 a.m. (−8)
Pacific Standard Time PST
International Date Line
West Australian Standard Time WAST
8:00 p.m. (+8)
China Coast Time CCT
Perth
20
A
Tōkyō
5
Manila
105°
5:00 a.m. (−7)
Mountain Standard Time MST
Easter I.
San Francisco
Anchorage
Magadan
7:00 p.m. (+7)
Beijing
Vancouver
China Time
Yakutsk
Singapore
19
Denver
Bangkok
6
Central Standard Time CST
Mexico City
Irkutsk
6:30 p.m.
6:30 p.m.
Galápagos Is.
NORTH AMERICA
Dhaka
5:30 p.m.
90°
6:00 a.m. (−6)
Norilsk
Chicago
North Pole
Novosibirsk
6:00 p.m. (+6)
ASIA
5:45 p.m.
Indian Time
Toronto
Omsk
Delhi
18
New York
Yekaterinburg
5:30 p.m.
5:30 p.m.
7
Eastern Standard Time EST
Izhevsk
Lima
Arctic Circle
Maldives
8:30 a.m.
Newfoundland
Moscow
Samara
4:30 p.m.
Karachi
(+5)
7:00 a.m. (−5)
Caracas
7:30 a.m.
Baku
3:30 p.m.
75°
Tehrān
5:00 p.m.
London
Berlin
SOUTH AMERICA
A
Azores
Riyadh
Seychelles
EUROPE
17
Manaus
8
Atlantic Standard Time AST
Buenos Aires
Algiers
Cairo
60°
8:00 a.m. (−4)
4:00 p.m. (+4)
Tropic of Cancer
Moscow Time MSK
Rio de Janeiro
Dakar
AFRICA
Nairobi
16
9
Baghdad Time BT
Accra
3:00 p.m. (+3)
9:00 a.m. (−3)
Equator
45°
Kinshasa
Johannesburg
Tropic of Capricorn
10
15
B
Eastern European Time EET
Azores Time AT
Coordinated Universal Time UTC/[2]
Central European Time CET/[1]
10:00 a.m. (−2)
2:00 p.m. (+2)
30°
14
11:00 a.m. (−1)
1:00 p.m. (+1)
11
15°
12:00 a.m. (±0)
15°
13
0°
12

KLETT-PERTHES

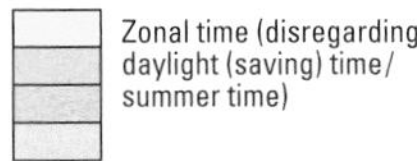

Zonal time (disregarding daylight (saving) time/summer time)

National time

[1] Middle European Time MET
Middle European Winter Time MEWT

[2] Western European Time WET
Greenwich Mean Time GMT

[3] New Zealand Standard Time NZST

Countries with their own time (at 12 a.m. UTC/GMT):

Afghanistan 4:30 p.m.
Australia:
Northern Territory 9:30 p.m.
South Australia 9:30 p.m.
India 5:30 p.m.
Iran 3:30 p.m.
Canada:
Newfoundland 8:30 a.m.
Cocos Islands 6:30 p.m.
French Polynesia:
Marquesas Islands 2:30 a.m.
Myanmar (Burma) 6:30 p.m.
Nepal 5:45 p.m.
New Zealand:
Chatham Islands 12:45 a.m.
Norfolk Island 11:30 p.m.
Sri Lanka 5:30 p.m.
Venezuela 7:30 a.m.

Numbers in the outer circle of the map indicate the difference in hours between each zone and Coordinated Universal Time (UTC), also known as Greenwich Mean Time. New York ("−5") is five hours behind London ("0") but three hours ahead of San Francisco ("−8") and five hours ahead of Hawaii ("−10"). Coordinated Universal Time (UTC), which is observed in London and Accra, is also used throughout Antarctica. Since Earth turns around its axis once in 24 hours, you would expect to have 24 different time zones that follow the meridians. However, the real delimitation of time zones on the land surface of the earth often follows political boundaries. Some countries and islands use a special national time. For example, the national time of India at 12 a.m. UTC is 4:30 p.m., while the time in Nepal to the north of India is 5:45 p.m. The International Date Line, which largely follows the 180th meridian, marks the line along which a calendar day has to be repeated if you cross it from west to east and skipped if you cross it from east to west.

The World from Washington, D.C.

1:200,000,000

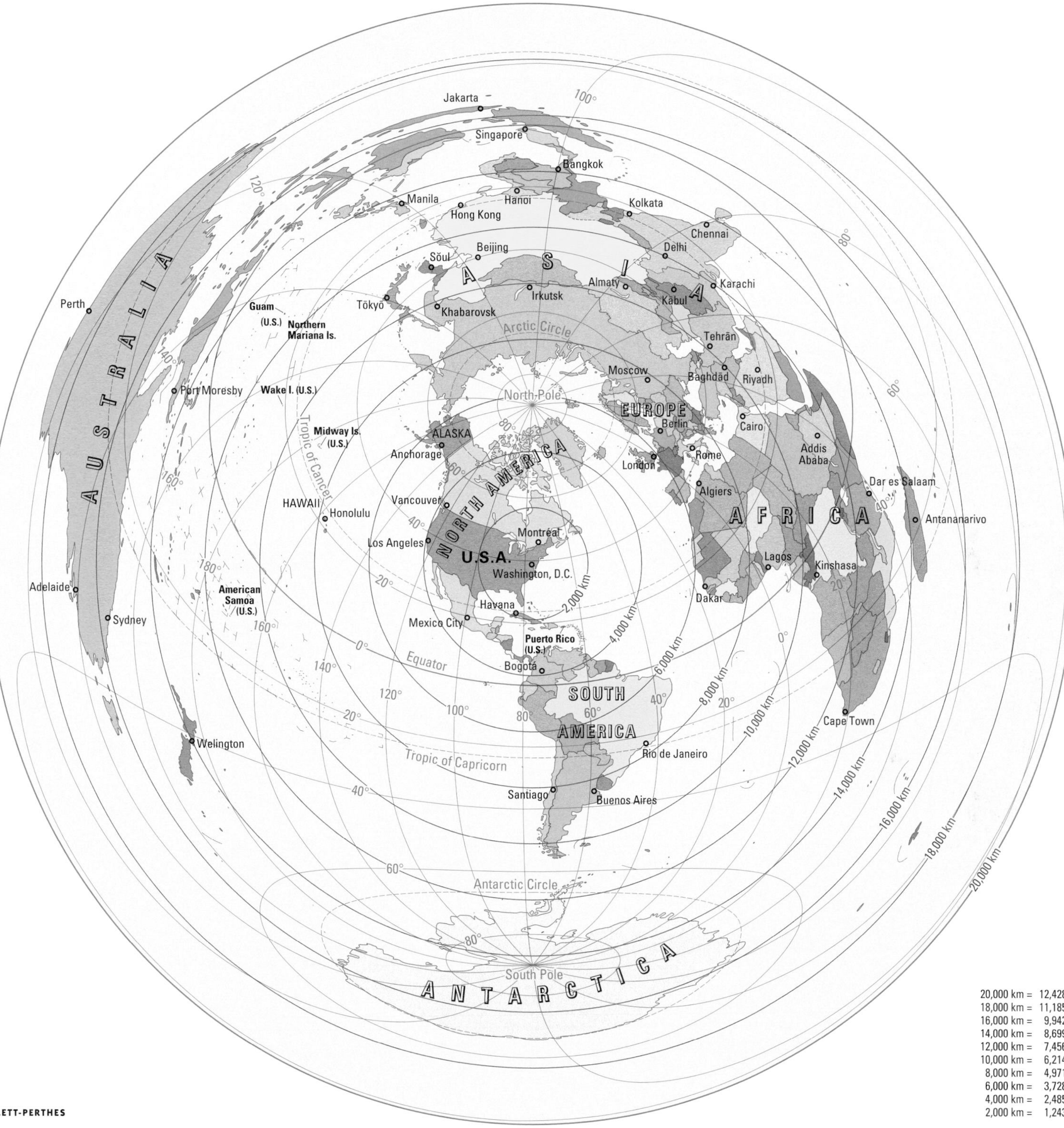

20,000 km =	12,428 mi
18,000 km =	11,185 mi
16,000 km =	9,942 mi
14,000 km =	8,699 mi
12,000 km =	7,456 mi
10,000 km =	6,214 mi
8,000 km =	4,971 mi
6,000 km =	3,728 mi
4,000 km =	2,485 mi
2,000 km =	1,243 mi

KLETT-PERTHES

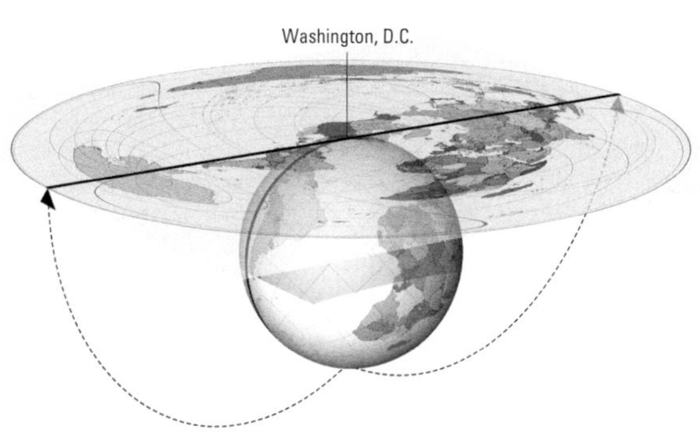

On this azimuthal equidistant projection, scale is constant along all straight lines through the map center or tangent point (where the projection plane touches the globe). Because this projection is tangent at Washington, D.C., where the latitude and longitude are 38.9° N and 77.0° W, you can easily compare distances from the national capital to any other place on Earth. To help you estimate the distance, the map includes concentric circles representing distances between 2,000 and 20,000 km, in 2,000 km increments (2,000 km is approximately 1,240 miles.) The outer circle represents Washington's antipode, that is, the point farthest away, on the other side of the world; in Washington's case, the antipode lies in the Indian Ocean, southwest of Australia. As with other azimuthal projections, straight lines through the tangent point (map center) also represent great circles, which divide Earth into two equal-size parts. Put differently, each diameter through the center of the map equals the circumference of the globe (see figure on the right).

A 160° B 140° C 120° D 100° E 80° F 60° G 40° H 20° J
ARCTIC
Beaufort Sea
Baffin Bay
G. of Alaska
Hudson Bay
Labrador Sea
Arctic Circle
London
Paris
Madrid
Toronto
Chicago
New York - Newark
Philadelphia
Los Angeles - Long Beach - Santa Ana
Tropic of Cancer
Sargasso Sea
Gulf of Mexico
Miami
ATLANTIC
Mexico City
Caribbean Sea
PACIFIC
Bogotá
Lagos
G. of Guinea
Equator
Lima
Belo Horizonte
Rio de Janeiro
São Paulo
OCEAN
Tropic of Capricorn
Santiago
Buenos Aires
OCEAN
Scotia Sea
Antarctic Circle
Bellingshausen Sea
Weddell Sea
Amundsen Sea

O C E A N
Laptev Sea
East Siberian Sea
Kara Sea
Barents Sea
Bering Sea
Sea of Okhotsk
St. Petersburg
Moscow
Sea of Japan
Beijing
Tianjin
Seoul
Tōkyō
Osaka-Kobe
İstanbul
Tehrān
Baghdād
Wuhan
Shanghai
P A C I F I C
Lahore
Cairo
Delhi
Dhaka
Riyadh
Karachi
Ahmadabad
Kolkata
Hong Kong
Mumbai
Hyderabad
Bay of Bengal
Arabian Sea
Bangalore
Chennai
Bangkok
South China Sea
Metro Manila
Hô Chi Minh City
O C E A N
Equator
Kinshasa
Jakarta
I N D I A N
O C E A N
Coral Sea
Tasman Sea
Ross Sea
Number of Persons
(per sq mile)
(per km²)
Over 2,500 | Over 1,000
1,250 to 2,500 | 500 to 1,000
250 to 1,250 | 100 to 500
62.5 to 250 | 25 to 100
12.5 to 62.5 | 5 to 25
2.5 to 12.5 | 1 to 5
Under 2.5 | Under 1
Urban agglomerations
■ Over 10 millions inhabitants
• 5 to 10 millions inhabitants
KLETT-PERTHES
L 40° M 60° N 80° O 100° P 120° Q 140° R 160° S 180° T

World: Population 2050 · Urbanization

1:160,000,000

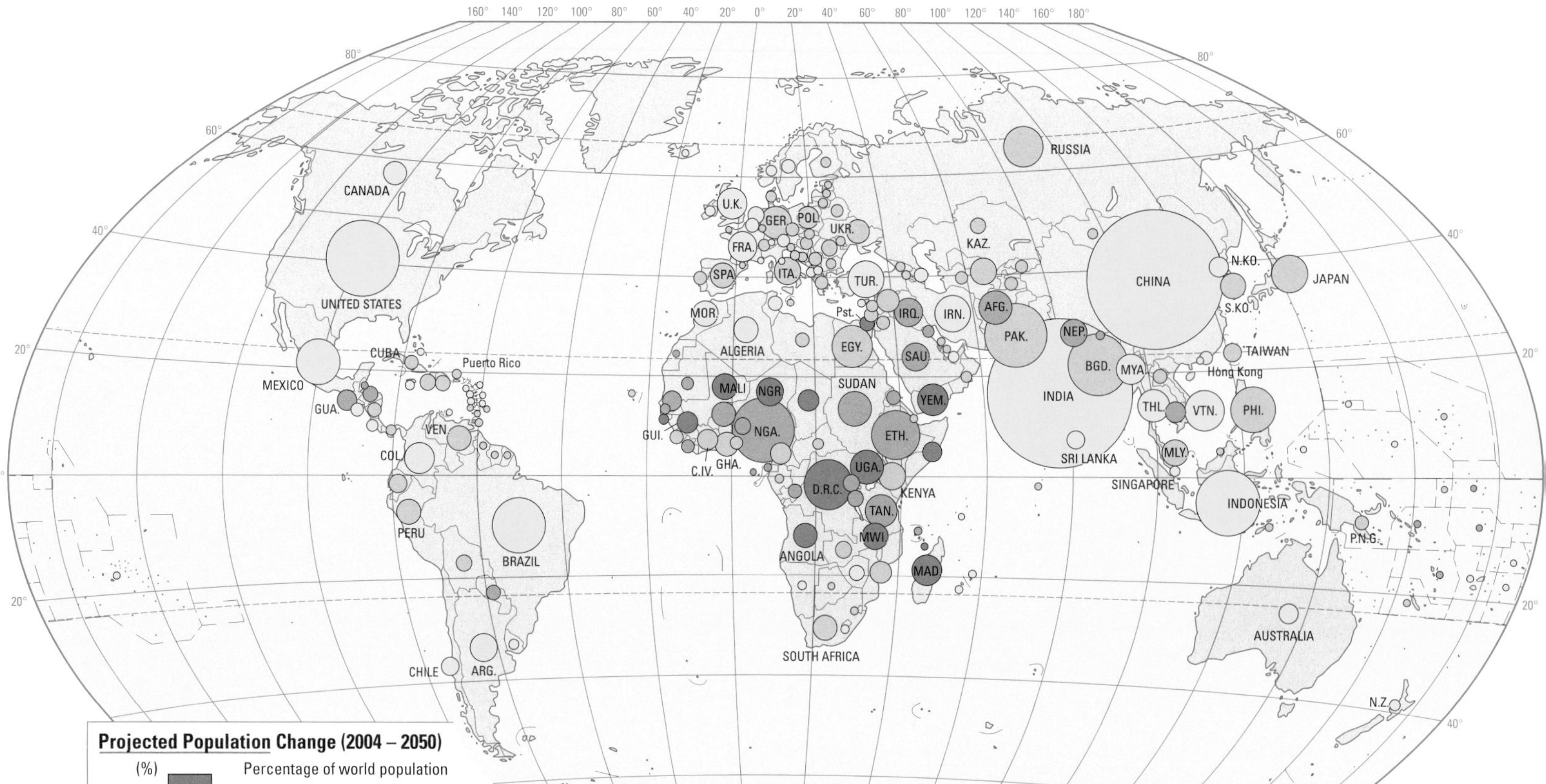

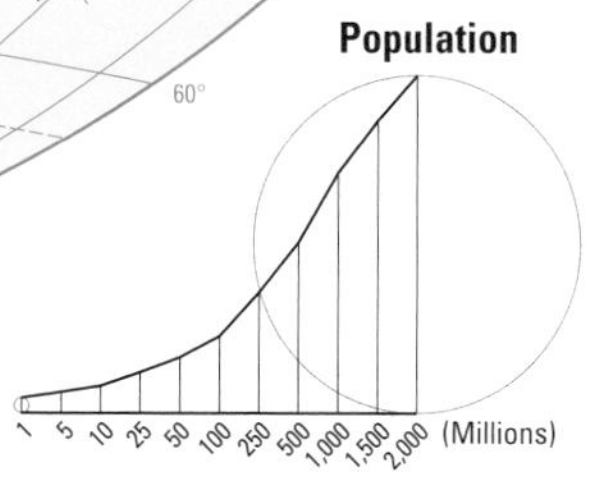

160° 140° 120° 100° 80° 60° 40° 20° 0° 20° 40° 60° 80° 100° 120° 140° 160° 180°

80° 60° 40° 20° 0° 20° 40° 60° 80°

RUSSIA
CANADA
U.K.
GER.
POL.
UKR.
FRA.
KAZ.
JAPAN
N.KO.
CHINA
SPA.
ITA.
TUR.
S.KO.
UNITED STATES
MOR.
Pst.
IRQ.
IRN.
AFG.
PAK.
NEP.
ALGERIA
EGY.
SAU.
TAIWAN
BGD.
MYA.
Hong Kong
CUBA
Puerto Rico
MEXICO
MALI
NGR.
SUDAN
YEM.
INDIA
THL.
VTN.
PHI.
GUA.
VEN.
GUI.
NGA.
ETH.
COL.
C.IV.
GHA.
UGA.
SRI LANKA
MLY.
D.R.C.
KENYA
SINGAPORE
INDONESIA
PERU
TAN.
BRAZIL
MWI.
P.N.G.
ANGOLA
MAD.
AUSTRALIA
CHILE
ARG.
SOUTH AFRICA
N.Z.

Projected Population Change (2004 – 2050)

(%)	Percentage of world population
Over 200	III
100 to 200	IIIIIIII
50 to 100	IIIIIIIIIIII
0 to 50	45
Under 0	IIIIIIIIIIII

KLETT-PERTHES

Population

1 5 10 25 50 100 250 500 1,000 1,500 2,000 (Millions)

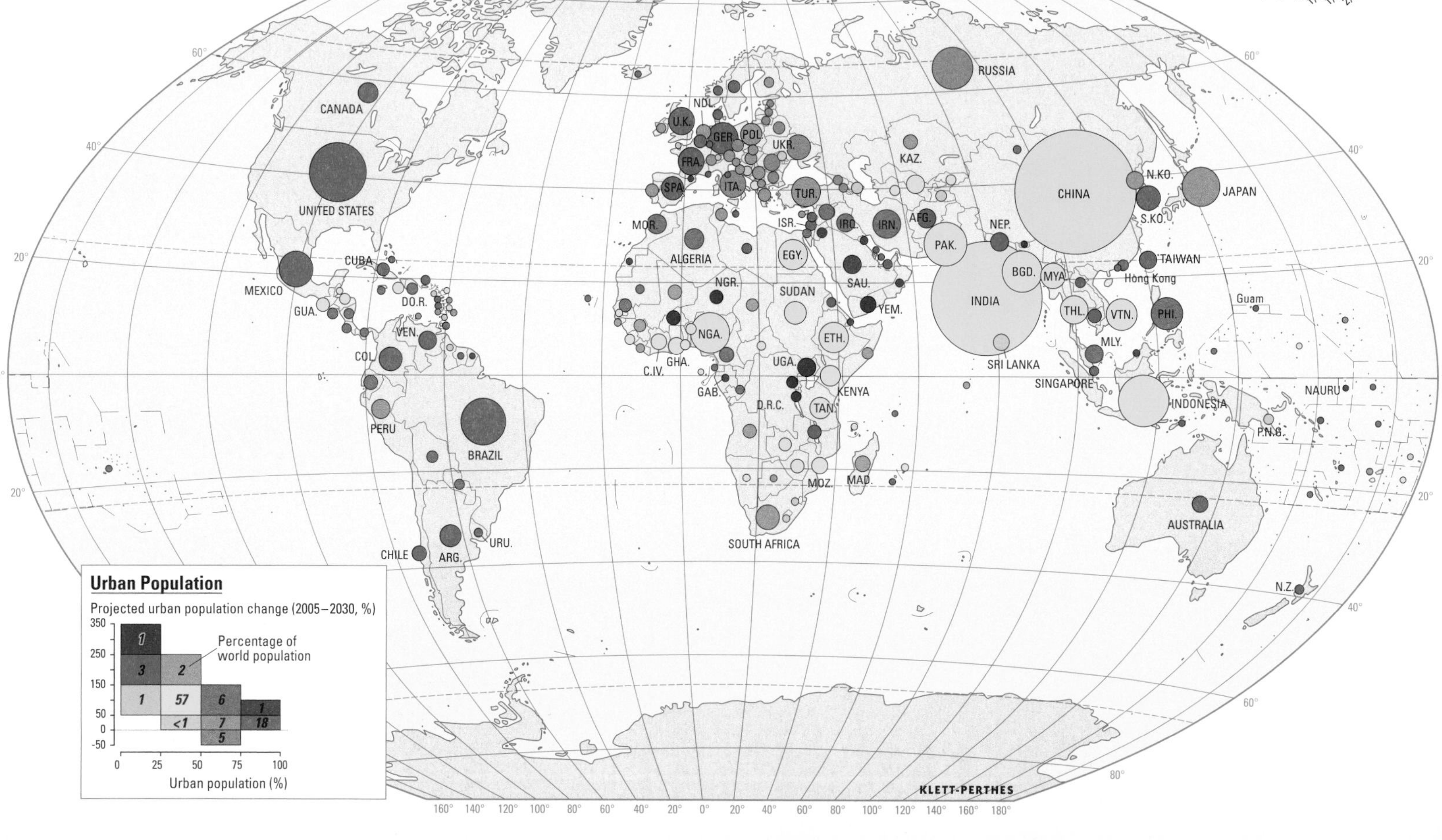

RUSSIA
CANADA
NDL.
U.K.
GER.
POL.
UKR.
FRA.
KAZ.
N.KO.
CHINA
JAPAN
SPA.
ITA.
TUR.
S.KO.
UNITED STATES
MOR.
ISR.
IRQ.
IRN.
AFG.
NEP.
ALGERIA
EGY.
PAK.
TAIWAN
CUBA
MEXICO
NGR.
SAU.
BGD.
MYA.
Hong Kong
DO.R.
SUDAN
INDIA
Guam
GUA.
YEM.
THL.
VTN.
PHI.
VEN.
NGA.
ETH.
COL.
GHA.
MLY.
C.IV.
UGA.
SRI LANKA
SINGAPORE
GAB.
KENYA
NAURU
D.R.C.
TAN.
INDONESIA
PERU
BRAZIL
P.N.G.
MOZ.
MAD.
AUSTRALIA
URU.
SOUTH AFRICA
CHILE
ARG.
N.Z.

Urban Population

Projected urban population change (2005–2030, %)

Percentage of world population

Projected urban population change (%)	0–25	25–50	50–75	75–100
250 to 350	1			
150 to 250	3	2		
50 to 150	1	57	6	
0 to 50		<1	7	1 / 18
-50 to 0			5	

Urban population (%)

KLETT-PERTHES

Population

(Millions) 1,500 1,000 500 250 100 50 25 10 5 1

Natural Population Development

		Percentage of world population
High increase (BR > 30, DR > 15)		IIIII
Highest increase (BR > 30, DR < 15)		IIIIIIIIII
Medium increase (BR = 20 to 30, DR < 15)		IIIIIIIIIIIIIIIIIIIIIIIIIIIIIIIIII
Low increase (BR < 20, DR < 15)		IIIIIIIIIIIIIIIIIIIIIIIIIIIIIIIIIIII
Stagnation (BR = DR)		IIIIIIII
Low decrease (BR < DR)		IIII

Average Annual Net Migration Rate (2000 – 2005)

	(‰)	Percentage of world population
Immigration	Over 10	I
	5 to 10	II
	2.5 to 5	IIIIIII
	0 to 2.5	IIIIIIIIIIIII
Emigration	−2.5 to 0	IIIIIIIIIIIIIIIIIIIIIIIIIIIIIIIIIIIIIIIIIIIIIIIIIIIIIIIIIIIIIIIIIIIIIIIIII
	−5 to −2.5	IIIIII
	−10 to −5	I
	Under −10	

Migratory movement

Width of the arrows gives only a rough indication of the size of movement

No data

World: Life Expectancy · Education

1:160,000,000

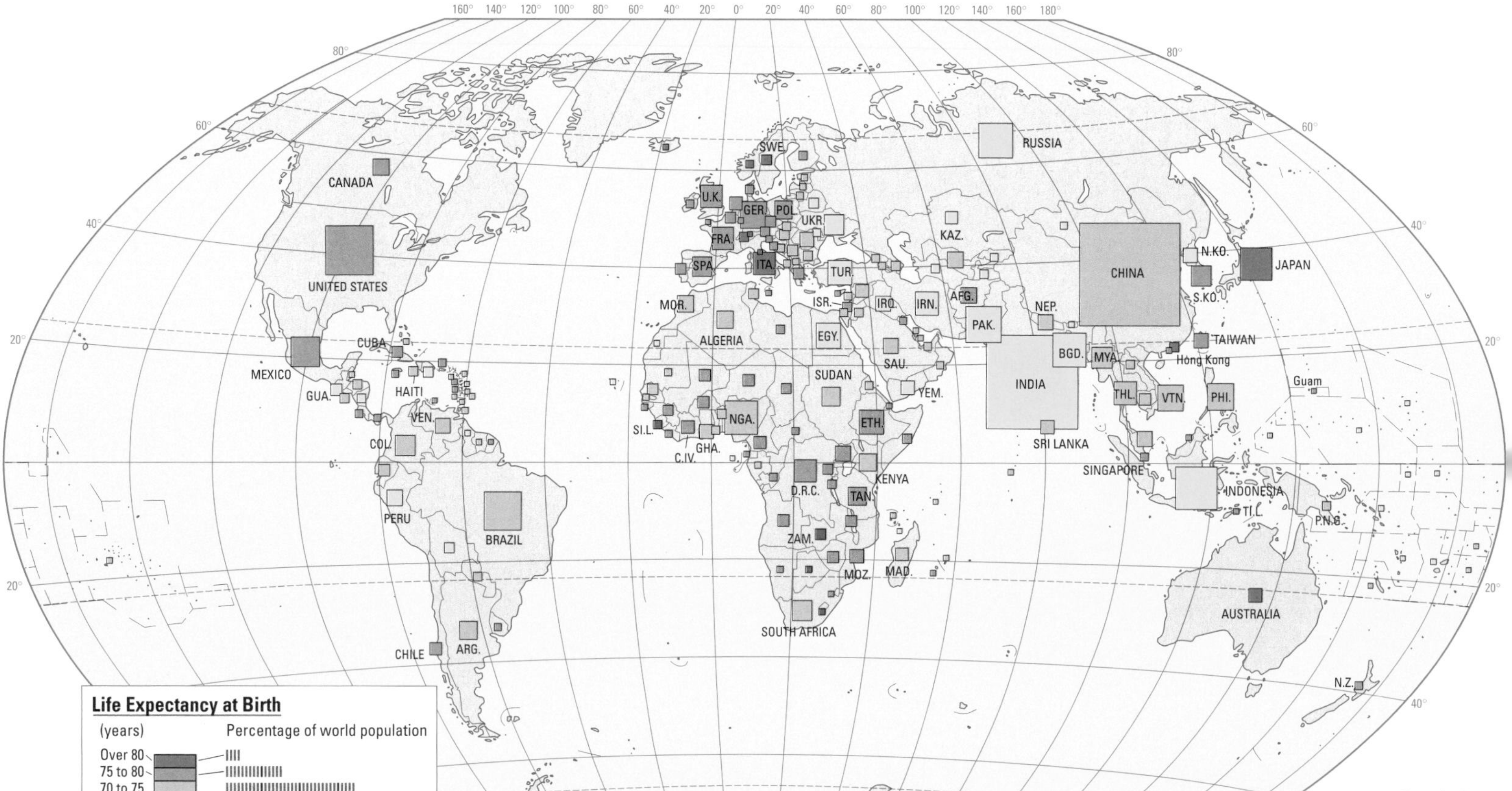

Life Expectancy at Birth

(years)	Percentage of world population
Over 80	IIII
75 to 80	IIIIIIIIIIIIII
70 to 75	IIIIIIIIIIIIIIIIIIIIIIIIIIIIIIIIIIII
67	
60 to 70	IIIIIIIIIIIIIIIIIIIIIIIIIIIIIIIIIIII
50 to 60	IIIIIII
40 to 50	IIIIII
Under 40	

KLETT-PERTHES

Population

1, 5, 10, 25, 50, 100, 250, 500, 1,000, 1,500 (Millions)

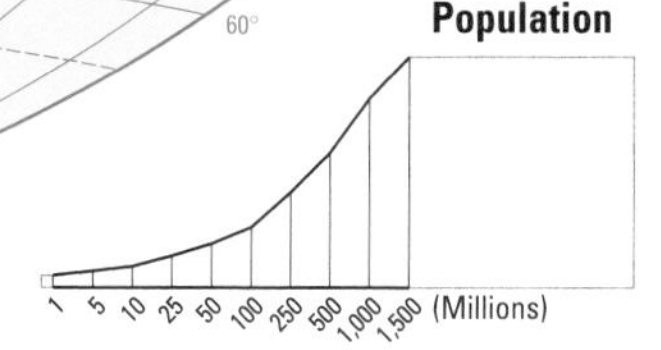

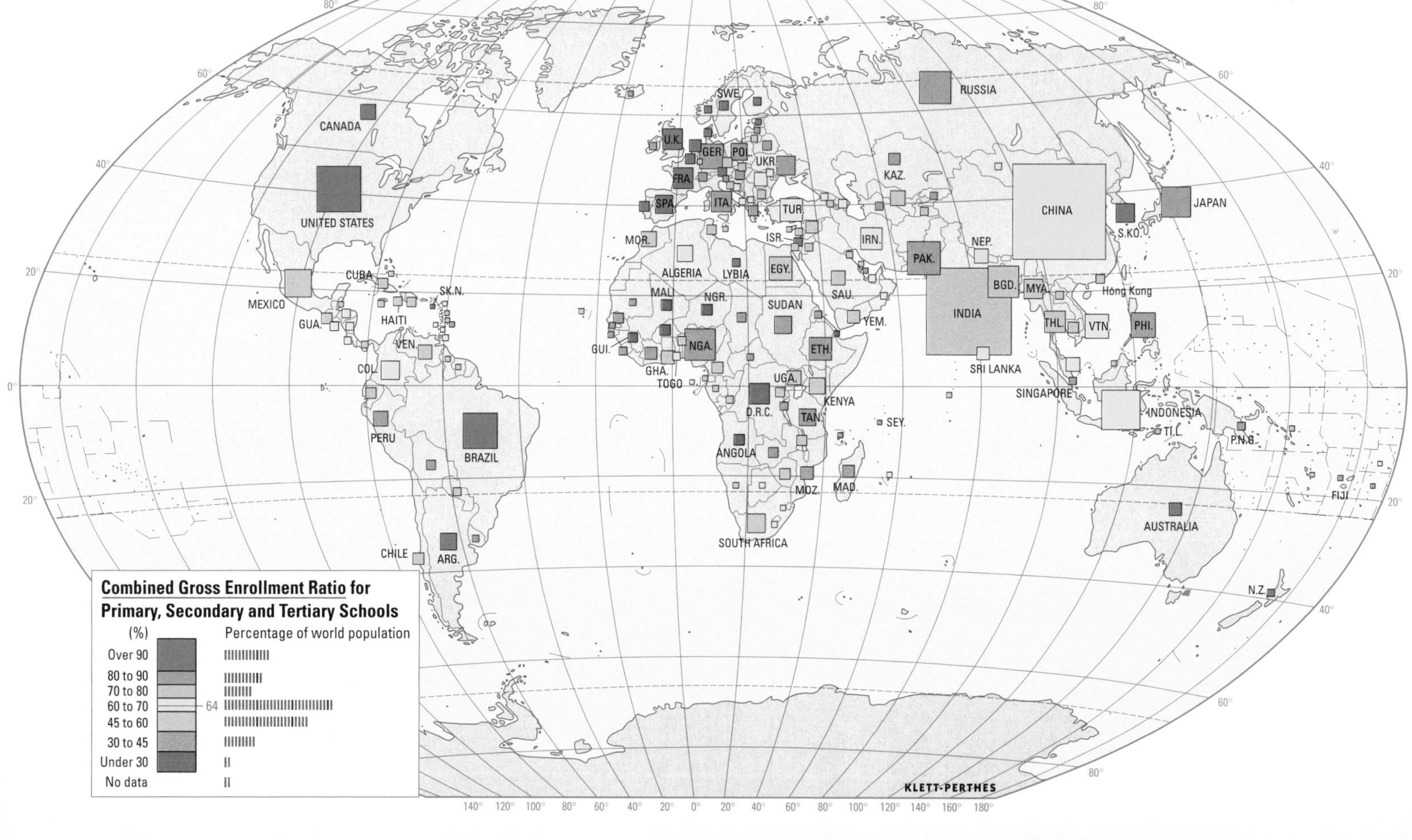

Combined Gross Enrollment Ratio for Primary, Secondary and Tertiary Schools

(%)	Percentage of world population
Over 90	IIIIIIIIIIIII
80 to 90	IIIIIIIIIII
70 to 80	IIIIIIII
64	
60 to 70	IIIIIIIIIIIIIIIIIIIIIIIIIIIIIIIIIIIIII
45 to 60	IIIIIIIIIIIIIIIIIIIIIIIIIIIIIIIII
30 to 45	IIIIIIIII
Under 30	II
No data	II

KLETT-PERTHES

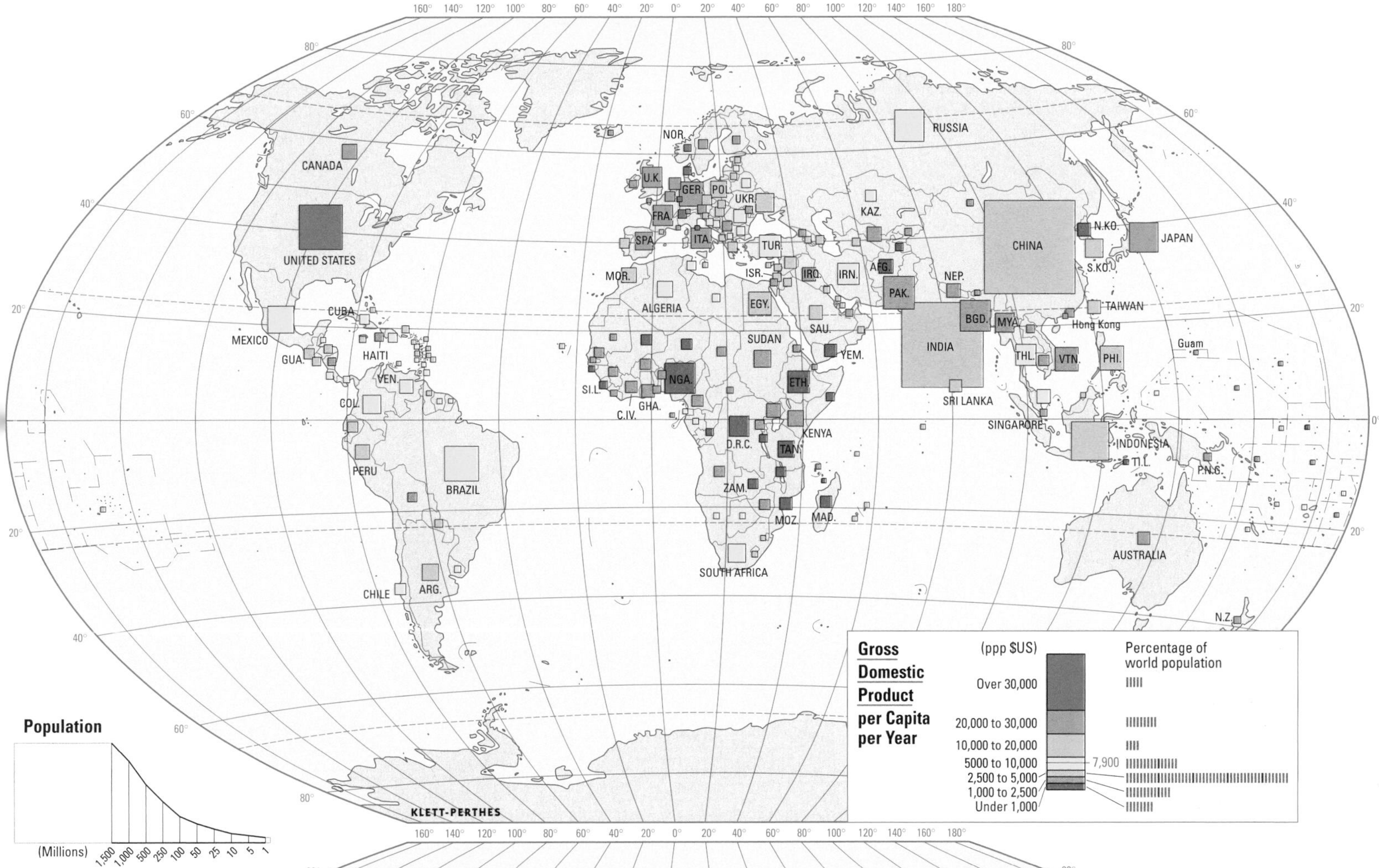

Gross Domestic Product per Capita per Year

(ppp $US) — Percentage of world population

- Over 30,000
- 20,000 to 30,000
- 10,000 to 20,000
- 5000 to 10,000 — 7,900
- 2,500 to 5,000
- 1,000 to 2,500
- Under 1,000

Population

(Millions) 1,500 1,000 500 250 100 50 25 10 5 1

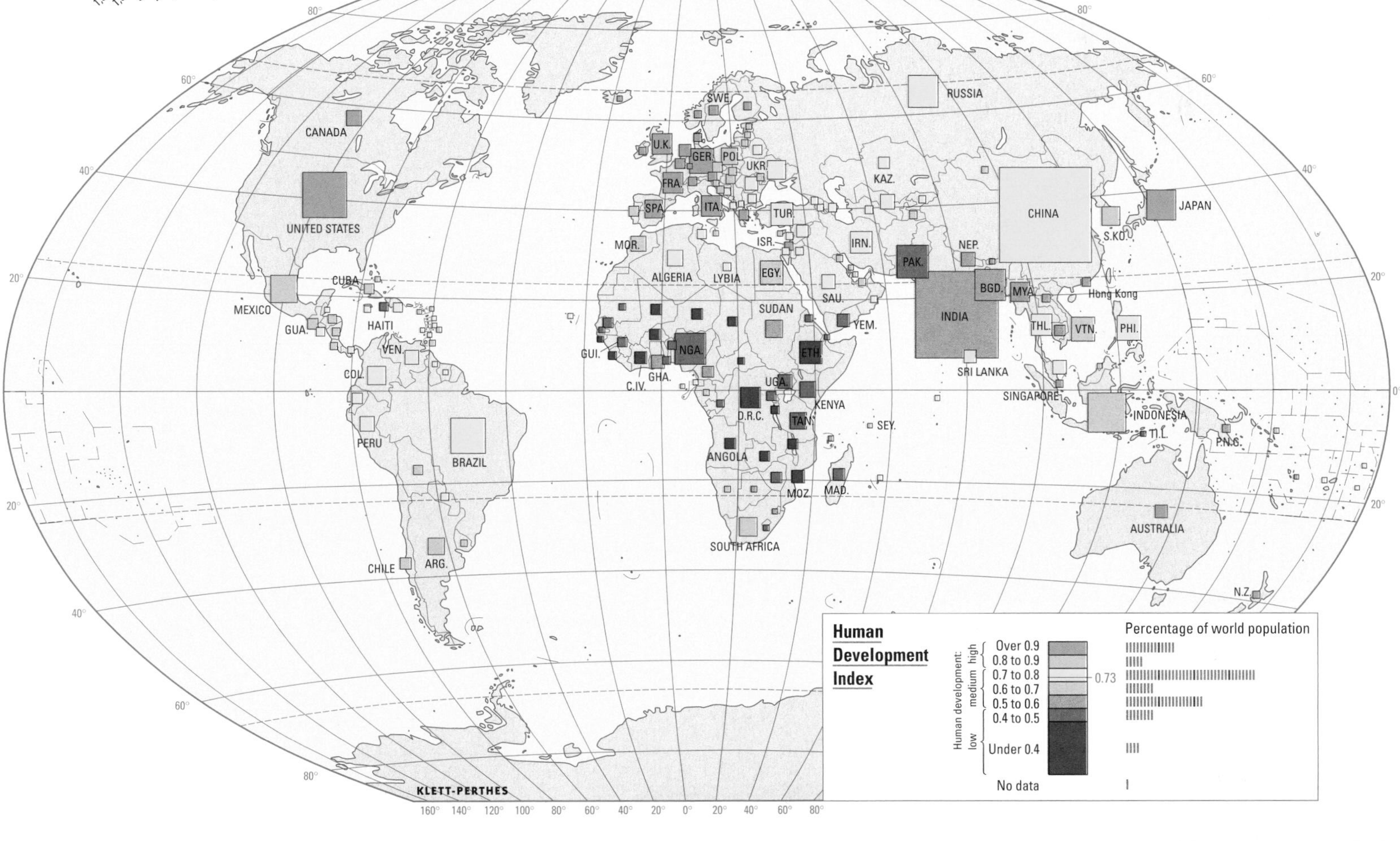

Human Development Index

Human development: high / medium / low — Percentage of world population

- high: Over 0.9
- high: 0.8 to 0.9
- medium: 0.7 to 0.8 — 0.73
- medium: 0.6 to 0.7
- medium: 0.5 to 0.6
- low: 0.4 to 0.5
- low: Under 0.4
- No data

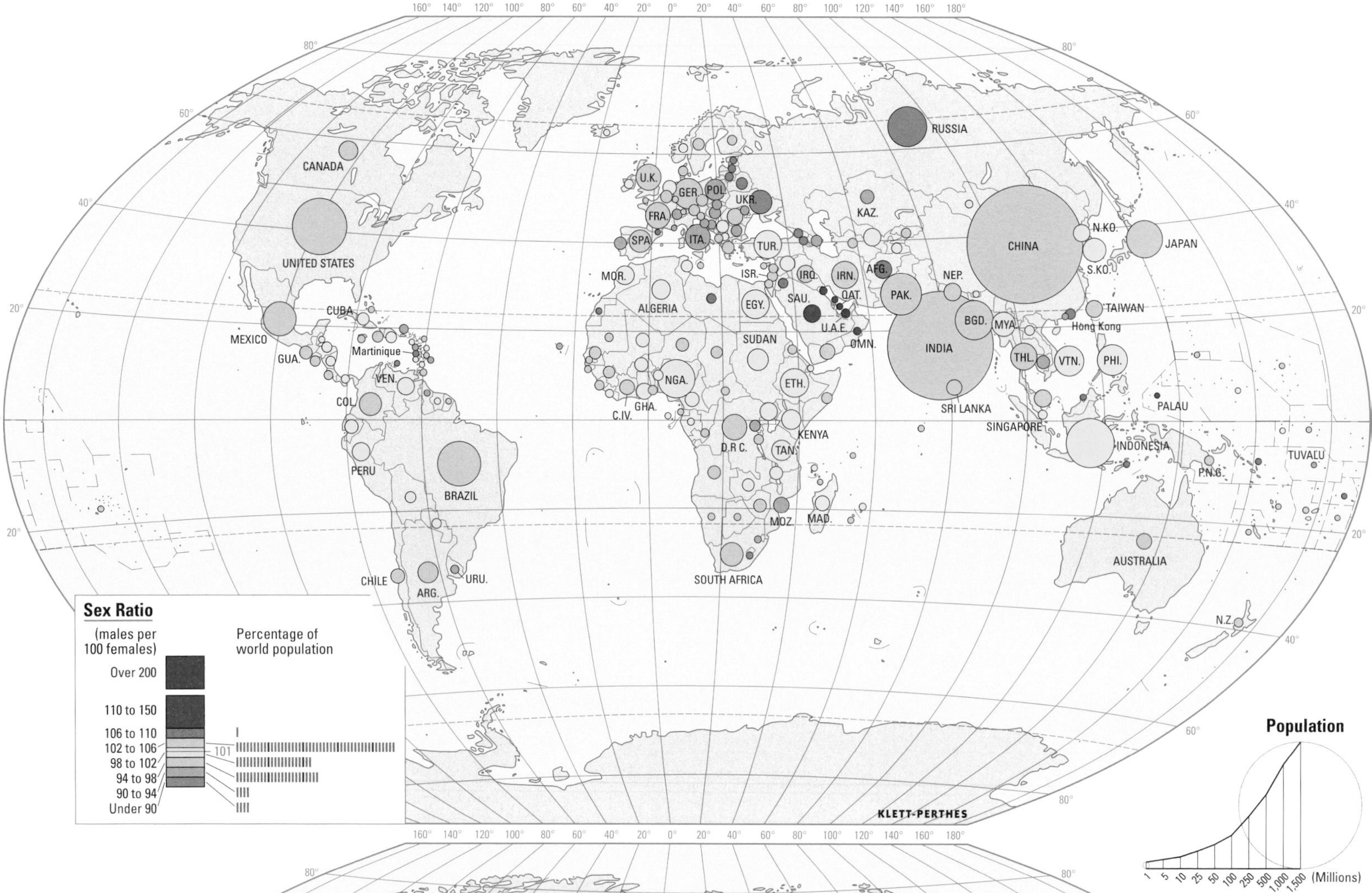

World: Male/Female Ratio · Population by Age

1:160,000,000

CANADA
UNITED STATES
MEXICO
CUBA
GUA.
Martinique
VEN.
COL.
PERU
BRAZIL
CHILE
ARG.
URU.
U.K.
GER.
POL.
UKR.
FRA.
SPA.
ITA.
TUR.
MOR.
ALGERIA
ISR.
EGY.
IRQ.
IRN.
SAU.
QAT.
U.A.E.
OMN.
AFG.
PAK.
NEP.
KAZ.
RUSSIA
CHINA
N.KO.
S.KO.
JAPAN
TAIWAN
Hong Kong
BGD.
MYA.
INDIA
SRI LANKA
THL.
VTN.
PHI.
SINGAPORE
INDONESIA
PALAU
P.N.G.
TUVALU
AUSTRALIA
N.Z.
SUDAN
ETH.
NGA.
GHA.
C.IV.
D.R.C.
KENYA
TAN.
MOZ.
MAD.
SOUTH AFRICA

Sex Ratio

(males per 100 females)

Over 200
110 to 150
106 to 110
102 to 106
98 to 102
94 to 98
90 to 94
Under 90

101

Percentage of world population

KLETT-PERTHES

Population

1, 5, 10, 25, 50, 100, 250, 500, 1,000, 1,500 (Millions)

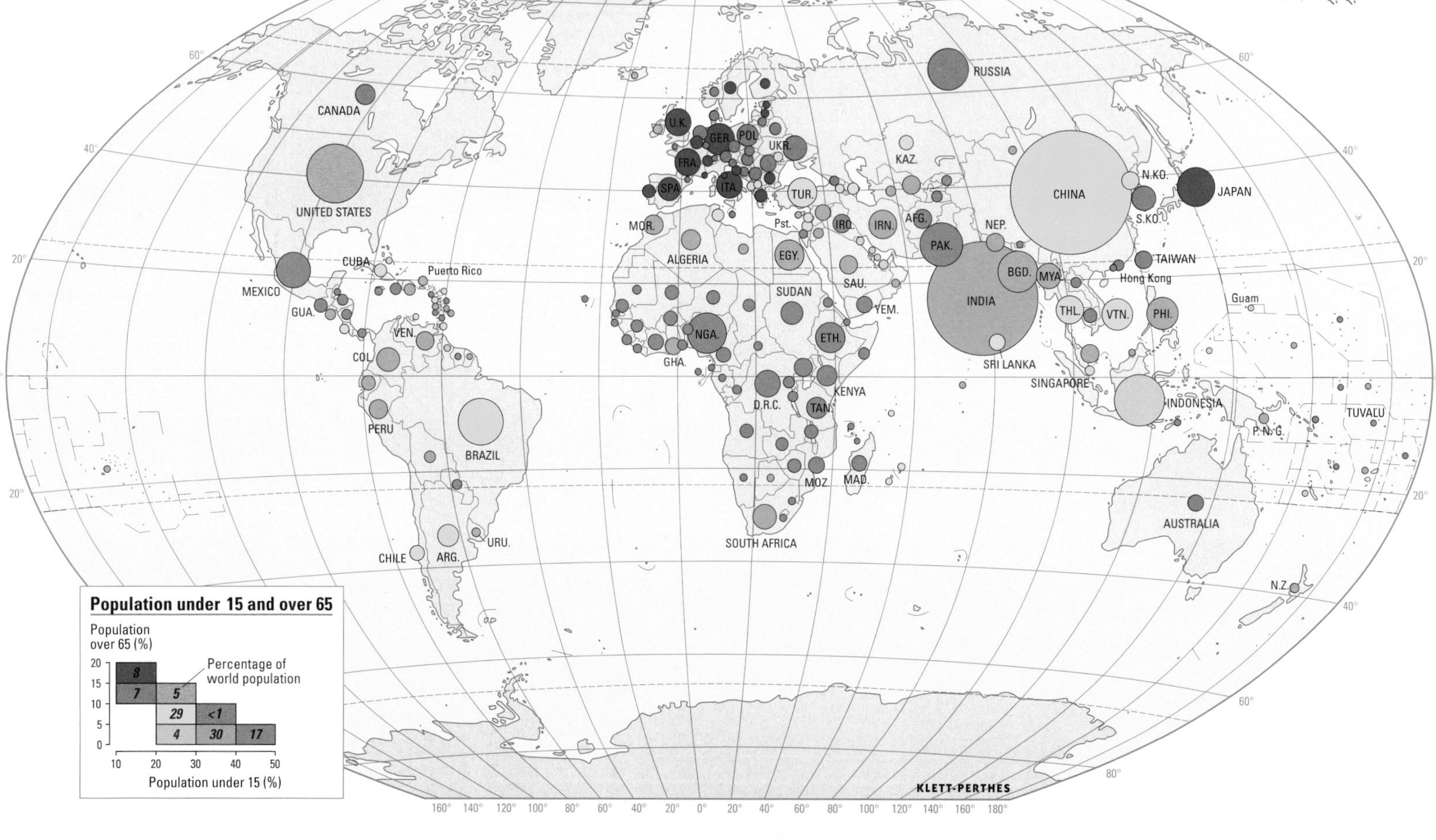

CANADA
UNITED STATES
MEXICO
CUBA
Puerto Rico
GUA.
VEN.
COL.
PERU
BRAZIL
CHILE
ARG.
URU.
U.K.
GER.
POL.
UKR.
FRA.
SPA.
ITA.
TUR.
MOR.
ALGERIA
Pst.
EGY.
IRQ.
IRN.
SAU.
YEM.
AFG.
PAK.
NEP.
KAZ.
RUSSIA
CHINA
N.KO.
S.KO.
JAPAN
TAIWAN
Hong Kong
BGD.
MYA.
INDIA
SRI LANKA
THL.
VTN.
PHI.
Guam
SINGAPORE
INDONESIA
P.N.G.
TUVALU
AUSTRALIA
N.Z.
SUDAN
ETH.
NGA.
GHA.
D.R.C.
KENYA
TAN.
MOZ.
MAD.
SOUTH AFRICA

Population under 15 and over 65

Population over 65 (%)

Percentage of world population

Population over 65 (%)	10–20	20–30	30–40	40–50
15–20	8			
10–15	7	5		
5–10		29	<1	
0–5		4	30	17

Population under 15 (%)

KLETT-PERTHES

Infant Mortality Rate

(‰)	Percentage of world population
Over 150	IIIIII
100 to 150	IIIIIIIIII
60 to 100	IIIIIIIIIIII
30 to 60	56 IIIIIIIIIIIIIIIIIIIIIIIIIIIIIIIIII
10 to 30	IIIIIIIIIIIIIIIIIIIIIIIIIIIIII
5 to 10	IIIIIII
Under 5	I

Number of physicians per 10,000 population
- Over 30
- 10 to 30
- 2 to 10
- Under 2

No data

Adult Population Ages 15 to 49 with HIV/AIDS

(%)	Percentage of world population
Over 15	I
5 to 15	IIIII
1.5 to 5	IIIII
0.5 to 1.5	1.1 IIIIIIIIIIIIIIIIIIIIIIII
0.15 to 0.5	IIIIIIII
0.05 to 0.15	IIIIIIIIIIIIIIIIIIIIIIII
Under 0.05	IIIIIIIII

Spread of the epidemic

1985 to 1990 / 1975 / 1977 to 1980 — Focus and approximately year of outbreak of the epidemic

Path of the epidemic

No data IIIIII

World: Employment by Sector · Employment of Women

1:160,000,000

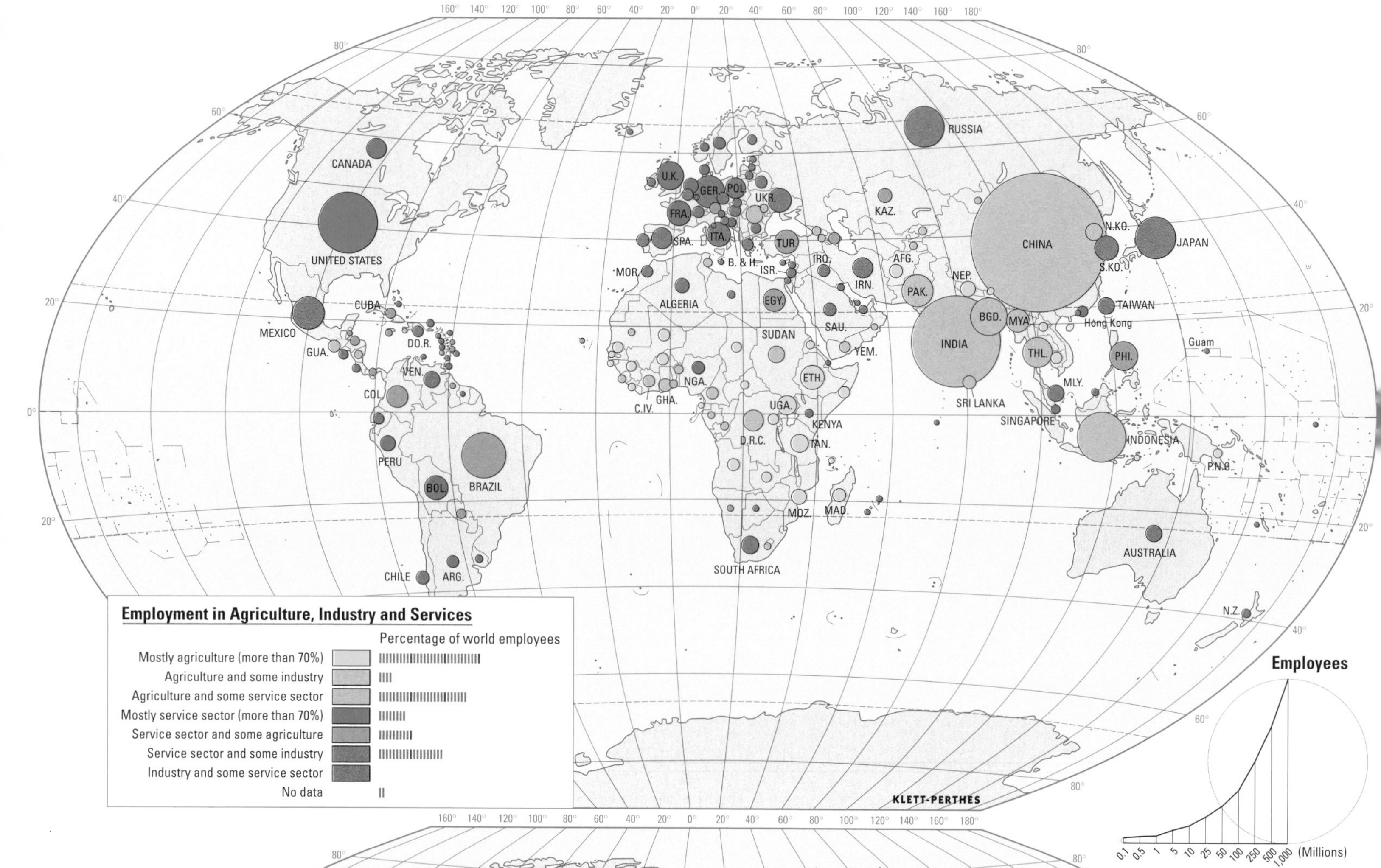

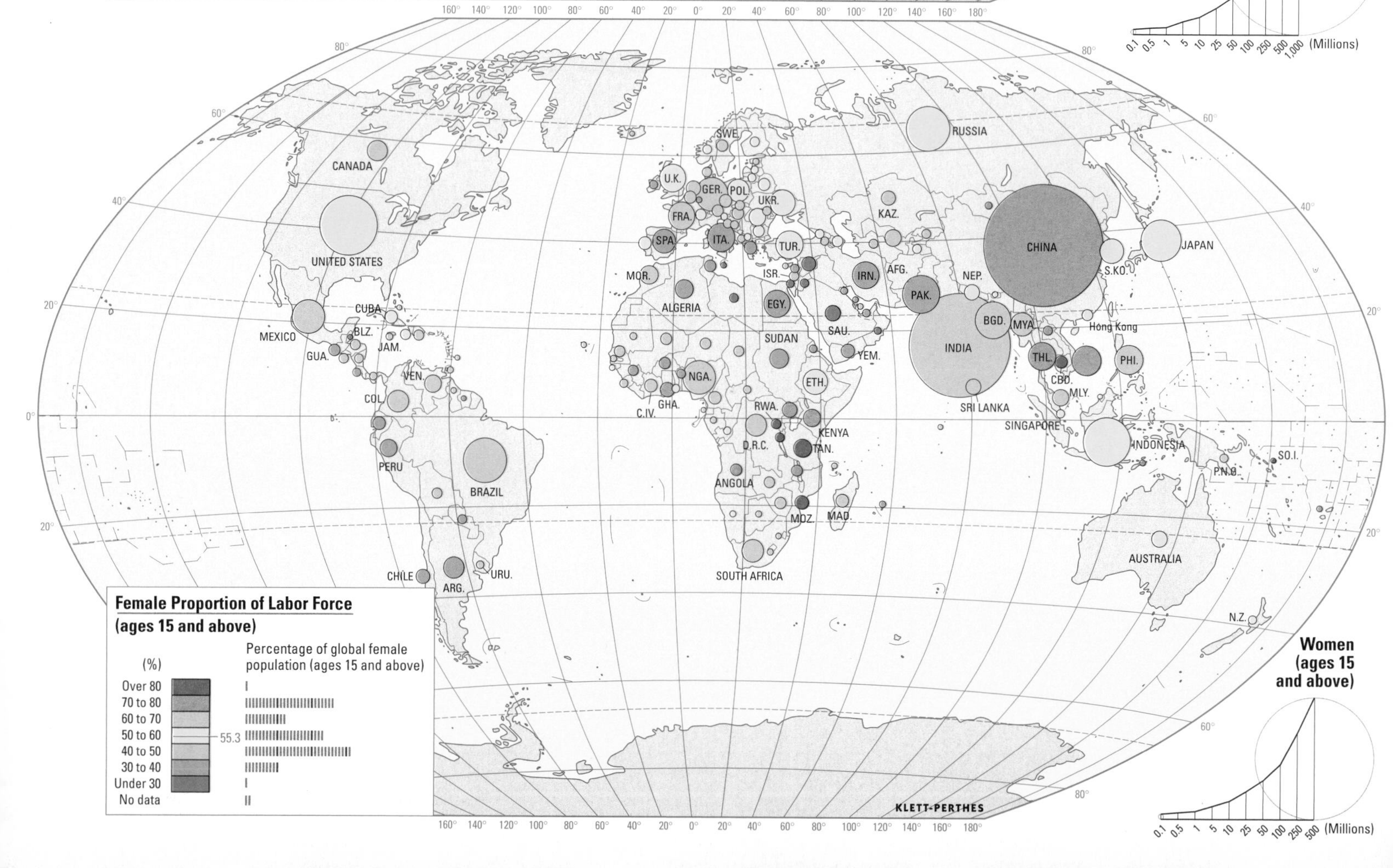

Employment in Agriculture, Industry and Services

	Percentage of world employees
Mostly agriculture (more than 70%)	IIIIIIIIIIIIIIIIIIIIIIIIIIIIII
Agriculture and some industry	IIII
Agriculture and some service sector	IIIIIIIIIIIIIIIIIIIIIIIIII
Mostly service sector (more than 70%)	IIIIIII
Service sector and some agriculture	IIIIIIIII
Service sector and some industry	IIIIIIIIIIIIIIIIIII
Industry and some service sector	
No data	II

Employees

0.1 0.5 1 5 10 25 50 100 250 500 1,000 (Millions)

CANADA, UNITED STATES, MEXICO, CUBA, GUA., DO.R., VEN., COL., PERU, BRAZIL, BOL., CHILE, ARG., U.K., GER., POL., FRA., UKR., ITA., SPA., TUR., B. & H., ISR., IRQ., IRN., MOR., ALGERIA, EGY., SAU., YEM., SUDAN, ETH., NGA., GHA., C.IV., UGA., KENYA, D.R.C., TAN., MOZ., MAD., SOUTH AFRICA, RUSSIA, KAZ., AFG., PAK., NEP., INDIA, SRI LANKA, BGD., MYA., THL., CHINA, N.KO., S.KO., JAPAN, TAIWAN, Hong Kong, PHI., MLY., SINGAPORE, INDONESIA, P.N.G., Guam, AUSTRALIA, N.Z.

KLETT-PERTHES

Female Proportion of Labor Force (ages 15 and above)

(%)	Percentage of global female population (ages 15 and above)
Over 80	I
70 to 80	IIIIIIIIIIIIIIIIIIIIIIIIIIIIII
60 to 70	IIIIIIIIIII
50 to 60	55.3 IIIIIIIIIIIIIIIIIIIIIIIIII
40 to 50	IIIIIIIIIIIIIIIIIIIIIIIIIIIIIIIIIII
30 to 40	IIIIIIIIII
Under 30	I
No data	II

Women (ages 15 and above)

0.1 0.5 1 5 10 25 50 100 250 500 (Millions)

CANADA, UNITED STATES, MEXICO, CUBA, BLZ., GUA., JAM., VEN., COL., PERU, BRAZIL, CHILE, ARG., URU., SWE., U.K., GER., POL., FRA., UKR., SPA., ITA., TUR., ISR., MOR., ALGERIA, EGY., SAU., YEM., SUDAN, ETH., NGA., GHA., C.IV., RWA., KENYA, D.R.C., TAN., ANGOLA, MOZ., MAD., SOUTH AFRICA, RUSSIA, KAZ., AFG., IRN., PAK., NEP., INDIA, SRI LANKA, BGD., MYA., THL., CBD., MLY., SINGAPORE, CHINA, S.KO., JAPAN, Hong Kong, PHI., INDONESIA, P.N.G., SO.I., AUSTRALIA, N.Z.

KLETT-PERTHES

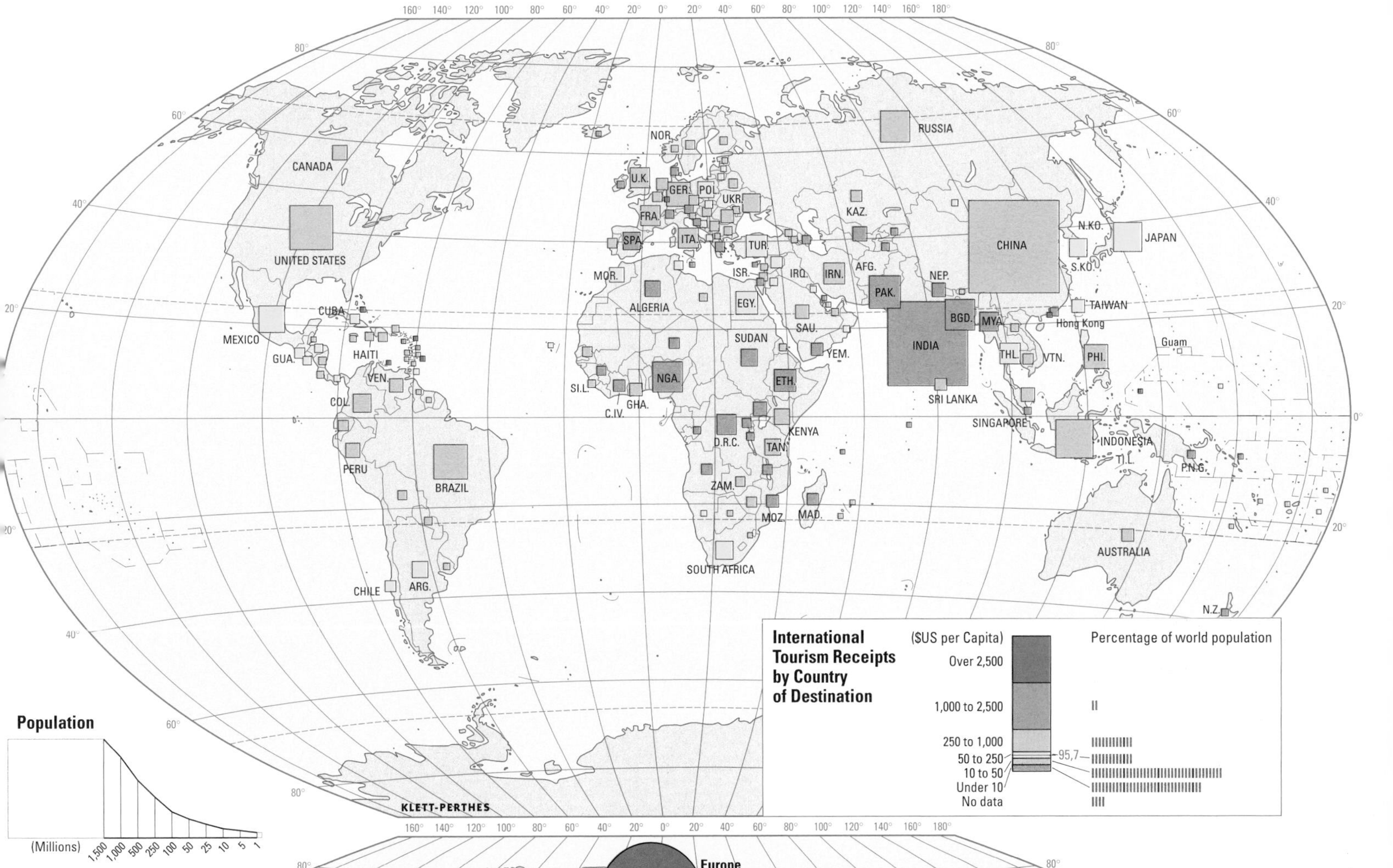

International Tourism Receipts by Country of Destination

($US per Capita)
Over 2,500
1,000 to 2,500
250 to 1,000
50 to 250
10 to 50
Under 10
No data
95,7

Percentage of world population

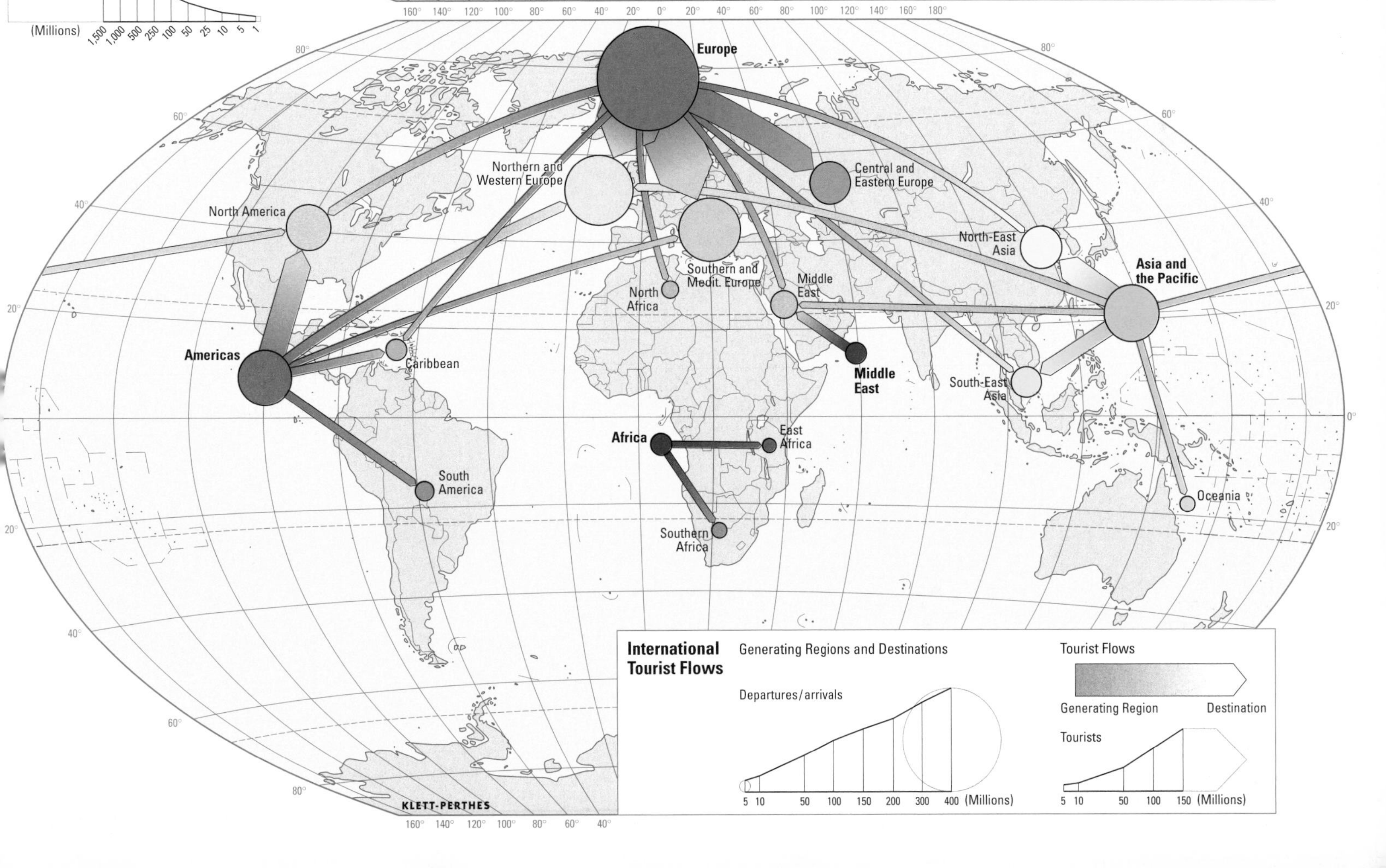

Population

(Millions) 1,500 1,000 500 250 100 50 25 10 5 1

International Tourist Flows

Generating Regions and Destinations

Departures/arrivals

5 10 50 100 150 200 300 400 (Millions)

Tourist Flows

Generating Region Destination

Tourists

5 10 50 100 150 (Millions)

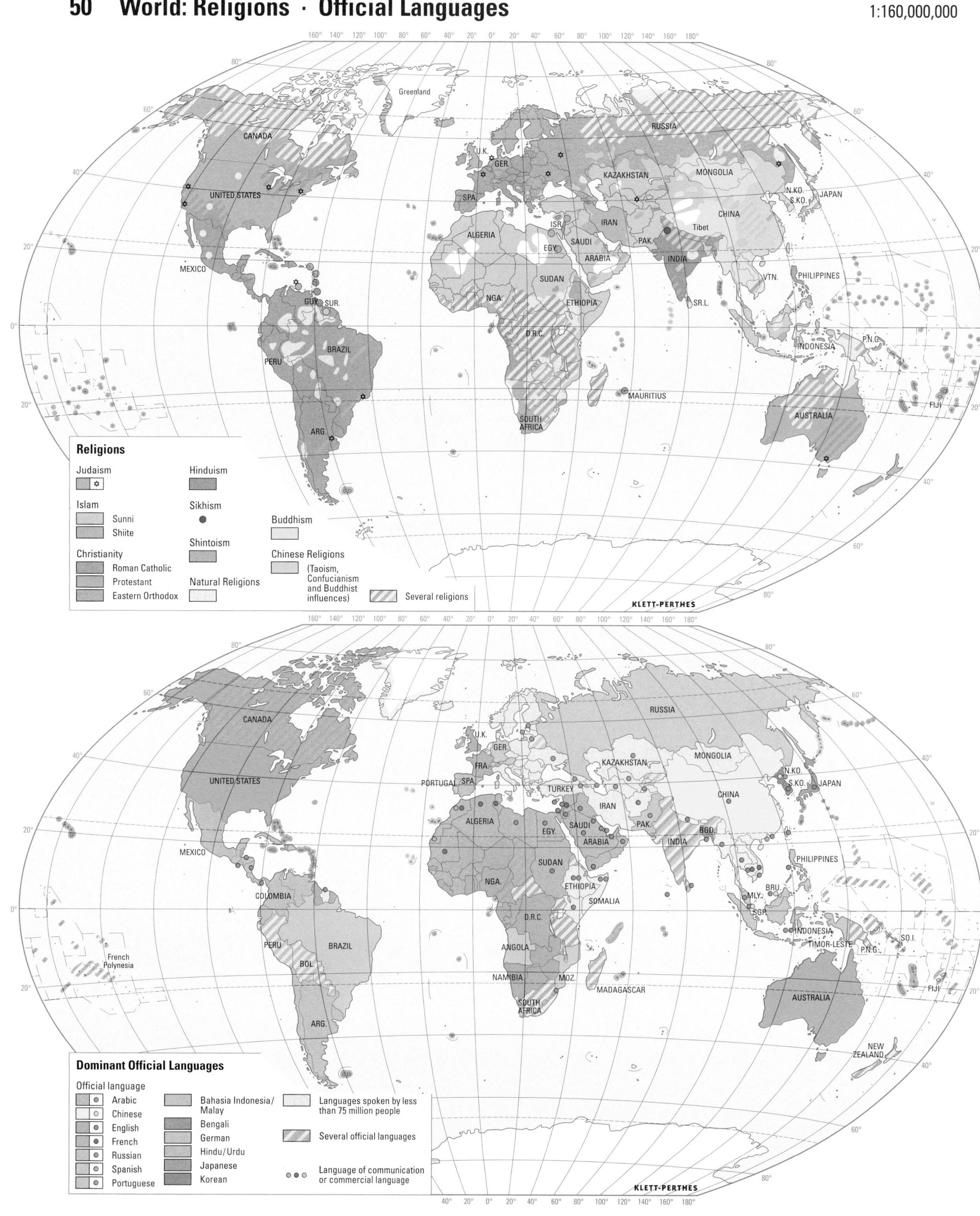

Greenland
CANADA
UNITED STATES
MEXICO
GUY.
SUR.
PERU
BRAZIL
ARG.
RUSSIA
U.K.
GER.
SPA.
KAZAKHSTAN
MONGOLIA
N.KO.
S.KO.
JAPAN
CHINA
Tibet
ISR.
IRAN
PAK.
EGY.
SAUDI
ARABIA
INDIA
ALGERIA
SUDAN
NGA.
ETHIOPIA
D.R.C.
SR.L.
VTN.
PHILIPPINES
INDONESIA
P.N.G.
MAURITIUS
SOUTH AFRICA
AUSTRALIA
FIJI
Religions
Judaism
Hinduism
Islam
Sikhism
Sunni
Shiite
Buddhism
Shintoism
Christianity
Chinese Religions
Roman Catholic
(Taoism, Confucianism and Buddhist influences)
Protestant
Natural Religions
Eastern Orthodox
Several religions
KLETT-PERTHES
CANADA
UNITED STATES
MEXICO
COLOMBIA
PERU
BRAZIL
BOL.
ARG.
French Polynesia
U.K.
GER.
FRA.
PORTUGAL
SPA.
RUSSIA
KAZAKHSTAN
MONGOLIA
N.KO.
S.KO.
JAPAN
TURKEY
CHINA
IRAN
PAK.
BGD.
INDIA
SAUDI
ARABIA
EGY.
ALGERIA
SUDAN
NGA.
ETHIOPIA
SOMALIA
D.R.C.
ANGOLA
NAMIBIA
MOZ.
MADAGASCAR
SOUTH AFRICA
PHILIPPINES
BRU.
MLY.
SGP.
INDONESIA
TIMOR-LESTE
P.N.G.
SO.I.
FIJI
AUSTRALIA
NEW ZEALAND
Dominant Official Languages
Official language
Arabic
Chinese
English
French
Russian
Spanish
Portuguese
Bahasia Indonesia/ Malay
Bengali
German
Hindu/Urdu
Japanese
Korean
Languages spoken by less than 75 million people
Several official languages
Language of communication or commercial language
KLETT-PERTHES

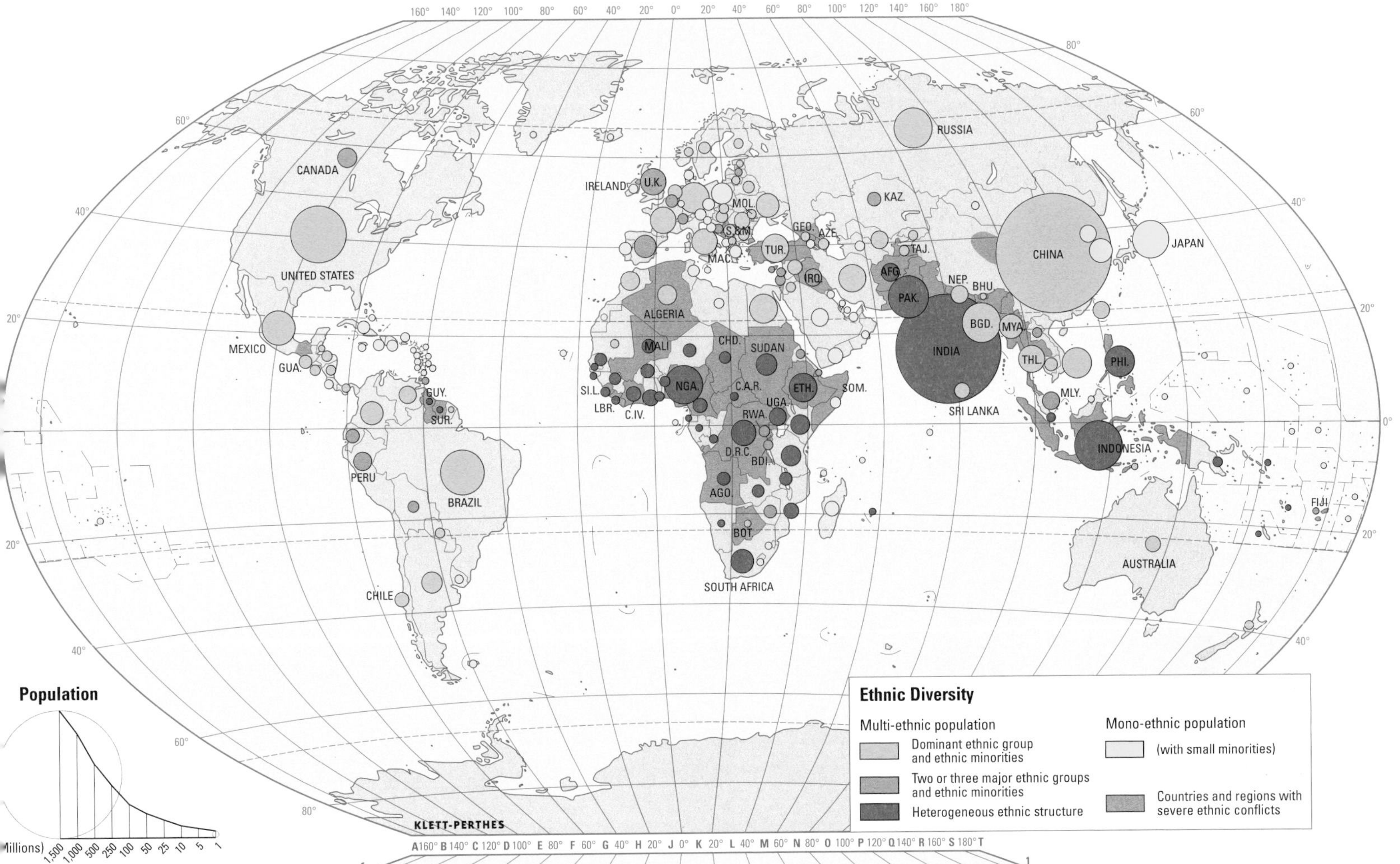

World: Ethnic Diversity · Cultural Regions

1:160,000,000

CANADA
UNITED STATES
MEXICO
GUA.
GUY.
SUR.
PERU
BRAZIL
CHILE
IRELAND
U.K.
MOL.
S.&M.
MAC.
TUR.
GEO.
AZE.
KAZ.
TAJ.
AFG.
PAK.
IRQ.
NEP
BHU.
BGD.
MYA.
INDIA
SRI LANKA
THL.
MLY.
PHI.
INDONESIA
CHINA
JAPAN
RUSSIA
ALGERIA
MALI
CHD.
SUDAN
S.L.
LBR.
C.I.V.
NGA.
C.A.R.
ETH.
SOM.
UGA.
RWA.
D.R.C.
BDI.
AGO.
BOT.
SOUTH AFRICA
AUSTRALIA
FIJI
KLETT-PERTHES

Population

(Millions) 1,500 1,000 500 250 100 50 25 10 5 1

Ethnic Diversity

Multi-ethnic population

- Dominant ethnic group and ethnic minorities
- Two or three major ethnic groups and ethnic minorities
- Heterogeneous ethnic structure

Mono-ethnic population

- (with small minorities)
- Countries and regions with severe ethnic conflicts

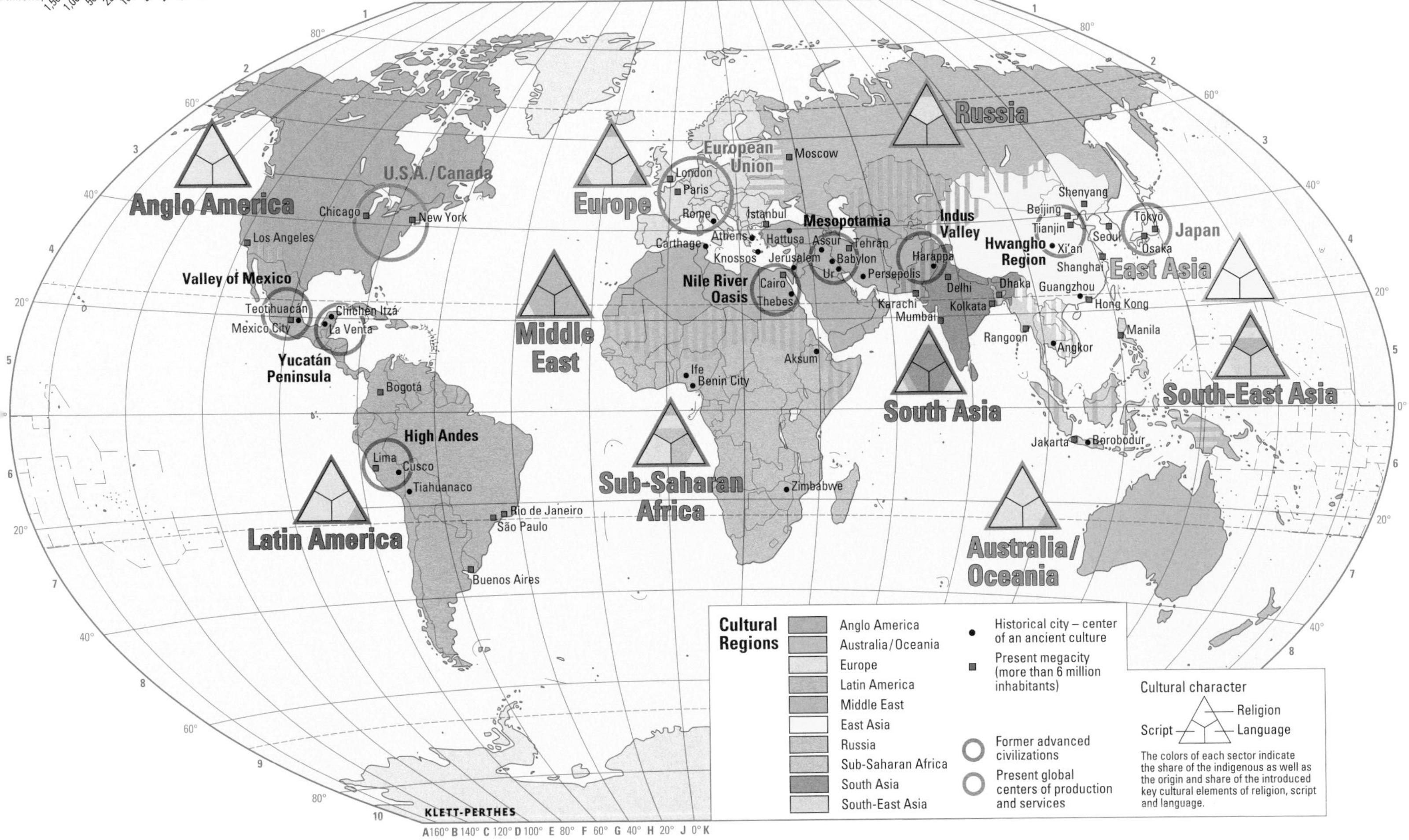

Anglo America
U.S.A./Canada
Chicago
New York
Los Angeles
Valley of Mexico
Teotihuacán
Mexico City
Chichén Itzá
La Venta
Yucatán Peninsula
Bogotá
High Andes
Lima
Cusco
Tiahuanaco
Rio de Janeiro
São Paulo
Buenos Aires
Latin America
Europe
European Union
London
Paris
Rome
Moscow
Istanbul
Athens
Knossos
Carthage
Hattusa
Jerusalem
Mesopotamia
Assur
Babylon
Ur
Tehran
Persepolis
Nile River Oasis
Cairo
Thebes
Middle East
Aksum
Ife
Benin City
Zimbabwe
Sub-Saharan Africa
Russia
Indus Valley
Harappa
Karachi
Mumbai
Delhi
Kolkata
Dhaka
South Asia
Hwangho Region
Shenyang
Beijing
Tianjin
Xi'an
Seoul
Tokyo
Osaka
Japan
Shanghai
Guangzhou
Hong Kong
East Asia
Rangoon
Angkor
Manila
Jakarta
Borobudur
South-East Asia
Australia/Oceania
KLETT-PERTHES

Cultural Regions

- Anglo America
- Australia/Oceania
- Europe
- Latin America
- Middle East
- East Asia
- Russia
- Sub-Saharan Africa
- South Asia
- South-East Asia

- Historical city – center of an ancient culture
- Present megacity (more than 6 million inhabitants)
- Former advanced civilizations
- Present global centers of production and services

Cultural character

Script – Religion – Language

The colors of each sector indicate the share of the indigenous as well as the origin and share of the introduced key cultural elements of religion, script and language.

1:160,000,000

Government Expenditures per Capita (2004)

($US)	Percentage of world population
Over 20,000	
10,000 to 20,000	IIIIIII
5,000 to 10,000	IIIII
2,500 to 5,000	III
1,000 to 2,500 (2,023)	IIIIII
500 to 1,000	IIIIIIIIII
250 to 500	IIIIIIIIIIIIIIIIIIIIIIIII
100 to 250	IIIIIIII
Under 100	IIIIIIIIIIIIIIIIIIIIIIIIIIIII
No data	I

Population

1, 5, 10, 25, 50, 100, 250, 500, 1,000, 1,500 (Millions)

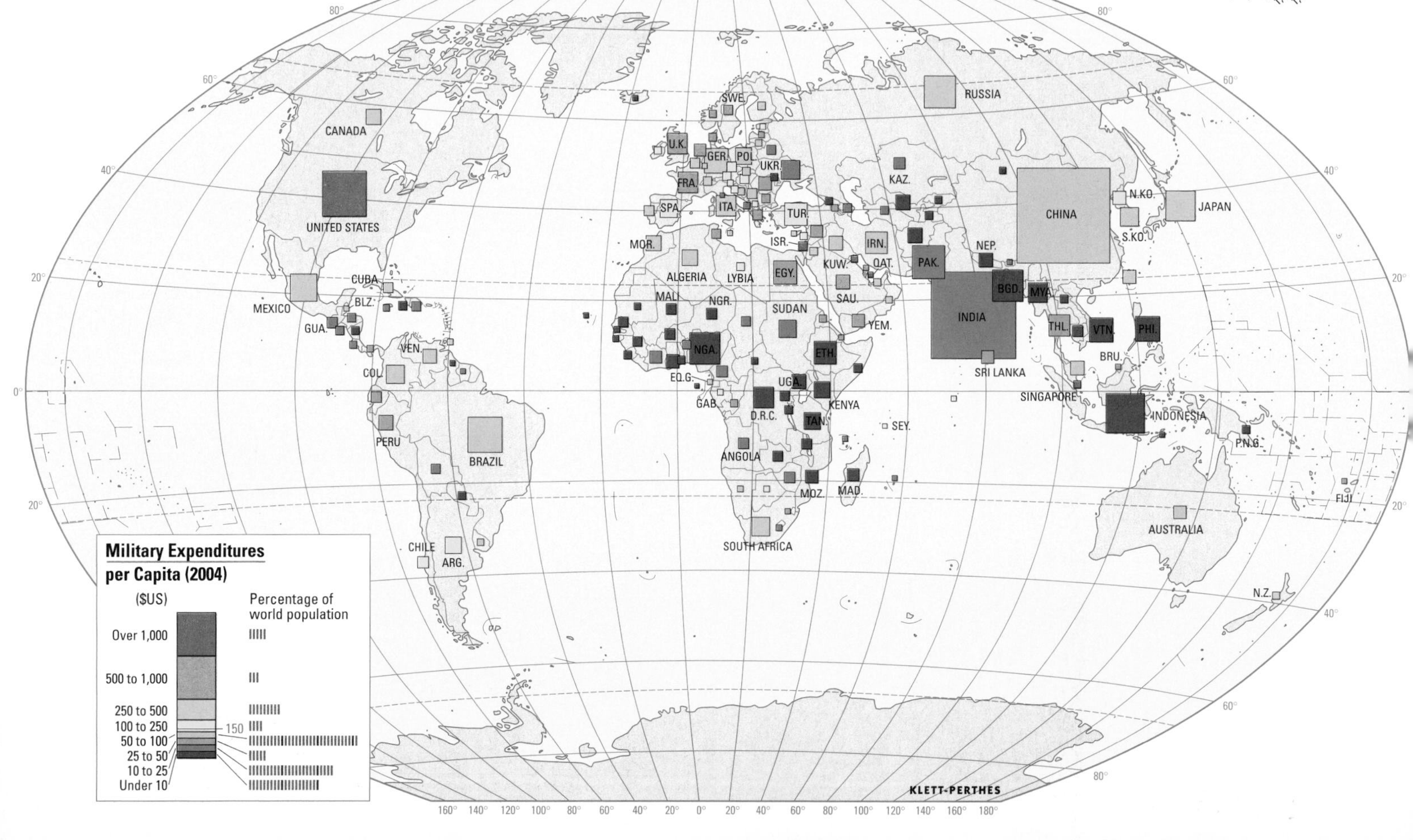

Military Expenditures per Capita (2004)

($US)	Percentage of world population
Over 1,000	IIIII
500 to 1,000	III
250 to 500	IIIIIIII
100 to 250 (150)	IIII
50 to 100	IIIIIIIIIIIIIIIIIIIIIIIIIIIIII
25 to 50	IIIII
10 to 25	IIIIIIIIIIIIIIIIIIIIIII
Under 10	IIIIIIIIIIIIIIIIIIIIII

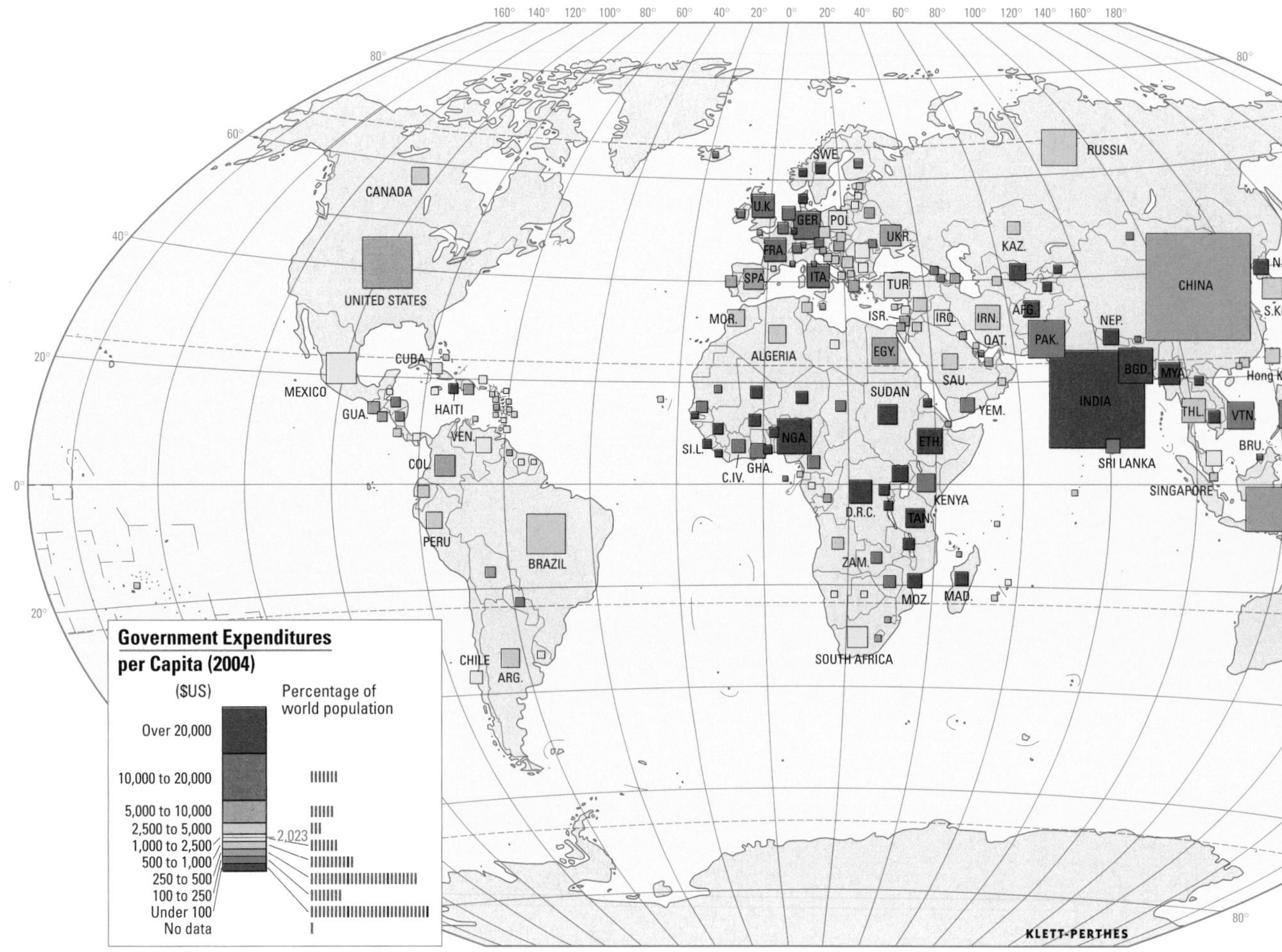

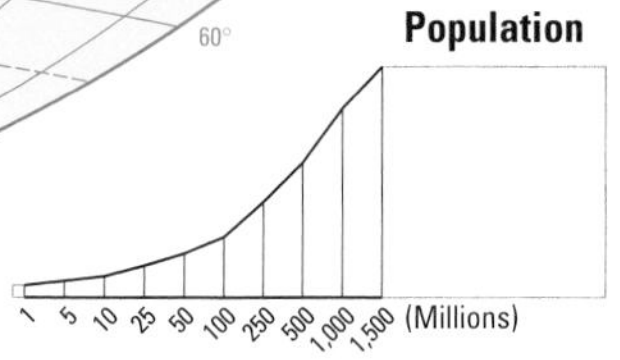

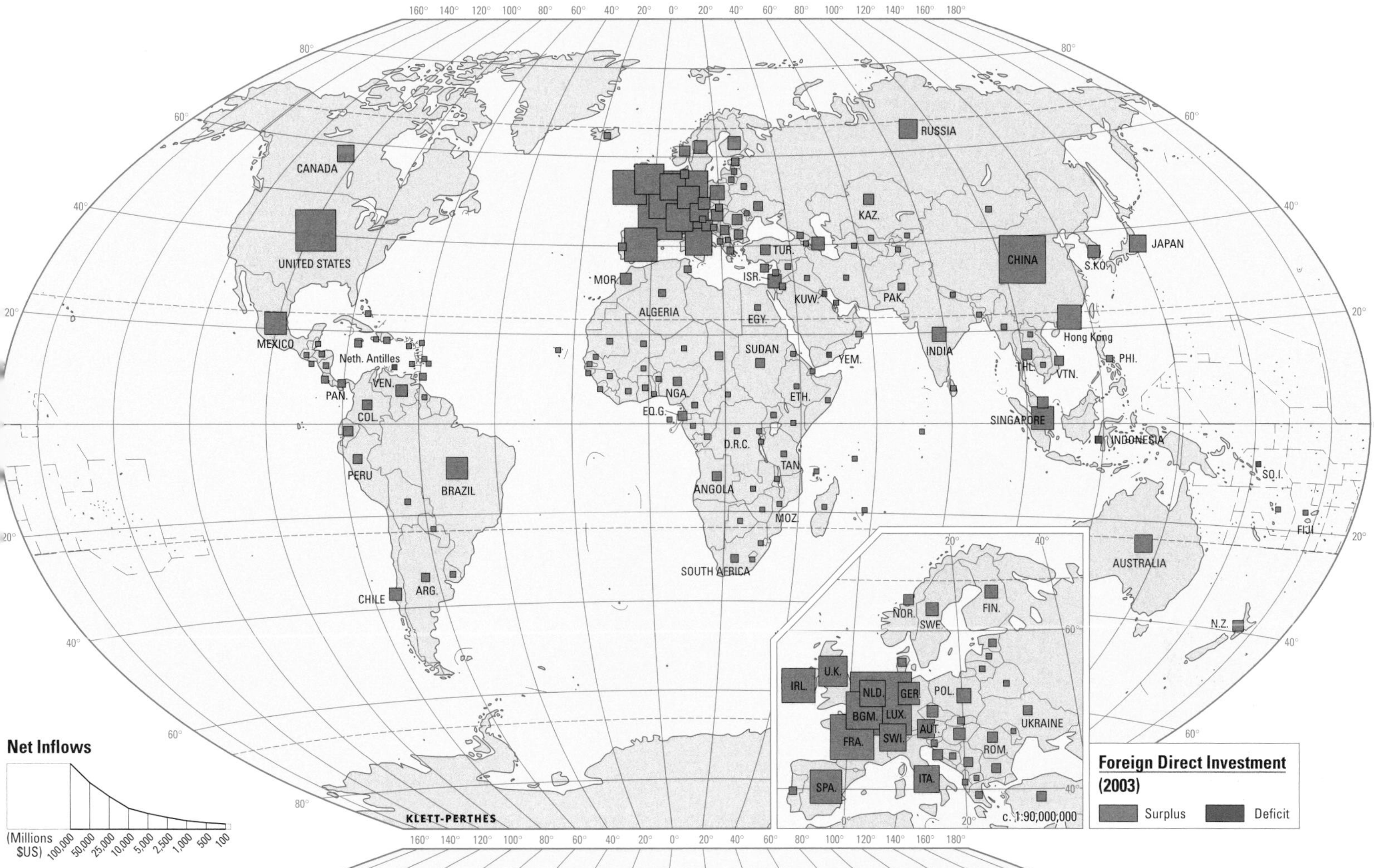

World: Foreign Direct Investment · Foreign Aid

1:160,000,000

Foreign Direct Investment (2003)

Surplus | Deficit

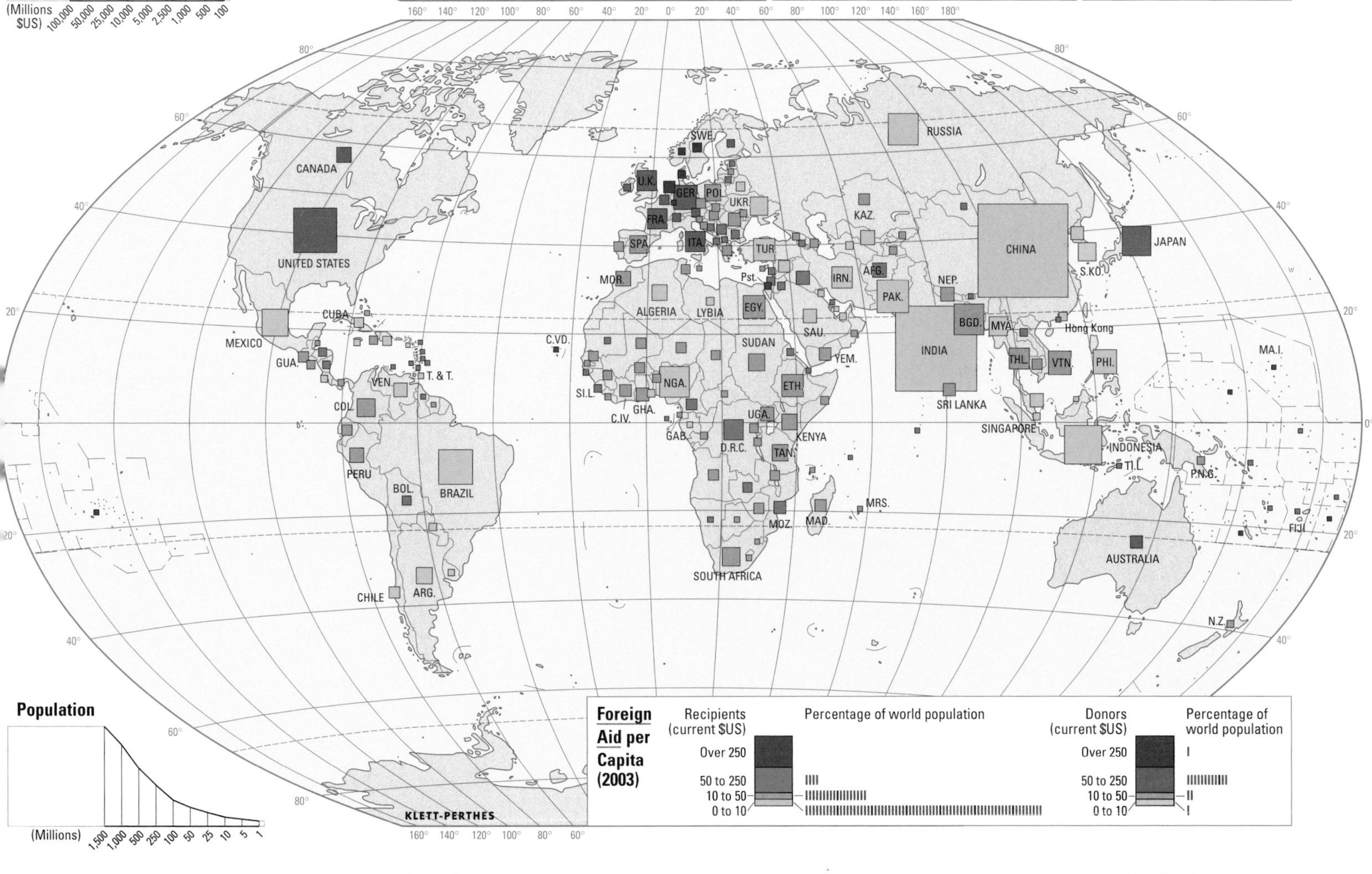

Net Inflows

(Millions $US) 100,000 50,000 25,000 10,000 5,000 2,500 1,000 500 100

Population

(Millions) 1,500 1,000 500 250 100 50 25 10 5 1

Foreign Aid per Capita (2003)

Recipients (current $US)	Percentage of world population	Donors (current $US)	Percentage of world population
Over 250		Over 250	I
50 to 250	IIII	50 to 250	IIIIIIIIIII
10 to 50	IIIIIIIIIIIIIIII	10 to 50	II
0 to 10	IIIIIIIIIIIIIIIIIIIIIIIIIIIIIIIIIIIIIIIIIIIIIIIIIIIIIIIIIIIIIIIIIIIIII	0 to 10	I

1:160,000,000

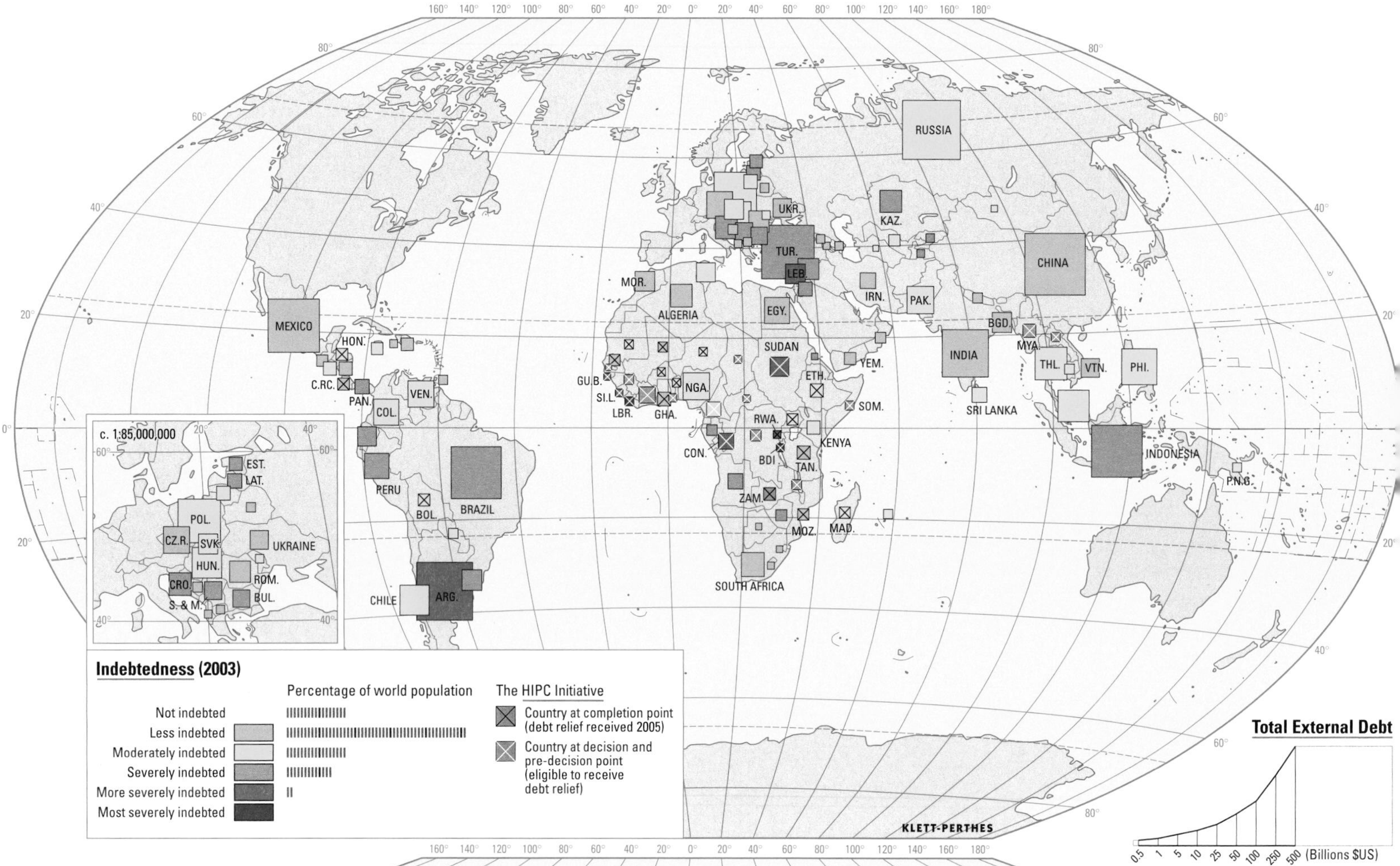

RUSSIA
UKR.
KAZ.
TUR.
LEB.
CHINA
MOR.
ALGERIA
IRN.
PAK.
EGY.
MEXICO
HON.
SUDAN
YEM.
BGD.
MYA.
INDIA
THL.
VTN.
PHI.
C.RC.
PAN.
VEN.
GU.B.
SI.L.
LBR.
GHA.
NGA.
ETH.
SOM.
SRI LANKA
COL
RWA.
CON.
KENYA
BDI
TAN.
INDONESIA
P.N.G.
PERU
BRAZIL
BOL.
ZAM.
MOZ.
MAD.
CHILE
ARG.
SOUTH AFRICA

c. 1:85,000,000
EST.
LAT.
POL.
CZ.R.
SVK
UKRAINE
HUN.
ROM.
CRO.
S. & M.
BUL.

Indebtedness (2003)

		Percentage of world population
Not indebted		IIIIIIIIIIIIIIII
Less indebted	▢	IIIIIIIIIIIIIIIIIIIIIIIIIIIIIIIIIIIIIIIIIIIIIIIIIIII
Moderately indebted	▢	IIIIIIIIIIIIIIII
Severely indebted	▢	IIIIIIIIIIIII
More severely indebted	▢	II
Most severely indebted	▢	

The HIPC Initiative
- Country at completion point (debt relief received 2005)
- Country at decision and pre-decision point (eligible to receive debt relief)

KLETT-PERTHES

Total External Debt

0.5 1 5 10 25 50 100 250 500 (Billions $US)

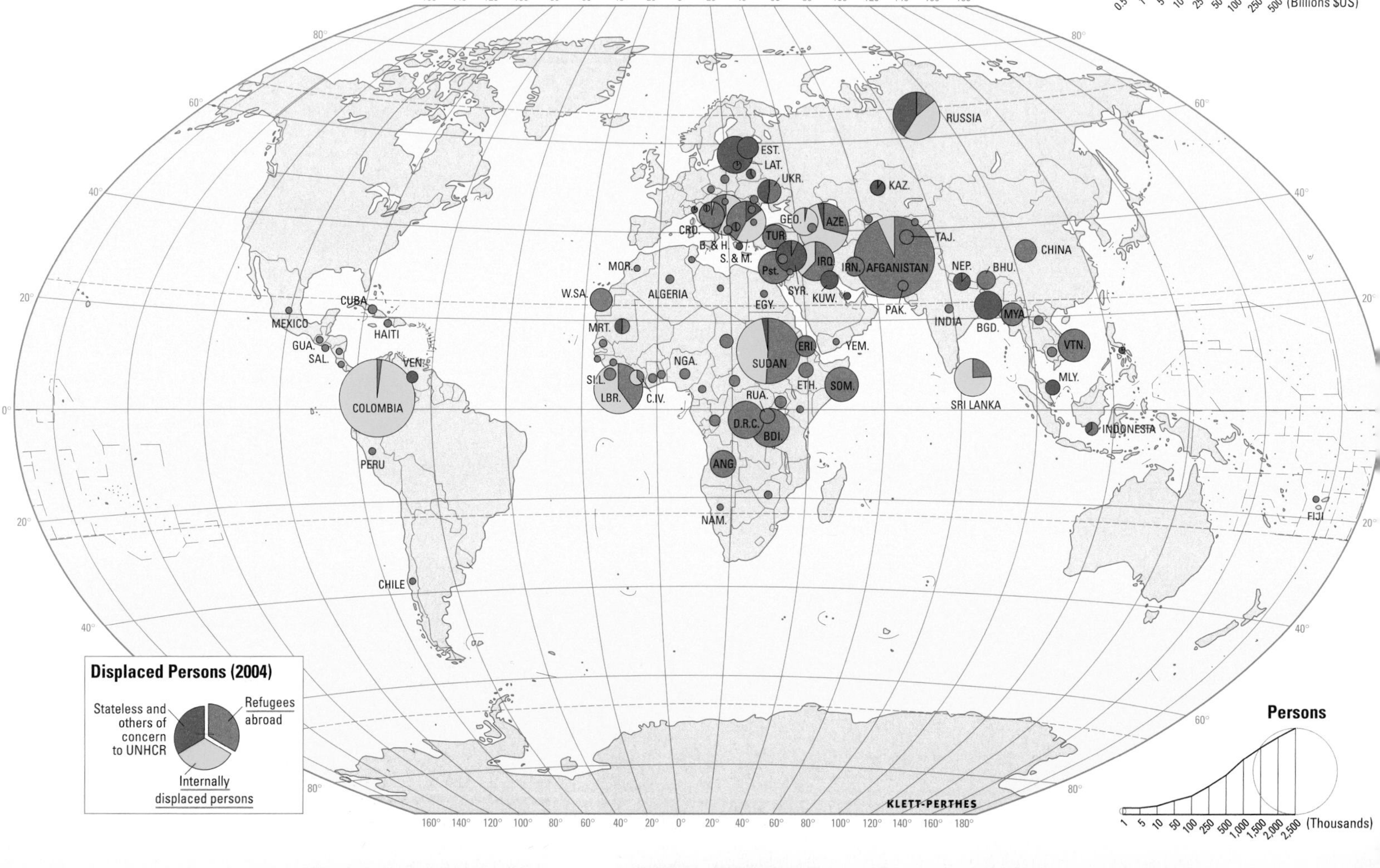

RUSSIA
EST.
LAT.
UKR.
KAZ.
CRO.
GEO.
AZE.
B. & H.
S. & M.
TUR
TAJ.
MOR.
Pst.
IRQ.
IRN.
AFGANISTAN
NEP.
BHU.
CHINA
W.SA.
ALGERIA
SYR.
KUW.
EGY.
PAK.
INDIA
BGD.
MYA.
CUBA
MEXICO
HAITI
MRT.
ERI.
YEM.
VTN.
GUA.
SAL.
VEN.
NGA.
SUDAN
SOM.
MLY.
SI.L.
LBR.
C.IV.
ETH.
SRI LANKA
COLOMBIA
RUA.
D.R.C.
BDI.
INDONESIA
PERU
ANG.
NAM.
FIJI
CHILE

Displaced Persons (2004)

Stateless and others of concern to UNHCR

Refugees abroad

Internally displaced persons

KLETT-PERTHES

Persons

1 5 10 50 100 250 500 1,000 1,500 2,000 2,500 (Thousands)

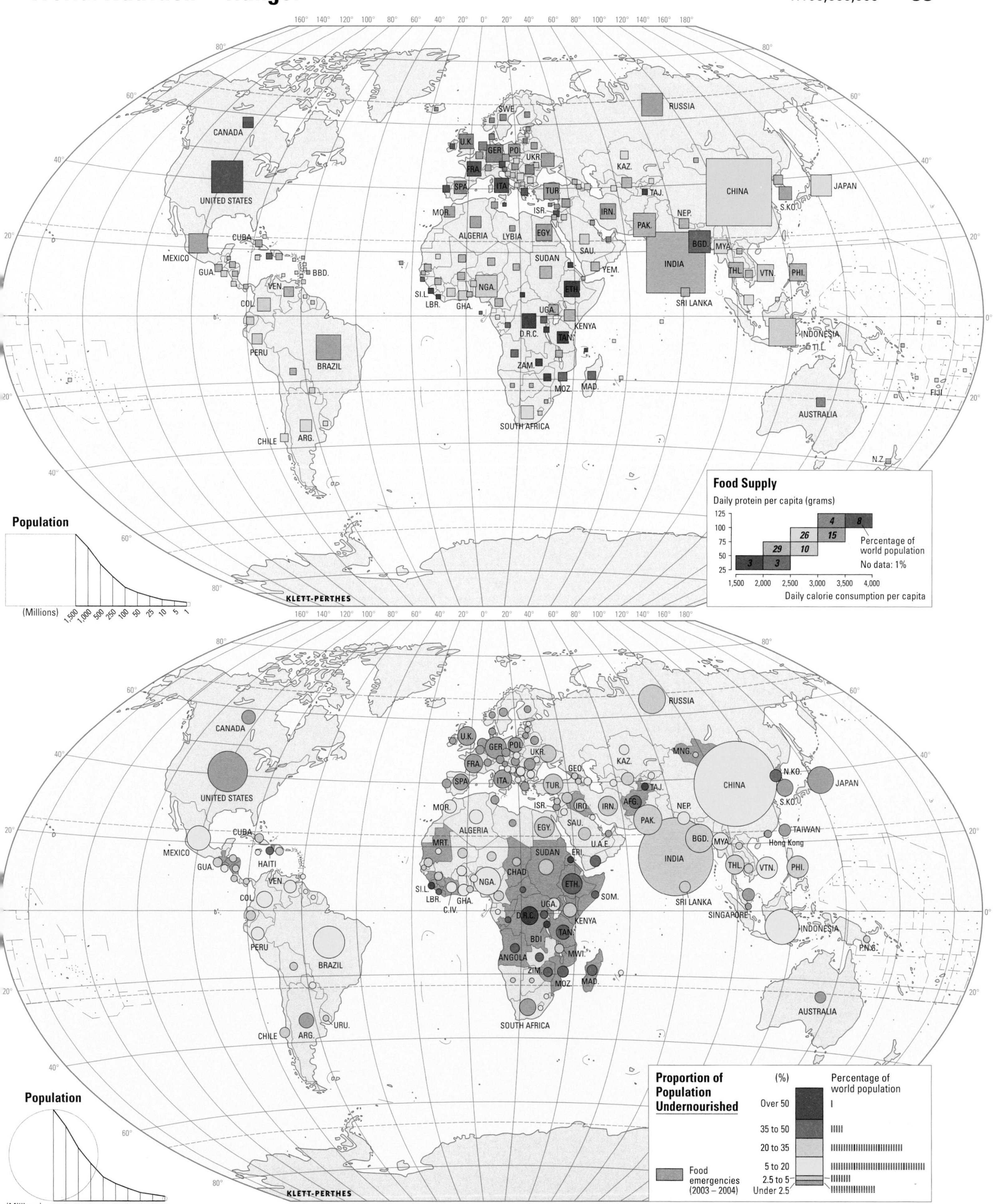

RUSSIA
CANADA
SWE.
U.K.
GER.
POL.
UKR.
FRA.
SPA.
ITA.
TUR.
KAZ.
TAJ.
CHINA
JAPAN
S.KO.
UNITED STATES
MOR.
ISR.
IRN.
NEP.
PAK.
ALGERIA
LYBIA
EGY.
BGD.
MYA.
CUBA
MEXICO
SAU.
INDIA
GUA.
BBD.
SUDAN
YEM.
THL.
VTN.
PHI.
VEN.
NGA.
ETH.
COL.
SI.L.
LBR.
GHA.
SRI LANKA
UGA.
KENYA
D.R.C.
TAN.
INDONESIA
TI.L.
PERU
BRAZIL
ZAM.
MOZ.
MAD.
FIJI
AUSTRALIA
SOUTH AFRICA
CHILE
ARG.
N.Z.
Food Supply
Daily protein per capita (grams)
125
100
75
50
25
1,500
2,000
2,500
3,000
3,500
4,000
Daily calorie consumption per capita
3
3
29
10
26
15
4
8
Percentage of world population
No data: 1%
Population
(Millions)
1,500
1,000
500
250
100
50
25
10
5
1
KLETT-PERTHES
MNG.
N.KO.
GEO.
IRQ.
AFG.
TAIWAN
Hong Kong
U.A.E.
MRT.
ERI.
HAITI
CHAD
SOM.
C.IV.
SINGAPORE
BDI
MWI.
ANGOLA
ZIM.
P.N.G.
URU.
Proportion of Population Undernourished
(%)
Percentage of world population
Over 50
35 to 50
20 to 35
5 to 20
2.5 to 5
Under 2.5
Food emergencies (2003 – 2004)
Population
(Millions)
1,500
1,000
500
250
100
50
25
10
5
1
KLETT-PERTHES

1:160,000,000

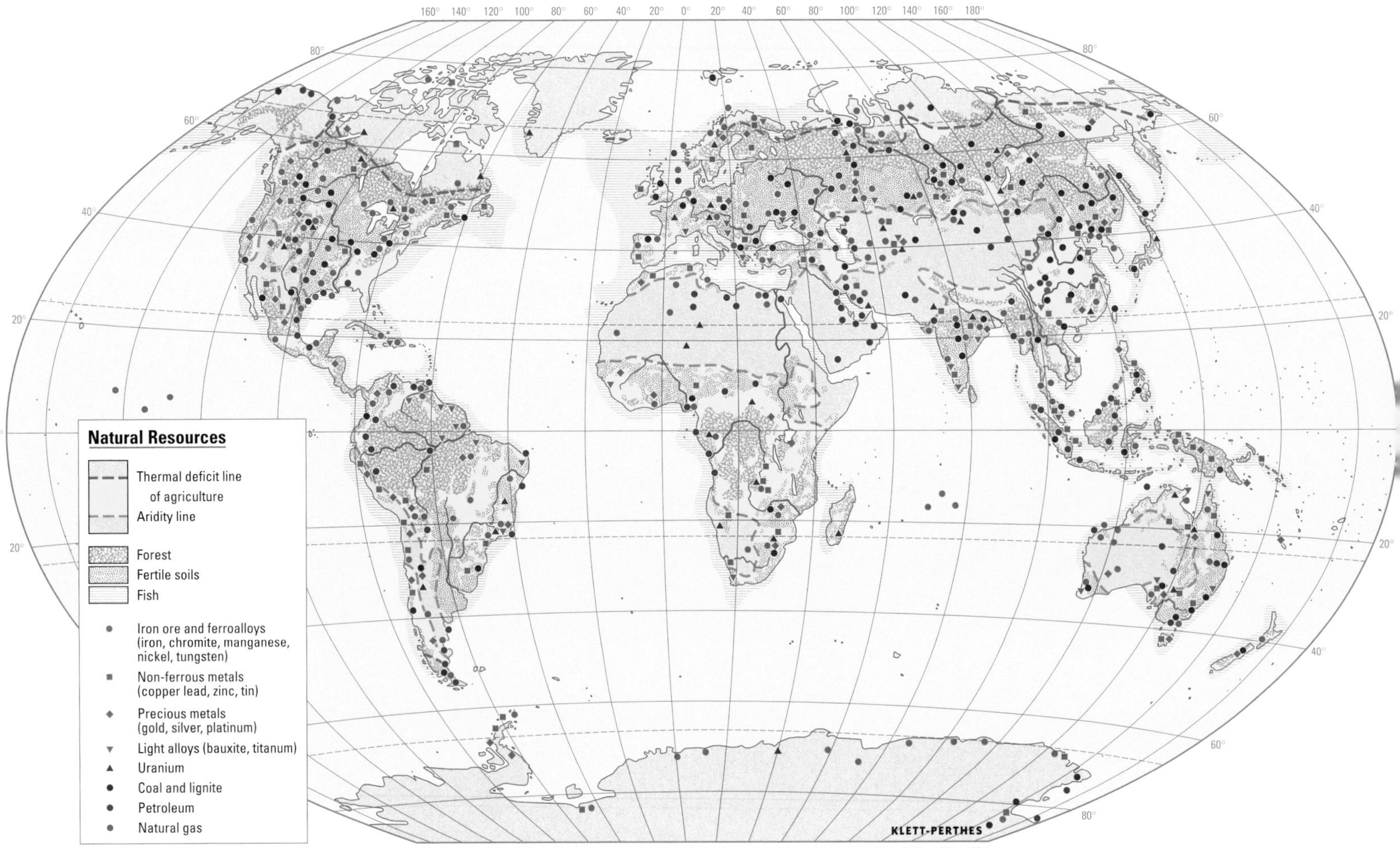

Natural Resources

- Thermal deficit line of agriculture
- Aridity line
- Forest
- Fertile soils
- Fish
- Iron ore and ferroalloys (iron, chromite, manganese, nickel, tungsten)
- Non-ferrous metals (copper lead, zinc, tin)
- Precious metals (gold, silver, platinum)
- Light alloys (bauxite, titanum)
- Uranium
- Coal and lignite
- Petroleum
- Natural gas

KLETT-PERTHES

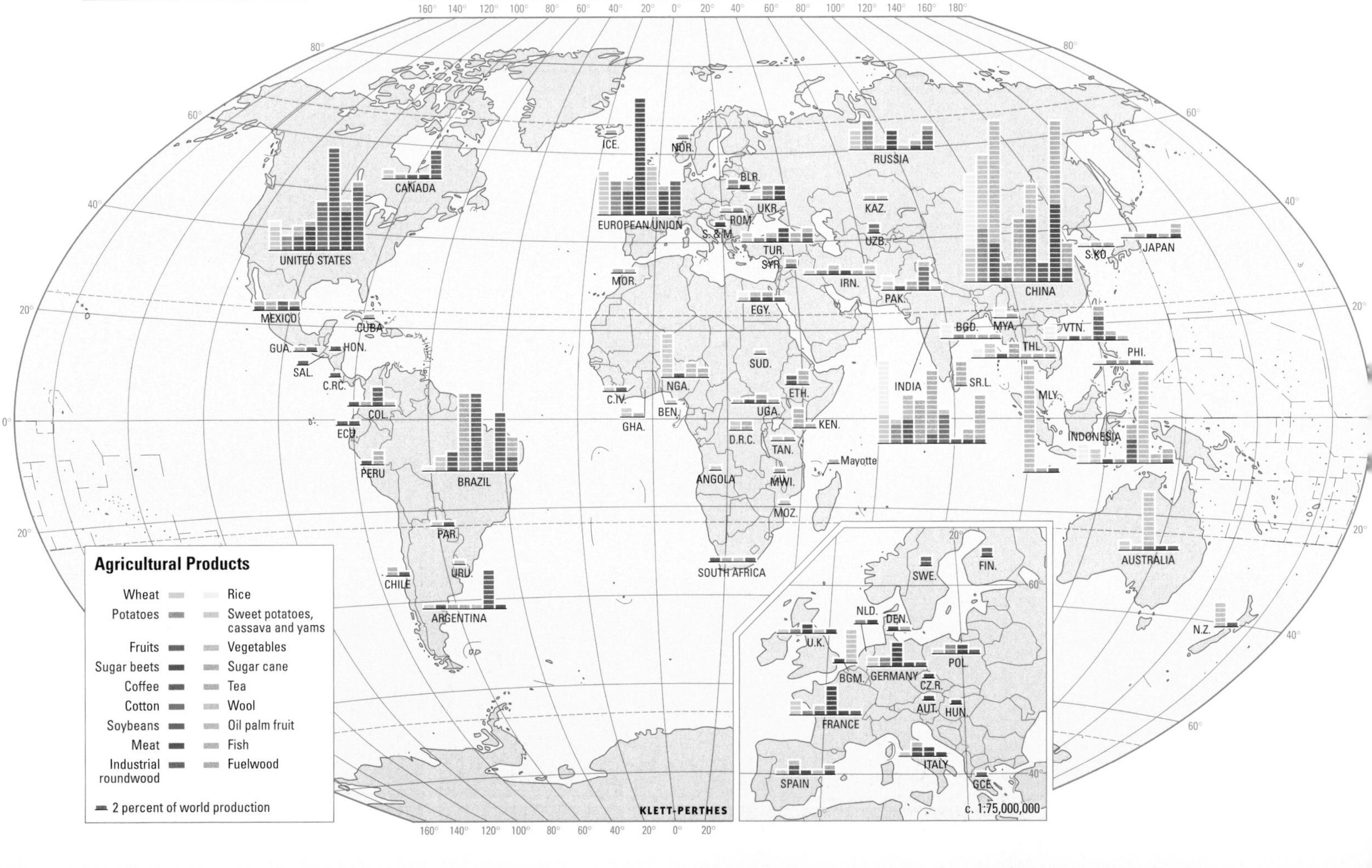

UNITED STATES, CANADA, MEXICO, CUBA, GUA., HON., SAL., C.R., COL., ECU., PERU, BRAZIL, PAR., URU., CHILE, ARGENTINA, ICE., NOR., EUROPEAN UNION, BLR., UKR., ROM., S. & M., TUR., SYR., MOR., EGY., RUSSIA, KAZ., UZB., IRN., PAK., CHINA, S.KO., JAPAN, BGD., MYA., VTN., THL., PHI., INDIA, SR.L., MLY., INDONESIA, AUSTRALIA, N.Z., SUD., ETH., NGA., C.IV., BEN., GHA., UGA., KEN., D.R.C., TAN., Mayotte, ANGOLA, MWI., MOZ., SOUTH AFRICA

SWE., FIN., NLD., DEN., U.K., POL., BGM., GERMANY, CZ.R., AUT., HUN., FRANCE, ITALY, SPAIN, GCE.

c. 1:75,000,000

Agricultural Products

Wheat	Rice
Potatoes	Sweet potatoes, cassava and yams
Fruits	Vegetables
Sugar beets	Sugar cane
Coffee	Tea
Cotton	Wool
Soybeans	Oil palm fruit
Meat	Fish
Industrial roundwood	Fuelwood

2 percent of world production

KLETT-PERTHES

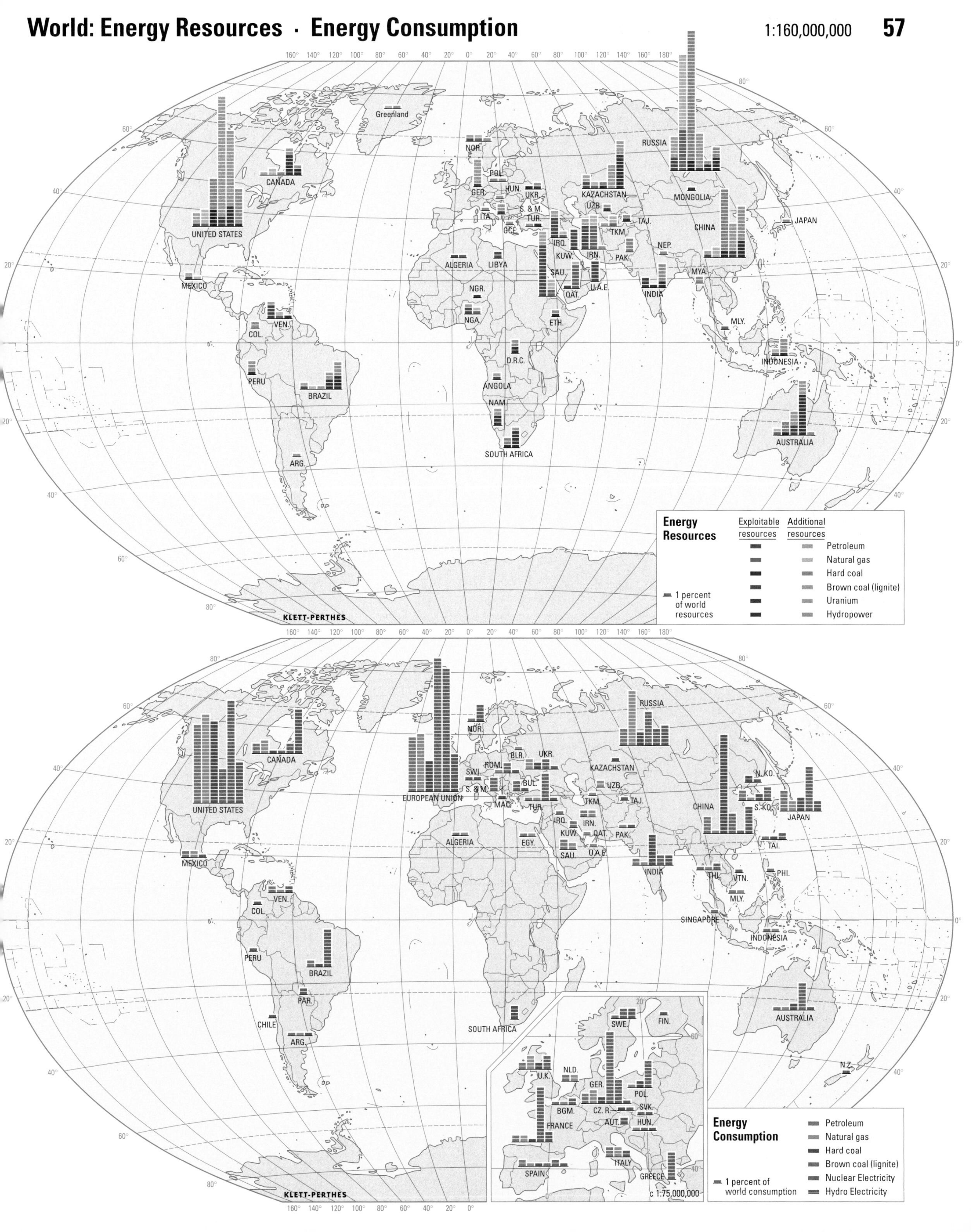
Greenland
NOR.
CANADA
UNITED STATES
MEXICO
POL.
GER.
HUN.
UKR.
ITA.
S. & M.
TUR.
GCE.
RUSSIA
KAZAKHSTAN
UZB.
TKM.
TAJ.
MONGOLIA
CHINA
JAPAN
IRQ.
KUW.
IRN.
PAK.
NEP.
SAU.
QAT.
U.A.E.
INDIA
MYA.
ALGERIA
LIBYA
NGR.
NGA.
ETH.
MLY.
INDONESIA
VEN.
COL.
PERU
BRAZIL
D.R.C.
ANGOLA
NAM.
SOUTH AFRICA
AUSTRALIA
ARG.
Energy Resources
Exploitable resources
Additional resources
Petroleum
Natural gas
Hard coal
Brown coal (lignite)
Uranium
Hydropower
1 percent of world resources
KLETT-PERTHES
EUROPEAN UNION
SWI.
ROM.
BLR.
BUL.
MAC.
S.K.O.
N. KO.
TAI.
PHI.
THL.
VTN.
SINGAPORE
EGY.
PAR.
CHILE
N.Z.
SWE.
FIN.
U.K.
NLD.
GER.
POL.
BGM.
CZ. R.
SVK.
AUT.
FRANCE
ITALY
SPAIN
GREECE
c 1:75,000,000
Energy Consumption
Petroleum
Natural gas
Hard coal
Brown coal (lignite)
Nuclear Electricity
Hydro Electricity
1 percent of world consumption
KLETT-PERTHES

World: Export Concentration · Trade in Agricultural Products

1:160,000,000

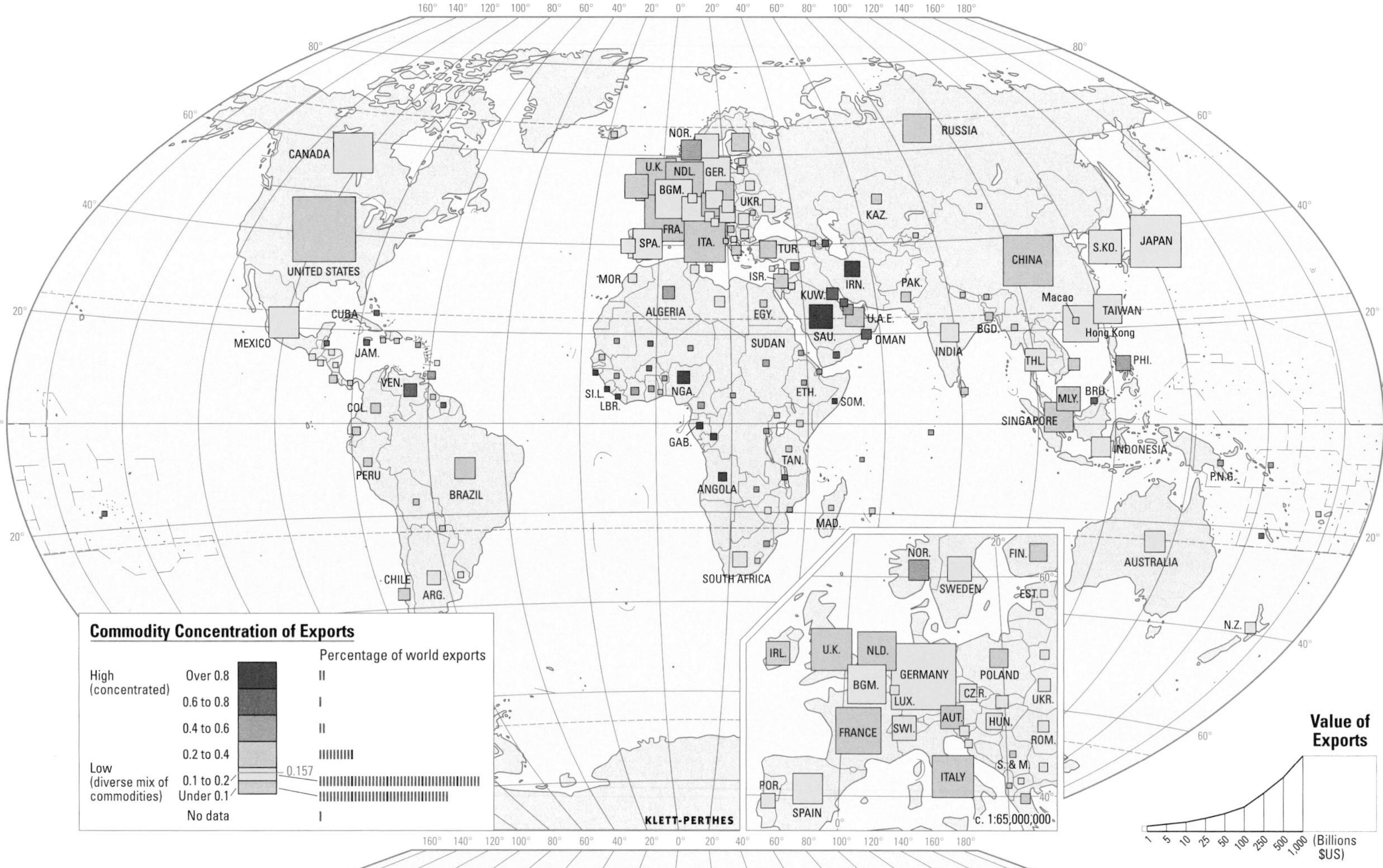

Commodity Concentration of Exports

		Percentage of world exports
High (concentrated)	Over 0.8	II
	0.6 to 0.8	I
	0.4 to 0.6	II
	0.2 to 0.4	IIIIIIIII
Low (diverse mix of commodities)	0.1 to 0.2 (0.157)	IIIIIIIIIIIIIIIIIIIIIIIIIIIIIIIIIIIIIIIIIIIIIIIIIII
	Under 0.1	IIIIIIIIIIIIIIIIIIIIIIIIIIIIIIIIIIIIIII
	No data	I

c. 1:65,000,000

Value of Exports

1 5 10 25 50 100 250 500 1,000 (Billions $US)

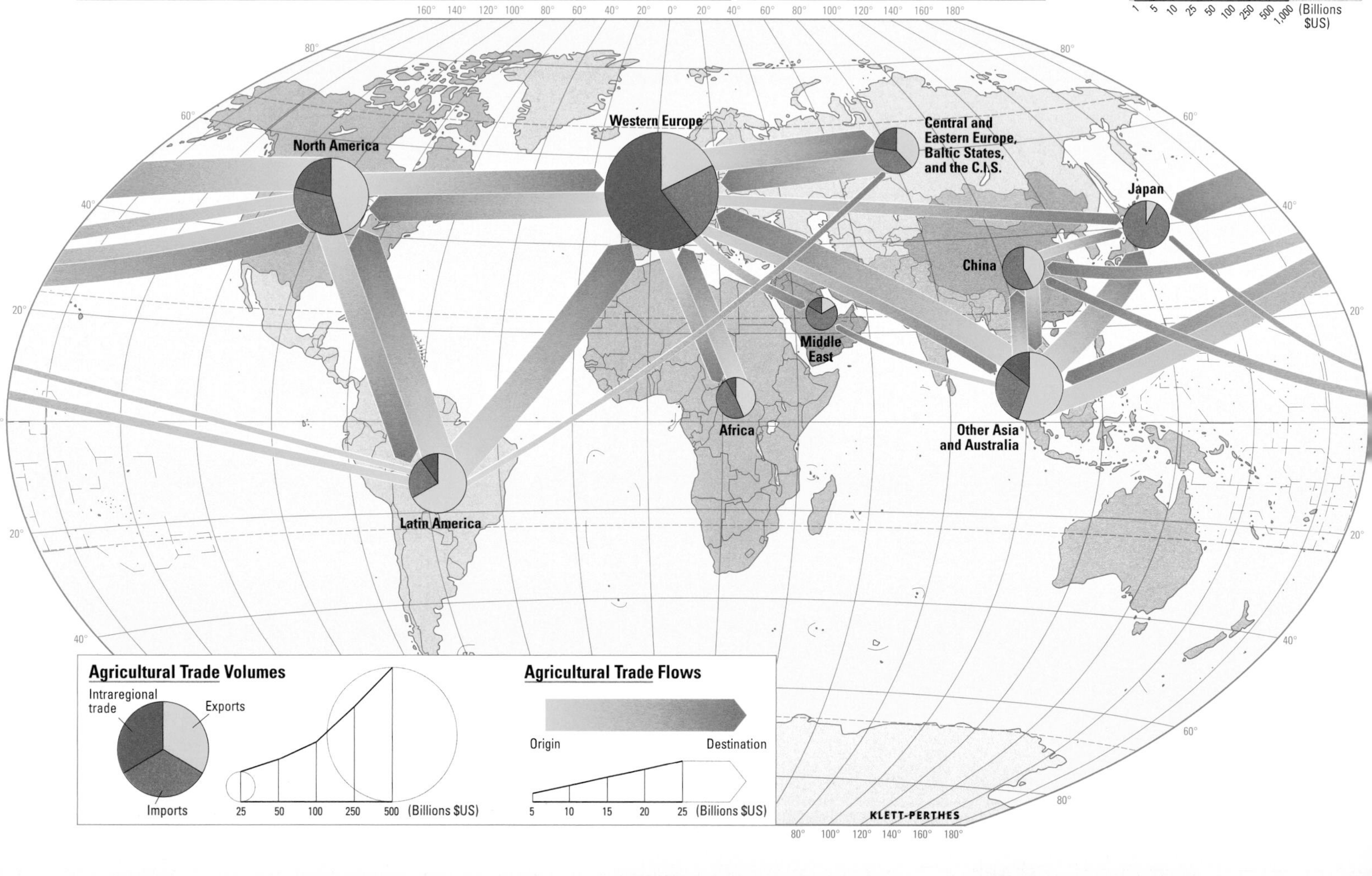

Western Europe

North America

Central and Eastern Europe, Baltic States, and the C.I.S.

Japan

China

Middle East

Africa

Other Asia and Australia

Latin America

Agricultural Trade Volumes

Intraregional trade

Exports

Imports

25 50 100 250 500 (Billions $US)

Agricultural Trade Flows

Origin

Destination

5 10 15 20 25 (Billions $US)

North America
Western Europe
Central and Eastern Europe, Baltic States, and the C.I.S.
Japan
China
Middle East
Africa
Other Asia and Australia
Latin America
Mining Trade Volumes
Intraregional trade
Exports
Imports
50 100 250 500 (Billions $US)
Mining Trade Flows
Origin
Destination
10 20 30 40 50 60 70 (Billions $US)
KLETT-PERTHES

North America
Western Europe
Central and Eastern Europe, Baltic States, and the C.I.S.
Japan
China
Middle East
Africa
Other Asia and Australia
Latin America
Trade Volumes of Manufactured Goods
Intraregional trade
Exports
Imports
100 250 500 1,000 2,500 5,000 (Billions $US)
Trade Flows of Manufactured Goods
Origin
Destination
50 100 150 200 250 300 (Billions $US)
KLETT-PERTHES

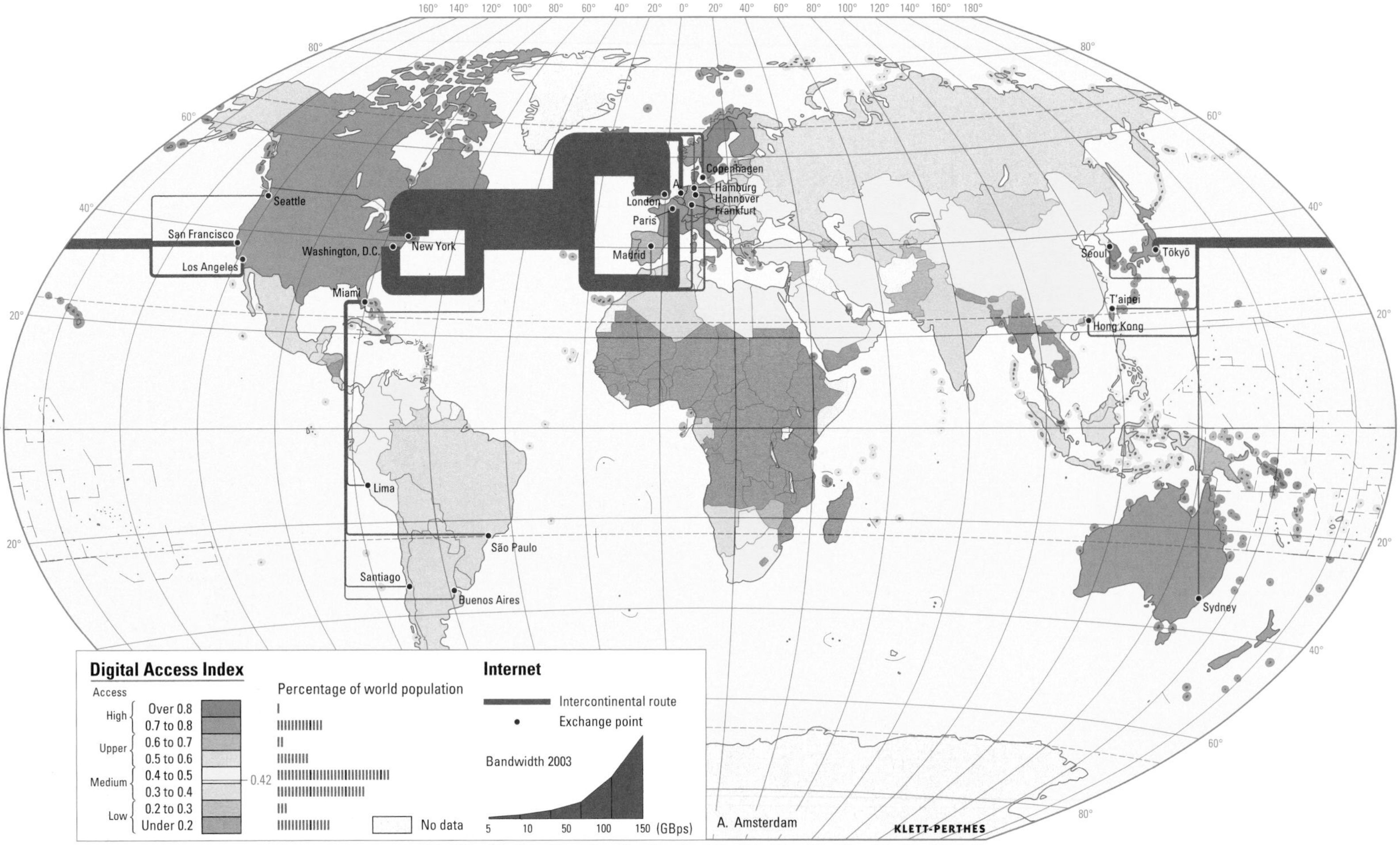

World: Telecommunication · Carbon Dioxide Emission

1:160,000,000

Seattle
San Francisco
Los Angeles
Washington, D.C.
New York
Miami
Lima
São Paulo
Santiago
Buenos Aires
Copenhagen
Hamburg
Hannover
Frankfurt
London
Paris
Madrid
A
Seoul
Tōkyō
T'aipei
Hong Kong
Sydney

Digital Access Index

Access		Percentage of world population
High	Over 0.8	I
	0.7 to 0.8	IIIIIIIIIIII
Upper	0.6 to 0.7	II
	0.5 to 0.6	IIIIIIII
Medium	0.4 to 0.5 (0.42)	IIIIIIIIIIIIIIIIIIIIIIIIIIIIII
	0.3 to 0.4	IIIIIIIIIIIIIIIIIIIIIII
Low	0.2 to 0.3	III
	Under 0.2	IIIIIIIIIIIIII

No data

Internet

Intercontinental route

Exchange point

Bandwidth 2003

5 10 50 100 150 (GBps)

A. Amsterdam

KLETT-PERTHES

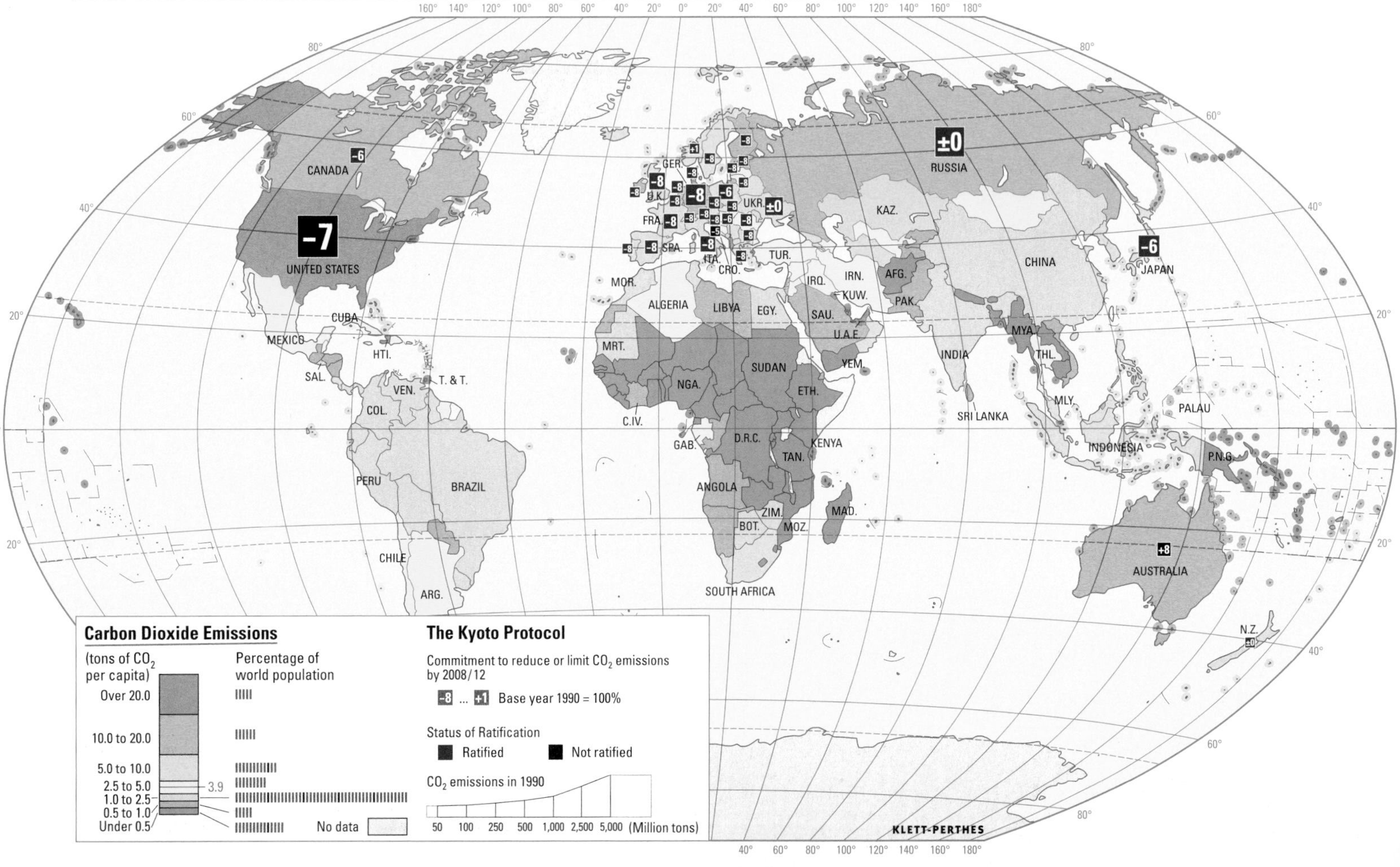

CANADA
UNITED STATES
MEXICO
CUBA
HTI.
SAL.
VEN.
T. & T.
COL.
PERU
BRAZIL
CHILE
ARG.
GER.
U.K.
FRA.
SPA.
ITA.
CRO.
UKR.
TUR.
RUSSIA
KAZ.
MOR.
ALGERIA
LIBYA
EGY.
IRQ.
IRN.
KUW.
SAU.
U.A.E.
YEM.
AFG.
PAK.
INDIA
SRI LANKA
CHINA
JAPAN
MYA.
THL.
MLY.
INDONESIA
PALAU
P.N.G.
AUSTRALIA
N.Z.
MRT.
NGA.
SUDAN
ETH.
C.IV.
GAB.
D.R.C.
KENYA
TAN.
ANGOLA
ZIM.
MOZ.
BOT.
MAD.
SOUTH AFRICA

−6 −7 ±0 −8 −6 +8 ±0 +1

Carbon Dioxide Emissions

(tons of CO_2 per capita)	Percentage of world population
Over 20.0	IIIII
10.0 to 20.0	IIIIII
5.0 to 10.0	IIIIIIIIIIIII
2.5 to 5.0 (3.9)	IIIIIIIII
1.0 to 2.5	IIIIIIIIIIIIIIIIIIIIIIIIIIIIIIIIIIIIIIIIIIIIII
0.5 to 1.0	IIIII
Under 0.5	IIIIIIIIIIIII

No data

The Kyoto Protocol

Commitment to reduce or limit CO_2 emissions by 2008/12

−8 ... +1 Base year 1990 = 100%

Status of Ratification

Ratified   Not ratified

CO_2 emissions in 1990

50 100 250 500 1,000 2,500 5,000 (Million tons)

KLETT-PERTHES

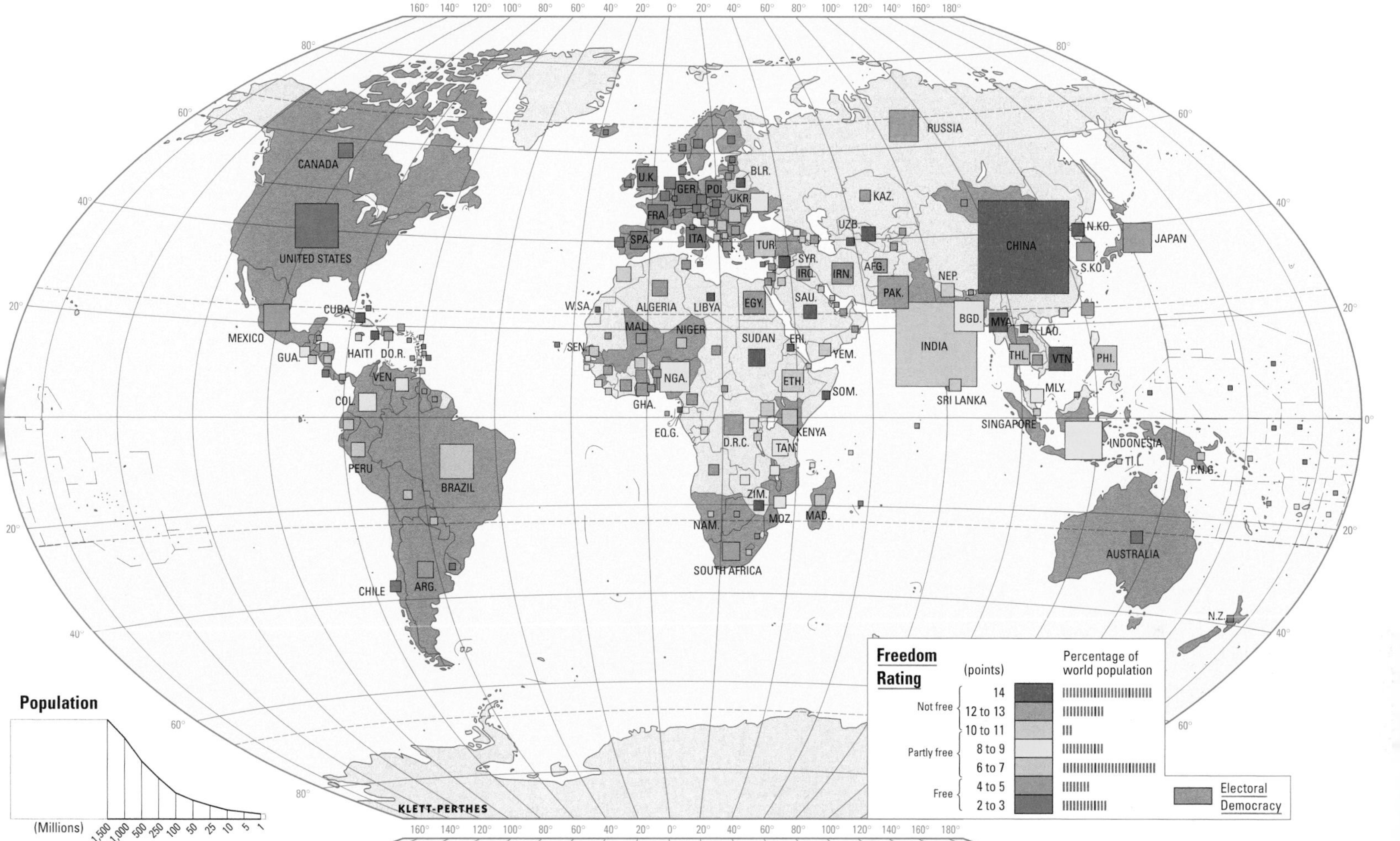

CANADA
UNITED STATES
MEXICO
CUBA
GUA.
HAITI
DO.R.
VEN.
COL.
PERU
BRAZIL
CHILE
ARG.
U.K.
GER.
POL.
BLR.
UKR.
FRA.
SPA.
ITA.
TUR.
SYR.
IRQ.
IRN.
AFG.
PAK.
KAZ.
UZB.
RUSSIA
CHINA
N.KO.
S.KO.
JAPAN
NEP.
INDIA
BGD.
MYA.
LAO.
THL.
VTN.
PHI.
MLY.
SRI LANKA
SINGAPORE
INDONESIA
T.L.
P.N.G.
AUSTRALIA
N.Z.
W.SA.
ALGERIA
LIBYA
EGY.
SAU.
YEM.
MALI
NIGER
SUDAN
ERI.
ETH.
SOM.
SEN.
NGA.
GHA.
EQ.G.
D.R.C.
KENYA
TAN.
ZIM.
MOZ.
MAD.
NAM.
SOUTH AFRICA

Population

(Millions) 1,500 1,000 500 250 100 50 25 10 5 1

Freedom Rating

	(points)		Percentage of world population
Not free	14		IIIIIIIIIIIIIIIIIIIIIIIIII
	12 to 13		IIIIIIIIIIII
	10 to 11		III
Partly free	8 to 9		IIIIIIIIIIII
	6 to 7		IIIIIIIIIIIIIIIIIIIIIIIIIIII
Free	4 to 5		IIIIIIII
	2 to 3		IIIIIIIIIIIIII

Electoral Democracy

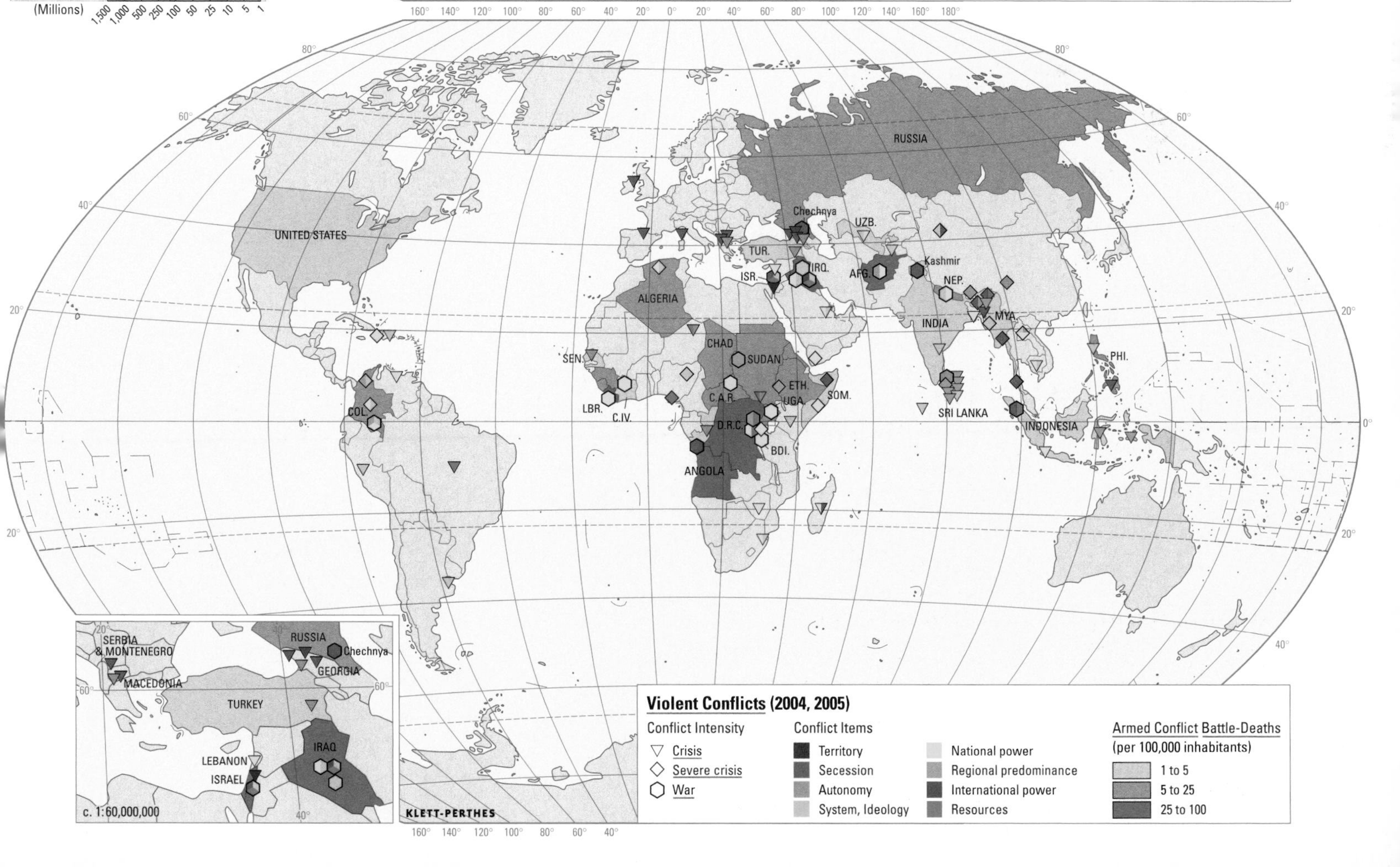

KLETT-PERTHES

RUSSIA
Chechnya
UZB.
UNITED STATES
TUR.
ISR.
IRQ.
AFG.
Kashmir
NEP.
INDIA
MYA.
ALGERIA
CHAD
SUDAN
SEN.
ETH.
SOM.
C.A.R.
UGA.
LBR.
C.I.V.
D.R.C.
BDI.
ANGOLA
COL.
SRI LANKA
INDONESIA
PHI.

SERBIA & MONTENEGRO
MACEDONIA
RUSSIA
Chechnya
GEORGIA
TURKEY
LEBANON
ISRAEL
IRAQ
c. 1:60,000,000

KLETT-PERTHES

Violent Conflicts (2004, 2005)

Conflict Intensity	Conflict Items		Armed Conflict Battle-Deaths (per 100,000 inhabitants)
▽ Crisis	Territory	National power	1 to 5
◇ Severe crisis	Secession	Regional predominance	5 to 25
⬡ War	Autonomy	International power	25 to 100
	System, Ideology	Resources	

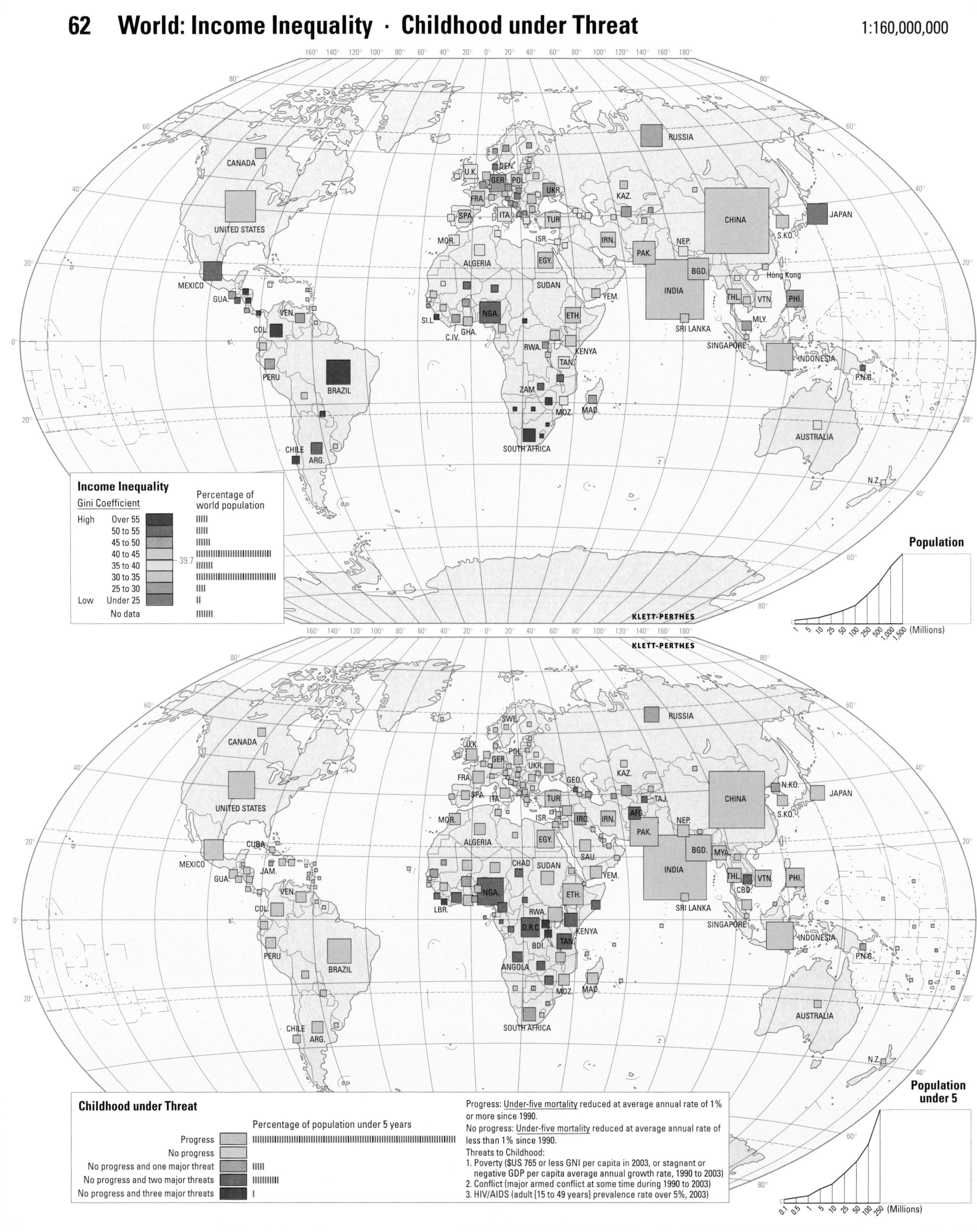

62 World: Income Inequality · Childhood under Threat
1:160,000,000
RUSSIA
CANADA
DEN.
U.K.
GER.
POL.
UKR.
FRA.
KAZ.
SPA.
ITA.
TUR.
CHINA
JAPAN
UNITED STATES
MOR.
ISR.
IRN.
NEP.
S.KO.
ALGERIA
EGY.
PAK.
BGD.
Hong Kong
MEXICO
SUDAN
YEM.
INDIA
GUA.
THL.
VTN.
PHI.
VEN.
NGA.
ETH.
SI.L.
GHA.
C.IV.
COL.
SRI LANKA
MLY.
SINGAPORE
RWA.
KENYA
TAN.
INDONESIA
PERU
BRAZIL
P.N.G.
ZAM.
MOZ.
MAD.
AUSTRALIA
CHILE
ARG.
SOUTH AFRICA
N.Z.
Income Inequality
Gini Coefficient
Percentage of world population
High
Over 55
50 to 55
45 to 50
40 to 45
35 to 40
30 to 35
25 to 30
Low
Under 25
No data
39.7
KLETT-PERTHES
Population
1 5 10 25 50 100 250 500 1,000 1,500 (Millions)
SWE.
N.KO.
GEO.
TAJ.
AFG.
IRQ.
CUBA
JAM.
SAU.
MYA.
CHAD
CBD.
LBR.
D.R.C.
BDI.
ANGOLA
Childhood under Threat
Percentage of population under 5 years
Progress
No progress
No progress and one major threat
No progress and two major threats
No progress and three major threats
Progress: Under-five mortality reduced at average annual rate of 1% or more since 1990.
No progress: Under-five mortality reduced at average annual rate of less than 1% since 1990.
Threats to Childhood:
1. Poverty ($US 765 or less GNI per capita in 2003, or stagnant or negative GDP per capita average annual growth rate, 1990 to 2003)
2. Conflict (major armed conflict at some time during 1990 to 2003)
3. HIV/AIDS (adult [15 to 49 years] prevalence rate over 5%, 2003)
Population under 5
0.1 0.5 1 5 10 25 50 100 250 (Millions)

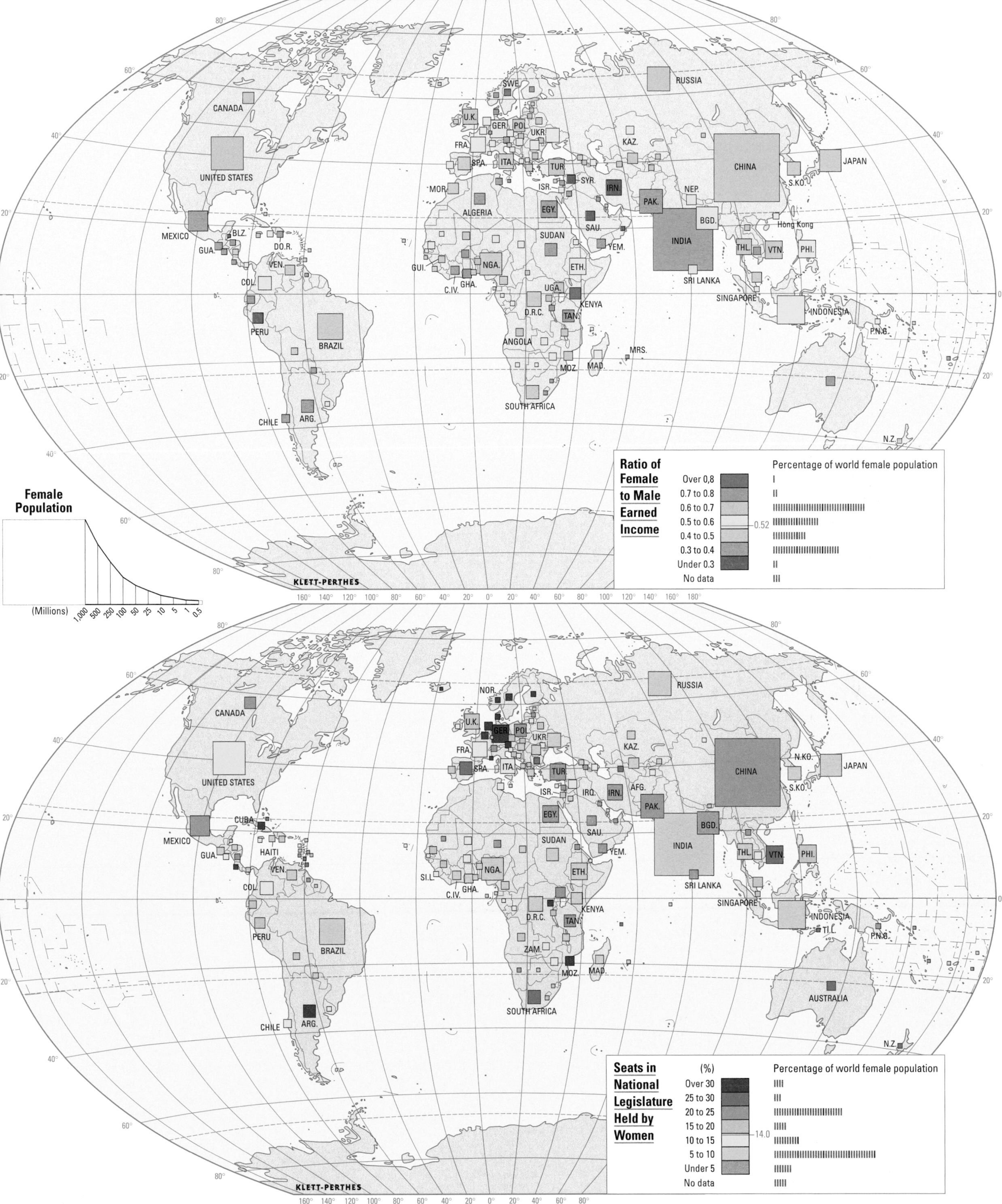
RUSSIA
CANADA
UNITED STATES
MEXICO
CHINA
JAPAN
INDIA
BRAZIL
INDONESIA
SOUTH AFRICA
KLETT-PERTHES
Ratio of Female to Male Earned Income
Over 0,8
0.7 to 0.8
0.6 to 0.7
0.5 to 0.6
0.4 to 0.5
0.3 to 0.4
Under 0.3
No data
0.52
Percentage of world female population
Female Population
(Millions)
1,000
500
250
100
50
25
10
5
1
0.5
Seats in National Legislature Held by Women
(%)
Over 30
25 to 30
20 to 25
15 to 20
10 to 15
5 to 10
Under 5
No data
14.0
AUSTRALIA

1:160,000,000

Political Organizations

NATO	North Atlantic Treaty Organization, founded 1948 (Headquarters in Washington, D.C.)
NATO	Partnership for Peace Program
CIS	Commonwealth of Independent States, founded 1991 (Headquarters in Minsk)
LAS	League of Arab States, founded 1945 (Headquarters in Cairo)
AU	African Union, founded 2000 (Headquarters in Addis Ababa)
OAS	Organization of American States, founded 1948 (Headquarters in Washington, D.C.)
ANZUS	Australia-New Zealand-U.S. Treaty, founded 1952 (Headquarters in Canberra)

Economic Organizations

ASEAN	Association of Southeast Asian Nations, founded 1967 (Headquarters in Jakarta)
EU	European Union, founded 1957/1958 (Headquarters in Brussels)
ECOWAS	Economic Community of West African States, founded 1975 (Headquarters in Abuja)
G8	Group of Eight, began 1975
MERCOSUR	Mercado Común del Cono Sur, founded 1991 (Headquarters in Montevideo)
NAFTA	North American Free Trade Agreement, signed 1992
OECD	Organization for Economic Cooperation and Development, founded 1961 (Headquarters in Paris)
OPEC	Organization of Petroleum Exporting Countries, founded 1960 (Headquarters in Vienna)
SADC	Southern African Development Community, founded 1992 (Headquarters in Gaborone)

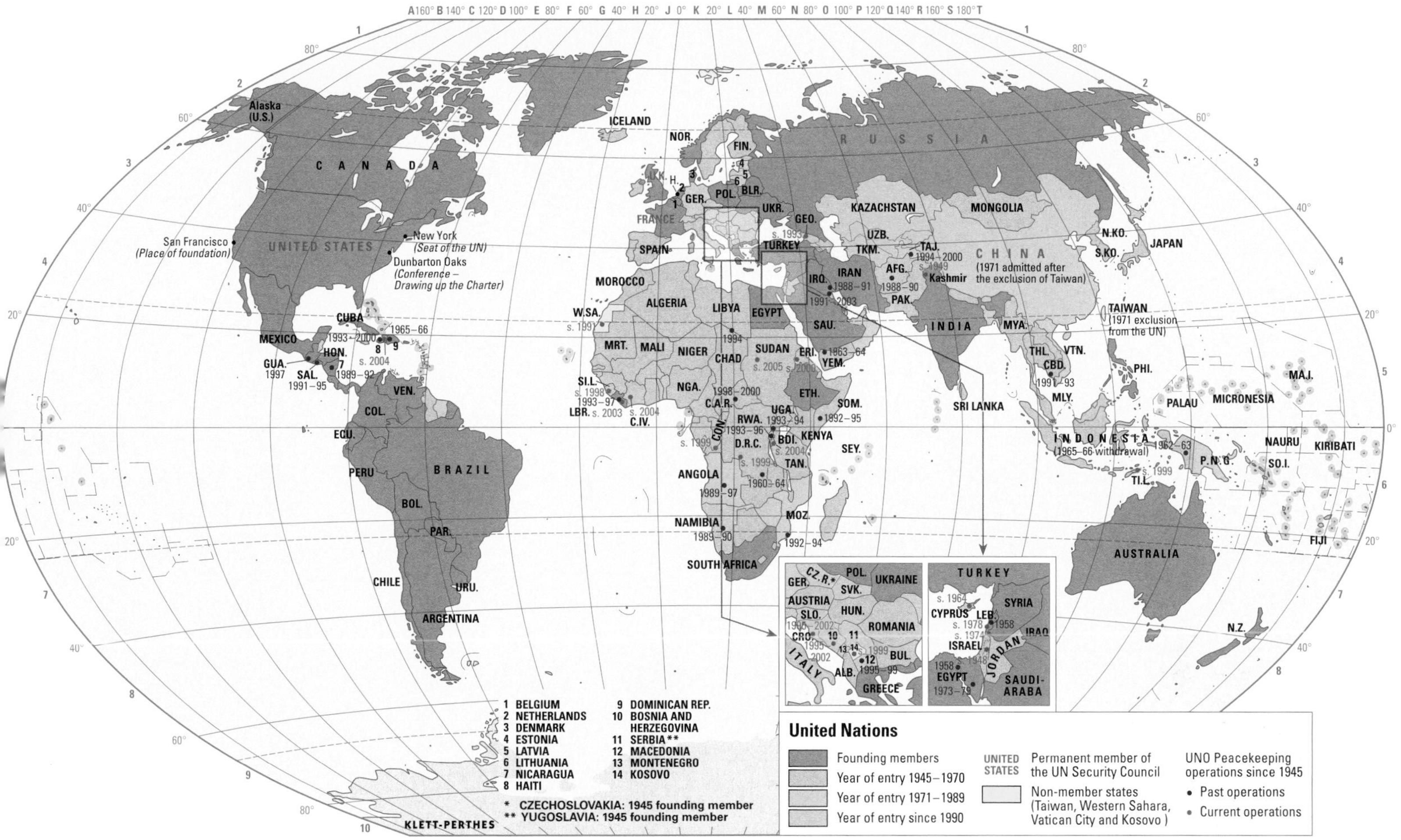

World: United Nations · Europe: European Union

1:160,000,000

San Francisco (Place of foundation)

New York (Seat of the UN)

Dunbarton Oaks (Conference – Drawing up the Charter)

CHINA (1971 admitted after the exclusion of Taiwan)

TAIWAN (1971 exclusion from the UN)

INDONESIA (1965–66 withdrawal)

1 BELGIUM
2 NETHERLANDS
3 DENMARK
4 ESTONIA
5 LATVIA
6 LITHUANIA
7 NICARAGUA
8 HAITI
9 DOMINICAN REP.
10 BOSNIA AND HERZEGOVINA
11 SERBIA**
12 MACEDONIA
13 MONTENEGRO
14 KOSOVO

* CZECHOSLOVAKIA: 1945 founding member
** YUGOSLAVIA: 1945 founding member

KLETT-PERTHES

United Nations

- Founding members
- Year of entry 1945–1970
- Year of entry 1971–1989
- Year of entry since 1990

UNITED STATES — Permanent member of the UN Security Council

Non-member states (Taiwan, Western Sahara, Vatican City and Kosovo)

UNO Peacekeeping operations since 1945
- Past operations
- Current operations

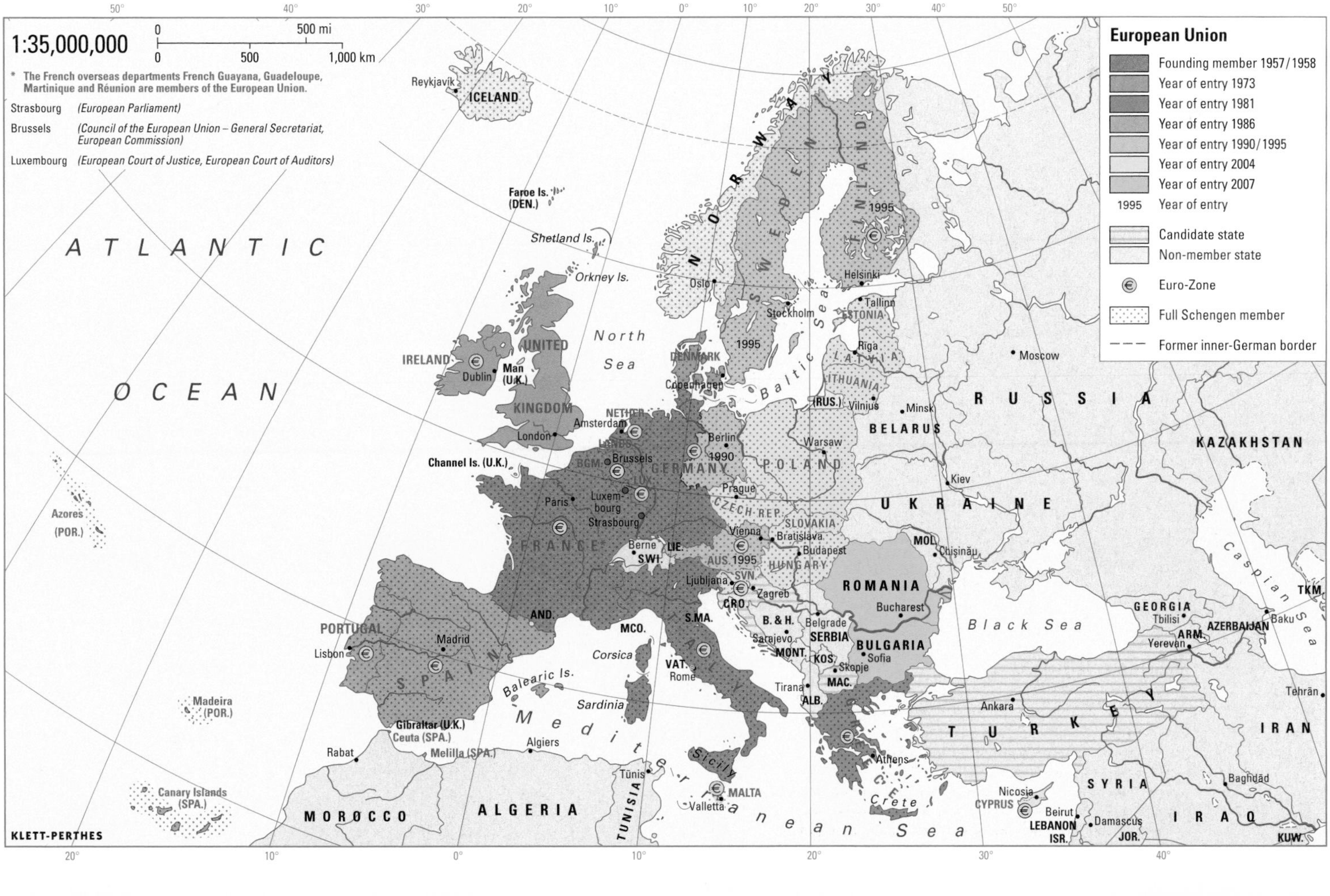

1:35,000,000

0 – 500 mi; 0 – 500 – 1,000 km

* The French overseas departments French Guayana, Guadeloupe, Martinique and Réunion are members of the European Union.

Strasbourg (European Parliament)

Brussels (Council of the European Union – General Secretariat, European Commission)

Luxembourg (European Court of Justice, European Court of Auditors)

European Union

- Founding member 1957/1958
- Year of entry 1973
- Year of entry 1981
- Year of entry 1986
- Year of entry 1990/1995
- Year of entry 2004
- Year of entry 2007
- 1995 Year of entry
- Candidate state
- Non-member state
- Euro-Zone
- Full Schengen member
- Former inner-German border

ATLANTIC OCEAN · North Sea · Baltic Sea · Black Sea · Caspian Sea · Mediterranean Sea

KLETT-PERTHES

A 160° B 140° C 120° D 100° E 80° F 60° G 40° H 20° J
80°
60°
40°
20°
0°
U.S.
Mt. McKinley
C A N A D A
Greenland
Northice
L. Superior
Missouri
Mississippi
Death Valley
U N I T E D
S T A T E S
MEXICO CITY
Great Britain
Mont Blanc
Sevilla
Ifrān
L. Maracaibo
Amazon
Ucayali
B R A Z I L
SÃO PAULO
Rivadavia
Aconcagua
Salinas Chicas
Sarmiento
Tierra del Fuego
Alexander I.
Vinson Massif
NORTH AMERICA
Total area: 9,530,000 sq mi/24,683,000 km²
Population: 527,041,000
Countries: 23
Canada 3,855,081 sq mi/9,984,670 km²
United States 305,826,000
Mexico City 17,309,000
Greenland 836,326 sq mi/2,166,086 km²
Lake Superior 31,700 sq mi/82,103 km²
Mississippi-Missouri 3,989 mi/6,420 km
Mount McKinley 20,320 ft/6,194 m
Death Valley –282 ft/–86 m
Death Valley 134°F/57°C
Northice –87°F/–66°C
EUROPE
Total area: 3,916,000 sq mi/10,142,000 km²
Population: 695,609,000
Countries: 45
Russia (European part) About 25% of 6,592,812 sq mi/17,075,400 km²
Russia (European part) About 75% of 142,499,000
Moscow 12,410,000
Great Britain 84,587 sq mi/219,081 km²
Lake Ladoga 7,002 sq mi/18,135 km²
Volga 2,194 mi/3,531 km
Mont Blanc 15,771 ft/4,807 m
Caspian Sea (surface) –92 ft/–28 m
Sevilla 122°F/50°C
Ust'-Shchugër –67°F/–55°C
AFRICA
Total area: 11,683,000 sq mi/30,260,000 km²
Population: 965,136,000
Countries: 54
Sudan 967,493 sq mi/2,505,810 km²
Nigeria 148,093,000
Cairo 10,834,000
Madagascar 226,657 sq mi/587,041 km²
Lake Victoria 26,828 sq mi/69,484 km²
Nile 4,145 mi/6,671 km
Kilimanjaro 19,331 ft/5,892 m
Lake Asālē (surface) –515 ft/–157 m
Al-'Azīzīyah 136°F/57,8°C
Ifrān –11°F/–24°C
SOUTH AMERICA
Total area: 6,815,000 sq mi/17,650,000 km²
Population: 383,999,000
Countries: 12
Brazil 3,300,153 sq mi/8,547,404 km²
Brazil 191,791,000
São Paulo 19,037,000
Tierra del Fuego 18,148 sq mi/47,000 km²
Lake Maracaibo 5,217 sq mi/13,512 km²
Amazon 4,000 mi/6,437 km
Aconcagua 22,841 ft/6,962 m
Salinas Chicas –138 ft/–42 m
Rivadavia 120°F/49°C
Sarmiento –27°F/–33°C
Largest country
Most populous country
Largest urban agglomeration
Largest island
Largest lake
Longest river
Highest elevation
Lowest elevation
Place with the highest recorded temperature
Place with the lowest recorded temperature

The Continents

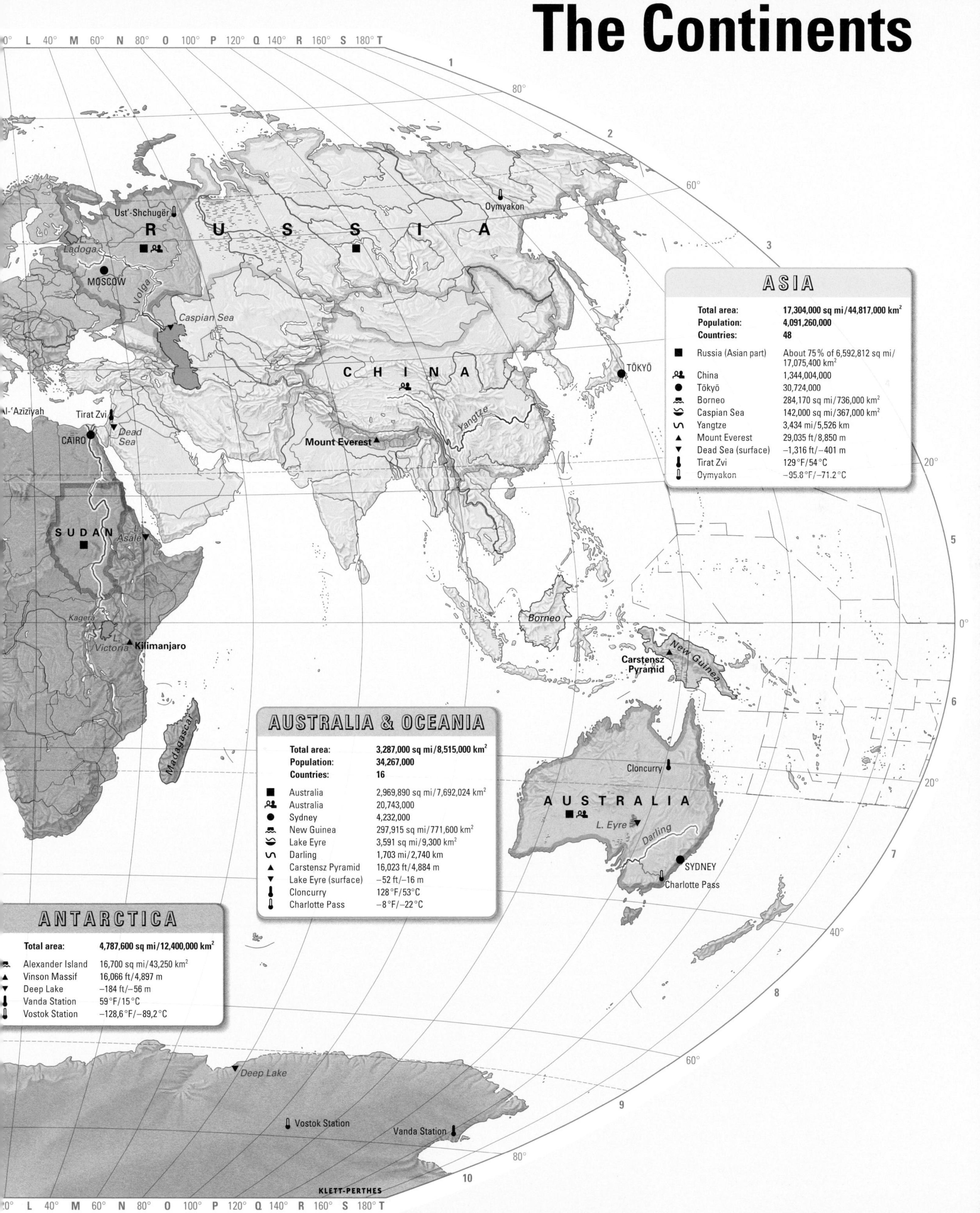

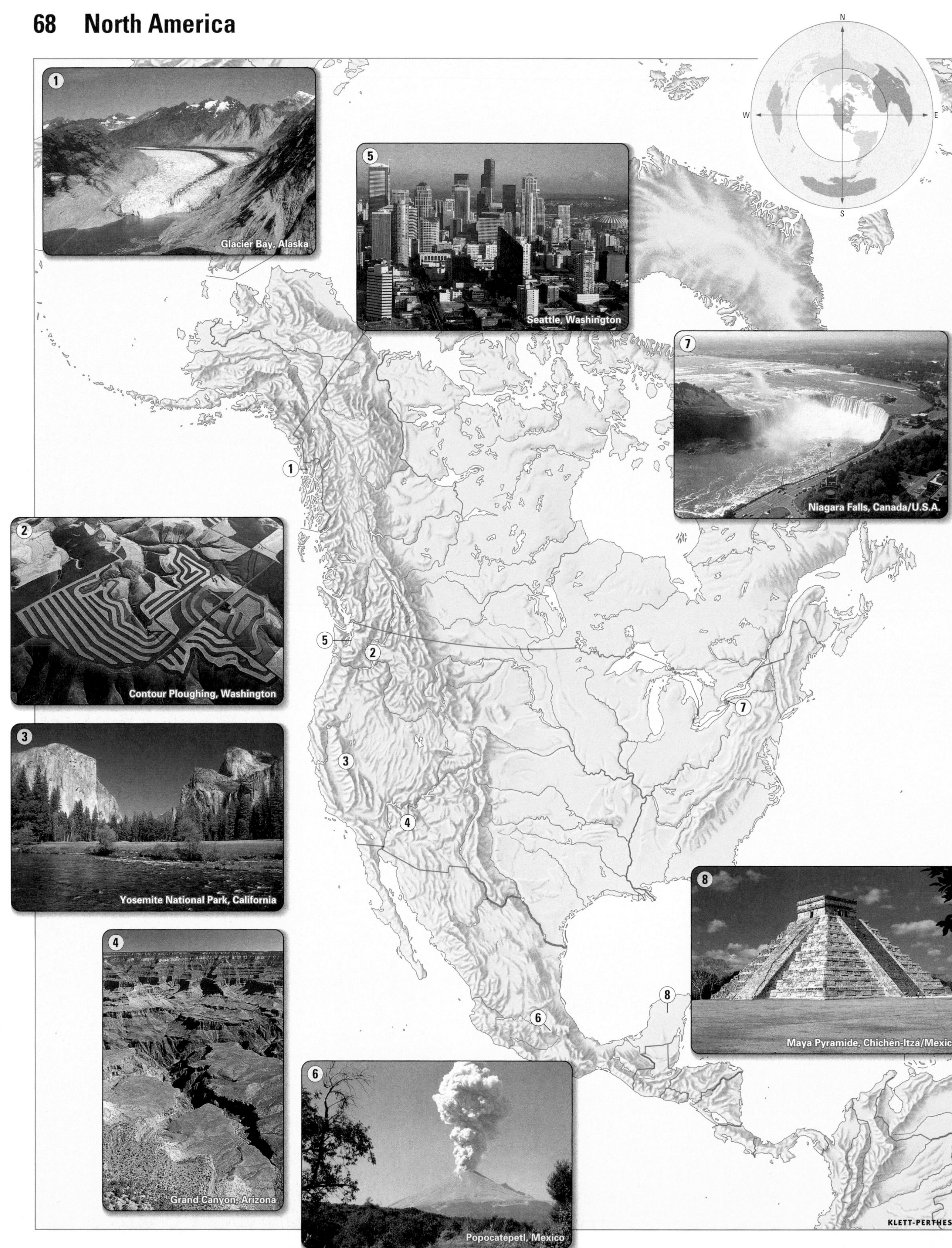

1 Glacier Bay, Alaska

2 Contour Ploughing, Washington

3 Yosemite National Park, California

4 Grand Canyon, Arizona

5 Seattle, Washington

6 Popocatépetl, Mexico

7 Niagara Falls, Canada/U.S.A.

8 Maya Pyramide, Chichén-Itzá/Mexico

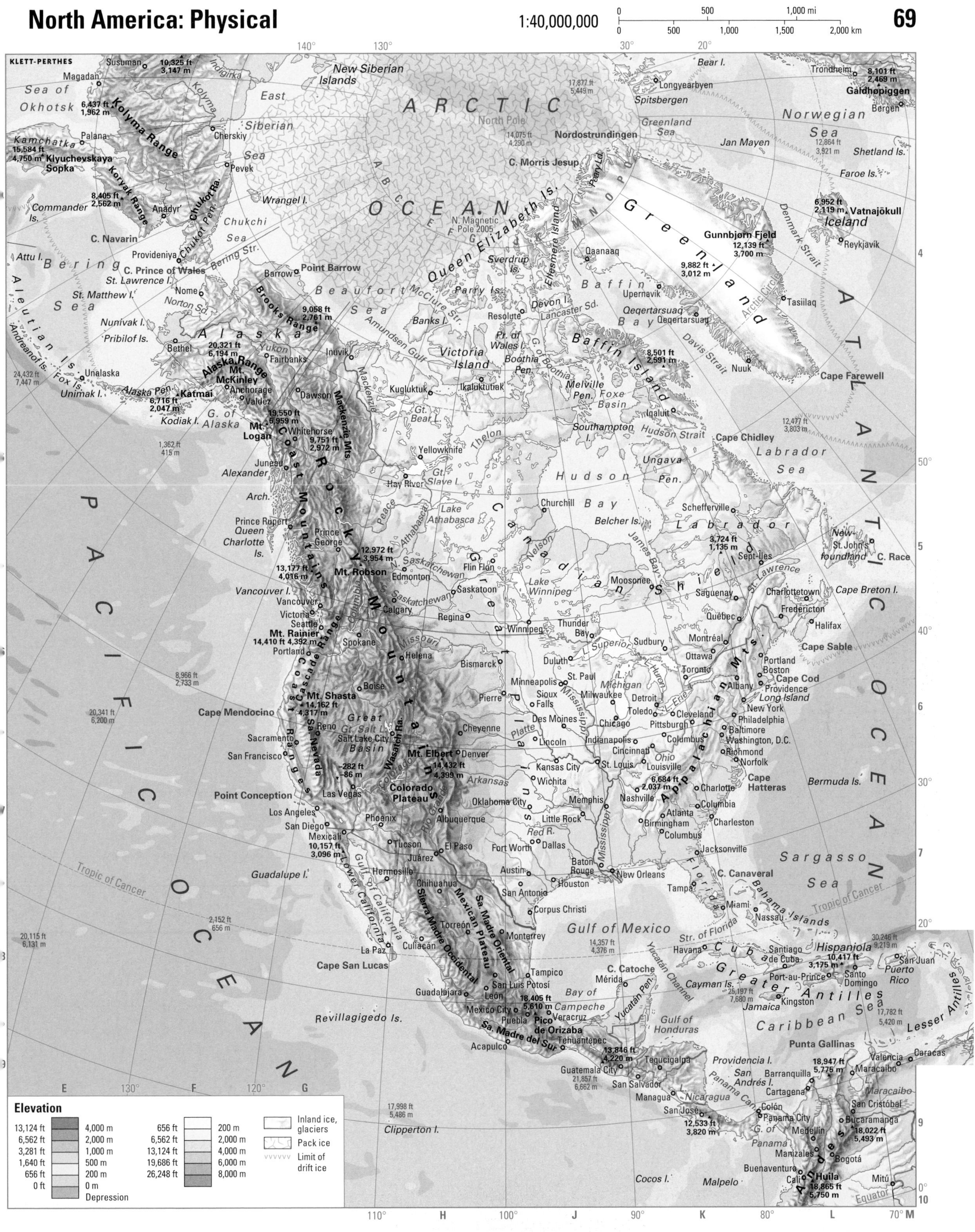

0 500 1,000 mi
0 500 1,000 1,500 2,000 km
KLETT-PERTHES
ARCTIC OCEAN
North Pole
N. Magnetic Pole 2005
New Siberian Islands
East Siberian Sea
Sea of Okhotsk
Kolyma Range
Kamchatka
Klyuchevskaya Sopka
15,584 ft 4,750 m
Koryak Range
Chukot Ra.
Chukchi Sea
Wrangel I.
Bering Sea
Bering Str.
Aleutian Is.
Andreanof Is.
Fox Is.
Unimak I.
Commander Is.
Attu I.
C. Navarin
Providenıya
C. Prince of Wales
St. Lawrence I.
St. Matthew I.
Nunivak I.
Pribilof Is.
Norton Sd.
Nome
Point Barrow
Barrow
Beaufort Sea
Brooks Range
9,058 ft 2,761 m
Alaska
Alaska Range
Mt. McKinley
20,321 ft 6,194 m
Fairbanks
Bethel
Unalaska
Alaska Pen.
Katmai
6,716 ft 2,047 m
Kodiak I.
G. of Alaska
Anchorage
Valdez
Mt. Logan
19,550 ft 5,959 m
Whitehorse
Dawson
Inuvik
Mackenzie Mts.
9,751 ft 2,972 m
Juneau
Alexander Arch.
Coast Mountains
Rocky Mountains
Prince Rupert
Queen Charlotte Is.
Prince George
Mt. Robson
12,972 ft 3,954 m
13,177 ft 4,016 m
Vancouver I.
Vancouver
Victoria
Seattle
Mt. Rainier
14,410 ft 4,392 m
Cascade Range
Portland
Spokane
Helena
Missouri
Coast Ranges
Mt. Shasta
14,162 ft 4,317 m
Boise
Cape Mendocino
Great Basin
Gt. Salt L.
Salt Lake City
Reno
Sierra Nevada
Sacramento
San Francisco
Wasatch Ra.
Mt. Elbert
14,432 ft 4,399 m
Denver
Cheyenne
-282 ft -86 m
Las Vegas
Colorado Plateau
Point Conception
Los Angeles
San Diego
Mexicali
10,157 ft 3,096 m
Phoenix
Tucson
Albuquerque
El Paso
Juárez
Rio Grande
Guadalupe I.
Hermosillo
Gulf of California
Lower California
Chihuahua
Sierra Madre Occidental
Mexican Plateau
Sa. Madre Oriental
Torreón
Monterrey
La Paz
Culiacán
Cape San Lucas
Revillagigedo Is.
Guadalajara
San Luis Potosí
León
Mexico City
Puebla
Pico de Orizaba
18,405 ft 5,610 m
Veracruz
Sa. Madre del Sur
Acapulco
Tehuantepec
Tampico
Bay of Campeche
Mérida
C. Catoche
Yucatán Pen.
Yucatán Channel
Gulf of Honduras
Guatemala City
13,846 ft 4,220 m
Tegucigalpa
San Salvador
Managua
Nicaragua
San José
12,533 ft 3,820 m
Panama Canal
Colón
Panama City
G. of Panama
Clipperton I.
Cocos I.
Malpelo
Providencia I.
San Andrés I.
Barranquilla
Cartagena
18,947 ft 5,775 m
Maracaibo
Caracas
Valencia
San Cristóbal
Bucaramanga
18,022 ft 5,493 m
Medellín
Manizales
Bogotá
Buenaventura
Cali
Huila
18,865 ft 5,750 m
Andes
Mitú
Equator
Punta Gallinas
Caribbean Sea
Lesser Antilles
Greater Antilles
Jamaica
Kingston
Cayman Is.
Cuba
Havana
Santiago de Cuba
Hispaniola
10,417 ft 3,175 m
Port-au-Prince
Santo Domingo
San Juan
Puerto Rico
Str. of Florida
Bahama Islands
Nassau
Miami
Florida
Tampa
C. Canaveral
Jacksonville
Sargasso Sea
Tropic of Cancer
Gulf of Mexico
Corpus Christi
Houston
San Antonio
Austin
Baton Rouge
New Orleans
Fort Worth
Dallas
Red R.
Little Rock
Oklahoma City
Memphis
Mississippi
Arkansas
Wichita
Kansas City
St. Louis
Louisville
Nashville
6,684 ft 2,037 m
Appalachian Mts.
Atlanta
Birmingham
Columbus
Charleston
Columbia
Charlotte
Cape Hatteras
Bermuda Is.
Norfolk
Richmond
Washington, D.C.
Baltimore
Philadelphia
New York
Long Island
Providence
Boston
Cape Cod
Albany
Portland
Lincoln
Platte
Great Plains
Des Moines
Sioux Falls
Pierre
Bismarck
Minneapolis
St. Paul
Milwaukee
Chicago
Indianapolis
Cincinnati
Ohio
Columbus
Pittsburgh
Cleveland
Toledo
Detroit
L. Michigan
L. Huron
L. Erie
Toronto
L. Superior
Duluth
Thunder Bay
Sudbury
Ottawa
Montréal
Québec
St. Lawrence
Saguenay
Fredericton
Charlottetown
Halifax
Cape Sable
Cape Breton I.
Newfoundland
St. John's
C. Race
Sept-Îles
Labrador
3,724 ft 1,135 m
Schefferville
Canadian Shield
James Bay
Moosonee
Belcher Is.
Hudson Bay
Churchill
Nelson
Lake Winnipeg
Winnipeg
Regina
Saskatoon
Saskatchewan
N. Saskatchewan
Calgary
Edmonton
Flin Flon
Lake Athabasca
Athabasca
Peace
Hay River
Gt. Slave L.
Yellowknife
Gt. Bear L.
Thelon
Mackenzie
Kugluktuk
Ikaluktutiak
Victoria Island
Banks I.
Amundsen Gulf
McClure Str.
Parry Is.
Prince of Wales I.
Boothia Pen.
G. of Boothia
Melville Pen.
Foxe Basin
Southampton I.
Hudson Strait
Ungava Pen.
Iqaluit
Baffin Island
8,501 ft 2,591 m
Cape Chidley
Labrador Sea
Davis Strait
Baffin Bay
Lancaster Sd.
Devon I.
Resolute
Sverdrup Is.
Queen Elizabeth Is.
Ellesmere Island
Peary Ld.
C. Morris Jesup
Nordostrundingen
Qaanaaq
Upernavik
Qeqertarsuaq
Greenland
9,882 ft 3,012 m
Gunnbjørn Fjeld
12,139 ft 3,700 m
Tasiilaq
Nuuk
Arctic Circle
Cape Farewell
Denmark Strait
Greenland Sea
Spitsbergen
Longyearbyen
Bear I.
Jan Mayen
Norwegian Sea
Iceland
Vatnajökull
6,952 ft 2,119 m
Reykjavík
Faroe Is.
Shetland Is.
Bergen
Trondheim
Galdhøpiggen
8,101 ft 2,469 m
ATLANTIC OCEAN
PACIFIC OCEAN
Magadan
Susuman
10,325 ft 3,147 m
Indigirka
Kolyma
6,437 ft 1,962 m
Palana
Cherskiy
Pevek
Anadyr'
8,405 ft 2,562 m
Chukot Pen.
Elevation
13,124 ft 4,000 m
6,562 ft 2,000 m
3,281 ft 1,000 m
1,640 ft 500 m
656 ft 200 m
0 ft 0 m
Depression
656 ft 200 m
6,562 ft 2,000 m
13,124 ft 4,000 m
19,686 ft 6,000 m
26,248 ft 8,000 m
Inland ice, glaciers
Pack ice
Limit of drift ice

1:40,000,000
0 500 1,000 mi
0 500 1,000 1,500 2,000 km
KLETT-PERTHES
ARCTIC OCEAN
North Pole
PACIFIC OCEAN
ATLANTIC OCEAN
Sea of Okhotsk
East Siberian Sea
Bering Sea
Chukchi Sea
Beaufort Sea
Greenland Sea
Norwegian Sea
Labrador Sea
Baffin Bay
Hudson Bay
Gulf of Mexico
Caribbean Sea
Sargasso Sea
Kolyma Range
Koryak Range
Chukot Ra.
Brooks Range
Alaska Range
Alaska
Rocky Mountains
Coast Mountains
Mackenzie Mts.
Cascade Range
Coast Ranges
Sa. Nevada
Great Basin
Colorado Plateau
Great Plains
Canadian Shield
Appalachian Mts.
Sierra Madre Occidental
Sa. Madre Oriental
Mexican Plateau
Sa. Madre del Sur
Greenland
Baffin Island
Victoria Island
Queen Elizabeth Is.
Iceland
Labrador
Andes
Greater Antilles
Bahama Islands
Tropic of Cancer
Arctic Circle
Edmonton
Calgary
Vancouver
Seattle
Portland
San Francisco
Los Angeles
San Diego
Denver
Winnipeg
Minneapolis
Chicago
Detroit
Toronto
Montréal
Québec
Boston
New York
Philadelphia
Washington, D.C.
Atlanta
Dallas
Houston
New Orleans
Miami
Havana
Mexico City
Guadalajara
Guatemala City
Caracas
Bogotá
Land Cover
(Explanations on page 32)
Natural Vegetation
Evergreen needleleaf forests
Evergreen broadleaf forests
Deciduous needleleaf forests
Deciduous broadleaf forests
Mixed forests
Closed shrublands
Open shrublands
Woody savannas
Savannas
Grasslands
Permanent wetlands
Developed and Mosaic Lands
Croplands
Cropland/natural vegetation mosaic
Urban and built-up lands
Non-Vegetated Lands
Snow and ice
Barren or sparsely vegetated
Water bodies
No data

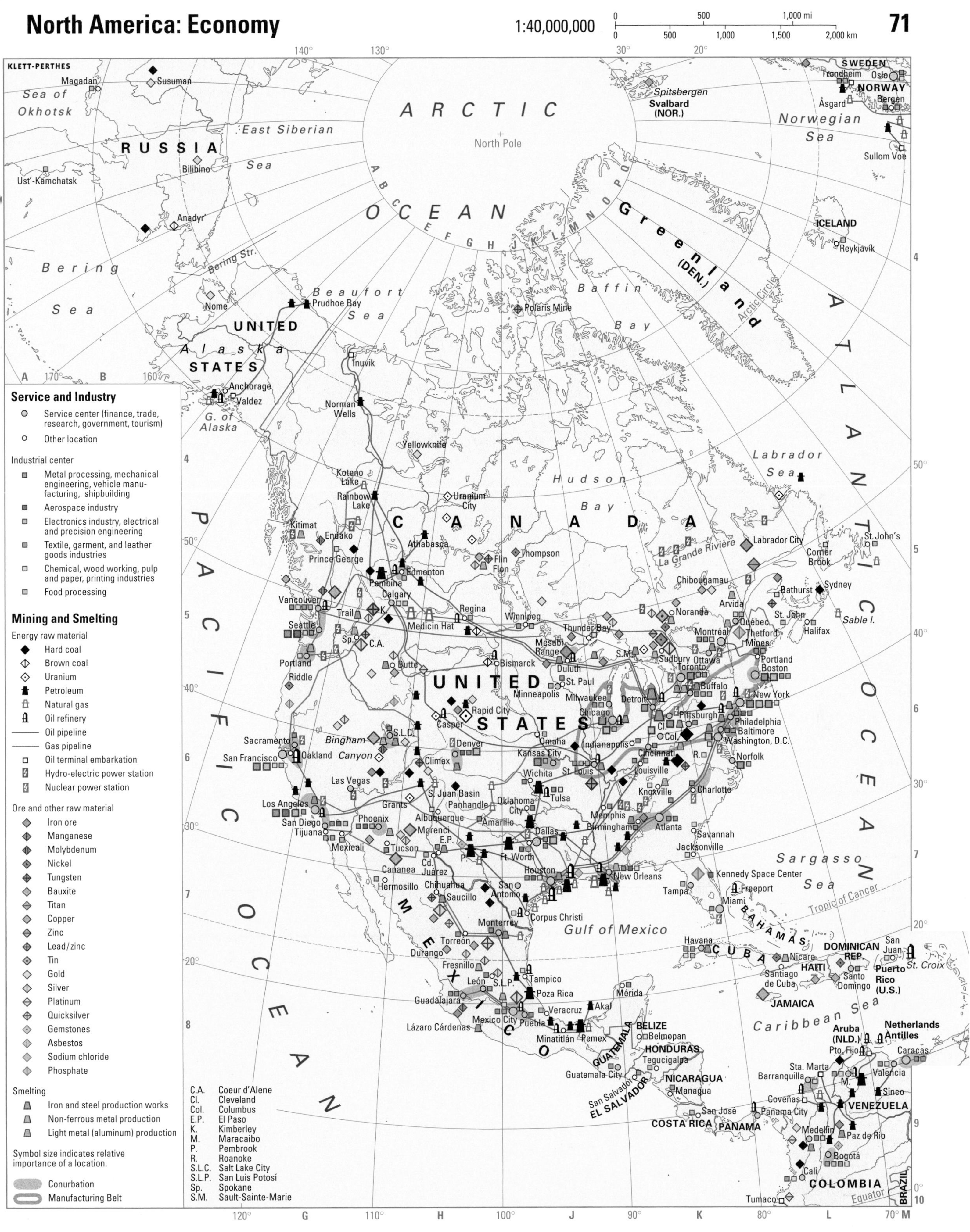

1:40,000,000
0 500 1,000 mi
0 500 1,000 1,500 2,000 km
KLETT-PERTHES
Service and Industry
Service center (finance, trade, research, government, tourism)
Other location
Industrial center
Metal processing, mechanical engineering, vehicle manufacturing, shipbuilding
Aerospace industry
Electronics industry, electrical and precision engineering
Textile, garment, and leather goods industries
Chemical, wood working, pulp and paper, printing industries
Food processing
Mining and Smelting
Energy raw material
Hard coal
Brown coal
Uranium
Petroleum
Natural gas
Oil refinery
Oil pipeline
Gas pipeline
Oil terminal embarkation
Hydro-electric power station
Nuclear power station
Ore and other raw material
Iron ore
Manganese
Molybdenum
Nickel
Tungsten
Bauxite
Titan
Copper
Zinc
Lead/zinc
Tin
Gold
Silver
Platinum
Quicksilver
Gemstones
Asbestos
Sodium chloride
Phosphate
Smelting
Iron and steel production works
Non-ferrous metal production
Light metal (aluminum) production
Symbol size indicates relative importance of a location.
Conurbation
Manufacturing Belt
C.A. Coeur d'Alene
Cl. Cleveland
Col. Columbus
E.P. El Paso
K. Kimberley
M. Maracaibo
P. Pembrook
R. Roanoke
S.L.C. Salt Lake City
S.L.P. San Luis Potosí
Sp. Spokane
S.M. Sault-Sainte-Marie
ARCTIC OCEAN
North Pole
RUSSIA
Sea of Okhotsk
East Siberian Sea
Bering Sea
Bering Str.
Beaufort Sea
UNITED STATES
Alaska
G. of Alaska
Greenland (DEN.)
Baffin Bay
Arctic Circle
Hudson Bay
Labrador Sea
CANADA
ATLANTIC OCEAN
PACIFIC OCEAN
Norwegian Sea
Svalbard (NOR.)
Spitsbergen
ICELAND
SWEDEN
NORWAY
UNITED STATES
MEXICO
Gulf of Mexico
Sargasso Sea
Tropic of Cancer
BAHAMAS
CUBA
HAITI
DOMINICAN REP.
Puerto Rico (U.S.)
JAMAICA
Caribbean Sea
BELIZE
GUATEMALA
HONDURAS
EL SALVADOR
NICARAGUA
COSTA RICA
PANAMA
COLOMBIA
VENEZUELA
BRAZIL
Aruba (NLD.)
Netherlands Antilles
Equator
Magadan
Susuman
Bilibino
Ust'-Kamchatsk
Anadyr'
Nome
Prudhoe Bay
Inuvik
Anchorage
Valdez
Norman Wells
Polaris Mine
Yellowknife
Koteno Lake
Rainbow Lake
Uranium City
Kitimat
Endako
Athabasca
Prince George
Flin Flon
Thompson
Edmonton
Pembina
Calgary
Vancouver
Trail
Regina
Winnipeg
Medicin Hat
Seattle
Sp.
C.A.
Portland
Riddle
Butte
Bismarck
Thunder Bay
Mesabi Range
Duluth
St. Paul
Minneapolis
Milwaukee
Chicago
Detroit
S.M.
Sudbury
Ottawa
Toronto
Buffalo
Montréal
Québec
Thetford Mines
Noranda
Chibougamau
Arvida
La Grande Rivière
Labrador City
St. John's
Corner Brook
Sydney
Bathurst
St. John
Halifax
Sable I.
Portland
Boston
New York
Philadelphia
Baltimore
Washington, D.C.
Pittsburgh
Cl.
Col.
Indianapolis
Cincinnati
R.
Norfolk
Louisville
Knoxville
Charlotte
Atlanta
Savannah
Jacksonville
Kennedy Space Center
Freeport
Tampa
Miami
Rapid City
Casper
Omaha
Kansas City
Denver
Climax
Wichita
St. Louis
Tulsa
Oklahoma City
Memphis
Birmingham
Sacramento
San Francisco
Oakland
Bingham Canyon
S.L.C.
Las Vegas
Grants
S. Juan Basin
Panhandle
Amarillo
Dallas
Ft. Worth
Los Angeles
San Diego
Tijuana
Mexicali
Phoenix
Tucson
Albuquerque
Morenci
E.P.
P.
Cd. Juárez
Cananea
Hermosillo
Chihuahua
Saucillo
San Antonio
Houston
New Orleans
Corpus Christi
Monterrey
Torreón
Durango
Fresnillo
Tampico
S.L.P.
León
Guadalajara
Poza Rica
Mérida
Veracruz
Akal
Mexico City
Puebla
Lázaro Cárdenas
Minatitlán
Pemex
Belmopan
Guatemala City
Tegucigalpa
San Salvador
Managua
San José
Panama City
Havana
Santiago de Cuba
Nicaro
Santo Domingo
San Juan
St. Croix
Pto. Fijo
Caracas
Sta. Marta
Barranquilla
M.
Valencia
Coveñas
Sinco
Medellín
Paz de Río
Bogotá
Cali
Tumaco
Trondheim
Oslo
Åsgard
Bergen
Sullom Voe
Reykjavík

1:40,000,000

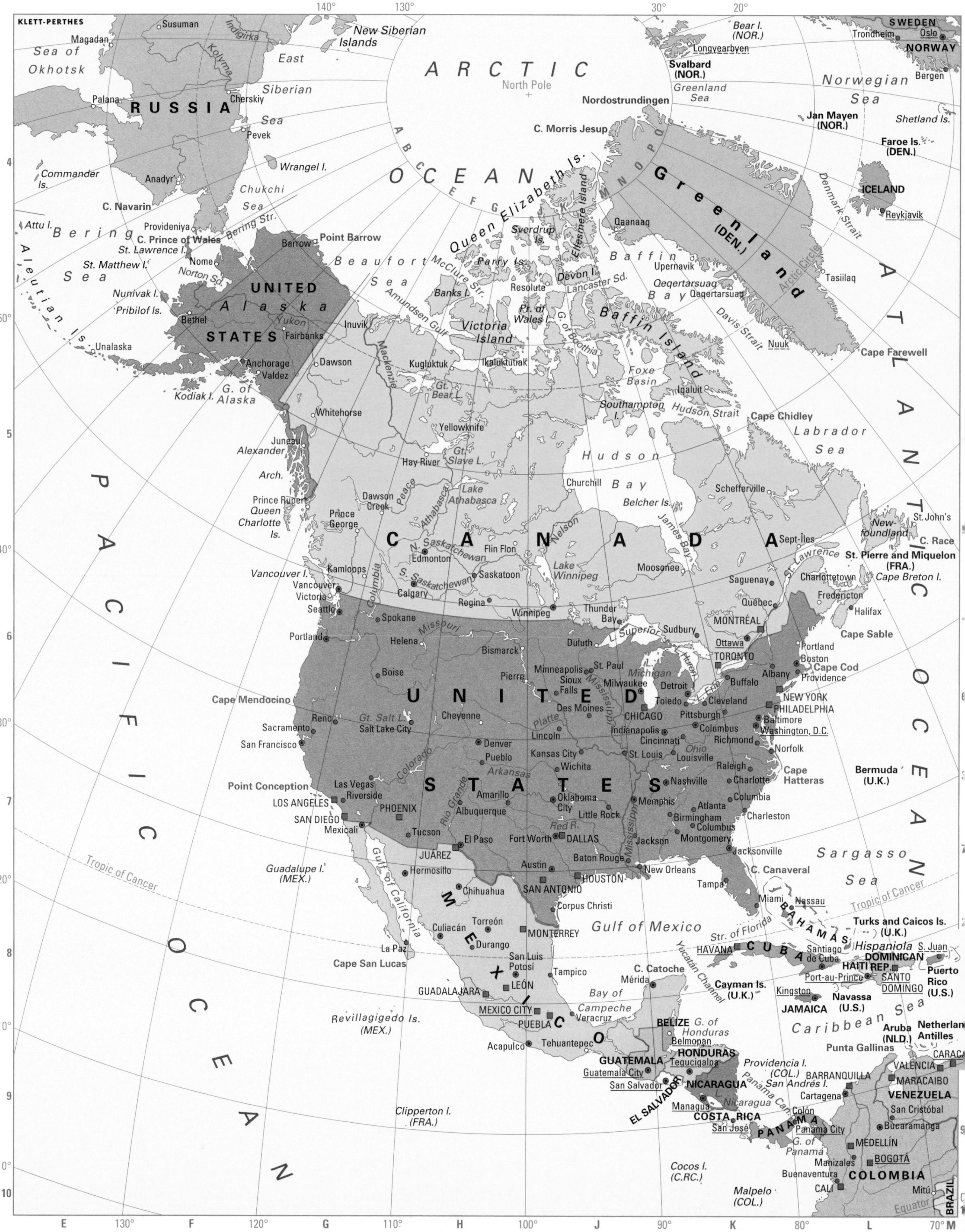

0 500 1,000 mi
0 500 1,000 1,500 2,000 km

KLETT-PERTHES

ARCTIC OCEAN
North Pole
PACIFIC OCEAN
ATLANTIC OCEAN

RUSSIA
Susuman
Magadan
Sea of Okhotsk
Palana
Cherskiy
Pevek
Anadyr'
Commander Is.
C. Navarin
Provideniya
Attu I.
Bering Sea
Aleutian Is.
Indigirka
Kolyma
New Siberian Islands
East Siberian Sea
Wrangel I.
Chukchi Sea
Bering Str.
C. Prince of Wales
St. Lawrence I.
St. Matthew I.
Nome
Norton Sd.
Nunivak I.
Pribilof Is.
Bethel
Unalaska
Kodiak I.
G. of Alaska
Barrow
Point Barrow
Beaufort Sea
UNITED STATES
Alaska
Yukon
Fairbanks
Anchorage
Valdez
Inuvik
Dawson
Whitehorse
Juneau
Alexander Arch.
Prince Rupert
Queen Charlotte Is.
Vancouver I.
Vancouver
Victoria
Seattle

Queen Elizabeth Is.
Sverdrup Is.
Ellesmere Island
Parry Is.
McClure Str.
Banks I.
Amundsen Gulf
Victoria Island
Resolute
Devon I.
Lancaster Sd.
Pr. of Wales I.
G. of Boothia
Baffin Island
Baffin Bay
Kugluktuk
Ikaluktutiak
Mackenzie
Gt. Bear L.
Yellowknife
Gt. Slave L.
Hay River
Foxe Basin
Iqaluit
Southampton I.
Hudson Strait
Hudson Bay
Churchill
Belcher Is.
James Bay
Cape Chidley
Labrador Sea
Schefferville
Dawson Creek
Peace
Athabasca
Lake Athabasca
Prince George
CANADA
N. Saskatchewan
Edmonton
Flin Flon
Nelson
Kamloops
Columbia
S. Saskatchewan
Saskatoon
Calgary
Regina
Lake Winnipeg
Winnipeg
Moosonee
Thunder Bay
L. Superior
Sudbury
Saguenay
Québec
MONTRÉAL
Ottawa
TORONTO
St. Lawrence
Sept-Îles
Newfoundland
St. John's
C. Race
St. Pierre and Miquelon (FRA.)
Charlottetown
Cape Breton I.
Fredericton
Halifax
Cape Sable

C. Morris Jesup
Nordostrundingen
Greenland (DEN.)
Qaanaaq
Upernavik
Qeqertarsuaq
Davis Strait
Nuuk
Arctic Circle
Tasiilaq
Cape Farewell
Denmark Strait
ICELAND
Reykjavík
Svalbard (NOR.)
Longyearbyen
Bear I. (NOR.)
Greenland Sea
Jan Mayen (NOR.)
Norwegian Sea
SWEDEN
NORWAY
Trondheim
Oslo
Bergen
Shetland Is.
Faroe Is. (DEN.)

UNITED STATES
Spokane
Missouri
Portland
Helena
Bismarck
Duluth
Boise
Pierre
Minneapolis
St. Paul
Sioux Falls
Mississippi
L. Michigan
Milwaukee
L. Huron
Detroit
Toledo
Erie
Cleveland
Buffalo
Albany
Portland
Boston
Cape Cod
Providence
NEW YORK
PHILADELPHIA
Baltimore
Washington, D.C.
Norfolk
Cape Mendocino
Reno
Gt. Salt L.
Salt Lake City
Cheyenne
Platte
Des Moines
CHICAGO
Pittsburgh
Sacramento
San Francisco
Denver
Lincoln
Indianapolis
Columbus
Cincinnati
Richmond
Ohio
Colorado
Pueblo
Kansas City
St. Louis
Louisville
Wichita
Arkansas
Raleigh
Cape Hatteras
Nashville
Charlotte
Point Conception
Las Vegas
Riverside
LOS ANGELES
SAN DIEGO
Mexicali
PHOENIX
Amarillo
Albuquerque
Rio Grande
Oklahoma City
Little Rock
Memphis
Atlanta
Birmingham
Columbus
Columbia
Charleston
Tucson
El Paso
Fort Worth
Red R.
DALLAS
Jackson
Montgomery
Jacksonville
Baton Rouge
Austin
SAN ANTONIO
HOUSTON
New Orleans
C. Canaveral
Tampa
Miami
Corpus Christi
Bermuda (U.K.)
Sargasso Sea
Tropic of Cancer

Guadalupe I. (MEX.)
JUÁREZ
Hermosillo
Gulf of California
Chihuahua
MEXICO
Torreón
Culiacán
MONTERREY
Durango
La Paz
Cape San Lucas
San Luis Potosí
Tampico
LEÓN
GUADALAJARA
MEXICO CITY
PUEBLA
Veracruz
Bay of Campeche
Revillagigedo Is. (MEX.)
Acapulco
Tehuantepec
Gulf of Mexico
Str. of Florida
Yucatán Channel
C. Catoche
Mérida
BELIZE
Belmopan
G. of Honduras
HONDURAS
Tegucigalpa
GUATEMALA
Guatemala City
San Salvador
EL SALVADOR
NICARAGUA
Managua
Nicaragua Can.
Providencia I. (COL.)
San Andrés I.
COSTA RICA
San José
PANAMA
Panama Can.
Colón
Panama City
G. of Panamá
Clipperton I. (FRA.)
Cocos I. (C.R.)
Malpelo (COL.)
Nassau
BAHAMAS
Turks and Caicos Is. (U.K.)
HAVANA
CUBA
Santiago de Cuba
Hispaniola
HAITI
Port-au-Prince
DOMINICAN REP.
SANTO DOMINGO
San Juan
Puerto Rico (U.S.)
Cayman Is. (U.K.)
Kingston
JAMAICA
Navassa (U.S.)
Caribbean Sea
Aruba (NLD.)
Netherlands Antilles
Punta Gallinas
BARRANQUILLA
Cartagena
CARACAS
VALENCIA
MARACAIBO
VENEZUELA
San Cristóbal
Bucaramanga
MEDELLÍN
BOGOTÁ
Manizales
Buenaventura
CALI
COLOMBIA
Mitú
BRAZIL
Equator

140° 130° 30° 20°
4 5 6 7 8 9 10
50° 40° 30° 20° 10° 0°
E 130° F 120° G 110° H 100° J 90° K 80° L 70° M

North America: Ethnic Groups

1:40,000,000

North America: Climate

1:40,000,000

0 500 1,000 mi
0 500 1,000 1,500 2,000 km

Climate	Station	Altitude	Precipitation	Temperature
Cs	San Francisco	5 m 16 ft	500 mm 19.7 in.	13.7 °C 56.7 °F
Do	Washington, D.C.	20 m 66 ft	971 mm 38.2 in.	13.7 °C 56.7 °F
Dc	Winnipeg	239 m 784 ft	504 mm 19.8 in.	2.4 °C 36.3 °F
Eo	Yakutat	9 m 30 ft	3,783 mm 148.9 in.	3.9 °C 39.0 °F
Ec	Churchill	29 m 95 ft	414 mm 16.3 in.	−7.1 °C 19.2 °F
FT	Qaanaaq/Thule	77 m 253 ft	124 mm 4.9 in.	−11.2 °C 11.8 °F
FI	Eismitte	3,012 m 9,882 ft	0 mm 0 in.	−30.2 °C −22.4 °F
Cr	New Orleans	9 m 30 ft	1,530 mm 60.2 in.	20.8 °C 69.4 °F
Cw	Mexico City	2,308 m 7,572 ft	894 mm 35.2 in.	16.5 °C 35.2 °F
BS	Denver	1,625 m 5,332 ft	395 mm 15.6 in.	10.1 °C 50.2 °F
BW	Phoenix	337 m 1,106 ft	195 mm 7.7 in.	22.3 °C 72.1 °F
Ar	Sabana de la Mar	3 m 10 ft	2,263 mm 89.1 in.	25.0 °C 77.0 °F
Am	Miami	4 m 13 ft	1,445 mm 56.9 in.	24.4 °C 75.9 °F
Aw	Tegucigalpa	1,007 m 3,304 ft	887 mm 34.9 in.	21.5 °C 70.7 °F

Climate Diagrams (by H. Walter)

2,263 mm 89.1 in. 25.0 °C 77.0 °F — Annual averages of precipitation and air temperature

1 3 6 9 12 Months

3 m 10 ft Altitude

Precipitation curve

Temperature curve

Dry season

Climatic Regions (Modified Koeppen System based on Trewartha; cf. p. 18/19)

Polar Climates
- FI Perpetual frost climate
- FT Tundra climate

Boreal Climates
- Eo Oceanic boreal climate
- Ec Continental boreal climate

Temperate Climates
- Do Oceanic temperate climate
- Dc Continental temperate climate

Subtropical Climates
- Cr Subtropical rain climate
- Cw Subtropical summer rain climate
- Cs Subtropical winter rain climate

Dry Climates
- BS Steppe climate
- BW Desert climate
- BM Marine dry climate

Tropical Rainy Climates
- Ar Tropical rainy climate
- Am Tropical monsoon rain climate
- Aw Tropical summer rain climate

• Meteorological station with climate diagram

ARCTIC OCEAN
Bear I.
Spitsbergen
Norwegian Sea
Greenland Sea
Jan Mayen
Greenland
Qaanaaq/Thule
Eismitte
Queen Elizabeth Is.
Ellesmere Island
Sverdrup Is.
Parry Is.
Devon I.
Lancaster Sd.
Baffin Bay
Qeqertarsuaq
Davis Strait
Baffin Island
Beaufort Sea
McClure Str.
Banks I.
Amundsen Gulf
Victoria Island
Pr. of Wales I.
G. of Boothia
Foxe Basin
Southampton I.
Hudson Strait
Labrador Sea
Hudson Bay
Churchill
Belcher Is.
James Bay
Newfoundland
Cape Breton I.
St. Lawrence
ATLANTIC OCEAN
Bering Str.
Bering Sea
St. Lawrence I.
St. Matthew I.
Norton Sd.
Nunivak I.
Pribilof Is.
Attu I.
Aleutian Is.
Andreanof Is.
Fox Is.
Unimak I.
Kodiak I.
Gulf of Alaska
Yakutat
Yukon
Mackenzie
Gt. Bear L.
Gt. Slave L.
Lake Athabasca
Athabasca
Peace
Alexander Arch.
Queen Charlotte Is.
Vancouver I.
Columbia
N. Saskatchewan
S. Saskatchewan
Nelson
Lake Winnipeg
Winnipeg
Missouri
L. Superior
L. Huron
L. Michigan
L. Erie
Mississippi
Long Island
Washington, D.C.
Gt. Salt L.
Platte
San Francisco
Denver
Colorado
Rio Grande
Arkansas
Ohio
Bermuda Is.
Phoenix
Red R.
Mississippi
New Orleans
Sargasso Sea
Bahama Islands (Ar/Aw/Am)
Tropic of Cancer
Miami
Gulf of California
Gulf of Mexico
Str. of Florida
Cuba
Yucatán Channel
Sabana de la Mar
Puerto R.
Hispaniola
Greater Antilles
Cayman Is.
Jamaica
PACIFIC OCEAN
Revillagigedo Is.
Bay of Campeche
Mexico City
Gulf of Honduras
Caribbean Sea
Tegucigalpa
Providencia I.
San Andrés I.
Nicaragua
Maracaibo
G. of Panama
Cocos I.
Malpelo

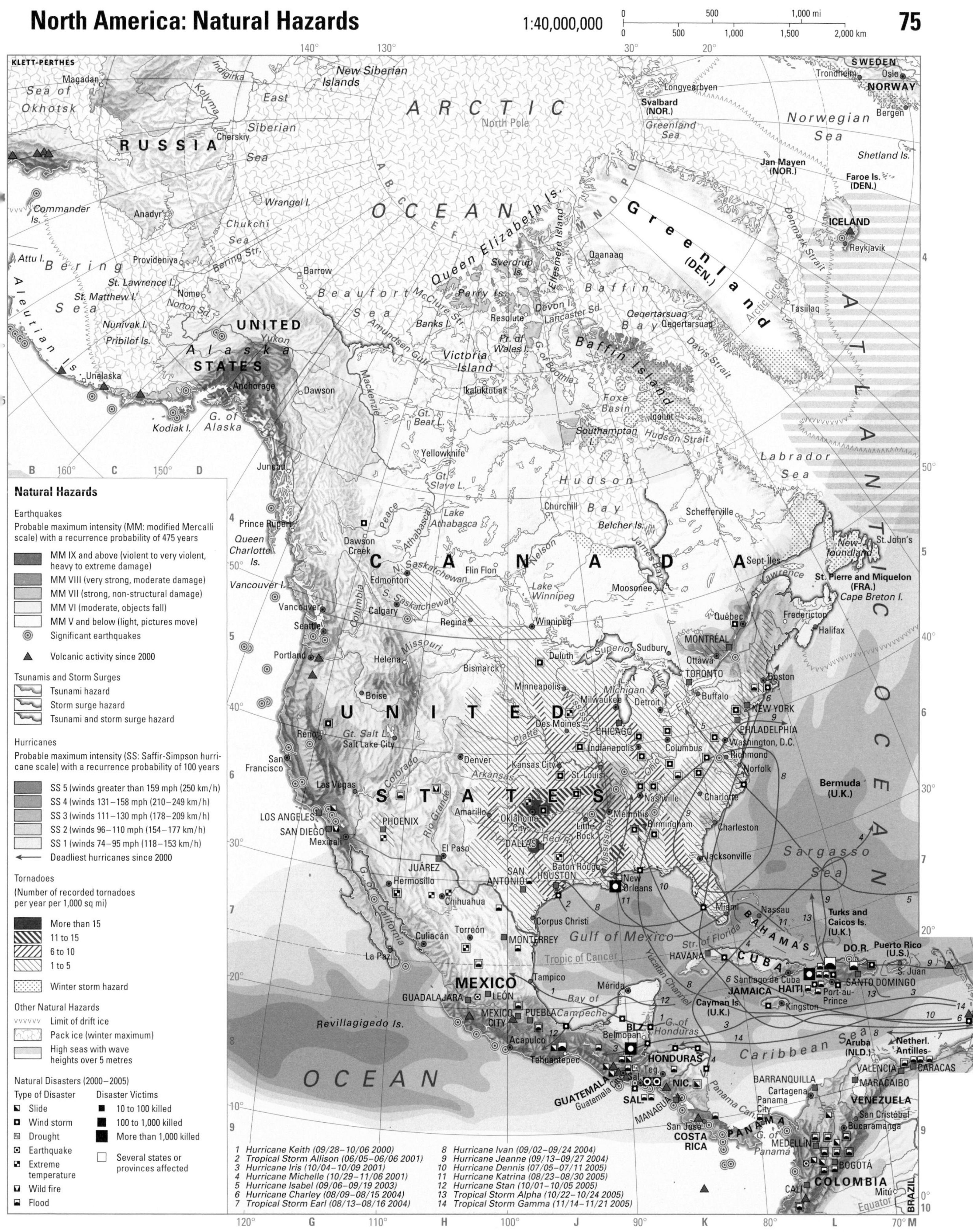
0 500 1,000 mi
0 500 1,000 1,500 2,000 km
KLETT-PERTHES
ARCTIC OCEAN
Greenland (DEN.)
UNITED STATES
CANADA
MEXICO
ATLANTIC OCEAN
OCEAN
Gulf of Mexico
Caribbean Sea
Hudson Bay
Baffin Bay
Labrador Sea
Bering Sea
Sargasso Sea
Natural Hazards
Earthquakes
Probable maximum intensity (MM: modified Mercalli scale) with a recurrence probability of 475 years
MM IX and above (violent to very violent, heavy to extreme damage)
MM VIII (very strong, moderate damage)
MM VII (strong, non-structural damage)
MM VI (moderate, objects fall)
MM V and below (light, pictures move)
Significant earthquakes
Volcanic activity since 2000
Tsunamis and Storm Surges
Tsunami hazard
Storm surge hazard
Tsunami and storm surge hazard
Hurricanes
Probable maximum intensity (SS: Saffir-Simpson hurricane scale) with a recurrence probability of 100 years
SS 5 (winds greater than 159 mph (250 km/h)
SS 4 (winds 131–158 mph (210–249 km/h)
SS 3 (winds 111–130 mph (178–209 km/h)
SS 2 (winds 96–110 mph (154–177 km/h)
SS 1 (winds 74–95 mph (118–153 km/h)
Deadliest hurricanes since 2000
Tornadoes
(Number of recorded tornadoes per year per 1,000 sq mi)
More than 15
11 to 15
6 to 10
1 to 5
Winter storm hazard
Other Natural Hazards
Limit of drift ice
Pack ice (winter maximum)
High seas with wave heights over 5 metres
Natural Disasters (2000–2005)
Type of Disaster
Slide
Wind storm
Drought
Earthquake
Extreme temperature
Wild fire
Flood
Disaster Victims
10 to 100 killed
100 to 1,000 killed
More than 1,000 killed
Several states or provinces affected
1 Hurricane Keith (09/28–10/06 2000)
2 Tropical Storm Allison (06/05–06/06 2001)
3 Hurricane Iris (10/04–10/09 2001)
4 Hurricane Michelle (10/29–11/06 2001)
5 Hurricane Isabel (09/06–09/19 2003)
6 Hurricane Charley (08/09–08/15 2004)
7 Tropical Storm Earl (08/13–08/16 2004)
8 Hurricane Ivan (09/02–09/24 2004)
9 Hurricane Jeanne (09/13–09/27 2004)
10 Hurricane Dennis (07/05–07/11 2005)
11 Hurricane Katrina (08/23–08/30 2005)
12 Hurricane Stan (10/01–10/05 2005)
13 Tropical Storm Alpha (10/22–10/24 2005)
14 Tropical Storm Gamma (11/14–11/21 2005)

ARCTIC OCEAN
Bering Sea
PACIFIC OCEAN
Beaufort Sea
Gulf of Alaska
Chukchi Sea
Koryak Range
Chukot Range
Brooks Range
Alaska Range
Kuskokwim Mts.
Aleutian Ra.
Mackenzie Mts.
Coast Mountains
Rocky Mountains
Cascade Ra.
Coast Ra.
Bitterroot Ra.
Mt. Logan 19,550 ft 5,959 m
Mt. McKinley 20,321 ft 6,194 m
Mt. Saint Elias 18,008 ft 5,489 m
Mt. Robson 12,972 ft 3,954 m
Mt. Waddington 13,177 ft 4,016 m
Mt. Rainier 14,410 ft 4,392 m
Mt. St Helens 8,364 ft 2,550 m
Mt. Shasta 14,162 ft 4,317 m
Grand Teton 13,770 ft 4,197 m
Borah Peak 12,662 ft 3,859 m
Mt. Assiniboine 11,870 ft 3,618 m
Mt. Isto 9,058 ft 2,761 m
Keele Peak 9,751 ft 2,972 m
Mt. Sylvia 9,652 ft 2,942 m
Mt. Ratz 10,289 ft 3,136 m
Mt. Veniaminof 8,225 ft 2,507 m
Golden Hinde 7,201 ft 2,195 m
Ledyanaya 8,405 ft 2,562 m
Alexander Arch.
Vancouver Island
Queen Charlotte Is.
Kodiak I.
Alaska Pen.
Seward Pen.
Banks Island
Victoria Island
Queen Elizabeth
Melville
Prince Patrick I.
Wrangel I.
Anchorage
Fairbanks
Juneau
Whitehorse
Yellowknife
Dawson
Inuvik
Edmonton
Calgary
Vancouver
Victoria
Seattle
Portland
Spokane
Kamloops
Prince George
Jasper
Lethbridge
Saskatoon
Great Falls
Helena
Billings
Boise
Idaho Falls
Elevation
13,124 ft 4,000 m
6,562 ft 2,000 m
3,281 ft 1,000 m
1,640 ft 500 m
656 ft 200 m
0 ft 0 m
Depression
656 ft 200 m
6,562 ft 2,000 m
13,124 ft 4,000 m
19,686 ft 6,000 m
26,248 ft 8,000 m
Inland ice, glaciers

90 91

1:20,000,000

0 200 400 mi
0 200 400 600 km

Nordostrundingen
C. Morris Jesup
Peary Land
Greenland Sea
Jan Mayen
Danmarkshavn
King Frederik VIII Land
Faroe Is.
Great Britain
Hebrides
Lincoln Sea
Cape Columbia
Ellesmere Island
Knud Rasmussen Land
Greenland
King Christian X Land
Ittoqqortoormiit
Arctic Circle
Akureyri
Vatnajökull 6,952 ft 2,119 m
Iceland
Reykjavík
Denmark Strait
Gunnbjørn Fjeld 12,139 ft 3,700 m
Axel Heiberg Island
Sverdrup Islands
Ellef Ringnes I.
Amund Ringnes I.
Norwegian Bay
Qaanaaq/Thule
Dundas
Melville Bay
9,882 ft 3,012 m
King Christian IX Land
Grise Fiord
Jones Sound
Upernavik
Tasiilaq
Bathurst I.
Cornwallis I.
Devon I.
6,299 ft 1,920 m
Baffin Bay
Nuugssuaq
Ilulissat
Qeqertarsuaq
Resolute
Lancaster Sound
Cape Liverpool
Bylot I.
6,401 ft 1,951 m
Kangerlussuaq
King Frederik VI Coast
Prince of Wales Island
Somerset I.
Brodeur Pen.
Arctic Bay
Gulf of Boothia
Clyde River
Sisimiut
Davis Strait
Baffin Island
Home Bay
Nuuk (Godthåb)
7,546 ft 2,300 m
Boothia Pen.
8,501 ft 2,591 m
Penny Highland
Cumberland Pen.
Cape Dyer
Qaqortoq
Ivittuut
Cape Farewell
King William I.
Melville Pen.
Prince Charles I.
Cumberland Sd.
Queen Maud Gulf
Foxe Basin
3,750 ft 1,143 m
Hall Pen.
Labrador Sea
12,477 ft 3,803 m
Repulse Bay
Foxe Pen.
Iqaluit/Frobisher Bay
Meta Incognita Pen.
Frobisher Bay
Resolution I.
Foxe Channel
Southampton I.
Hudson Strait
Cape Chidley
ATLANTIC
Roes Welcome Sd.
C. Wolstenholme
Akpatok I.
Coats Island
Rankin Inlet
Mansel I.
Ungava Peninsula
5,233 ft 1,595 m
Ungava Bay
Nain
Kuujjuaq/Fort Chimo
3,773 ft 1,150 m
Port Hope Simpson
Arviat
Ottawa Is.
Hudson Bay
Inukjuak/Port Harrison
L. Melville
Happy Valley-Goose Bay
Cape Churchill
Churchill
Schefferville
Smallwood Res.
Labrador (Nunatsiavut)
Grand Falls-Windsor
Gander
St. John's
Newfoundland
Avalon Pen.
Cape Race
Belcher Is.
Labrador City
Corner Brook
2,671 ft 814 m
167 ft 51 m
Lynn Lake
Nelson
Thompson
Winisk
Chisasibi
Mt. Otish 3,724 ft 1,135 m
Laurentian Highlands
Île d'Anticosti
St-Pierre
Sept-Îles
Gulf of St. Lawrence
Cabot Str.
James Bay
Akimiski I.
Lake Mistassini
4,160 ft 1,268 m
C. Gaspé
Îles de la Madeleine
Sydney
Cape Breton I.
Severn
Canadian Shield
St. Lawrence
Charlottetown
Lake Winnipeg
Moosonee
Mts. Notre-Dame
Sable I.
Chibougamau
Saguenay
3,875 ft 1,181 m
Fredericton
Halifax
Albany
Québec
St. John
Manitoba
Winnipeg
Nipigon
Timmins
Trois-Rivières
Cape Sable
Gulf of Maine
Assiniboine
L. of the Woods
Thunder Bay
Montréal
Augusta
Red R.
2,301 ft 701 m
Lake Superior
Sudbury
Ottawa
Montpelier
Portland
Grand Forks
Sault Sainte Marie
5,344 ft 1,629 m
Adirondack Mts.
Appalachian Mts.
Concord
OCEAN
Kingston
Duluth
Georgian Bay
Cape Cod
Fargo
Bismarck
Lake Huron
Albany
Boston
Toronto
L. Ontario
Providence
Hartford
St. Paul
Minneapolis
Green Bay
L. Michigan
Hamilton
Buffalo
Hudson
Long Island
New York
Missouri
Mississippi
Sioux Falls
Lansing
Detroit
Milwaukee
Madison
Grand Rapids
L. Erie
Erie
Philadelphia
Trenton
KLETT-PERTHES

100° V 95° 95 W 90° 98 X 85° Y 80° 99 Z 75° a 70° b 65° c 60° d

RUSSIA
ARCTIC OCEAN
Bering Sea
Aleutian Is.
Gulf of Anadyr
Chukchi Sea
Beaufort Sea
UNITED STATES
Alaska
Gulf of Alaska
PACIFIC OCEAN
Yukon Territory
Northwest Territories
British Columbia
Alberta
Saskatchewan
Washington
Oregon
Idaho
Montana
Wyoming
California
Anchorage
Fairbanks
Juneau
Whitehorse
Dawson
Inuvik
Yellowknife
Vancouver
Victoria
Surrey
Abbotsford
Kelowna
Kamloops
Prince George
Prince Rupert
Edmonton
Calgary
Red Deer
Lethbridge
Medicine Hat
Saskatoon
Fort McMurray
Seattle
Tacoma
Spokane
Portland
Salem
Eugene
Boise
Wrangel I.
Banks Island
Prince Patrick I.
Queen Charlotte Is.
Vancouver Island
Kodiak I.
Alexander Arch.

1:20,000,000
0 200 400 mi
0 200 400 600 km
Nordostrundingen
Morris Jesup
Greenland Sea
Jan Mayen (NOR.)
Danmarkshavn
Faroe Is. (DEN.)
UNITED KINGDOM
Great Britain
Hebrides
Daneborg
Lincoln Sea
Cape Columbia
National Park
of North and
East Greenland
Arctic Circle
Seyðisfjörður
Ittoqqortoormiit
Akureyri
ICELAND
Reykjavík
Denmark Strait
Greenland (DEN.)
Ellesmere Island
Axel Heiberg Island
Sverdrup Islands
Ellef Ringnes I.
Amund Ringnes I.
Norwegian Bay
Qaanaaq/ Thule
Dundas
Melville Bay
Grise Fiord
Jones Sound
Upernavik
Tasiilaq
Baffin Bay
Uummannaq
Ilulissat
Qasigiannguit
Bathurst I.
Cornwallis I.
Devon I.
Cape Liverpool
Bylot I.
Resolute
Lancaster Sound
Sirmilik Nat. Park
Pond Inlet
Qeqertarsuaq
Aasiaat
Kangerlussuaq
Somerset I.
Prince of Wales Island
Arctic Bay
Clyde River
Sisimiut
Gulf of Boothia
Baffin Island
Davis Strait
Maniitsoq
Home Bay
Nuuk (Godthåb)
Narsaq
Cape Dyer
Cape Farewell
Auyuittuq Nat. Park
Qaqortoq
Paamiut
Ivittuut
Nanortalik
Igloolik
Nunavut
King William I.
Prince Charles I.
Pangnirtung
Cumberland Sd.
Gjoa Haven
Oqsuqtooq
Foxe Basin
Labrador Sea
Repulse Bay
Iqaluit/ Frobisher Bay
Frobisher Bay
Ukkusiksalik Nat. Park
Foxe Channel
Cape Dorset
Resolution I.
Southampton I.
Hudson Strait
Cape Chidley
ATLANTIC
Qamani'tuaq/ Baker Lake
Coral Harbour
Roes Welcome Sd.
C. Wolstenholme
Ivujivik
Akpatok I.
Kangirsuk/ Payne
Ungava Bay
Coats Island
Rankin Inlet
Mansel I.
Nain
Hopedale
Rigolet
Newfoundland and Labrador
Kuujjuaq Fort Chimo
Arviat
Ottawa Is.
Hudson Bay
Inukjuak/ Port Harrison
Port Hope Simpson
L. Melville
St. Anthony
Happy Valley-Goose Bay
Schefferville
Smallwood Res.
Bonavista
Gander
St. John's
Cape Churchill
Churchill
Wapusk Nat. Park
CANADA
Grand Falls-Windsor
Newfoundland
Belcher Is.
Harrington Harbour
Labrador City
Corner Brook
Cape Race
York Factory
Kuujjuarapik/ Poste-de-la-Baleine
Stephenville
Lynn Lake
Nelson
Gillam
Gagnon
Havre-St-Pierre
St-Pierre
St. Pierre and Miquelon (FRA.)
Île d'Anticosti
Thompson
Winisk
Chisasibi
Port-Menier
Gulf of St. Lawrence
Channel-Port-aux-Basques
Manitoba
Québec
Sept-Îles
Gaspé
C. Gaspé
Cabot Str.
Flin Flon
Snow Lake
Severn
James Bay
Akimiski I.
Lake Mistassini
Baie-Comeau
Îles de la Madeleine
Glace Bay
Sydney
Prince Edward I.
Charlottetown
Cape Breton I.
The Pas
Lake Winnipeg
Waskaganish
Chibougamau
Bathurst
Moosonee
Summerside
New Brunswick
Moncton
Truro
Nova Scotia
Sable I.
Saguenay
Dartmouth
Ontario
Rivière-du-Loup
Fredericton
Halifax
Presque Isle
Québec
Lévis
Nakina
Albany
Kapuskasing
Rouyn-Noranda
Senneterre
La Tuque
St. John
Timmins
Val-d'Or
Shawinigan
Trois-Rivières
Maine
Bangor
Yarmouth
Winnipeg
Kenora
Dryden
Nipigon
White River
Drummondville
Sherbrooke
Cape Sable
Gulf of Maine
Lake of the Woods
Fort Frances
Thunder Bay
MONTRÉAL
Hull-Gatineau
Laval
Longueuil
Augusta
Sudbury
North Bay
Ottawa
Pembroke
Vermont
Montpelier
Portland
OCEAN
Grand Forks
Red R.
Lake Superior
Sault Sainte Marie
New Hampshire
Minot
North Dakota
Bemidji
Virginia
Marquette
Ironwood
Sault Sainte Marie
Parry Sound
Kingston
Georgian Bay
Concord
Manchester
Minnesota
Duluth
Superior
Peterborough
Watertown
Albany
Nashua
Cape Cod
Bismarck
Fargo
Fergus Falls
Michigan
Alpena
L. Huron
Barrie
Oshawa
Utica
Springfield
Boston
Providence
Saint Cloud
TORONTO
Mississauga
Syracuse
Rhode I.
Aberdeen
St. Paul
Wisconsin
Menominee
Green Bay
Cadillac
L. Ontario
Rochester
Hartford
Watertown
Minneapolis
Appleton
Saginaw
Hamilton
Buffalo
Binghamton
Ct.
New Haven
Long Island
South Dakota
Bloomington
Eau Claire
Mankato
La Crosse
Sarnia
London
Huron
Grand Rapids
Flint
Detroit
Scranton
Allentown
NEW YORK
Newark
Sioux Falls
Rochester
Madison
Milwaukee
Lansing
Windsor
L. Erie
Erie
Pennsylvania
New Jersey
PHILADELPHIA
Trenton
Iowa
KLETT-PERTHES

95
98
99

A 130° B 125° C 84 120° D 115° E 85 110° F 105° G 100° 86 H 95° J

Golden Hinde 7,201 ft 2,195 m
Courtenay
Vancouver
Vancouver I.
Victoria
Kamloops
Kelowna
Banff
11,870 ft Mt. 3,618 m Assiniboine
Calgary
Saskatoon
Lake Winnipeg
L. Winnipegosis
South Saskatchewan
Medicine Hat
Lethbridge
Regina
Qu'Appelle
Lake Manitoba
Brandon
Assiniboine
Winnipeg
Kenora
L. of the Woods
Seattle
Olympia
14,410 ft 4,392 m Mt. Rainier
8,364 ft 2,550 m Mt. St. Helens
Astoria
Portland
Columbia
Spokane
Columbia Basin
Kennewick
Kalispell
Missoula
Helena
Butte
Great Falls
Missouri
Minot
Souris
Red R.
Grand Forks
Bismarck
Fargo
Duluth
Salem
Eugene
Bend
Yellowstone
Billings
Lake Oahe
Saint Cloud
Mississippi
St Paul
Minneapolis
Bitterroot Range
12,662 ft 3,859 m Borah Peak
Boise
Snake
Idaho Falls
Grand Teton 13,770 ft 4,197 m
13,175 ft 4,016 m
Black Hills 7,242 ft 2,207 m
Rapid City
Custer
Pierre
Medford
Klamath Falls
9,002 ft 2,744 m
Mt. Shasta 14,162 ft 4,317 m
Cape Mendocino
Redding
Pocatello
Casper
Missouri
Sioux Falls
Sioux City
Black Rock Desert
Great Salt Lake
Ogden
Salt Lake City
Uinta Mts. 13,528 ft 4,123 m
Provo
Cheyenne
Fort Collins
North Platte
Omaha
Des Moines
Cedar Rapids
Reno
Carson City
Sacramento
Sacramento
San Francisco
Stockton
San Jose
S. Joaquin
Great Basin
Wheeler Peak 13,061 ft 3,982 m
Longs Peak 14,255 ft 4,345 m
Front Ra.
Denver
Colorado
Mt. Elbert 14,432 ft 4,399 m
Colorado Springs
Pueblo
Platte
Lincoln
Kansas City
Kansas
Missouri
Topeka
Kansas City
Jefferson City
Cedar City
Wasatch Ra.
Fresno
Mt. Whitney 14,495 ft 4,418 m
Death Valley -282 ft -86 m
Las Vegas
Lake Powell
Sangre de Cristo Mts.
Blanca Peak 14,360 ft 4,377 m
Dodge City
Arkansas
Wichita
Springfield
L. Mead
Grand Canyon
Colorado Plateau
Durango
2,340 ft 713 m
Bakersfield
Mojave Desert
Point Conception
Santa Barbara
Channel Islands
12,663 ft 3,860 m
Flagstaff
Santa Fe
Tulsa
Fayetteville
Boston Mts.
Los Angeles
Riverside
Albuquerque
Oklahoma City
Amarillo
Fort Smith
2,900 ft 884 m
Ouachita Mts.
Little Rock
San Diego
Phoenix
Lawton
Tijuana
Mexicali
Yuma
Gila
Colorado
Sierra Blanca Peak 12,003 ft 3,659 m
Sacramento Mts.
Llano Estacado
Lubbock
Wichita Falls
Tucson
Plano
Greenville
Longview
Shreveport
Dallas
Fort Worth
10,157 ft 3,096 m
Cerro de la Encantada
Nogales
El Paso
Rio Grande
Rio Bravo del Norte
Odessa
Pecos
Waco
Trinity
Red R.
Isla Ángel de la Guarda
Guadalupe I.
7,743 ft 2,360 m
Edwards Plateau
Austin
Brazos
Lake Charles
Beaumont
Tiburón
Cedros I.
Hermosillo
Yaqui
Colorado
Houston
San Antonio
Galveston
Pta. Sta. Eugenia
Acuña
Chihuahua
Piedras Negras
Eagle Pass
Ciudad Obregón
Creel
Laredo
Corpus Christi
Monclova
Los Mochis
Co. Mohinora 10,830 ft 3,300 m
Cd. Constitución
Torreón
Reynosa
Brownsville
Matamoros
Monterrey
Saltillo
Culiacán
La Paz
7,894 ft 2,406 m
San José del Cabo
Cape San Lucas
Durango
Cerro Peña Nevada 12,021 ft 3,664 m
Ciudad Victoria
Mazatlán
Tropic of Cancer
Islas Tres Marías
Tepic
Aguascalientes
San Luis Potosí
Tampico
9,800 ft 2,987 m
León
Puerto Vallarta
Cape Corrientes
Guadalajara
Rio Grande de Santiago
Revillagigedo Islands
Bay of Campeche
Nevado de Colima 14,600 ft 4,450 m
Uruapan
Morelia
Mexico City (Cd. de México)
Popocatépetl 17,887 ft 5,452 m
Puebla
Pico de Orizaba 18,405 ft 5,610 m
Veracruz
Manzanillo
Lázaro Cárdenas
Oaxaca
Coatzacoalcos
Villahermosa
Rocky Mountains
Great Plains
Coast Ranges
Cascade Range
Sierra Nevada
Lower California
Gulf of California
Sierra Madre Occidental
Mexican Plateau
Sierra Madre Oriental
Gulf of Mexico
PACIFIC OCEAN

45° 40° 35° 30° 25° 20°
2 3 4 5 6 7 8

Elevation

ft	m	ft	m
13,124 ft	4,000 m	656 ft	200 m
6,562 ft	2,000 m	6,562 ft	2,000 m
3,281 ft	1,000 m	13,124 ft	4,000 m
1,640 ft	500 m	19,686 ft	6,000 m
656 ft	200 m	26,248 ft	8,000 m
0 ft	0 m		
	Depression		

E 110° F 102

1:15,000,000
0 200 400 mi
0 200 400 600 km
K 87 85° L 80° M 75° 88 N 70° O 65° 89 P 60° Q 55° R
Canadian Shield
James Bay
Moosonee
Albany
Lake Mistassini
Chibougamau
Laurentian Highlands
Sept-Îles
Anticosti I.
Gulf of St. Lawrence
Newfoundland
Avalon Pen.
Cape Race
St-Pierre
Cabot Strait
C. Gaspé
1,268 m
4,160 ft
Mts. Notre-Dame
St. Lawrence
Rimouski
Magdalene Is.
Saguenay
3,875 ft
1,181 m
Senneterre
Lake Nipigon
Thunder Bay
Timmins
Québec
Charlottetown
Sydney
Cape Breton Island
Moncton
Fredericton
St. John
Bay of Fundy
Halifax
Sable I.
Lake Superior
Trois-Rivières
Sault Sainte Marie
Sudbury
North Bay
Montréal
Sherbrooke
Marquette
Ottawa
Georgian Bay
Lake Huron
Augusta
Gulf of Maine
Cape Sable
Montpelier
Adirondack Mts.
5,344 ft
1,629 m
White Mts.
Portland
Kingston
Concord
Green Bay
Lake Michigan
Barrie
Toronto
Lake Ontario
Hamilton
Albany
Boston
Cape Cod
Rochester
Saginaw
London
Buffalo
Hudson
Providence
Nantucket I.
Milwaukee
Lansing
Hartford
New Haven
Madison
Grand Rapids
Detroit
Lake Erie
Erie
Scranton
New York
Long Island
Chicago
Toledo
Cleveland
Trenton
South Bend
Harrisburg
Fort Wayne
Pittsburgh
Philadelphia
Peoria
Columbus
Baltimore
Dover
Indianapolis
Washington, D.C.
Annapolis
Spruce Knob
4,861 ft
1,482 m
Springfield
Cincinnati
Ohio
Charleston
Chesapeake Bay
Frankfort
Richmond
Evansville
Louisville
Newport News
Norfolk
Chesapeake
Allegheny Mts.
Appalachian Mts.
Greensboro
Raleigh
Nashville
Knoxville
Mt. Mitchell
6,684 ft
2,037 m
C. Hatteras
Charlotte
Fayetteville
Memphis
Chattanooga
Greenville
Wilmington
Tennessee
Columbia
Hamilton
Bermuda Is.
Birmingham
Atlanta
Piedmont
Charleston
Mississippi
Macon
Greenville
Columbus
Savannah
Jackson
Montgomery
ATLANTIC OCEAN
Mobile
Pensacola
Tallahassee
Jacksonville
Baton Rouge
Sargasso Sea
New Orleans
Cape San Blas
Apalachee Bay
Florida
Orlando
Cape Canaveral
Tampa
Saint Petersburg
Bahamas
West Palm Beach
Gd. Bahama I.
Great Abaco
Cape Coral
Fort Lauderdale
Eleuthera I.
Miami
Nassau
Cat I.
Cape Sable
Straits of Florida
Florida Keys
207 ft
63 m
Mt. Alvernia
San Salvador
Andros I.
Long Island
Gulf of Mexico
Acklins I.
Caicos Is.
Grand Turk (Cockburn Town)
Turks Is.
Havana (La Habana)
Santa Clara
Cuba
Great Inagua
Pinar del Río
Camagüey
Holguín
Cape Maisí
30,246 ft
9,219 m
Mona Passage
Anegada Passage
St-Barthélemy
Yucatán Channel
Cape San Antonio
C. Catoche
Isla de la Juventud
Windward Passage
Santiago de Cuba
San Juan
Sa. Maestra
Manzanillo
Pico Turquino
6,476 ft
1,974 m
Cap-Haïtien
10,417 ft
3,175 m
Santiago
P. Duarte
Santo Domingo
Co. de Punta
4,390 ft
1,338 m
Charlotte Amalie
St-Martin
Basseterre
Lesser Antilles
Mérida
Cancún
Ponce
Puerto Rico
St. Croix
Chichén-Itzá
Cozumel I.
The Bluff
141 ft
43 m
Grand Cayman
Cayman Is.
25,197 ft
7,680 m
Port-au-Prince
8,793 ft
2,680 m
La Selle
Hispaniola
Campeche
Yucatán Pen.
Georgetown
Jamaica
Caribbean Sea
Greater Antilles
Kingston
Blue Mtn. Peak
7,401 ft
2,256 m
Chetumal
KLETT-PERTHES
K 85° 103 L 80° M 75° N 70° O 65° P
2 3 4 5 6 7 8
45° 40° 35° 30° 25° 20° 15°

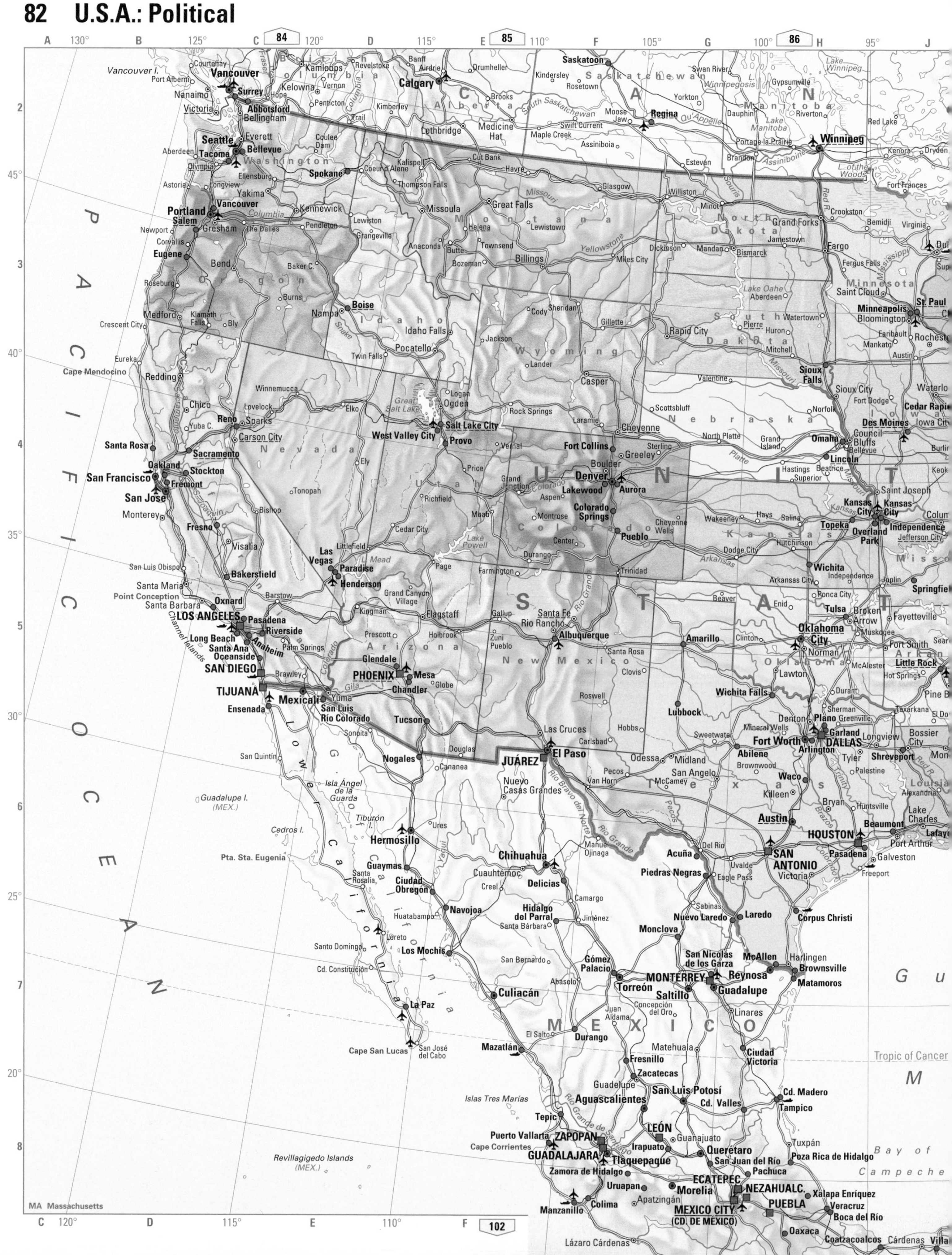
A
130°
B
125°
C
84
120°
D
115°
E
85
110°
F
105°
G
100°
86
H
95°
J
2
45°
3
40°
4
35°
5
30°
6
25°
7
20°
8
P
A
C
I
F
I
C
O
C
E
A
N
Vancouver I.
Port Alberni
Nanaimo
Victoria
Vancouver
Surrey
Abbotsford
Bellingham
Courtenay
Kamloops
Revelstoke
Kelowna
Vernon
Penticton
Hope
Trail
Kimberley
Banff
Airdrie
Calgary
Drumheller
Brooks
Lethbridge
Medicine Hat
Kindersley
Saskatoon
Rosetown
Swift Current
Moose Jaw
Regina
Yorkton
Swan River
Lake Winnipegosis
Gypsumville
Lake Winnipeg
Dauphin
Riverton
Lake Manitoba
Portage-la-Prairie
Winnipeg
Brandon
Estevan
Assiniboia
Maple Creek
Red Lake
Kenora
Dryden
Fort Frances
L. of the Woods
C
A
N
Alberta
Saskatchewan
Manitoba
Seattle
Everett
Bellevue
Tacoma
Aberdeen
Olympia
Washington
Coulee Dam
Ellensburg
Spokane
Coeur d'Alene
Kalispell
Cut Bank
Havre
Glasgow
Williston
Minot
Grand Forks
Crookston
Bemidji
Virginia
Duluth
Astoria
Longview
Yakima
Kennewick
Portland
Vancouver
Salem
Gresham
The Dalles
Pendleton
Lewiston
Grangeville
Thompson Falls
Missoula
Great Falls
Montana
Helena
Lewistown
Townsend
Anaconda
Butte
Bozeman
Billings
Miles City
Dickinson
Mandan
Bismarck
Jamestown
Fargo
Fergus Falls
North Dakota
Newport
Corvallis
Eugene
Bend
Baker C.
Oregon
Roseburg
Burns
Boise
Nampa
Idaho
Idaho Falls
Pocatello
Twin Falls
Cody
Sheridan
Gillette
Rapid City
Lake Oahe
Aberdeen
Watertown
Saint Cloud
Minneapolis
St. Paul
Bloomington
Minnesota
Pierre
Huron
Mitchell
South Dakota
Faribault
Mankato
Rochester
Austin
Medford
Klamath Falls
Bly
Crescent City
Eureka
Cape Mendocino
Redding
Chico
Yuba C.
Jackson
Wyoming
Lander
Casper
Valentine
Sioux Falls
Sioux City
Fort Dodge
Waterloo
Cedar Rapids
Winnemucca
Lovelock
Elko
Logan
Ogden
Great Salt Lake
Salt Lake City
West Valley City
Provo
Rock Springs
Laramie
Cheyenne
Scottsbluff
Nebraska
North Platte
Grand Island
Norfolk
Omaha
Council Bluffs
Bellevue
Des Moines
Iowa City
Reno
Sparks
Carson City
Nevada
Santa Rosa
Sacramento
Oakland
Stockton
San Francisco
Fremont
San Jose
Monterey
Ely
Vernal
Fort Collins
Greeley
Sterling
Boulder
Denver
Lakewood
Aurora
Lincoln
Hastings
Beatrice
Superior
Saint Joseph
Kansas City
Topeka
Overland Park
Independence
Jefferson City
Tonopah
Price
Grand Junction
Aspen
Colorado Springs
Pueblo
Montrose
Colorado
Richfield
Utah
Moab
Bishop
Fresno
Visalia
Cedar City
Lake Powell
Center
Durango
Cheyenne Wells
Wakeeney
Hays
Salina
Kansas
Hutchinson
Dodge City
Wichita
Independence
Arkansas City
Joplin
Springfield
Las Vegas
Paradise
Henderson
Littlefield
L. Mead
Page
Farmington
Trinidad
San Luis Obispo
Bakersfield
Santa Maria
Point Conception
Santa Barbara
Oxnard
Barstow
Grand Canyon Village
Kingman
Flagstaff
Gallup
Santa Fe
Rio Rancho
Albuquerque
Amarillo
Beaver
Enid
Ponca City
Tulsa
Broken Arrow
Fayetteville
Oklahoma City
Muskogee
Fort Smith
Norman
McAlester
Little Rock
Hot Springs
LOS ANGELES
Pasadena
Riverside
Long Beach
Santa Ana
Anaheim
Oceanside
Palm Springs
SAN DIEGO
Channel Islands
Prescott
Holbrook
Arizona
Zuni Pueblo
New Mexico
Santa Rosa
Clovis
Clinton
Lawton
Oklahoma
Glendale
PHOENIX
Mesa
Chandler
Globe
Brawley
TIJUANA
Mexicali
Yuma
San Luis Río Colorado
Ensenada
Roswell
Lubbock
Wichita Falls
Durant
Sherman
Denton
Plano
Greenville
Texarkana
Pine Bluff
El Dorado
Tucson
Sonoita
Las Cruces
Carlsbad
Hobbs
Sweetwater
Mineral Wells
Fort Worth
Arlington
Garland
DALLAS
Longview
Bossier City
Shreveport
Monroe
Douglas
Nogales
Cananea
JUÁREZ
El Paso
Odessa
Midland
Abilene
Brownwood
Tyler
Palestine
San Quintín
Isla Ángel de la Guarda
Nuevo Casas Grandes
Pecos
Van Horn
McCamey
San Angelo
Texas
Waco
Killeen
Bryan
Huntsville
Alexandria
Lake Charles
Lafayette
Guadalupe I. (MEX.)
Cedros I.
Tiburón I.
Ures
Hermosillo
Austin
HOUSTON
Beaumont
Port Arthur
Pasadena
Galveston
Pta. Sta. Eugenia
Guaymas
Chihuahua
Manuel Ojinaga
Acuña
Del Rio
SAN ANTONIO
Uvalde
Victoria
Freeport
Santa Rosalía
Ciudad Obregón
Cuauhtémoc
Delicias
Creel
Piedras Negras
Eagle Pass
Navojoa
Huatabampo
Hidalgo del Parral
Santa Bárbara
Camargo
Jiménez
Sabinas
Nuevo Laredo
Laredo
Corpus Christi
Monclova
Loreto
Los Mochis
Santo Domingo
Cd. Constitución
San Bernardo
Gómez Palacio
Torreón
Abasolo
San Nicolás de los Garza
MONTERREY
Saltillo
Guadalupe
McAllen
Reynosa
Harlingen
Brownsville
Matamoros
G
La Paz
Culiacán
Juan Aldama
Concepción del Oro
Linares
MEXICO
Cape San Lucas
San José del Cabo
El Salto
Durango
Matehuala
Mazatlán
Ciudad Victoria
Fresnillo
Zacatecas
Tropic of Cancer
M
Islas Tres Marías
Guadelupe
Aguascalientes
San Luis Potosí
Cd. Valles
Cd. Madero
Tampico
Tepic
Puerto Vallarta
Cape Corrientes
ZAPOPAN
GUADALAJARA
Tlaquepaque
LEÓN
Guanajuato
Irapuato
Querétaro
San Juan del Río
Tuxpán
Poza Rica de Hidalgo
Bay of Campeche
Revillagigedo Islands (MEX.)
Zamora de Hidalgo
Pachuca
Uruapan
Morelia
ECATEPEC
NEZAHUALC.
Xalapa Enríquez
Veracruz
Boca del Río
Manzanillo
Colima
Apatzingán
MEXICO CITY (CD. DE MÉXICO)
PUEBLA
Oaxaca
Lázaro Cárdenas
Coatzacoalcos
Cárdenas
Villa
MA Massachusetts
C
120°
D
115°
E
110°
F
102

1:15,000,000
0 200 400 mi
0 200 400 600 km
87
88
89
103
KLETT-PERTHES
ATLANTIC OCEAN
Sargasso Sea
Gulf of St. Lawrence
Gulf of Maine
James Bay
Lake Superior
Lake Michigan
Lake Huron
Lake Ontario
Lake Erie
Georgian Bay
Cabot Strait
Bay of Fundy
Chesapeake Bay
Apalachee Bay
Straits of Florida
Florida Keys
Windward Passage
Mona Passage
Anegada Passage
Yucatán Channel
Yucatán Pen.
Lesser Antilles
Greater Antilles
Caribbean
Hispaniola
Newfoundland
Newfoundland and Labrador
Avalon Pen.
Cape Race
St. Pierre and Miquelon (FRA.)
St-Pierre
Channel-Port-aux-Basques
Stephenville
Anticosti I.
Port-Menier
Sept-Îles
C. Gaspé
Gaspé
Magdalene Is.
Prince Edward I.
Charlottetown
Cape Breton Island
Glace Bay
Sydney
Sable I.
Nova Scotia
Halifax
Dartmouth
Truro
Amherst
Moncton
Summerside
New Brunswick
Fredericton
St. John
Yarmouth
Cape Sable
Campbellton
Bathurst
Edmundston
Rimouski
Presque Isle
Baie-Comeau
Rivière-du-Loup
Saguenay
Alma
Chibougamau
Lake Mistassini
Québec
Lévis
La Tuque
Shawinigan
Trois-Rivières
Drummondville
Sherbrooke
MONTREAL
Laval
Longueuil
Hull-Gatineau
Ottawa
Mont-Laurier
Pembroke
Kingston
Peterborough
Barrie
Oshawa
Markham
TORONTO
Mississauga
Hamilton
St. Catharines
London
Sarnia
Parry Sound
Owen Sound
North Bay
Sudbury
Sault Sainte Marie
Timmins
Rouyn-Noranda
Val-d'Or
Senneterre
Cochrane
Kapuskasing
Hearst
Moosonee
Waskaganish
Fort Albany
Nakina
Marathon
White River
Thunder Bay
Lake Nipigon
Québec
Ontario
Bangor
Augusta
Lewiston
Portland
Maine
Burlington
Montpelier
Vermont
New Hampshire
Concord
Manchester
Nashua
Lowell
Worcester
Boston
Springfield
Cape Cod
New Bedford
Providence
Rhode I.
Nantucket I.
Hartford
Connecticut
New Haven
Albany
Utica
Syracuse
Rochester
Buffalo
Watertown
Binghamton
New York
NEW YORK
Yonkers
Newark
Long Island
Trenton
Scranton
Williamsport
Allentown
Pennsylvania
PHILADELPHIA
New Jersey
Atlantic City
Dover
Delaware
Harrisburg
York
Altoona
Erie
Olean
Pittsburgh
Baltimore
Annapolis
Maryland
Washington, D.C.
Wheeling
Parkersburg
West Virginia
Charleston
Huntington
Charlottesville
Richmond
Virginia
Newport News
Virginia Beach
Norfolk
Portsmouth
Chesapeake
Elizabeth City
Lynchburg
Roanoke
Bluefield
Danville
Winston-Salem
Greensboro
Durham
Raleigh
High Point
Greenville
C. Hatteras
North Carolina
Charlotte
Gastonia
Fayetteville
Jacksonville
Wilmington
Asheville
Spartanburg
Greenville
Anderson
Columbia
Florence
South Carolina
Georgetown
North Charleston
Charleston
Athens-Clarke
Augusta
Atlanta
Macon
Georgia
Columbus
Savannah
Brunswick
Albany
Valdosta
Jacksonville
Saint Augustine
Tallahassee
Gainesville
Ocala
Daytona Beach
Orlando
Cape Canaveral
Melbourne
Clearwater
Tampa
Saint Petersburg
Sarasota
Fort Pierce
Port Saint Lucie
West Palm Beach
Cape Coral
Fort Myers
Fort Lauderdale
Hollywood
Hialeah
Miami
Cape Sable
Key West
Cape San Blas
Panama City
Pensacola
Mobile
Biloxi
Gulfport
Metairie
New Orleans
Hattiesburg
McComb
Jackson
Meridian
Mississippi
Tuscaloosa
Alabama
Montgomery
Dothan
Birmingham
Winona
Tupelo
Gadsden
Huntsville
Decatur
Rome
Chattanooga
Corinth
Memphis
Jackson
Tennessee
Tullahoma
Columbia
Nashville
Clarksville
Murfreesboro
Knoxville
Oak Ridge
Johnson City
Paducah
Bowling Green
Kentucky
Owensboro
Evansville
Louisville
Frankfort
Lexington
Cincinnati
Hamilton
Dayton
Columbus
Springfield
Ohio
Mansfield
Akron
Canton
Youngstown
Parma
Cleveland
Toledo
Lima
Windsor
Detroit
Ann Arbor
Jackson
Lansing
Flint
Saginaw
Grand Rapids
Cadillac
Alpena
Menominee
Green Bay
Appleton
Sheboygan
Milwaukee
Racine
Kenosha
CHICAGO
Elgin
Aurora
Joliet
Rockford
South Bend
Fort Wayne
Muncie
Indiana
Lafayette
Indianapolis
Terre Haute
Vincennes
Champaign
Peoria
Springfield
Illinois
Alton
Saint Louis
Carbondale
Marquette
Ironwood
Hamilton
Bermuda (U.K.)
BAHAMAS
Coopers Town
Marsh Harbour
Great Abaco
Freeport
Gd. Bahama I.
Eleuthera I.
Nassau
Andros I.
Cat I.
San Salvador
Long Island
Clarence Town
Acklins I.
Great Inagua
Turks and Caicos Is. (U.K.)
Grand Turk (Cockburn Town)
HAVANA (LA HABANA)
Matanzas
Cárdenas
Artemisa
Santa Clara
Consolación del Sur
Colón
Cienfuegos
Ciego de Avila
Pinar del Rio
Sancti Spíritus
Nueva Gerona
Isla de la Juventud
Cape San Antonio
Camagüey
Nuevitas
Puerto Padre
Holguín
Las Tunas
Bayamo
Manzanillo
Mayarí
Moa
Baracoa
Cape Maisí
Guantánamo
Santiago de Cuba
CUBA
Cayman Islands (U.K.)
Georgetown
JAMAICA
Montego Bay
Kingston
Portmore
Navassa (U.S.)
HAITI
Cap-Haïtien
Gonaïves
Saint-Marc
Jérémie
Les Cayes
Carrefour
Delmas
Port-au-Prince
DOMINICAN REP.
Puerto Plata
Santiago
La Vega
San Francisco de Macorís
La Romana
San Cristóbal
SANTO DOMINGO
Mayagüez
Bayamón
San Juan
Ponce
Puerto Rico (U.S.)
British Virgin Is. (U.K.)
Charlotte Amalie
Virgin Islands, U.S.
St. Croix
Anguilla (U.K.)
(Guad.)
(Neth. Antilles)
Basseterre
SAINT KITTS AND NEVIS
C. Catoche
Progreso
Tizimín
Mérida
Valladolid
Chichén-Itzá
Cancún
Playa del Carmen
Cozumel
Cozumel I.
Chetumal
Orange Walk
BELIZE
Francisco Escárcega
Gulf of Mexico

A
128°
B
124°
C
120°
D
2
52°
3
48°
4
44°
U.S.
Alaska
Behm Canal
Portland Canal
4,595 ft
1,400 m
Shedin Pk.
8,750 ft
2,667 m
Skeena Mts.
Omineca Mts.
Omineca
Skeena
Babine
Hazelton Mts.
Babine Range
Gitanmaax Ind. Res.
Gitsegukla Ind. Res.
Nass
Lachkaltsap Ind. Res.
New Hazelton
Takla Lake
Williston Lake
Mt. Crysdale
7,950 ft
2,423 m
Peace
Fort St. John
Hudson Hope
Chetwynd
Dawson Creek
Spirit River
Fairview
Peace
Smoky
Mackenzie
Pine Pass
2,851 ft
869 m
Murray
Tumbler Ridge
Beaverlodge
Sexsmith
Grande-Prairie
Valley
Sturgeon Lake Ind. Res.
Dundas Island
Mt. McNeil
4,550 ft
1,387 m
Seven Sisters Peaks
9,040 ft
2,755 m
Mt. Cronin
7,822 ft
2,384 m
6,792 ft
2,070 m
Nation
Nechako
Sentinel Peak
8,200 ft
2,499 m
Tsimpsean Ind. Res.
Terrace
Prince Rupert
Skeena
Smithers
Bulkley
Babine Lake
Plateau
Parsnip
Wapiti
Houston
Burns Lake
Stuart Lake
Fort St. James
Salmon
Crooked
Kakwa
Simonette
Little Smoky
Porcher Island
Dolphin Island Ind. Res.
Kitimat
Pitt Island
Greenville Ch.
Douglas Ch.
Atna Peak
9,050 ft
2,758 m
Francois
British
Ootsa Lake
Fraser Lake
Nechako
Stony Creek Ind. Res.
Vanderhoof
Prince George
Willow River
McGregor
Mount Sir Alexander
10,740 ft
3,274 m
Grande Cache
Berland
Banks Island
Hawkesbury I.
Gribbell I.
Micheal Peak
7,451 ft
2,271 m
Willow
Bowron
11,140 ft
3,395 m
Cariboo Mts.
Fraser
McBride
Wildhay
Athabasca
Hinton
5,500 ft
1,676 m
Princess Royal Island
Caamaño Sound
Eutsuk Lake
Natalkuz Lake
West Road
5,758 ft
1,755 m
Nazko
Fraser
Quesnel
Wells
12,972 ft
3,954 m
Mount Robson
Jasper
Aristazabal Island
Dean
Kalone Peak
8,390 ft
2,545 m
Columbia
Quesnel
Quesnel Lake
Mount Sir Wilfrid Laurier
Valemount
Jasper National
Laredo Sound
Ocean Falls
Bella Coola
Bella Coola
11,500 ft
3,505 m
Canoe
Milbanke Sound
Bella Bella Ind. Res.
Hunter Island
Coast Mountains
Fraser Plateau
Williams Lake
Clearwater
Blue River
Thompson
Mt. Columbia
12,294 ft
3,747 m
Kinbasket Lake
Calvert Island
Mt. Buxton
3,250 ft
991 m
Owenkeno Lake
Chilko
Stone Ind. Res.
Chilcotin
Alkali Lake Ind. Res.
Smith Sound
Mount Waddington
13,177 ft
4,016 m
Klinaklini
Homathko
Chilko Lake
100 Mile House
Clearwater
Monashee Mountains
Mt. Sir Sandford
11,556 ft
3,522 m
Selkirk
Queen Charlotte Str.
Good Hope Mtn.
10,630 ft
3,240 m
7,625 ft
2,324 m
Mt. Bowman
Baldy Mtn.
7,500 ft
2,286 m
Revelstoke
Barrière
Adams Lake
Mt. Revelstoke Nat. Park
Glacier Nat. P.
Port Hardy
6,100 ft
1,859 m
Knight Inlet
Bute Inlet
Bridge
Bralorne
Clinton
Kamloops Ind. Res.
Shuswap
Revelstoke
Port McNeill
Quatsino Sound
Port Alice
4,600 ft
1,402 m
Lillooet
Lillooet
Thompson
Ashcroft
Kamloops
Salmon Arm
Mt. Odin
9,750 ft
2,972 m
Upper Arrow Lake
Gott Peak
9,700 ft
2,956 m
Okanagan Ind. Res.
Vernon
6,880 ft
2,097 m
Checleset Bay
Tahsis
Campbell River
Jervis Inlet
Squamish
Whistler
Wedge Mtn.
9,527 ft
2,904 m
Lytton
Merritt
Douglas Lake Ind. Res.
Okanagan Lake
Nakusp
Lower Arrow Lake
Kootenay Lake
Nootka Island
Vancouver
Courtenay
Golden Hinde
7,201 ft
2,195 m
Powell River
Squamish
Harrison Lake
Kelowna
Nootka Sound
Cumberland
Strait of Georgia
Sechelt
Summerland
Kettle
Midway Ra.
7,930 ft
2,417 m
Slocan
Island
Port Alberni
Parksville
North Vancouver
Vancouver
Burnaby
Princeton
Penticton Ind. Res.
Penticton
Cascade Range
Tofino
Nanaimo
Surrey
Chilliwack
Hope
7,201 ft
2,195 m
Oliver
Osoyoos Ind. Res.
Castlegar
Pacific
Ucluelet
Barkley Sound
Ladysmith
White Rock
Abbotsford
Keremeos
Osoyoos
Grand Forks
Trail
Rim Nat. Park
Duncan
Lummi Ind. Res.
Lynden
Bellingham
Mt. Baker
10,777 ft
3,285 m
North Cascades Nat. P.
Okanogan Ra.
Methow
Mt. Bonaparte
7,257 ft
2,212 m
Colville
Sidney
Port Renfrew
Saanich
Victoria
Anacortes
Omak
Okanogan
Kettle River Ra.
F. D. Roosevelt Lake
6,837 ft
2,084 m
Makah Ind. Res.
Strait of Juan de Fuca
Oak Harbor
Mt. Vernon
Colville Ind. Res.
Sekiu
Port Townsend
Tulalip Ind. Res.
Port Angeles
Olympic Nat. P.
Port Gamble Ind. Res.
Marysville
Glacier Peak
10,541 ft
3,213 m
Lake Chelan
Columbia
Spokane Ind. Res.
Newport
Mt. Olympus
7,966 ft
2,428 m
Everett
Coulee Dam
Port Madison Ind. Res.
Bellevue
Chelan
PACIFIC
Quinault Ind. Res.
Bremerton
Seattle
Leavenworth
Banks Lake
Wilbur
Davenport
Spokane
Kent
Mt. Stuart
9,415 ft
2,870 m
Wenatchee
Medical Lake
Cheney
Coeur d'Alene Ind. Res.
Shelton
Tacoma
Federal Way
Ephrata
Odessa
Puyallup
Washington
Hoquiam
Elma
Olympia
Lakewood
Mount Rainier Nat. P.
Cle Elum
Moses Lake
Grays Harbor
Aberdeen
Ellensburg
Potholes Res.
Ritzville
Mt. Rainier
14,410 ft
4,392 m
Yakima
Othello
Willapa Bay
South Bend
Centralia
Chehalis
Selah
Pullman
Morton
Yakima
Snake
Long Beach
3,110 ft
948 m
Cowlitz
Toppenish
Richland
Pomeroy
Astoria
Seaside
Mt. St. Helens
8,364 ft
2,550 m
Mt. Adams
12,277 ft
3,742 m
Yakima Ind. Res.
Sunnyside
Prosser
Pasco
Kennewick
Dayton
Walla Walla
6,387 ft
1,947 m
Lewiston
OCEAN
Longview
Lewis
3,283 ft
1001 m
St. Helens
Goldendale
UNITED
Columbia
Milton-Freewater
White Salmon
Hillsboro
Vancouver
Camas
Hood River
Arlington
Hermiston
Pendleton
Umatilla Ind. Res.
Tillamook
Portland
Gresham
The Dalles
Mt. Hood
11,240 ft
3,428 m
Pilot Rock
Blue Mountains
McMinnville
Heppner
La Grande
Woodburn
Silverton
Wallowa Mts.
Eagle Cap
Lincoln C.
Dallas
Salem
Deschutes
Warm Springs Ind. Res.
5,112 ft
1,558 m
N. F. John Day
John Day
Oregon
Willamette
Newport
Toledo
Mt. Jefferson
10,497 ft
3,199 m
Corvallis
Albany
Mill City
Madras
Baker C.
Powder
Lebanon
4,097 ft
1,249 m
Sweet Home
A
128°
B
124°
C
120°
D

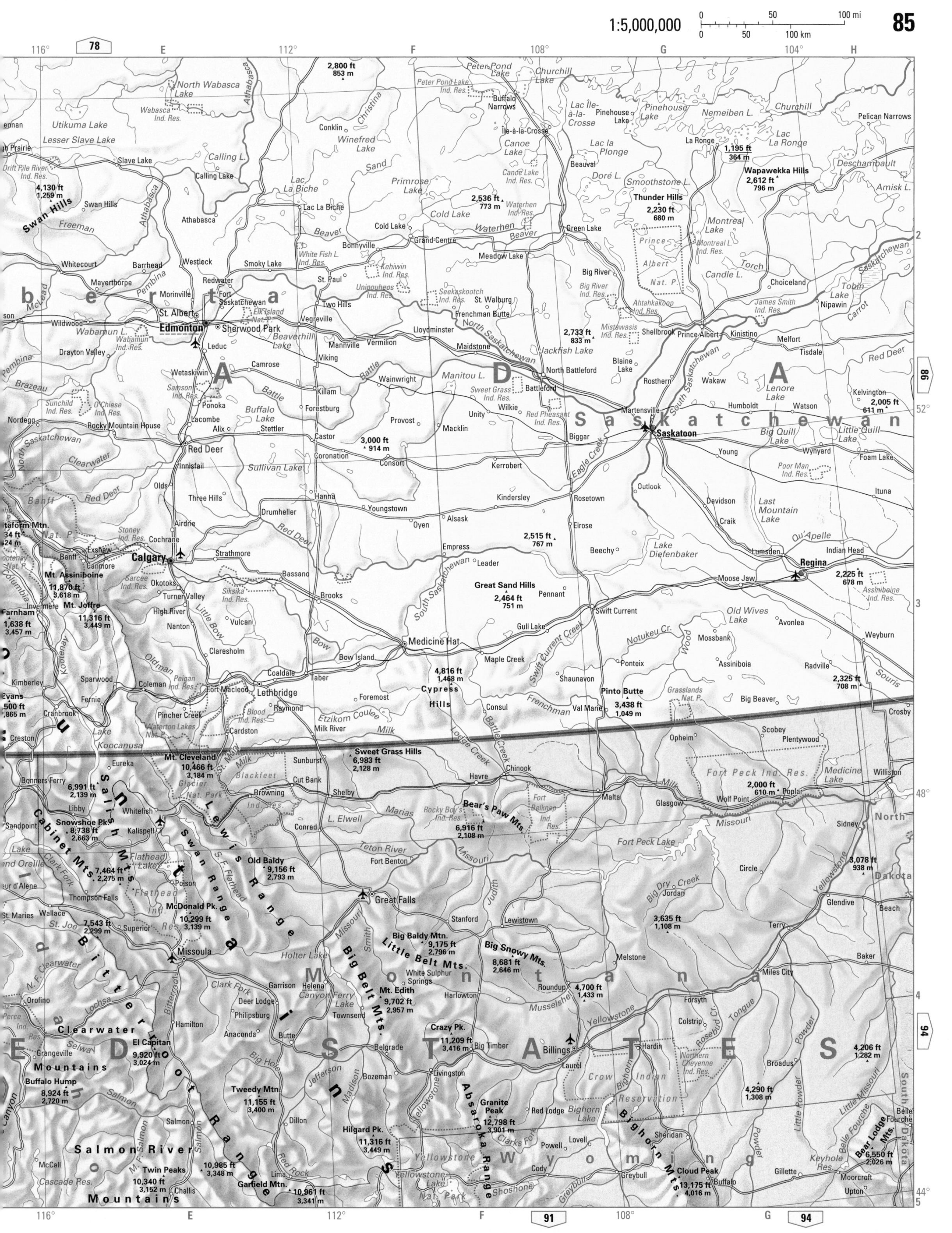
1:5,000,000
0 50 100 mi
0 50 100 km
116° 78 E 112° F 108° G 104° H
North Wabasca Lake
Wabasca Ind. Res.
Athabasca
Utikuma Lake
Lesser Slave Lake
Slave Lake
Calling L.
Calling Lake
Drift Pile River Ind. Res.
4,130 ft 1,259 m
Swan Hills
Freeman
Athabasca
Whitecourt
Barrhead
Westlock
Smoky Lake
Redwater
Mayerthorpe
Pembina
Morinville
Fort Saskatchewan
St. Albert
Edmonton
Sherwood Park
Elk Island Nat. P.
Wildwood
Wabamun L.
Wabamun Ind. Res.
Leduc
Drayton Valley
Beaverhill Lake
Wetaskiwin
Camrose
Samson Ind. Res.
Ponoka
Brazeau
Sunchild Ind. Res.
O'Chiese Ind. Res.
Nordegg
Lacombe
Rocky Mountain House
Alix
Stettler
Buffalo Lake
Red Deer
Innisfail
Clearwater
North Saskatchewan
Sullivan Lake
Olds
Three Hills
Banff
Red Deer
Drumheller
Airdrie
Stoney Ind. Res.
Cochrane
Exshaw
Banff
Canmore
Calgary
Strathmore
Mt. Assiniboine 11,870 ft 3,618 m
Sarcee Ind. Res.
Okotoks
Mt. Joffre 11,316 ft 3,449 m
Turner Valley
Siksika Ind. Res.
Bassano
Brooks
High River
Nanton
Vulcan
Little Bow
Claresholm
Farnham 11,638 ft 3,457 m
Kootenay
Oldman
Kimberley
Sparwood
Fernie
Coleman
Peigan Ind. Res.
Fort Macleod
Lethbridge
Coaldale
Taber
Bow Island
Bow
Medicine Hat
Pincher Creek
Raymond
Blood Ind. Res.
Waterton Lakes Nat. P.
Cardston
Cranbrook
Creston
Lake Koocanusa
Milk River
Etzikom Coulee
Milk
Foremost
Cypress Hills
4,816 ft 1,468 m
Conklin
Christina
Winefred Lake
Sand
Lac La Biche
Primrose Lake
Cold Lake
Beaver
Bonnyville
Grand Centre
White Fish L. Ind. Res.
Kehiwin Ind. Res.
St. Paul
Unipouheos Ind. Res.
Two Hills
Vegreville
Mannville
Vermilion
Viking
Battle
Killam
Forestburg
Wainwright
Provost
Castor
Coronation
Consort
3,000 ft 914 m
Hanna
Youngstown
Oyen
Alsask
Empress
Leader
South Saskatchewan
Lloydminster
Maidstone
2,800 ft 853 m
Peter Pond Lake
Peter Pond Lake Ind. Res.
Buffalo Narrows
Churchill Lake
Île-à-la-Crosse
Canoe Lake
Canoe Lake Ind. Res.
2,536 ft 773 m
Waterhen Ind. Res.
Waterhen
Meadow Lake
Seekaskootch Ind. Res.
St. Walburg
Frenchman Butte
North Saskatchewan
Manitou L.
Sweet Grass Ind. Res.
Battleford
North Battleford
Unity
Wilkie
Red Pheasant Ind. Res.
Macklin
Kerrobert
Kindersley
Rosetown
Biggar
Eagle Creek
2,515 ft 767 m
Elrose
Beechy
Great Sand Hills 2,464 ft 751 m
Pennant
Swift Current
Gull Lake
Maple Creek
Swift Current Creek
Shaunavon
Frenchman
Consul
Val Marie
Pinto Butte 3,438 ft 1,049 m
Lac Île-à-la-Crosse
Pinehouse Lake
Lac la Plonge
Beauval
Doré L.
Green Lake
Smoothstone L.
Thunder Hills 2,230 ft 680 m
Prince Albert Nat. P.
Big River
Big River Ind. Res.
Ahtahkakoop Ind. Res.
2,733 ft 833 m
Mistawasis Ind. Res.
Shellbrook
Jackfish Lake
Blaine Lake
Rosthern
Martensville
Saskatoon
Saskatchewan
Outlook
Young
Davidson
Craik
Lake Diefenbaker
Moose Jaw
Regina
Lumsden
Qu'Appelle
Old Wives Lake
Notukeu Cr.
Wood
Mossbank
Ponteix
Assiniboia
Grasslands Nat. P.
Pinehouse Lake
Nemeiben L.
La Ronge
Lac La Ronge
1,195 ft 364 m
Wapawekka Hills 2,612 ft 796 m
Montreal Lake
Montreal L. Ind. Res.
Candle L.
Torch
Prince Albert
Kinistino
James Smith Ind. Res.
South Saskatchewan
Wakaw
Humboldt
Lenore Lake
Watson
Big Quill Lake
Little Quill Lake
Wynyard
Poor Man Ind. Res.
Last Mountain Lake
Churchill
Pelican Narrows
Deschambault L.
Amisk L.
Choiceland
Tobin Lake
Nipawin
Carrot
Saskatchewan
Melfort
Tisdale
Red Deer
Kelvington 2,005 ft 611 m
Foam Lake
Ituna
Indian Head
2,225 ft 678 m
Assiniboine Ind. Res.
Avonlea
Weyburn
Radville
2,325 ft 708 m
Souris
Big Beaver
Crosby
C A N A D A
Alberta
Opheim
Scobey
Plentywood
Fort Peck Ind. Res.
Medicine Lake
Williston
2,000 ft 610 m
Poplar
Wolf Point
Glasgow
Missouri
Milk
Malta
Sidney
North Dakota
Fort Peck Lake
3,078 ft 938 m
Circle
Yellowstone
Big Dry Creek
Jordan
Glendive
Beach
3,635 ft 1,108 m
Terry
Baker
Melstone
Miles City
Forsyth
Colstrip
Rosebud Cr.
Tongue
Powder
Hardin
Northern Cheyenne Ind. Res.
Broadus
4,206 ft 1,282 m
Crow Indian Reservation
Bighorn
4,290 ft 1,308 m
Little Powder
Little Missouri
Belle Fourche
South Dakota
Bear Lodge Mts. 6,550 ft 2,026 m
Keyhole Res.
Gillette
Moorcroft
Upton
Sheridan
Bighorn Mts.
Cloud Peak 13,175 ft 4,016 m
Buffalo
Bighorn Lake
Red Lodge
Lovell
Powell
Cody
Greybull
Shoshone
Wyoming
Sweet Grass Hills 6,983 ft 2,128 m
Sunburst
Cut Bank
Shelby
Havre
Chinook
Lodge Creek
Battle Creek
Bear's Paw Mts.
Rocky Boy's Ind. Res.
6,916 ft 2,108 m
Fort Belknap Ind. Res.
Marias
Conrad
L. Elwell
Teton River
Fort Benton
Missouri
Great Falls
Judith
Stanford
Lewistown
Big Snowy Mts. 8,681 ft 2,646 m
Big Baldy Mtn. 9,175 ft 2,796 m
Little Belt Mts.
White Sulphur Springs
Mt. Edith 9,702 ft 2,957 m
Big Belt Mts.
Smith
Harlowton
Roundup
4,700 ft 1,433 m
Musselshell
Yellowstone
Billings
Laurel
Crazy Pk. 11,209 ft 3,416 m
Big Timber
Livingston
Bozeman
Belgrade
Absaroka Range
Granite Peak 12,798 ft 3,901 m
Clarks Fork
Yellowstone Lake
Yellowstone Nat. Park
Hilgard Pk. 11,316 ft 3,449 m
Madison
Jefferson
Mt. Cleveland 10,466 ft 3,184 m
Blackfeet Glacier Nat. Park
Browning
Eureka
Whitefish
Kalispell
Flathead Lake
Lewis Range
Swan Range
S. F. Flathead
Old Baldy 9,156 ft 2,793 m
McDonald Pk. 10,299 ft 3,139 m
Flathead Ind. Res.
Polson
Salish Mts.
Bonners Ferry
6,991 ft 2,139 m
Libby
Cabinet Mts.
Snowshoe Pk. 8,738 ft 2,663 m
Sandpoint
7,464 ft 2,275 m
Clark Fork
Thompson Falls
St. Maries
Wallace
St. Joe
7,543 ft 2,299 m
Superior
Missoula
N. F. Clearwater
Holter Lake
Helena
Canyon Ferry Lake
Townsend
Garrison
Deer Lodge
Philipsburg
Anaconda
Butte
Clark Fork
Bitterroot
Hamilton
Orofino
Lochsa
Clearwater Mountains
Selway
El Capitan 9,920 ft 3,024 m
Grangeville
Buffalo Hump 8,924 ft 2,720 m
Bitterroot Range
Big Hole
Tweedy Mtn. 11,155 ft 3,400 m
Dillon
Salmon
Salmon River Mountains
M. F. Salmon
McCall
Cascade Res.
Twin Peaks 10,340 ft 3,152 m
Challis
10,985 ft 3,348 m
Garfield Mtn.
Lima
Red Rock
10,961 ft 3,341 m
Montana
Idaho
U N I T E D S T A T E S
52° 48° 44°
2 3 4 5
86
94
116° E 112° F 91 108° G 94

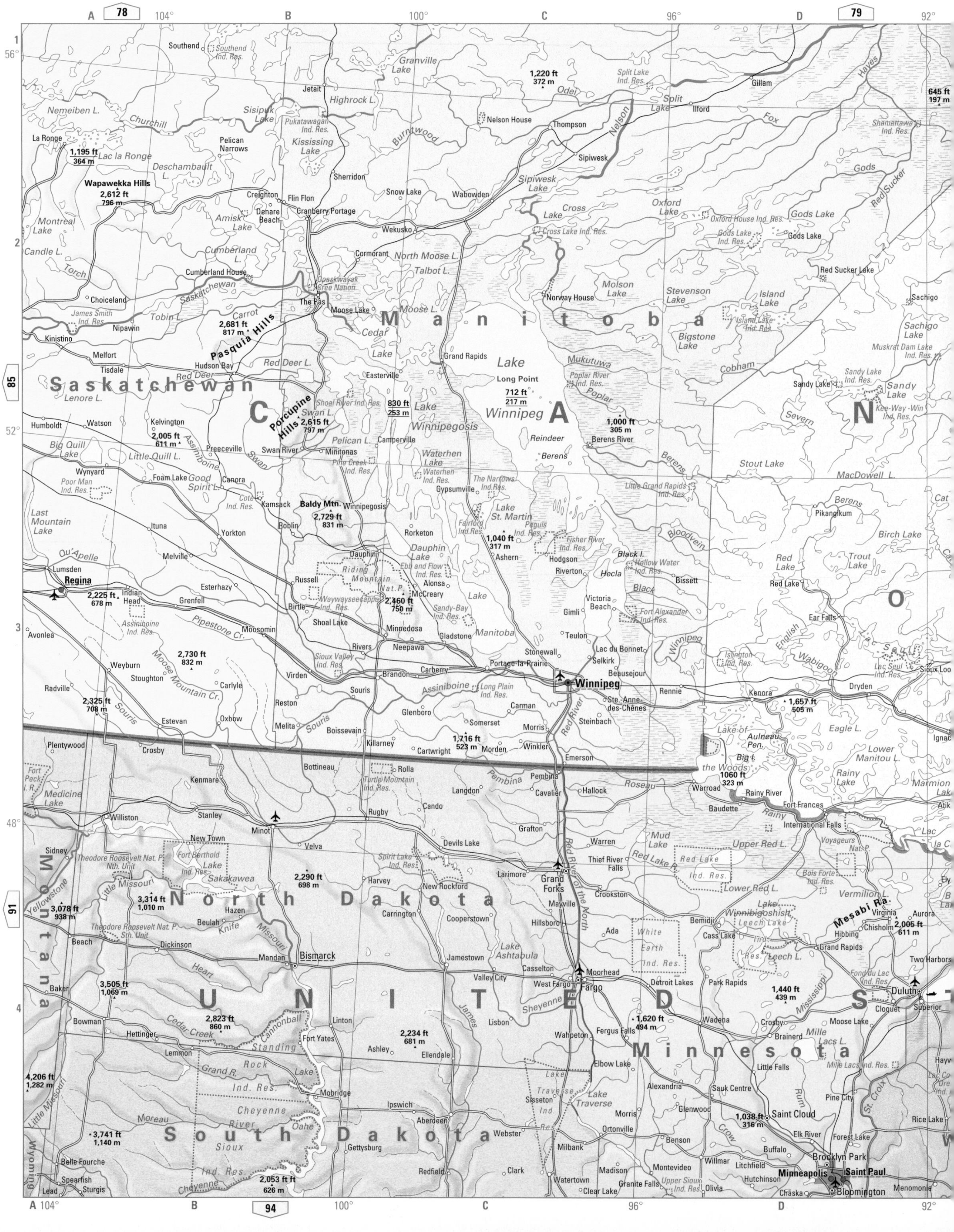

A 78 104° B 100° C 96° D 79 92°

Southend
Southend Ind. Res.
Granville Lake
1,220 ft 372 m
Split Lake Ind. Res.
Gillam
Hayes
645 ft 197 m
Jetait
Highrock L.
Odei
Split Lake
Ilford
Nemeiben L.
Sisipuk Lake
Churchill
Pukatawagan Ind. Res.
Nelson House
Thompson
Nelson
Fox
Shamattawa Ind. Res.
La Ronge
Pelican Narrows
Kississing Lake
Burntwood
1,195 ft 364 m
Lac la Ronge
Sipiwesk
Deschambault L.
Sherridon
Gods
Wapawekka Hills
2,612 ft 796 m
Creighton
Flin Flon
Snow Lake
Wabowden
Sipiwesk Lake
Red Sucker
Oxford Lake
Montreal Lake
Amisk Lake
Denare Beach
Cranberry Portage
Cross Lake
Oxford House Ind. Res.
Gods Lake
Gods Lake Ind. Res.
Gods Lake
Wekusko
Cross Lake Ind. Res.
Candle L.
Cumberland L.
Cormorant
North Moose L.
Talbot L.
Torch
Cumberland House
Opaskwayak Cree Nation
Molson Lake
Red Sucker Lake
Saskatchewan
Choiceland
The Pas
Norway House
Stevenson Lake
Island Lake
Sachigo
James Smith Ind. Res.
Tobin L.
Carrot
Moose Lake
Moose L.
Island Lake Ind. Res.
Sachigo Lake
Nipawin
2,681 ft 817 m
Pasquia Hills
Cedar
Manitoba
Kinistino
Lake
Bigstone Lake
Muskrat Dam Lake Ind. Res.
Melfort
Grand Rapids
Lake
Mukutuwa
Hudson Bay
Red Deer L.
Cobham
Tisdale
Red Deer
Easterville
Long Point
Poplar River Ind. Res.
Sandy Lake Ind. Res.
Sandy Lake
Sandy Lake
Saskatchewan
Lenore L.
712 ft 217 m
Poplar
Shoal River Ind. Res.
Swan L.
Porcupine Hills
830 ft 253 m
Lake
Winnipeg
Kee-Way-Win Ind. Res.
Severn
C
A
N
Humboldt
Watson
Kelvington
2,615 ft 797 m
Winnipegosis
1,000 ft 305 m
2,005 ft 611 m
Reindeer
Berens River
Pelican L.
Camperville
Berens
Big Quill Lake
Little Quill L.
Assiniboine
Preeceville
Swan River
Minitonas
Stout Lake
Swan
Pine Creek Ind. Res.
Waterhen Lake
Wynyard
Waterhen Ind. Res.
The Narrows Ind. Res.
Berens
MacDowell L.
Foam Lake
Good Spirit L.
Canora
Gypsumville
Little Grand Rapids Ind. Res.
Poor Man Ind. Res.
Cote Ind. Res.
Kamsack
Baldy Mtn.
Winnipegosis
Lake St. Martin
Berens
Pikangikum
Cat
2,729 ft 831 m
Last Mountain Lake
Ituna
Yorkton
Roblin
Rorketon
Fairford Ind. Res.
Peguis Ind. Res.
Fisher River Ind. Res.
Bloodvein
Birch Lake
1,040 ft 317 m
Dauphin Lake
Ashern
Hodgson
Qu'Appelle
Melville
Dauphin
Black I.
Red Lake
Trout Lake
Lumsden
Riding Mountain Nat. P.
Ebb and Flow Ind. Res.
Hollow Water Ind. Res.
Regina
Russell
Riverton
Hecla
Bissett
Red Lake
2,225 ft 678 m
Indian Head
Esterhazy
Alonsa
Black
McCreary
Victoria Beach
O
Waywayseecappo Ind. Res.
Lake
Grenfell
Birtle
2,460 ft 750 m
Sandy-Bay Ind. Res.
Gimli
Fort Alexander Ind. Res.
Ear Falls
Assiniboine Ind. Res.
Pipestone Cr.
Shoal Lake
Avonlea
Moosomin
Minnedosa
Gladstone
Manitoba
Teulon
English
Lac Seul
Moose Mountain Cr.
Rivers
Neepawa
Lac du Bonnet
Winnipeg
2,730 ft 832 m
Sioux Valley Ind. Res.
Stonewall
Selkirk
Islington Ind. Res.
Wabigoon
Weyburn
Stoughton
Carlyle
Virden
Brandon
Carberry
Portage-la-Prairie
Beausejour
Lac Seul Ind. Res.
Sioux Lookout
Winnipeg
Radville
Souris
Assiniboine
Long Plain Ind. Res.
Rennie
Kenora
Dryden
2,325 ft 708 m
Souris
Carman
Ste. Anne-des-Chênes
1,657 ft 505 m
Reston
Red River
Glenboro
Steinbach
Estevan
Oxbow
Melita
Souris
Somerset
Lake of the Woods
Aulneau Pen.
Eagle L.
Boissevain
Morris
Ignace
Plentywood
Crosby
Killarney
1,716 ft 523 m
Cartwright
Morden
Winkler
Big I.
Lower Manitou L.
Emerson
Fort Peck I. R.
Bottineau
Rolla
1060 ft 323 m
Rainy Lake
Kenmare
Turtle Mountain Ind. Res.
Pembina
Pembina
Cavalier
Hallock
Roseau
Warroad
Rainy River
Marmion Lake
Medicine Lake
Langdon
Cando
Baudette
Fort Frances
Atikokan
Williston
Stanley
Minot
Rugby
Rainy
International Falls
Grafton
Lac la Croix
New Town
Velva
Devils Lake
Warren
Mud Lake
Upper Red L.
Voyageurs Nat. P.
Sidney
Theodore Roosevelt Nat. P. Nth. Unit
Fort Berthold Lake Ind. Res.
Spirit Lake Ind. Res.
Thief River Falls
Red Lake R.
Red Lake Ind. Res.
Bois Forte Ind. Res.
Ely
Sakakawea
Harvey
Larimore
Grand Forks
Red River of the North
Lower Red L.
2,290 ft 698 m
New Rockford
Vermilion L.
Montana
Yellowstone
Little Missouri
3,314 ft 1,010 m
North Dakota
Crookston
Mesabi Ra.
Aurora
3,078 ft 938 m
Hazen
Carrington
Mayville
Lake Winnibigoshish
Virginia
Beulah
Knife
Missouri
Cooperstown
Bemidji
Leech Lake Ind. Res.
Chisholm
2,005 ft 611 m
Theodore Roosevelt Nat. P. Sth. Unit
Hillsboro
Ada
White Earth Ind. Res.
Cass Lake
Hibbing
Beach
Dickinson
Mandan
Bismarck
Jamestown
Lake Ashtabula
Leech L.
Grand Rapids
Two Harbors
Heart
Valley City
Casselton
Moorhead
Fond du Lac Ind. Res.
Baker
3,505 ft 1,069 m
West Fargo
Fargo
Detroit Lakes
Park Rapids
1,440 ft 439 m
Duluth
Superior
UNITED STATES
Sheyenne
Mississippi
Cloquet
Bowman
2,823 ft 860 m
Cedar Creek
Cannonball
Linton
Lisbon
1,620 ft 494 m
Wadena
Crosby
Moose Lake
Hettinger
Standing Rock Ind. Res.
Fort Yates
2,234 ft 681 m
Wahpeton
Fergus Falls
Brainerd
Mille Lacs L.
Lemmon
Ashley
Ellendale
James
Minnesota
Grand R.
Lake
Elbow Lake
Little Falls
Mille Lacs Ind. Res.
4,206 ft 1,282 m
Mobridge
Lake Traverse Ind. Res.
Alexandria
Sauk Centre
Rum
Little Missouri
Cheyenne River
Oahe
Ipswich
Sisseton
Traverse
Morris
Glenwood
Pine City
St. Croix
Moreau
Aberdeen
1,038 ft 316 m
Saint Cloud
Rice Lake
3,741 ft 1,140 m
South Dakota
Webster
Ortonville
Benson
Crow
Elk River
Forest Lake
Sioux
Gettysburg
Milbank
Buffalo
Brooklyn Park
Wyoming
Belle Fourche
Ind. Res.
Redfield
Clark
Madison
Montevideo
Willmar
Litchfield
Minneapolis
Saint Paul
Spearfish
Lead
Sturgis
Cheyenne
2,053 ft 626 m
Watertown
Clear Lake
Granite Falls
Upper Sioux Ind. Res.
Olivia
Hutchinson
Chaska
Bloomington
Menomonie

85 91 1 2 3 4 56° 52° 48°

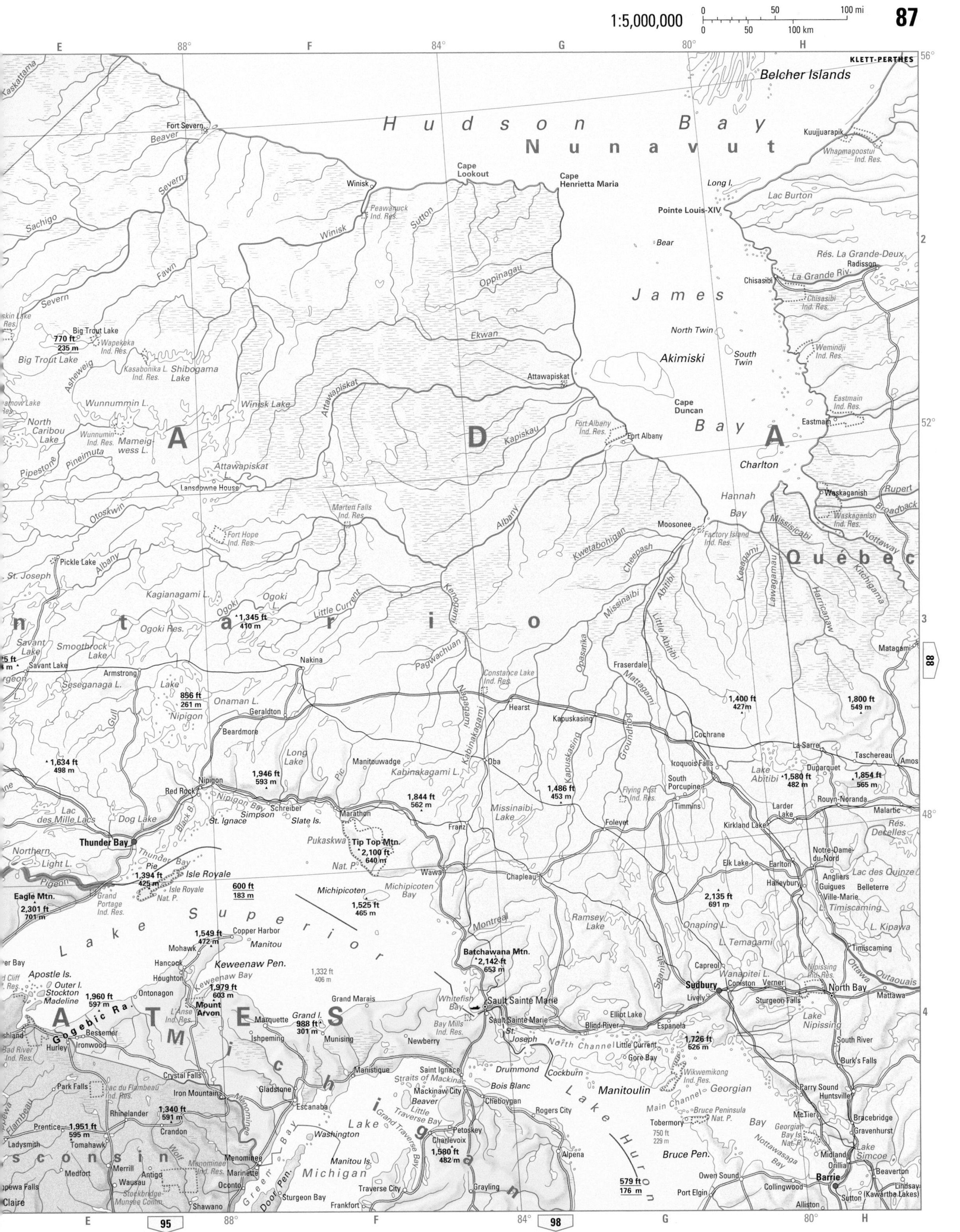
KLETT-PERTHES
Hudson Bay
Nunavut
Belcher Islands
Kuujjuarapik
Whapmagoostui Ind. Res.
Fort Severn
Beaver
Severn
Sachigo
Winisk
Peawanuck Ind. Res.
Sutton
Cape Lookout
Cape Henrietta Maria
Long I.
Lac Burton
Pointe Louis-XIV
Bear
Rés. La Grande-Deux
Radisson
Chisasibi
La Grande Riv.
Chisasibi Ind. Res.
James Bay
North Twin
South Twin
Akimiski
Wemindji Ind. Res.
Oppinagau
Ekwan
Fawn
Big Trout Lake
770 ft
235 m
Wapekeka Ind. Res.
Asheweig
Kasabonika L. Ind. Res.
Shibogama Lake
Attawapiskat
Winisk Lake
Wunnummin L.
North Caribou Lake
Wunnumin Ind. Res.
Mameigwess L.
Pipestone
Pineimuta
Attawapiskat L.
Lansdowne House
Cape Duncan
Eastmain
Eastmain Ind. Res.
Fort Albany Ind. Res.
Fort Albany
Kapiskau
CANADA
Charlton
Hannah Bay
Waskaganish
Waskaganish Ind. Res.
Rupert
Broadback
Nottaway
Moosonee
Factory Island Ind. Res.
Missisicabi
Québec
Otoskwin
Marten Falls Ind. Res.
Fort Hope Ind. Res.
Albany
Kwetabohigan
Cheepash
Kesagami
Lawagamau
Harricanaw
Kitchigama
Pickle Lake
St. Joseph
Kagianagami L.
Ogoki
Ogoki L.
1,345 ft
410 m
Ogoki Res.
Little Current
Kenogami
Missinaibi
Abitibi
Little Abitibi
Ontario
Savant Lake
Smoothrock Lake
Armstrong
Nakina
Pagwachuan
Opasatika
Fraserdale
Mattagami
Matagami
Seseganaga L.
Lake Nipigon
856 ft
261 m
Onaman L.
Geraldton
Constance Lake Ind. Res.
Nagagami
Hearst
Kapuskasing
Groundhog
1,400 ft
427 m
1,800 ft
549 m
Gull
Beardmore
Long Lake
Manitouwadge
Kabinakagami
Kabinakagami L.
Oba
Cochrane
La Sarre
Taschereau
Amos
1,634 ft
498 m
Nipigon
Red Rock
Nipigon Bay
1,946 ft
593 m
Pic
1,844 ft
562 m
1,486 ft
453 m
Iroquois Falls
South Porcupine
Lake Abitibi
1,580 ft
482 m
Duparquet
1,854 ft
565 m
Rouyn-Noranda
Malartic
Flying Post Ind. Res.
Timmins
Larder Lake
Lac des Mille Lacs
Dog Lake
Black B.
Simpson
Schreiber
Slate Is.
Marathon
St. Ignace
Missinaibi Lake
Franz
Foleyet
Kirkland Lake
Rés. Decelles
Thunder Bay
Northern Light L.
Pukaskwa Nat. P.
Tip Top Mtn.
2,100 ft
640 m
Notre-Dame-du-Nord
Pigeon
Pie
1,394 ft
425 m
Isle Royale
Isle Royale Nat. P.
Grand Portage Ind. Res.
600 ft
183 m
Wawa
Chapleau
Elk Lake
Earlton
Haileybury
Angliers
Guigues
Ville-Marie
Lac des Quinze
Belleterre
L. Timiscaming
Eagle Mtn.
2,301 ft
701 m
Michipicoten
Michipicoten Bay
1,525 ft
465 m
2,135 ft
691 m
Lake Superior
1,549 ft
472 m
Copper Harbor
Manitou
Montreal
Ramsey Lake
Onaping L.
L. Temagami
L. Kipawa
Timiscaming
Batchawana Mtn.
2,142 ft
653 m
Mohawk
Hancock
Keweenaw Pen.
Keweenaw Bay
Houghton
Apostle Is.
Outer I.
Stockton
Madeline
1,960 ft
597 m
Ontonagon
1,979 ft
603 m
Mount Arvon
L'Anse Ind. Res.
1,332 ft
406 m
Spanish
Capreol
Wanapitei L.
Nipissing Ind. Res.
Ottawa
Outaouais
Grand Marais
Whitefish Bay
Sault Sainte Marie
Sudbury
Coniston
Verner
North Bay
Mattawa
Lively
Sturgeon Falls
Lake Nipissing
Gogebic Ra.
Bessemer
Hurley
Ironwood
Bad River Ind. Res.
Marquette
Ishpeming
Grand I.
988 ft
301 m
Munising
Bay Mills Ind. Res.
Newberry
St. Joseph
Elliot Lake
Blind River
Espanola
1,726 ft
526 m
North Channel
Little Current
Gore Bay
South River
Burk's Falls
UNITED STATES
Michigan
Crystal Falls
Park Falls
Lac du Flambeau Ind. Res.
Iron Mountain
Manistique
Saint Ignace
Straits of Mackinac
Mackinaw City
Drummond
Cockburn
Wikwemikong Ind. Res.
Manitoulin
Georgian Bay
Bois Blanc
Cheboygan
Beaver
Little Traverse Bay
Gladstone
Escanaba
Flambeau
Rhinelander
1,340 ft
591 m
Menominee
Rogers City
Main Channel
Bruce Peninsula Nat. P.
Tobermory
750 ft
229 m
Parry Sound
Huntsville
McTier
Bracebridge
Gravenhurst
Prentice
1,951 ft
595 m
Crandon
Grand Traverse Bay
Washington
Petoskey
Charlevoix
1,580 ft
482 m
Lake Huron
Georgian Bay Is. Nat. P.
Nottawasaga Bay
Lake Simcoe
Ladysmith
Tomahawk
Wolf
Menominee Ind. Res.
Manitou Is.
Alpena
Bruce Pen.
Midland
Orillia
Wisconsin
Medford
Merrill
Antigo
Wausau
Menominee
Marinette
Green Bay
Door Pen.
Lake Michigan
Owen Sound
Collingwood
Beaverton
Barrie
Lindsay (Kawartha Lakes)
Sutton
Stockbridge-Munsee Comm.
Oconto
Traverse City
Grayling
579 ft
176 m
Port Elgin
Alliston
Claire
Shawano
Sturgeon Bay
Frankfort
E
F
G
H
88°
84°
80°
56°
52°
48°
2
3
4
88
95
98

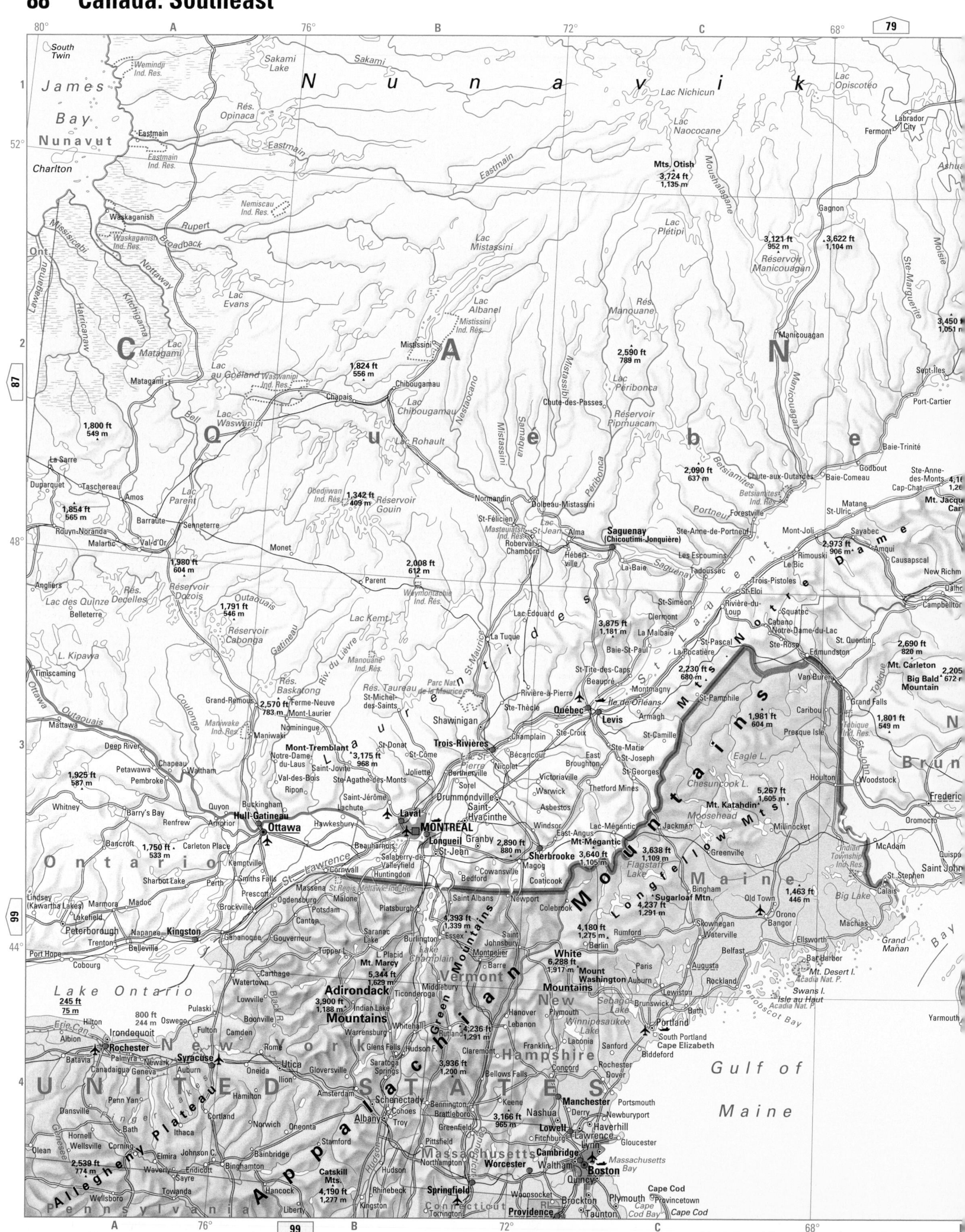
80°
A
76°
B
72°
C
68°
79
87
99
1
2
3
4
52°
48°
44°
South Twin
Wemindji Ind. Res.
James Bay
Nunavut
Eastmain
Eastmain Ind. Res.
Charlton
Sakami Lake
Sakami
Nunavik
Lac Nichicun
Lac Opiscotéo
Labrador City
Fermont
Rés. Opinaca
Eastmain
Lac Naococane
Mts. Otish
3,724 ft
1,135 m
Mouchalagane
Nemiscau Ind. Res.
Waskaganish
Waskaganish Ind. Res.
Rupert
Broadback
Missisicabi
Nottaway
Ont.
Lac Mistassini
Lac Plétipi
Gagnon
3,121 ft
952 m
3,622 ft
1,104 m
Réservoir Manicouagan
Moisie
Ste-Marguerite
Lawagamau
Harricanaw
Kitchigama
Lac Evans
Lac Albanel
Mistissini Ind. Rés.
Rés. Manouane
3,450 ft
1,051 m
Lac Matagami
Mistissini
Canada
Manicouagan
2,590 ft
789 m
Matagami
Lac au Goéland
Waswanipi Ind. Res.
1,824 ft
556 m
Chibougamau
Chapais
Lac Chibougamau
Nestaocano
Mistassibi
Lac Péribonca
Sept-Îles
Port-Cartier
Bell
Lac Waswanipi
1,800 ft
549 m
Lac Rohault
Mistassini
Samaqua
Chute-des-Passes
Réservoir Pipmuacan
Québec
La Sarre
2,090 ft
637 m
Betsiamites
Chute-aux-Outardes
Baie-Trinité
Godbout
Baie-Comeau
Ste-Anne-des-Monts
Cap-Chat
Duparquet
Taschereau
Amos
Lac Parent
Obedjiwan Ind. Rés.
1,342 ft
409 m
Réservoir Gouin
Normandin
Dolbeau-Mistassini
Péribonca
Betsiamites Ind. Res.
Forestville
Matane
St-Ulric
Mt. Jacques Cartier
1,854 ft
565 m
Barraute
Senneterre
St-Félicien
Mashteuiatsh Ind. Rés.
Lac St-Jean
Alma
Saguenay (Chicoutimi-Jonquière)
Portneuf
Ste-Anne-de-Portneuf
Mont-Joli
Sayabec
Rouyn-Noranda
Malartic
Val-d'Or
Monet
Roberval
Chambord
Hébertville
Les Escoumins
2,973 ft
906 m
Amqui
Causapscal
Rimouski
Le Bic
1,980 ft
604 m
Réservoir Dozois
2,008 ft
612 m
La-Baie
Saguenay
Tadoussac
New Richmond
Angliers
Rés. Decelles
Parent
Weymontachie Ind. Rés.
Trois-Pistoles
St-Éloi
Lac des Quinze
Belleterre
Outaouais
1,791 ft
546 m
Réservoir Cabonga
Lac Kemt
Lac Édouard
St-Siméon
Rivière-du-Loup
Squatec
Campbellton
Dalhousie
3,875 ft
1,181 m
Clermont
La Malbaie
Cabano
Notre-Dame-du-Lac
Ste-Rose
St. Quentin
2,690 ft
820 m
L. Kipawa
Gatineau
Riv. du Lièvre
Manouane Ind. Rés.
La Tuque
St-Maurice
Baie-St-Paul
St-Pascal
La Pocatière
Edmundston
Mt. Carleton
Big Bald Mountain
2,205 ft
672 m
Timiscaming
Rés. Baskatong
Rés. Taureau
Parc Nat. de la Mauricie
St-Tite-des-Caps
Beaupré
2,230 ft
680 m
Van Buren
Tobique
Ottawa
Coulonge
Grand-Remous
2,570 ft
783 m
Ferme-Neuve
Mont-Laurier
St-Michel-des-Saints
Rivière-à-Pierre
Ste-Thècle
Québec
Île de Orléans
Montmagny
St-Pamphile
Grand Falls
Outaouais
Mattawa
Maniwaki Ind. Res.
Maniwaki
Nominingue
Shawinigan
Lévis
Armagh
1,981 ft
604 m
Caribou
1,801 ft
549 m
Tobique Ind. Res.
Deep River
Mont-Tremblant
3,175 ft
968 m
Notre-Dame-du-Laus
St-Donat
St-Côme
Trois-Rivières
Champlain
Ste-Croix
St-Camille
Presque Isle
Chapeau
Petawawa
Pembroke
Waltham
Val-des-Bois
Saint-Jovite
Ste-Agathe-des-Monts
Joliette
Lac St-Pierre
Berthierville
Bécancour
Nicolet
Sorel
Ste-Marie
St-Joseph
East Broughton
St-Georges
Eagle L.
Brunswick
1,925 ft
587 m
Ripon
Drummondville
Victoriaville
Warwick
Thetford Mines
Chesuncook L.
Houlton
Woodstock
Fredericton
Whitney
Barry's Bay
Renfrew
Quyon
Buckingham
Hull-Gatineau
Arnprior
Ottawa
Saint-Jérôme
Lachute
Hawkesbury
Laval
MONTRÉAL
Saint-Hyacinthe
Asbestos
5,267 ft
1,605 m
Mt. Katahdin
Moosehead Lake
Millinocket
Oromocto
Bancroft
1,750 ft
533 m
Carleton Place
Beauharnois
Longueuil
Granby
Windsor
East-Angus
Lac-Mégantic
Mt-Mégantic
Jackman
Longfellow Mts.
Indian Township Ind. Res.
McAdam
Ontario
Kemptville
Salaberry-de-Valleyfield
St-Jean
2,890 ft
880 m
Sherbrooke
3,640 ft
1,105 m
3,638 ft
1,109 m
Greenville
Sharbot Lake
Perth
Smiths Falls
St. Lawrence
Cornwall
Huntingdon
Cowansville
Magog
Coaticook
Flagstaff Lake
Maine
Bingham
St. Stephen
Calais
Saint John
Quispamsis
Lindsay (Kawartha Lakes)
Marmora
Madoc
Prescott
Massena
St. Regis Mohawk Ind. Res.
Malone
Bedford
Saint Albans
Newport
Colebrook
Sugarloaf Mtn.
4,237 ft
1,291 m
Old Town
1,463 ft
446 m
Big Lake
Lakefield
Brockville
Ogdensburg
Potsdam
Plattsburgh
4,393 ft
1,339 m
Green Mountains
Orono
Bangor
Machias
Peterborough
Napanee
Kingston
Canton
Saranac Lake
Burlington
Essex
Saint Johnsbury
4,180 ft
1,275 m
Berlin
Rumford
Skowhegan
Waterville
Ellsworth
Grand Manan
Bay of Fundy
Trenton
Belleville
Gananoque
Gouverneur
Tupper L.
Lake Placid
Lake Champlain
Montpelier
Barre
White Mountains
6,288 ft
1,917 m
Mount Washington
Belfast
Port Hope
Cobourg
Mt. Marcy
5,344 ft
1,629 m
Vermont
Paris
Augusta
Bar Harbor
Mt. Desert I.
Acadia Nat. P.
Carthage
Watertown
Adirondack Mountains
Ticonderoga
Middlebury
Auburn
Rockland
Lake Ontario
245 ft
75 m
Lowville
3,900 ft
1,188 m
Indian Lake
Lewiston
Swans I.
Isle au Haut
Acadia Nat. P.
Pulaski
800 ft
244 m
Oswego
Black R.
Boonville
Hanover
Lebanon
New Hampshire
Plymouth
Sebago Lake
Brunswick
Bath
Penobscot Bay
Yarmouth
Hilton
Erie Canal
Albion
Irondequoit
Rochester
Fulton
Camden
Whitehall
Warrensburg
Rutland
4,236 ft
1,291 m
Winnipesaukee Lake
Portland
South Portland
Cape Elizabeth
Batavia
Palmyra
Newark
Syracuse
New York
Rome
Glens Falls
Hudson F.
Claremont
Franklin
Laconia
Sanford
Biddeford
Canandaigua
Geneva
Auburn
Oneida
Utica
Saratoga Springs
3,936 ft
1,200 m
Bellows Falls
Concord
Rochester
Dover
Gulf of Maine
Ilion
Gloversville
UNITED STATES
Hamilton
Amsterdam
Schenectady
Keene
Manchester
Portsmouth
Dansville
Penn Yan
Finger Lakes
Cortland
Cohoes
Troy
Albany
Bennington
Brattleboro
Nashua
Derry
Newburyport
Bath
Norwich
Oneonta
Greenfield
3,166 ft
965 m
Lowell
Haverhill
Hornell
Wellsville
Corning
Ithaca
Allegheny Plateau
Stamford
Pittsfield
Fitchburg
Lawrence
Lynn
Gloucester
Olean
Genesee
Elmira
Johnson C.
Bainbridge
Appalachian Mountains
Massachusetts
Northampton
Worcester
Cambridge
Waltham
Boston
Massachusetts Bay
2,539 ft
774 m
Waverly
Endicott
Sayre
Binghamton
Hudson
Catskill Mts.
4,190 ft
1,277 m
Quincy
Cape Cod
Provincetown
Towanda
Wellsboro
Pennsylvania
Hancock
Liberty
Kingston
Rhinebeck
Springfield
Connecticut
Torrington
Woonsocket
Providence
Brockton
Taunton
Plymouth
Cape Cod Bay
Cape Cod
A
76°
99
B
72°
C
68°

Labrador
(Nunatsiavut)
Newfoundland and Labrador
Mealy Mountains
Churchill Falls
Happy Valley-Goose Bay
Port Hope Simpson
Belle Isle
Cape Bauld
St. Anthony
Red Bay
Forteau
Blanc-Sablon
Strait of Belle Isle
St-Augustin
Grey Islands
Englee
Long Range Mountains
Harrington Harbour
Natashquan
La Romaine
Havre-St-Pierre
Rivière-au-Tonnerre
Détroit de Jacques-Cartier
Port-Menier
Île d'Anticosti
Baie-du-Renard
Détroit d'Honguedo
Gaspé
Parc National du Canada Forillon
Chandler
Gulf of Saint Lawrence
Îles de la Madeleine
Île du Havre Aubert
Cap-aux-Meules
Brion
Miscou
Île Lamèque
Shippagan
Tracadie-Sheila
Horse Is.
White Bay
Baie Verte
New World I.
Fogo
Funk I.
Notre Dame Bay
Gros Morne Nat. P.
Springdale
Deer Lake
Lewisporte
Gander
Badger
Bishop's Falls
Grand Falls-Windsor
Gambo
Bonavista Bay
Bonavista
Terra Nova Nat. P.
Corner Brook
Grand Lake
Lewis Hills
Stephenville
Newfoundland
Clarenville-Shoal Harbour
St. George's Bay
Blue Hills of Couteau
Maelpaeg Res.
St. Alban's
Trinity Bay
Carbonear
Bay Roberts
St. John's
Conception Bay South
Mt. Pearl
Merasheen I.
C. Ray
Channel-Port aux Basques
Burgeo
Harbour Breton
Fortune Bay
Placentia Bay
Dunville
Avalon Pen.
Marystown
Grand Bank
Miquelon
St. Pierre and Miquelon (FRA.)
St-Pierre
St. Mary's Bay
Cape Race
Cabot Strait
St. Paul
C. North
White Hill
Cape Breton Highlands Nat. P.
Prince Edward Island
Prince Edward Island Nat. P.
Tignish
Summerside
Charlottetown
Souris
Georgetown
Northumberland Strait
Moncton
Shediac
Riverview
Sackville
Port Elgin
Amherst
Sussex
Fundy Nat. P.
Pictou
Antigonish
New Glasgow
Truro
Nova Scotia
Inverness
Sydney Mines
Sydney
Glace Bay
Baddeck
Whycocomagh Ind. Res.
Bras d'Or Lake
Eskasoni Ind. Res.
Cape Breton
Cape Breton Island
Port Hawkesbury
I. Madame
Str. of Canso
Kentville
Windsor
Indian Brook Ind. Res.
Sheet Harbour
Dartmouth
Halifax
Bridgewater
Liverpool
Sable I.
Sable
ATLANTIC OCEAN
KLETT-PERTHES

84
92
A
B
C
D
124°
120°
116°
48°
44°
40°
1
2
3
4
British Columbia
CANADA
Washington
Oregon
UNITED
Nevada
California
Idaho
PACIFIC OCEAN
Vancouver Island
Vancouver
Burnaby
Surrey
Chilliwack
Abbotsford
Hope
Princeton
Penticton
Nelson
Fernie
Cranbrook
Castlegar
Trail
Salmo
Creston
Tofino
Port Alberni
Parksville
Nanaimo
Ucluelet
Pacific Rim Nat. Park
Barkley Sound
Ladysmith
Duncan
Port Renfrew
Sidney
Saanich
Victoria
Strait of Georgia
Strait of Juan de Fuca
Makah Ind. Res.
Sekiu
Oak Harbor
Port Townsend
Port Angeles
Olympic Nat. P.
Mt. Olympus
7,966 ft
2,428 m
Lynden
Bellingham
Anacortes
Mt. Vernon
Mt. Baker
10,777 ft
3,285 m
Keremeos
Oliver
Osoyoos
7,201 ft
2,195 m
North Cascades Nat. P.
Okanogan Ra.
Mt. Bonaparte
7,257 ft
2,212 m
Grand Forks
Kettle River Ra.
Monashee Mts.
Selkirk Mts
Mt. Evans
9,500 ft
2,865 m
Marysville
Everett
Glacier Peak
10,541 ft
3,213 m
Lake Chelan
Chelan
Omak
Colville
Colville Ind. Res.
F. D. Roosevelt Lake
Spokane Ind. Res.
6,837 ft
2,084 m
Priest Lake
Bonners Ferry
Sandpoint
Newport
Bellevue
Seattle
Kent
Federal Way
Tacoma
Puyallup
Lakewood
Bremerton
Shelton
Quinault Ind. Res.
Hoquiam
Elma
Aberdeen
Olympia
Grays Harbor
Willapa Bay
South Bend
Long Beach
Centralia
Chehalis
Leavenworth
Mt. Stuart
9,415 ft
2,870 m
Cle Elum
Wenatchee
Ephrata
Coulee Dam
Grand Coulee
Banks Lake
Wilbur
Davenport
Spokane
Medical Lake
Cheney
Odessa
Coeur d'Alene
Coeur d'Alene Ind. Res.
Post Falls
L. Pend Oreille
Mt. Rainier
14,410 ft
4,392 m
Mount Rainier Nat. P.
Ellensburg
Potholes Res.
Moses Lake
Ritzville
Othello
St. Maries
St. Joe
Palouse
Pullman
Moscow
Morton
3,110 ft
948 m
Cowlitz
Yakima
Selah
Yakima Ind. Res.
Toppenish
Sunnyside
Richland
Prosser
Pasco
Kennewick
Mt. St. Helens
8,366 ft
2,550 m
Mt. Adams
12,277 ft
3,742 m
Astoria
Seaside
Longview
3,283 ft
1001 m
St. Helens
Lewis
Hillsboro
Vancouver
Portland
Camas
Tillamook
White Salmon
Hood River
The Dalles
Goldendale
Arlington
Gresham
Mt. Hood
11,240 ft
3,428 m
McMinnville
Woodburn
Silverton
Salem
Dallas
Lincoln City
Newport
Toledo
Corvallis
Albany
Lebanon
Mill City
Warm Springs Ind. Res.
10,497 ft
3,199 m
Mt. Jefferson
Madras
4,097 ft
1,249 m
Sweet Home
Junction C.
Florence
Eugene
Springfield
10,358 ft
3,157 m
Redmond
Prineville
Bend
Cottage Grove
Drain
Reedsport
Oakridge
Umpqua
5,960 ft
1,817 m
Coos Bay
Coquille
Myrtle Point
Roseburg
Myrtle Creek
Cape Blanco
Port Orford
Rogue
Crater Lake Nat. Park
Mt. Thielson
9,182 ft
2,799 m
8,926 ft
2,721 m
Crescent
7,984 ft
2,433 m
Fremont Mts.
Grants Pass
Gold Beach
5,098 ft
1,554 m
Brookings
Mt. McLoughlin
9,495 ft
2,894 m
Medford
Ashland
Upper Klamath Lake
Klamath Falls
Bly
Gearhart Mtn.
8,364 ft
2,549 m
Summer Lake
Lake Albert
8,017 ft
2,444 m
Lakeview
Heppner
Pilot Rock
Pendleton
Hermiston
Umatilla Ind. Res.
Milton-Freewater
Walla Walla
Columbia
Dayton
Pomeroy
6,387 ft
1,947 m
Blue Mountains
Gde. Ronde
La Grande
Joseph
Wallowa Mts.
Eagle Cap
9,595 ft
2,924 m
Powder
Baker C.
Hells Canyon
Snake
5,112 ft
1,558 m
N.F. John Day
John Day
Deschutes
6,871 ft
2,094 m
Canyon City
Strawberry Mtn.
9,038 ft
2,755 m
Seneca
Crooked
6,385 ft
1,940 m
Great Sandy Desert
Harney Basin
Burns
Malheur
Malheur Lake
Harney Lake
Steens Mtn.
9,721 ft
2,963 m
Cascade Res.
Weiser
Payette
Ontario
Vale
Nyssa
Emmett
Caldwell
Boise
Nampa
Lake Owyhee
Owyhee
Jordan Valley
Owyhee Mts.
8,403 ft
2,561 m
Mountain Home
Bruneau
Gooding
Jerome
Buhl
Twin Falls
Burley
Snake R.
Lewiston
Nez Perce Ind. Res.
Orofino
Clearwater Mountains
N.F. Clearwater
Lochsa
Selway
Grangeville
Buffalo Hump
8,924 ft
2,720 m
Salmon
Salmon River Mountains
McCall
M.F. Salmon
10,340 ft
3,152 m
10,985 ft
3,348 m
Twin Peaks
Challis
Sawtooth Ra.
Lost River
Borah Peak
12,662 ft
3,859 m
Payette
Hyndman Peak
12,078 ft
3,681 m
Ketchum
Hailey
Big Lost R.
Craters of the Moon Nat. Mon.
American
Bitterroot
El Capitan
9,920 ft
3,024 m
Hamilton
Missoula
Philipsburg
Clark Fork
Superior
7,543 ft
2,299 m
Wallace
Thompson Falls
7,464 ft
2,275 m
Polson
Flathead Ind. Res.
McDonald Peak
10,299 ft
3,139 m
Flathead Lake
Kalispell
Whitefish
Swan Ra.
Salish Mts.
Cabinet Mts.
Libby
Snowshoe Peak
8,738 ft
2,663 m
6,991 ft
2,139 m
Eureka
Lake Koocanusa
10,466 ft
3,184 m
Mt. Cleveland
Glacier
Waterton Lakes Nat. P.
Coleman
Pincher Creek
Fort Macleod
Point St. George
Crescent City
Redwood Nat. P.
Yurok Ind. Res.
Hoopa Valley Ind. Res.
Yreka
Klamath
Clear Lake
Lava Beds Nat. Mon.
Goose Lake
Crane Mtn.
8,456 ft
2,577 m
Upper Alkali Lake
Middle Alkali Lake
Lower Alkali Lake
Warner Mts.
9,906 ft
3,019 m
Alturas
Weed
Mt. Shasta
14,162 ft
4,317 m
McKinleyville
Arcata
Eureka
Humboldt Bay
Fortuna
Rio Dell
9,002 ft
2,744 m
Clair Engle Lake
Weaverville
Shasta Lake
Shasta Lake
Burney
Redding
Lassen Volcanic Nat. P.
Cape Mendocino
Punta Gorda
4,088 ft
1,246 m
10,457 ft
3,187 m
Chester
Eagle Lake
Susanville
Honey Lake
Lake Almanor
Red Bluff
8,090 ft
2,466 m
Corning
Round Valley Ind. Res.
Orland
Quincy
8,370 ft
2,552 m
Paradise
Chico
Portola
Willows
Oroville
Fort Bragg
Mendocino
Willits
Ukiah
Clear Lake
Williams
Colusa
Grass Valley
Yuba City
Marysville
Lakeport
Point Arena
4,721 ft
1,439 m
Cloverdale
Healdsburg
Lake Berryessa
Woodland
Davis
Auburn
Roseville
Sacramento
Vacaville
Fairfield
Napa
Santa Rosa
Petaluma
S. Pablo Bay
Vallejo
Concord
Point Reyers
San Rafael
Stockton
Lodi
Ione
Stanislaus
Sonora
Yosemite Nat. P.
Mono Lake
Truckee
Squaw Valley
Lake Tahoe
South Lake Tahoe
6,230 ft
1,899 m
Freel Peak
10,880 ft
3,316 m
Incline Village-Crystal Bay
Carson City
Carson
Minden
Reno
Sparks
Sun Valley
Fernley
Silver Springs
Fallon
Fallon Ind. Res.
Yerington
Schurz
Walker River Ind. Res.
Walker Lake
Mt. Grant
10,912 ft
3,426 m
Hawthorne
Mina
Gabbs
Pyramid Lake
Pyramid Lake Ind. Res.
3,793 ft
1,156 m
Lovelock
Carson Sink
Stillwater Mts.
Humboldt Ra.
East Ra.
8,461 ft
2,579 m
9,050 ft
2,758 m
Gerlach-Empire
Rye Patch Res.
Black Rock Desert
Duffer Pk.
9,458 ft
2,883 m
Quinn
McDermitt
Fort McDermitt Ind. Res.
Santa Rosa Ra.
Granite Peak
9,779 ft
2,981 m
S. F. Owyhee
10,440 ft
3,182 m
Duck Valley Ind. Res.
Owyhee
Winnemucca
Humboldt
9,833 ft
2,997 m
Battle Mountain
9,680 ft
2,950 m
Carlin
Independence Mts.
Elko
Wells
Spring Creek
Matterhorn
10,839 ft
3,304 m
Pilot Peak
10,715 ft
3,266 m
West Wendover
Spruce Mtn.
10,263 ft
3,128 m
Ruby Mts.
11,249 ft
3,429 m
Shoshone Ra.
9,162 ft
2,792 m
Cortez Mts.
Mt. Callahan
10,187 ft
3,105 m
Cold Springs
Austin
Eureka
Diamond Mts.
10,614 ft
3,235 m
Cherry Creek
McGill
Ely
Egan Range
Schell Creek Range
11,890 ft
3,624 m
Haystack
12,100 ft
3,688 m
Deep Creek Ra.
Goshute Ind. Res.
10,313 ft
3,143 m
Shoshone Mts.
Reese
Toiyabe Ra.
Big Smokey Valley
Toquima Ra.
Mt. Jefferson
11,949 ft
3,642 m
Monitor Ra.
10,745 ft
3,275 m
Pancake Ra.
Currant Mtn.
11,513 ft
3,509 m
White River
Grant Ra.
Troy Peak
11,267 ft
3,434
Great Basin Nat. P.
Wheeler Pk.
13,061 ft
3,982 m
Snake Range
9,725 ft
2,964 m
9,783 ft
2,982 m
Tonopah
Warm Springs
Great
Salt
Des
Oakley
Cache Pk.
10,353 ft
3,155 m
Sierra Nevada
Cascade Range
Coast Ranges
KLETT-PERTHES

1:5,000,000
0 50 100 mi
0 50 100 km
112°
E
85
108°
F
104°
G
100° H
Lethbridge
4,816 ft
1,468 m
Shaunavon
Radville
Oxbow
Melita
Boissevain
Killarney
Foremost
Cypress Hills
Etzikom Coulee
Saskatchewan
Pinto Butte
3,438 ft
1,049 m
Souris
Estevan
Manitoba
Rolla
Alberta
CANADA
Consul
Frenchman
Val Marie
Grasslands Nat. P.
Big Beaver
2,325 ft
708 m
Bottineau
Turtle Mountain Ind. Res.
Milk River
Milk
Crosby
1
Sunburst
Sweet Grass Hills
6,983 ft
2,128 m
Lodge Creek
Battle Creek
Opheim
Scobey
Plentywood
Kenmare
Rugby
Cut Bank
Chinook
Fort Peck Ind. Res.
Medicine Lake
Shelby
Havre
Malta
Milk
2,000 ft
610 m
Poplar
Williston
Stanley
Minot
Velva
48°
Marias
L. Elwell
Rocky Boy's Ind. Res.
Bear's Paw Mts.
Fort Belknap Ind. Res.
Glasgow
Wolf Point
Missouri
Fort Berthold Ind. Res.
New Town
Lake Sakakawea
Harvey
2,290 ft
698 m
Conrad
6,916 ft
2,108 m
Sidney
Theodore Roosevelt Nat. P. N. Unit
Teton River
Missouri
Fort Benton
Little Missouri
North Dakota
3,314 ft
1,010 m
Fort Peck Lake
Great Falls
Big Dry Creek
Jordan
Circle
Beulah
Hazen
Knife
3,078 ft
938 m
Theodore Roosevelt Nat. P. S. Unit
Judith
Stanford
Lewistown
Glendive
Beach
Dickinson
Mandan
Bismarck
Big Baldy Mtn.
9,175 ft
2,796 m
Missouri
Little Belt Mts.
Big Belt Mts.
Smith
Montana
Big Snowy Mts.
8,681 ft
2,646 m
3,635 ft
1,108 m
Terry
Heart
Holter Lake
Melstone
3,505 ft
1,069 m
2,823 ft
860 m
Cannonball
Linton
Helena
Garrison
Canyon Ferry L.
White Sulphur Springs
Roundup
4,700 ft
1,433 m
Miles City
Baker
Fort Yates
Deer Lodge
Mt. Edith
9,702 ft
2,957 m
Harlowton
Yellowstone
Bowman
Hettinger
Cedar Creek
Standing
2
Townsend
Musselshell
Forsyth
Lemmon
Rock
Lake
Crazy Pk.
11,209 ft
3,416 m
Colstrip
Rosebud Cr.
Tongue
Grand R.
Ind. Res.
Mobridge
Butte
Belgrade
Big Timber
Billings
Laurel
Hardin
Powder
Cheyenne
Oahe
Jefferson
Madison
Bozeman
Livingston
Crow
Bighorn
Indian
Northern Cheyenne Ind. Res.
Moreau
River
Absaroka Range
Broadus
4,206 ft
1,282 m
Sioux
Dillon
Red Lodge
Granite Pk.
12,798 ft
3,901 m
Reservation
4,290 ft
1,308 m
Little Powder
3,741 ft
1,140 m
Ind. Res.
Bighorn Lake
Bighorn Mts.
Little Missouri
Hilgard Pk.
11,316 ft
3,449 m
Clarks F.
Sheridan
Belle Fourche
2,053 ft
626 m
Powell
Lovell
Bear Lodge Mts.
South Dakota
Pierre
Red Rock
Yellowstone
Powder
Keyhole Res.
Spearfish
Sturgis
1,570 ft
479 m
Garfield Mtn.
10,961 ft
3,341 m
Yellowstone Lake
Shoshone
Cody
Greybull
13,175 ft
4,016 m
Cloud Peak
Buffalo
Gillette
6,550 ft
2,026 m
Lead
Rapid City
Philip
Bad R.
44°
Nat. Park
Moorcroft
Upton
Black Hills
Mt. Rushmore Nat. Memorial
White R.
Ashton
Worland
Newcastle
7,242 ft
2,207 m
Grand Teton Nat. Park
Francs Pk.
13,153 ft
4,009 m
Wind Cave Nat. P.
Badlands Nat. P.
Pine Ridge
Rexburg
Gd. Teton
13,770 ft
4,197 m
9,872 ft
3,009 m
Owl Creek Mts.
Thermopolis
Hot Springs
3,410 ft
1,039 m
Rosebud Ind. Res.
Rosebud
6,410 ft
1,954 m
Idaho Falls
Jackson
Doubletop Peak
11,740 ft
3,578 m
Wind River
Boysen Res.
Midwest
Edgemont
Martin
Pine Ridge
Valentine
94
UNITED STATES
Wind River Range
Gannett Peak
13,804 ft
4,207 m
Wind
Ind. Res.
Riverton
Casper
Douglas
Lusk
Chadron
Gordon
Blackfoot
Fort Hall
Blackfoot Res.
Wyoming Ra.
Pinedale
Lander
Mills
6,135 ft
1,870 m
Pocatello
Wyoming
8,244 ft
2,513 m
Glendo Res.
Niobrara
3,400 ft
1,036 m
American Falls
McCammon
Soda Springs
11,378 ft
3,480 m
Wyoming Peak
9,554 ft
3,034 m
Laramie Mts.
Laramie Peak
10,297 ft
3,131 m
Alliance
4,203 ft
1,281 m
Thedford
3
Meade Peak
Green Mts.
9,215 ft
2,812 m
Pathfinder Res.
Shirley Mts.
Sweetwater
Torrington
Malad City
Montpelier
Seminoe Res.
9,151 ft
2,789 m
Wheatland
Scottsbluff
Nebraska
Preston
Wasatch Range
8,685 ft
2,647 m
Basin
Hanna
Hogback Mtn.
5,063 ft
1,543 m
Gering
Bridgeport
Richmond
Bear Lake
Kemmerer
Green River
Rawlins
North Platte
Lake McConaughy
Tremonton
Logan
Wellsville
Rock Springs
Green River
Medicine Bow Pk.
12,013 ft
3,661 m
Horse Creek
Brigham City
Lyman
Saratoga
Laramie
Kimball
Sidney
Ogallala
North Platte
9,764 ft
2,976 m
Evanston
Wyoming Basin
Cheyenne
Great Salt Lake
212 ft
283 m
Ogden
Flaming Gorge Res.
11,007 ft
3,354 m
Park Range
Medicine Bow Mts.
Julesburg
Grant
3,025 ft
922 m
Layton
Bountiful
13,528 ft
4,123 m
Mt. Zirkel
12,180 ft
3,712 m
Sterling
Imperial
Salt Lake City
Kings Peak
Uinta Mountains
Rocky Mountain Nat. Park
Fort Collins
Windsor
West Valley City
Sandy
West Jordan
Dinosaur Nat. Mon.
Craig
Estes Park
South Platte
American Fork
Vernal
Yampa
Steamboat Springs
Loveland
Greeley
Brush
Yuma
Wray
40°
Lehi
Orem
Provo
Uintah
Roosevelt
14,255 ft
4,345 m
Longmont
Fort Lupton
Fort Morgan
Utah Lake
Springville
Duchesne
White River
Granby
Boulder
Brighton
Beaver Creek
Spanish Fork
Santaquin
West Tavaputs Plateau
Meeker
Sheep Mtn.
12,248 ft
3,733 m
Gore Ra.
13,534 ft
4,351 m
Denver
Lakewood
Aurora
Colby
Mt. Nebo
11,928 ft
3,636 m
Nephi
Ouray
Goodland
Helper
East Tavaputs Plateau
Roan Plateau
Rifle
White River Plateau
Avon
6,005 ft
1,830 m
Parker
Burlington
Price
10,450 ft
3,185 m
Roan Cliffs
Colorado
Glenwood Springs
Mt. Lincoln
14,286 ft
4,354 m
Castle Rock
Limon
Oakley
Ephraim
Leadville
4,039 ft
1,231 m
Delta
Manti
Grand Junction
Fruita
Aspen
Mt. Elbert
14,433 ft
4,399 m
Sawatch Ra.
Woodland Park
Calhan
Big Sandy Creek
Kansas
4
San Rafael
Green River
Colorado Nat. Mon.
Gunnison
11,234 ft
3,424 m
Pikes Peak
14,108 ft
4,300 m
Colorado Springs
Cheyenne Wells
Fillmore
Salina
Colorado
Fountain
Scott City
Richfield
Mt. Marvine
11,610 ft
3,536 m
Sevier
Arches Nat. P.
Uncompahgre Plateau
Delta
Black Canyon of the Gunnison Nat. Mon.
Gunnison
Salida
Cañon City
Eads
Moab
Mt. Peale
12,721 ft
3,875 m
9,731 ft
2,966 m
Florence
Pueblo
Ordway
Delano Peak
12,173 ft
3,710 m
Dirty Devil
Capitol Reef Nat. P.
Canyonlands Nat. P.
Montrose
Naturita
14,309 ft
4,361 m
Uncompahgre Peak
14,294 ft
4,356 m
Arkansas
Rocky Ford
La Junta
Las Animas
Lamar
Arkansas
112°
E
93
108°
F
104°
G

PACIFIC OCEAN
San Francisco
Oakland
Sacramento
San Jose
Fresno
Bakersfield
LOS ANGELES
SAN DIEGO
TIJUANA
Reno
Las Vegas
Hawaiian Islands
UNITED STATES
Hawaii
Kauai
Oahu
Honolulu
Molokai
Maui
Lanai
Kahoolawe
Hawaii (Big Island)
1:5,000,000
Hawaii: East

1:5,000,000
0 50 100 mi
0 50 100 km
93
112° E 108° F 104° G
91
Oakley
Cache Pk.
10,353 ft
3,155 m
Malad City
Preston
Bear Lake
Richmond
Logan
Wellsville
Tremonton
Brigham City
9,764 ft
2,976 m
Ogden
Great Salt Lake
4,209 ft
1,283 m
Roy
Layton
Bountiful
Salt Lake City
West Valley City
West Jordan
Sandy
Wendover
Great Salt Lake Desert
Lehi
American Fork
Orem
Provo
Utah Lake
Springville
Spanish Fork
Santaquin
Mt. Nebo
11,928 ft
3,636 m
Nephi
Mt. Haystack
12,100 ft
3,688 m
Sevier Desert
Sevier Lake
Delta
9,725 ft
2,964 m
Wasatch Range
Kemmerer
Evanston
Lyman
Green River
Rock Springs
Flaming Gorge Res.
Wyoming Basin
Wyoming
Seminoe Res.
8,685 ft
2,647 m
Hanna
Rawlins
Saratoga
North Platte
Medicine Bow Pk.
12,013 ft
3,661 m
Medicine Bow Mts.
11,007 ft
3,354 m
Park Range
Mt. Zirkel
12,180 ft
3,712 m
Laramie
Horse Creek
Cheyenne
Scottsbluff
Gering
Bridgeport
5,063 ft
1,543 m
Hogback Mtn.
North Platte
Nebraska
Sidney
L. McConaughy
Kimball
Julesburg
1
13,528 ft
4,123 m
Kings Peak
Uinta Mountains
Dinosaur Nat. Mon.
Yampa
Craig
Vernal
Roosevelt
Duchesne
Uintah and Ouray Ind. Res.
West Tavaputs Plateau
Helper
Price
10,450 ft
3,185 m
East Tavaputs Plateau
Roan Cliffs
Roan Plateau
White River
Meeker
Rifle
Steamboat Springs
Rocky Mountain Nat. Park
Estes Park
Granby
14,255 ft
4,345 m
Sheep Mtn.
12,248 ft
3,733 m
13,534 ft
4,351 m
Gore Ra.
White River Plateau
Avon
Glenwood Springs
Rocky Mountains
Fort Collins
Windsor
Loveland
Greeley
Longmont
Fort Lupton
Brighton
Boulder
Denver
Aurora
Lakewood
Parker
Castle Rock
Sterling
South Platte
Brush
Fort Morgan
Yuma
Wray
40°
6,005 ft
1,830 m
Burlington
Limon
Ephraim
Manti
Salina
Fillmore
Richfield
S. Rafael
Green River
Grand Junction
Fruita
Colorado Nat. Mon.
11,234 ft
3,424 m
Colorado
Mt. Lincoln
14,286 ft
4,354 m
Leadville
Aspen
Mt. Elbert
14,433 ft
4,399 m
Sawatch Ra.
Woodland Park
Calhan
Pikes Peak
14,108 ft
4,300 m
Colorado Springs
Fountain
Cheyenne Wells
Big Sandy Creek
Eads
94
Mt. Marvine
11,610 ft
3,536 m
Arches Nat. P.
Moab
Mt. Peale
12,721 ft
3,875 m
9,731 ft
2,966 m
Uncompahgre Plateau
Delta
Gunnison
Black Canyon of the Gunnison Nat. Park
Montrose
Salida
Arkansas
Cañon City
Florence
Pueblo
Ordway
Las Animas
Lamar
2
Milford
12,173 ft
3,710 m
Delano Peak
Beaver
Capitol Reef Nat. P.
Mt. Ellen
11,522 ft
3,540 m
Dirty Devil
Canyonlands Nat. P.
United States
Uncompahgre Peak
14,309 ft
4,361 m
Naturita
Ouray
14,294 ft
4,356 m
Great Sand Dunes Nat. Mon.
12,349 ft
3,764 m
La Junta
4,052 ft
1,235 m
9,783 ft
2,982 m
Mt. Dutton
10,800 ft
3,292 m
Little Salt L.
Parowan
Panguitch
11,360 ft
3,463 m
Monticello
Mt. Wilson
14,246 ft
4,342 m
Silverton
Center
Monte Vista
Walsenburg
Blanca Peak
14,360 ft
4,377 m
Springfield
Purgatoire
Cedar City
Brian Head
11,316 ft
3,446 m
Bryce Canyon Nat. Park
Zion Nat. P.
Dolores
Blanding
Natural Bridges Nat. Mon.
13,300 ft
4,054 m
Alamosa
San Luis Valley
San Juan Mts.
Aguilar
Lake Powell
Cortez
Mesa Verde Nat. P.
Durango
Trinidad
Cimarron
Bluff
9,970 ft
3,041 m
Antonito
Raton
Oklahoma
Boise City
Washington
St. George
Hurricane
Kanab
Navajo Mtn.
10,388 ft
3,166 m
San Juan
Ute Mountain Ind. Res.
Southern Ute Ind. Res.
Navajo Lake
Chama
11,403 ft
3,476 m
13,160 ft
4,011 m
Rio Grande
Jicarilla Apache Ind. Res.
Laughlin Peak
8,820 ft
2,688 m
6,062 ft
1,848 m
Littlefield
Colorado City
Fredonia
Kaibab Ind. Res.
Page
Mt. Bangs
8,350 ft
2,545 m
Shiprock
Kirtland
Aztec
Bloomfield
Farmington
Wheeler Peak
Taos
Springer
Clayton
Carrizo Creek
Colorado Plateau
Kayenta
9,833 ft
2,861 m
Chuska Mts.
Chaco
Rio Chama
Sangre de Cristo Range
Ute Creek
Dalhart
36°
Grand Canyon Nat. Park
8,029 ft
2,447 m
Pt. Imperial
8,803 ft
2,683 m
1,640 ft
500 m
Grand Canyon
Tubac
8,075 ft
2,466 m
Navajo Indian Reservation
Newcomb
Chicoma Mtn.
11,562 ft
3,524 m
San Juan Pueblo
Chimayo
Española
Nambe Pueblo
13,101 ft
3,993 m
Los Alamos
Canadian
Roy
Mora
Grand Canyon Village
Havasupai Ind. Res.
Chinle
Canyon de Chelly Nat. Mon.
Hopi Ind. Res.
Polacca
Cochiti Pueblo
Santa Fe
Jemez Pueblo
Las Vegas
Painted Desert
Coconino Plateau
Hualapai Ind. Res.
Cataract Creek
Fort Defiance
Window Rock
Ganado
Zia Pueblo
San Felipe Pueblo
Santo Domingo Pueblo
Bernalillo
Tucumcari
Wupatki Nat. Mon.
Humphreys Pk.
12,663 ft
3,860 m
Pueblo Colorado Wash
Gallup
Thoreau
Mt. Taylor
11,303 ft
3,445 m
Rio Rancho
10,679 ft
3,255 m
Pecos
5,150 ft
1,570 ft
Seligman
Chambers
9,255 ft
2,821 m
Zuni Mts.
Zuni
Zuni Pueblo Ind. Res.
Grants
Laguna
Albuquerque
Moriarty
Santa Rosa
Isleta Pueblo
Los Lunas
Ash Fork
Williams
Flagstaff
Winslow
Holbrook
Petrified Forest Nat. Park
El Malpais Nat. Mon.
Acoma Pueblo
Belen
Willard
Vaughn
Fort Sumner
Clovis
Farwell
Portales
Hualapai Mts.
7,499 ft
2,286 m
Sedona
7,743 ft
2,360 m
Cottonwood
Camp Verde
Prescott Valley
Prescott
Mogollon Plateau
Snowflake
Saint Johns
Little Colorado
New Mexico
3
Arizona
Show Low
8,077 ft
2,462 m
Payson
Springerville
Alegros Mtn.
10,244 ft
3,122 m
Magdalena
Socorro
South Baldy
10,783 ft
3,287 m
Rio Grande
Llano Estacado
Fort Apache Ind. Res.
Cibecue
Eagar
Baldy Peak
11,590 ft
3,533 m
Carrizozo
Wickenburg
12,003 ft
3,659 m
Roswell
96
5,683 ft
1,732 m
Peoria
Scottsdale
Salt River Ind. Res.
Salt River
Glendale
Mesa
Chandler
PHOENIX
Avondale
San Carlos Ind. Res.
San Carlos
Globe
Superior
Whitewater Baldy
10,695 ft
3,320 m
Mogollon Mts.
San Francisco
Black Ra.
10,011 ft
3,051 m
8,958 ft
2,730 m
San Andres Mts.
Tularosa Valley
Ruidoso
Mescalero Ind. Res.
Rio Hondo
Hagerman
Tularosa
Alamogordo
Sacramento Mts.
Truth or Consequences
Lovington
Kofa Mts.
Gila River Ind. Res.
Florence
Hayden
Morenci
Clifton
Bylas
Artesia
Hobbs
Maricopa
Casa Grande
Gila Bend
Coolidge
Safford
Silver City
Santa Clara Pueblo
Bayard
White Sands Nat. Mon.
Gila
Eunice
Eloy
4,373 ft
1,333 m
Mt. Graham
10,717 ft
3,265 m
Duncan
Carlsbad
Loving
Guadalupe Mts.
Carlsbad Caverns Nat. Park
Las Cruces
8,920 ft
2,719 m
32°
San Manuel
9,157 ft
2,791 m
Marana
San Pedro
Santa Cruz
Bowie
Lordsburg
Oro Valley
Tohono O'odham Nation
Willcox
Deming
7,402 ft
2,256 m
Anthony
Chaparral
Kermit
Organ Pipe Cactus Nat. Mon.
Saguaro Nat. P.
Tucson
Ajo
Mt. Ajo
4,808 ft
1,465 m
Sells
Pascua Yaqui Ind. Res.
Green Valley
Benson
Chiricahua Mts.
9,795 ft
2,986 m
El Paso
Sunland Park
Socorro
JUÁREZ
San Elizario
Fabens
Guadalupe Peak
8,749 ft
2,667 m
Guadalupe Mts. Nat. Park
Pecos
Sa. del Pinacate
4,560 ft
1,390 m
Sonoita
Desierto de Altar
Tombstone
Animas Pk.
8,532 ft
2,600 m
Puerto Palomas
Samalayuca
Fort Hancock
Texas
4
Sierra Vista
9,466 ft
2,885 m
Bisbee
Douglas
Agua Prieta
La. de Guzmán
Rio Bravo del Norte
Rio Grande
Porvenir
Van Horn
Eagle Mts.
7,497 ft
2,285 m
Nogales
El Cozón
5,470 ft
1,667 m
Sonora
Mexico
Chihuahua
Ascensión
El Barreal
Bahía de Adair
Puerto Peñasco
D 102 112° E 108° 96 F 104° G

91 86 85 91 93 96

1:5,000,000

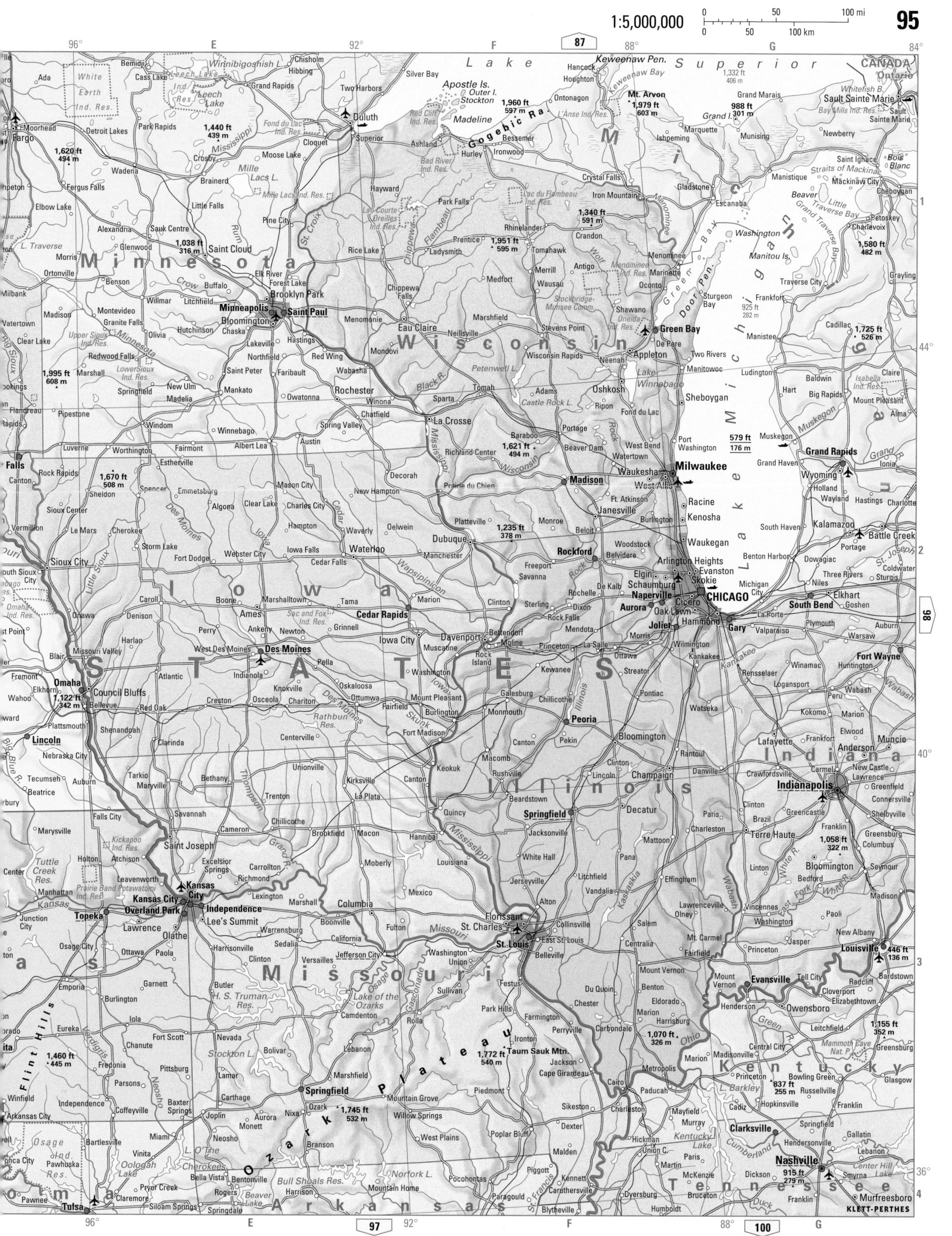
0
50
100 mi
0
50
100 km
96°
E
92°
F
87
88°
G
84°
Lake Superior
Keweenaw Pen.
CANADA
Ontario
Apostle Is.
Gogebic Ra.
Mt. Arvon
1,979 ft
603 m
Sault Sainte Marie
Straits of Mackinac
Minnesota
Wisconsin
Michigan
Iowa
Illinois
Indiana
Missouri
Kentucky
Tennessee
Arkansas
Ozark Plateau
Flint Hills
UNITED STATES
Lake Michigan
Green Bay
Door Pen.
Duluth
Superior
Fargo
Moorhead
Minneapolis
Saint Paul
Saint Cloud
Rochester
La Crosse
Eau Claire
Wausau
Green Bay
Appleton
Oshkosh
Lake Winnebago
Sheboygan
Milwaukee
Madison
Racine
Kenosha
Waukegan
Rockford
Dubuque
Waterloo
Cedar Rapids
Iowa City
Davenport
Des Moines
Sioux City
Omaha
Council Bluffs
Lincoln
CHICAGO
Evanston
Skokie
Naperville
Aurora
Joliet
Gary
South Bend
Grand Rapids
Kalamazoo
Battle Creek
Fort Wayne
Peoria
Bloomington
Champaign
Springfield
Decatur
Indianapolis
Terre Haute
Bloomington
Louisville
Evansville
Owensboro
Bowling Green
Clarksville
Nashville
Murfreesboro
St. Louis
St. Charles
Florissant
Columbia
Jefferson City
Kansas City
Overland Park
Independence
Lee's Summit
Topeka
Saint Joseph
Springfield
Joplin
Tulsa
Taum Sauk Mtn.
1,772 ft
540 m
Mississippi
Missouri
Ohio
Wabash
Illinois
Des Moines
Lake of the Ozarks
Bull Shoals Res.
Kentucky Lake
L. Barkley
Mammoth Cave Nat. P.
36°
40°
44°
1
2
3
4
96
97
100
88°
KLETT-PERTHES

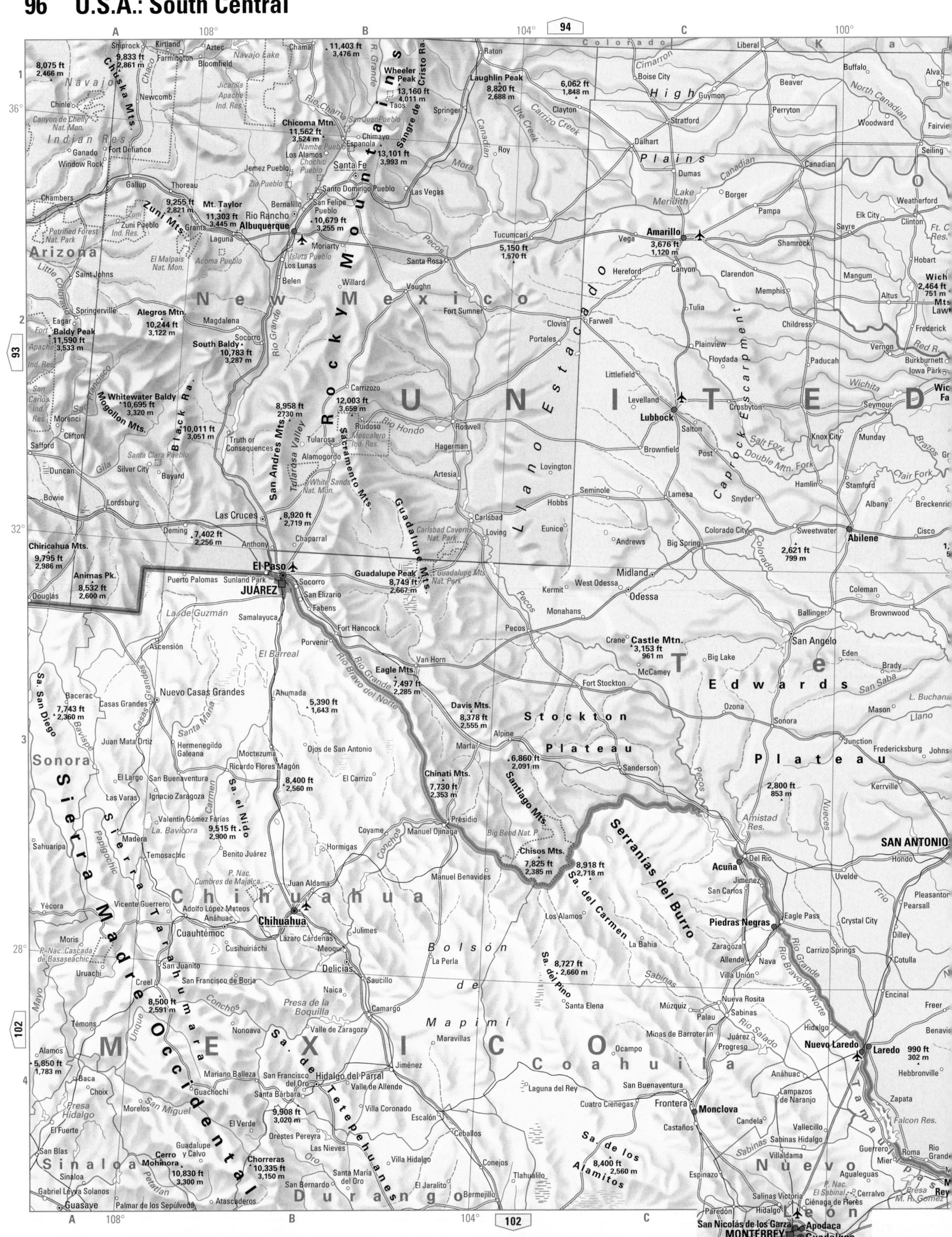
A
108°
B
104°
94
C
100°
1
2
3
4
36°
32°
28°
93
102
Colorado
Kansas
Arizona
New Mexico
UNITED
STATES
MEXICO
Sonora
Chihuahua
Coahuila
Durango
Sinaloa
Nuevo León
Shiprock
Kirtland
Farmington
Aztec
Bloomfield
Navajo Lake
Chama
11,403 ft
3,476 m
8,075 ft
2,466 m
9,833 ft
2,861 m
Chuska Mts.
Navajo Indian Res.
Newcomb
Jicarilla Apache Ind. Res.
Chaco
Wheeler Peak
13,160 ft
4,011 m
Taos
Sangre de Cristo Ra.
Raton
Laughlin Peak
8,820 ft
2,688 m
6,062 ft
1,848 m
Cimarron
Boise City
Liberal
Buffalo
Alva
Beaver
High Plains
Guymon
Clayton
Carrizo Creek
Ute Creek
Springer
Stratford
Perryton
Woodward
North Canadian
Chinle
Canyon de Chelly Nat. Mon.
Ganado
Fort Defiance
Window Rock
Chicoma Mtn.
11,562 ft
3,524 m
Chimayo
Espanola
Los Alamos
Nambe Pueblo
Chochiti Pueblo
San Juan Pueblo
13,101 ft
3,993 m
Rio Chama
Rio Grande
Canadian
Mora
Roy
Dalhart
Dumas
Canadian
Seiling
Jemez Pueblo
Santa Fe
Zia Pueblo
Santo Domingo Pueblo
Las Vegas
Rocky Mountains
Gallup
Thoreau
Chambers
9,255 ft
2,821 m
Mt. Taylor
11,303 ft
3,445 m
Zuni Mts.
Zuni
Zuni Pueblo
Zuni Ind. Res.
Grants
Rio Rancho
Bernalillo
San Felipe Pueblo
10,679 ft
3,255 m
Albuquerque
Laguna
Petrified Forest Nat. Park
Moriarty
Isleta Pueblo
Los Lunas
Acoma Pueblo
El Malpais Nat. Mon.
Lake Meridith
Borger
Pampa
Weatherford
Elk City
Clinton
Sayre
Amarillo
3,676 ft
1,120 m
Vega
Tucumcari
5,150 ft
1,570 ft
Pecos
Santa Rosa
Shamrock
Hereford
Canyon
Clarendon
Hobart
Mangum
Memphis
Altus
Little Colorado
Saint Johns
Belen
Willard
Vaughn
Springerville
Eagar
Alegros Mtn.
10,244 ft
3,122 m
Magdalena
Socorro
Baldy Peak
11,590 ft
3,533 m
Fort Apache Ind. Res.
South Baldy
10,783 ft
3,287 m
Fort Sumner
Clovis
Farwell
Portales
Tulia
Childress
Frederick
Plainview
Floydada
Paducah
Vernon
Red R.
Burkburnett
Iowa Park
Llano Estacado
Caprock Escarpment
Littlefield
San Carlos Ind. Res.
Francisco
Whitewater Baldy
10,695 ft
3,320 m
Mogollon Mts.
Black Ra.
Carrizozo
12,003 ft
3,659 m
8,958 ft
2730 m
Ruidoso
Mescalero Ind. Res.
Rio Hondo
Levelland
Lubbock
Crosbyton
Seymour
Wichita
Morenci
Clifton
10,011 ft
3,051 m
Safford
Truth or Consequences
San Andres Mts.
Tularosa Valley
Tularosa
Sacramento Mts.
Roswell
Hagerman
Salton
Brownfield
Post
Salt Fork
Double Mtn. Fork
Knox City
Munday
Brazos
Santa Clara Pueblo
Gila
Silver City
Bayard
Duncan
Alamogordo
White Sands Nat. Mon.
Artesia
Lovington
Hamlin
Stamford
Clear Fork
Snyder
Albany
Breckenridge
Bowie
Lordsburg
Guadalupe Mts.
Seminole
Hobbs
Lamesa
Las Cruces
8,920 ft
2,719 m
Carlsbad
Carlsbad Caverns Nat. Park
Loving
Eunice
Andrews
Big Spring
Colorado City
Sweetwater
Abilene
Cisco
2,621 ft
799 m
Colorado
Chiricahua Mts.
9,795 ft
2,986 m
Deming
7,402 ft
2,256 m
Anthony
Chaparral
Animas Pk.
8,532 ft
2,600 m
Douglas
El Paso
Puerto Palomas
Sunland Park
Juárez
Socorro
San Elizario
Fabens
Guadalupe Peak
8,749 ft
2,667 m
Guadalupe Mts. Nat. Park
Kermit
West Odessa
Midland
Odessa
Monahans
Coleman
Brownwood
Ballinger
Laguna de Guzmán
Samalayuca
Fort Hancock
Pecos
Pecos
Porvenir
Crane
Castle Mtn.
3,153 ft
961 m
McCamey
Big Lake
San Angelo
Eden
Brady
San Saba
Ascensión
El Barreal
Rio Grande
Rio Bravo del Norte
Van Horn
Eagle Mts.
7,497 ft
2,285 m
Fort Stockton
Edwards Plateau
Stockton Plateau
Sa. San Diego
Bacerac
7,743 ft
2,360 m
Casas Grandes
Nuevo Casas Grandes
Ahumada
5,390 ft
1,643 m
Davis Mts.
8,378 ft
2,555 m
Ozona
Mason
Llano
L. Buchanan
Sonora
Junction
Fredericksburg
Johnson
Bavispe
Santa María
Juan Mata Ortiz
Hermenegildo Galeana
Moctezuma
Ojos de San Antonio
Alpine
Marfa
6,860 ft
2,091 m
Sanderson
Ricardo Flores Magón
El Largo
San Buenaventura
8,400 ft
2,560 m
El Carrizo
Chinati Mts.
7,730 ft
2,353 m
Santiago Mts.
Kerrville
2,800 ft
853 m
Las Varas
Ignacio Zaragoza
Carmen
Sa. el Nido
Valentín Gómez Farías
La. Bavícora
9,515 ft
2,900 m
Presidio
Coyame
Manuel Ojinaga
Big Bend Nat. P.
Serranías del Burro
Amistad Res.
Nueces
Sierra Madre Occidental
Papigochic
Madera
Sahuaripa
Temosachic
Benito Juárez
Hormigas
Conchos
Chisos Mts.
7,825 ft
2,385 m
8,918 ft
2,718 m
Del Rio
Acuña
San Antonio
Hondo
Uvalde
Jiménez
San Carlos
Frio
Pleasanton
Pearsall
P. Nac. Cumbres de Majalca
Juan Aldama
Manuel Benavides
Sa. del Carmen
Yécora
Vicente Guerrero
Adolfo López Mateos
Anáhuac
Chihuahua
Los Alamos
Eagle Pass
Piedras Negras
Crystal City
Dilley
Moris
P. Nac. Cascada de Basaseachic
Cuauhtémoc
Cusihuiriáchi
Lázaro Cárdenas
Meoqui
Julimes
Bolsón de Mapimí
La Bahia
Zaragoza
Allende
Nava
Carrizo Springs
Cotulla
Sierra Tarahumara
San Juanito
Uruachi
Delicias
La Perla
Sa. del Pino
8,727 ft
2,660 m
Villa Unión
Creel
San Francisco de Borja
Saucillo
Sabinas
Encinal
Mayo
Conchos
Naica
8,500 ft
2,591 m
Presa de la Boquilla
Santa Elena
Múzquiz
Nueva Rosita
Sabinas
Palau
Freer
Témoris
Unique
Camargo
Nonoava
Valle de Zaragoza
Maravillas
Minas de Barroterán
Rio Salado
Hidalgo
Benavides
Juárez
Progreso
Nuevo Laredo
Laredo
990 ft
302 m
Sa. de Tepehuanes
Alamos
5,850 ft
1,783 m
Mariano Balleza
San Francisco del Oro
Hidalgo del Parral
Jiménez
Ocampo
Hebbronville
Baca
Choix
Guachochi
Santa Bárbara
Valle de Allende
San Buenaventura
Anáhuac
Lampazos de Naranjo
Zapata
Presa Hidalgo
Morelos
San Miguel
9,908 ft
3,020 m
Villa Coronado
Laguna del Rey
Cuatro Ciénegas
Frontera
Monclova
Candela
Falcon Res.
El Fuerte
El Verde
Escalón
Castaños
Vallecillo
Orestes Pereyra
Ceballos
Sabinas Hidalgo
Villaldama
San Blas
Guadalupe y Calvo
Las Nieves
Sa. de los Alamitos
8,400 ft
2,560 m
Guerrero
Roma
Rio Grande City
Mier
Cerro Mohinora
10,830 ft
3,300 m
Chorreras
10,335 ft
3,150 m
Oro
Villa Hidalgo
Conejos
Tlahualilo
Sinaloa
Petatlán
Santa María del Oro
El Jaralito
Espinazo
Agualeguas
Cerralvo
P. Nac. El Sabinal
Ciénaga de Flores
Presa M. R. Gómez
Gabriel Leyva Solanos
San Bernardo
Bermejillo
Salinas Victoria
Guasave
Palmar de los Sepúlveda
Atascaderos
Paredón
Hidalgo
San Nicolás de los Garza
Monterrey
Apodaca
Guadalupe
P. N. Cumbres de Monterrey
Tamaulipas
Wichita Mts.
2,464 ft
751 m
Lawton
Fairview
Ft. Cobb Res.

D 96° E 95 92° F 98 88° G

Arkansas City Coffeyville Joplin Aurora Nixa Ozark Willow Springs Poplar Bluff Dexter Sikeston Kentucky Mayfield Murray Clarksville Springfield
Baxter Springs Monett Neosho Missouri Hickman Hendersonville
Blackwell Ponca City Osage Ind. Res. Miami L. O' The Cherokees Branson Bull Shoals Res. West Plains Malden Kentucky Lake Cumberland Nashville
Tonkawa Pawhuska Res. Bartlesville Vinita Oologah Lake Norfork L. Mountain Home Piggott Union C. Martin Paris Dickson 915 ft 279 m 36°
Enid Pawnee Pryor Creek Bella Vista Bentonville Pocohontas Kennett McKenzie Franklin
Perry Keystone Lake Tulsa Claremore Siloam Springs Rogers Beaver Lake Harrison Paragould Caruthersville Dyersburg Bruceton
Stillwater Sapulpa Broken Arrow Springdale White R. St. Francis Blytheville Tennessee
Guthrie Cushing Bristow Wagoner Tahlequah Fayetteville 2,697 ft 822 m Marshall Jonesboro Humboldt Lexington Duck Columbia
Oklahoma Muskogee Tenkiller Lake Boston Mts. Batesville Black R. Trumann Osceola Brownsville Jackson Lewisburg
Edmond Okmulgee Ozark Greers Ferry Lake Newport Covington Hatchie
1,207 ft 364 m Oklahoma City Midwest City Henryetta Sallisaw Van Buren Bald Knob Millington Lawrenceburg Pulaski
Moore Shawnee Eufaula Fort Smith 2,837 ft 839 m Russellville Searcy West Memphis Memphis Bartlett Bolivar Selmer Savannah
Norman Seminole R. S. Kerr Res. Morrilton Conway Wynne Forrest City Germantown Pickwick L. Wilson L. Athens
Chickasha Holdenville Eufaula Res. Poteau Arkansas Southaven Corinth Florence
Washita Canadian McAlester Waldron Jacksonville Brinkley Hernando Holly Springs Muscle Shoals Wheeler Lake Decatur
Wilburton 2,681 ft 817 m Ouachita Mts. Little Rock North Little Rock Tunica Booneville Tennessee
Pauls Valley Ada Kiamichi Hot Springs Nat. P. Benton Helena New Albany Russellville Hartselle
Mena L. Ouachita Hot Springs Stuttgart White R. Oxford 1,074 ft 327 m Cullmann
1,414 ft 431 m Atoka Malvern Arkansas Mississippi Tombigbee Tupelo Haleyville
Ardmore Antlers Pine Bluff Clarksdale Bruce
Madill Durant Hugo Little R. Arkadelphia Aberdeen Jasper
Texoma Red R. Idabel De Queen Gurdon Fordyce Grenada West Point
Gainesville Denison Paris Ashdown Hope Monticello McGehee Cleveland Winona Eupora Columbus Starkville
Sherman Bonham Camden Warren Indianola Greenwood Northport Tuscaloosa
STATES Texarkana Texarkana Magnolia Ouachita Saline Lake Village Leland Greenville Kosciusko Louisville Centreville
Denton McKinney Commerce W. Patman L. El Dorado Crossett Mississippi Black Warrior
Lewisville Plano Greenville Sulphur Springs Mount Pleasant Springhill Lake Providence Rolling Fork Yazoo Yazoo City Philadelphia Eutaw Marion 100
Irving Garland Vivian Bastrop Big Black R. Canton Mississippi Choctaw Ind. Res. Alabama
Fort Worth Arlington DALLAS Terrell Marshall Bossier C. Monroe Minden Ruston Tallulah Clinton Ross Barnett Res. Meridian Demopolis Selma
Weatherford Sabine Longview Shreveport 535 ft 163 m Rayville Vicksburg Jackson Forest York Linden
Waxahachie Tyler Kilgore Jonesboro Winnsboro 32°
Cleburne Ennis Cedar Creek Res. Athens Carthage Columbia Tombigbee Thomasville Camden
Corsicana 764 ft 233 m Henderson Mansfield Coushatta Crystal Springs Mendenhall Waynesboro
Hillsboro Jacksonville Winnfield Laurel Jackson Monroeville
Palestine Rusk Natchitoches Jonesville Ferriday Brookhaven
Mexia Nacogdoches San Augustine Toledo Bend Res. Many Red River Natchez Columbia Hattiesburg Alabama
Waco McGregor Lufkin Sam Rayburn Res. 463 ft 141 m Alexandria McComb Pearl Mobile Atmore
Marlin Crockett Trinity Diboll Neches Marksville Woodville Bay Minette Escambia FL
Temple Leesville Lecompte Wiggins Lucedale Pascagoula
Killeen Lake Livingston Jasper Louisiana Bogalusa Mobile Daphne
Cameron Hearne Huntsville Woodville De Ridder Oakdale Jackson Poplarville Pensacola
Little R. Bryan Livingston Sabine Ville Platte Opelousas Baton Rouge Picayune Ocean Springs Mobile Bay
Georgetown Rockdale College Station Eunice Hammond Covington Gulfport Biloxi Pascagoula Santa Rosa
Taylor Brazos Silsbee Kinder Lafayette Plaquemine Lake Pontchartrain Slidell Mississippi Sound Dauphin
Round Rock Caldwell Navasota Conroe Cleveland Jennings Saint Martinville 3
Austin Colorado Giddings Beaumont Orange Sulphur Lake Charles Crowley New Iberia Donaldsonville Laplace New Orleans Chandeleur Sound
Brenham The Woodlands Nederland Abbeville Metairie Chandeleur Is.
Lockhart La Grange Spring Liberty Port Arthur Sabine Lake Intracoastal Waterway Thibodaux
San Marcos New Braunfels Columbus HOUSTON Pasadena White L. Franklin Morgan City Houma Breton Sound
Gonzales Sugar Land Baytown Galveston Bay Marsh Atchafalaya Bay Mississippi River Delta
Seguin Guadalupe Eagle Lake Richmond League City Texas City Grand Isle Buras
Wharton Alvin Hitchcock Galveston Caillou Bay Barataria Bay
Yoakum El Campo Angleton Isles Dernieres Timbalier
Cuero Lake Jackson Galveston
Edna Bay City Freeport
San Antonio Victoria Palacios
Goliad Port Lavaca Matagorda Pen.
Tres Palacios Bay 28°
Beeville Refugio
George West Matagorda
Mathis Sinton Portland San Jose
Port Aransas
Robstown Corpus Christi Gulf of
Baffin Bay 4
Padre I.
Laguna Madre Mexico
Raymondville
Harlingen
Weslaco San Benito
Rio Bravo Brownsville
Matamoros

KLETT-PERTHES

D 96° E 92° 102 F 88° G

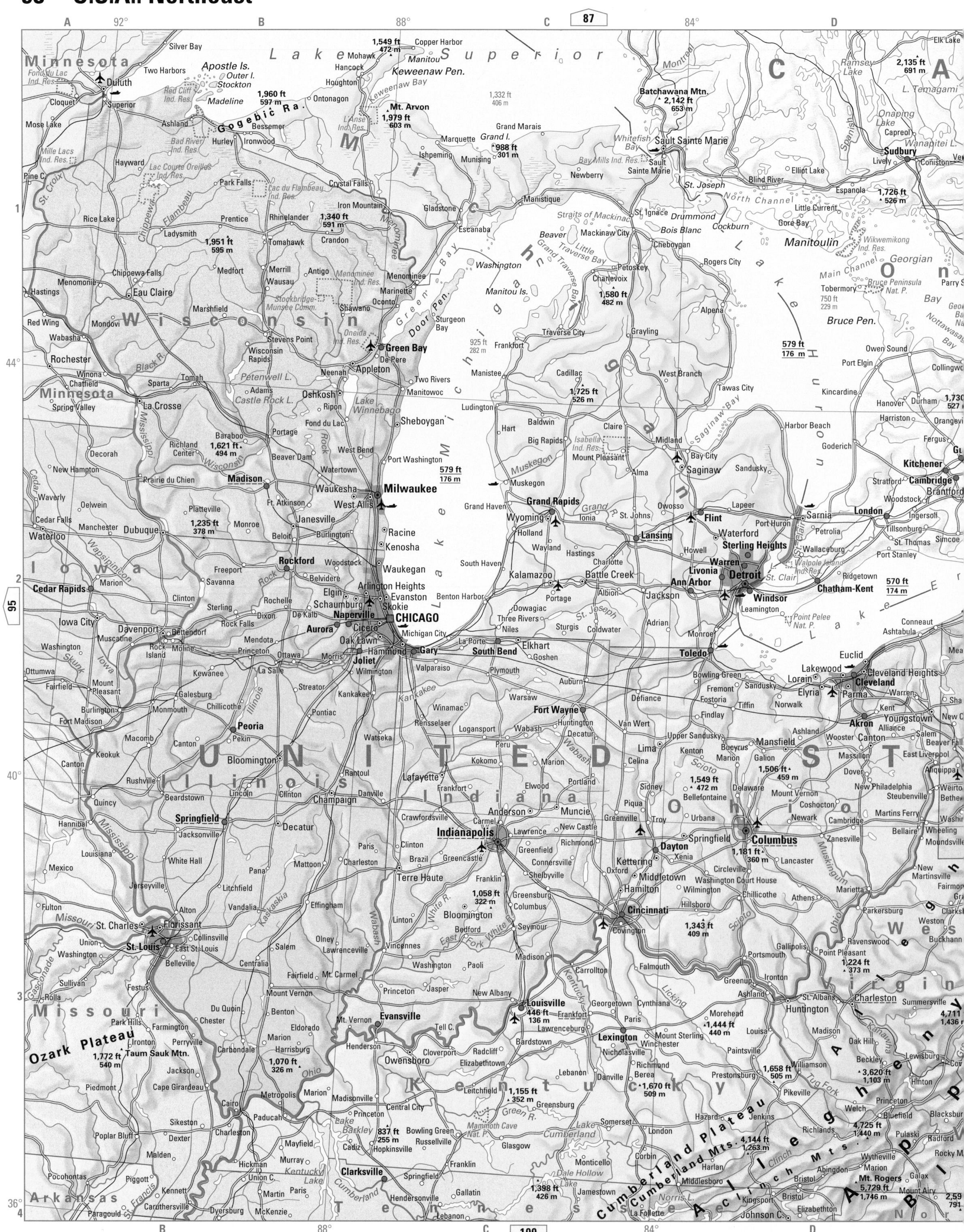

A
B
C
D
92°
88°
84°
44°
40°
36°
1
2
3
4
Lake Superior
Silver Bay
Two Harbors
Apostle Is.
Outer I.
Stockton
Red Cliff Ind. Res.
Madeline
Duluth
Superior
Cloquet
Fond du Lac Ind. Res.
Minnesota
Mose Lake
Ashland
Gogebic Ra.
Bessemer
Hurley
Ironwood
Bad River Ind. Res.
Mille Lacs Ind. Res.
Hayward
Lac Courte Oreilles Ind. Res.
Park Falls
Lac du Flambeau Ind. Res.
Pine C.
St. Croix
Rice Lake
Chippewa
Flambeau
Prentice
Rhinelander
Ladysmith
Tomahawk
Crandon
Medford
Merrill
Antigo
Menominee Ind. Res.
Wausau
Chippewa Falls
Menomonie
Eau Claire
Hastings
Stockbridge-Munsee Comm.
Shawano
Marshfield
Red Wing
Mondovi
Wisconsin
Wabasha
Stevens Point
Oneida Ind. Res.
Green Bay
De Pere
Appleton
Neenah
Wisconsin Rapids
Rochester
Winona
Chatfield
Black R.
Petenwell L.
Castle Rock L.
Adams
Tomah
Sparta
La Crosse
Spring Valley
Oshkosh
Ripon
Lake Winnebago
Fond du Lac
Sheboygan
Baraboo
1,621 ft
494 m
Richland Center
Portage
Decorah
West Bend
Beaver Dam
Port Washington
New Hampton
Watertown
Madison
Prairie du Chien
Waukesha
Milwaukee
West Allis
Ft. Atkinson
Waverly
Oelwein
Platteville
Janesville
Cedar Falls
Manchester
Dubuque
1,235 ft
378 m
Monroe
Beloit
Burlington
Racine
Kenosha
Waterloo
Wapsipinicon
Iowa
Freeport
Rockford
Woodstock
Waukegan
Cedar Rapids
Marion
Savanna
Belvidere
Elgin
Arlington Heights
Evanston
Skokie
Schaumburg
Clinton
Sterling
Rochelle
De Kalb
Naperville
CHICAGO
Iowa City
Dixon
Aurora
Cicero
Davenport
Bettendorf
Rock Falls
Mendota
Oak Lawn
Michigan City
Muscatine
Rock Island
Moline
Princeton
Ottawa
Morris
Hammond
Gary
Washington
Joliet
Wilmington
Ottumwa
Kewanee
La Salle
Fairfield
Mount Pleasant
Galesburg
Streator
Kankakee
Burlington
Chillicothe
Fort Madison
Monmouth
Pontiac
Peoria
Pekin
Macomb
Canton
Keokuk
Bloomington
UNITED STATES
Rantoul
Canton
Rushville
Illinois
Lincoln
Clinton
Champaign
Danville
Quincy
Beardstown
Hannibal
Springfield
Jacksonville
Decatur
Louisiana
White Hall
Mexico
Pana
Mattoon
Charleston
Paris
Jerseyville
Litchfield
Effingham
Alton
Vandalia
Fulton
St. Charles
Florissant
Collinsville
St. Louis
East St. Louis
Union
Washington
Belleville
Salem
Olney
Lawrenceville
Centralia
Fairfield
Mt. Carmel
Sullivan
Festus
Rolla
Gasconade
Missouri
Mount Vernon
Benton
Du Quoin
Chester
Park Hills
Farmington
Eldorado
Ozark Plateau
Ironton
Perryville
Carbondale
Marion
Harrisburg
1,772 ft
540 m
Taum Sauk Mtn.
Jackson
1,070 ft
326 m
Ohio
Piedmont
Cape Girardeau
Metropolis
Cairo
Paducah
Sikeston
Poplar Bluff
Dexter
Charleston
Malden
Mayfield
Murray
Hickman
Union C.
Kentucky Lake
Pocohontas
Piggott
Kennett
Martin
Paris
Arkansas
Caruthersville
Dyersburg
McKenzie
Paragould
Mohawk
Hancock
Houghton
Copper Harbor
Manitou
Keweenaw Pen.
Keweenaw Bay
1,549 ft
472 m
1,960 ft
597 m
Ontonagon
Mt. Arvon
1,979 ft
603 m
L'Anse Ind. Res.
Marquette
Ishpeming
Munising
Grand I.
988 ft
301 m
Grand Marais
1,332 ft
406 m
Crystal Falls
Iron Mountain
1,340 ft
591 m
Gladstone
Escanaba
Manistique
Menominee
Marinette
Oconto
Green Bay
Door Pen.
Sturgeon Bay
Washington
Manitou Is.
Beaver
Straits of Mackinac
Mackinaw City
Little Traverse Bay
Grand Traverse Bay
Petoskey
Charlevoix
1,580 ft
482 m
Traverse City
Frankfort
925 ft
282 m
Manistee
Cadillac
1,725 ft
526 m
Ludington
Lake Michigan
Two Rivers
Manitowoc
579 ft
176 m
Hart
Baldwin
Big Rapids
Isabella Ind. Res.
Mount Pleasant
Muskegon
Grand Haven
Grand Rapids
Wyoming
Holland
Wayland
Hastings
South Haven
Kalamazoo
Portage
Benton Harbor
Dowagiac
Three Rivers
Niles
Sturgis
Coldwater
St. Joseph
La Porte
South Bend
Elkhart
Goshen
Valparaiso
Plymouth
Warsaw
Winamac
Rensselaer
Logansport
Fort Wayne
Huntington
Wabash
Peru
Kokomo
Lafayette
Frankfort
Elwood
Indiana
Anderson
Muncie
Carmel
Indianapolis
Crawfordsville
New Castle
Richmond
Greenfield
Connersville
Shelbyville
Clinton
Brazil
Greencastle
Terre Haute
Franklin
1,058 ft
322 m
Bloomington
Linton
Greensburg
Columbus
Bedford
Seymour
Vincennes
Washington
Paoli
Madison
Jasper
New Albany
Louisville
446 ft
136 m
Frankfort
Evansville
Mt. Vernon
Tell C.
Henderson
Owensboro
Cloverport
Radcliff
Elizabethtown
Lawrenceburg
Bardstown
Lexington
Nicholasville
Kentucky
Leitchfield
1,155 ft
352 m
Greensburg
Green R.
Danville
Richmond
Berea
1,670 ft
509 m
Lebanon
Madisonville
Central City
Princeton
Lake Barkley
837 ft
255 m
Bowling Green
Russellville
Mammoth Cave Nat. P.
Cadiz
Hopkinsville
Glasgow
Somerset
Cumberland
London
Clarksville
Springfield
Franklin
Monticello
Dale Hollow Lake
1,398 ft
426 m
Gallatin
Jamestown
Hendersonville
Lebanon
Tennessee
Sault Sainte Marie
Whitefish Bay
Bay Mills Ind. Res.
Newberry
St. Ignace
Drummond
Bois Blanc
Cheboygan
Cockburn
Rogers City
Alpena
Grayling
West Branch
Tawas City
Saginaw Bay
Claire
Midland
Bay City
Saginaw
Alma
Sandusky
Owosso
Lapeer
Flint
St. Johns
Ionia
Lansing
Charlotte
Battle Creek
Albion
Jackson
Howell
Waterford
Sterling Heights
Warren
Livonia
Ann Arbor
Detroit
Windsor
Adrian
Monroe
Toledo
Port Huron
Sarnia
Lake St. Clair
Walpole Island Ind. Res.
Bowling Green
Fremont
Sandusky
Auburn
Defiance
Fostoria
Tiffin
Findlay
Van Wert
Upper Sandusky
Lima
Bucyrus
Kenton
Marion
Celina
Galion
Mansfield
Sidney
1,549 ft
472 m
Bellefontaine
Delaware
Piqua
Urbana
Greenville
Troy
Springfield
Columbus
Dayton
Xenia
Kettering
Oxford
Middletown
Hamilton
1,181 ft
360 m
Lancaster
Circleville
Washington Court House
Wilmington
Chillicothe
Cincinnati
Covington
Hillsboro
1,343 ft
409 m
Portsmouth
Falmouth
Carrollton
Georgetown
Cynthiana
Paris
Mount Sterling
Winchester
Morehead
1,444 ft
440 m
Ashland
Greenup
Ironton
Batchawana Mtn.
2,142 ft
653 m
Montreal
Ramsey Lake
2,135 ft
691 m
L. Temagami
Onaping Lake
Capreol
Wanapitei L.
Sudbury
Lively
Coniston
Elliot Lake
Blind River
St. Joseph
North Channel
Espanola
1,726 ft
526 m
Little Current
Gore Bay
Manitoulin
Wikwemikong Ind. Res.
Main Channel
Georgian Bay
Tobermory
Bruce Peninsula Nat. P.
750 ft
229 m
Bruce Pen.
Lake Huron
579 ft
176 m
Owen Sound
Port Elgin
Kincardine
Hanover
Durham
Harriston
Harbor Beach
Goderich
Kitchener
Cambridge
Stratford
Woodstock
Brantford
London
Ingersoll
Tillsonburg
St. Thomas
Simcoe
Petrolia
Wallaceburg
Port Stanley
Ridgetown
Chatham-Kent
570 ft
174 m
Leamington
Point Pelee Nat. P.
Lake Erie
Conneaut
Ashtabula
Euclid
Lakewood
Cleveland Heights
Lorain
Cleveland
Elyria
Parma
Norwalk
Kent
Akron
Youngstown
Canton
Alliance
Ashland
Wooster
Salem
Massillon
Dover
New Philadelphia
1,506 ft
459 m
Mount Vernon
Coshocton
Newark
Cambridge
Zanesville
Muskingum
Steubenville
Martins Ferry
Wheeling
Bellaire
Moundsville
Marietta
Athens
Parkersburg
Ravenswood
Gallipolis
Point Pleasant
1,224 ft
373 m
West Virginia
Charleston
St. Albans
Huntington
Madison
Louisa
Oak Hill
Beckley
Paintsville
Prestonsburg
1,658 ft
505 m
Williamson
3,620 ft
1,103 m
Pikeville
Tug Fork
Welch
Princeton
Bluefield
Hazard
Jenkins
Richlands
4,725 ft
1,440 m
Cumberland Plateau
Cumberland Mts.
4,144 ft
1,263 m
Clinch Mts.
Allegheny
Harlan
Middlesboro
Corbin
Wytheville
Marion
Abingdon
Mt. Rogers
5,729 ft
1,746 m
Bristol
Kingsport
Johnson C.
Elizabethton
La Follette
Norris L.
Galax
Mount Airy
Radford
Pulaski
Blacksburg
Lewisburg
Hinton
Summersville
Appalachian
Blue Ridge
Elk Lake
Canada
Ontario

87
95
100

1:5,000,000
0
50
100 mi
0
50
100 km
E
76°
F
88
72°
G
H
ATLANTIC
OCEAN
Gulf of
Maine
Québec
Maine
New
Brunswick
New
Hampshire
Vermont
Massachusetts
Connecticut
Rhode
Island
New York
Pennsylvania
New
Jersey
Delaware
Maryland
Virginia
Carolina
Lake Ontario
Adirondack
Mountains
Green Mountains
White
Mountains
Longfellow Mts
Appalachian Mountains
Blue Ridge
Laurentides
St. Lawrence
Lake Champlain
Long Island
Long Island Sound
Cape Cod
Cape Cod Bay
Massachusetts Bay
Nantucket Sound
Martha's Vineyard
Nantucket
Block Island
Montauk Point
Delaware Bay
Cape May
Cape May Point
Delmarva
Peninsula
Chesapeake Bay
Assateague
Parramore
Cape Charles
Cape Henry
Currituck Sound
Penobscot Bay
Mt. Desert I.
Swans I.
Isle au Haut
Moosehead Lake
Chesuncook L.
Eagle L.
Flagstaff L.
Winnipesaukee Lake
Sebago L.
Mt. Katahdin
5,267 ft
1,605 m
Mt. Washington
6,288 ft
1,917 m
Mt. Marcy
5,344 ft
1,629 m
Sugarloaf Mtn.
4,237 ft
1,291 m
Mt-Mégantic
3,640 ft
1,105 m
Catskill Mts.
4,190 ft
1,277 m
Blue Knob
3,136 ft
956 m
Mont-Tremblant
3,175 ft
968 m
Shenandoah Mts.
Shenandoah Nat. P.
MONTRÉAL
Ottawa
Québec
Lévis
Trois-Rivières
Laval
Longueuil
Sherbrooke
Kingston
TORONTO
Missisauga
Markham
Oshawa
Whitby
Hamilton
Buffalo
Niagara Falls
Rochester
Syracuse
Utica
Albany
Schenectady
Binghamton
Scranton
Wilkes-Barre
Allentown
Bethlehem
Reading
Harrisburg
Lancaster
PHILADELPHIA
Trenton
Camden
Wilmington
Baltimore
Washington, D.C.
Arlington
Alexandria
Richmond
Hampton
Newport News
Norfolk
Portsmouth
Virginia Beach
Chesapeake
NEW YORK
Jersey City
Newark
Elizabeth
Paterson
Yonkers
Stamford
Bridgeport
New Haven
Waterbury
Hartford
Springfield
Worcester
Providence
Boston
Cambridge
Lowell
Manchester
Nashua
Portland
Bangor
Augusta
Burlington
Montpelier
Concord
Edmundston
Presque Isle
Houlton
Calais
St. Stephen
Woodstock
KLETT-PERTHES
101
76°
F
72°
G
44°
40°
36°
1
2
3
4

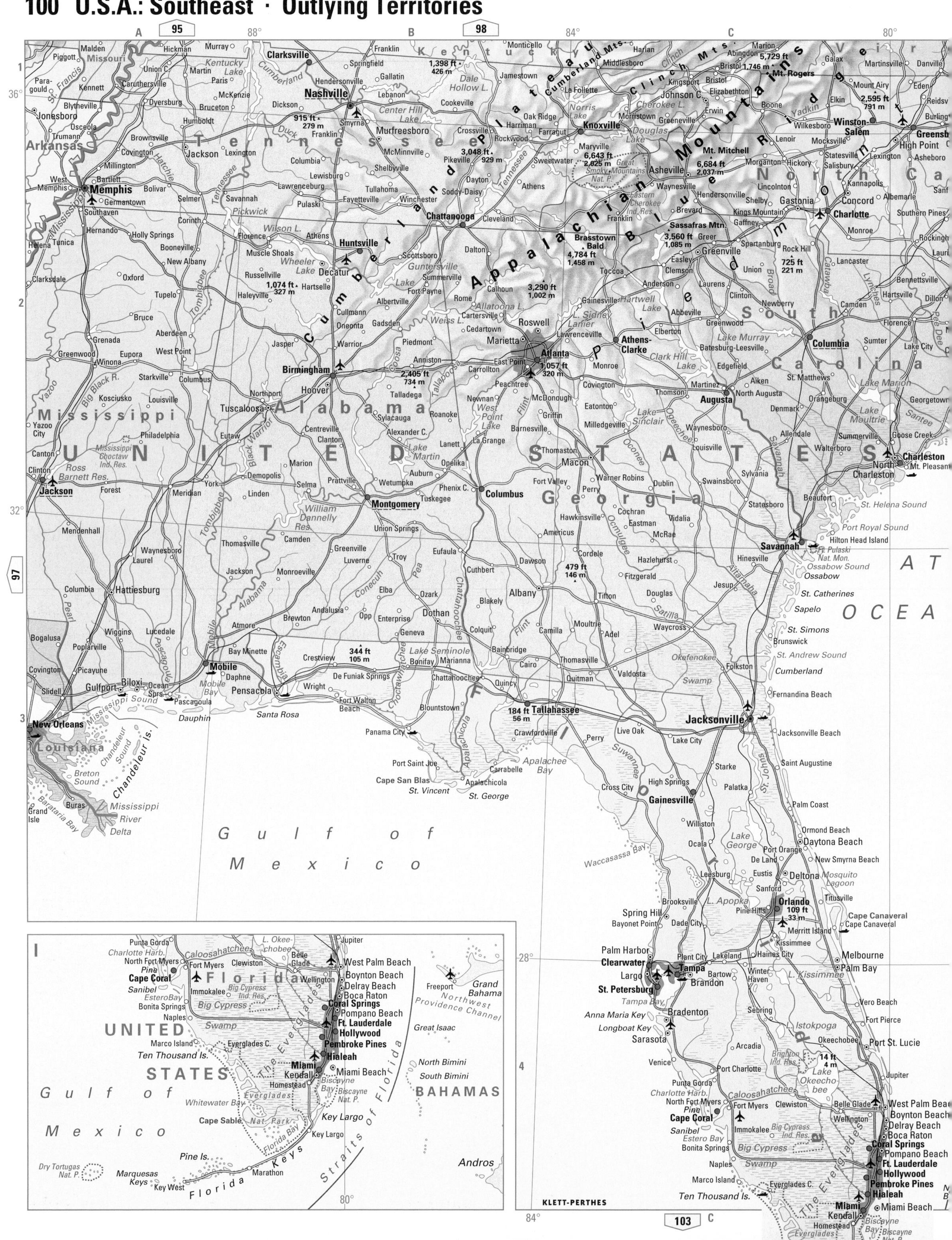

95
98
97
103
A
B
C
88°
84°
80°
36°
32°
28°
1
2
3
4
Kentucky
Tennessee
North Carolina
South Carolina
Georgia
Alabama
Mississippi
Arkansas
Missouri
Louisiana
Florida
Virginia
UNITED STATES
Cumberland Plateau
Cumberland Mts.
Clinch Mts.
Appalachian Mountains
Blue Ridge
Piedmont
Great Smoky Mountains Nat. P.
Nashville
Clarksville
Memphis
Knoxville
Chattanooga
Huntsville
Birmingham
Montgomery
Atlanta
Athens-Clarke
Augusta
Columbia
Charleston
Charlotte
Greenville
Asheville
Winston-Salem
Savannah
Columbus
Macon
Mobile
Jackson
Tallahassee
Jacksonville
Gainesville
Orlando
Tampa
St. Petersburg
Clearwater
New Orleans
Pensacola
Gulfport
Biloxi
Mt. Mitchell
6,684 ft
2,037 m
Mt. Rogers
5,729 ft
Brasstown Bald
4,784 ft
1,458 m
Sassafras Mtn.
3,560 ft
1,085 m
Lake Okeechobee
Okefenokee Swamp
Big Cypress Swamp
The Everglades
Gulf of Mexico
ATLANTIC OCEAN
Straits of Florida
Florida Keys
BAHAMAS
Grand Bahama
Andros
Key West
Key Largo
Miami
Miami Beach
Hialeah
Ft. Lauderdale
Hollywood
Pembroke Pines
Coral Springs
Pompano Beach
Boca Raton
Delray Beach
Boynton Beach
West Palm Beach
Cape Coral
Cape Canaveral
Daytona Beach
Melbourne
Palm Bay
Port St. Lucie
Sarasota
Bradenton
Mississippi River Delta
Chandeleur Is.
KLETT-PERTHES

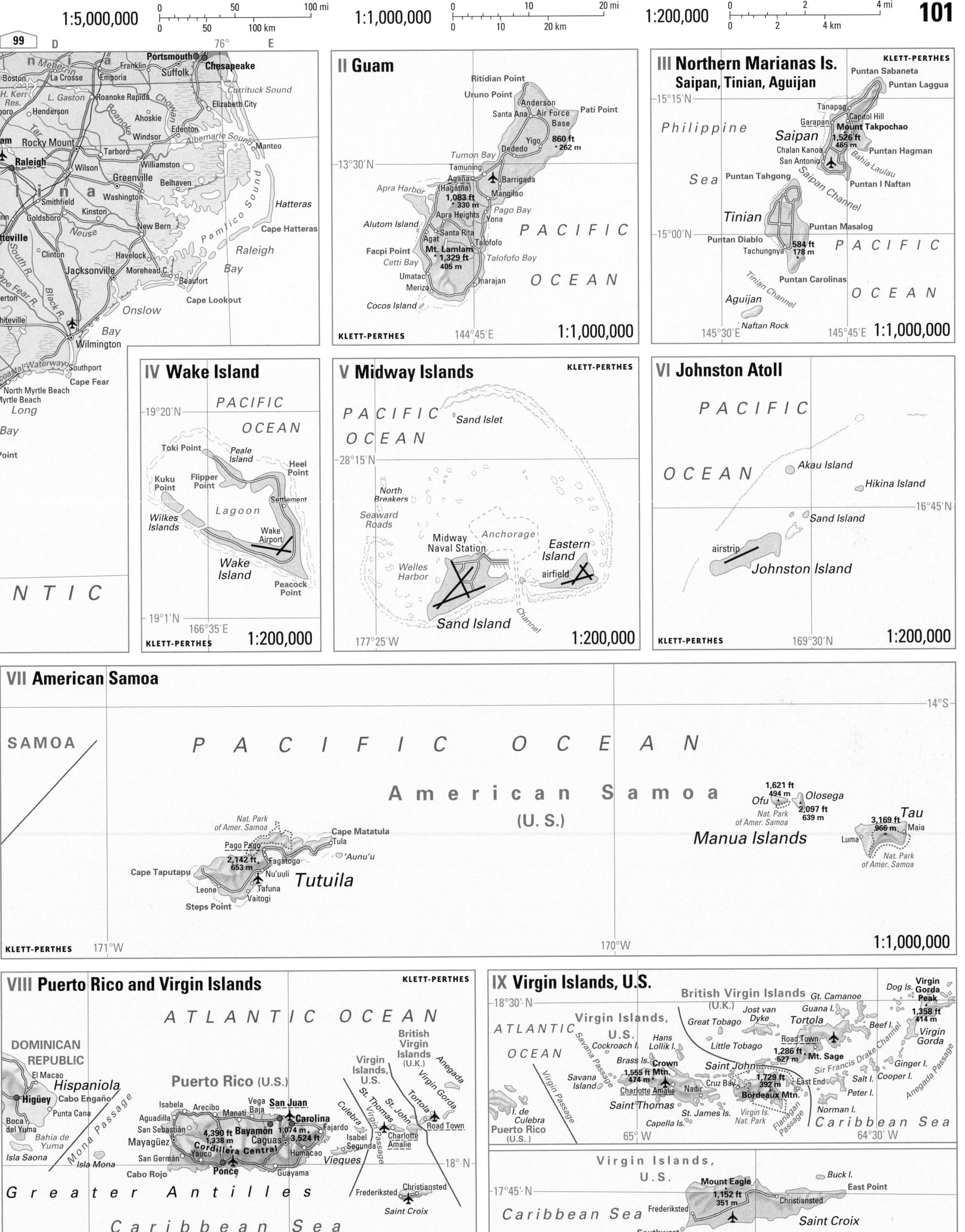
1:5,000,000
1:1,000,000
1:200,000
II Guam
III Northern Marianas Is.
Saipan, Tinian, Aguijan
IV Wake Island
V Midway Islands
VI Johnston Atoll
VII American Samoa
VIII Puerto Rico and Virgin Islands
IX Virgin Islands, U.S.
PACIFIC OCEAN
ATLANTIC OCEAN
Caribbean Sea
Greater Antilles
American Samoa (U.S.)
Manua Islands
Tutuila
Puerto Rico (U.S.)
Hispaniola
DOMINICAN REPUBLIC
British Virgin Islands (U.K.)
Saint Croix
Saint Thomas
Saint John
KLETT-PERTHES

A 120° 92 B 115° C 110° 93 D 105° E 94 100° F 95° 95 G 90° 98 H

P A C I F I C O C E A N

G u l f o f M e x i c o

Bay of Campeche

Gulf of Tehuantepec

Tropic of Cancer

UNITED STATES

MEXICO

Sierra Madre Occidental

Sierra Madre Oriental

Sierra Madre del Sur

Sierra Madre

Edwards Plateau

Yucatán Pen.

Lower California

G. of California

LOS ANGELES
Pasadena
Oxnard
Long Beach
Anaheim
Santa Ana
Oceanside
SAN DIEGO
TIJUANA
Ensenada
Mexicali
Riverside
Palm Springs
Barstow
Brawley
Yuma
San Luis Río Colorado
PHOENIX
Mesa
Glendale
Chandler
Tucson
Nogales
Flagstaff
Kingman
Prescott
Holbrook
Gallup
Farmington
Albuquerque
Rio Rancho
Santa Fe
Santa Rosa
Sierra Blanca Peak 12,003 ft 3,659 m
Roswell
Las Cruces
Carlsbad
Hobbs
El Paso
JUÁREZ
Douglas
Cananea
Hermosillo
Guaymas
Ciudad Obregón
Navojoa
Huatabampo
Los Mochis
Chihuahua
Cuauhtémoc
Creel
Delicias
Camargo
Hidalgo del Parral
Santa Bárbara
Jiménez
Co. Mohinora 10,827 ft 3,300 m
Culiacán
Gómez Palacio
Torreón
Durango
Mazatlán
Tepic
Puerto Vallarta
Cape Corrientes
ZAPOPAN
GUADALAJARA
Tlaquepaque
Aguascalientes
LEÓN
Irapuato
Guanajuato
Querétaro
Zacatecas
Fresnillo
S. Luis Potosí
Morelia
Uruapan
Apatzingán
Colima
Manzanillo
Nevado de Colima 14,600 ft 4,450 m
Lázaro Cárdenas
Acapulco
Chilpancingo
Iguala
Cuernavaca
Toluca
MEXICO CITY (CD. DE MÉXICO)
ECATEPEC
NEZAHUALCÓYOTEL
PUEBLA
Popocatépetl 17,888 ft 5,452 m
Pico de Orizaba 18,406 ft 5,610 m
Pachuca
Xalapa Enríquez
Veracruz
Boca del Río
Tehuacán
Oaxaca
Coatzacoalcos
Villahermosa
Cárdenas
Juchitán
Tehuantepec
Salina Cruz
Tuxtla Gutiérrez
San Cristóbal de las Casas
Tonalá
Tapachula
Campeche
Cd. del Carmen
Mérida
Progreso
Chichén-Itzá
Valladolid
Cancún
Cozumel
Chetumal
Belize City
BELIZE
Guatemala C. (Cd. de Guatemala)
Quezaltenango
Mixco
Villa Nueva
San Salvador
EL SALVADOR
Nueva San Salvador
Santa Ana
San Miguel
Tegucigalpa
San Pedro Sula
Choloma
El Progreso
Managua
León
Chinandega
Masaya
Monterrey
Saltillo
Guadalupe
Reynosa
Matamoros
Brownsville
McAllen
Harlingen
Nuevo Laredo
Laredo
Monclova
Piedras Negras
Acuña
Del Rio
Eagle Pass
Cd. Victoria
Cd. Madero
Tampico
Cd. Valles
Tuxpán
Poza Rica de Hidalgo
SAN ANTONIO
Austin
HOUSTON
Galveston
Corpus Christi
Victoria
DALLAS
Fort Worth
Arlington
Garland
Plano
Denton
Waco
Abilene
San Angelo
Midland
Odessa
Lubbock
Amarillo
Wichita Falls
Lawton
Oklahoma City
Norman
Tulsa
Wichita
Fort Smith
Little Rock
Memphis
Nashville
Shreveport
Jackson
Baton Rouge
New Orleans
Metairie
Lafayette
Beaumont
Mobile
Biloxi
Gulfport
Hattiesburg
Birmingham
Revillagigedo Islands (MEX.)
Clipperton I. (FRA.)
Islas Tres Marías
Guadalupe I.
Cedros I.
Cocos I. (C.RC.)
Cape San Lucas
La Paz
San José del Cabo

C 110° D 105° E 100° F 95° G 90° H

1:15,000,000
0 200 400 mi
0 200 400 600 km
J K L M N O P
99
112
113
85° 80° 75° 70° 65° 60° 55°
30° 25° 20° 15° 10°
2 3 4 5 6 7 8
ATLANTIC OCEAN
Sargasso Sea
Caribbean Sea
Greater Antilles
Lesser Antilles
Hamilton
Bermuda (U.K.)
Charleston
Huntington
West Virginia
Lexington
Charlottesville
Maryland
Chesapeake Bay
Richmond
Lynchburg
Newport News
Norfolk
Virginia Beach
Bluefield
Roanoke
Danville
Portsmouth
Chesapeake
Johnson City
Winston-Salem
Greensboro
Elizabeth City
Oak Ridge
Mt. Mitchell
6,683 ft
2,037 m
Durham
Raleigh
Knoxville
High Point
Greenville
Asheville
North Carolina
Charlotte
C. Hatteras
Gastonia
Fayetteville
Spartanburg
Jacksonville
Greenville
Wilmington
Anderson
South Carolina
Florence
Athens-Clarke
Columbia
Atlanta
Georgetown
North Charleston
Augusta
Charleston
Macon
Georgia
Columbus
Savannah
Albany
Brunswick
Valdosta
Tallahassee
Jacksonville
Saint Augustine
Gainesville
Apalachee Bay
Ocala
Daytona Beach
Orlando
Cape Canaveral
Clearwater
Tampa
Melbourne
Saint Petersburg
Fort Pierce
Sarasota
Port Saint Lucie
Coopers Town
West Palm Beach
Cape Coral
Marsh Harbour
Gd. Bahama I.
Freeport
Fort Myers
Great Abaco
Hialeah
Fort Lauderdale
Hollywood
Miami
Eleuthera I.
Cape Sable
BAHAMAS
Nassau
Cat I.
Mt. Alvernia
207 ft
63 m
Florida Keys
Straits of Florida
Key West
Andros I.
San Salvador
HAVANA (LA HABANA)
Matanzas
Long Island
Clarence Town
Artemisa
Cárdenas
Santa Clara
Acklins I.
Turks and Caicos Is. (U.K.)
Colón
Pinar del Río
Consolación del Sur
Cienfuegos
Morón
Ciego de Ávila
Grand Turk (Cockburn Town)
Nueva Gerona
Nuevitas
Puerto Padre
CUBA
Sancti Spíritus
Florida
Great Inagua
Isla de la Juventud
Camagüey
Holguín
Moa
Cape Maisí
Windward Passage
Las Tunas
Baracoa
Bayamo
Mayarí
Manzanillo
Sa. Maestra
Guantánamo
Cap-Haïtien
Puerto Plata
DOMINICAN REP.
30,246 ft
9,219 m
Pico Turquino
6,477 ft
1,974 m
Santiago de Cuba
The Bluff
141 ft
43 m
Gonaïves
Santiago
10,417 ft
3,175 m
San Francisco de Macorís
HAITI
La Vega
P. Duarte
La Romana
Cayman Is. (U.K.)
25,197 ft
7,680 m
Georgetown
Grand Cayman
Saint-Marc
Jérémie
Carrefour
Delmas
San Cristóbal
SANTO DOMINGO
Port-au-Prince
La Selle
8,793 ft
2,680 m
Les Cayes
Hispaniola
Montego Bay
JAMAICA
Kingston
Blue Mtn. Peak
7,402 ft
2,256 m
Spanish Town
Portmore
Navassa (U.S.)
Mona Passage
San Juan
Bayamón
Mayagüez
Ponce
Puerto Rico (U.S.)
Virgin Islands, U.S.
British Virgin Is.
Anegada Passage
Charlotte Amalie
St. Croix
Anguilla (U.K.)
St. Maarten (Neth. Ant.)/St-Martin (FRA.)
St-Barthélemy (FRA.)
Barbuda
Basseterre
(Neth. Antilles)
SAINT KITTS AND NEVIS
St. John's
ANTIGUA AND BARBUDA
Plymouth
Montserrat (U.K.)
Pointe-à-Pitre
4,813 ft
1,467 m
Soufrière
Guadeloupe (FRA.)
Basse-Terre
Marie-Galante
DOMINICA
Roseau
Mt. Pelée
4,583 ft
1,397 m
Fort-de-France
Martinique (FRA.)
SAINT LUCIA
Castries
BARBADOS
SAINT VINCENT AND THE GRENADINES
Kingstown
Bridgetown
Mt. St. Cathrine
2,756 ft
840 m
GRENADA
St. George's
Tobago
Blanquilla
Aruba (NLD.)
Netherlands Antilles
Curaçao
Bonaire
Oranjestad
Willemstad
Punta Gallinas
La Asunción
Margarita
Carúpano
Port of Spain
TRINIDAD AND TOBAGO
Trinidad
Chaguanas
San Fernando
Guajira Pen.
G. of Venezuela
Punta Fijo
Ríohacha
Coro
Catia la Mar
CARACAS
Cumaná
8,517 ft
2,596 m
Santa Marta
Maicao
San Felipe
Puerto Cabello
Barcelona
Puerto la Cruz
Co. Turimiquire
Maturín
Tucupita
BARRANQUILLA
Pico Cristóbal Colón
18,947 ft
5,775 m
MARACAIBO
Barquisimeto
Maracay
Petare
Ciénaga
Soledad
Cabimas
VALENCIA
San Juan de los Morros
6,336 ft
1,931 m
El Tigre
Ciudad Guayana
Cartagena
Valledupar
Lake Maracaibo
Acarigua
Ciudad Bolívar
Upata
Trujillo
San Carlos
El Carmen de Bolívar
San Carlos del Zulia
Valera
Guanare
Calabozo
Orinoco
Guri Res.
Gulf of Darién
Sincelejo
Pico Bolívar
Barinas
San Fernando de Apure
Apure
Ciudad Piar
Mérida
16,428 ft
5,007 m
El Dorado
Ocaña
Montería
Turbo
Cúcuta
VENEZUELA
GUYANA
Cauca
Magdalena
San Cristóbal
Auyán Tepuy
8,399 ft
2,560 m
Mt. Roraima
9,219 ft
2,810 m
Mahdia
Bucaramanga
Caroní
Barrancabermeja
Floridablanca
Arauca
Meta
Puerto Carreño
7,497 ft
2,285 m
Co Yaví
Santa Elena de Uairén
Bello
Puerto Berrío
Cocuy
18,022 ft
5,493 m
MEDELLÍN
Envigado
Puerto Ayacucho
Guiana Highlands
Itagüí
COLOMBIA
La Dorada
Puerto Nariño
Lethem
Quibdó
Manizales
Tunja
Yopal
Orocué
Puerto Inírida
San Fernando de Atabapo
BRAZIL
Roraima
Pereira
Ibagué
BOGOTÁ
Guaviare
Boa Vista
13,944 ft
4,250 m
Armenia
Girardot
Villavicencio
Caracaraí
Puerto Lempira
Coco
C. Gracias á Dios
6,529 ft
1,990 m
Puerto Cabezas
Providencia I. (COL.)
NICARAGUA
Rama
San Andrés
San Andrés I.
Bluefields
L. Nicaragua
San Carlos
COSTA RICA
Alajuela
Limón
Cartago
San José
Cerro Cirripó
12,533 ft
3,820 m
Volcán Barú
11,401 ft
3,475 m
Bocas del Toro
Panama Canal
Punta Manzanillo
El Porvenir
Colón
Panama City (Panamá)
San Miguelito
PANAMA
La Palma
Puerto Armuelles
David
Chitré
Gulf of Panama
Santiago
Azuero Pen.
Punta Mala
Coiba

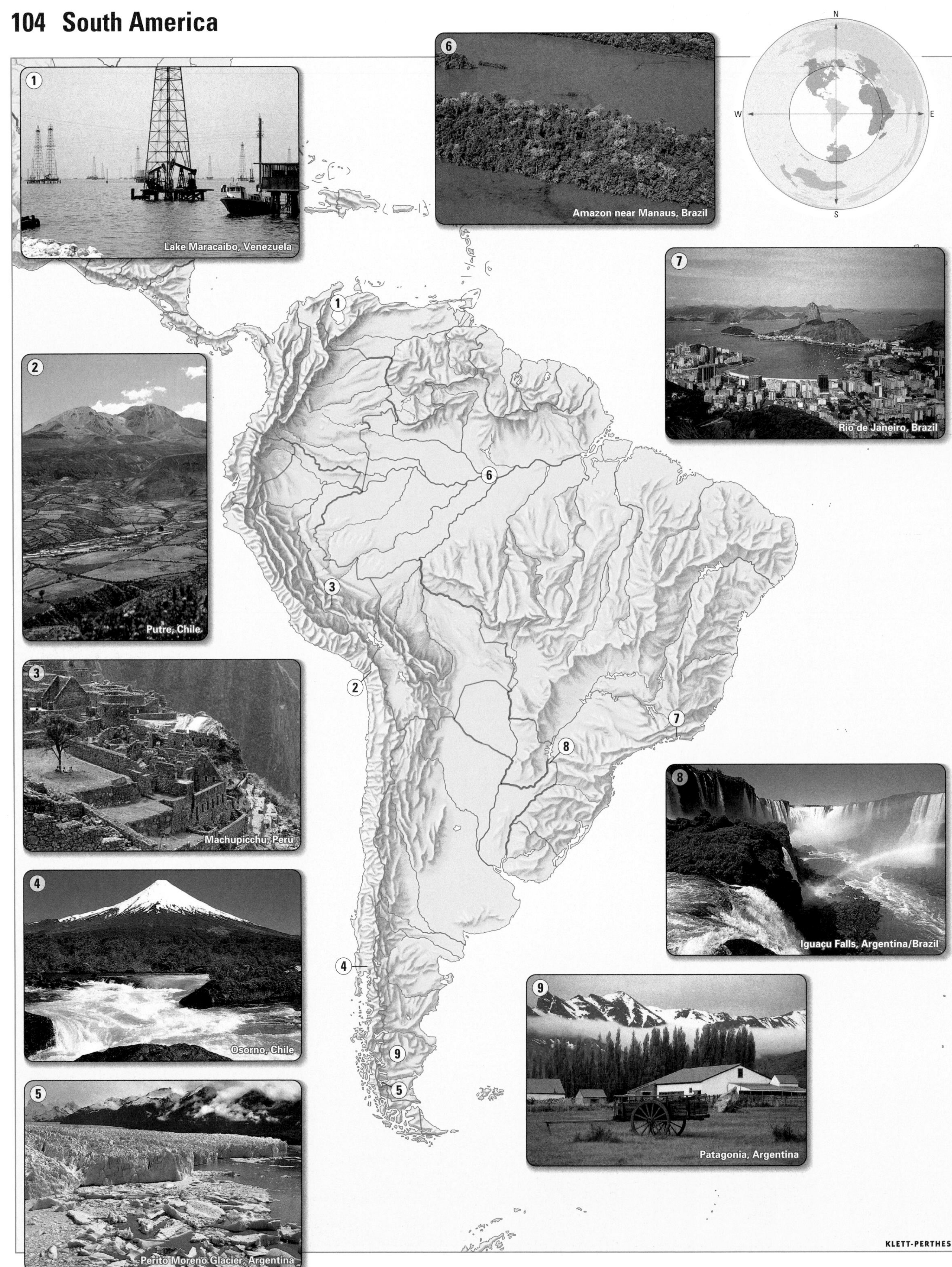

1 Lake Maracaibo, Venezuela

2 Putre, Chile

3 Machupicchu, Peru

4 Osorno, Chile

5 Perito Moreno Glacier, Argentina

6 Amazon near Manaus, Brazil

7 Rio de Janeiro, Brazil

8 Iguaçu Falls, Argentina/Brazil

9 Patagonia, Argentina

0 500 1,000 mi
0 500 1,000 1,500 2,000 km

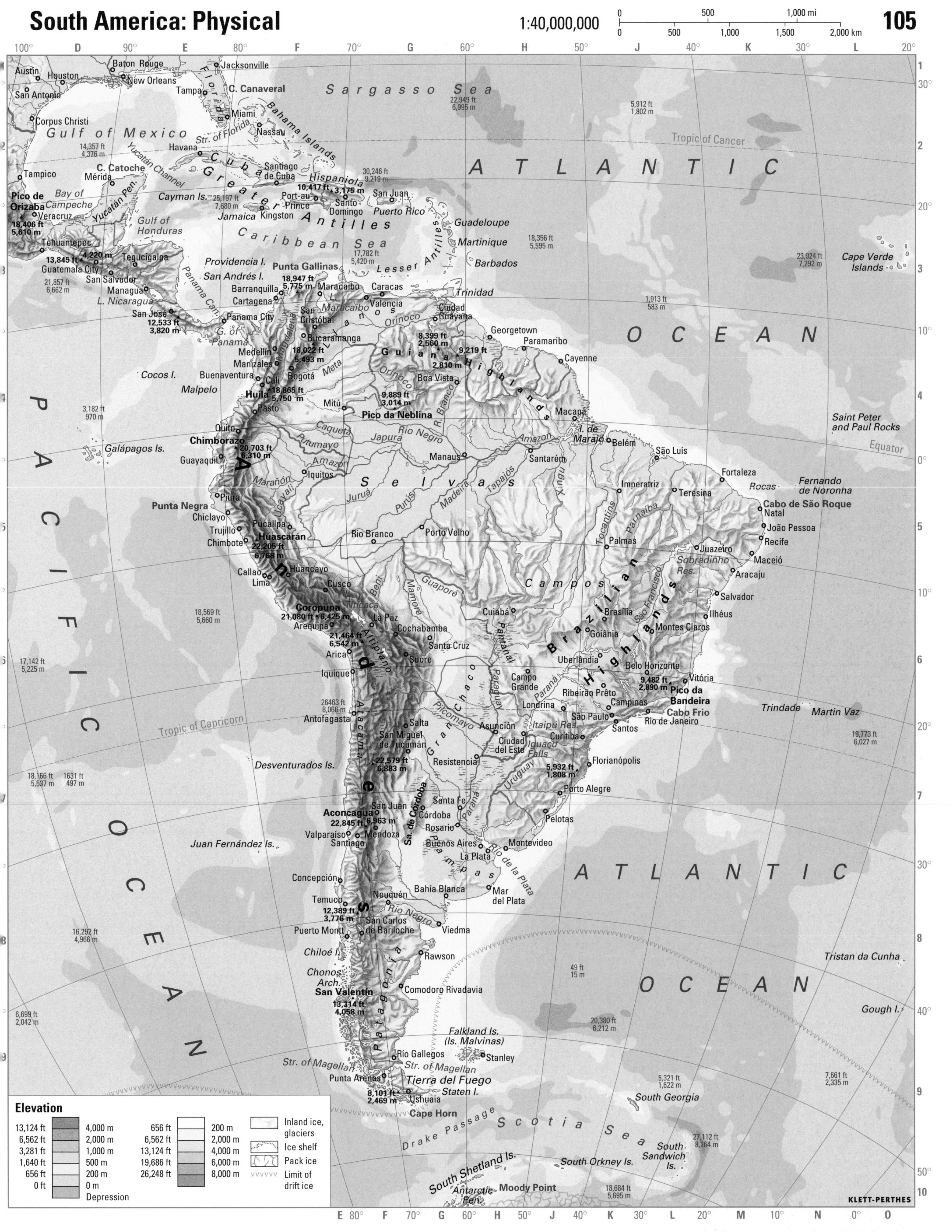

1:40,000,000

0 500 1,000 mi
0 500 1,000 1,500 2,000 km
Jacksonville
New Orleans
San Antonio
Houston
Tampa
Florida
Miami
Sargasso Sea
Bahama Islands
Str. of Florida
Gulf of Mexico
Havana
Cuba
Tropic of Cancer
Yucatán Channel
Greater Antilles
Hispaniola
ATLANTIC
Bay of Campeche
Yucatán
Cayman Is.
Puerto Rico
Jamaica
Gulf of Honduras
Caribbean Sea
Guadeloupe
Martinique
Lesser Antilles
Barbados
Providencia I.
San Andrés I.
Guatemala City
Panama Can.
Maracaibo
Caracas
Trinidad
L. Nicaragua
Llanos
Orinoco
Cape Verde Islands
G. of Panama
Magdalena
OCEAN
Bogotá
Meta
Guiana Highlands
Cocos I.
Malpelo
PACIFIC OCEAN
Quito
Caquetá
Putumayo
Japurá
Rio Negro
R. Branco
Amazon
I. de Marajó
Saint Peter and Paul Rocks
Galápagos Is.
Equator
Andes
Marañón
Selvas
Xingu
Ucayali
Juruá
Purus
Madeira
Tapajós
Rocas
Fernando de Noronha
Tocantins
Parnaíba
Sobradinho Res.
Lima
Campos
Beni
Mamoré
Guaporé
L. Titicaca
Brazilian Highlands
São Francisco
Brasília
Goiânia
Altiplano
Pantanal
Belo Horizonte
Paraguay
Paraná
Vitória
Gran Chaco
Pilcomayo
Trindade
Martin Vaz
São Paulo
Rio de Janeiro
Tropic of Capricorn
Atacama
Itaipú Res.
Curitiba
Desventurados Is.
Uruguay
Porto Alegre
Sa. de Córdoba
Córdoba
Juan Fernández Is.
Santiago
Buenos Aires
Montevideo
Río de la Plata
Pampas
ATLANTIC
Río Negro
Chiloé I.
Chonos Arch.
Patagonia
OCEAN
Tristan da Cunha
Gough I.
Falkland Is. (Is. Malvinas)
Str. of Magellan
Tierra del Fuego
Staten I.
South Georgia
Drake Passage
Scotia Sea
South Sandwich Is.
South Orkney Is.
South Shetland Is.
Antarctic Pen.
Land Cover
(Explanations on page 32)
Natural Vegetation
Evergreen needleleaf forests
Evergreen broadleaf forests
Deciduous needleleaf forests
Deciduous broadleaf forests
Mixed forests
Closed shrublands
Open shrublands
Woody savannas
Savannas
Grasslands
Permanent wetlands
Developed and Mosaic Lands
Croplands
Cropland/natural vegetation mosaic
Urban and built-up lands
Non-Vegetated Lands
Snow and ice
Barren or sparsely vegetated
Water bodies
No data
KLETT-PERTHES

1:40,000,000
0 500 1,000 mi
0 500 1,000 1,500 2,000 km
Sargasso Sea
Gulf of Mexico
ATLANTIC OCEAN
PACIFIC OCEAN
Caribbean Sea
Tropic of Cancer
Equator
Tropic of Capricorn
Drake Passage
Scotia Sea
UNITED STATES
MEXICO
CUBA
BAHAMAS
HAITI
DOMINICAN REP.
Puerto Rico (U.S.)
JAMAICA
BELIZE
GUATEMALA
HONDURAS
EL SALVADOR
NICARAGUA
COSTA RICA
PANAMA
Aruba (NLD.)
Neth. Antilles
TRINIDAD AND TOBAGO
VENEZUELA
GUYANA
SURINAME
French Guiana
COLOMBIA
ECUADOR
PERU
BRAZIL
BOLIVIA
PARAGUAY
CHILE
ARGENTINA
URUGUAY
Houston
San Antonio
New Orleans
Jacksonville
Tampa
Miami
Freeport
Corpus Christi
Havana
Tampico
Mérida
Veracruz
Akal
Minatitlán
Pemex
Belmopan
Tegucigalpa
Guatemala City
San Salvador
Managua
San José
Nicaro
Santiago de Cuba
Santo Domingo
San Juan
St. Croix
Sta. Marta
Barranquilla
Pto. Fijo
Caracas
M.
Valencia
Maturín
Port of Spain
Coveñas
Panama City
Sinco
El Tigre
Cd. Guayana
Cerro Bolívar
Georgetown
Paramaribo
Medellín
Paz del Río
Bogotá
Cali
Tumaco
Esmeraldas
Quito
Orito
Amapá
Serra do Navio
Macapá
Pôrto Trombetas
Belém
São Luís
Manaus
Guayaquil
Capahua
Iquitos
Fortaleza
Itaituba
Marabá
Carajás
Serra Pelada
Agulha
Bayovár
Pucallpa
Porto Velho
João Pessoa
Recife
Chimbote
Cerro de Pasco
La Oroya
Maceió
Senhor do Bonfim
Aracaju
Lima
Cusco
Niquelândia
Salvador
Pisco
Marcona
Puno
Cuiabá
Brasília
La Paz
Ilo
Oruro
Santa Cruz
Corumbá
Diamantina
Arica
Itabira
Iquique
Potosí
Belo Horizonte
Vitória
Chuquicamata
Poços de Caldas
V.R.
São Paulo
Campo Durán
Antofagasta
Itaipú
Santos
Rio de Janeiro
Jujuy
Asunción
Curitiba
El Salvador
Resistencia
Blumenau
Copiapó
Porto Alegre
La Senena
Córdoba
Santa Fe
Rio Grande
Santiago
Rosario
Valparaíso
Mendoza
Montevideo
El Teniente
Buenos Aires
Concepción
Mar del Plata
Bahía Blanca
Valdivia
Neuquén
Puerto Madryn
Comodoro Rivadavia
El Turbio
Río Gallegos
Service and Industry
Service center (finance, trade, research, government, tourism)
Other location
Industrial center
Metal processing, mechanical engineering, vehicle manufacturing, shipbuilding
Aerospace industry
Electronics industry, electrical and precision engineering
Textile, garment, and leather goods industries
Chemical, wood working, pulp and paper, printing industries
Food processing
Mining and Smelting
Energy raw material
Hard coal
Uranium
Petroleum
Natural gas
Oil refinery
Oil pipeline
Gas pipeline
Oil terminal embarkation
Hydro-electric power station
Nuclear power station
Ore and other raw materials
Iron ore
Chromite
Manganese
Nickel
Tungsten
Bauxite
Copper
Antimony
Lead/zinc
Tin
Bismuth
Gold
Silver
Platinum
Gemstones
Sodium chloride
Phosphate
Salpeter
Smelting
Iron and steel production works
Non-ferrous metal production
Light metal (aluminum) production
Conurbation
Symbol size indicates relative importance of a location.
B. Barcelona
M. Maracaibo
V.R. Volta Redonda
KLETT-PERTHES

1:40,000,000

UNITED STATES
HOUSTON
SAN ANTONIO
Austin
Baton Rouge
New Orleans
Jacksonville
Tampa
C. Canaveral
Miami
Nassau
Corpus Christi
Sargasso Sea
Gulf of Mexico
Str. of Florida
BAHAMAS
Tropic of Cancer
MEXICO
HAVANA
CUBA
Yucatán Channel
Turks and Caicos Is. (U.K.)
Virgin Islands, U.S.
British Virgin Is. (U.K.)
ATLANTIC
Tampico
C. Catoche
Mérida
Cayman Is. (U.K.)
Santiago de Cuba
Hispaniola
HAITI
DOMINICAN REP.
San Juan
Bay of Campeche
Port-au-Prince
SANTO DOMINGO
Puerto Rico (U.S.)
Anguilla (U.K.)
ANTIGUA AND BARBUDA
Veracruz
BELIZE
G. of Honduras
Belmopan
Kingston
JAMAICA
Navassa (U.S.)
SAINT KITTS AND NEVIS
Montserrat (U.K.)
Guadeloupe (FRA.)
DOMINICA
Martinique (FRA.)
GUATEMALA
Caribbean Sea
Tehuantepec
HONDURAS
Tegucigalpa
Guatemala City
Providencia I. (COL.)
Aruba (NLD.)
Neth. Antilles
ST. LUCIA
ST. VINCENT AND THE GRENADINES
BARBADOS
GRENADA
CAPE VERDE
Praia
San Salvador
EL SALVADOR
NICARAGUA
Managua
L. Nicaragua
Panama Can.
San Andrés I.
Punta Gallinas
BARRANQUILLA
Cartagena
MARACAIBO
L. Maracaibo
CARACAS
VALENCIA
Port of Spain
TRINIDAD AND TOBAGO
San José
COSTA RICA
Panama City
PANAMA
G. of Panama
San Cristóbal
Orinoco
Ciudad Guayana
VENEZUELA
GUYANA
Georgetown
Paramaribo
OCEAN
MEDELLÍN
Bucaramanga
Manizales
BOGOTÁ
Cayenne
French Guiana
SURINAME
Cocos I. (C.RC.)
Malpelo (COL.)
Buenaventura
CALI
COLOMBIA
Meta
Magdalena
Boa Vista
R. Branco
Mitú
Macapá
Pasto
QUITO
ECUADOR
Caquetá
Putumayo
Japurá
Rio Negro
Amazon
Saint Peter and Paul Rocks
PACIFIC OCEAN
Galápagos Is. (ECU.)
GUAYAQUIL
MANAUS
Santarém
BELÉM
São Luís
Equator
(BRA.)
Marañón
Iquitos
Xingu
Tapajós
Madeira
Purús
Juruá
Ucayali
Imperatriz
Teresina
FORTALEZA
Rocas
Fernando de Noronha
Piura
Punta Negra
Chiclayo
PERU
Tocantins
Parnaíba
Cabo de São Roque
Natal
João Pessoa
RECIFE
Trujillo
Chimbote
Pucallpa
Rio Branco
Porto Velho
BRAZIL
Palmas
Juazeiro
Sobradinho Res.
Maceió
Aracaju
Callao
LIMA
Huancayo
Cusco
Beni
Mamoré
Guaporé
São Francisco
SALVADOR
L. Titicaca
La Paz
Cochabamba
Cuiabá
BRASÍLIA
Montes Claros
Ilhéus
Arequipa
SANTA CRUZ
GOIÂNIA
BOLIVIA
Arica
Sucre
Uberlândia
BELO HORIZONTE
Iquique
Campo Grande
Paraguay
Paraná
Ribeirão Prêto
Vitória
PARAGUAY
Campinas
Londrina
SÃO PAULO
Cabo Frio
Trindade
Martin Vaz (BRA.)
Tropic of Capricorn
Antofagasta
Pilcomayo
Salta
Itaipú Res.
Santos
RIO DE JANEIRO
Asunción
Ciudad del Este
CURITIBA
Desventurados Is. (CHL.)
San Miguel de Tucumán
Resistencia
Florianópolis
CHILE
Uruguay
PORTO ALEGRE
ARGENTINA
San Juan
Santa Fe
CÓRDOBA
Pelotas
Valparaíso
Mendoza
Rosario
URUGUAY
Juan Fernández Is. (CHL.)
SANTIAGO
BUENOS AIRES
MONTEVIDEO
La Plata
Río de la Plata
Concepción
Bahía Blanca
Mar del Plata
Temuco
Neuquén
Río Negro
Viedma
Puerto Montt
San Carlos de Bariloche
Chiloé I.
Rawson
Tristan da Cunha (U.K.)
Chonos Arch.
Comodoro Rivadavia
Gough I.
Falkland Is. (Is. Malvinas) (U.K.)
Río Gallegos
Stanley
Str. of Magellan
Punta Arenas
Tierra del Fuego
Staten I.
Ushuaia
South Georgia and the South Sandwich Is. (U.K.)
Cape Horn
Drake Passage
Scotia Sea
South Shetland Is.
South Orkney Is.
Moody Point
KLETT-PERTHES

South America: Ethnic Groups

1:40,000,000

1:40,000,000
0 500 1,000 mi
0 500 1,000 1,500 2,000 km
KLETT-PERTHES
Climate Diagrams (by H. Walter)
2,263 mm 25.0 °C 89.1 in. 77.0 °F Annual averages of precipitation and air temperature
1 3 6 9 12 Months
3 m 10 ft Altitude
Precipitation curve
Temperature curve
Dry season
Ar 2,853 mm 26.2 °C 112.3 in. 79.2 °F Iquitos 126 m 413 ft
Am 2,573 mm 26.6 °C 101.3 in. 80.0 °F Macapá 15 m 49 ft
Aw 1,555 mm 20.7 °C 61.2 in. 69.3 °F Brasília 1,158 m 3,799 ft
Aw 912 mm 27.4 °C 35.9 in. 81.3 °F Barranquilla 21 m 69 ft
As 1,595 mm 26.0 °C 62.8 in. 78.8 °F Aracaju 5 m 16 ft
BS 564 mm 27.6 °C 22.2 in. 81.7 °F Maracaibo 65 m 213 ft
BS 235 mm 12.8 °C 9.3 in. 55.0 °F Com. Rivadavia 46 m 151 ft
BW 1 mm 18.7 °C 0.04 in. 65.7 °F Arica 58 m 190 ft
Cs 301 mm 14.3 °C 11.9 in. 57.7 °F Santiago 520 m 1,706 ft
Cw 757 mm 16.4 °C 29.8 in. 61.5 °F Salta 1,221 m 4,006 ft
Cr 1,173 mm 17.5 °C 46.2 in. 63.5 °F Buenos Aires 25 m 82 ft
Do 1,705 mm 10.1 °C 67.1 in. 50.2 °F Puerto Montt 85 m 279 ft
Eo 723 mm 6.3 °C 28.5 in. 43.3 °F Balmaceda 520 m 1,706 ft
FT 524 mm 5.7 °C 20.6 in. 42.3 °F Ushuaia 14 m 46 ft
Climatic Regions
(Modified Koeppen System based on Trewartha; cf. p. 18/19)
Tropical Rainy Climates
Ar Tropical rainy climate
Am Tropical monsoon rain climate
Aw Tropical summer rain climate
As Tropical winter rain climate
Dry Climates
BS Steppe climate
BW Desert climate
BM Marine dry climate
Subtropical Climates
Cr Subtropical rain climate
Cw Subtropical summer rain climate
Cs Subtropical winter rain climate
Temperate Climates
Do Oceanic temperate climate
Dc Continental temperate climate
Boreal Climates
Eo Oceanic boreal climate
Polar Climates
FT Tundra climate
FI Perpetual frost climate
Meteorological station with climate diagram
Sargasso Sea
Gulf of Mexico
Tropic of Cancer
Str. of Florida
Bahama Islands (Ar/Aw/Am)
Cuba
Greater Antilles
Hispaniola
Bay of Campeche
Cayman Is.
Jamaica
Puerto Rico
Gulf of Honduras
Caribbean Sea
Guadeloupe
Martinique
Barbados
Lesser Antilles
Providencia I.
San Andrés I.
Trinidad
L. Nicaragua
G. of Panama
Cocos I.
Malpelo
Galápagos Is. (BS/Aw)
PACIFIC OCEAN
ATLANTIC OCEAN
Saint Peter and Paul Rocks
Equator
Rocas
Fernando de Noronha
Sobradinho Res.
Itaipú Res.
Trindade
Martin Vaz
Tropic of Capricorn
Rio de la Plata
Chiloé I.
Chonos Arch.
Falkland Is. (Is. Malvinas)
Str. of Magellan
Tierra del Fuego
Staten I.
Drake Passage
Scotia Sea
South Georgia
South Orkney Is.
South Sandwich Is.
South Shetland Is.
Magdalena
Orinoco
Meta
Caquetá
Putumayo
Japurá
Rio Negro
R. Branco
Amazon
Marañón
Ucayali
Juruá
Purus
Madeira
Tapajós
Xingu
Tocantins
Parnaíba
São Francisco
Beni
Mamoré
Guaporé
Titicaca
Pilcomayo
Paraguay
Paraná
Uruguay
Barranquilla
Maracaibo
Macapá
Iquitos
Aracaju
Brasília
Arica
Salta
Santiago
Buenos Aires
Puerto Montt
Balmaceda
Comodoro Rivadavia
Ushuaia

1:40,000,000

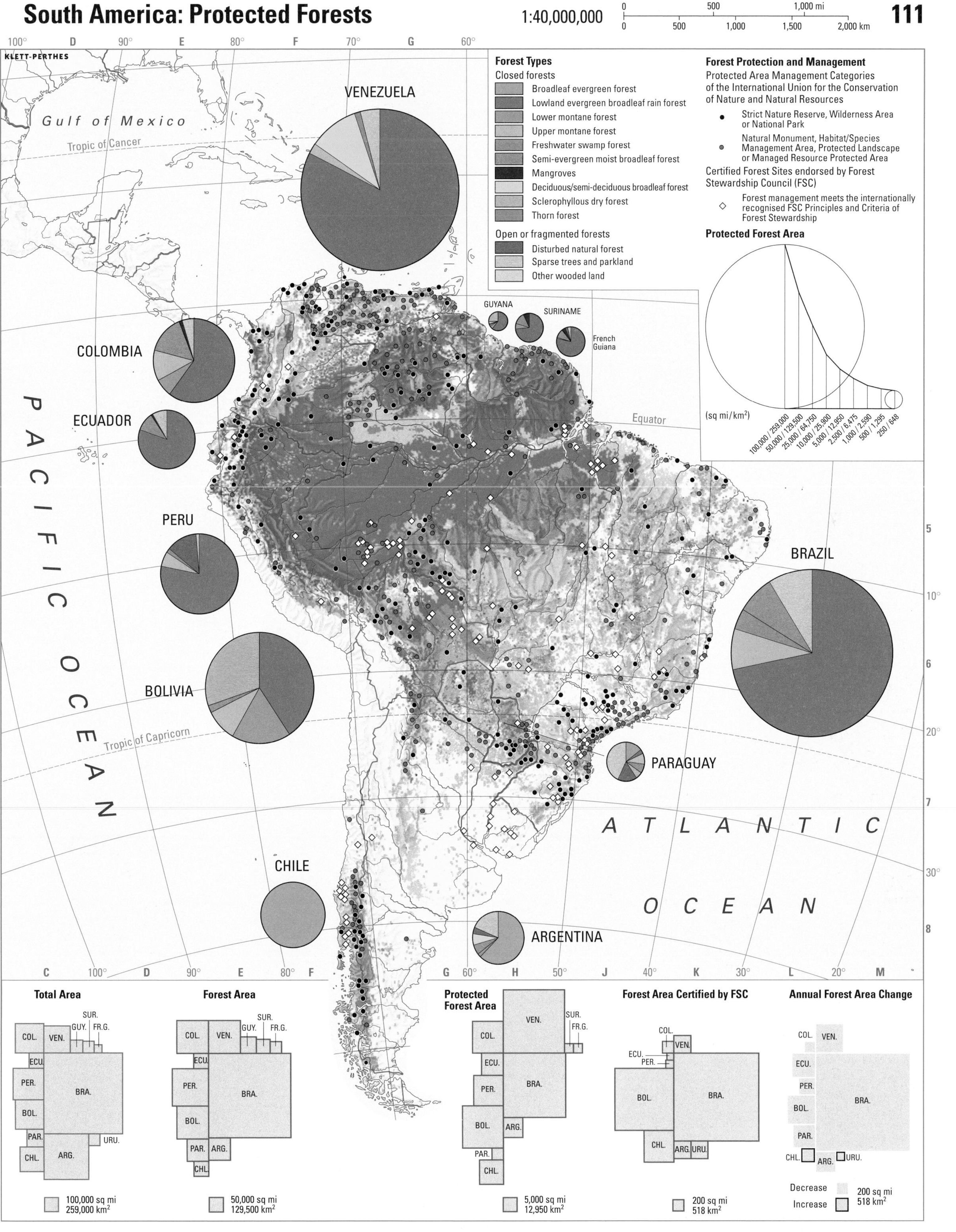

0 500 1,000 mi
0 500 1,000 1,500 2,000 km
KLETT-PERTHES
Forest Types
Closed forests
Broadleaf evergreen forest
Lowland evergreen broadleaf rain forest
Lower montane forest
Upper montane forest
Freshwater swamp forest
Semi-evergreen moist broadleaf forest
Mangroves
Deciduous/semi-deciduous broadleaf forest
Sclerophyllous dry forest
Thorn forest
Open or fragmented forests
Disturbed natural forest
Sparse trees and parkland
Other wooded land
Forest Protection and Management
Protected Area Management Categories of the International Union for the Conservation of Nature and Natural Resources
Strict Nature Reserve, Wilderness Area or National Park
Natural Monument, Habitat/Species Management Area, Protected Landscape or Managed Resource Protected Area
Certified Forest Sites endorsed by Forest Stewardship Council (FSC)
Forest management meets the internationally recognised FSC Principles and Criteria of Forest Stewardship
Protected Forest Area
(sq mi/km²)
100,000 / 259,000
50,000 / 129,500
25,000 / 64,750
10,000 / 25,900
5,000 / 12,950
2,500 / 6,475
1,000 / 2,590
500 / 1,295
250 / 648
Gulf of Mexico
Tropic of Cancer
Equator
Tropic of Capricorn
PACIFIC OCEAN
ATLANTIC OCEAN
VENEZUELA
COLOMBIA
ECUADOR
PERU
BOLIVIA
CHILE
ARGENTINA
PARAGUAY
BRAZIL
GUYANA
SURINAME
French Guiana
Total Area
Forest Area
Protected Forest Area
Forest Area Certified by FSC
Annual Forest Area Change
COL. VEN. GUY. SUR. FR.G. ECU. PER. BRA. BOL. PAR. URU. CHL. ARG.
100,000 sq mi 259,000 km²
50,000 sq mi 129,500 km²
5,000 sq mi 12,950 km²
200 sq mi 518 km²
Decrease
Increase
200 sq mi 518 km²

102
103
Caribbean Sea
PACIFIC
OCEAN
Galápagos Is.
(ECU.)
Marchena
5,601 ft
1,707 m
Volcano Wolf
San Salvador
Santa Cruz
Fernandina
Pto. Ayora
Pto. Baquerizo Moreno
Puerto Villamil
Isabela
Cristóbal
Santa Maria
Española
Equator
Cocos I.
(C.RC.)
Malpelo
(COL.)
Providencia I.
(COL.)
San Andrés
San Andrés I.
N. S. S.
San S.
Soyapango
San Miguel
EL SALVADOR
La Unión
Estelí
Choluteca
NICARAGUA
6,529 ft
1,990 m
Chinandega
Matagalpa
León
Boaco
Rama
MANAGUA
Masaya
Granada
Bluefields
L. Nicaragua
San Carlos
Liberia
COSTA RICA
Limón
Puntarenas
Alajuela
Pen. de Nicoya
Cabo Blanco
San José
Cartago
Cerro Cirripó
12,533 ft
3,820 m
Volcán Barú
11,401 ft
3,475 m
Puerto Armuelles
David
Bocas del Toro
Colón
Panama Canal
Punta Manzanilla
El Porvenir
San Miguelito
Arraiján
Panama City
(Panamá)
PANAMA
Gulf of Panama
Santiago
Chitré
Azuero Pen.
Coiba
Punta Mala
La Palma
Gulf of Darién
El Carmen de Bolívar
Santa Marta
BARRANQUILLA
Ciénaga
Cartagena
Soledad
18,947 ft
5,775 m
Pico Cristóbal Colón
Valledupar
Riohacha
Punta Gallinas
Guajira Pen.
Maicao
MARACAIBO
Cabimas
Lake Maracaibo
Sincelejo
Montería
Turbo
Ocaña
Cúcuta
San Cristóbal
Bucaramanga
Floridablanca
Barrancabermeja
Cocuy
18,022 ft
5,493 m
Bello
MEDELLÍN
Envigado
Itagüí
Puerto Berrío
La Dorada
Tunja
Yopal
Quibdó
Manizales
Pereira
Armenia
Ibagué
BOGOTÁ
Girardot
Villavicencio
13,944 ft
4,250 m
Buenaventura
Tuluá
Buga
Palmira
CALI
Jamundí
14,961 ft
4,560 m
Neiva
Huila
18,865 ft
5,750 m
Popayán
COLOMBIA
Cordillera Occidental
Cordillera Central
Cordillera Oriental
Magdalena
Cauca
Meta
Orocué
Guaviare
San José del Guaviare
Vaupés
Mitú
Tumaco
Pasto
Mocoa
Florencia
San Lorenzo
Ipiales
Tulcán
Puerto Asís
Punta Galera
Esmeraldas
Ibarra
Santo Domingo de los Colorados
QUITO
Puerto Francisco de Orellana
Cotopaxi
19,348 ft
5,897 m
Tena
ECUADOR
Portoviejo
Manta
Quevedo
Chimborazo
6,310 m
20,703 ft
Ambato
Puyo
Babahoyo
Riobamba
GUAYAQUIL
Milagro
Macas
Pta. Sta. Elena
Salinas
Eloy Alfaro
Gulf of Guayaquil
Puná I.
Azogues
Cuenca
Machala
Tumbes
Loja
Zamora
12,907 ft
3,934 m
Talara
Sullana
Paita
Cerro Viejo
Chulucanas
Piura
Jaén
Punta Negra
Lambayeque
Chiclayo
Cajamarca
Pacasmayo
Trujillo
Chimbote
Huallanca
22,205 ft
6,768 m
Huascarán
Huaraz
Barranca
Huacho
LIMA
Callao
La Oroya
Chosica
Huancayo
Huancavelica
Chincha Alta
Pisco
Ayacucho
Ica
Punta Carreta
Nazca
Puquio
Chala
Andes
Cordillera Central
Cordillera Occidental
Cordillera Oriental
Marañón
Yurimaguas
Moyobamba
Chachapoyas
Tarapoto
Juanjuí
Orellana
Ucayali
Huallaga
Pucallpa
Uchiza
Tingo María
Huánuco
Cerro de Pasco
PERU
Iquitos
Napo
Putumayo
Caquetá
Araracuara
Requena
Leticia
Tabatinga
Benjamin Constant
Amazon
Quillabamba
Machupicchu
20,575 ft
6,271 m
Salcantay
Cusco
Abancay
Sicuani
Sandia
Juliaca
Puerto Acosta
L. Titicaca
21,080 ft
6,425 m
Coropuna
19,932 ft
6,075 m
Chachani
Arequipa
Puno
Mollendo
Moquegua
Ilo
Tacna
Arica
Iquique
CHILE
Altiplano
Ancohuma
21,087 ft
6,427 m
El Alto
La Paz
Illimani
21,201 ft
6,462 m
Guaqui
Viacha
BOLIVIA
Quillacollo
Sacaba
Cochabamba
21,464 ft
6,542 m
Sajama
Putre
Oruro
Llallagua
L. Poopó
Salar de Uyuni
Uyuni
20,263 ft
6,176 m
Aucanquilcha
Chuquicamata
Tocopilla
19,751 ft
6,020 m
Potosí
Sucre
Tarija
Tupiza
Villazón
Yacuiba
Challapata
Aiquile
Cabezas
Montero
SANTA CR
Aruba
(NLD.)
Oranj.
Netherlands Antilles
Bonaire
Willemstad
Curaçao
Gulf of Venezuela
Punto Fijo
Coro
San Felipe
Puerto Cabello
Catia la Mar
CARACAS
Petare
Maracay
VALENCIA
Barquisimeto
Valera
Trujillo
San Carlos del Zulia
6,336 ft
1,931 m
S. Carlos
San Juan de los Morros
Acarigua
Guanare
Mérida
Pico Bolívar
16,428 ft
5,007 m
Barinas
Apure
San Fernando de Apure
Calabozo
Barcelona
Cumaná
Carúpano
Margarita
Blanquilla
Pto. la Cruz
El Tigre
Ciudad Bolívar
Orinoco
Ciudad Piar
Maturín
VENEZUELA
Arauca
Puerto Carreño
Puerto Ayacucho
7,497 ft
2,285 m
Co. Yaví
Puerto Nariño
Puerto Inírida
San Fernando de Atabapo
Guiana
Casiquiare
R. Negro
San Carlos de Río Negro
9,889 ft
3,014 m
Pico da Neblina
S. Gabriel da Cachoeira
Santa Isabel do Rio Negro
Japurá
Fonte Boa
Tefé
São Paulo de Olivença
Carauari
Juruá
Eirunepé
Amazonas
Lábrea
Cruzeiro do Sul
Tarauacá
Acre
Purús
Boca do Acre
Sena Madureira
Rio Branco
Porto Velho
Ariquemes
Guayaramerín
Guajará-Mirim
Riberalta
Cobija
Puerto Maldonado
Beni
Mamoré
Santa Ana
Apolo
Rurrenabaque
San Borja
San Ignacio
Trinidad
Todos Santos
Ascensión
Pilcomayo
KLETT-PERTHES

1:15,000,000
0 200 400 mi
0 200 400 600 km
60° H 55° J 50° K 45° L 40° M
ATLANTIC
OCEAN
Mt. St. Cathrine
GRENADA
Saint George's
Tobago
TRINIDAD AND TOBAGO
Trinidad
San Fernando
Tucupita
Mabaruma
Matthews Ridge
Anna Regina
El Dorado
Vreed-en-Hoop
Georgetown
Paradise
Bartica
New Amsterdam
Fort Wellington
Corriverton
Linden
Nieuw Nickerie
Totness
Paramaribo
Nieuw Amsterdam
Groningen
Lelydorp
Albina
Onverwacht
Brokopondo
Mt. Roraima
9,219 ft
2,810 m
Mahdia
St-Laurent-du-Maroni
Kourou
Cayenne
Matoury
SURINAME
Juliana Top
4,036 ft
1,230 m
Maripasoula
Bellevue de l'Inini
2,792 ft
851 m
French Guiana
Diapoque
Highlands
Boa Vista
Lethem
2,389 ft
728 m
Essequibo
2,973 ft
906 m
Tumucumaque Mts.
Calçoene
Amapá
Maracá I.
Caracaraí
Amapá
Serra do Navio
Porto Grande
Macapá
Porto Santana
Caviana I.
Ilha de Marajó
Soure
Baía de Marajó
Laranjal do Jari
Balbina Res.
Óbidos
Alenquer
Almeirim
Breves
Ananindeua
Vigia
Bragança
BELÉM
Castanhal
Abaetetuba
Cametá
Amazon
Rio Negro
MANAUS
Itacoatiara
Manacapuru
Parintins
Santarém
Maués
Altamira
Xingu
Tocantins
Paragominas
Tucuruí
São Luís
Baía de São Marcos
Primeira Cruz
Tutóia
Parnaíba
Ponta Jericoacoara
Camocim
São Bernardo
Santa Inês
Itapipoca
Sobral
FORTALEZA
Caucaia
Maranguape
Maracanaú
Itaituba
Borba
Purus
Iriri
Pará
Serra dos Carajás
Bacabal
Açailândia
Pedreiras
Codó
Caxias
Piripiri
Serra da Ibiapaba
Campo Maior
Aracati
Maranhão
Timon
Teresina
Ceará
Mossoró
Madeira
Manicoré
Tapajós
Marabá
Imperatriz
Carajás
Araguatins
Barra do Corda
Crateús
2,379 ft
725 m
Macau
Jacaré-a-Canga
São Félix do Xingu
Tocantinópolis
Rocas
Fernando de Noronha (BRA.)
Cabo de São Roque
Rio Grande do Norte
Natal
Parnamirim
Araguaína
Carolina
Floriano
Iguatu
Caicó
Picos
Crato
Juazeiro do Norte
Patos
Redenção
Conceição do Araguaia
Balsas
Piauí
3,576 ft
1,090 m
Campina Grande
Paraíba
João Pessoa
Santa Rita
Salgueiro
Serra Talhada
Pernambuco
Caruaru
Olinda
RECIFE
Jaboatão
Garanhuns
Roosevelt
Juruena
Araguaia
Miracema de Tocantins
Alto Parnaíba
Petrolina
Juazeiro
Paulo Afonso
Rio Largo
Alagoas
Maceió
Arapiraca
Ji-Paraná
Cacaol
Porto Nacional
Palmas
Corrente
Sobradinho Res.
Senhor do Bonfim
São Francisco
Sergipe
Mato Grosso
Tocantins
Xingu
Dianópolis
Barra
Nossa Senhora do Socorro
Aracaju
São Cristovão
Estância
Sinop
São Félix do Araguaia
Vilhena
Gurupi
Barreiras
Sa. Geral de Goiás
Taguatinga
Bahia
Ibotirama
Alagoinhas
Feira de Santana
Camaçari
Porangatu
Candeias
SALVADOR
Itaparica
Bom Jesus da Lapa
Pico das Almas
6,070 ft
1,850 m
Guaporé
2,592 ft
790 m
Diamantino
2,825 ft
861 m
Posse
Nazaré
Mato Grosso
Tangará da Serra
2,930 ft
893 m
Uruaçu
5,505 ft
1,678 m
Brumado
Jequié
Aruanã
Cuiabá
Várzea Grande
Goiás
Vitória da Conquista
Itabuna
Ilhéus
San Ignacio de Velasco
Cáceres
Barra do Garças
BRASÍLIA
Formosa
Januária
Serra do Espinhaço
San Matías
Poconé
Aragarças
Rondonópolis
Anápolis
Iporá
Trindade
GOIÂNIA
Aparecida de Goiânia
Luziânia
Minas
Itapetinga
Canavieiras
Almenara
Eunápolis
San José
Alto Araguaia
Mineiros
Jataí
Rio Verde
Paracatu
Montes Claros
Pirapora
Jequitinhonha
Porto Seguro
Araçuaí
Pantanal
Catalão
Itumbiara
Gerais
Teixeira de Freitas
Puerto Suárez
Mato
Rio Verde
Corinto
Teófilo Otôni
Nanuque
Caravelas
Diamantina
Caçumba
Corumbá
Ituiutaba
Araguari
Uberlândia
Patos de Minas
Curvelo
Governador Valadares
Capitán Pablo Lagerenza
Grosso
Paranaíba
Uberaba
Araxá
Sete Lagoas
Espírito Santo
São Mateus
PARAGUAY
Aquidauana
Campo Grande
Santa Fe do Sul
Jales
Contagem
Ipatinga
Linhares
General Eugenio A. Garay
do Sul
São Paulo
Franca
Divinópolis
Betim
Sabará
Caratinga
Colatina
Paraguay
Fuerte Olimpo
Três Lagoas
São José do Rio Preto
Barretos
Passos
Conselheiro Lafaiete
BELO HORIZONTE
Vitória
Serra
Vila Velha
Araçatuba
114
115
60° H 55° J 50° K 45° L 40° M 35° N
1 2 3 4 5 6 7
10° 5° 0° 5° 10° 15°

PACIFIC
OCEAN
Tropic of Capricorn
Antofagasta
Calama
Tocopilla
Punta Angamos
Taltal
Chañaral
Caldera
Copiapó
Huasco
Vallenar
La Serena
Coquimbo
Ovalle
Illapel
Viña del Mar
Valparaíso
Quilpué
San Antonio
SANTIAGO
Puente Alto
San Bernardo
Rancagua
San Fernando
Curicó
Constitución
Talca
Cauquenes
Linares
Chillán
Talcahuano
Concepción
Coronel
Lebu
Los Angeles
Angol
Temuco
Valdivia
Osorno
Puerto Montt
Ancud
Castro
Chiloé I.
Quellón
Chonos Arch.
Taitao Pen.
Gulf of Peñas
Campana I.
Wellington I.
Madre de Dios I.
Queen Adelaide Arch.
Strait of Magellan
Cabo Deseado
Santa Inés I.
Desventurados Is. (CHL.)
Juan Fernández Is. (CHL.)
Robinson Crusoe
Alejandro Selkirk
BOLIVIA
Tarija
Tupiza
Villazón
La Quiaca
Yacuíba
Tartagal
Bermejo
San Ramón de la Nueva Orán
Embarcación
Jujuy
San Salvador de Jujuy
Salta
San Pedro
Metán
Tucumán
San Miguel de Tucumán
Santiago del Estero
Catamarca
San Fernando del Valle de Catamarca
La Rioja
San Juan
Mendoza
San Luis
Córdoba
CÓRDOBA
Villa María
Río Cuarto
Rosario
Santa Fe
Paraná
Entre Ríos
Corrientes
Resistencia
Formosa
Posadas
Misiones
BUENOS AIRES
S. JUSTO
Lomas de Zamora
La Plata
Mar del Plata
Tandil
Necochea
Bahía Blanca
La Pampa
Santa Rosa
Neuquén
General Roca
Río Negro
Viedma
San Carlos de Bariloche
Gulf of San Matías
Valdés Pen.
Puerto Madryn
Trelew
Rawson
Chubut
Comodoro Rivadavia
Gulf of San Jorge
Santa Cruz
Puerto Deseado
Puerto San Julián
Puerto Santa Cruz
Río Gallegos
Bahía Grande
Punta Arenas
Tierra del Fuego
Río Grande
Ushuaia
Staten I.
Cape Horn
Falkland Islands (Is. Malvinas) (U. K.)
West Falkland
East Falkland
Stanley
PARAGUAY
Asunción
Encarnación
Gran Chaco
URUGUAY
MONTEVIDEO
Salto
Paysandú
Rivera
Tacuarembó
Punta del Este
Río de la Plata
Cordillera de la Costa
Atacama Desert
Aconcagua 22,845 ft 6,963 m
Ojos del Salado 22,573 ft 6,880 m
Llullaillaco 22,058 ft 6,723 m
ARGENTINA
PATAGONIA
Cordillera Patagónica
Andes
O

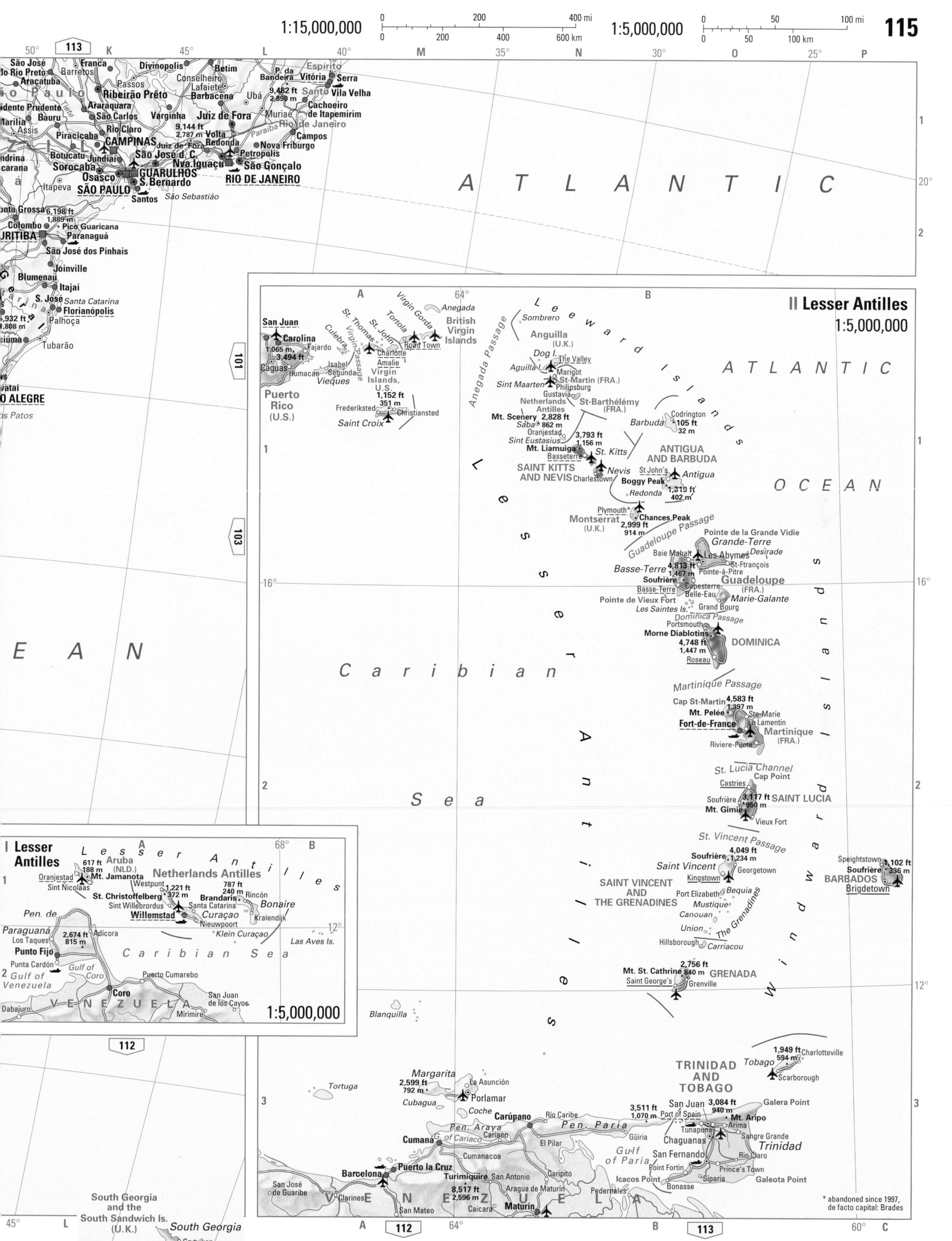
1:15,000,000
1:5,000,000
II Lesser Antilles
1:5,000,000
I Lesser Antilles
1:5,000,000
ATLANTIC
ATLANTIC OCEAN
EAN
Caribbean Sea
Leeward Islands
Lesser Antilles
Windward Islands
São José do Rio Preto
Franca
Divinópolis
Betim
Araçatuba
Barretos
Passos
Conselheiro Lafaiete
Ribeirão Prêto
Barbacena
Ubá
Presidente Prudente
Araraquara
São Carlos
Varginha
Juiz de Fora
Marília
Bauru
Assis
Piracicaba
Rio Claro
CAMPINAS
Jundiaí
Botucatu
Sorocaba
Osasco
GUARULHOS
S. Bernardo
SÃO PAULO
Santos
São Sebastião
Itapeva
Volta Redonda
São José d. C.
Nva.Iguaçu
Petrópolis
Nova Friburgo
Campos
São Gonçalo
RIO DE JANEIRO
Muriaé
Rio de Janeiro
Cachoeiro de Itapemirim
Vitória
Serra
Vila Velha
Espírito Santo
P. da Bandeira
9,482 ft
2,890 m
9,144 ft
2,787 m
Ponta Grossa
6,198 ft
1,889 m
Pico Guaricana
Colombo
CURITIBA
Paranaguá
São José dos Pinhais
Joinville
Blumenau
Itajaí
S. José
Santa Catarina
Florianópolis
Palhoça
Tubarão
PORTO ALEGRE
Lagoa dos Patos
San Juan
Carolina
Caguas
Fajardo
Humacao
1,065 m
3,494 ft
Puerto Rico (U.S.)
Culebra
Vieques
Isabel Segunda
Virgin Passage
St. Thomas
St. John
Tortola
Virgin Gorda
Anegada
British Virgin Islands
Road Town
Charlotte Amalie
Virgin Islands, U.S.
1,152 ft
351 m
Frederiksted
Christiansted
Saint Croix
Anegada Passage
Sombrero
Anguilla (U.K.)
Dog I.
The Valley
Aguilla I.
Marigot
St-Martin (FRA.)
Sint Maarten
Philipsburg
Gustavia
St-Barthélémy (FRA.)
Netherlands Antilles
Mt. Scenery
2,828 ft
862 m
Saba
Oranjestad
Sint Eustasius
3,793 ft
1,156 m
Mt. Liamuiga
Basseterre
St. Kitts
SAINT KITTS AND NEVIS
Nevis
Charlestown
Barbuda
Codrington
105 ft
32 m
ANTIGUA AND BARBUDA
St John's
Antigua
Boggy Peak
1,319 ft
402 m
Redonda
Plymouth*
Chances Peak
Montserrat (U.K.)
2,999 ft
914 m
Guadeloupe Passage
Pointe de la Grande Vidie
Grande-Terre
Baie Mahalt
Les Abymes
Desirade
Basse-Terre
4,813 ft
1,467 m
St-Ftrançois
Pointe-à-Pitre
Soufrière
Guadeloupe (FRA.)
Capesterre
Basse-Terre
Belle-Eau
Pointe de Vieux Fort
Marie-Galante
Grand Bourg
Les Saintes Is.
Dominica Passage
Portsmouth
Morne Diablotins
4,748 ft
1,447 m
DOMINICA
Roseau
Martinique Passage
Cap St-Martin
4,583 ft
1,397 m
Mt. Pelée
Ste-Marie
Fort-de-France
Le Lamentin
Martinique (FRA.)
Riviere-Pilote
St. Lucia Channel
Cap Point
Castries
Soufrière
3,117 ft
950 m
Mt. Gimie
SAINT LUCIA
Vieux Fort
St. Vincent Passage
Soufrière
4,049 ft
1,234 m
Saint Vincent
Kingstown
Georgetown
SAINT VINCENT AND THE GRENADINES
Port Elizabeth
Bequia
Mustique
Canouan
Union
The Grenadines
Hillsborough
Carriacou
Speightstown
1,102 ft
336 m
Soufrière
BARBADOS
Bridgetown
2,756 ft
840 m
Mt. St. Cathrine
GRENADA
Saint George's
Grenville
Blanquilla
Tortuga
Margarita
2,599 ft
792 m
La Asunción
Porlamar
Cubagua
Coche
Carúpano
Pen. Araya
Golfo de Cariaco
Cariaco
Cumana
Cumanacoa
Río Caribe
Pen. Paria
El Pilar
Güiria
Gulf of Paria
Barcelona
Puerto la Cruz
Turimiquire
San Antonio
8,517 ft
2,596 m
Caripito
Aragua de Maturín
San José de Guaribe
Clarines
San Mateo
Caicara
Maturín
Pedernales
VENEZUELA
Tobago
1,949 ft
594 m
Charlotteville
Scarborough
TRINIDAD AND TOBAGO
3,511 ft
1,070 m
San Juan
Port of Spain
3,084 ft
940 m
Mt. Aripo
Galera Point
Tunapuna
Arima
Chaguanas
Sangre Grande
Trinidad
San Fernando
Rio Claro
Point Fortin
Icacos Point
Bonasse
Siparia
Prince's Town
Galeota Point
* abandoned since 1997, de facto capital: Brades
Aruba (NLD.)
617 ft
188 m
Oranjestad
Mt. Jamanota
Sint Nicolaas
Netherlands Antilles
Westpunt
1,221 ft
372 m
St. Christoffelberg
Sint Willebrordus
787 ft
240 m
Brandaris
Rincón
Bonaire
Santa Catarina
Curaçao
Willemstad
Nieuwpoort
Kralendijk
Klein Curaçao
Las Aves Is.
Pen. de Paraguaná
2,674 ft
815 m
Adicora
Los Taques
Punto Fijo
Punta Cardón
Gulf of Venezuela
Gulf of Coro
Puerto Cumarebo
Coro
San Juan de los Cayos
Dabajuro
Mirimire
South Georgia and the South Sandwich Is. (U.K.)
South Georgia
Grytviken
113
101
103
112
113

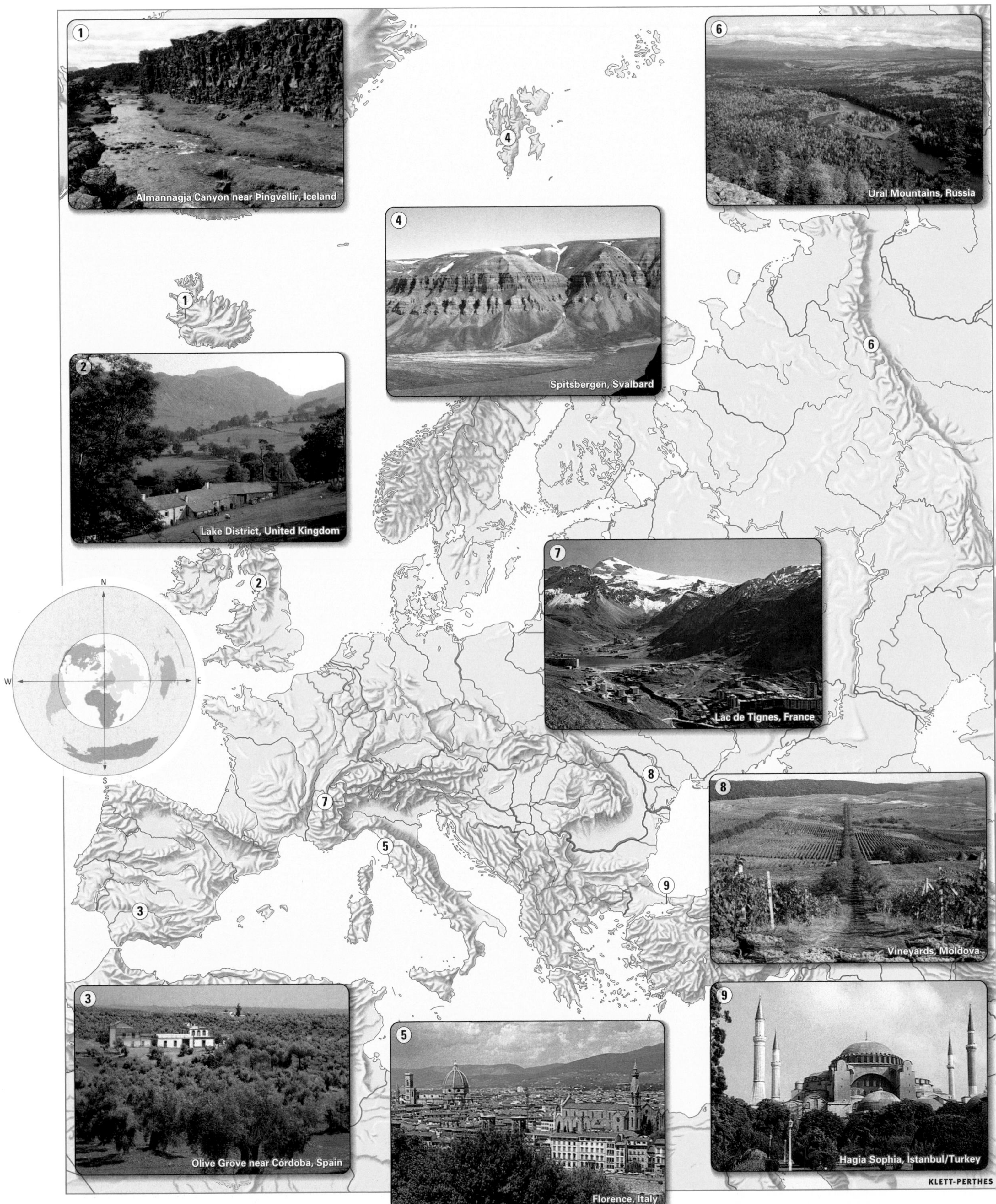

KLETT-PERTHES

1:25,000,000

ARCTIC OCEAN
Greenland
Greenland Sea
Norwegian Sea
Barents Sea
Kara Sea
North Sea
Baltic Sea
ATLANTIC OCEAN
Bay of Biscay
Mediterranean Sea
Black Sea
Caspian Sea
Adriatic Sea
Tyrrhenian Sea
Ionian Sea
Aegean Sea
Denmark Strait
Iceland
Spitsbergen
Novaya Zemlya
Scandinavia
British Isles
Great Britain
Ireland
Iberian Peninsula
Alps
Pyrenees
Carpathian Mts.
Caucasus
Ural Mountains
North Russian Ridge
Central Russian Upland
Volga Heights
Valday Hills
Timan Ridge
West Siberian Plain
Anatolia
Balkan Mts.
Dinaric Alps
Apennines
Atlas
Sahara
Elevation
6,562 ft 2,000 m
3,281 ft 1,000 m
1,640 ft 500 m
656 ft 200 m
328 ft 100 m
0 ft 0 m
Depression
656 ft 200 m
6,562 ft 2,000 m
13,124 ft 4,000 m
Inland ice, glaciers
Pack ice
Limit of drift ice
KLETT-PERTHES

1:25,000,000

0 500 1000 mi
0 500 1000 1500 km

0 200 400 600 mi
0 200 400 600 800 km
Service and Industry
Service center (finance, trade, research, government, tourism)
Other location
Industrial center
Metal processing, mechanical engineering, vehicle manufacturing, shipbuilding
Electronics industry, electrical and precision engineering
Textile, garment, and leather goods industries
Chemical, wood working, pulp and paper, printing industries
Food processing
Conurbation
Mining and Smelting
Energy raw material
Hard coal
Brown coal
Uranium
Petroleum
Natural gas
Oil refinery
Oil pipeline
Gas pipeline
Oil terminal embarkation
Hydro-electric power station
Nuclear power station (selection)
Ore and other raw materials
Iron ore
Chromite
Cobalt
Manganese
Nickel
Tungsten
Bauxite
Titanium
Copper
Lead/zinc
Tin
Gold
Silver
Platinum
Mercury
Gemstones
Graphite
Sulfur
Sodium chloride
Potassium
Phosphate
Smelting
Iron and steel production works
Non-ferrous metal production
Light metal (aluminum) production
Symbol size indicates relative importance of a location.
Am. Amsterdam
Ant. Antwerp
Br. Bussels
Col. Cologne
Dn. Dnipropetrovs'k
Dr. Dresden
Fl. Florence
Fr. Frankfurt/Main
Han. Hannover
Hu. Hunedoara
I. Ingolstadt
K. Krasnodar
L. Leeds
Lj. Ljubljana
Man. Manchester
N.Ch. Naberezhnyye Chelny
Nu. Nuremberg
Ri. Rijeka
Ro. Rotterdam
Tr. Trieste
Yek. Yekaterinburg
Z. Zaporizhzhya
ARCTIC OCEAN
Kara Sea
Barents Sea
Norwegian Sea
ATLANTIC OCEAN
North Sea
Black Sea
Caspian Sea
Mediterranean Sea
Red Sea
ICELAND
UNITED KINGDOM
IRELAND
NORWAY
SWEDEN
FINLAND
RUSSIA
ESTONIA
LATVIA
LITHUANIA
BELARUS
UKRAINE
KAZAKHSTAN
POL.
GER.
DENMARK
FRANCE
SPAIN
PORTUGAL
ITALY
AUSTRIA
SWI.
HUNGARY
ROM.
BUL.
SERBIA
GREECE
TURKEY
GEO.
ARM.
AZERBAIJAN
IRAN
IRAQ
SYR.
LEBANON
ISRAEL
JORDAN
CYPRUS
MALTA
SAUDI ARABIA
EGYPT
LIBYA
TUNISIA
ALGERIA
MOROCCO
Svalbard (NOR.)
Faroe Is. (DEN.)
KLETT-PERTHES

1:25,000,000

0 200 400 600 mi
0 200 400 600 800 km

60° A 50° B 40° C 30° D 20° E 10° F 0° G 10° H 20° J 30° K 40° L 50° M 60° N 70° O 80° P 90° Q 100°

ARCTIC OCEAN
Nordostrundingen
Baffin Bay
Qeqertarsuaq
Greenland (DEN.)
Franz Josef Land
C. Karlsen
Dikson
Noril'sk
Yenisey
Kara Sea
Novaya Zemlya
Gulf of Ob'
Longyearbyen
Svalbard (NOR.)
Greenland Sea
Barents Sea
Tasiilaq
Ittoqqortoormiit
Bear I. (NOR.)
Kara Str.
Vorkuta
Salekhard
Denmark Strait
Jan Mayen (NOR.)
North Cape
Kolguyev I.
Vadsø
C. Kanin Nos
Nar'yan-Mar
Khanty-Mansiysk
Reykjavík
ICELAND
Norwegian Sea
Tromsø
Inari L.
Murmansk
Pechora
Ob'
Lapland
Kirovsk
Lofoten
Bodø
Arctic Circle
Rovaniemi
White Sea
Mezen'
Ukhta
Arkhangel'sk
Severodvinsk
Onega
Serov
Luleå
Oulu
Karelia
Vychegda
North. Dvina
Berezniki
Nizhniy Tagil
Syktyvkar
Faroe Is. (DEN.)
Trondheim
Umeå
RUSSIA
YEKATERINBURG
Ålesund
Gulf of Bothnia
Vaasa
L. Onega
Kotlas
Kama
Shetland Is.
Sognefj.
Sundsvall
FINLAND
SWEDEN
NORWAY
Petrozavodsk
Sukhona
PERM'
Rockall
Orkney Is.
Bergen
Tampere
Kirov
CHELYABINSK
British Isles
Hebrides
Klarälven
Gävle
Turku
Helsinki
L. Ladoga
Vologda
Izhevsk
ATLANTIC OCEAN
Oslo
Åland Is.
G. of Finland
ST. PETERSBURG
Rybinsk Res.
Yoshkar-Ola
Vyatka
UFA
Stavanger
Stockholm
Tallinn
KAZAN'
Naberezhnyye Chelny
Ural
Scotland
Aberdeen
Kristiansand
Saaremaa
ESTONIA
Vel. Novgorod
Yaroslavl'
Glasgow
UNITED KINGDOM
Edinburgh
Skagerrak
Norrköping
L. Peipus
Ivanovo
NIZHNIY NOVGOROD
Orenburg
Belfast
Göteborg
Tver'
Volga
Kattegat
Riga
SAMARA
North Sea
Gotland
LATVIA
MOSCOW
Ufyanovsk
IRELAND
Newcastle
Western Dvina
Dublin
Irish Sea
England
COPENHAGEN
Baltic Sea
Ryazan'
Penza
DENMARK
Malmö
LITHUANIA
Smolensk
Cork
Manchester
Kaunas
Vitsyebsk
Tula
Tambov
Saratov
Oral
Wales
Bornholm
(Russia)
Vilnius
Oka
Birmingham
Kaliningrad
MINSK
Dnieper
Orël
NETHERLANDS
Amsterdam
HAMBURG
Gdańsk
Bryansk
Land's End
Bristol
LONDON
Bremen
Elbe
Szczecin
BELARUS
Kursk
Voronezh
KAZAKHSTAN
Greenwich
Rotterdam
Hannover
BERLIN
POLAND
Homyel'
English Channel
Lille
Brussels
GERMANY
Poznań
Vistula
Don
Channel Is. (U.K.)
Le Havre
BELGIUM
Düsseldorf
Oder
Łódź
WARSAW
Brest
Atyraū
Cologne
Leipzig
Dresden
Zhytomyr
KIEV
KHARKIV
VOLGOGRAD
LUX.
Wrocław
Lublin
Rennes
Luxembourg
Frankfurt
PRAGUE
UKRAINE
Volga
PARIS
Meuse
Luhans'k
Strasbourg
Rhine
Stuttgart
CZECH REP.
Kraków
L'viv
Vinnytsya
DONETS'K
Astrakhan'
Nantes
Loire
Seine
Danube
Brno
SLOVAKIA
Dniester
DNIPROPETROVS'K
ROSTOV-NA-DONU
Bay of Biscay
Dijon
MUNICH
VIENNA
Bratislava
Kryvyy Rih
Mariupol'
Aqtau
C. Finisterre
FRANCE
Berne
LIE.
AUSTRIA
BUDAPEST
Tisza
MOLDOVA
Chişinău
Sea of Azov
Kuban'
Stavropol'
Caspian Sea
Gijón
SWITZERLAND
Graz
HUNGARY
Iaşi
Mykolayiv
Groznyy
Makhachkala
Vigo
Lyon
Transylvania
Prut
ODESA
Krasnodar
Bordeaux
Turin
MILAN
Ljubljana
SLOVENIA
Zagreb
Timişoara
Galaţi
Crimea
Vladikavkaz
Bilbao
Venice
ROMANIA
Novorossiysk
Porto
Toulouse
Montpellier
CROATIA
Sava
Sevastopol'
Sochi
GEORGIA
BAKU
Valladolid
Ebro
Bologna
BOSNIA AND HERZEGOVINA
BELGRADE
Wallachia
Constanţa
Sukhumi
TBILISI
AZERBAIJAN
PORTUGAL
AND.
Nice
Genoa
SERBIA
BUCHAREST
Black Sea
Kura
Gancə
Aragón
Marseille
MCO.
Ligurian Sea
Florence
Split
Niš
ARMENIA
Tejo
MADRID
Zaragoza
S.MA.
Sarajevo
BULGARIA
Varna
YEREVAN
Catalonia
Corsica (FRA.)
Adriatic Sea
MONTENEGRO
Prishtina
Danube
SOFIA
Bosporus
Trabzon
Aras
Lisbon
SPAIN
BARCELONA
ITALY
Podgorica
KOSOVO
Samsun
Erzurum
Naxçıvan
Valencia
Balearic Is.
Menorca
VAT.
ROME
Tirana
ALBANIA
Skopje
MAC.
ISTANBUL
Kizilirmak
L. Van
TABRIZ
Seville
Córdoba
NAPLES
Bari
ANKARA
Sivas
L. Urmia
Andalusia
Murcia
Palma de M.
Mallorca
Tyrrhenian Sea
Thessaloniki
BURSA
Kayseri
Diyarbakır
Van
Orūmīyeh
Ibiza
Sardinia
GREECE
Eskişehir
TURKEY
Tigris
Kurdistan
IRAN
Str. of Gibraltar
Málaga
Malatya
Tanger
Gibraltar (U.K.)
Cagliari
Anatolia
Gaziantep
Şanlıurfa
Mediterranean Sea
Str. of Sicily
Ionian Sea
Ionian Is.
Euboea
Aegean Sea
IZMIR
Konya
MOSUL
Kirkūk
RABAT
Melilla (SPA.)
Oran
ALGIERS
Palermo
ADANA
Euphrates
Kermānshāh
Fez
Annaba
Sicily
Patras
Athens
Mersin
ALEPPO
Oujda
Constantine
Tūnis
Catania
Antalya
SYRIA
BAGHDĀD
Mulūyah
Sousse
Rhodes
Nicosia
Ḩimş
MOROCCO
MALTA
Valletta
IRAQ
TUNISIA
Sfax
Crete
CYPRUS
BEIRUT
LEBANON
DAMASCUS
Al-Aghwāt
G. of Gabès
Jarbah
ISRAEL
Béchar
Tughghūrt
Tel Aviv-Yafo
AMMAN
ALGERIA
TRIPOLI
Jerusalem
Dead Sea
Ghazzah
Miṣrātah
Benghazi
JORDAN
Gulf of Sirte
ALEXANDRIA
Port Said
Surt
SAUDI ARABIA
Suez
Elat
Ḩā'il
GIZA
CAIRO
Tabūk
Buraydah
Sīwah
Al-Fayyūm
LIBYA
EGYPT
Al-Minyā
Red Sea

AND.	ANDORRA
LIE.	LIECHTENSTEIN
LUX.	LUXEMBOURG
MAC.	MACEDONIA
MCO.	MONACO
S.MA.	SAN MARINO
VAT.	VATICAN CITY

Palestine:
1 West Bank
2 Gaza Strip

F 0° G 10° H 20° J 30° K 40° L

KLETT-PERTHES

Europe: Ethnic Groups

1:25,000,000

1:25,000,000

0 200 400 600 mi
0 200 400 600 800 km

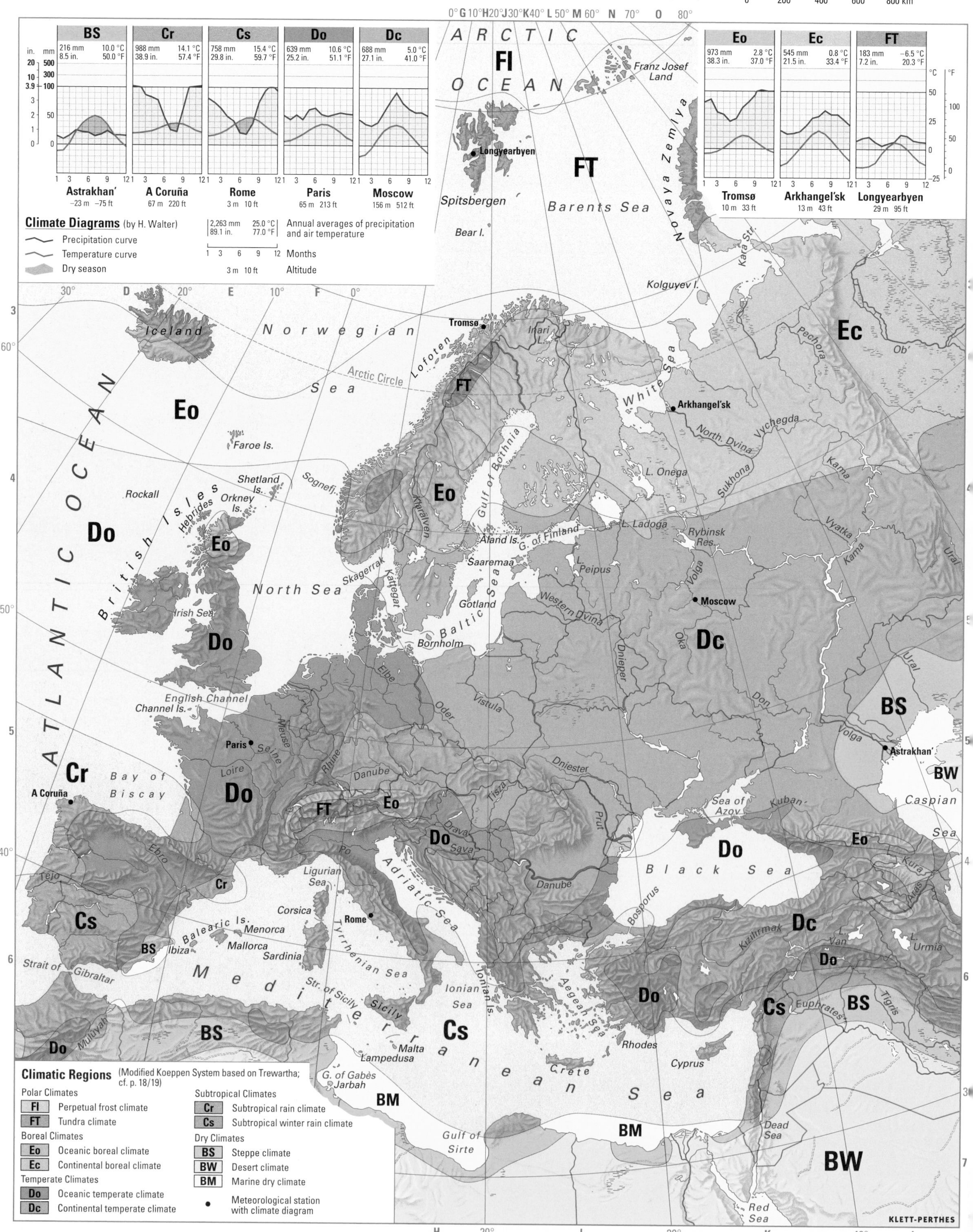

1:18,000,000
0 200 400 mi
0 200 400 600 km
Tourism
Vacation areas
Mainly summer guests
Moderate tourism
Mass tourism
Summer and winter guests
Moderate tourism
Mass tourism
Harz Popular vacation area, national or international
Air tourism
Important airport
City tourism
Major cities with international city tourism
Over 1 million inh.
Over 100,000 inh.
ATLANTIC OCEAN
North Sea
Bay of Biscay
Mediterranean Sea
Black Sea
Baltic Sea
NORWAY
SWEDEN
FINLAND
ESTONIA
LATVIA
LITHUANIA
RUSSIA
BELARUS
UKRAINE
MOLDOVA
ROMANIA
POLAND
DENMARK
UNITED KINGDOM
IRELAND
NETHERLANDS
BELGIUM
LUX.
GERMANY
CZECH REP.
SLOVAKIA
HUNGARY
AUSTRIA
SWITZERLAND
LIE.
FRANCE
SPAIN
PORTUGAL
AND.
MCO.
ITALY
S.MA.
VAT.
SLOVENIA
CROATIA
BOSNIA AND HERZEGOVINA
SERBIA
MONTENEGRO
KOSOVO
ALBANIA
MACEDONIA
BULGARIA
GREECE
TURKEY
MOROCCO
ALGERIA
TUNISIA
MALTA
Bergen
Oslo
Stockholm
Helsinki
St. Petersburg
Tallinn
Riga
Vilnius
Minsk
Moscow
Kiev
Copenhagen
Hamburg
Lübeck
Berlin
Hannover
Dresden
Gdańsk
Warsaw
Kraków
Prague
Vienna
Budapest
Bucharest
Belgrade
Sofia
İstanbul
Ankara
İzmir
Antalya
Athens
Edinburgh
Glasgow
Dublin
Leeds
Manchester
Birmingham
London
Amsterdam
Rotterdam
Bruges
Ghent
Brussels
Düsseldorf
Cologne
Frankfurt
Heidelberg
Stuttgart
Strasbourg
Munich
Salzburg
Paris
Bordeaux
Lyon
Geneva
Marseille
Nice
Turin
Milan
Genoa
Verona
Venezia
Florence
Rome
Naples
Palermo
Zagreb
Madrid
Barcelona
Bilbao
Lisbon
Valencia
Benidorm
Seville
Córdoba
Granada
Tanger
Rabat
Algiers
Tunis
Odesa
Sevastopol
Dnipropetrovs'k
Lviv
Canary Islands
La Palma
Tenerife
Lanzarote
Hierro
La Gomera
Gran Canaria
Fuerteventura
Balearic Islands
Mallorca
Menorca
Ibiza
Corsica
Sardinia
Sicily
Crete
Rhodes
Costa Brava
Costa Dorada
Costa Blanca
Costa del Sol
Costa de la Luz
Côte d'Azur
Riviera
Alps
Pyrenees
Dolomites
KLETT-PERTHES
1960
Railroad station
to Valencia
to Alicante
harbour
castillo
city hall and tourist information
Benidorm
Playa de Levante
Mediterranean Sea
Sierra Helada
Punta de Pinet
1:45,000
0 0.5 mi
0 500 m
2000
Railroad station
racetrack
stadium
Plaza Toros
new building area planned
new building area
to the expressway
Playa de Poniente
La Cala
Benidorm 1960 and 2000
From a fishing village to a tourist city on the Costa Blanca
Old village centre until 1952
First hotels and guesthouses
Houses outside the village centre (farmhouses, holiday villas)
Sandy beach
Built-up area (mainly hotels, guesthouses, restaurants, shops)
Gardens
Park
Roads
Hotel with grounds
Apartment house
Campsite
Restaurant, nightclub, discotheque (selection)
Railroad

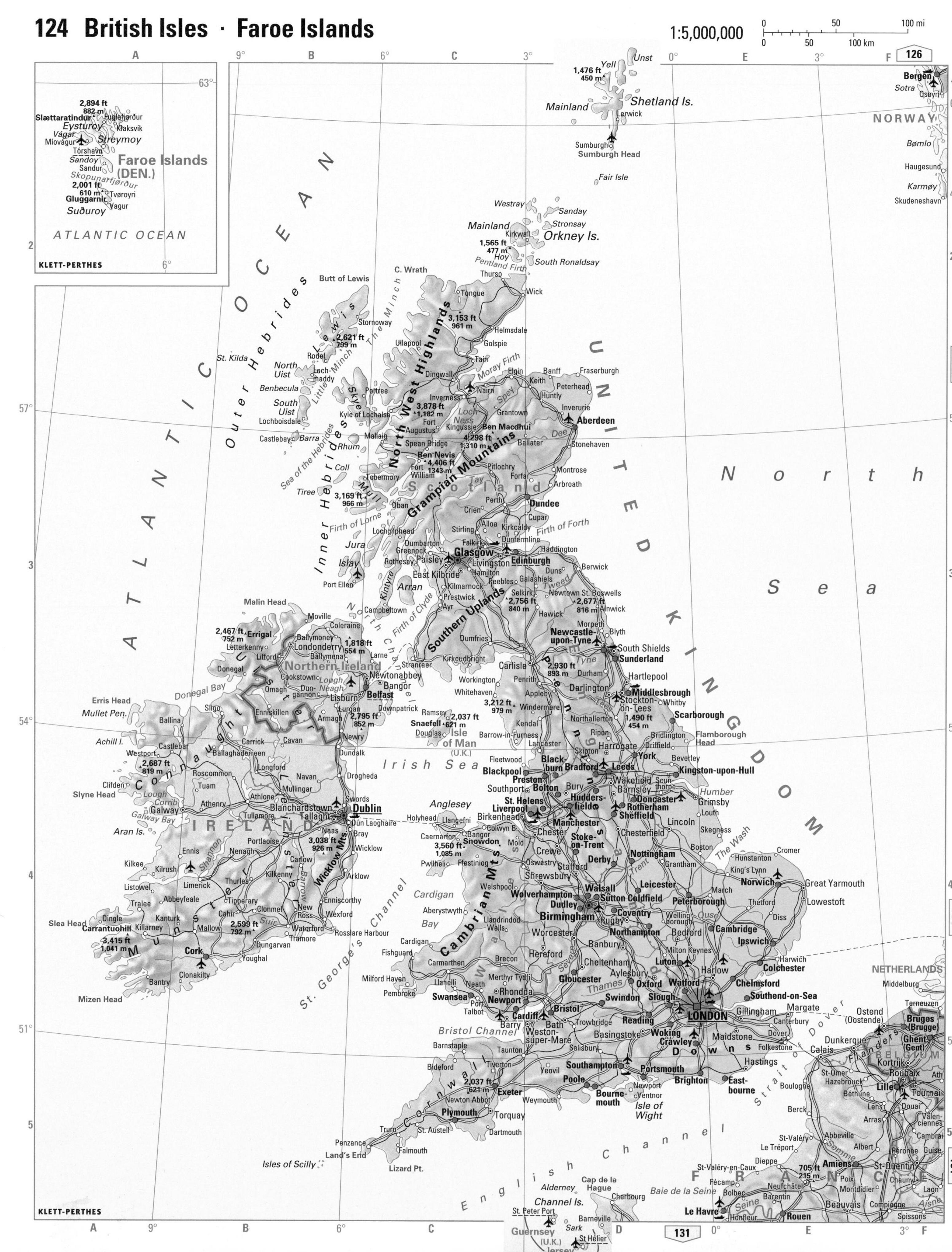
1:5,000,000
0 50 100 mi
0 50 100 km
A B C D E F
9° 6° 3° 0° 3°
126
131
Faroe Islands (DEN.)
2,894 ft 882 m
Slættaratindur
Fuglafjørður
Eysturoy
Klaksvík
Vágar
Miðvágur
Streymoy
Tórshavn
Sandoy
Sandur
Skopunarfjørður
2,001 ft 610 m
Gluggarnir
Tvøroyri
Vagur
Suðuroy
ATLANTIC OCEAN
63°
6°
KLETT-PERTHES
ATLANTIC OCEAN
Yell
Unst
1,476 ft 450 m
Mainland
Shetland Is.
Lerwick
Sumburgh
Sumburgh Head
Fair Isle
Westray
Sanday
Stronsay
Mainland
Kirkwall
Orkney Is.
1,565 ft 477 m
Hoy
Pentland Firth
South Ronaldsay
Thurso
Wick
Butt of Lewis
C. Wrath
Tongue
Outer Hebrides
Lewis
Stornoway
2,621 ft 799 m
The Minch
3,153 ft 961 m
Helmsdale
Golspie
Ullapool
North West Highlands
St. Kilda
Rodel
North Uist
Lochmaddy
Little Minch
Tain
Moray Firth
Elgin
Banff
Fraserburgh
Dingwall
Keith
Peterhead
Benbecula
Skye
Portree
Nairn
Spey
Huntly
Inverness
South Uist
Kyle of Lochalsh
3,878 ft 1,182 m
Loch Ness
Grantown
Inverurie
Aberdeen
Lochboisdale
Fort Augustus
Kingussie
Ben Macdhui
Castlebay
Barra
Mallaig
4,298 ft 1,310 m
Dee
Rhum
Spean Bridge
Ballater
Stonehaven
Inner Hebrides
Sea of the Hebrides
Ben Nevis
4,406 ft 1343 m
Fort William
Grampian Mountains
Coll
Tobermory
Pitlochry
Montrose
Tay
Forfar
Tiree
3,169 ft 966 m
Mull
Scotland
Arbroath
Oban
Perth
Dundee
Crieff
Firth of Lorne
Cupar
Alloa
Kirkcaldy
Firth of Forth
Lochgilphead
Stirling
Jura
Dunfermline
Falkirk
Haddington
Dumbarton
Greenock
Glasgow
Edinburgh
Islay
Rothesay
Paisley
Livingston
Berwick
East Kilbride
Hamilton
Duns
Port Ellen
Kintyre
Arran
Kilmarnock
Peebles
Galashiels
Tweed
Prestwick
Selkirk
Newtown St. Boswells
Campbeltown
Ayr
2,756 ft 840 m
2,677 ft 816 m
Alnwick
Firth of Clyde
Southern Uplands
Hawick
North Channel
Morpeth
Malin Head
Moville
Coleraine
Newcastle-upon-Tyne
Blyth
2,467 ft 752 m
Errigal
Ballymoney
1,818 ft 554 m
Dumfries
South Shields
Letterkenny
Londonderry
Sunderland
Lifford
Ballymena
Larne
Kirkcudbright
Tyne
Northern Ireland
Stranraer
Carlisle
2,930 ft 893 m
Durham
Hartlepool
Donegal
Cookstown
Lough Neagh
Newtonabbey
Penrith
Donegal Bay
Omagh
Dungannon
Bangor
Belfast
Workington
Darlington
Middlesbrough
Whitehaven
Appleby
Stockton-on-Tees
Whitby
Erris Head
Enniskillen
Lisburn
Downpatrick
Ramsey
3,212 ft 979 m
Windermere
Tees
Mullet Pen.
Sligo
Lurgan
2,037 ft
Northallerton
1,490 ft 454 m
Scarborough
Ballina
Armagh
2,795 ft 852 m
Snaefell 621 m
Isle of Man (U.K.)
Kendal
Douglas
Ripon
Bridlington
Flamborough Head
Achill I.
Castlebar
Carrick
Cavan
Newry
Barrow-in-Furness
Lancaster
Driffield
Ulster
Connaught
Westport
Ballaghaderreen
Dundalk
Skipton
Harrogate
York
Beverley
2,687 ft 819 m
Longford
Fleetwood
Black-burn
Bradford
Leeds
Roscommon
Navan
Drogheda
Irish Sea
Blackpool
Preston
Wakefield
Kingston-upon-Hull
Clifden
Tuam
Mullingar
Southport
Bolton
Bury
Barnsley
Scunthorpe
Humber
Slyne Head
Lough Corrib
Athlone
Leinster
Swords
Anglesey
St. Helens
Hudders-field
Doncaster
Grimsby
Galway
Athenry
Blanchardstown
Dublin
Liverpool
Rotherham
Louth
Galway Bay
Tullamore
Tallaght
Dún Laoghaire
Holyhead
Llangefni
Birkenhead
Manchester
Sheffield
Lincoln
Aran Is.
IRELAND
Naas
Bray
Colwyn B.
Chester
Chesterfield
Skegness
Portlaoise
3,038 ft 926 m
Caernarfon
Bangor
Snowdon
Stoke-on-Trent
Shannon
Wicklow
3,560 ft 1,085 m
Mold
Crewe
Nottingham
Boston
The Wash
Hunstanton
Cromer
Kilkee
Ennis
Nenagh
Carlow
Wicklow Mts.
Pwllheli
Ffestiniog
Oswestry
Stafford
Derby
Grantham
King's Lynn
Kilrush
Barrow
Arklow
Shrewsbury
Trent
Norwich
Great Yarmouth
Listowel
Limerick
Thurles
Kilkenny
Walsall
Leicester
Munster
Cardigan Bay
Welshpool
Wolverhampton
Sutton Coldfield
Peterborough
March
Tralee
Abbeyfeale
Tipperary
Enniscorthy
Aberystwyth
Dudley
Thetford
Lowestoft
Clonmel
New Ross
Wexford
Birmingham
Coventry
Ouse
Slea Head
Dingle
Kanturk
Cahir
Suir
Llandrindod Wells
Rugby
Welling-borough
Diss
Carrantuohill
Killarney
Mallow
2,599 ft 792 m
Waterford
Rosslare Harbour
Cambrian Mts.
Worcester
Northampton
Bedford
Cambridge
3,415 ft 1,041 m
Tramore
Cardigan
Ipswich
Cork
Dungarvan
Fishguard
Hereford
Banbury
Milton Keynes
Harwich
Youghal
St. George's Channel
Wales
Brecon
Severn
Cheltenham
Luton
Colchester
Carmarthen
Aylesbury
Harlow
Bantry
Clonakilty
Milford Haven
Merthyr Tydfil
Gloucester
Oxford
Watford
Chelmsford
Mizen Head
Llanelli
Neath
Thames
Pembroke
Swansea
Rhondda
Swindon
Slough
Southend-on-Sea
Newport
Port Talbot
Cardiff
Bristol
LONDON
Gillingham
Margate
Barry
Bath
Trowbridge
Reading
Canterbury
Bristol Channel
Weston-super-Mare
Basingstoke
Woking
Crawley
Maidstone
Dover
Folkestone
Barnstaple
Taunton
Salisbury
Downs
Strait of Dover
Bideford
Tiverton
Yeovil
Southampton
Portsmouth
Brighton
Hastings
Eastbourne
Cornwall
2,037 ft 621 m
Exeter
Poole
Bournemouth
Newport
Ventnor
Isle of Wight
Newton Abbot
Weymouth
Plymouth
Torquay
Truro
St. Austell
Dartmouth
Penzance
Land's End
Falmouth
Lizard Pt.
Isles of Scilly
English Channel
Alderney
Cap de la Hague
Channel Is.
Cherbourg
Baie de la Seine
St. Peter Port
Guernsey (U.K.)
Sark
Barneville
St. Hélier
Jersey
UNITED KINGDOM
North Sea
Bergen
Sotra
Osøyro
NORWAY
Bømlo
Haugesund
Karmøy
Skudeneshavn
NETHERLANDS
Middelburg
Terneuzen
Ostend (Oostende)
Bruges (Brugge)
Ghent (Gent)
Dunkerque
Calais
Flanders
BELGIUM
Kortrijk
Roubaix
St-Omer
Hazebrouck
Lille
Béthune
Tournai
Boulogne
Lens
Douai
Arras
Valenciennes
Berck
Cambrai
St-Valéry
Abbeville
Le Tréport
Somme
Albert
Péronne
Guise
Dieppe
Amiens
St-Quentin
705 ft 215 m
St-Valéry-en-Caux
Fécamp
Bolbec
Neufchâtel
Poix
Montdidier
Chauny
Laon
FRANCE
Barentin
Le Havre
Seine
Honfleur
Rouen
Beauvais
Compiègne
Aisne
Soissons
57°
54°
51°
1 2 3 4 5

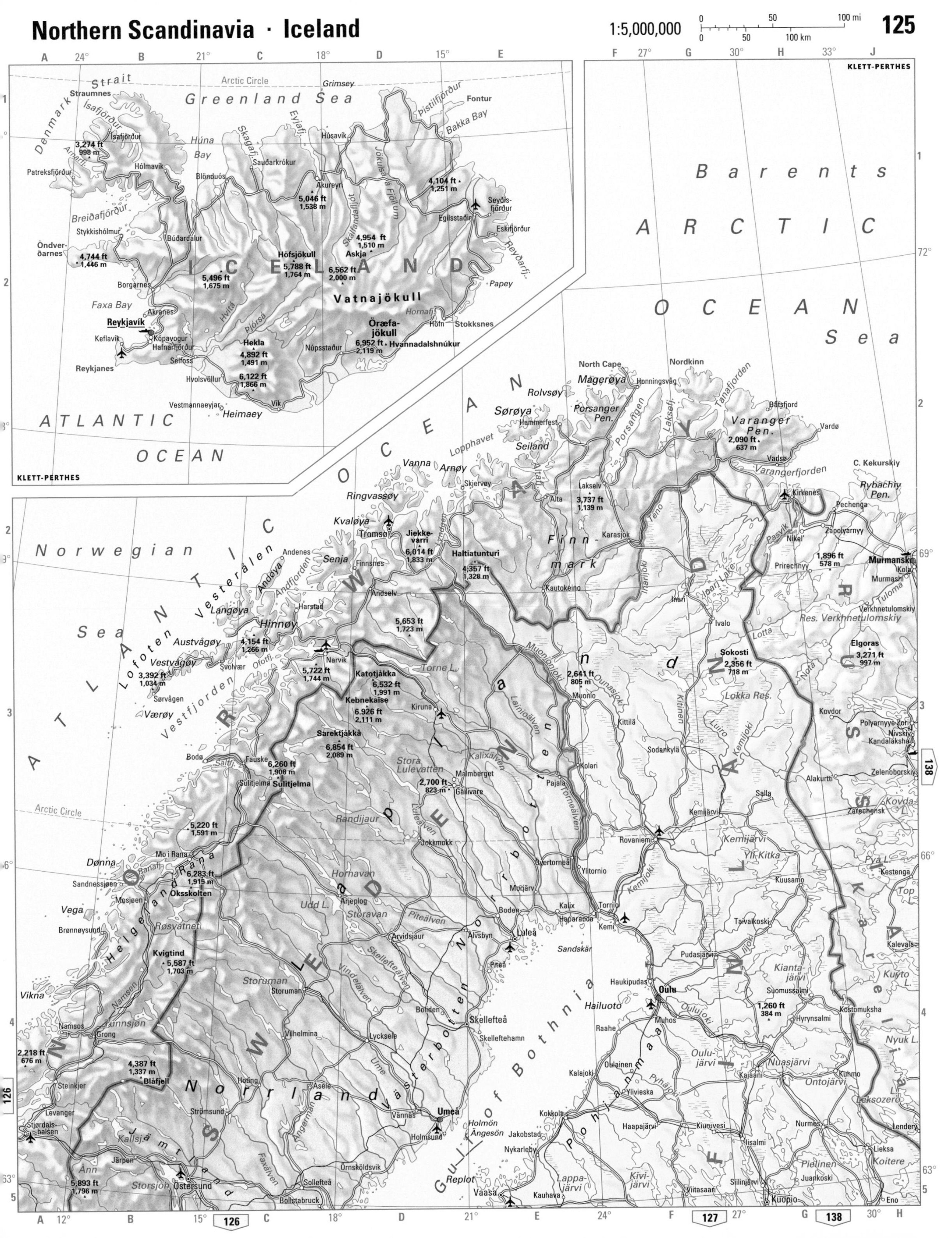
0 50 100 mi
0 50 100 km
KLETT-PERTHES
Denmark Strait
Arctic Circle
Greenland Sea
Grimsey
Straumnes
Ísafjörður
Ísafjörður
3,274 ft
998 m
Arnarfj.
Patreksfjörður
Hólmavík
Húna Bay
Skagafj.
Sauðárkrókur
Blönduós
Húsavík
Eyjafj.
Akureyri
5,046 ft
1,538 m
Jökulsá á Fjöllum
Skjálfandafljót
Þistilfjörður
Fontur
Bakka Bay
4,104 ft
1,251 m
Seyðisfjörður
Egilsstaðir
Eskifjörður
Reyðarfj.
Breiðafjörður
Stykkishólmur
Búðardalur
Öndverðarnes
4,744 ft
1,446 m
ICELAND
Hofsjökull
5,788 ft
1,764 m
5,496 ft
1,675 m
4,954 ft
1,510 m
Askja
6,562 ft
2,000 m
Vatnajökull
Papey
Borgarnes
Faxa Bay
Akranes
Reykjavík
Kópavogur
Hafnarfjörður
Keflavík
Hvítá
Þjórsá
Hornafj.
Höfn
Stokksnes
Öræfajökull
6,952 ft
2,119 m
Hvannadalshnúkur
Hekla
4,892 ft
1,491 m
Núpsstaður
Selfoss
Reykjanes
Hvolsvöllur
6,122 ft
1,866 m
Vík
Vestmannaeyjar
Heimaey
ATLANTIC OCEAN
Barents Sea
ARCTIC OCEAN
North Cape
Nordkinn
Magerøya
Honningsvåg
Tanafjorden
Rolvsøy
Sørøya
Hammerfest
Porsanger Pen.
Porsangen
Laksefj.
Båtsfjord
Varanger Pen.
2,090 ft
637 m
Vardø
Vadsø
Varangerfjorden
Seiland
Loppahavet
Vanna
Arnøy
Altafj.
Skjervøy
Lakselv
3,737 ft
1,139 m
Alta
C. Kekurskiy
Rybachiy Pen.
Kirkenes
Pechenga
Ringvassøy
Kvaløya
Tromsø
Jiekkevarri
6,014 ft
1,833 m
Lyngen
Haltiatunturi
4,357 ft
1,328 m
Finnmark
Karasjok
Teno
Pasvik
Nikel'
Zapolyarnyy
Norwegian Sea
Andenes
Senja
Finnsnes
Vesterålen
Andøya
Andfjorden
Kautokeino
Inarijoki
Inari Lake
Inari
1,896 ft
578 m
Prirechnyy
Murmansk
Kola
Murmashi
Tuloma
Verkhnetulomskiy
Res. Verkhnetulomskiy
Andselv
Harstad
Langøya
Hinnøy
5,653 ft
1,723 m
Ivalo
Lotta
Austvågøy
4,154 ft
1,266 m
Narvik
Lofoten
Vestvågøy
Svolvær
Ofotfj.
Torne L.
Muonionjoki
Sokosti
2,356 ft
718 m
Elgoras
3,271 ft
997 m
3,392 ft
1,034 m
Sørvågen
Værøy
Vestfjorden
5,722 ft
1,744 m
Katotjåkka
6,532 ft
1,991 m
Kebnekaise
6,926 ft
2,111 m
Kiruna
Lainioälven
2,641 ft
805 m
Ounasjoki
Muonio
Kittilä
Kitinen
Lokka Res.
Luiro
Kemijoki
Nota
Kovdor
Polyarnyye Zori
Nivskiy
Kandalaksha
Sarektjåkkå
6,854 ft
2,089 m
Bodø
Saltfj.
Fauske
6,260 ft
1,908 m
Sulitjelma
Sulitjelma
Stora Lulevatten
Kalixälven
Malmberget
2,700 ft
823 m
Gällivare
Pajala
Torneälven
Kolari
Sodankylä
Alakurtti
Zelenoborskiy
Salla
Kovda L.
Zarechensk
Arctic Circle
5,220 ft
1,591 m
Randijaur
Luleälven
Jokkmokk
Rovaniemi
Kemijärvi
Kemijärvi
Yli-Kitka
Pya L.
Kestenga
Dønna
Mo i Rana
Ranafj.
Rana
6,283 ft
1,915 m
Oksskolten
Sandnessjøen
Hornavan
Övertorneå
Ylitornio
Kemijoki
Kuusamo
Top L.
Mosjøen
Mourjärvi
Vega
Udd L.
Arjeplog
Storavan
Piteälven
Boden
Kalix
Haparanda
Tornio
Kemi
Taivalkoski
Brønnøysund
Røsvatnet
Arvidsjaur
Älvsbyn
Luleå
Sandskär
Kalevala
Helgeland
Kvigtind
5,587 ft
1,703 m
Skellefteälven
Vindelälven
Piteå
Pudasjärvi
Iijoki
Kiantajärvi
Kuyto L.
Storuman
Storuman
Haukipudas
Oulu
Suomussalmi
Vikna
Namsen
Boliden
Hailuoto
Oulujoki
1,260 ft
384 m
Kostomuksha
Namsos
Tunnsjøen
Grong
Skellefteå
Muhos
Hyrynsalmi
Vilhelmina
Lycksele
Skelleftehamn
Raahe
Nyuk L.
2,218 ft
676 m
4,387 ft
1,337 m
Bläfjell
Ume
Västerbotten
Norrbotten
Gulf of Bothnia
Kalajoki
Oulainen
Pyhäjoki
Oulujärvi
Kajaani
Nuasjärvi
Kuhmo
Ontojärvi
Steinkjer
Hoting
Norrland
Åsele
Ylivieska
Leksozero L.
Levanger
Strömsund
Ångermanälven
Vännäs
Umeå
Kokkola
Pohjanmaa
Stjørdalshalsen
Holmön
Ängesön
Holmsund
Jakobstad
Haapajärvi
Kiuruvesi
Nurmes
Lendery
Kallsjön
Jämtland
Nykarleby
Iisalmi
Lieksa
Koitere
Järpen
Ånn
Faxälven
Örnsköldsvik
Pielinen
5,893 ft
1,796 m
Storsjön
Östersund
Sollefteå
Replot
Lappajärvi
Kivijärvi
Siilinjärvi
Juankoski
Bollstabruck
Vaasa
Kauhava
Viitasaari
Kuopio
Eno
NORWAY
SWEDEN
FINLAND
LAPLAND
RUSSIA
Karelia
126
127
138

KLETT-PERTHES
0°
A
3°
B
6°
C
9°
D
12°
E
15°
F
18°
125
G
63°
60°
57°
54°
1
2
3
4
5
124
128
ATLANTIC
OCEAN
North
Sea
German
Bight
Skagerrak
Kattegat
Baltic
Gulf of Bothnia
Åland Strait
NORWAY
SWEDEN
DENMARK
GERMANY
NETHERLANDS
POLAND
Norrland
Jämtland
Ångermanland
Västerbotten
Härjedalen
Hälsingland
Svealand
Götaland
Småland
Skåne
Jylland
Fyn
Sjælland
Pomerania
Hardanger-vidda
Jotunheimen
Jostedalsbreen
Telemark
Trondheim
Kristiansund
Molde
Ålesund
Åndalsnes
Sunndalsøra
Oppdal
Ulsberg
Røros
Tynset
Dombås
Snøhetta
7,500 ft
2,286 m
Galdhøpiggen
8,101 ft
2,469 m
Glittertind
8,088 ft
2,465 m
Otta
Florø
Førde
Høyanger
Leikanger
Øvre Årdal
Sognefjorden
Nordfjord
Nordfjordeid
Ørsta
Gurskøy
Bremanger-landet
Indre Solund
Radøy
Sotra
Bergen
Os
Voss
Geilo
6,106 ft
1,861 m
Lofthus
Odda
Husnes
Leirvik
Bømlo
Etne
Sauda
Haugesund
Karmøy
Skudeneshavn
Stavanger
Sandnes
Nærbø
Egersund
Flekkefjord
Farsund
Lindesnes
Mandal
Lyngdal
Vennesla
Kristiansand
Grimstad
Arendal
Risør
Kragerø
Larvik
Sandefjord
Tønsberg
Horten
Skien
Porsgrunn
Drangedal
Dalen
Gvarv
Notodden
Kongsberg
Drammen
Rjukan
Gausta
6,178 ft
1,883 m
Haukeligrend
Bykle
Ruven
4,771 ft
1,454 m
Tonstad
Evje
Sira
Otra
Oslo
Ski
Askim
Moss
Sarpsborg
Fredrikstad
Halden
Strömstad
Jessheim
Lørenskog
Fetsund
Nesoddtangen
Kongsvinger
Elverum
Hamar
Brumunddal
Gjøvik
Raufoss
Lillehammer
Fagernes
Brandbu
Hønefoss
Tyrifjorden
Mjøsa
Glomma
Lågen
Begna
Hallingdal
Numedalslågen
Rødberg
Geithus
Koppang
Femunden
Trysilelva
Steinkjer
Levanger
Stjørdalshalsen
Orkanger
Brekstad
Trondheimsfjord
Frøya
Hitra
Smøla
Namsos
Grong
Tunnsjøen
2,218 ft
676 m
Blåfjell
4,387 ft
1,337 m
Vilhelmina
Lycksele
Boliden
Hoting
Åsele
Vännäs
Umeå
Holmsund
Strömsund
Kallsjön
Järpen
Östersund
Storsjön
Åre
5,893 ft
1,796 m
Örnsköldsvik
Sollefteå
Bollstabruk
Kramfors
Härnösand
Hemsö
Timrå
Sundsvall
Bräcke
Ånge
Ljungan
Hede
Sveg
Ljusnan
Ljusdal
Hudiksvall
Bollnäs
Söderhamn
Särna
Österdalälven
Västerdalälven
3,100 ft
945 m
Älvdalen
Orsa
Mora
Siljan
Leksand
Malung
Falun
Borlänge
Sandviken
Gävle
Hofors
Hedesunda
Gräsö
Tierp
Säter
Avesta
Fagersta
Ludvika
Smedjebacken
Östhammar
Hallstavik
Väddö
Åland Is.
Åland
Godby
Mariehamn
Björkö
Lemland
Uppsala
Norrtälje
Märsta
Sala
Enköping
Västerås
Köping
Frövi
Hällefors
Lindesberg
915 ft
279 m
Kristinehamn
Filipstad
Hagfors
Torsby
Sunne
Arvika
Årjäng
Karlstad
Kil
Skoghall
Säffle
Åmål
Ed
Mellerud
Vänern
Örebro
Eskilstuna
Hjälmaren
Mälaren
Sollentuna
Täby
Lidingö
Huddinge
Södertälje
Stockholm
Nynäshamn
Nyköping
Oxelösund
Flen
Katrineholm
Hallsberg
Laxå
Norrköping
Linköping
Motala
Mjölby
Ödeshög
Valdemarsvik
Västervik
Mariestad
Töreboda
Skövde
Lidköping
Skara
Vänersborg
Trollhättan
Uddevalla
Vårgårda
Falköping
Vättern
Orust
Tjörn
Kungälv
Göteborg
Alingsås
Lerum
Borås
Kinna
Kungsbacka
Göta Älv
Jönköping
Tranås
Sommen
Kisa
Nässjö
Mariannelund
Hultsfred
Vetlanda
Emån
Värnamo
Lammhult
Oskarshamn
Mönsterås
Gislaved
Varberg
Falkenberg
Hyltebruk
Bolmen
Ljungby
Växjö
Nybro
Kalmar
Öland
Borgholm
Färjestaden
Emmaboda
Halmstad
Lagan
Åsnen
Älmhult
741 ft
226 m
Markaryd
Ängelholm
Hässleholm
Karlshamn
Ronneby
Karlskrona
Kristianstad
Helsingborg
Helsingør
Hillerød
Eslöv
Lund
Malmö
Trelleborg
Ystad
Simrishamn
COPENHAGEN
(KØBENHAVN)
Køge
Roskilde
Ringsted
Sorø
Slagelse
Korsør
Kalundborg
Næstved
469 ft
143 m
Stege
Møn
Nykøbing
Falster
Lolland
Nakskov
Rødby
Gedser
Great Belt
Lange-land
Samsø
Visby
Gotland
Slite
Hemse
Fårösund
Fårö
Gotska Sandön
Skagen
Hirtshals
Hjørring
Frederikshavn
Brønderslev
Nørresundby
Aalborg
Læsø
Hanstholm
Thisted
Thyborøn
Skive
Hobro
Randers
Viborg
Holstebro
Ringkøbing
Herning
Silkeborg
Århus
Grenå
568 ft
173 m
Yding Skovhøj
Skjern
Billund
Horsens
Vejle
Esbjerg
Ribe
Kolding
Odense
Nyborg
Svendborg
Haderslev
Aabenraa
Tønder
Rømø
Sylt
Westerland
North Frisian Is.
Als
Sønderborg
Flensburg
Schleswig
Husum
Eckernförde
Rendsburg
Kiel
Heide
Neumünster
Plön
Itzehoe
Heligoland
Cuxhaven
Norderney
Borkum
East Frisian Is.
West Frisian Is.
Emden
Wilhelmshaven
Bremerhaven
Bremervörde
Leer
Papenburg
Oldenburg
Leeuwarden
Groningen
Assen
Heerenveen
Stade
Elmshorn
Norderstedt
HAMBURG
Geesthacht
Bad Segeberg
Lübeck
Neustadt
Bad Doberan
Wismar
Schwerin
Parchim
Güstrow
Rostock
Waren
Malchin
Demmin
Greifswald
Stralsund
Barth
Bergen
Rügen
Sassnitz
C. Arkona
528 ft
161 m
Fehmarn
Burg
Anklam
Neubrandenburg
Ahlbeck
Usedom
Wolin
Świnoujście
Kamień Pomorski
Gryfice
Płoty
Świdwin
Białogard
Kołobrzeg
Koszalin
Sławno
Darłowo
Ustka
Słupsk
Bytów
Miastko
Łeba
Lębork
Władysławowo
Hel
Gdynia
Sopot
Gdańsk
Gdańsk Bay
Tczew
Starogard Gdański
Czersk
Kościerzyna
1,079 ft
329 m
Malbork
Elbląg
Nowy Dwór
Braniewo
Kaliningrad
Baltiysk
Mamonovo
Bagrationovsk
Zelenogradsk
Pionerskiy
Lidzbark Warmiński
Bartoszyce
Dobre Miasto
Morąg
Bornholm
Rønne
Neksø
532 ft
162 m
Pomeranian Bay
Liepāja
Klaipėda
Curonian Spit
Curonian Lagoon

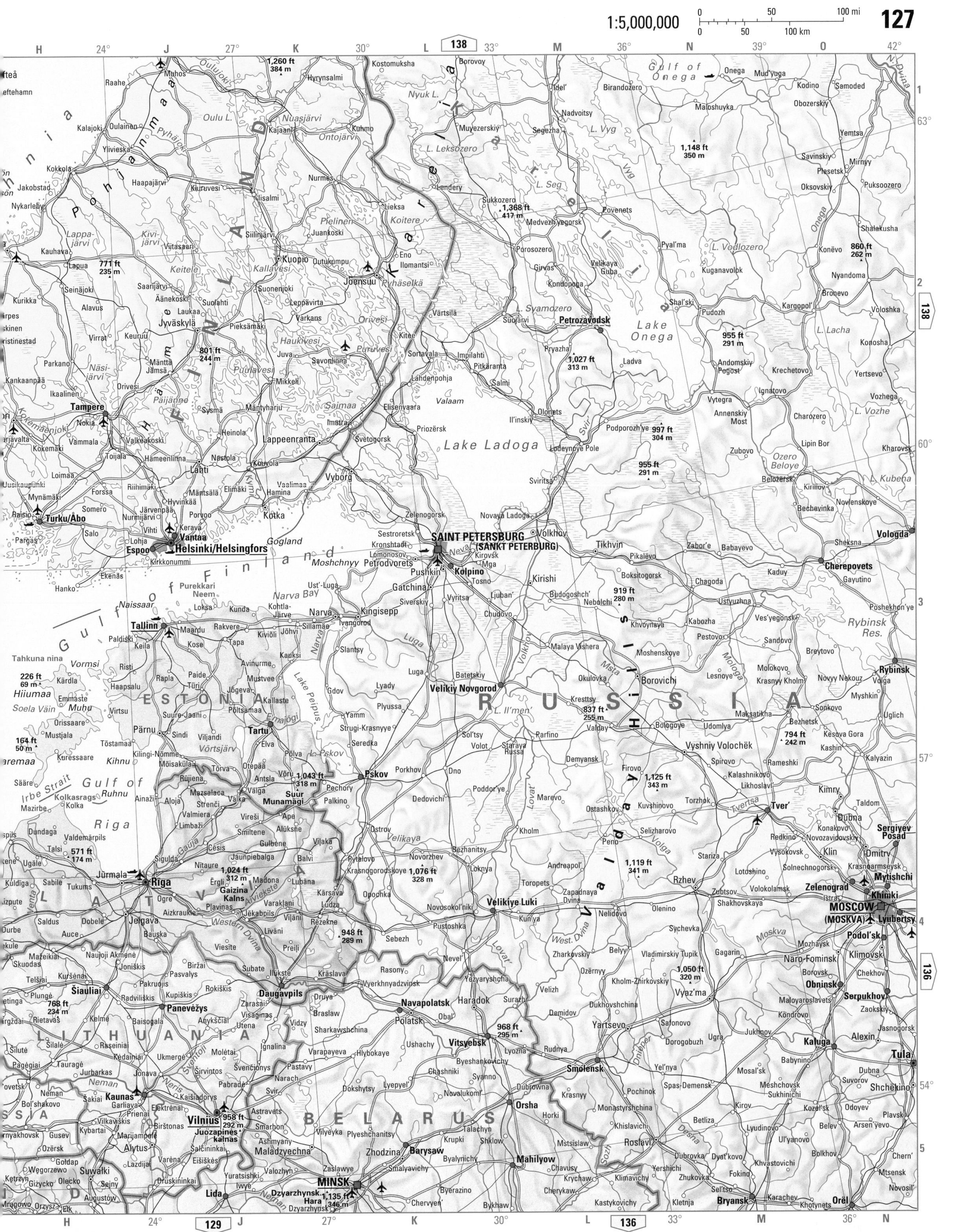
1:5,000,000
0 50 100 mi
0 50 100 km
H 24° J 27° K 30° L 138 33° M 36° N 39° O 42°
1
2
3
4
5
63°
60°
57°
54°
138
136
FINLAND
Pohjanmaa
Karelia
Gulf of Bothnia
Gulf of Onega
Onega
Mud'yuga
Kodino
Samoded
Obozerskiy
Maloshuyka
Yemtsa
Savinskiy
Plesetsk
Mirnyy
Oksovskiy
Puksoozero
Shalakusha
860 ft
262 m
Konëvo
Nyandoma
Bronevo
Kargopol'
Voloshka
L. Lacha
Konosha
Yertsevo
Krechetovo
Vozhega
L. Vozhe
Charozero
Lipin Bor
Kharovsk
Ozero Beloye
Belozërsk
Kirillov
L. Kubena
Novlenskoye
Bechevinka
Vologda
Sheksna
Cherepovets
Gayutino
Kaduy
Poshekhon'ye
Rybinsk Res.
Rybinsk
Breytovo
Molokovo
Krasnyy Kholm
Novyy Nekouz
Volga
Myshkin
Uglich
Sonkovo
Bezhetsk
Kesova Gora
794 ft
242 m
Kashin
Kalyazin
Rameshki
Kimry
Taldom
Dubna
Sergiyev Posad
Dmitrov
Krasnoarmeysk
Mytishchi
Khimki
Zelenograd
MOSCOW
(MOSKVA)
Lyubertsy
Podol'sk
Klimovsk
Chekhov
Serpukhov
Obninsk
Zaoksky
Jasnogorsk
Aleksin
Tula
Shchëkino
Plavsk
Odoyev
Arsen'yevo
Belev
Bolkhov
Chern'
Mtsensk
Novosil'
Orël
Khotynets
Karachev
Bryansk
Kostomuksha
Borovoy
Nyuk L.
Ideľ
Birandozero
Nadvoitsy
Segezha
L. Vyg
Vyg
1,148 ft
350 m
Muyezerskiy
L. Leksozero
Lendery
L. Seg
Sukkozero
1,368 ft
417 m
Medvezh'yegorsk
Povenets
Porosozero
Girvas
Velikaya Guba
Kondopoga
Pyal'ma
L. Vodlozero
Kuganavolok
Shal'ski
Pudozh
L. Syamozero
Suojarvi
Petrozavodsk
Lake Onega
955 ft
291 m
Pryazha
1,027 ft
313 m
Ladva
Andomskiy Pogost
Vytegra
Ignatovo
Annenskiy Most
Podporozh'ye
997 ft
304 m
Svir'
Olonets
Il'inskiy
Lodeynoye Pole
Zubovo
Svirtsa
Novaya Ladoga
Volkhov
Tikhvin
Zabor'e
Babayevo
Pikalëvo
Boksitogorsk
Chagoda
Kirishi
Budogoshch'
919 ft
280 m
Nebolchi
Ustyuzhna
Ves'yegonsk
Khvoynaya
Kabozha
Pestovo
Sandovo
Malaya Vishera
Moshenskoye
Okulovka
Msta
Borovichi
Lesnoye
Mologa
Krestsy
837 ft
255 m
Valday
Bologoye
Udomlya
Maksatikha
Vyshniy Volochëk
Spirovo
Kalashnikovo
Likhoslavl'
Torzhok
Tver'
Tvertsa
Konakovo
Novozavidovskiy
Redkino
Klin
Vysokovsk
Solnechnogorsk
Lotoshino
Volokolamsk
Stariza
Rzhev
Zubtsov
Shakhovskaya
Sychevka
Olenino
Nelidovo
Zapadnaya Dvina
Mozhaysk
Naro-Fominsk
Borovsk
Gagarin
Vladimirskiy Tupik
1,050 ft
320 m
Kholm-Zhirkovskiy
Vyaz'ma
Maloyaroslavets
Kondrovo
Kaluga
Yukhnov
Safonovo
Yartsevo
Dorogobuzh
Ugra
Babynino
Dubna
Suvorov
Mosal'sk
Meshchovsk
Sukhinichi
Kozel'sk
Spas-Demensk
Yel'nya
Kirov
Lyudinovo
Ul'yanovo
Khvastovichi
Betliza
Desna
Roslavl'
Dubrovka
Dyat'kovo
Fokino
Zhukovka
Sel'tso
Kletnja
Kostykovichi
Yershichi
Klimavichy
Mstsislaw
Pochinok
Monastyrshchina
Khislavichi
Smolensk
Rudnya
Dnieper
Krasnyy
Horki
Dubrowna
Orsha
Lyozna
Vitsyebsk
Byeshankovichy
Syanno
Chashniki
Novalukoml'
Lyepyel'
Dokshytsy
Krupki
Barysaw
Shklow
Byalynichy
Mahilyow
Chavusy
Krychaw
Cherykaw
Sozh
Byerazino
Chervyen'
Bykhaw
MINSK
Dzyarzhynsk
Hara
1,135 ft
346 m
Zaslawye
Smalyavichy
Zhodzina
Maladzyechna
Ashmyany
Smarhon
Vilyeyka
Plyeshchanitsy
Astravets
BELARUS
Narach
Svir
Pastavy
Hlybokaye
Ushachy
Varapayeva
Sharkawshchina
Braslaw
Polatsk
Navapolatsk
Obal'
Haradok
Surazh
968 ft
295 m
Demidov
Dukhovshchina
Velizh
Yezyaryshcha
Vyerkhnyadzvinsk
Rasony
Druya
Nevel'
Lovat'
Pustoshka
Kun'ya
Velikiye Luki
West. Dvina
Zharkovskiy
Belyy
Ozërnyy
Novosokol'niki
Sebezh
Opochka
Toropets
Andreapol'
Zapadnaya Dvina
1,119 ft
341 m
Peno
Selizharovo
Kuvshinovo
Ostashkov
Valdai Hills
1,125 ft
343 m
Firovo
Demyansk
Marevo
Kholm
Bezhanitsy
Loknya
Novorzhev
1,076 ft
328 m
Krasnogorodskoye
Pytalovo
Ostrov
Velikaya
Dedovichi
Porkhov
Dno
Poddor'ye
Staraya Russa
Parfino
L. Il'men'
RUSSIA
Velikiy Novgorod
Batetskiy
Sol'tsy
Volot
Shimsk
Chudovo
Lyuban'
Tosno
Volkhov
Pskov
Pechory
Palkino
Seredka
Strugi-Krasnyye
Plyussa
Lyady
Yamm
Gdov
Slantsy
Luga
Lake Peipus
Narva
Ivangorod
Kingisepp
Sillamäe
Jõhvi
Kiviõli
Kohtla-Järve
Kunda
Rakvere
Tapa
Kose
Maardu
Tallinn
Keila
Paldiski
Narva Bay
Ust'-Luga
Volosovo
Gatchina
Siverskiy
Vyritsa
Pushkin
Kolpino
Kirovsk
Mga
Petrodvorets
Lomonosov
Kronshtadt
Sestroretsk
Zelenogorsk
SAINT PETERSBURG
(SANKT PETERBURG)
Neva
Moshchnyy
Gogland
Gulf of Finland
Purekkari Neem
Loksa
Naissaar
Vyborg
Svetogorsk
Imatra
Priozërsk
Lake Ladoga
Valaam
Elisenvaara
Lahdenpohja
Sortavala
Impilahti
Pitkäranta
Salmi
Kitee
Värtsilä
Joensuu
Pyhäselkä
Ilomantsi
Eno
Outokumpu
Kuopio
Kallavesi
Lieksa
Koitere
Pielinen
Juankoski
Nurmes
Kuhmo
Ontojärvi
Nuasjärvi
Kajaani
Oulu L.
Oulujoki
Muhos
Hyrynsalmi
1,260 ft
384 m
Raahe
Kalajoki
Oulainen
Pyhäjoki
Ylivieska
Kokkola
Jakobstad
Nykarleby
Haapajärvi
Kiuruvesi
Iisalmi
Siilinjärvi
Kivijärvi
Vitasaari
Lappajärvi
Kauhava
Lapua
771 ft
235 m
Keitele
Seinäjoki
Saarijärvi
Äänekoski
Suolahti
Suonenjoki
Leppävirta
Varkaus
Orivesi
Kurikka
Alavus
Laukaa
Jyväskylä
Pieksämäki
Haukivesi
Puruvesi
Savonlinna
Juva
Virrat
Keuruu
Mänttä
801 ft
244 m
Jämsä
Puulavesi
Mikkeli
Parkano
Näsijärvi
Kankaanpää
Ikaalinen
Orivesi
Tampere
Päijänne
Sysmä
Mäntyharju
Saimaa
Nokia
Kokemäenjoki
Vammala
Kokemäki
Valkeakoski
Heinola
Lappeenranta
Toijala
Hämeenlinna
Nastola
Lahti
Kouvola
Loimaa
Riihimäki
Kymi
Vaalimaa
Hamina
Forssa
Mäntsälä
Elimäki
Mynämäki
Hyvinkää
Uusikaupunki
Raisio
Turku/Åbo
Somero
Järvenpää
Nurmijärvi
Porvoo
Kotka
Kerava
Vantaa
Vihti
Lohja
Salo
Pargas
Espoo
Helsinki/Helsingfors
Kirkkonummi
Ekenäs
Hanko
Tahkuna nina
Vormsi
226 ft
69 m
Kärdla
Hiiumaa
Emmaste
Soela Väin
Muhu
Risti
Rapla
Paide
Türi
Haapsalu
ESTONIA
Jõgeva
Mustvee
Kallaste
Põltsamaa
Suure-Jaani
Virtsu
Pärnu
Viljandi
Emajõgi
Tartu
Elva
Võrtsjärv
Sindi
Orissaare
Mustjala
164 ft
50 m
Tõstamaa
Kuressaare
Kihnu
Kilingi-Nõmme
Mõisaküla
Tõrva
Otepää
Põlva
L. Pskov
Rüjiena
Antsla
Võru
1,043 ft
318 m
Suur Munamägi
Valga
Valka
Mazsalaca
Strenči
Ainaži
Aloja
Valmiera
Limbaži
Vireši
Ape
Alūksne
Smiltene
Gulbene
Cēsis
Gauja
Vilaka
Jaunpiebalga
Balvi
Sigulda
Nītaure
1,024 ft
312 m
Madona
Lubāna
Gaizina Kalns
Ērgli
Kārsava
Rēzekne
Ludza
Varakļāni
Viļāni
Aiviekste
Pļaviņas
Jēkabpils
Aizkraukle
Ogre
Riga
Jūrmala
LATVIA
Gulf of Riga
Irbe Strait
Kolkasrags
Kolka
Mazirbe
Ruhnu
Sääre
Dundaga
Valdemārpils
Talsi
571 ft
174 m
Ugāle
Venta
Kuldīga
Sabile
Tukums
Saldus
Dobele
Jelgava
Bauska
Auce
Livāni
948 ft
289 m
Preiļi
Western Dvina
Viesīte
Subate
Ilūkste
Krāslava
Daugavpils
Biržai
Pasvalys
Rokiškis
Naujoji Akmenė
Joniškis
Mažeikiai
Skuodas
Kuršėnai
Telšiai
Šiauliai
Pakruojis
Radviliškis
Kupiškis
Panevėžys
Zarasai
Visaginas
Utena
Anykščiai
Ignalina
Plungė
768 ft
234 m
Rietavas
Kelmė
Baisogala
LITHUANIA
Šilutė
Šilalė
Raseiniai
Kėdainiai
Ukmergė
Molėtai
Švenčionys
Šventoji
Širvintos
Pagėgiai
Tauragė
Jurbarkas
Jonava
Neris
Pabradė
Neman
Kaunas
Garliava
Kaišiadorys
Vilnius
958 ft
292 m
Juozapinės kalnas
Šakiai
Prienai
Elektrėnai
Vilkaviškis
Birštonas
Kybartai
Marijampolė
Alytus
Šalčininkai
Varėna
Eišiškės
Lazdijai
Druskininkai
Gusev
Ozërsk
Sovetsk
Neman
Bol'shakovo
Chernyakhovsk
Gołdap
Suwałki
Węgorzewo
Olecko
Sejny
Giżycko
Kętrzyn
Augustów
Mrągowo
Orzysz
Ełk
Lida
Iwye
Yuratsishki
Valozhyn
Neman

126
124
131
131
132

LITHUANIA
LATVIA
RUSSIA
BELARUS
POLAND
UKRAINE
SLOVAKIA
HUNGARY
ROMANIA
MOLDOVA
SERBIA
CROATIA
Baltic Sea
Black Sea
Courland Spit
Courland Lagoon
Gdańsk Bay
Mazury
Beskids
Carpathian Mts
Transylvanian Alps
Muntii Apuseni
Great Hungarian Plain
Western Dvina
Neman
Vistula
Pripet
Dnieper
Desna
Kiev Reservoir
Southern Bug
Dniester
Prut
Siret
Danube
Tisza
Mureș
Someș
Bug
Narew
Pilica
Wieprz
San
Sluch
Horyn
Ubarts
Berezina
Sozh
Dnistrovs'kyy Lyman
Lake Yalpuh
Zmiyinyy
Klaipėda
Šiauliai
Panevėžys
Kaunas
Vilnius
Daugavpils
Liepāja
Kaliningrad
Gdańsk
Gdynia
Elbląg
Olsztyn
Białystok
Hrodna
Lida
MINSK
Navapolatsk
Polatsk
Vitsyebsk
Orsha
Mahilyow
Babruysk
Barysaw
Maladzyechna
Baranavichy
Salihorsk
Slutsk
Homyel'
Mazyr
Pinsk
Brest
Smolensk
Roslavl'
WARSAW (WARSZAWA)
Łódź
Radom
Lublin
Kielce
Częstochowa
Kraków
Katowice
Bytom
Chorzów
Gliwice
Zabrze
Sosnowiec
Tarnów
Rzeszów
Płock
Toruń
Bydgoszcz
Włocławek
Grudziądz
Siedlce
L'viv
Ternopil'
Luts'k
Rivne
Zhytomyr
KIEV (KYYIV)
Chernihiv
Bila Tserkva
Vinnytsya
Khmel'nyts'kyy
Ivano-Frankivs'k
Chernivtsi
Uzhhorod
Košice
Prešov
Miskolc
Nyíregyháza
Debrecen
BUDAPEST
Székesfehérvár
Kecskemét
Szeged
Pécs
Győr
Bratislava
Satu Mare
Baia Mare
Oradea
Cluj-Napoca
Târgu Mureș
Arad
Timișoara
Sibiu
Brașov
Bacău
Iași
Botoșani
Suceava
Piatra-Neamț
Focșani
Galați
Brăila
Buzău
Chișinău
Bălți
Tiraspol
Tighina (Bendery)
ODESA
Izmayil
Hoverla 6,762 ft 2,061 m
Gerlachovský štít 8,711 ft 2,655 m
Moldoveanu 8,347 ft 2,544 m

1:5,000,000
0 50 100 mi
0 50 100 km
131
KLETT-PERTHES
ATLANTIC OCEAN
Bay of Biscay
FRANCE
Gascony
Languedoc
Pyrenees
ANDORRA
Andorra la Vella
Cantabrian Mountains
Asturias
Cantabria
Basque Country
Navarra
La Rioja
Galicia
Castile and León
Old Castile
New Castile
Castile-La Mancha
La Mancha
Extremadura
Andalusia
Sierra Morena
Sierra Nevada
Sierra de Gredos
Sierra de Guadarrama
Serranía de Cuenca
Sa. de Gata
Sierra de la Demanda
Aragon
Catalonia
Valencian Community
Murcia
SPAIN
PORTUGAL
Minho
Alentejo
Algarve
Estremadura
Beira
MADRID
Móstoles
Leganés
Getafe
Fuenlabrada
Alcobendas
Alcalá de Henares
Torrejón de Ardoz
Aranjuez
Toledo
Guadalajara
BARCELONA
L'Hospitalet de Llobregat
Badalona
Sabadell
Terrassa
Mataró
Tarragona
Lleida/Lérida
Girona
Zaragoza
Valencia
Castellón de la Plana
Sagunto
Torrent
Alicante
Elche
Murcia
Cartagena
Almería
Granada
Málaga
Marbella
Córdoba
Jaén
Seville (Sevilla)
Dos Hermanas
Huelva
Cádiz
Jerez de la Frontera
Algeciras
Gibraltar (U.K.)
Ceuta (SPA.)
Tanger (Tanjah)
MOROCCO
Strait of Gibraltar
Badajoz
Mérida
Cáceres
Salamanca
Valladolid
Burgos
León
Oviedo
Gijón
Santander
Bilbao
Donostia/San Sebastián
Vitoria/Gasteiz
Pamplona/Iruña
Logroño
A Coruña
Santiago de Compostela
Lugo
Ourense
Vigo
Pontevedra
Ferrol
Lisbon (Lisboa)
Amadora
Setúbal
Porto
Vila Nova de Gaia
Braga
Coimbra
Albacete
Ciudad Real
Cuenca
Teruel
Soria
Segovia
Ávila
Palencia
Zamora
Huesca
Picos de Europa 8,688 ft 2,648 m
Aneto 11,168 ft 3,404 m
Monte Perdido 11,008 ft 3,355 m
Vignemale 10,821 ft 3,298 m
Mulhacén 11,424 ft 3,482 m
Pico del Teide 12,199 ft 3,718 m
Pico 7,717 ft 2,352 m
Pico Ruivo 6,109 ft 1,862 m
Costa Brava
Costa Dorada
Costa Blanca
Costa del Sol
Gulf of Valencia
Gulf of Cádiz
Bay of Setúbal
Mediterranean Sea
Balearic Islands
Mallorca
Menorca
Ibiza
Formentera
Cabrera
Palma de M.
Mahón
Alborán
C. Ortegal
C. Finisterre
C. de Peñas
C. Trafalgar
C. de Gata
C. Nao
C. Tortosa
C. Creus
C. da Roca
Cape Saint Vincent
Ebro
Duero
Douro
Tagus
Tejo
Guadiana
Guadalquivir
Júcar
Segura
Miño
Azores
PORTUGAL
ATLANTIC OCEAN
Corvo
Flores
Graciosa
Terceira
Faial
Pico
São Jorge
São Miguel
Santa Maria
Ponta Delgada
Angra do Heroísmo
1:3,000,000
0 20 mi
0 20 km
Madeira
Porto Santo
Funchal
Ilhas Desertas
1:6,000,000
0 50 mi
0 50 km
Canary Islands
SPAIN
La Palma
La Gomera
Hierro
Tenerife
Gran Canaria
Fuerteventura
Lanzarote
Alegranza
Graciosa
Isla de Lobos
Santa Cruz de Tenerife
San Cristóbal de la Laguna
Las Palmas
Western Sahara
ATLANTIC OCEAN

1:5,000,000

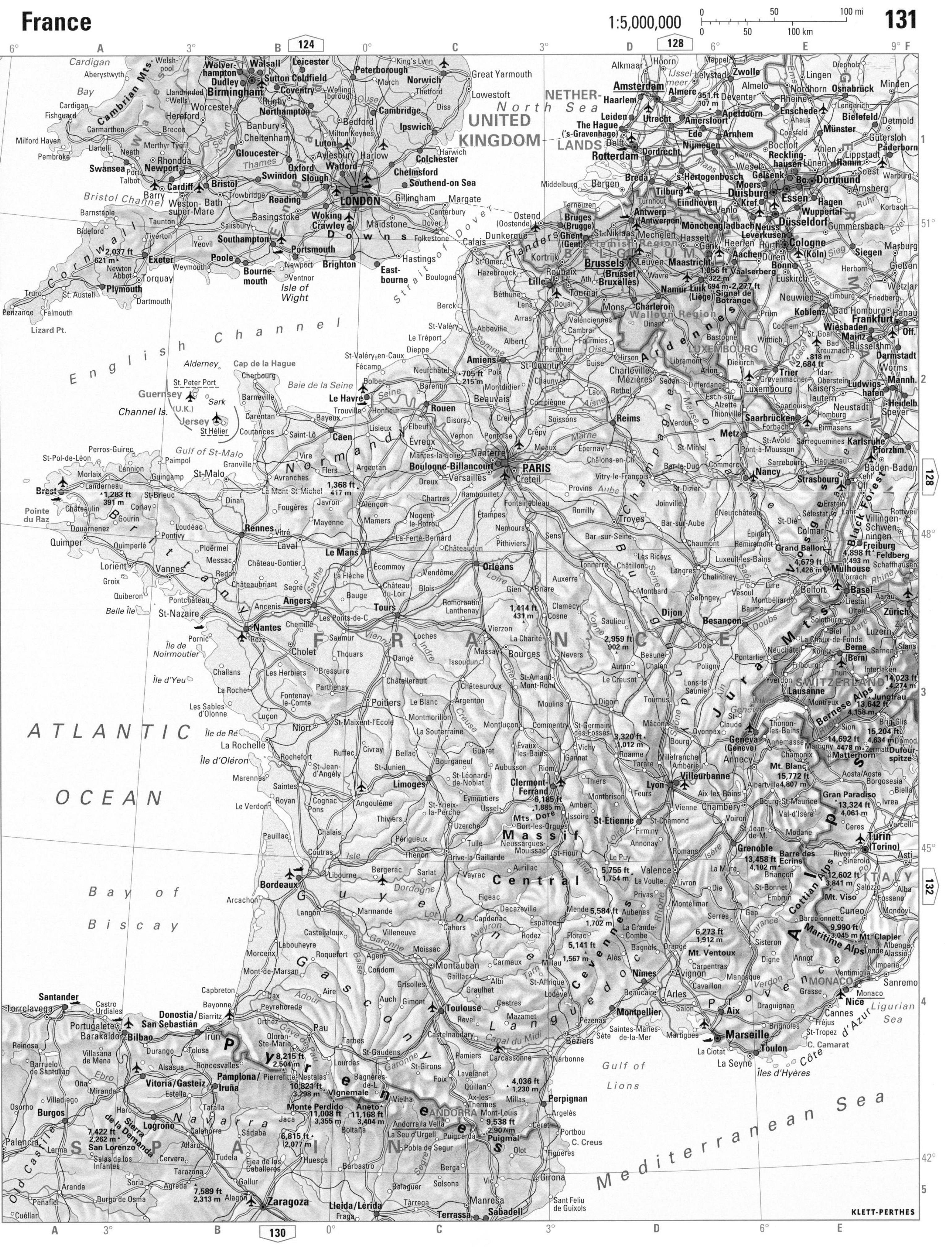
0 50 100 mi
0 50 100 km
A B C D E F
6° 3° 0° 3° 6° 9°
51° 48° 45° 42°
1 2 3 4 5
124
128
130
132
North Sea
UNITED KINGDOM
NETHERLANDS
BELGIUM
LUXEMBOURG
GERMANY
SWITZERLAND
ITALY
MONACO
ANDORRA
SPAIN
FRANCE
English Channel
Channel Is.
Strait of Dover
ATLANTIC OCEAN
Bay of Biscay
Gulf of Lions
Mediterranean Sea
Ligurian Sea
Bristol Channel
Cardigan Bay
Cambrian Mts.
Cornwall
Downs
Isle of Wight
Lizard Pt.
Alderney
Guernsey
Jersey
Sark
St. Peter Port
St Hélier
Cap de la Hague
Baie de la Seine
Gulf of St-Malo
Pointe du Raz
Belle Île
Île de Noirmoutier
Île d'Yeu
Île de Ré
Île d'Oléron
Normandy
Brittany
Flanders
Flemish Region
Walloon Region
Ardennes
Champagne
Lorraine
Vosges
Burgundy
Jura Mts.
Black Forest
Bernese Alps
Alps
Cottian Alps
Maritime Alps
Massif Central
Cevennes
Languedoc
Provence
Guyenne
Gascony
Pyrenees
Navarra
Old Castile
Sierra de la Demanda
Mts. Dore
Mt. Blanc 15,772 ft 4,807 m
Matterhorn
Jungfrau 13,642 ft 4,158 m
Gran Paradiso 13,324 ft 4,061 m
Barre des Ecrins 13,458 ft 4,102 m
Mt. Viso 12,602 ft 3,841 m
Mt. Ventoux 6,273 ft 1,912 m
Aneto 11,168 ft 3,404 m
Monte Perdido 11,008 ft 3,355 m
Vignemale 10,821 ft 3,298 m
Puigmal 9,538 ft 2,907 m
Grand Ballon 4,679 ft 1,426 m
Feldberg 4,898 ft 1,493 m
Signal de Botrange 2,277 ft 694 m
Vaalserberg 1,056 ft 322 m
Seine
Loire
Rhône
Garonne
Dordogne
Rhine
Marne
Oise
Somme
Meuse
Moselle
Saône
Allier
Vienne
Lot
Tarn
Thames
Severn
Ebro
London
Birmingham
Bristol
Cardiff
Swansea
Plymouth
Southampton
Portsmouth
Brighton
Oxford
Cambridge
Norwich
Ipswich
Dover
Folkestone
Amsterdam
The Hague ('s-Gravenhage)
Rotterdam
Utrecht
Antwerp (Antwerpen)
Brussels (Brussel/Bruxelles)
Ghent (Gent)
Bruges (Brugge)
Liège
Maastricht
Aachen
Cologne (Köln)
Düsseldorf
Essen
Dortmund
Frankfurt
Mainz
Wiesbaden
Koblenz
Trier
Saarbrücken
Karlsruhe
Strasbourg
Freiburg
Basel
Zürich
Bern (Bern)
Lausanne
Geneva (Genève)
Turin (Torino)
Nice
Monaco
Sanremo
Marseille
Toulon
Aix
Avignon
Nîmes
Montpellier
Perpignan
Béziers
Narbonne
Carcassonne
Toulouse
Bordeaux
Pau
Biarritz
Bayonne
Donostia/San Sebastián
Bilbao
Santander
Vitoria/Gasteiz
Pamplona/Iruña
Logroño
Burgos
Zaragoza
Huesca
Lleida/Lérida
Girona
Sabadell
Terrassa
Andorra la Vella
Lyon
Villeurbanne
St-Étienne
Grenoble
Chambéry
Annecy
Valence
Clermont-Ferrand
Limoges
Poitiers
Tours
Orléans
Bourges
Dijon
Besançon
Mulhouse
Colmar
Nancy
Metz
Reims
Troyes
Amiens
Rouen
Le Havre
Caen
Cherbourg
Paris
Versailles
Boulogne-Billancourt
Nanterre
Créteil
Lille
Roubaix
Dunkerque
Calais
Boulogne
Le Mans
Angers
Nantes
St-Nazaire
Rennes
Brest
Quimper
Lorient
Vannes
St-Malo
La Rochelle
Niort
Angoulême
Périgueux
Montauban
Luxembourg
KLETT-PERTHES

1:5,000,000

0 50 100 mi
0 50 100 km

128
129
131
176
177

A B C D E
9° 12° 15° 18°
45° 42° 39° 36°
1 2 3 4 5

Pontarlier Köniz Berne (Bern) Erlbourg Thun Sarnen Stans Schwyz Glarus Altdorf Chur Davos
Yverdon Lausanne Montreux Interlaken Jungfrau Bernese Alps 14,023 ft 4,274 m 4,158 m 13,642 ft Andermatt
Thonon-les-Bains Sion Brig-Glis Martigny Zermatt Chamonix 15,204 ft 14,692 ft 4,634 m 4,478 m Matterhorn Dufourspitze Domodossola
Mt. Blanc 15,772 ft 4,807 m Aosta/Aoste Valle d'Aosta/Vallee d'Aoste Verbania L. Maggiore Locarno Bellinzona Lugano L. Como Lecco
Bourg-St-Maurice Val-d'Isère Gran Paradiso 13,324 ft 4,061 m Ceres Modane Borgosesia Biella Ivrea Busto Arsizio Varese Como Monza Bergamo Brescia
Rhaetian Alps Similaun 11,831 ft 3,606 m Meran Mals St. Moritz Ortles 12,812 ft 3,905 m Bormio Bernina 13,285 ft 4,049 m Sondrio Chiavenna Malè
Bergamo Alps Oglio Garda Trento Riva Rovereto 7,333 ft 2,235 m Schio Marmolada 10,965 ft 3,342 m Dolomites Mezzolombardo
4,498 ft 1,371 m Brenner Sterzing Alto Adige South Tyrol Brixen Bruneck Bozen/Bolzano Cortina d'Ampezzo Pieve di Cadore Belluno Feltre Vittorio Pordenone
Gross-glockner 12,461 ft 3,798 m Tauern Lienz Greifenburg Spittal St. Veit Klagenfurt Villach Graz Wolfsberg Leibnitz Mur Maribor Slovenj Gradec 5,063 ft 1,543 m Velenje Ptuj
Friuli Gemona Udine Tolmin Gorizia Monfalcone Portogruaro Spilimbergo Venezia Giulia 9,397 ft 2,864 m Triglav Karawanken Jesenice Julian Alps Kranj Ljubljana Vrhnika Celje Trbovlje Krapina
Nova Gorica Karst Postojna Trieste Koper Pivka Snežnik 5,893 ft 1,796 m Novo Mesto Trebnje Sava Samobor Zagreb Sesvete Velika Gorica Ivanić-Grad Kutina Bjelovar Koprivnica Đurđevac Varaždin Čakovec
Milan (Milano) Novara Vercelli Turin (Torino) Casale Monf. Vigevano Pavia Asti Alessandria Voghera Piacenza Cremona Lombardy Treviglio Desenzano Manerbio Verona Vicenza Padua (Padova) Treviso Venice (Venezia) Chioggia Castelfranco Bassano Conegliano S. Donà di P. Veneto Legnago Villafranca Mantova (Mantua) Rovigo Adige 1,972 ft 601 m
Gulf of Venice Poreč Rovinj Istria Pazin Labin Pula Rt Kamenjak Opatija Rijeka Vel. Risnjak 5,013 ft 1,528 m Crikvenica Krk Senj Cres Rab Lošinj Mali Lošinj
Briançon Pinerolo Rivoli Cottian Alps Mt. Viso 12,602 ft 3,841 m Saluzzo Fossano Alba Cuneo Mondovì Barcelonnette Acqui Terme Novi Ligure 5,902 ft 1,799 m Savona Genoa (Genova) Chiavari Rapallo
9,990 ft 3,045 m Mt. Clapier Maritime Alps Tende Annot Ventimiglia Albenga Alassio Imperia San Remo Monaco MONACO Nice Grasse Cannes Fréjus Côte d'Azur FRANCE
Fidenza Bobbio Parma Reggio nell'Em. Carpi Modena Ferrara Argenta Comacchio Bologna Sassuolo Castelnovo ne'Monti Borgo Imola Lugo Faenza Ravenna Cervia Forlì Cesena Rimini San Marino SAN MARINO Pesaro Fano Urbino
7,103 ft 2,165 m La Spezia Carrara Massa Viareggio Pisa Lucca Pistoia Prato Florence (Firenze) Empoli Livorno Gorgona Volterra Montevarchi Arezzo Siena Cecina Cortona Montepulciano
Apennines Tuscany Umbria Marches Lazio Abruzzi Molise Campania Apulia Basilicata Calabria
Gulf of Genoa Ligurian Sea Capraia Piombino Portoferraio Elba Follonica Pianosa Montecristo Grosseto Orbetello Giglio 2,083 ft 635 m Giannutri Manciano
Senigallia Ancona Iesi Civitanova Marche Macerata Fermo San Benedetto Ascoli Piceno Giulianova Teramo Gran Sasso d'Italia 9,554 ft 2,912 m Pescara Chieti Penne L'Aquila Antrodoco Rieti Spoleto Foligno Assisi Perugia L. Trasimeno Fabriano Città di Castello Orvieto Montefiascone L. Bolsena Terni 5,702 ft 1,738 m
Viterbo Tarquinia Civitavecchia Rome (Roma) VATICAN CITY Fiumicino Marino Velletri Aprilia Anzio Latina 5,040 ft 1,536 m Terracina C. Circeo Gaeta Formia Sessa Aurunca Cassino Frosinone Sora Avezzano Sulmona 2,793 m 9,164 ft Lanciano Vasto Termoli Larino Isernia Campobasso Liri
C. Corse L'Île Rousse Calvi Bastia Mte. Cinto 8,878 ft 2,706 m Corte C. Rosso (FRA.) Corsica Ajaccio 7,008 ft 2,136 m Sartène Porto-Vecchio Bonifacio Str. of Bonifacio
Asinara La Maddalena Tempio Pausania 4,469 ft 1,362 m Olbia Porto Torres Sassari Alghero Ozieri Siniscola Bosa Macomer Nuoro Dorgali Sardinia Monti del Gennargentu 6,017 ft 1,834 m Oristano Tortolì Terralba Mandas Guspini Villacidro Muravera Iglesias Quartu Sant'Elena S. Pietro Carbonia Cagliari Sant'Antioco C. Carbonara Gulf of Cagliari C. Teulada
Tremiti Is. Pianosa Palagruža 3,465 ft 1,056 m Vieste San Severo Testa del Gargano Manfredonia Gulf of Manfredonia Lucera Foggia San Bartolomeo Cerignola Barletta Bisceglie Molfetta Andria Bari Mola di Bari Monopoli Altamura Gioia del C. Martina Franca Ostuni Brindisi Taranto Manduria Lecce Galatina Nardo Gallipoli Gagliano del Capo C. Santa Maria di Leuca Matera Francavilla
Pontine Is. Benevento Ariano Irpino Melfi Venosa Caserta 4,203 ft 1,281 m Avellino Pozzuoli Naples (Napoli) Vesuvius Pompei Ischia Torre del Greco Sorrento Capri Salerno Eboli Battipaglia Avigliano Potenza Tricarico Capaccio Agropoli Sala Consilina Marsico Nuovo Bernalda Montalbano Ionico Sant'Arcangelo Sapri Lauria 7,451 ft 2,271 m Castrovillari Gulf of Taranto
Tyrrhenian Sea Belvedere Marittimo Corigliano Calabro Rossano Cetraro Fuscaldo Paola Cosenza San Giovanni in Fiore Crotone Amantea Cutro Lamezia Catanzaro C. Rizzuto Pizzo Tropea Vibo Valentia Gioia Tauro Palmi Taurianova Siderno Villa San Giovanni 6,418 ft 1,956 m Reggio di Cal. Melito di Porto Salvo C. Spartivento
Stromboli Lipari Is. Salina Lipari Vulcano Ustica Milazzo Messina Str. of Messina
C. San Vito Egadi Is. Trapani Palermo Bagheria Monreale Alcamo Termini Imerese Cefalù Sant'Agata di Militello Patti Barcellona Mistretta 6,493 ft 1,979 m Gangi Monte Etna 10,903 ft 3,323 m Bronte Adrano Taormina Acireale Catania Paternò Marsala Castelvetrano Corleone Mazara del Vallo Sciacca Caltanissetta Enna Sicily Porto Empedocle Agrigento Piazza Armerina Riesi Lentini Palma di Montechiaro Caltagirone Licata Gela Vizzini Augusta Syracuse (Siracusa) Vittoria Ragusa Modica Avola Noto Pozzallo Pachino C. Passero
Strait of Otranto Ionian Sea
Mediterranean Sea Str. of Sicily Pantelleria Linosa Lampedusa Gozo MALTA Valletta Malta 830 ft 253 m Ta'Dmejrek
Jālīṭā Ra's al-Abyad Bizerte (Binzart) Ra's al-Jabal C. Side Manzil Bū Ruqaybah Zambra C. Bon G. of Tunis Māṭir Ariana (Aryanah) Carthage Tūnis Bin 'Arūs 2,090 ft 637 m Qulaybīyah Manzil Tamīm Zaghwān Nābul Al-Ḥammāmāt
'Annābah Ṭabarqah Al-Qal'ah At-Ṭarif Dariyah Qālmah 3,947 ft 1,203 m Mujarridah Mts. Bājah Majāz al-Bāb Tabursuq Al-Fahs Dundubah ALGERIA Sūq Ahrās Sadrātah TUNISIA Al-Kāf Silyānah Madawrush Al-Wīnzah Ad-Dahmānī Tajirwin Makthar Sbikha 'Ayn al-Bayḍā'
Zalaegerszeg Keszthely Balaton Siófok Fonyód Sió Paks Tamási Kiskőrös Csongrád Kiskunhalas Szekszárd Dombóvár 2,238 ft 682 m Baja Komló Kaposvár HUNGARY Nagykanizsa Lenart Murska Sobota Pécs Siklós Mohács Barcs Subotica Sombor Virovitica Drava Valpovo Apatin Vrbas Srbobran Vojvodina Temerin Novi Sad Našice Osijek Vukovar Vinkovci Bačka Palanka Đakovo Slavonski Brod Požega Daruvar Velika Sisak Karlovac Vrginmost Ogulin
CROATIA Bosanski Novi Bos. Gradiška Prijedor Bos. Krupa Bihać Banja Luka Derventa Doboj Brčko Mitrovica Šabac Bijeljina Tuzla 2,254 ft 687 m Loznica Zvornik SERBIA Teslić Sanski Most Zavidovići Srnetica Kladanj Jajce Travnik Zenica Vareš 5,043 ft 1,537 m Srebrenica Kleкovača 6,434 ft 1,961 m BOSNIA AND HERZEGOVINA Federation of B. & H. Sarajevo Bjelašnica 6,782 ft 2,067 m Goražde Višegrad Konjic Visoko Bugojno Gornji Vakuf Pale Foča
Dinaric Alps Velebit Gospić Karlobag Pag 5,768 ft 1,758 m Dinara 6,007 ft 1,831 m Knin Dalmatia Zadar Ugljan Pašman Dugi Otok Šali Kornat 4,951 ft 1,509 m Šibenik Primošten Trogir Split Livno Imotski Sinj Jablanica 7,303 ft 2,226 m Mostar Nevesinje 6,126 ft 1,867 m Durmitor 8,275 ft 2,522 m Pljevlja Šolta Brač Makarska Hvar Vis Korčula Ploče Pelješac Metković Trebinje Lastovo Mljet Dubrovnik Nikšić MONTENEGRO Podgorica Kotor Lake Scutari Bar
Adriatic Sea Danube Sava Kupa Una Vrbas Bosna Drina Neretva Tisza

KLETT-PERTHES

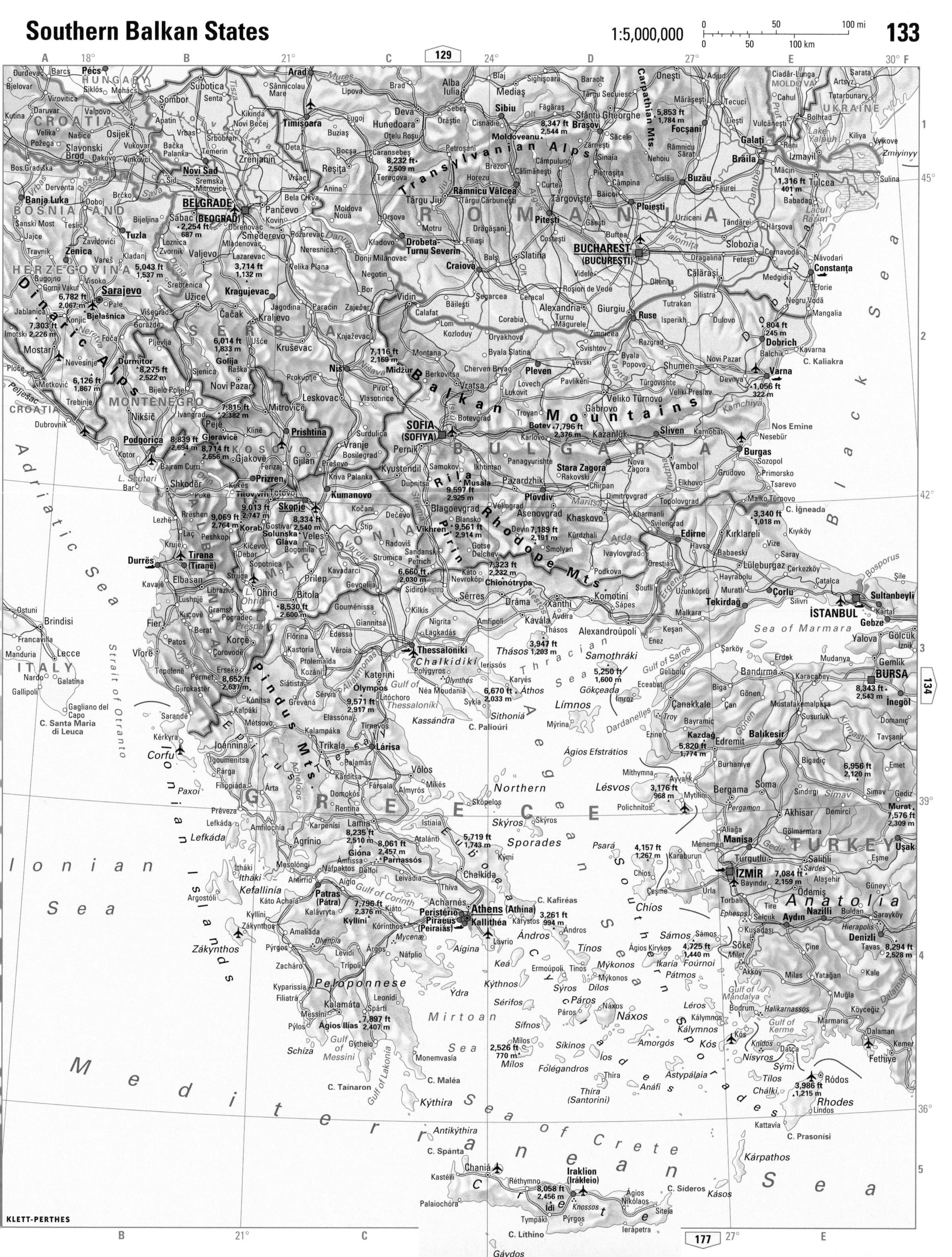

129
134
177

KLETT-PERTHES

129
136
133

UKRAINE
MOLDOVA
ROMANIA
BULGARIA
GREECE
TURKEY

Black Sea
Sea of Azov
Sea of Marmara
Mediterranean Sea
Gulf of Antalya

Krym
Transylvanian Alps
Carpathian Mts.
Balkan Mountains
Küre Dağları
Pontine Mountains
Taurus Mountains
Anatolia

Chişinău
Odesa
Mykolayiv
Kherson
Melitopol'
Mariupol'
Simferopol'
Sevastopol'
Kerch
Novorossiysk
Bucharest (Bucureşti)
Constanţa
Varna
Burgas
Edirne
İstanbul
Bursa
İzmir
Ankara
Konya
Kayseri
Adana
Mersin
Antalya
Aleppo (Halab)

KLETT-PERTHES

152
152

1:5,000,000

0 50 100 mi
0 50 100 km
137
148
153
RUSSIA
GEORGIA
ARMENIA
AZERBAIJAN
KAZAKHSTAN
IRAN
IRAQ
Caspian Sea
Caspian Depression
Kalmykia/Khalmg-Tangch
Chërnyye Zemli
Yergeni Heights
Caucasus
Lesser Caucasus
Doğu Toroslar
Qareh Dāgh
ROSTOV-NA-DONU
Taganrog
Bataysk
Novocherkassk
Volgodonsk
Krasnodar
Armavir
Stavropol'
Nevinnomyssk
Cherkessk
Pyatigorsk
Kislovodsk
Nal'chik
Vladikavkaz
Nazran'
Groznyy
Makhachkala
Khasavyurt
Kaspiysk
Derbent
Elista
Astrakhan'
Budënnovsk
Maykop
Sochi
Tuapse
Aqua/Sokhumi
Batumi
Kutaisi
Poti
TBILISI
Rustavi
Gyumri
Vanadzor
YEREVAN
Lake Sevan
Gäncä
Mingäçevir
Sumqayıt
BAKU (BAKI)
Xankändi (Step'anakert)
Naxçıvan
Trabzon
Rize
Erzurum
Erzincan
Kars
Ağri
Van
Lake Van
Muş
Bingöl
Elâzığ
Diyarbakır
Batman
Siverek
Şanlıurfa
Mardin
Kızıltepe
Al-Qāmishlī
Al-Ḥasakah
MOSUL (AL-MAWṢIL)
Arbīl (Irbil)
Orūmīyeh
Lake Urmia
TABRĪZ
Ardabīl
Rasht
Zanjān
Qazvīn
Mahābād
Saqqez
Miāndowāb
Marāgheh
Khvoy
El'brus 18,511 ft 5,642 m
Kazbek 16,559 ft 5,047 m
Ararat 16,946 ft 5,165 m
Bazardüzü Dağı 14,653 ft 4,466 m
Süphan Dağı 13,314 ft 4,058 m
Kaçkar Dağı 12,901 ft 3,932 m
Aragats Lerr 13,419 ft 4,090 m
Gamış Dağı 12,218 ft 3,724 m
Kūh-e Hājī Ebrāhīm 11,811 ft 3,600 m
39°
42°
45°
48°
51°
36°
F
G
H
J
K
1
2
3
4
5

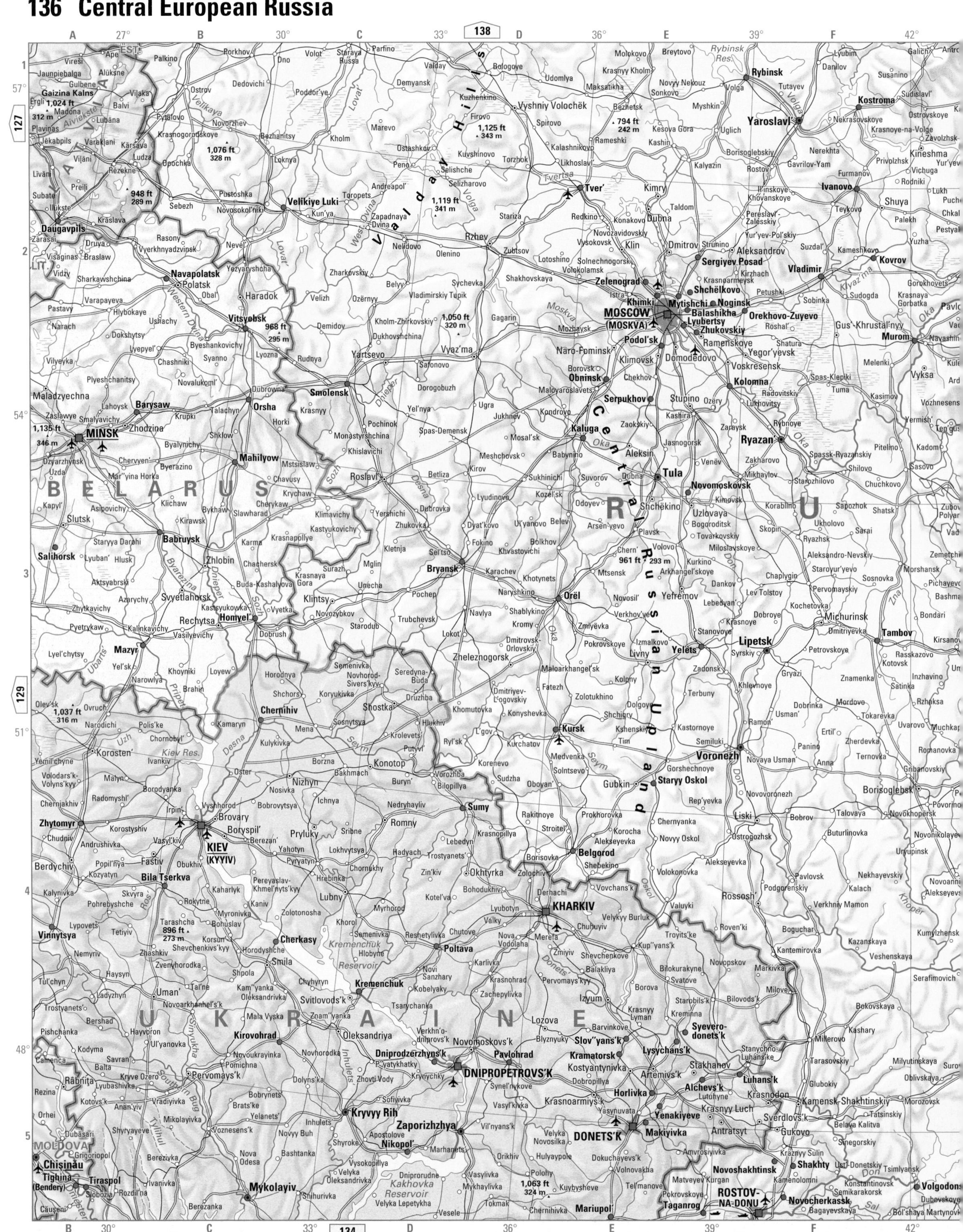
A
27°
B
30°
C
33°
138
D
36°
E
39°
F
42°
127
129
57°
54°
51°
48°
134
BELARUS
UKRAINE
RU
LAT.
LIT.
MOLDOVA
Valday Hills
Central Russian Upland
MOSCOW
(MOSKVA)
MINSK
KIEV
(KYYIV)
KHARKIV
DNIPROPETROVS'K
DONETS'K
ROSTOV-NA-DONU
Chişinău
Daugavpils
Rybinsk
Yaroslavl'
Kostroma
Ivanovo
Vladimir
Kovrov
Tver'
Rzhev
Velikiye Luki
Navapolatsk
Polatsk
Vitsyebsk
Smolensk
Orsha
Barysaw
Mahilyow
Babruysk
Homyel'
Mazyr
Salihorsk
Bryansk
Orël
Kaluga
Tula
Obninsk
Serpukhov
Kolomna
Ryazan'
Murom
Novomoskovsk
Lipetsk
Tambov
Yelets
Kursk
Voronezh
Staryy Oskol
Belgorod
Sumy
Chernihiv
Zhytomyr
Bila Tserkva
Vinnytsya
Cherkasy
Poltava
Kremenchuk
Kirovohrad
Mykolayiv
Kryvyy Rih
Zaporizhzhya
Nikopol'
Dniprodzerzhyns'k
Pavlohrad
Kramatorsk
Slov"yans'k
Lysychans'k
Syeverodonets'k
Luhans'k
Alchevs'k
Horlivka
Yenakiyeve
Makiyivka
Mariupol'
Taganrog
Novocherkassk
Shakhty
Novoshakhtinsk
Volgodonsk
Tiraspol
Sergiyev Posad
Zelenograd
Mytishchi
Shchëlkovo
Balashikha
Noginsk
Lyubertsy
Zhukovskiy
Orekhovo-Zuyevo
Podol'sk
Khimki
Vyshniy Volochëk
Kremenchuk Reservoir
Kakhovka Reservoir
Kiev Res.
Rybinsk Res.
Volga
Oka
Don
Dnieper
Desna
Western Dvina
Pripet
Southern Bug
Donets
Seym
Moskva
Klyaz'ma
Khoper
Gaizina Kalns
1,024 ft
312 m
1,076 ft
328 m
948 ft
289 m
1,125 ft
343 m
794 ft
242 m
1,119 ft
341 m
968 ft
295 m
1,050 ft
320 m
1,135 ft
346 m
961 ft
293 m
1,037 ft
316 m
896 ft
273 m
1,063 ft
324 m

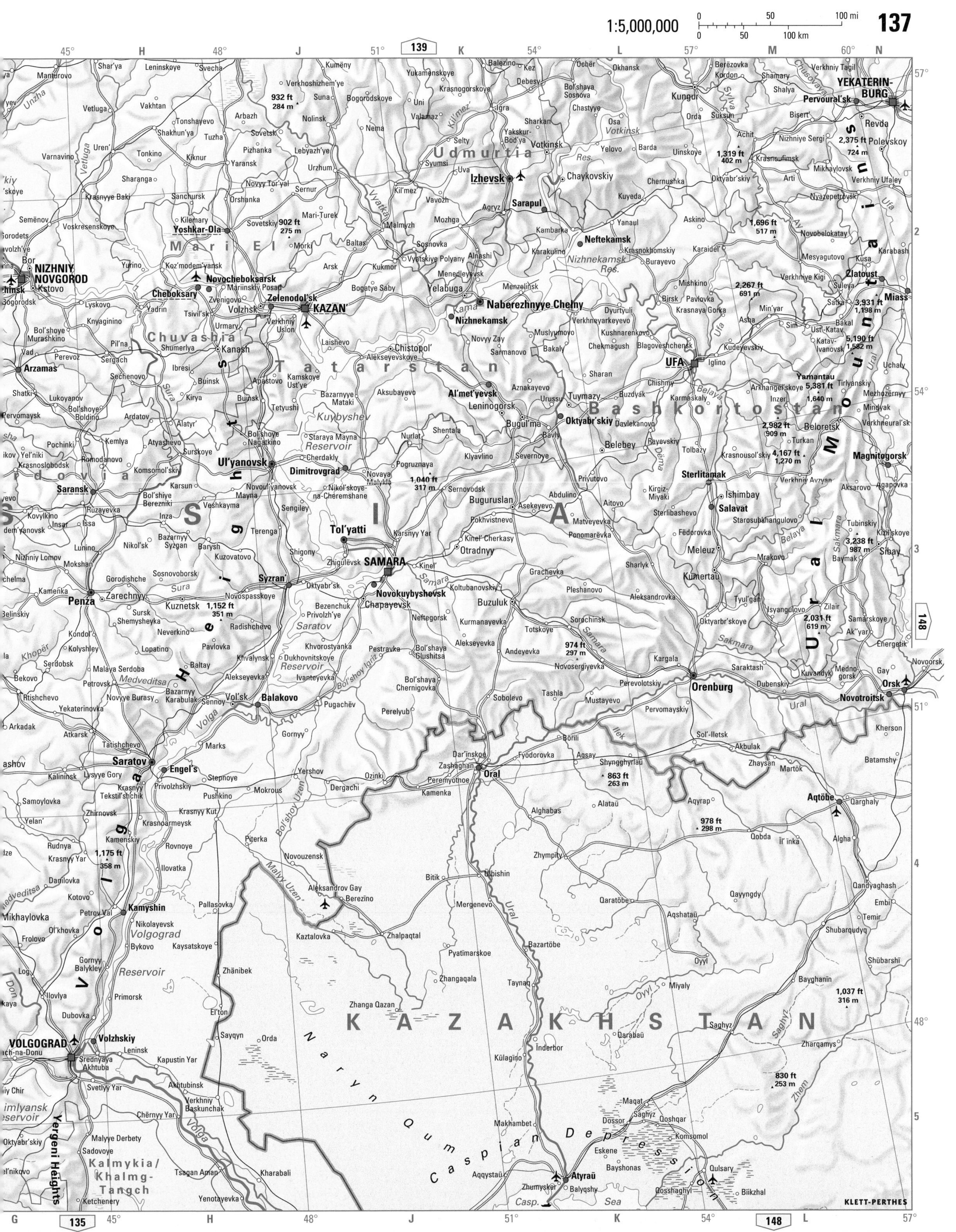
1:5,000,000
0 50 100 mi
0 50 100 km
139
135
148
Udmurtia
Mari El
Chuvashia
Tatarstan
Bashkortostan
Mordovia
RUSSIA
Volga Heights
Ural Mountains
Volga
KAZAKHSTAN
Caspian Depression
Naryn Qum
Kalmykia/Khalmg-Tangch
Yergeni Heights
YEKATERINBURG
NIZHNIY NOVGOROD
KAZAN'
SAMARA
UFA
VOLGOGRAD
Izhevsk
Sarapul
Votkinsk
Neftekamsk
Naberezhnyye Chelny
Nizhnekamsk
Yelabuga
Al'met'yevsk
Leninogorsk
Bugul'ma
Oktyabr'skiy
Belebey
Sterlitamak
Salavat
Ishimbay
Meleuz
Kumertau
Orenburg
Orsk
Novotroitsk
Magnitogorsk
Beloretsk
Zlatoust
Miass
Kungur
Pervoural'sk
Revda
Polevskoy
Yoshkar-Ola
Cheboksary
Novocheboksarsk
Zelenodol'sk
Kstovo
Arzamas
Kanash
Chistopol'
Dimitrovgrad
Ul'yanovsk
Saransk
Penza
Kuznetsk
Syzran'
Tol'yatti
Novokuybyshevsk
Chapayevsk
Otradnyy
Buguruslan
Buzuluk
Balakovo
Vol'sk
Saratov
Engel's
Kamyshin
Volzhskiy
Oral
Aqtöbe
Atyraū
Kuybyshev Reservoir
Saratov Reservoir
Volgograd Reservoir
Tsimlyansk Reservoir
Nizhnekamsk Res.
Votkinsk Res.
Caspian Sea
Kama
Vyatka
Belaya
Ural
Samara
Sakmara
Sura
Khopër
Medveditsa
Malyy Uzen'
Bol'shoy Uzen'
Ilek
Oyyl
Saghyz
Zhem
Don
932 ft 284 m
902 ft 275 m
1,319 ft 402 m
2,375 ft 724 m
1,696 ft 517 m
2,267 ft 691 m
3,931 ft 1,198 m
5,190 ft 1,582 m
5,381 ft 1,640 m
2,982 ft 909 m
4,167 ft 1,270 m
3,238 ft 987 m
2,031 ft 619 m
1,040 ft 317 m
1,152 ft 351 m
974 ft 297 m
863 ft 263 m
978 ft 298 m
1,175 ft 358 m
1,037 ft 316 m
830 ft 253 m
KLETT-PERTHES

A 21° B 24° C 125 27° D 30° E 33° F 36° G 39° H 42° J

KLETT-PERTHES

Lappland
Barents Sea
Kola Pen.
Murmanskiy Bereg
White Sea
Gulf of Bothnia
Gulf of Finland
Dvina Bay
Gulf of Onega
Kandalaksha Gulf
Karelskiy Bereg
Karelia
Norrbotten
SWEDEN
FINLAND
Pohjanmaa
Häme
ESTONIA
LATVIA
RU
Valday Hills
Lake Ladoga
Lake Onega
Rybinsk Res.

Kiruna
Malmberget
Gällivare
Pajala
Kolari
Muonio
Kittilä
Inari
Ivalo
Inari Lake
Sokosti
2,356 ft
718 m
2,641 ft
805 m
Lokka Res.
Sodankylä
Övertorneå
Ylitornio
Morjärv
Boden
Kalix
Luleå
Haparanda
Tornio
Kemi
Rovaniemi
Kemijärvi
Salla
Sandskär
Yli-Kitka
Kuusamo
Taivalkoski
Ii
Haukipudas
Pudasjärvi
Oulu
Hailuoto
Raahe
Muhos
Kiantajärvi
Suomussalmi
1,260 ft
384 m
Kalajoki
Oulainen
Oulu L.
Hyrynsalmi
Kokkola
Ylivieska
Kajaani
Nuasjärvi
Haapajärvi
Kuhmo
Ontojärvi
Kiuruvesi
Lappajärvi
Kivijärvi
Iisalmi
Nurmes
771 ft
235 m
Viitasaari
Siilinjärvi
Juankoski
Lieska
Pielinen
Alavus
Saarijärvi
Keitele
Kuopio
Äänekoski
Suolahti
Kallavesi
Outukumpu
Koitere
Virrat
Keuruu
Laukaa
Suonenjoki
Eno
Jyväskylä
Leppävirta
Joensuu
Ilomantsi
Pyhäselkä
Mänttä
Jämsä
Pieksämäki
Varkaus
801 ft
244 m
Orivesi
Haukivesi
Juva
Puruvesi
Värtsilä
Sysmä
Mikkeli
Savonlinna
Kitee
Valkeakoski
Päijänne
Hämeenlinna
Heinola
Mäntyharju
Saimaa
Lahti
Nastola
Riihimäki
Imatra
Lappeenranta
Hyvinkää
Mäntsälä
Kouvola
Elimäki
Nurmijärvi
Järvenpää
Kerava
Porvoo
Hamina
Vaalimaa
Vantaa
Kotka
Helsinki/Helsingfors
Gogland
Purekkari Neem
Loksa
Maardu
Kunda
Kose
Tapa
Rakvere
Kiviõli
Jõhvi
Sillamäe
Narva Bay
Kohtla-Järve
Paide
Avinurme
Kauksi
Türi
Mustvee
Põltsamaa
Jõgeva
Suure-Jaani
Kallaste
Viljandi
Võrtsjärv
Tartu
Emajõgi
Elva
Tõrva
Otepää
Põlva
Valga
Võru
Valka
Antsla
1,043 ft
318 m
Suur Munamägi
Vireši
Ape
Lake Peipus
L. Pskov
Pechory
Pskov
Porkhov
Dno

Priozërsk
Valaam
Elisenvaara
Lahdenpohja
Sortavala
Impilahti
Pitkäranta
Salmi
Svetogorsk
Vyborg
Zelenogorsk
Sestroretsk
Kronshtadt
Lomonosov
Petrodvorets
SAINT PETERSBURG (SANKT PETERBURG)
Neva
Pushkin
Kolpino
Kirovsk
Volkhov
Novaya Ladoga
Ust'-Luga
Ivangorod
Narva
Kingisepp
Gatchina
Mga
Tosno
Siverskiy
Vyritsa
Slantsy
Luga
Lyuban'
Kirishi
Gdov
Lyady
Chudovo
Budogoshch'
Batetskiy
Yamm
Plyussa
Strugi-Krasnyye
Seredka
Velikiy Novgorod
Malaya Vishera
L. Il'men'
Sol'tsy
Staraya Russa
Volot
Parfino
Kresttsy
Okulovka
837 ft
255 m
Msta
Volkhov

Murmansk
Severomorsk
Polyarnyy
Teriberka
Kola
Murmashi
Tuloma
Res. Verkhnetulomskiy
Verkhnetulomskiy
Lotta
Prirechnyy
1,896 ft
578 m
3,271 ft
997 m
Elgoras
Olenegorsk
Lovozero
L. Lovozero
Monchegorsk
Imandra L.
Khibiny
3,908 ft
1,191 m
3,970 ft
1,210 m
Kirovsk
Apatity
L. Umbozero
Kovdor
Polyarnyye Zori
Afrikanda
Nivskiy
Kandalaksha
Alakurtti
Zelenoborskiy
Kovda L.
Zarechensk
Umba
Chupa
Loukhi
Pya L.
Kestenga
Top L.
Ambarnyy
Kalevala
Kuyto L.
Krivoy Porog
Kem
Solovets Is.
Kostomuksha
Yushkozero
Borovoy
Nyuk L.
Belomorsk
Idel'
Muyezerskiy
Leksozero
Virandozero
Nadvoitsy
Segezha
L. Vyg
Vyg
Lendery
Sukkozero
L. Seg
1,368 ft
417 m
Medvezh'yegorsk
Povenets
Porosozero
Girvas
Velikaya Guba
Suojärvi
Kondopoga
L. Syamozero
Petrozavodsk
Pryazha
1,027 ft
313 m
Ladva
Il'inskiy
Olonets
Svir'
Podporozh'ye
Lodeynoye Pole
Svirits
997 ft
304 m
955 ft
291 m
Tikhvin
Pikalëvo
Boksitogorsk
919 ft
280 m
Nebolchi
Khvoynaya
Borovichi
Moshenskoye
Lesnoye
Pestovo
Mologa
Kabozha
Ustyuzhna
Chagoda
Babayevo
Zabor'e
Ves'yegonsk
Sandovo
Breytovo
Molokovo

Teriberka
C. Svyatoy Nos
Gremikha
1,303 ft
397 m
Krasnoshchel'ye
Ponoy
C. Kanin Nos
C. Konush
Morzhovets
Mezensk Guba
Sosnovka
Kuzomen'
Pyalitsa
Kamen
Verkhnyaya Zolotitsa
748 ft
228 m
Kuloy
Pertominsk
Pinega
Severodvinsk
Arkhangel'sk
Novodvinsk
Kholmogory
Onega
Malen'ga
Maloshuyka
Mud'yuga
Kodino
Lomovoye
Samoded
Yemetsk
Northern Dvina
Obozerskiy
1,148 ft
350 m
Yemtsa
Savinskiy
Mirnyy
Bereznik
Plesetsk
Puksoozero
Oksovskiy
Pyal'ma
Kuganavolok
L. Vodlozero
Konëvo
Shalakusha
Shenkursk
Vaga
860 ft
262 m
Shal'skiy
Pudozh
Bronevo
Nyandoma
955 ft
291 m
Andomskiy Pogost
Kargopol'
Voloshka
L. Lacha
Ust'-Shonosha
Vel'sk
Vytegra
Krechetovo
Ignatovo
Konosha
Solginskiy
Kuloy
Oktyabr'skiy
Annenskiy Most
Yertsevo
L. Vozhe
Vozhega
Kubena
Verkhovazh'ye
Zubovo
Charozero
Tarnogskiy Gorodok
Ozero Beloye
Lipin Bor
Belozërsk
Syamzha
Tot'ma
Kirillov
Kharovsk
L. Kubena
Bechevinka
Chekshino
Imeni Babushkina
Novlenskoye
Sokol
Kadnikov
Shuyskoye
Sukhona
Cherepovets
Kaduy
Sheksna
Vologda
Soligalich
Kostroma
Gayutino
Gryazovets
965 ft
294 m
Chukhloma
Vokhtoga
Parfen'yevo
Poshekhon'ye
Lyubim
Buy
Antropovo
Galich

2 3 4 5
66° 63° 60°
125 127

C 27° D 30° E 33° F 136 36° G 39° H 42°

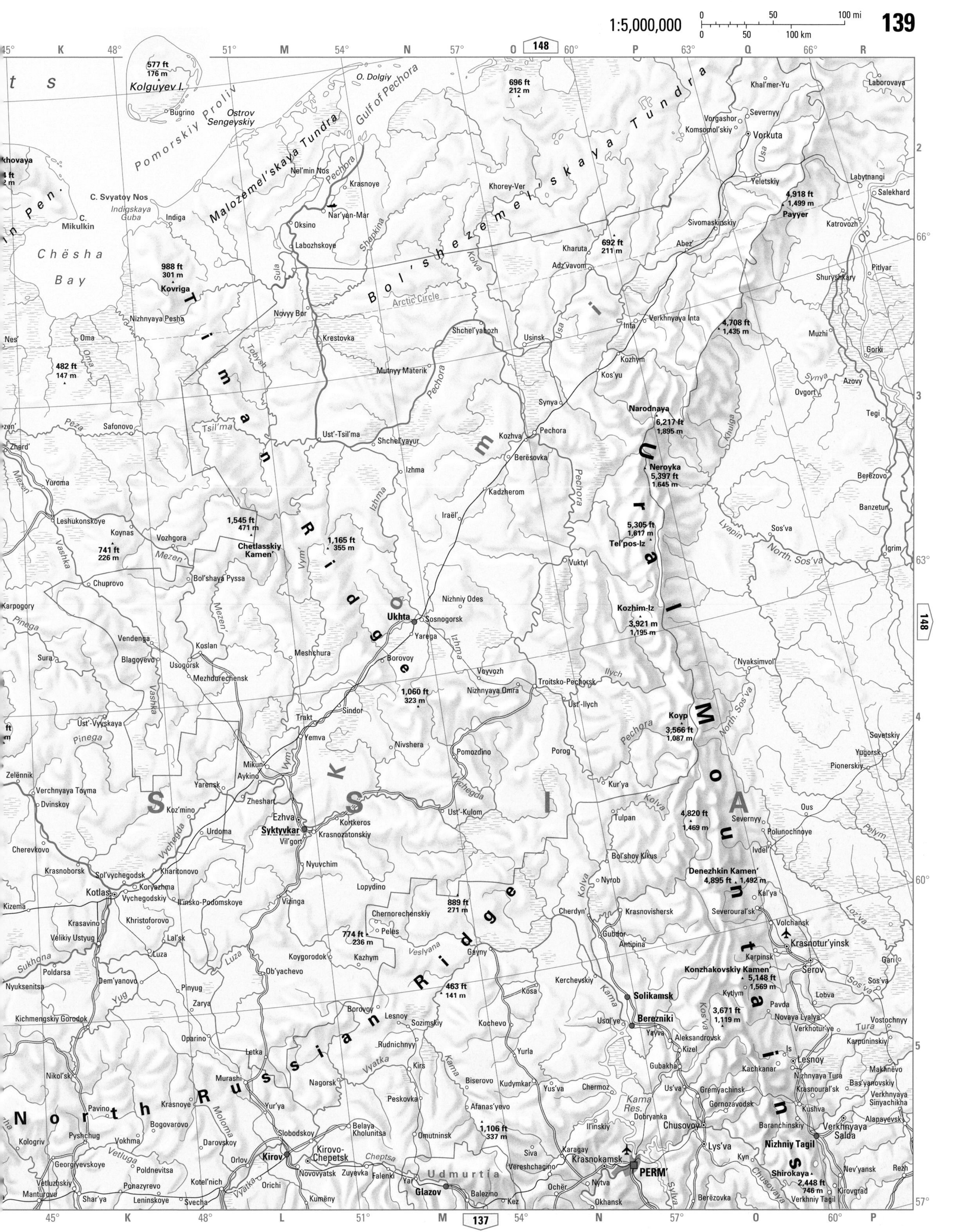
1:5,000,000
0 50 100 mi
0 50 100 km
148
137
Kolguyev I.
577 ft
176 m
Bugrino
Ostrov Sengeyskiy
Pomorskiy Proliv
O. Dolgiy
Gulf of Pechora
Malozemel'skaya Tundra
Bol'shezemel'skaya Tundra
Nel'min Nos
Krasnoye
Pechora
Nar'yan-Mar
Oksino
Labozhskoye
Shapkina
C. Svyatoy Nos
Indigskaya Guba
Indiga
C. Mikulkin
Chësha Bay
988 ft
301 m
Kovriga
Sula
Novyy Bor
Nizhnyaya Pesha
Oma
Nes'
482 ft
147 m
Krestovka
Tobysh
Timan Ridge
Mutnyy Materik
Arctic Circle
Shchel'yabozh
Usinsk
Usa
Inta
Verkhnyaya Inta
4,708 ft
1,435 m
Kozhym
Kos'yu
Synya
Narodnaya
6,217 ft
1,895 m
696 ft
212 m
Khorey-Ver
692 ft
211 m
Kharuta
Adz'vavom
Abez'
Sivomaskinskiy
Kolva
Khal'mer-Yu
Laborovaya
Vorgashor
Severnyy
Komsomol'skiy
Vorkuta
Yeletskiy
4,918 ft
1,499 m
Payyer
Labytnangi
Salekhard
Katrovozh
Ob
Pitlyar
Shuryshkary
Muzhi
Gorki
Synya
Ovgort
Azovy
Tegi
Khulga
Berëzovo
Banzetur
Lyapin
Sos'va
North. Sos'va
Igrim
Safonovo
Peza
Tsil'ma
Ust'-Tsil'ma
Shchel'yayur
Kozhva
Pechora
Berësovka
Izhma
Kadzherom
Iraël'
Neroyka
5,397 ft
1,645 m
5,305 ft
1,617 m
Tel'pos-Iz
Zherd'
Mezen'
Yuroma
Leshukonskoye
Koynas
741 ft
226 m
Vashka
Vozhgora
1,545 ft
471 m
Chetlasskiy Kamen'
1,165 ft
355 m
Vym'
Chuprovo
Bol'shaya Pyssa
Karpogory
Pinega
Vendenga
Koslan
Sura
Blagoyevo
Usogorsk
Mezhdurechensk
Meshchura
Ukhta
Sosnogorsk
Yarega
Borovoy
Nizhniy Odes
Vuktyl
Kozhim-Iz
3,921 m
1,195 m
Ural Mountains
Nyaksimvol'
Ilych
Voyvozh
Nizhnyaya Omra
Troitsko-Pechorsk
Ust'-Ilych
1,060 ft
323 m
Sindor
Trakt
Yemva
Nivshera
Pomozdino
Porog
Koyp
3,566 ft
1,087 m
Pechora
North. Sos'va
Sovetskiy
Yugorsk
Pionerskiy
Ust'-Vyyskaya
Mikun'
Aykino
Zelënnik
Verchnyaya Toyma
Dvinskoy
Yarensk
Koz'mino
Zheshart
Ezhva
Syktyvkar
Vil'gort
Kortkeros
Krasnozatonskiy
Ust'-Kulom
Vychegda
Kur'ya
Kolva
Tulpan
4,820 ft
1,469 m
Severnyy
Ous
Polunochnoye
Pelym
Ivdel'
Urdoma
Cherevkovo
Nyuvchim
Krasnoborsk
Sol'vychegodsk
Kharitonovo
Kotlas
Koryazhma
Vychegodskiy
Il'insko-Podomskoye
Lopydino
Vizinga
Bol'shoy Kikus
Nyrob
Denezhkin Kamen'
4,895 ft
1,492 m
Kal'ya
Kizema
Krasavino
Velikiy Ustyug
Khristoforovo
Lal'sk
Sukhona
Luza
889 ft
271 m
Chernorechenskiy
774 ft
236 m
Peles
Kazhym
Veslyana
Gayny
Koygorodok
Cherdyn'
Krasnovishersk
Severoural'sk
Volchansk
Krasnotur'yinsk
Gubdor
Antipina
Karpinsk
Konzhakovskiy Kamen'
5,148 ft
1,569 m
Serov
Gari
Sos'va
Poldarsa
Nyuksenitsa
Dem'yanovo
Ob'yachevo
Pinyug
Zarya
Yug
463 ft
141 m
Kerchevskiy
Kosa
Solikamsk
Kama
Kytlym
3,671 ft
1,119 m
Pavda
Lobva
Novaya Lyalya
Verkhotur'ye
Vostochnyy
Tura
Kichmengskiy Gorodok
Oparino
Borovoy
Lesnoy
Sozimskiy
Kochevo
Usol'ye
Berezniki
Yayva
Aleksandrovsk
Kizel
Karpunınskiy
Letka
Rudnichnyy
Yurla
Gubakha
Is
Lesnoy
Kachkanar
Makhnëvo
Nizhnyaya Tura
Krasnoural'sk
Bas'yanovskiy
Verkhnyaya Sinyachikha
Nikol'sk
Murashi
Kirs
Vyatka
Biserovo
Kudymkar
Yus'va
Chermoz
Us'va
Gremyachinsk
Gornozavodsk
Kushva
Alapayevsk
North Russian Ridge
Nagorsk
Peskovka
Kama Res.
Dobryanka
Chusovoy
Baranchinskiy
Verkhnyaya Salda
Pavino
Krasnoye
Yur'ya
Afanas'yevo
Molonga
Bogovarovo
Pyshchug
Slobodskoy
Belaya Kholunitsa
1,106 ft
337 m
Il'inskiy
Lys'va
Nizhniy Tagil
Kologriv
Vokhma
Darovskoy
Omutninsk
Siva
Karagay
Krasnokamsk
Vetluga
Kirov
Kirovo-Chepetsk
Cheptsa
Vereshchagino
PERM'
Kyn
Georgiyevskoye
Poldnevitsa
Orlov
Novovyatsk
Zuyevka
Falenki
Udmurtia
Nytva
Chusovaya
Shirokaya
2,448 ft
746 m
Nev'yansk
Rezh
Vetluzhskiy
Ponazyrevo
Kotel'nich
Orichi
Yar
Sylva
Verkhniy Tagil
Kirovgrad
Manturovo
Shar'ya
Leninskoye
Svecha
Kumëny
Glazov
Balezino
Kez
Ochër
Okhansk
Berëzovka
45°
48°
51°
54°
57°
60°
63°
66°
K
L
M
N
O
P
Q
R
2
3
4
5
57°
60°
63°
66°

1
North Passage, Arctic Ocean
2
Sher-Dor Madrassah, Samarqand/Uzbekistan
3
Negev Desert, Israel
4
Plateau of Tibet, China
5
Türgen and Kharkhiraa Mountains, Mongolia
6
Rice Field, Sri Lanka
7
Mount Fuji, Japan
8
Karst Mountains near Guilin, China
N
W
E
S
KLETT-PERTHES

0 500 1,000 mi

0 500 1,000 1,500 2,000 km

Elevation

ft	m	ft	m
13,124 ft	4,000 m	656 ft	200 m
6,562 ft	2,000 m	6,562 ft	2,000 m
3,281 ft	1,000 m	13,124 ft	4,000 m
1,640 ft	500 m	19,686 ft	6,000 m
656 ft	200 m	26,248 ft	8,000 m
0 ft	0 m		
	Depression		

Inland ice, glaciers

Pack ice

Limit of drift ice

KLETT-PERTHES

1:45,000,000

0 500 1,000 mi
0 500 1,000 1,500 2,000 km
KLETT-PERTHES
ATLANTIC OCEAN
ARCTIC OCEAN
North Pole
PACIFIC OCEAN
INDIAN OCEAN
Greenland Sea
Norwegian Sea
North Sea
Barents Sea
Kara Sea
Laptev Sea
East Siberian Sea
Chukchi Sea
Bering Sea
Sea of Okhotsk
Sea of Japan
Yellow Sea
East China Sea
South China Sea
Arabian Sea
Bay of Bengal
Andaman Sea
Baltic Sea
White Sea
Black Sea
Caspian Sea
Aral Sea
Mediterr. Sea
Red Sea
Persian Gulf
G. of Oman
Gulf of Aden
Gulf of Thailand
Sulu Sea
Celebes Sea
Molucca Sea
Banda Sea
Java Sea
British Isles
Shetland Is.
Spitsbergen
Bear I.
Franz Josef Land
Severnaya Zemlya
New Siberian Islands
Wrangel I.
St. Lawrence I.
Fox Is.
Aleutian Is.
Commander Is.
Novaya Zemlya
Kolguyev I.
Kola Pen.
Peary Ld.
Arctic Circle
Alaska
Alaska Pen.
Bering Str.
Chukot Pen.
Chukot Ra.
Koryak Ra.
Kolyma Ra.
Cherskiy Range
Verkhoyansk Range
Kamchatka
Kurile Is.
Sakhalin
Hokkaido
Honshu
Shikoku
Kyushu
Ryukyu Is.
Taiwan
Luzon
Mindoro
Panay
Negros
Palawan
Mindanao
Manila
Moluccas
Scandinavia
Karelia
London
Paris
Berlin
Loire
Rhine
Alps
Carpathian Mts.
St. Petersburg
Moscow
Kiev
Dnieper
Danube
Volga
Don
Crimea
Donets'k
Ural Mts.
Ural
Yekaterinburg
West Siberian Plain
Siberia
Yakutia
Ob
G. of Ob
Irtysh
Yenisey
Lower Tunguska
Central Siberian Plateau
Putoran Mts.
Taymyr Pen.
Indigirka
Kolyma
Lena
Aldan
Angara
Lake Baykal
Stanovoy Ra.
Dzhugdzhur Ra.
Sikhote-Alin Ra.
Amur
Yablonovyy Ra.
Eastern Sayan
Western Sayan
Altay Mts.
Khangay
Novokuznetsk
Qaraghandy
L. Balqash
Dzungaria
Gobi
Inner Mongolia
Gt. Khingan Ra.
Manchuria
Songhua
Korea
Seoul
Tōkyō
Osaka
Beijing
Jinan
Great Plain of China
Yellow R.
Xi'an
Shanghai
Chengdu
Red Basin
Yangtze
Guangzhou
Hainan
Pontine Mts.
Anatolia
Taurus Mts.
Caucasus
Caspian Depr.
Ustyurt Plateau
Turan Lowland
Syr Darya
Amu Darya
Almaty
Tashkent
Tien Shan
Sinkiang
Tarim
Lop Nur
Takla Makan Desert
Altun Shan
Qaidam Pendi
Kunlun Shan
Tibet
Nyainqêntanglha Shan
Himalayas
Pamir
Hindu Kush
Karakoram Ra.
Kashmir
Kābul
Punjab
Indus
Balūchistān
Delhi
Hindustan
Ganges
Brahmaputra
India
Deccan
Western Ghats
Eastern Ghats
Mumbai
Chennai
Kolkata
Karachi
Tropic of Cancer
Ceylon
Laccadive Is.
Andaman Is.
Nicobar Is.
Arakan Yoma
Salween
Mekong
Rangoon
Bangkok
Hô Chi Minh City
Malay Pen.
Sumatra
Mentawai Is.
Borneo (Kalimantan)
Makassar Str.
Celebes (Sulawesi)
Equator
Greater Sunda Is.
Lesser Sunda Is.
Jakarta
Java
Bali
Flores
Sumba
Cairo
Sinai Pen.
Mesopotamia
Tigris
Euphrates
Baghdād
Tehrān
Elburz Mts.
Zagros Mts.
Iranian Plateau
Arabian Peninsula
Al-Hijāz
Najd
Riyadh
Ar-Rub' al-Khālī
Hadramawt
Socotra
Somali Pen.
Shebele
30° 40° 140° 150°
50° J 60° K 70° L 80° M 90°
N 100° O 110° P 120° Q
A B C D E F G H J K L M N Q R S T U V W X
Land Cover (Explanations on p. 32)
Natural Vegetation
Evergreen needleleaf forests
Evergreen broadleaf forests
Deciduous needleleaf forests
Deciduous broadleaf forests
Mixed forests
Closed shrublands
Open shrublands
Woody savannas
Savannas
Grasslands
Permanent wetlands
Developed and Mosaic Lands
Croplands
Cropland/natural vegetation mosaic
Urban and built-up lands
Non-Vegetated Lands
Snow and ice
Barren or sparsely vegetated
Water bodies
No data

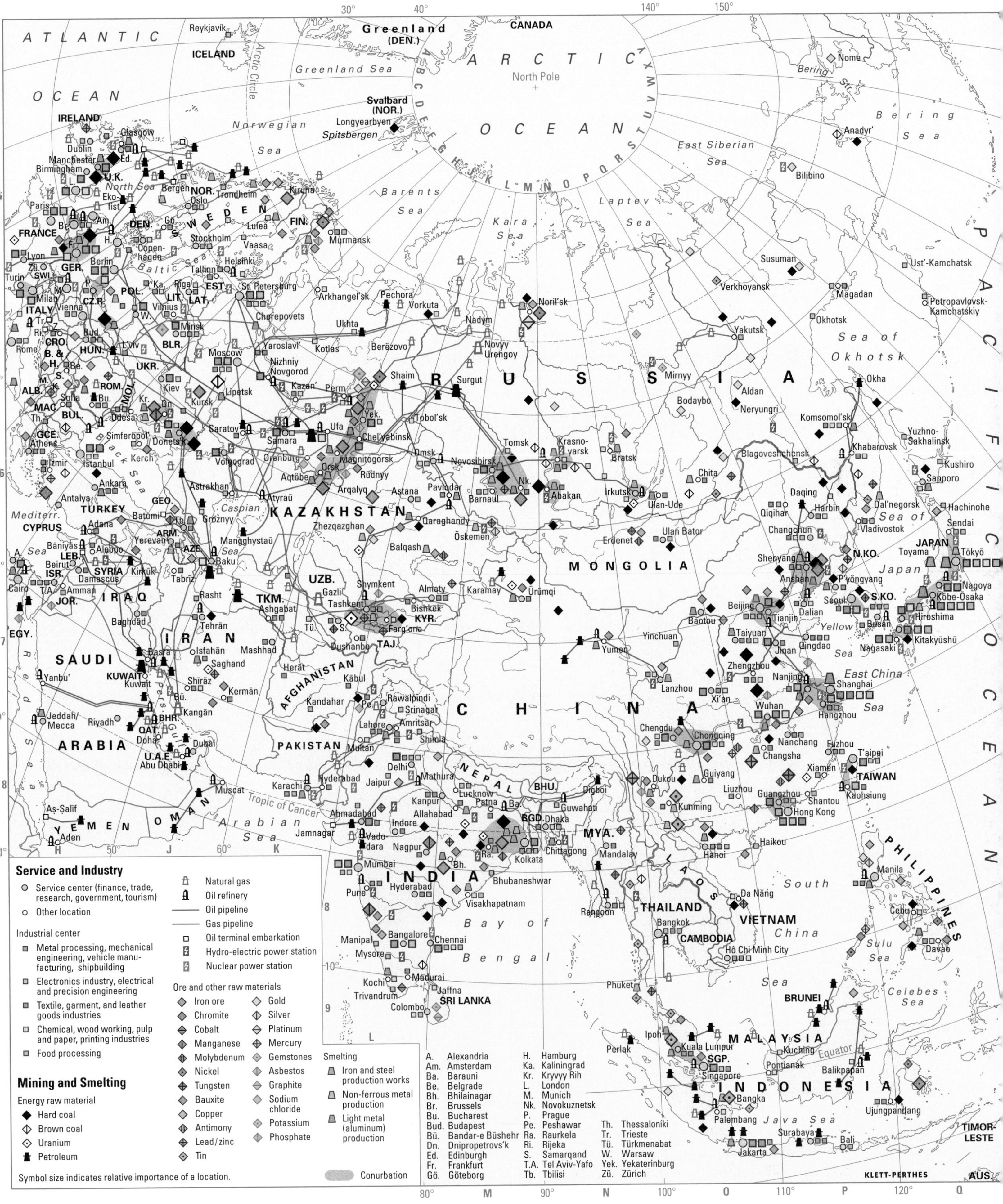

Asia: Economy

1:45,000,000

0 500 1,000 mi
0 500 1,000 1,500 2,000 km

Service and Industry

- Service center (finance, trade, research, government, tourism)
- Other location

Industrial center

- Metal processing, mechanical engineering, vehicle manufacturing, shipbuilding
- Electronics industry, electrical and precision engineering
- Textile, garment, and leather goods industries
- Chemical, wood working, pulp and paper, printing industries
- Food processing

- Natural gas
- Oil refinery
- Oil pipeline
- Gas pipeline
- Oil terminal embarkation
- Hydro-electric power station
- Nuclear power station

Mining and Smelting

Energy raw material

- Hard coal
- Brown coal
- Uranium
- Petroleum

Ore and other raw materials

- Iron ore
- Chromite
- Cobalt
- Manganese
- Molybdenum
- Nickel
- Tungsten
- Bauxite
- Copper
- Antimony
- Lead/zinc
- Tin
- Gold
- Silver
- Platinum
- Mercury
- Gemstones
- Asbestos
- Graphite
- Sodium chloride
- Potassium
- Phosphate

Smelting

- Iron and steel production works
- Non-ferrous metal production
- Light metal (aluminum) production

Conurbation

Symbol size indicates relative importance of a location.

A.	Alexandria	H.	Hamburg		
Am.	Amsterdam	Ka.	Kaliningrad		
Ba.	Barauni	Kr.	Kryvyy Rih		
Be.	Belgrade	L.	London		
Bh.	Bhilainagar	M.	Munich		
Br.	Brussels	Nk.	Novokuznetsk		
Bu.	Bucharest	P.	Prague		
Bud.	Budapest	Pe.	Peshawar	Th.	Thessaloníki
Bü.	Bandar-e Būshehr	Ra.	Raurkela	Tr.	Trieste
Dn.	Dnipropetrovs'k	Ri.	Rijeka	Tü.	Türkmenabat
Ed.	Edinburgh	S.	Samarqand	W.	Warsaw
Fr.	Frankfurt	T.A.	Tel Aviv-Yafo	Yek.	Yekaterinburg
Gö.	Göteborg	Tb.	Tbilisi	Zü.	Zürich

KLETT-PERTHES

1:45,000,000

0 500 1,000 mi
0 500 1,000 1,500 2,000 km

KLETT-PERTHES

Abbr.	Country
ARM.	ARMENIA
AUT.	AUSTRIA
AZE.	AZERBAIJAN
B. & H.	BOSNIA AND HERZEGOVINA
BGM.	BELGIUM
BHU.	BHUTAN
BUL.	BULGARIA
CRO.	CROATIA
CZ.R.	CZECH REPUBLIC
DJI.	DJIBOUTI
EST.	ESTONIA
GEO.	GEORGIA
HUN.	HUNGARY
K.	KOSOVO
LIE.	LIECHTENSTEIN
LIT.	LITHUANIA
LUX.	LUXEMBOURG
M.	MONTENEGRO
MAC.	MACEDONIA
MOL.	MOLDOVA
NLD.	NETHERLANDS
QAT.	QATAR
SERB.	SERBIA
SVK.	SLOVAKIA
SVN.	SLOVENIA
SWI.	SWITZERLAND
U.A.E.	UNITED ARAB EMIRATES

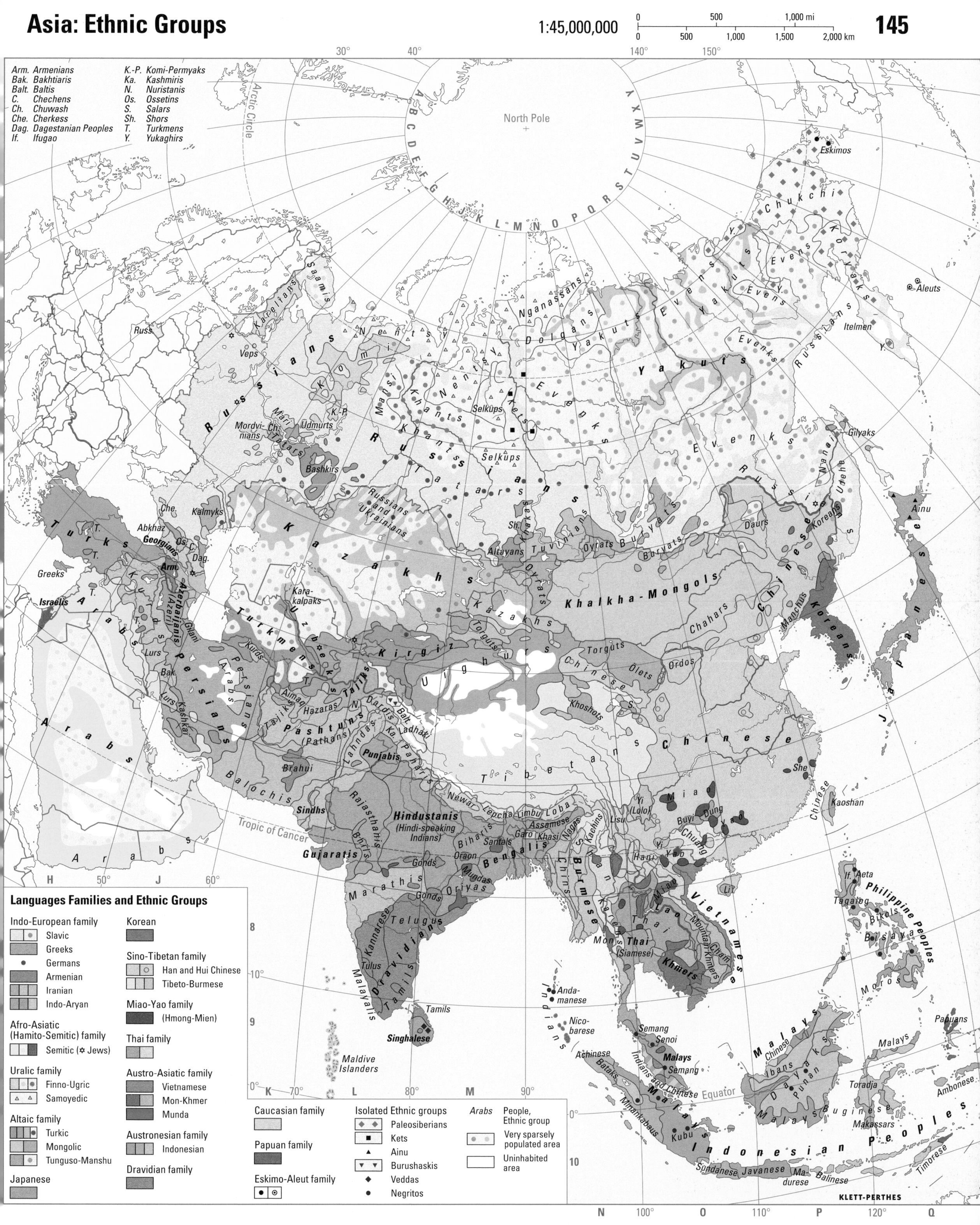

0 500 1,000 mi
0 500 1,000 1,500 2,000 km
Arm. Armenians
Bak. Bakhtiaris
Balt. Baltis
C. Chechens
Ch. Chuwash
Che. Cherkess
Dag. Dagestanian Peoples
If. Ifugao
K.-P. Komi-Permyaks
Ka. Kashmiris
N. Nuristanis
Os. Ossetins
S. Salars
Sh. Shors
T. Turkmens
Y. Yukaghirs
North Pole
Arctic Circle
Tropic of Cancer
Equator
Eskimos
Chukchi
Koryaks
Aleuts
Itelmen
Evens
Yakuts
Evenks
Russians
Gilyaks
Nanai
Udehe
Ainu
Japanese
Koreans
Chinese
Manchus
Daurs
Buryats
Khalkha-Mongols
Chahars
Ordos
Ölets
Torguts
Khoshots
Oyrats
Tuvinians
Altayans
Khakas
Kets
Selkups
Nentsy
Nganasans
Dolgans
Khants
Mansi
Komi
Saamis
Karelians
Russ
Veps
Mari
Mordvinians
Udmurts
Tatars
Bashkirs
Russians and Ukrainians
Kazakhs
Kalmyks
Abkhaz
Georgians
Turks
Greeks
Kurds
Azerbaijanis (Azeri)
Israelis
Arabs
Lurs
Gilani
Persians
Kashkai
Karakalpaks
Turkmens
Uzbeks
Kirgiz
Tajiks
Uighurs
Aimaq
Hazaras
Dardis
Pashtuns (Pathans)
Lahndas
Ladhaki
Paharis
Punjabis
Brahui
Balochis
Sindhs
Tibetans
Hindustanis (Hindi-speaking Indians)
Rajasthanis
Bhils
Gujaratis
Biharis
Santals
Newar
Lepcha
Limbu
Loba
Assamese
Garo
Khasi
Nagas
Kachins
Lisu
Yi (Lolo)
Miao
Buyi
Dung
Yao
Chuang
Hani
She
Kaoshan
Bengalis
Oraon
Mundas
Gonds
Marathis
Oriyas
Telugus
Kannarese
Dravidians
Tulus
Malayalis
Tamils
Singhalese
Maldive Islanders
Andamanese
Nicobarese
Indians
Chins
Burmese
Shan
Karens
Mon
Thai (Siamese)
Lao
Khmers
Vietnamese
Mountain Khmers
Cham
Li
Semang
Senoi
Malays
Achinese
Bataks
Minankabaus
Kubu
Indians and Chinese
Ibans
Dayaks
Punan
Aeta
Tagalog
Bikols
Bisayas
Philippine Peoples
Moros
Papuans
Toradja
Buginese
Makassars
Amboinese
Indonesian Peoples
Sundanese
Javanese
Madurese
Balinese
Timorese
Languages Families and Ethnic Groups
Indo-European family
Slavic
Greeks
Germans
Armenian
Iranian
Indo-Aryan
Afro-Asiatic (Hamito-Semitic) family
Semitic (✡ Jews)
Uralic family
Finno-Ugric
Samoyedic
Altaic family
Turkic
Mongolic
Tunguso-Manshu
Japanese
Korean
Sino-Tibetan family
Han and Hui Chinese
Tibeto-Burmese
Miao-Yao family (Hmong-Mien)
Thai family
Austro-Asiatic family
Vietnamese
Mon-Khmer
Munda
Austronesian family
Indonesian
Dravidian family
Caucasian family
Papuan family
Eskimo-Aleut family
Isolated Ethnic groups
Paleosiberians
Kets
Ainu
Burushaskis
Veddas
Negritos
Arabs People, Ethnic group
Very sparsely populated area
Uninhabited area
KLETT-PERTHES

1:45,000,000

0 500 1,000 mi
0 500 1,000 1,500 2,000 km

Climate Diagrams (by H. Walter)

Climate	Station	Altitude	Annual precipitation	Annual mean temperature
Cr	Tōkyō	6 m 20 ft	1,410 mm 55.5 in.	15.6 °C 60.1 °F
Cw	Kunming	1,892 m 6,208 ft	1,008 mm 39.7 in.	14.5 °C 58.1 °F
Cs	Jerusalem	809 m 2,654 ft	642 mm 25.3 in.	16.5 °C 61.7 °F
Do	Zhengzhou	111 m 364 ft	666 mm 26.2 in.	14.2 °C 57.6 °F
Dc	Petropavl	140 m 459 ft	366 mm 14.4 in.	1.5 °C 33.8 °F
Eo	Simushir Island	25 m 82 ft	1,630 mm 64.2 in.	2.8 °C 37.0 °F
Ec	Verkhoyansk	137 m 449 ft	177 mm 7.0 in.	−15.1 °C 4.8 °F
FT	Dikson	20 m 66 ft	351 mm 13.8 in.	−11.9 °C 10.6 °F
BS	Tehrān	1,191 m 3,908 ft	218 mm 8.6 in.	16.9 °C 62.4 °F
BW	Riyadh	612 m 2,008 ft	118 mm 4.6 in.	25.6 °C 78.1 °F
BW	Dalandzadgad	1,465 m 4,807 ft	126 mm 5.0 in.	4.3 °C 39.7 °F
Ar	Singapore	16 m 52 ft	2,091 mm 82.3 in.	27.3 °C 81.1 °F
Am	Dawei	17 m 56 ft	5,500 mm 216.5 in.	26.5 °C 79.7 °F
Aw	Kolkata	6 m 20 ft	1,739 mm 68.5 in.	26.9 °C 80.4 °F
As	Hambantota	20 m 66 ft	1,045 mm 41.1 in.	27.2°C 81.0 °F

Months: 1 3 6 9 12

Climate Diagrams (by H. Walter)

2,263 mm 89.1 in. — 25.0 °C 77.0 °F — Annual averages of precipitation and air temperature

1 3 6 9 12 — Months

3 m 10 ft — Altitude

Precipitation curve

Temperature curve

Dry season

ARCTIC OCEAN, Chukchi Sea, Wrangel I., East Siberian Sea, New Siberian Islands, Laptev Sea, Kara Sea, Barents Sea, Novaya Zemlya, Kolguyev I., White Sea, G. of Ob, Ob, Yenisei, Lena, Indigirka, Kolyma, Aldan, Lower Tunguska, Angara, Arctic Circle, Lake Baykal, Amur, Songhua, Sea of Okhotsk, Sakhalin, Kurile Is., Aleutian Is., Commander Is., Alaska, PACIFIC OCEAN, Hokkaido, Honshu, Sea of Japan, Shikoku, Kyushu, Yellow Sea, East China Sea, Ryukyu Is., Taiwan, Luzon, Mindoro, Negros, Palawan, Mindanao, Sulu Sea, Celebes Sea, Molucca Sea, Moluccas, Celebes (Sulawesi), Banda Sea, Makassar Str., Borneo (Kalimantan), Greater Sunda Is., Lesser Sunda Is., Java Sea, Java, Bali, Flores, Sumba, Sumatra, Mentawai Is., Equator, South China Sea, Hainan, Gulf of Thailand, Mekong, Salween, Yangtze, Yellow R., Brahmaputra, Ganges, Indus, Bay of Bengal, Andaman Sea, Andaman Is., Nicobar Is., Ceylon (Aw/Ar/As/Am), Arabian Sea, Tropic of Cancer, G. of Oman, Persian Gulf, Red Sea, Euphrates, Tigris, Mediterr. Sea, Black Sea, Danube, Volga, Ural, Caspian Sea, Aral Sea, Syr Darya, Amu Darya, L. Balqash, Irtysh, Tarim, Lop Nur

Climatic Regions

(Modified Koeppen System based on Trewartha; cf. p. 18/19)

Tropical Rainy Climates
- Ar — Tropical rainy climate
- Am — Tropical monsoon rain climate
- Aw — Tropical summer rain climate
- As — Tropical winter rain climate

Dry Climates
- BS — Steppe climate
- BW — Desert climate
- BM — Marine dry climate

Subtropical Climates
- Cr — Subtropical rain climate
- Cw — Subtropical summer rain climate
- Cs — Subtropical winter rain climate

Temperate Climates
- Do — Oceanic temperate climate
- Dc — Continental temperate climate

Boreal Climates
- Eo — Oceanic boreal climate
- Ec — Continental boreal climate

Polar Climates
- FT — Tundra climate

● Meteorological station with climate diagram

KLETT-PERTHES

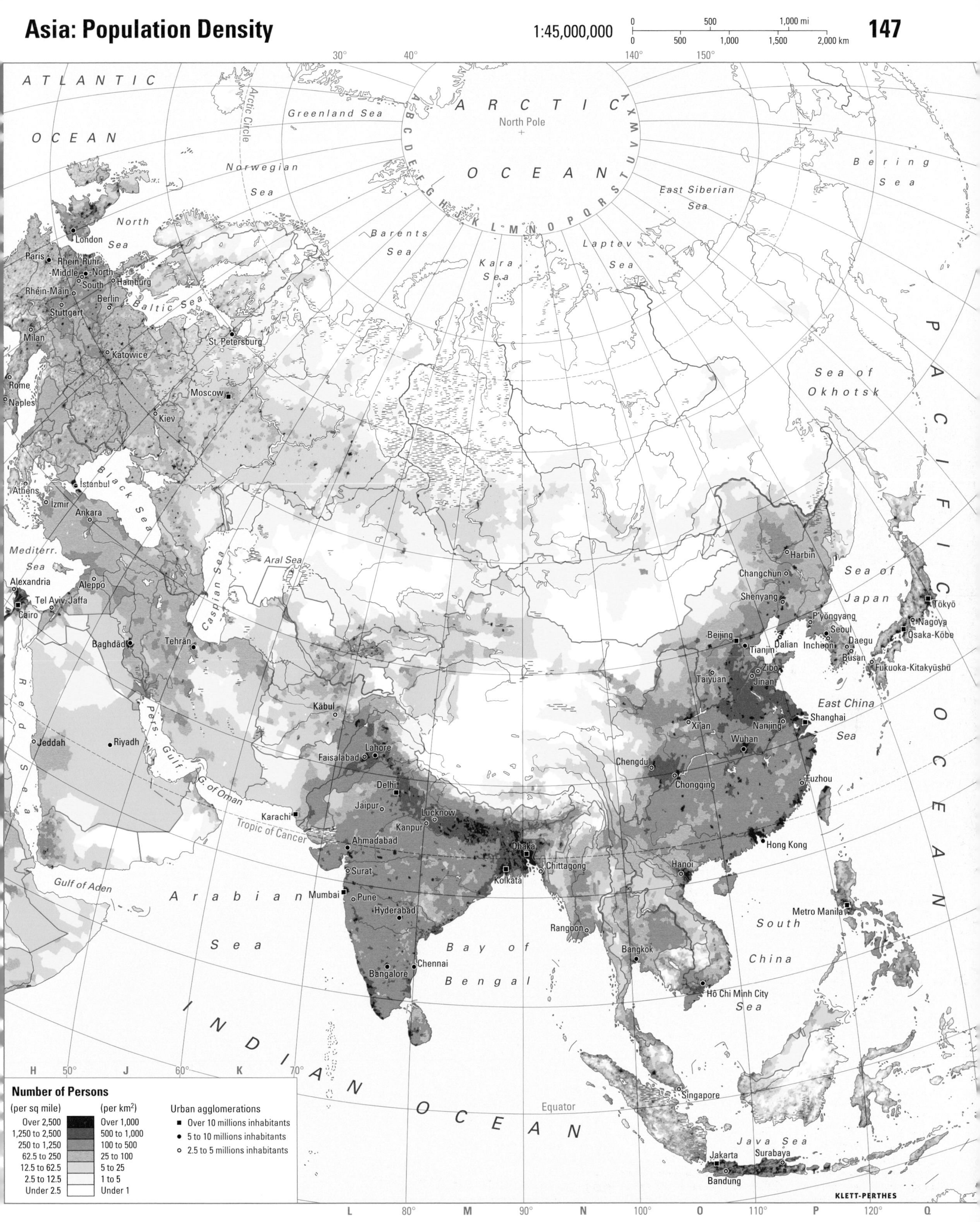
1:45,000,000
0 500 1,000 mi
0 500 1,000 1,500 2,000 km
ATLANTIC OCEAN
ARCTIC OCEAN
North Pole
Greenland Sea
Norwegian Sea
North Sea
Barents Sea
Kara Sea
Laptev Sea
East Siberian Sea
Bering Sea
Sea of Okhotsk
Sea of Japan
PACIFIC OCEAN
East China Sea
South China Sea
Java Sea
Bay of Bengal
Arabian Sea
INDIAN OCEAN
Baltic Sea
Black Sea
Caspian Sea
Aral Sea
Mediterr. Sea
Red Sea
Pers. Gulf
G. of Oman
Gulf of Aden
Arctic Circle
Tropic of Cancer
Equator
London
Paris
Rhein-Ruhr-Middle
Rhein-Ruhr-North
Rhein-Ruhr-South
Hamburg
Rhein-Main
Berlin
Stuttgart
Milan
Katowice
St. Petersburg
Rome
Naples
Moscow
Kiev
Athens
İstanbul
İzmir
Ankara
Alexandria
Cairo
Tel Aviv-Jaffa
Aleppo
Baghdād
Tehrān
Jeddah
Riyadh
Kābul
Lahore
Faisalabad
Karachi
Delhi
Jaipur
Lucknow
Kanpur
Ahmadabad
Surat
Mumbai
Pune
Hyderabad
Bangalore
Chennai
Dhaka
Kolkata
Chittagong
Rangoon
Bangkok
Hanoi
Hô Chi Minh City
Singapore
Jakarta
Bandung
Surabaya
Metro Manila
Hong Kong
Fuzhou
Chongqing
Chengdu
Wuhan
Nanjing
Shanghai
Xi'an
Taiyuan
Jinan
Zibo
Tianjin
Beijing
Dalian
Shenyang
Changchun
Harbin
P'yŏngyang
Seoul
Inch'ŏn
Daegu
Busan
Tōkyō
Nagoya
Ōsaka-Kōbe
Fukuoka-Kitakyūshū
30° 40° 140° 150°
50° 60° 70° 80° 90° 100° 110° 120°
A B C D E F G H J K L M N O P Q R S T U V W X
H J K L M N O P Q
Number of Persons
(per sq mile) (per km²)
Over 2,500 Over 1,000
1,250 to 2,500 500 to 1,000
250 to 1,250 100 to 500
62.5 to 250 25 to 100
12.5 to 62.5 5 to 25
2.5 to 12.5 1 to 5
Under 2.5 Under 1
Urban agglomerations
Over 10 millions inhabitants
5 to 10 millions inhabitants
2.5 to 5 millions inhabitants
KLETT-PERTHES

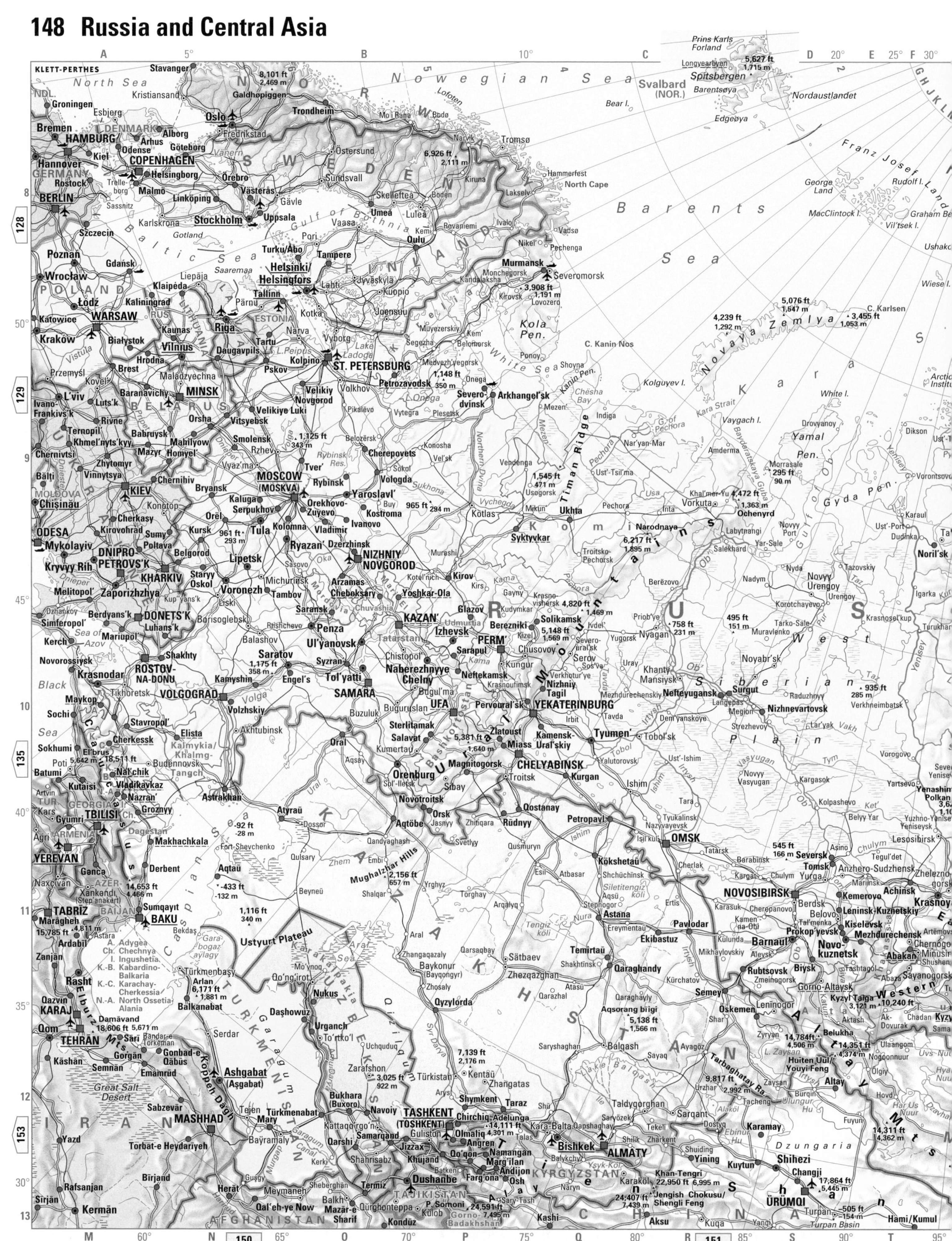

KLETT-PERTHES
Norwegian Sea
Barents Sea
Kara Sea
North Sea
Baltic Sea
White Sea
Black Sea
Caspian Sea
Aral Sea
Sea of Azov
Gulf of Bothnia
Svalbard (NOR.)
Spitsbergen
Nordaustlandet
Franz Josef Land
Novaya Zemlya
Kola Pen.
Yamal Pen.
Gyda Pen.
West Siberian Plain
Ural Mountains
Timan Ridge
Ustyurt Plateau
Mughalzhar Hills
Qizilqum
Garagum
Kopet Dagh
Elburz Mts.
Tien Shan
Altay Mts.
Dzungaria
Tarbaghatay Ra.
Great Salt Desert
Turpan Basin
NORWAY
SWEDEN
FINLAND
DENMARK
GERMANY
POLAND
ESTONIA
LATVIA
LITHUANIA
BELARUS
UKRAINE
MOLDOVA
RUSSIA
GEORGIA
ARMENIA
AZERBAIJAN
KAZAKHSTAN
UZBEKISTAN
TURKMENISTAN
KYRGYZSTAN
TAJIKISTAN
AFGHANISTAN
IRAN
CHINA
MOSCOW (MOSKVA)
ST. PETERSBURG
HELSINKI/ HELSINGFORS
Stockholm
Oslo
COPENHAGEN
BERLIN
WARSAW
Tallinn
Riga
Vilnius
MINSK
KIEV
Chişinău
TBILISI
YEREVAN
BAKU
TEHRAN
Ashgabat (Aşgabat)
TASHKENT (TOSHKENT)
Dushanbe
Bishkek
ALMATY
Astana
NOVOSIBIRSK
YEKATERINBURG
CHELYABINSK
OMSK
KAZAN'
NIZHNIY NOVGOROD
SAMARA
VOLGOGRAD
ROSTOV-NA-DONU
KHARKIV
DNIPROPETROVS'K
DONETS'K
ODESA
PERM'
UFA
ÜRÜMQI
MASHHAD
TABRIZ
KARAJ
Murmansk
Arkhangel'sk
Vorkuta
Noril'sk
Surgut
Tyumen'
Orenburg
Saratov
Astrakhan
Barnaul
Semey
Qaraghandy
Bukhara (Buxoro)
Samarqand
Khujand
Andijon
Osh
Namangan
A. Adygea
Ch. Chechnya
I. Ingushetia
K.-B. Kabardino-Balkaria
K.-C. Karachay-Cherkessia
N.-A. North Ossetia-Alania
Damāvand 18,606 ft 5,671 m
El'brus 18,511 ft 5,642 m
Khan-Tengri 22,950 ft 6,995 m
Jengish Chokusu/ Shengli Feng 24,407 ft 7,439 m
Belukha 14,784 ft 4,506 m
Galdhøpiggen 8,101 ft 2,469 m
A 10°, 5°
B
C
D 20°
E 25°
F 30°
M 60°
N 150 65°
O 70°
P 75°
Q 80°
R 151 85°
S 90°
T 95°
128
129
135
153

ARCTIC OCEAN
Chukchi Sea
Cape Dezhnev
Uelen
Bering Strait
Nunivak
UNITED STATES
Saint Lawrence I.
Provideniya
Cape Chukotskiy
Chukot Pen.
3,799 ft 1,158 m
St. Matthew I.
Mys Shmidta
3,596 ft 1,096 m
Wrangel I.
De Long Str.
Egvekinot
Gulf of Anadyr'
Chukot Range
6,047 ft 1,843 m
East Siberian Sea
Cape Shelagskiy
Pevek
Beringovskiy
Cape Navarin
Anadyr'
Arctic Circle
Ayon I.
Shmidt I.
Komsomolets I.
Severnaya Zemlya
October Revolution I.
965 m
3,166 ft
Bol'shevik I.
3,068 ft 935 m
Malyy Taymyr
Vil'kitskiy Str.
C. Chelyuskin
New Siberian Is.
New Siberia
Bear Is.
Bilibino
6,080 ft 1,853 m
Ambarchik
Anyuy Ra.
5,824 ft 1,775 m
Markovo
Laptev Sea
Faddeyev I.
Kotel'nyy I.
1,227 ft 374 m
Lyakhov Is.
Little Lyakhov I.
Great Lyakhov I.
Bel'kovskiy I.
Sannikov Str.
Dmitri Laptev Str.
Cherskiy
Gt. Anyuy
Omolon
5,896 ft 1,797 m
Ledyanaya
8,406 ft 2,562 m
Koryak Range
Penzhina
4,931 ft 1,503 m
Kamenskoye
Pakhachi
Cape Olyutorskiy
Olyutorskiy Bay
3,429 ft 1,045 m
Korf
Bering Sea
Stolbovoy I.
Chokurdakh
Srednekolymsk
3,888 ft 1,185 m
Kolyma Range
Taymyr Pen.
1,146m
3,760 ft
Byrrang Mts.
Bol'shoy Begichev I.
L. Taymyr
Kosistyy
Ust'-Olenek
Tiksi
Nizhneyansk
Yana Bay
Indigirka
Belaya Gora
Severnyy
4,229 ft 1,289 m
Druzhina
Deputatskiy
Zyryanka
Evensk
Penzhina Gulf
Il'pyrskiy
Karaginskiy Bay
Karaginskiy I.
Commander Is.
Copper I.
Bering I.
1,719 ft 524 m
Olenëk
Verkhoyansk Range
Khatanga
Novorybnaya
Selennyakh
7,169 ft 2,185 m
8,311 ft 2,533 m
Pobeda
10,325 ft 3,147 m
Merenga
Gizhiga Gulf
Shelikhov Gulf
6,437 ft 1,962 m
Palana
8,590 ft 2,618 m
Central Range
Siktyakh
Cherskiy Range
Seymchan
Ust'-Kamchatsk
Klyuchi
Klyuchevskaya Sopka
15,585 ft 4,750 m
Tigil'
Batagay
Verkhoyansk
5,801 ft 1,768 m
7,838 ft 2,389 m
Susuman
Yagodnoye
8,485 ft 2,586 m
Ust'-Nera
Cape Tolstoy
Kamchatka
2,969 ft 905 m
Anabar
Kheta
Putoran Mts.
5,581 ft 1,701 m
Yessey
Oymyakon
9,708 ft 2,959 m
Magadan
Mil'kovo
Kronotskaya Sopka
11,339 ft 3,456 m
Petropavlovsk-Kamchatskiy
Yelizovo
Vilyuchinsk
Central Siberian Plateau
SAKHA
Zhigansk
Olenëk
7,530 ft 2,295 m
Mötykley
Kirovskiy
Udachnyy
Sangar
Khandyga
Aykhal
2,385 ft 727 m
Ekonda
Markha
Vilyuy
Aldan
Allakh-Yun'
Okhotsk
Oktyabr'skiy
Ozernovskiy
First Kurile Str.
Yakutsk
Nizhniy Bestyakh
Vilyuysk
Brindakit
Ust'-Maya
Severo-Kuril'sk
Paramushir I.
7,674 ft 2,339 m
Sea of Okhotsk
Tura
1,211 ft 369 m
Pokrovsk
Nyurba
Amga
Onekotan I.
Shiashkotan I.
2,913 ft 888 m
Chernyshevskiy
Mirnyy
Suntar
Vilyuy Res.
Maya
Nel'kan
6,253 ft 1,906 m
Ayan
Dzhugdzhur Ra.
Cape Yelizavety
Okha
Baykit
Olëkminsk
Lensk
Tommot
Chagda
Shantar Is.
Sakhalin Str.
Strelka-Chunya
Yerbogachën
Olëkma
Aldan
Simushir I.
Taimba
Vanavara
Lower Tunguska
5,584 ft 1,702 m
Vitim
Perevoz
Bol'shoy Nimnyr
Timpton
Gonam
2,412 m 7,914 ft
Nikolayevsk-na-Amure
Nogliki
5,279 ft 1,609 m
Pogibi
Sakhalin
Chumikan
7,822 ft 2,384 m
Lazarev
De-Kastri
Tatar Strait
Aleksandrovsk-Sakhalinskiy
Urup I.
Artëmovskiy
6,585 ft 2,007 m
Chul'man
Neryungri
Stanovoy Range
Uda
3,104 ft 946 m
Vitimskiy
Bodaybo
Novaya Chara
Nagornyy
Tynda
Ekimchan
Poronaysk
Uglegorsk
Makarov
Taëzhnyy
Ust'-Ilimsk
Kirensk
9,840 ft 2,999 m
Zeya Res.
Sofiysk
Berezovyy
Komsomol'sk-na-Amure
Pivan'
Amur
Amursk
Sikhote-Alin Range
Iturup I.
Kuril'sk
Kurile Islands
Ust'-Kut
8,458 ft 2,578 m
Novyy Uoyan
Taksimo
Upper Angara
Zheleznogorsk-Ilimskiy
Bratsk
Nizhnyaya-Poyma
Tayshet
Bratsk Reservoir
Severobaykal'sk
9,318 ft 2,840 m
6,424 ft 1,958 m
Yerofey Pavlovich
Skovorodino
Magdagachi
Tygda
Zeya
Fevral'sk
Bureya
Chegdomyn
8,662 ft 2,640 m
6,815 ft 2,077 m
Sovetskaya Gavan'
Il'inskiy
Kholmsk
Yuzhno-Sakhalinsk
Korsakov
Kunashir I.
Yuzhno-Kuril'sk
8,439 ft 2,572 m
Vitim Ra.
5,584 ft 1,702 m
Mogocha
Shimanovsk
Svobodnyy
Belogorsk
Mayskiy
6,595 ft 2,010 m
Gornozavodsk
C. Crillon
La Pérouse Strait
Abashiri
Nemuro
Tulun
Pik Grandioznyy
Kurumkan
Bukachacha
Shilka
Mohe
5,020 ft 1,530 m
Blagoveshchensk
Zavitinsk
Raychikhinsk
Birobidzhan
Khabarovsk
Svetlaya
Wakkanai
7,513 ft 2,290 m
Kushiro
Zima
2,922 m
Romanovka
Nerchinsk
Sretensk
Gornyy Zerentuy
Argun'
Yitulihe
Jagdaqi
Heihe
Vyazemskiy
Asahikawa
Obihiro
Hokkaido
Cheremkhovo
Ust'-Ordynskiy
Ust'-Barguzin
Baikal
Yablonovyy Ra.
Chita
Baley
Wuyiling
3,435 ft 1,047 m
Fujin
Bikin
Ebetsu
C. Erimo
Otaru
SAPPORO
Usol'ye-Sibirskoye
Angarsk
Ulan-Ude
Khilok
Olovyannaya
Nenjiang
Yichun
Hegang
Shuangyashan
Terney
Dal'negorsk
Muroran
Sayan
Irkutsk
Slyudyanka
Aginskoye
Krasnokamensk
Borzya
Great Khingan Range
Bei'an
Tangyuan
Jiamusi
Lesozavodsk
Rudnaya Pristan'
Hakodate
Okushiri
11,454 ft 3,491 m
Turt
Petrovsk-Zabaykal'skiy
Yakeshi
Zalantun
Hailun
Spassk-Dal'niy
Hachinohe
Munku-Sardyk
Hövsgöl Nuur
Zakamensk
Kyakhta
Khapcheranga
Onon
Manzhouli
Hailar
Hulun Nur
Qiqihar
Suihua
Jixi
L. Khanka
6,086 ft 1,855 m
Tsugaru Str.
Aomori
Sühbaatar
8,278 ft 2,523 m
DAQING
HARBIN
Ussuriysk
Morioka
Akita
Mörön
Darhan
Choybalsan
Yirxie
Anda
Mudanjiang
Vladivostok
Nakhodka
C. Povorotnyy
Chōkai-san
7,317 ft 2,230 m
JAPAN
Bulgan
Selenge
Erdenet
9,026 ft 2,751 m
5,738 ft 1,749 m
Ulanhot
CHINA
Manchuria
Yamagata
SENDAI
Ulan Bator (Ulaanbaatar)
Dzuunmod
Herlen Gol
Baicheng
JILIN
Yanji
Najin
Fukushima
Honshu
Niigata
Aizu-Wakamatsu
Tsetserleg
Öndörhaan
Baruun-Urt
Tongyu
CHANGCHUN
Baitou Shan/Paekdu-san
9,003 ft 2,744 m
Ch'ŏngjin
Sea of Japan
Sado
Utsunomiya
Mito
812 ft
905 m
Khangai Mts.
Karakorum (Harhorin)
Choyr
6,398 ft 1,950 m
Shuangliao
Liaoyuan
C.Suzu
Funabashi
TOKYO
MONGOLIA
Mandalgovĭ
Xilinhot
Tongliao
Kailu
Siping
Baishan
Hyesan
Kimch'aek
Nagano
Toyama
KAWASAKI
Chiba
YOKOHAMA
Bayanhongor
Arvayheer
Saynshand
6,657 ft 2,029 m
Linxi
Tonghua
SHENYANG
FUSHUN
Kanggye
NORTH KOREA
Kanazawa
Mt. Fuji
12,389 ft 3,776 m
12,983 ft 3,957 m
Govĭ Altayn Nuruu
Fuxin
Benxi
Hŭich'ŏn
Hamhŭng
Fukui
Gifu
NAGOYA
Izu Islands
Erenhot
Chifeng
ANSHAN
Panjin
Sinŭiju
Wŏnsan
KYŌTO
Chaoyang
Sonid Youqi
Dalandzadgad
Jinzhou
Yingkou
Dandong
P'yŏngsong
Ullung
Oki Is.
Tottori
OSAKA
Namp'o
P'YONGYANG
SOUTH KOREA
KOBE
Sakai
PACIFIC OCEAN
60° 90° 120° 150° 175° l 180° m 175° n 170° o
55° 50° 45° 40° 35°
100° V 105° W 110° X 115° Y 120° Z 125° a 130° b 135° c
1 2 3 4 5 6 7 8 9 10 11 12

A 25° B 30° 134 C 35° D 40° E 135 45° F 50° G 55° H 60° J 65° K 148 70°

133

Black Sea
Caspian Sea
Mediterranean Sea
Red Sea
Persian Gulf
Gulf of Oman
Gulf of Aden
Arabian Sea
INDIAN

BULGARIA
GREECE
TURKEY
CYPRUS
SYRIA
LEBANON
ISRAEL
JORDAN
IRAQ
KUWAIT
BAHRAIN
QATAR
UNITED ARAB EMIRATES
OMAN
YEMEN
SAUDI ARABIA
EGYPT
SUDAN
ERITREA
DJIBOUTI
ETHIOPIA
SOMALIA
KENYA
IRAN
AFGHANISTAN
PAKISTAN
TURKMENISTAN
UZBEKISTAN
KAZAKHSTAN
TAJIKISTAN
GEORGIA
ARMENIA
AZERBAIJAN
RUSSIA
MALDIVES

Thessaloníki
Edirne
Alexandroúpoli
İSTANBUL
Tekirdağ
Zonguldak
Gebze
İzmit
Edremit
BURSA
Eskişehir
Çankırı
Çorum
Samsun
Sinop
Cape İnce
İZMİR
Manisa
ANKARA
Kırıkkale
Amasya
Sivas
Athens (Athína)
Chíos
Aydın
Uşak
Afyon
Denizli
Isparta
Konya
Kayseri
Niğde
Malatya
Elâzığ
Antalya
Karaman
Taurus Mountains
Kahramanmaraş
Ródos
Rhodes
Alanya
Mersin
Tarsus
ADANA
Gaziantep
Iráklio
Crete
İskenderun
Şanlıurfa
Diyarbakır
Batman
Siirt
Van
Erzurum
Kars
Trabzon
Euphrates
Nicosia (Lefkosia/Lefkoşa)
Limassol (Lemesós)
Latakia (Al-Lādhiqīyah)
Tripoli (Țarābulus)
ALEPPO (HALAB)
Hamāh
Ar-Raqqah
Al-Qāmishlī
Al-Hasakah
MOSUL (AL-MAWṢIL)
Dahūk
Arbil (Irbīl)
Kirkūk
As-Sulaymānīyah
Hims
Dayr az-Zawr
BEIRUT (BAYRŪT)
DAMASCUS (DIMASHQ)
Haifa (Hefa)
Tel Aviv-Yafo
Irbid
AMMĀN ('AMMĀN)
Jerusalem (Yerushalayim/Al-Quds)
Be'er Sheva'
Ar-Ramādī
BAGHDĀD
Karbalā'
Al-Ḥillah
Al-Kūt
An-Najaf
Ad-Dīwānīyah
Al-'Amārah
As-Samāwah
An-Nāṣirīyah
BASRA (AL-BAṢRAH)
Marsá Maṭrūḥ
ALEXANDRIA (AL-ISKANDARĪYAH)
Port Said
Dumyāṭ
Damanhūr
Ṭanṭā
CAIRO (AL-QĀHIRAH)
GIZA (AL-JĪZAH)
Al-Fayyūm
Banī Suwayf
Suez (As-Suways)
Al-Ismā'īlīyah
Elat
Aqaba (Al-'Aqabah)
Sinai Pen.
J. Katrīnah
Al-Minyā
Asyūṭ
Sawhāj
Hurghada (Al-Ghurdaqah)
Qinā
Luxor (Al-Uqṣur)
Idfū
Aswān (Assuan)
Lake Nasser
Tabūk
Sakākah
'Ar'ar
Ḥā'il
Buraydah
'Unayzah
Medina (Al-Madīnah)
Yanbu'
An-Nafūd
Ad-Dahnā'
RIYADH (AR-RIYĀḌ)
Al-Kharj
Al-Hufūf
Al-Mubarraz
Ad-Dammām
Dhahran (Az-Zahrān)
Al-Jubayl
Manama (Al-Manāmah)
Doha (Ad-Dawḥah)
Abu Dhabi (Abū Ẓaby)
Dubai (Dubayy)
Ash-Shāriqah
Ra's al-Khaymah
Al-'Ayn
Ṣuḥār
Muscat (Masqaṭ)
Maṭraḥ
As-Sīb
Ṣūr
Ra's al-Hadd
Maṣīrah
Ẓufār
Ṣalālah
Kuria Muria Is.
Ar-Rub' al-Khālī
Najd
JEDDAH (JIDDAH)
MECCA (MAKKAH)
Aṭ-Ṭā'if
Al-Hawīyah
Al-Bāḥah
'Asīr
Abhā
Khamīs Mushayṭ
Najrān
Jīzān
Farasān Is.
SANAA (SAN'Ā')
Ṣa'dah
Dhamār
Ibb
Ta'izz
Aden ('Adan)
Al-Mukallā
Ḥaḍramawt
Say'ūn
Socotra (YEM.)
C. Guardafui
Port Sudan (Būr Sūdān)
Sawākin
'Aṭbarah
Ad-Dāmir
OMDURMAN (UMM DURMĀN)
KHARTOUM NORTH (AL-KHARṬŪM BAḤRĪ)
KHARTOUM (AL-KHARṬŪM)
Kassalā
Wad Madanī
Ad-Duwaym
Sinnār
Al-Qaḍārif
Kūstī
Ad-Damāzin
White Nile
Blue Nile
Nubian Desert
Wādī Ḥalfā
Dunqulā
Asmera
Mek'ele
Gonder
Bahir Dar
L. Tana
Desē
Kembolcha
Djibouti/Jibūtī
ADDIS ABABA (ADIS ABEBA)
Nazrēt
Dirē Dawa
Hārer
Jijiga
Jīma
Shashemenē
Awasa
Sodo
Ārba Minch
Hargeysa
Berbera
Burco
Boosaaso
Qardho
Garoowe
Gaalkacyo
Beledweyne
Baydhabo
MOGADISHU (MUQDISHO)
Marka
Jawhar
Lake Turkana
Marsabit
Wajir
Sochi
Sokhumi
Poti
Batumi
Kutaisi
TBILISI
Cherkessk
Pyatigorsk
Nal'chik
El'brus
Nazran'
Groznyy
Vladikavkaz
Makhachkala
Derbent
Budënnovsk
Gyumri
Gəncə
YEREVAN
Ararat
Sumqayıt
BAKU
Khvoy
TABRĪZ
Ardabīl
Orūmīyeh
Rasht
Zanjān
Qazvīn
KARAJ
TEHRĀN
Damāvand
Elburz Mts.
Sārī
Bābol
Gorgān
Gonbad-e Qābūs
Hamadān
Sanandaj
Kermānshāh
Borūjerd
Arāk
Qom
Kāshān
Khorramābād
Dezfūl
ISFAHAN (ESFAHĀN)
Ahvāz
Khorramshahr
Ābādān
Yāsūj
Shīrāz
Bandar-e Būshehr
Yazd
Kermān
Sīrjān
Bandar-e 'Abbās
Zāhedān
Great Salt Desert
Semnān
Mashhad
Sabzevār
Neyshābūr
Torbat-e Heydarīyeh
Bīrjand
Zābol
Īrānshahr
Chābahār
Baluchestan
Gwadar
Turbat
KARACHI
HYDERABAD
Quetta
Sukkur
Larkana
MULTAN
FAISALABAD
PESHAWAR
KABUL
Jalālābād
Herāt
Kandahār (Qandahār)
Mazār-e Sharīf
Kondūz
Balkh
Ashgabat (Aşgabat)
Türkmenbaşy
Balkanabat
Mary
Bayramaly
Türkmenabat
Dashowuz
Urganch
Nukus
Bukhara (Buxoro)
Samarqand
Qarshi
Navoiy
Jizzax
TASHKENT (TOSHKENT)
Dushanbe
Khujand
Shymkent
Qyzylorda
Baykonur (Bayqongyr)
Aqtaū
Beyneu
Aral Sea
Ustyurt Plateau
Qizilqum
Garagum
Koppeh Dāgh
Hindu Kush
Gujarat
Ahmadabad
Rajkot
Jamnagar
Porbandar
Junagadh
Bhavnagar
Surat
MUMBAI (BOMBAY)
Lakshadweep
Amindivi Is.
Laccadive Is.
Minicoy
Tropic of Cancer

KLETT-PERTHES

D 40° 177 E 45° F 50° G 55° H 60° J 65° K 70°

1:20,000,000
0 200 400 mi
0 200 400 600 km
M N O P Q R S T U V
149
155
156
A. K. Azad Kashmir
An. Anyang
Be. Bengbu
H. Haryana
Hu. Huaibei
Miz. Mizoram
N. Nagaland
Sa. Sanmenxia
Si. Sikkim
Tr. Tripura
Utt. Uttarakhand
Xi. Xianyang
Xu. Xuchang
Ya. Yancheng
Za. Zaozhuang
A.R. Autonomous Region
MONGOLIA
CHINA
INDIA
MYANMAR
THAILAND
CAMBODIA
VIETNAM
MALAYSIA
INDONESIA
SRI LANKA
BHUTAN
Bay of Bengal
South China Sea
Andaman Sea
Gulf of Thailand
Gulf of Tonkin
OCEAN
Himalayas
Kunlun Shan
Tian Shan
Qilian Shan
Altun Shan
Nyainqêntanglha Shan
Qin Ling
Takla Makan Desert
Tibet (A.R. Xizang)
A.R. Xinjiang Uygur
Inner Mongolia A.R.
Qinghai
Sichuan
Yunnan
Guangxi
Hainan
Malay Peninsula
Sumatra
Borneo (Kalimantan)
Ceylon
Andaman Islands
Andaman and Nicobar Is. (IND.)
Nicobar Islands
Paracel Islands (CHN.)
ALMATY
ÜRÜMQI
LANZHOU
BEIJING
TIANJIN
DALIAN
ANSHAN
SHIJIAZHUANG
TAIYUAN
BAOTOU
QINGDAO
JINAN
ZIBO
HANDAN
XUZHOU
ZHENGZHOU
LUOYANG
XI'AN
NANJING
WUXI
HEFEI
WUHAN
NANCHANG
CHANGSHA
CHONGQING
CHENGDU
GUIYANG
KUNMING
GUANGZHOU
SHANTOU
HONG KONG (XIANGGANG)
Macau (Aomen)
Lhasa
Thimphu
Kathmandu
DELHI
MEERUT
LUCKNOW
KANPUR
AGRA
JAIPUR
BHOPAL
PATNA
VARANASI (BENARES)
KOLKATA (CALCUTTA)
DHAKA
CHITTAGONG
NAGPUR
HYDERABAD
CHENNAI (MADRAS)
BANGALORE
PUNE
Colombo (Kolamba)
Mandalay
RANGOON (YANGON)
BANGKOK (KRUNG THEP)
Viangchan
HANOI (HÀ NOI)
Hai Phong
PHNUM PENH
HO CHI MINH CITY (THAN-PHÔ HÔ CHI MINH)
KUALA LUMPUR
SINGAPORE
MEDAN
Mt. Everest 29,036 ft 8,850 m
K2 28,252 ft 8,611 m
Kangchenjunga 28,210 ft 8,598 m

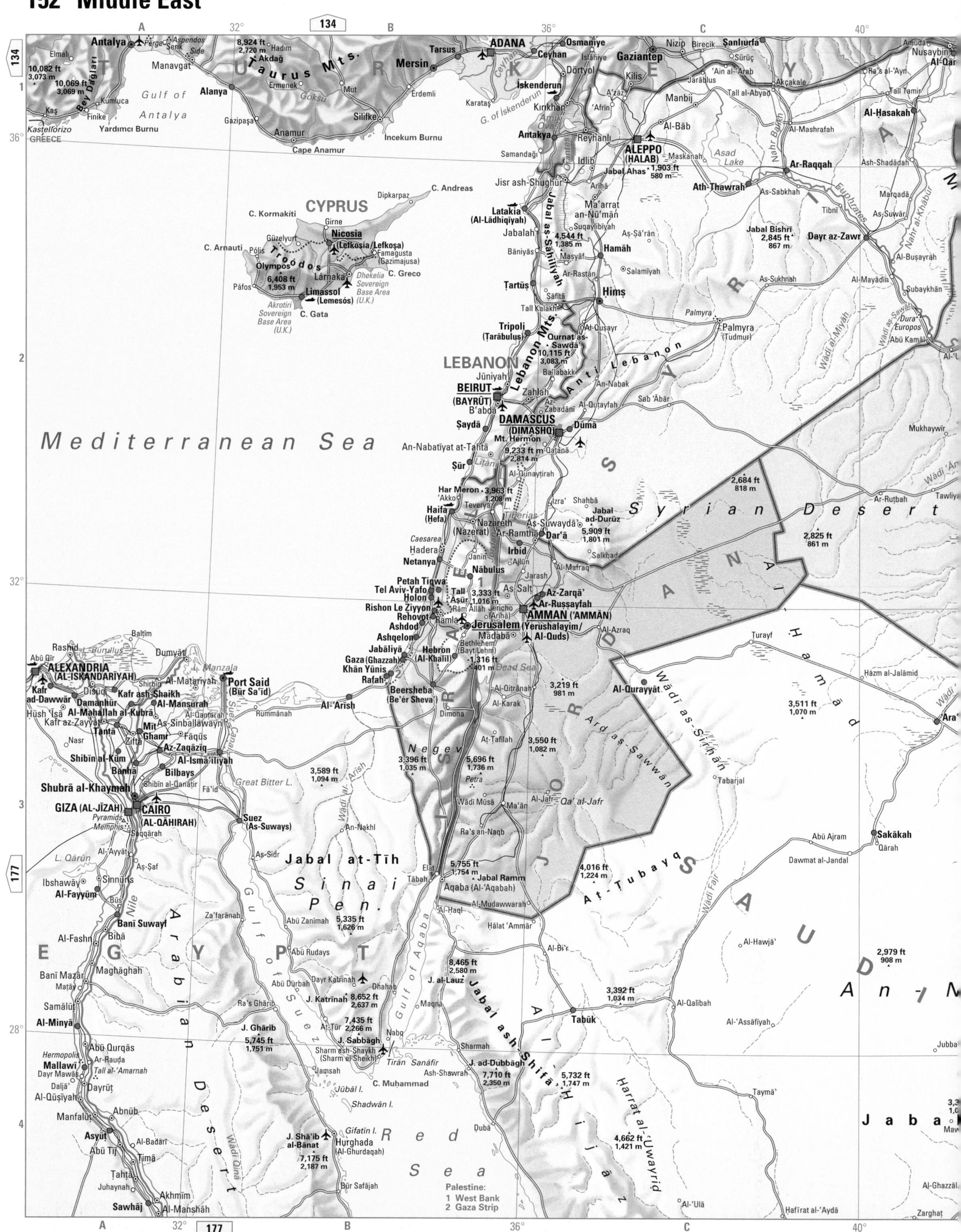

134
A
B
C
32°
36°
40°
1
2
3
4
28°
177
Antalya
Perge
Aspendos
Serik
Side
Elmalı
10,082 ft
3,073 m
10,069 ft
3,069 m
Bey Dağları
Kumluca
Kaş
Finike
Kastellorizo
GREECE
Yardımcı Burnu
Manavgat
Gulf of Antalya
Alanya
Gazipaşa
Anamur
Cape Anamur
8,924 ft
2,720 m
Hadim
Akdağ
Taurus Mts.
Ermenek
Göksu
Mut
Silifke
Erdemli
İncekum Burnu
Mersin
Tarsus
ADANA
Ceyhan
Osmaniye
Karataş
İskenderun
Dörtyol
İslahiye
Kırıkhan
G. of İskenderun
Antakya
Samandağı
Reyhanlı
Gaziantep
Kilis
A'zaz
'Afrin
Nizip
Birecik
Şanlıurfa
Sürüç
'Ain al-'Arab
Jarābulus
Akçakale
Tall al-Abyad
Manbij
Al-Bāb
ALEPPO
(HALAB)
Maskanah
Asad Lake
Jabal Ahas
1,903 ft
580 m
Idlib
Orontes
Ar-Raqqah
Ath-Thawrah
As-Sabkhah
Al-Mashrafah
Nahr Balīkh
Nusaybin
Amūda
Al-Qāmishlī
Ra's al-'Ayn
Tall Tamir
Al-Hasakah
Ash-Shadādah
Marqadā
Tibnī
As-Suwār
Euphrates
Nahr al-Khābūr
Jabal Bishrī
2,845 ft
867 m
Dayr az-Zawr
Al-Busayrah
Al-Mayādīn
Subaykhān
Dura-Europos
Abū Kamāl
Palmyra
(Tudmur)
Wādī al-Miyāh
As-Sukhnah
Jisr ash-Shughūr
Arīhā
Ma'arrat an-Nu'mān
Suqaylibīyah
Latakia
(Al-Lādhiqīyah)
Jabalah
Jabal as-Sahiliyah
4,544 ft
1,385 m
Bāniyās
Masyāf
Hamāh
As-Sa'rān
Salamīyah
Ar-Rastān
Tartūs
Hims
Sāfitā
Tall Kalakh
Tripoli
(Tarābulus)
Al-Qusayr
Qurnat as-Sawdā'
10,115 ft
3,083 m
Lebanon Mts.
LEBANON
Jūniyah
Ba'labakk
Anti Lebanon
BEIRUT
(BAYRŪT)
B'abdā
Zahlah
Az-Zabadānī
An-Nabak
Al-Qutayfah
Sab 'Ābār
Saydā
DAMASCUS
(DIMASHQ)
Dūmā
Mt. Hermon
9,233 ft
2,814 m
Qatanā
An-Nabatīyat at-Tahtā
Sūr
Lītānī
Al-Qunaytirah
Mukhaywir
CYPRUS
C. Andreas
Dipkarpaz
C. Kormakíti
Girne
Nicosia
(Lefkosia/Lefkoşa)
Famagusta
(Gazimajusa)
Güzelyurt
Pólis
C. Arnauti
Troodos
Olympos
6,408 ft
1,953 m
Lárnaka
Dhekelia Sovereign Base Area (U.K.)
C. Greco
Limassol
(Lemesós)
Páfos
Akrotiri Sovereign Base Area (U.K.)
C. Gata
Mediterranean Sea
Har Meron
3,963 ft
1,208 m
'Akko
Haifa
(Hefa)
Teverya
Tiberias
Nazareth
(Nazerat)
Caesarea
Hadera
Netanya
Janin
Nābulus
Izra'
Shahbā
Jabal ad-Durūz
5,909 ft
1,801 m
As-Suwaydā'
Ar-Ramthā
Dar'ā
Irbid
'Ajlūn
Salkhad
Al-Mafraq
Jarash
Syrian Desert
2,684 ft
818 m
2,825 ft
861 m
Ar-Rutbah
Tawliyah
Petah Tiqwa
Tel Aviv-Yafo
Holon
Rishon Le Ziyyon
Rehovot
Ramla
Ashdod
Ashqelon
Tall Asūr
3,333 ft
1,016 m
Rām Allāh
Jericho
(Arīhā)
As-Salt
Az-Zarqā'
Ar-Rusayfah
AMMAN ('AMMĀN)
Jerusalem (Yerushalayim/Al-Quds)
Mādabā
Bethlehem
(Bayt Lahm)
Hebron
(Al-Khalīl)
-1,316 ft
-401 m
Dead Sea
Al-Azraq
Jabāliyā
Gaza (Ghazzah)
Khān Yūnis
Rafah
Beersheba
(Be'er Sheva)
Dimona
Al-Qitrānah
Al-Karak
3,219 ft
981 m
Turayf
Al-Qurayyāt
Hamād
Hazm al-Jalāmid
3,511 ft
1,070 m
Wādī as-Sirhān
Ard as-Sawwān
At-Tafīlah
3,550 ft
1,082 m
Negev
3,396 ft
1,035 m
5,696 ft
1,736 m
Petra
Wādī Mūsā
Ma'ān
Al-Jafr
Qa' al-Jafr
Ra's an-Naqb
Tabarjal
JORDAN
ISRAEL
SYRIA
IRAQ
Sakākah
Qārah
Abū Ajram
Dawmat al-Jandal
5,755 ft
1,754 m
Jabal Ramm
4,016 ft
1,224 m
Elat
Tābah
Aqaba (Al-'Aqabah)
Al-Mudawwarah
At-Tubayq
Wādī Fajr
Al-Haql
Hālat 'Ammār
Al-Bi'r
Al-Hawjā'
2,979 ft
908 m
SAUDI ARABIA
An-Nafūd
Baltīm
Rashīd
Burullus
Dumyāt
L. Manzala
Port Said
(Būr Sa'īd)
Abū Qīr
ALEXANDRIA
(AL-ISKANDARĪYAH)
Kafr ad-Dawwār
Shirbīn
Al-Matarīyah
Disūq
Kafr ash-Shaikh
Damanhūr
Al-Mansūrah
Hūsh 'Īsā
Al-Mahallah al-Kubrā
Kafr az-Zayyāt
Al-Qantarah
As-Sinballāwayn
Tantā
Mīt Ghamr
Zifta
Fāqūs
Nasr
Az-Zaqāzīq
Shibīn al-Kūm
Banhā
Bilbays
Al-Ismā'īlīyah
Suez Canal
Rummānah
Al-'Arīsh
Shubrā al-Khaymah
Shibīn al-Qanātir
Fā'id
Great Bitter L.
GIZA (AL-JĪZAH)
CAIRO
(AL-QĀHIRAH)
Pyramids
Memphis
Saqqārah
Suez
(As-Suways)
3,589 ft
1,094 m
Wādī al-'Arīsh
An-Nakhl
Al-'Ayyāt
L. Qārūn
As-Saf
As-Sidr
Jabal at-Tīh
Sinai Pen.
Ibshawāy
Sinnūris
Al-Fayyūm
Būs
Nile
Banī Suwayf
Za'farānah
Abū Zanīmah
5,335 ft
1,626 m
Al-Fashn
Bibā
EGYPT
Abū Rudays
Banī Mazār
Maghāghah
Matāy
Samālūt
Al-Minyā
Arabian Desert
Gulf of Suez
Abū Durbah
Dayr Katrīnah
Dhahab
J. Katrīnah
8,652 ft
2,637 m
Ra's Ghārib
7,435 ft
2,266 m
At-Tūr
J. Sabbāgh
Maqnā
Nabq
J. Ghārib
5,745 ft
1,751 m
Sharm ash-Shaykh
(Sharm el-Sheikh)
Gulf of Aqaba
8,465 ft
2,580 m
J. al-Lauz
Jabal ash-Shifā
Tabūk
3,392 ft
1,034 m
Al-Qalībah
Al-'Assāfīyah
Tīrān
Sanāfir
Sharmah
J. ad-Dubbāgh
7,710 ft
2,350 m
Ash-Shawrah
5,732 ft
1,747 m
Jamsah
C. Muhammad
Jūbāl I.
Shadwān I.
Hermopolis
Abū Qurqās
Ar-Rauda
Mallawī
Tall al-'Amarnah
Dayr Mawās
Daljā'
Dayrūt
Al-Qūsīyah
Manfalūt
Abnūb
Asyūt
Al-Badārī
Abū Tīj
Tīmā
Tahtā
Juhaynah
Akhmīm
Sawhāj
Al-Manshāh
Wādī Qinā
Gifatīn I.
J. Shā'ib al-Banāt
7,175 ft
2,187 m
Hurghada
(Al-Ghurdaqah)
Red Sea
Būr Safājah
Dubā
Harrat al-'Uwayrid
4,662 ft
1,421 m
Hijāz
Al-'Ulā
Taymā'
Jubbah
Jabal
Al-Ghazzālah
Hafīrat al-'Aydā
Zarghat
Palestine:
1 West Bank
2 Gaza Strip

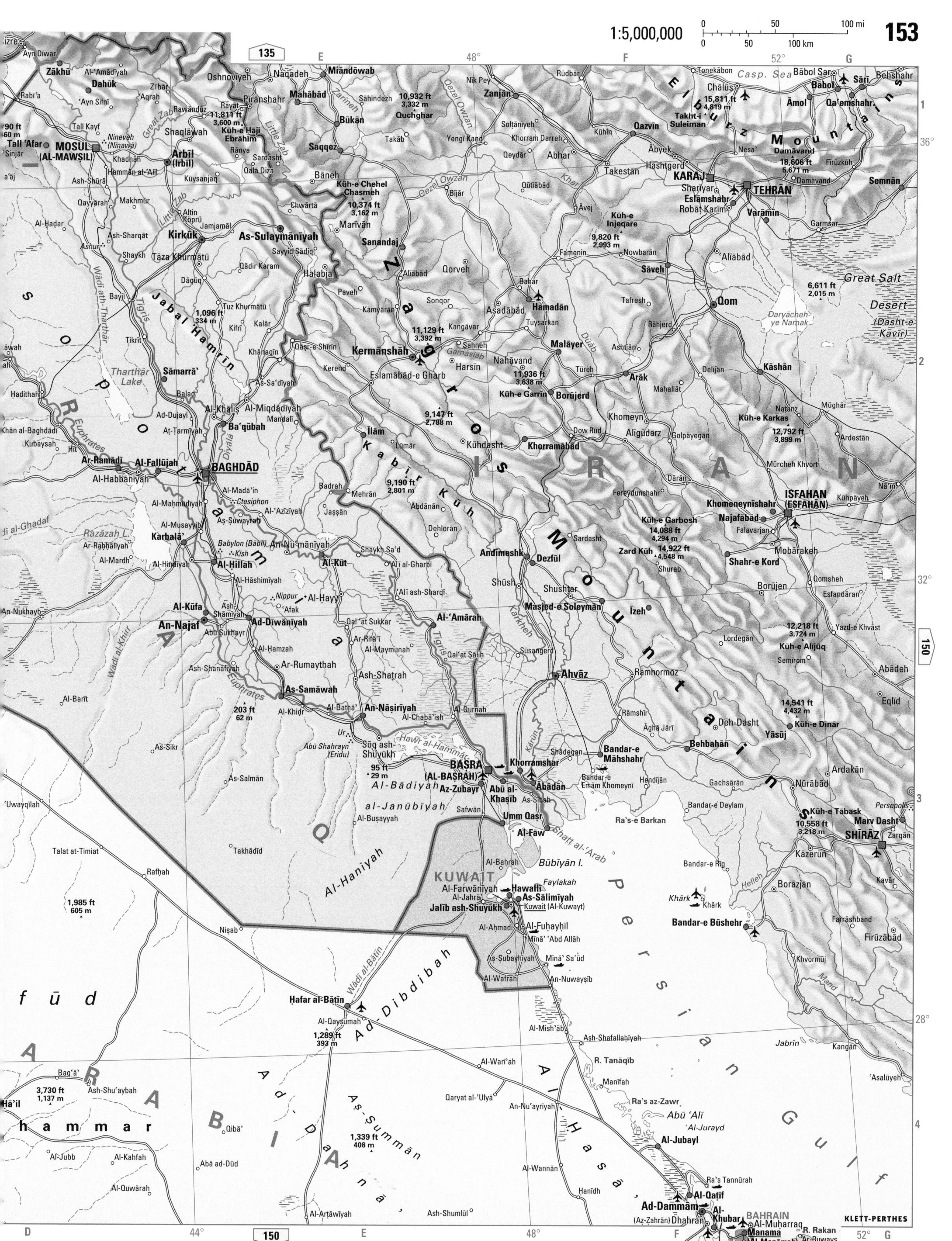

0 50 100 mi
0 50 100 km
135
150
E
F
G
D
48°
52°
44°
36°
32°
28°
Casp. Sea
Elburz Mountains
Zagros Mountains
IRAN
Great Salt Desert (Dasht-e Kavīr)
Daryācheh-ye Namak
Kabīr Kūh
Jabal Ḥamrīn
Persian Gulf
Shaṭṭ al-'Arab
Būbīyān I.
Faylakah
KUWAIT
BAHRAIN
Al-Bādiyah al-Janūbīyah
Al-Haniyah
Ad-Dibdibah
Ad-Dahnā'
Aṣ-Ṣummān
Al-Ḥasā'
Hawr al-Hammār
Tharthār Lake
Razāzah L.
Euphrates
Tigris
Great Zab
Little Zab
Diyala
Karkheh
Kārūn
Zakho
Dahūk
Mosul (Al-Mawṣil)
Nineveh (Nīnawā)
Tall 'Afar
Sinjār
Arbīl (Irbīl)
Rawāndūz
Kūh-e Hājī Ebrāhīm
11,811 ft
3,600 m
Rānya
Kūysanjaq
Qal'at Dīza
Sardasht
Piranshahr
Oshnovīyeh
Naqadeh
Miāndōwab
Mahābād
Būkān
Saqqez
Bāneh
Kūh-e Chehel Chasmeh
10,374 ft
3,162 m
Marīvān
Sanandaj
Chwārtā
As-Sulaymānīyah
Kirkūk
Altin Köprü
Jamjamāl
Ash-Sharqāṭ
Qayyārah
Makhmūr
Al-Ḥaḍar
Ashur
Shaykh
Ṭāza Khurmātū
Qādir Karam
Dāqūq
Ḥalabja
Sayyid Ṣādiq
Bayjī
Tuz Khurmātū
1,096 ft
334 m
Kifrī
Kalār
Tikrīt
Khānaqīn
Qaṣr-e Shīrīn
Kerend
Kermānshāh
Eslāmābād-e Gharb
Sāmarrā'
As-Sa'dīyah
Balad
Al-Khāliṣ
Al-Miqdādīyah
Mandalī
Ba'qūbah
Ad-Dujayl
Aṭ-Ṭarmīyah
Ḥadīthah
Khān al-Baghdādī
Kubaysah
Hīt
Ar-Ramādī
Al-Fallūjah
Al-Habbānīyah
BAGHDĀD
Al-Madā'in
Ctesiphon
Al-Maḥmūdīyah
Al-'Azīzīyah
Aṣ-Ṣuwayrah
Al-Musayyib
Karbalā'
Ar-Raḥḥālīyah
Babylon (Bābil)
Kish
Al-Hindīyah
Al-Ḥillah
An-Nu'mānīyah
Al-Kūt
Shaykh Sa'd
'Alī al-Gharbī
'Alī ash-Sharqī
Al-Hāshimīyah
Nippur
Al-Ḥayy
Afak
Al-Kūfa
An-Najaf
Ash-Shāmīyah
Ad-Dīwānīyah
Abū Sukhayr
Qal'at Sukkar
Ar-Rifā'ī
Al-Maymūnah
Al-'Amārah
Qal'at Ṣāliḥ
Al-Ḥamzah
Ar-Rumaythah
Ash-Shanāfīyah
Ash-Shaṭrah
As-Samāwah
An-Nāṣirīyah
Al-Baṭḥā'
Al-Khiḍr
Al-Chabā'ish
Al-Qurnah
203 ft
62 m
Ur
Sūq ash-Shuyūkh
Abū Shahrayn (Eridu)
Al-Barīt
As-Sikr
As-Salmān
95 ft
29 m
BAṢRA (AL-BAṢRAH)
Az-Zubayr
Abū al-Khaṣīb
Safwān
Umm Qaṣr
Al-Fāw
Al-Buṣayyah
Takhādīd
Rafḥah
'Uwayqīlah
Talat at-Timiat
1,985 ft
605 m
Niṣab
Al-Baḥrah
Al-Jahrā'
Al-Farwānīyah
Ḥawallī
As-Sālimīyah
Kuwait (Al-Kuwayt)
Jalīb ash-Shuyūkh
Al-Aḥmadī
Al-Fuḥayḥīl
Mīnā' 'Abd Allāh
Aṣ-Ṣubayḥīyah
Mīnā' Sa'ūd
Al-Wafrah
An-Nuwayṣīb
Wādī al-Bāṭin
Ḥafar al-Bāṭin
Al-Qayṣūmah
1,289 ft
393 m
Al-Mish'āb
Ash-Shafallaḥīyah
R. Tanāqīb
Manīfah
Al-Warī'ah
Qaryat al-'Ulyā
An-Nu'ayrīyah
Ra's az-Zawr
Abū 'Alī
Al-Jurayd
Al-Jubayl
Al-Wannān
Ḥanīdh
Ra's Tannūrah
Al-Qaṭīf
Ad-Dammām
Al-Khubar
(Aẓ-Ẓahrān) Dhahran
Al-Muḥarraq
Manama (Al-Manāmah)
Ar-Rifā'
400 ft
R. Rakan
Ar-Ruways
Ash-Shumlūl
Al-Arṭāwīyah
1,339 ft
408 m
Baq'ā'
Ash-Shu'aybah
3,730 ft
1,137 m
Ḥā'il
Qibā'
Al-Jubb
Al-Kahfah
Abā ad-Dūd
Al-Quwārah
ARABIA
Shammar
Nafūd
MESOPOTAMIA
Wādī al-Khirr
Wādī ath-Tharthār
An-Nukhayb
Ilām
Lūmār
Kūhdasht
9,147 ft
2,788 m
Badrah
Mehrān
9,190 ft
2,801 m
Jaṣṣān
Ābdānān
Dehlorān
Andīmeshk
Dezfūl
Shūsh
Shushtar
Masjed-e Soleymān
Īzeh
Sūsangerd
Ahvāz
Rāmhormoz
Rāmshīr
Āghā Jārī
Deh-Dasht
Behbahān
Yāsūj
Shādegān
Bandar-e Māhshahr
Khorramshahr
Ābādān
As-Sībah
Bandar-e Emām Khomeynī
Hendījān
Gachsārān
Ra's-e Barkan
Bandar-e Deylam
Bandar-e Rīg
Khārk
Bandar-e Būshehr
Helleh
Borāzjān
Kāzerūn
Farrāshband
Fīrūzābād
Khvormūj
Mand
Jabrīn
Kangān
'Asalūyeh
Nūrābād
Ardakān
Kūh-e Tābask
10,558 ft
3,218 m
SHĪRĀZ
Zargān
Marv Dasht
Persepolis
Kavār
Eqlīd
Abādeh
14,541 ft
4,432 m
Kūh-e Dīnār
12,218 ft
3,724 m
Kūh-e Alījūq
Semīrom
Yazd-e Khvāst
Lordegān
Borūjen
Qomsheh
Esfandāran
Shahr-e Kord
Mobārakeh
Falāvarjān
Najafābād
Khomeyneyshahr
ISFAHAN (EṢFAHĀN)
Kūhpāyeh
Nā'īn
Kūh-e Garbosh
14,088 ft
4,294 m
Zard Kūh
14,922 ft
4,548 m
Shurab
Sardasht
Fereydūnshahr
Dārān
Mūrcheh Khvort
Ardestān
Kūh-e Karkas
12,792 ft
3,899 m
Naṭanz
Mūghār
Khomeyn
Alīgūdarz
Golpāyegān
Dow Rūd
Khorramābād
Borūjerd
Kūh-e Garrīn
11,936 ft
3,638 m
Nahāvand
Harsīn
Gamasiāb
Ṣaḥneh
Kangāvar
11,129 ft
3,392 m
Kāmyārān
Sonqor
Paveh
Alīābād
Qorveh
Asadābād
Bahār
Hamadān
Tūysarkān
Malāyer
Ashtīān
Tūreh
Arāk
Mahallāt
Delījān
Kāshān
Dūāb
Rāhjerd
Tafresh
Qom
Sāveh
Nowbarān
Famenīn
Kūh-e Injeqare
9,820 ft
2,993 m
Āvej
Qūtīābād
Bījār
Qezel Owzan
Takestān
Qeydār
Abhar
Khorram Darreh
Solṭānīyeh
Yengī Kand
Takāb
Zanjān
Nīk Pey
Ṣāhīndezh
10,932 ft
3,332 m
Quchghar
Zarīneh
Rūdbār
Kūhīn
Qazvīn
Ābyek
Hashtgerd
KARAJ
Shahriyār
Eslāmshahr
Robāṭ Karīm
TEHRĀN
Varāmīn
Garmsar
Alīābād
Tonekābon
Chālūs
15,811 ft
4,819 m
Takht-i Suleiman
Bābol Sar
Bābol
Sārī
Behshahr
Āmol
Qa'emshahr
Damāvand
18,606 ft
5,671 m
Fīrūzkūh
Nesa'
Semnān
6,611 ft
2,015 m
KLETT-PERTHES

148
150
151
156
K A Z A K H S T A N
UZBEKISTAN
TURKMENISTAN
TAJIKISTAN
KYRGYZSTAN
AFGHANISTAN
PAKISTAN
INDIA
NEPAL
BHUTAN
BANGLADESH
MYANMAR
THAILAND
CAMBODIA
SRI LANKA
MALDIVES
C H I N A
M O N G O L I A
Arabian Sea
Bay of Bengal
Andaman Sea
Andaman Islands
Andaman and Nicobar Is. (IND.)
Lakshadweep (IND.)
Laccadive Is.
Amindivi Is.
Minicoy I.
Ceylon
Gulf of Kutch
G. of Mannar
Palk Str.
Mergui Archipelago
Gulf of Thailand
G. of Tonking
Takla Makan Desert
Thar Desert
Dzungaria
Turpan Basin
Lop Nur
Badain Jaran Shamo
Gobi
Tien Shan
Altay Mts
Western Sayan
Eastern Sayan
Khangai
Govĭ Altayn Nuruu
Pamir
Hindu Kush
Karakoram Ra.
Himalayas
Kunlun Shan
Altun Shan
Qilian Shan
Qin Ling
Nyainqêntanglha Shan
Western Ghats
Eastern Ghats
Arakan Yoma
Annam Plateau
Tarbaghatay Ra.
Qinghai
Sichuan
Yunnan
Guizhou
Gansu
A.R. Xinjiang Uygur
A.R. Xizang
Tibet
Huang He
Yangtze
Mekong
Salween
Brahmaputra
Ganges
Indus
Irrawaddy
Mt. Everest 29,036 ft 8,850 m
K2 28,252 ft 8,611 m
Kangchenjunga 28,210 ft 8,598 m
Dhaulagiri 26,795 ft 8,167 m
Nanga Parbat
Khan-Tengri 22,950 ft 6,995 m
Jengish Chokusu/ Shengli Feng 24,407 ft 7,439 m
Muztag Feng 25,339 ft 7,723 m
Kongur Shan 25,326 ft 7,719 m
Kula Kangri 24,784 ft 7,554 m
Hkakabo Razi 19,295 ft 5,881 m
Gongga Shan 24,791 ft 7,556 m
Nganglong Kangri 21,641 ft 6,596 m
Kailash (Kangrinboqê) 22,028 ft 6,714 m
Kamet 25,447 ft 7,756 m
Tonkin
ALMATY
Bishkek
TASHKENT (TOSHKENT)
Dushanbe
KABUL
Islamabad
RAWALPINDI
PESHAWAR
LAHORE
FAISALABAD
GUJRANWALA
MULTAN
Quetta
HYDERABAD
KARACHI
New Delhi
DELHI
MEERUT
JAIPUR
AGRA
LUCKNOW
KANPUR
VARANASI (BENARES)
PATNA
Kathmandu
Thimphu
DHAKA
KOLKATA (CALCUTTA)
CHITTAGONG
AHMADABAD
SURAT
MUMBAI (BOMBAY)
PUNE
NAGPUR
INDORE
BHOPAL
VADODARA
HYDERABAD
BANGALORE
CHENNAI (MADRAS)
Trivandrum (Thiruvananthapuram)
Vijayawada
Visakhapatnam
Bhubaneshwar
Cuttack
Sittwe (Akyab)
Mandalay
RANGOON (YANGON)
Naypyidaw
Mawlamyine
BANGKOK (KRUNG THEP)
PHNUM PENH
Viangchan
HANOI (HÀ NỘI)
Hai Phong
HO CHI MINH CITY
KUNMING
CHENGDU
CHONGQING
GUIYANG
LANZHOU
Xining
XI'AN
BAOTOU
Nanning
Lhasa
ÜRÜMQI
Kashi
Hotan
Ulan Bator (Ulaanbaatar)
Irkutsk
Karakorum (Harhorin)
Semey
Öskemen
Qaraghandy
Qyzylorda
Balqash
Taraz
Samarqand
Bukhara (Buxoro)
Urganch
Andijon
Namangan
Osh
Mazār-e Sharif
Kandahar/ Qandahar
Srinagar
Amritsar
Ludhiana
Chandigarh
Jodhpur
Ajmer
Gwalior
Allahabad
Jabalpur
Raipur
Ranchi
Jamshedpur
Madurai
Coimbatore
Kochi
Mysore
Salem
Mangalore
Jaffna
Trincomalee
Anuradhapura
Port Blair
Chiang Mai
Phnum Aoral
Tônlé Sap
Cape Comorin
C. Negrais
Ramree
Cheduba

1:20,000,000
0 200 400 mi
0 200 400 600 km
149
156
157
KLETT-PERTHES
A. R. Autonomous Region
H. Haryana
Hu. Huainan
Ji. Jingdezhen
Ma. Matsuyama
Miz. Mizoram
My. Mymensingh
N. Nagaland
Pa. Panjin
Pi. Pingdingshan
Pu. Punjab
Pu. Puyang
Sa. Sanmenxia
Sh. Shimonoseki
Si. Sikkim
Ta. Takamatsu
To. Tongling
Tr. Tripura
Utt. Uttarakhand
Wa. Wakayama
Xi. Xianyang
Xia. Xiangtan
Sea of Okhotsk
Sakhalin
Kurile Islands
Hokkaido
Honshu
Shikoku
Kyushu
Sea of Japan
NORTH KOREA
SOUTH KOREA
JAPAN
PACIFIC OCEAN
Yellow Sea
East China Sea
Philippine Sea
South China Sea
Ryukyu Islands
Izu Islands
Bonin Is. (JAP.)
Volcano Is. (JAP.)
Marcus I. (JAP.)
Okino Tori (JAP.)
Tropic of Cancer
Northern Mariana Is. (U.S.)
Mariana Islands
Guam (U.S.)
MICRONESIA
Caroline Is.
PALAU
TAIWAN
PHILIPPINES
Luzon
Mindoro
Palawan
Samar
Leyte
Negros
Great Khingan Range
Sikhote-Alin Range
Heilongjiang
Manchuria
Mongolia
Harbin
Changchun
Jilin
Shenyang
Fushun
Anshan
Dalian
Beijing
Tianjin
Shijiazhuang
Jinan
Qingdao
Zhengzhou
Xuzhou
Nanjing
Wuxi
Suzhou
Shanghai
Hefei
Hangzhou
Ningbo
Wuhan
Nanchang
Changsha
Fuzhou
Xiamen
Guangzhou
Hong Kong (Xianggang)
Macau (Aomen)
Shenzhen
Shantou
T'aipei
T'aichung
Kaohsiung
Vladivostok
Khabarovsk
Yuzhno-Sakhalinsk
P'yongyang
Seoul
Incheon
Suwon
Daejeon
Daegu
Ulsan
Busan
Gwangju
Sapporo
Sendai
Tokyo
Kawasaki
Yokohama
Nagoya
Kyoto
Kobe
Osaka
Hiroshima
Kitakyushu
Fukuoka
Kagoshima
Okinawa
Naha
Manila
Quezon City
Caloocan
Cebu
Mt. Fuji 12,389 ft 3,776 m
Yu Shan 12,966 ft 3,952 m
Mt. Pulog 9,610 ft 2,929 m
Mt. Lamlam 1,332 ft 406 m

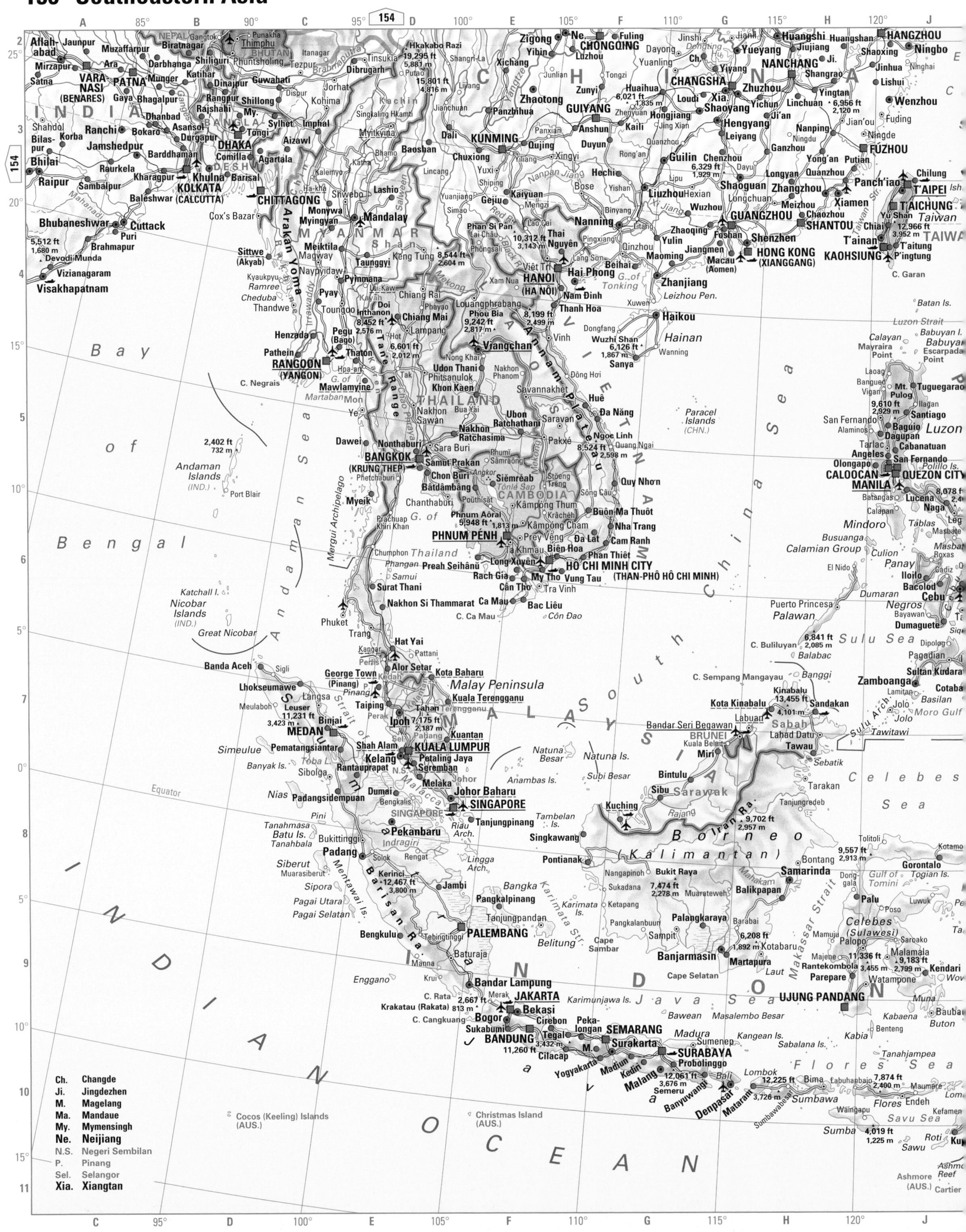
154
Bay of Bengal
Andaman Sea
South China Sea
INDIAN OCEAN
Java Sea
Celebes Sea
Sulu Sea
Flores Sea
Savu Sea
Gulf of Thailand
Gulf of Tonkin
Strait of Malacca
Makassar Strait
Malay Peninsula
Equator
INDIA
BANGLADESH
BHUTAN
NEPAL
CHINA
MYANMAR
THAILAND
LAOS
CAMBODIA
VIETNAM
MALAYSIA
BRUNEI
SINGAPORE
INDONESIA
Taiwan
Luzon
Mindoro
Palawan
Negros
Borneo (Kalimantan)
Celebes (Sulawesi)
Sumatra
Java
Bali
Lombok
Sumbawa
Flores
Sumba
Hainan
Andaman Islands (IND.)
Nicobar Islands (IND.)
Great Nicobar
Paracel Islands (CHN.)
Natuna Besar
Natuna Is.
Anambas Is.
Bangka
Belitung
Mentawai Is.
Siberut
Cocos (Keeling) Islands (AUS.)
Christmas Island (AUS.)
Ashmore Reef (AUS.)
Arakan Yoma
Annam Plateau
Tenasserim
Barisan Ra.
Iran Ra.
Mergui Archipelago
KOLKATA (CALCUTTA)
DHAKA
CHITTAGONG
RANGOON (YANGON)
Mandalay
BANGKOK (KRUNG THEP)
Chiang Mai
Vientiane
HANOI (HA NOI)
Hai Phong
PHNUM PENH
HO CHI MINH CITY (THAN-PHO HO CHI MINH)
KUALA LUMPUR
SINGAPORE
JAKARTA
BANDUNG
SEMARANG
SURABAYA
PALEMBANG
MEDAN
UJUNG PANDANG
MANILA
QUEZON CITY
CALOOCAN
HONG KONG (XIANGGANG)
Macau (Aomen)
GUANGZHOU
KUNMING
GUIYANG
CHONGQING
CHANGSHA
NANCHANG
HANGZHOU
FUZHOU
T'AIPEI
KAOHSIUNG
Kota Kinabalu
Bandar Seri Begawan
Kuching
Cebu
Zamboanga
Ch. Changde
Ji. Jingdezhen
M. Magelang
Ma. Mandaue
My. Mymensingh
Ne. Neijiang
N.S. Negeri Sembilan
P. Pinang
Sel. Selangor
Xia. Xiangtan

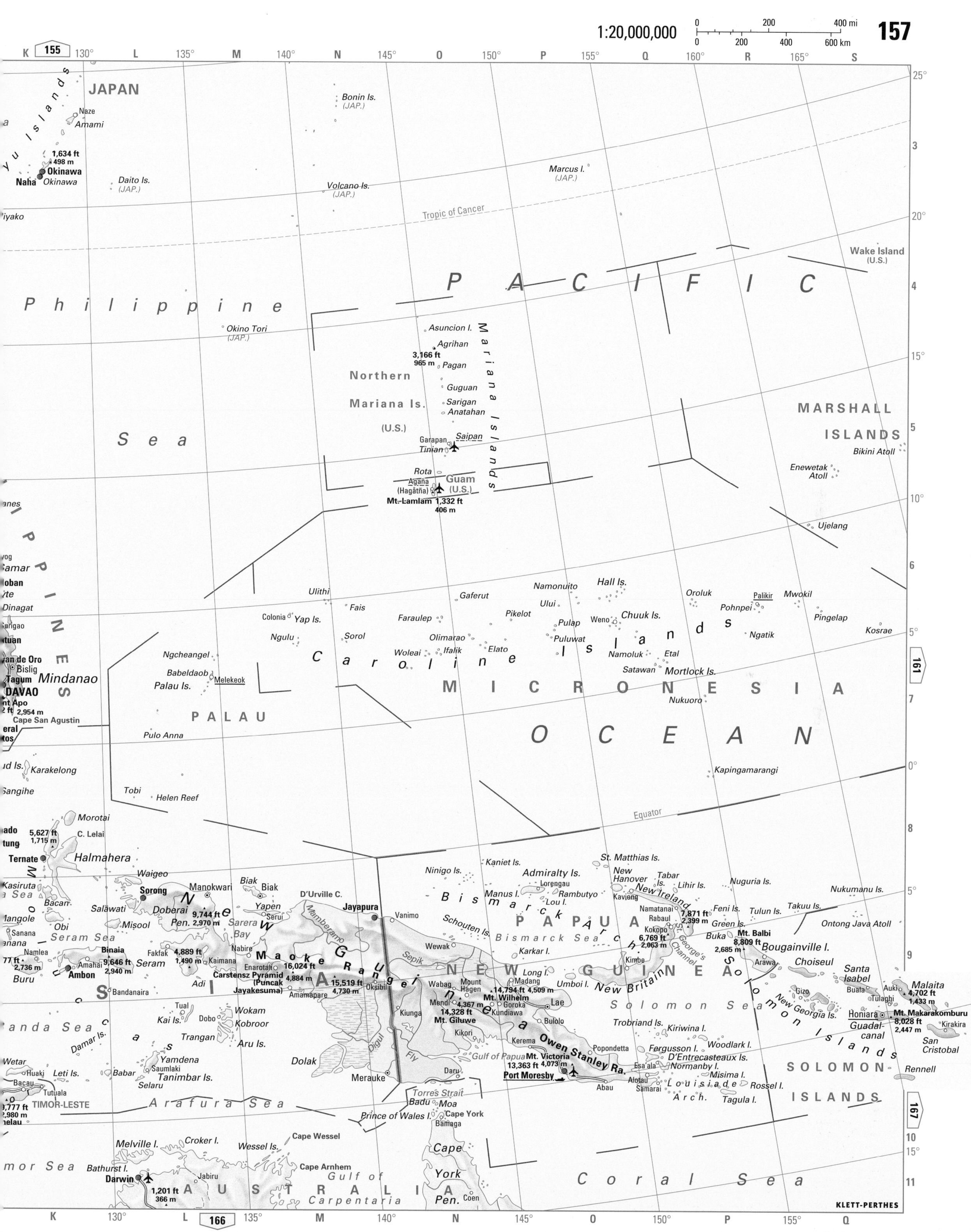
1:20,000,000
0 200 400 mi
0 200 400 600 km
155
130° 135° 140° 145° 150° 155° 160° 165°
JAPAN
Naze
Amami
1,634 ft
498 m
Okinawa
Naha
Daito Is.
(JAP.)
Bonin Is.
(JAP.)
Volcano Is.
(JAP.)
Marcus I.
(JAP.)
Tropic of Cancer
Wake Island
(U.S.)
P A C I F I C
Philippine
Sea
Okino Tori
(JAP.)
Asuncion I.
Agrihan
3,166 ft
965 m
Pagan
Northern
Mariana Is.
(U.S.)
Guguan
Sarigan
Anatahan
Mariana Islands
Garapan
Saipan
Tinian
Rota
Agana
(Hagåtña)
Guam
(U.S.)
Mt. Lamlam 1,332 ft
406 m
MARSHALL
ISLANDS
Bikini Atoll
Enewetak
Atoll
Ujelang
Ulithi
Gaferut
Namonuito
Hall Is.
Oroluk
Palikir
Mwokil
Colonia
Yap Is.
Fais
Faraulep
Pikelot
Ului
Pulap
Weno
Chuuk Is.
Pohnpei
Pingelap
Kosrae
Ngatik
Ngulu
Sorol
Olimarao
Puluwat
Woleai
Ifalik
Elato
Namoluk
Etal
Caroline Islands
Ngcheangel
Babeldaob
Melekeok
Palau Is.
Satawan
Mortlock Is.
MICRONESIA
Nukuoro
PALAU
Pulo Anna
OCEAN
Kapingamarangi
Tobi
Helen Reef
Equator
Mindanao
DAVAO
Tagum
Bislig
Cape San Agustin
Karakelong
Sangihe
Morotai
C. Lelai
5,627 ft
1,715 m
Halmahera
Ternate
Waigeo
Kasiruta
Sorong
Manokwari
Biak
Salawati
Doberai
Pen.
9,744 ft
2,970 m
Yapen
Serui
Sarera Bay
D'Urville C.
Jayapura
Vanimo
Mamberamo
Bacan
Obi
Misool
Sanana
Seram Sea
Namlea
Buru
Ambon
Amahai
Binaia
9,646 ft
2,940 m
Seram
Fakfak
4,889 ft
1,490 m
Kaimana
Nabire
Maoke Range
Enarotali
16,024 ft
4,884 m
Carstensz Pyramid
(Puncak Jayakesuma)
15,519 ft
4,730 m
Oksibil
Amamapare
Adi
Bandanaira
Tual
Kai Is.
Dobo
Wokam
Kobroor
Aru Is.
Trangan
Banda Sea
Damar Is.
Yamdena
Saumlaki
Tanimbar Is.
Babar
Wetar
Leti Is.
Selaru
TIMOR-LESTE
Arafura Sea
Dolak
Merauke
Digul
Fly
Sepik
Wewak
Ninigo Is.
Kaniet Is.
Admiralty Is.
Lorengau
Manus I.
Lou I.
Rambutyo
St. Matthias Is.
New Hanover
Kavieng
Tabar Is.
Lihir Is.
Nuguria Is.
New Ireland
Bismarck Arch.
Schouten Is.
Bismarck Sea
Karkar I.
Namatanai
Rabaul
Kokopo
7,871 ft
2,399 m
6,769 ft
2,063 m
Feni Is.
Green Is.
Tulun Is.
Takuu Is.
Nukumanu Is.
Ontong Java Atoll
St. George's Channel
Buka
Mt. Balbi
8,809 ft
2,685 m
Bougainville I.
Arawa
Choiseul
PAPUA NEW GUINEA
Kimbe
Long I.
Madang
Wabag
Mount Hagen
Mendi
14,794 ft
4,509 m
Mt. Wilhelm
Goroka
4,367 m
14,328 ft
Mt. Giluwe
Kundiawa
Kiunga
Umboi I.
New Britain
Lae
Bulolo
Kikori
Kerema
Solomon Sea
Solomon Islands
Trobriand Is.
Kiriwina I.
Woodlark I.
Owen Stanley Ra.
Popondetta
Fergusson I.
D'Entrecasteaux Is.
Normanby I.
Gulf of Papua
Mt. Victoria
13,363 ft
4,073 m
Port Moresby
Esa'ala
Alotau
Samarai
Abau
Misima I.
Louisiade Arch.
Rossel I.
Tagula I.
Santa Isabel
Malaita
4,702 ft
1,433 m
Buala
Auki
Tulaghi
Gizo
New Georgia Is.
Honiara
Mt. Makarakomburu
8,028 ft
2,447 m
Guadalcanal
Kirakira
San Cristobal
Rennell
SOLOMON
ISLANDS
Daru
Torres Strait
Badu
Moa
Prince of Wales I.
Cape York
Bamaga
Cape York Pen.
Coen
Melville I.
Croker I.
Wessel Is.
Cape Wessel
Cape Arnhem
Bathurst I.
Darwin
Jabiru
1,201 ft
366 m
Timor Sea
AUSTRALIA
Gulf of Carpentaria
Coral Sea
161
167
166
KLETT-PERTHES

Land Cover
(Explanations on page 32)
Natural Vegetation
Evergreen needleleaf forests
Evergreen broadleaf forests
Deciduous needleleaf forests
Deciduous broadleaf forests
Mixed forests
Closed shrublands
Open shrublands
Woody savannas
Savannas
Grasslands
Permanent wetlands
Developed and Mosaic Lands
Croplands
Cropland/natural vegetation mosaic
Urban and built-up lands
Non-Vegetated Lands
Snow and ice
Barren or sparsely vegetated
Water bodies
No data
Philippine Sea
South China Sea
INDIAN OCEAN
Australia
Great Australian Bight
Arafura Sea
Timor Sea
Banda Sea
Java Sea
Celebes Sea
Sulu Sea
Solomon Sea
Coral
Bay of Bengal
Andaman Sea
Great Sunda Is.
Lesser Sunda Is.
Moluccas
New Guinea
Great Barrier Reef
Great Dividing Range
Gt. Victoria Desert
Nullarbor Plain
Macdonnell Ra.
Arnhem Land
Cape York Pen.
Gulf of Carpentaria
Tasmania
Sydney
Melbourne
Adelaide
Perth
Brisbane
Borneo (Kalimantan)
Celebes (Sulawesi)
Sumatra
Java
Mindanao
Luzon
Taiwan
Hainan
Caroline
Micronesia
Melanesia
Bismarck Arch.
Halmahera
Timor
Flores
Sumba
Bali
Madura
Jakarta
Singapore
Bangkok
Rangoon
Kolkata
Manila
Guangzhou
Himalayas
Maoke Range
Austral. Alps
Equator
1
2
3
4
5
9

1:35,000,000

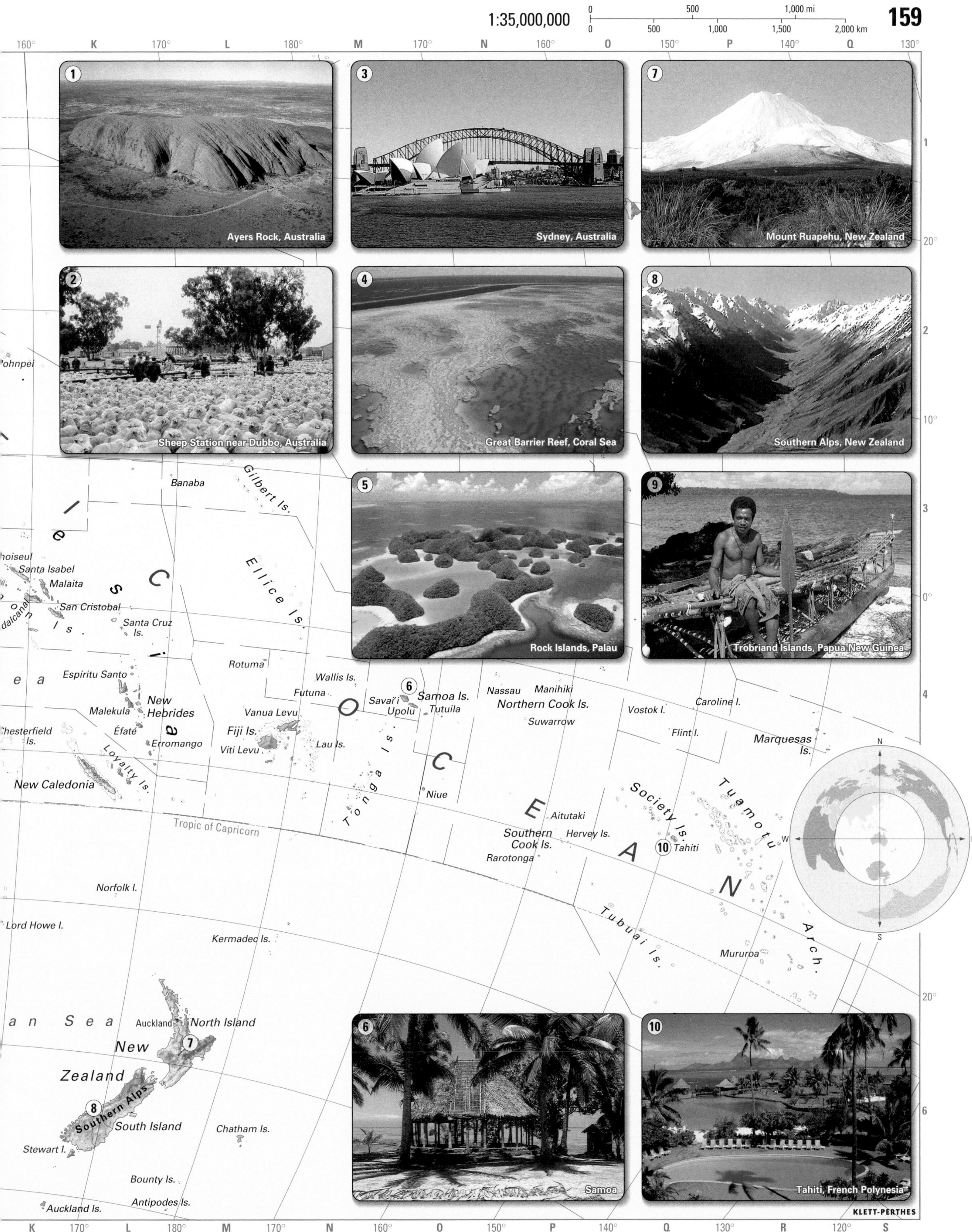

Ayers Rock, Australia
Sydney, Australia
Mount Ruapehu, New Zealand
Sheep Station near Dubbo, Australia
Great Barrier Reef, Coral Sea
Southern Alps, New Zealand
Rock Islands, Palau
Trobriand Islands, Papua New Guinea
Banaba
Gilbert Is.
Ellice Is.
Santa Isabel
Malaita
San Cristobal
Santa Cruz Is.
Rotuma
Espíritu Santo
Malekula
New Hebrides
Éfaté
Erromango
Wallis Is.
Futuna
Savai'i
Upolu
Samoa Is.
Tutuila
Nassau
Manihiki
Northern Cook Is.
Suwarrow
Vostok I.
Caroline I.
Flint I.
Marquesas Is.
Vanua Levu
Fiji Is.
Viti Levu
Lau Is.
Loyalty Is.
New Caledonia
Tonga Is.
Niue
Society Is.
Tuamotu Arch.
Aitutaki
Hervey Is.
Southern Cook Is.
Rarotonga
Tahiti
Tropic of Capricorn
Norfolk I.
Lord Howe I.
Kermadec Is.
Tubuai Is.
Mururoa
OCEAN
North Island
Auckland
New Zealand
Southern Alps
South Island
Stewart I.
Chatham Is.
Bounty Is.
Antipodes Is.
Auckland Is.
Samoa
Tahiti, French Polynesia
KLETT-PERTHES

B
90°
C
100°
D
110°
E
120°
F
130°
G
140°
H
150°
Mt. Everest
29,035 ft
8,850 m
NEP.
Kathmandu
Thimphu
BHU.
Himalayas
Brahmaputra
19,295 ft
5,881 m
Yangtze
CHANGSHA
NANCHANG
Wenzhou
GUIYANG
FUZHOU
JAPAN
Naha
Ryukyu Is.
T'AIPEI
Taiwan Str.
C H I N A
KUNMING
Xi Jiang
GUANGZHOU
SHANTOU
12,966 ft
3,952 m
TAIWAN
I N D I A
BANGLA-
DHAKA
DESH
Ganges
Nanning
HONG KONG
Macau
Daito Is.
(JAP.)
Bonin Is.
(JAP.)
Volcano Is.
(JAP.)
Marcus I.
(JAP.)
Okino Tori
(JAP.)
Mandalay
Salween
Arakan Yoma
KOLKATA
MYANMAR
HANOI
Hai Phong
8,199 ft
2,499 m
G. of Tonkin
9,242 ft
2,817 m
Vientiane
LAOS
Hainan
6,126 ft
1,867 m
9,610 ft
2,929 m
Luzon
Philippine Sea
Northern
Mariana Is.
(U.S.)
Saipan
Garapan
20°
Bay of
Bengal
RANGOON
THAILAND
Mekong
Huë
Da Năng
Paracel Is.
(CHN.)
MANILA
Guam (U.S.)
Agana
BANGKOK
Tônlé
Sap
CAMBODIA
PHNUM PENH
HÔ CHI MINH
CITY
Nha Trang
7,438 ft
2,267 m
18,238 ft
5,559 m
Mindoro
PHILIPPINES
Samar
Panay
Cebu
Negros
34,439 ft
10,497 m
Vityaz Depth
36,204 ft
11,035 m
Andaman Is.
(IND.)
Yap Is.
M I C R O N E S I A
Andaman
Sea
G. of
Thailand
South China Sea
Palawan
Sulu Sea
Zamboanga
Mt. Apo
9,692 ft
2,954 m
DAVAO
Mindanao
Palau
Is.
Melekeok
PALAU
Chuuk
Is.
Caroline
10°
Kinabalu
13,455 ft
4,101 m
Bandar Seri Begawan
BRUNEI
Sulu Arch.
Sangir
Is.
Celebes
Sea
Nicobar Is.
(IND.)
M A L A Y S I A
Malay Pen.
Manado
Molucca Sea
Halmahera
Melanesia
KUALA LUMPUR
Str. of Malacca
MEDAN
Sumatra
Kuching
9,702 ft
2,957 m
Borneo
(Kalimantan)
Samarinda
Makassar Str.
Moluccas
Biak
Admiralty
Is.
SINGAPORE
SINGAPORE
Pekanbaru
Pontianak
7,474 ft
2,278 m
10,863 ft
3,311 m
Celebes
(Sulawesi)
Seram
Jayapura
Bismarck
Arch.
Rabaul
New
Ireland
INDONESIA
Padang
Mentawai Is.
Banjarmasin
Buru
Ambon
16,024 ft
4,884 m
Carstensz
Pyramid
Maoke Range
New Guinea
Sepik
PAPUA
Mt. Wilhelm
14,794 ft
4,509 m
8,809 ft
2,685 m
New Britain
Bougainville
0°
PALEMBANG
Greater Sunda Is.
UJUNG PANDANG
11,336 ft
3,455 m
Buton
Banda Sea
Kai Is.
Aru
Is.
Lae
Solomon
Sea
Java Sea
Tanimbar
Is.
Dolak
NEW GUINEA
13,363 ft
4,073 m
Mt. Victoria
Port Moresby
Fly
JAKARTA
SEMARANG
Madura
SURABAYA
Lesser Sunda Is.
Dili
TIMOR-
LESTE
Arafura Sea
Torres Str.
C. York
Sunda Str.
BANDUNG
11,260 ft
3,432 m
Semeru
12,061 ft
3,676 m
Java
Bali
12,225 ft
3,726 m
9,354 ft
2,851 m
Flores
Sumba
Kupang
Melville I.
Darwin
C. Arnhem
Louisiade
Arch.
Timor
Sea
Ashmore
(AUS.)
Cartier
Arnhem
Land
Gulf of
Carpentaria
Cape
York
Pen.
Christmas I.
(AUS.)
Cairns
5,322 ft
1,622 m
Great Barrier Reef
Coral
Coral Sea
(AUS.)
Cocos Is.
(AUS.)
10°
Derby
Fitzroy
Flinders
Townsville
Mount Isa
Mackay
Port Hedland
5,023 ft
1,531 m
Macdonnell Ra.
Alice Springs
Rockhampton
North West Cape
4,111 ft
1,253 m
Ayers Rock
2,844 ft
867 m
Great Dividing Range
Fraser
AUSTRALIA
Carnarvon
4,708 ft
1,435 m
BRISB.
Gold
L. Eyre
Cooper Cr.
-39 ft
-12 m
Gt. Victoria Desert
20°
Geraldton
Broken Hill
Darling
5,276 ft
1,608 m
Nullarbor Plain
Ceduna
Port
Augusta
3,901 ft
1,189 m
Newcastle
SYDNEY
Wollongong
PERTH
Great
Australian Bight
ADELAIDE
Murray
Canberra
Mt. Kosciusko
7,310 ft
2,228 m
Austral. Alps
Kangaroo I.
Cape Leeuwin
Albany
Geelong
MELBOURNE
Tasman
18,605 ft
5,671 m
King I.
Bass Str.
5,305 ft
1,617 m
Tasmania
Hobart
South East Cape
INDIAN OCEAN
Elevation
13,124 ft
6,562 ft
3,281 ft
1,640 ft
656 ft
0 ft
4,000 m
2,000 m
1,000 m
500 m
200 m
0 m
Depression
656 ft
6,562 ft
13,124 ft
19,686 ft
26,248 ft
200 m
2,000 m
4,000 m
6,000 m
8,000 m
Inland ice,
glaciers
Reef
* free association
with New Zealand
BHU. BHUTAN
NEP. NEPAL
C 100°
D
110°
E
120°
F
130°
G
140°
H
150°
J
1
2
3
4
5
6

1:35,000,000

0 500 1,000 mi
0 500 1,000 1,500 2,000 km
PACIFIC OCEAN
UNITED STATES
Hawaiian Islands
Midway Is. (U.S.)
Tropic of Cancer
Oahu
Honolulu
Maui
Mauna Kea 13,796 ft 4,205 m
Hawaii
Wake I. (U.S.)
Johnston Atoll (U.S.)
Polynesia
Micronesia
Melanesia
Enewetak Atoll
Bikini Atoll
Ralik Chain
Ratak Chain
MARSHALL ISLANDS
Majuro
Delap-Uliga-Djarrit
Palikir
Pohnpei
Kosrae
Kingman Reef (U.S.)
Palmyra Atoll
Line Islands
Teraina
Tabuaeran
Kiritimati
Tarawa
Bairiki
Gilbert Is.
Yaren
NAURU
Banaba
KIRIBATI
Howland I. (U.S.)
Baker I.
Kanton
Phoenix Is.
Jarvis I. (U.S.)
Equator
SOLOMON ISLANDS
Santa Isabel
Malaita
Honiara
8,028 ft 2,447 m
San Cristobal
Santa Cruz Is.
TUVALU
Ellice Is.
Funafuti
Vaiaku
Malden I.
Atafu
Tokelau (N.Z.)
Starbuck I.
Northern Cook Is.
Penrhyn
Pukapuka
Rotuma
Wallis and Futuna (FRA.)
Wallis Is.
Futuna
Matā'utu
SAMOA
6,096 ft 1,858 m
Savai'i
Apia
Upolu
American Samoa (U.S.)
Tutuila
Pago Pago
Nassau
Manihiki
Vostok I.
Caroline I.
Flint I.
Suwarrow
Marquesas Is.
Espíritu Santo
6,165 ft 1,879 m
VANUATU
New Hebrides
Malekula
Port Vila
Efaté
Erromango
Vanua Levu
Viti Levu
Suva
FIJI
Lau Is.
TONGA
Tonga Is.
COOK ISLANDS*
Chesterfield Is.
5,341 ft 1,628 m
New Caledonia (FRA.)
Nouméa
Loyalty Is.
Alofi
NIUE*
Nuku'alofa
Society Is.
Tuamotu Arch.
Aitutaki
Hervey Is.
Southern Cook Is.
Papeete
7,352 ft 2,241 m
Tahiti
Avarua
Rarotonga
French Polynesia
Tropic of Capricorn
17,398 ft 5,303 m
35,702 ft 10,882 m
19,819 ft 6,041 m
Norfolk (AUS.)
International Date Line
Lord Howe I. (AUS.)
Kermadec Is. (N.Z.)
Tubuai Is.
Mururoa
North Cape
32,962 ft 10,047 m
3,570 ft 1,088 m
Rapa
Oeno I.
Adamstown
Pitcairn I.
Pitcairn (U.K.)
Tasman Sea
Auckland
Hamilton
North Island
East Cape
NEW ZEALAND
Mt. Ruapehu 9,177 ft 2,797 m
Wellington
Mt. Cook 12,349 ft 3,764 m
Southern Alps
Christchurch
South Island
Dunedin
Stewart I.
South West Cape
Monday
Sunday
Chatham Is. (N.Z.)
Maria Theresa Reef
Bounty Is. (N.Z.)
Antipodes Is.
Auckland Is. (N.Z.)
14,271 ft 4,350 m
20,751 ft 6,325 m
24,002 ft 7,316 m
25,216 ft 7,686 m
KLETT-PERTHES

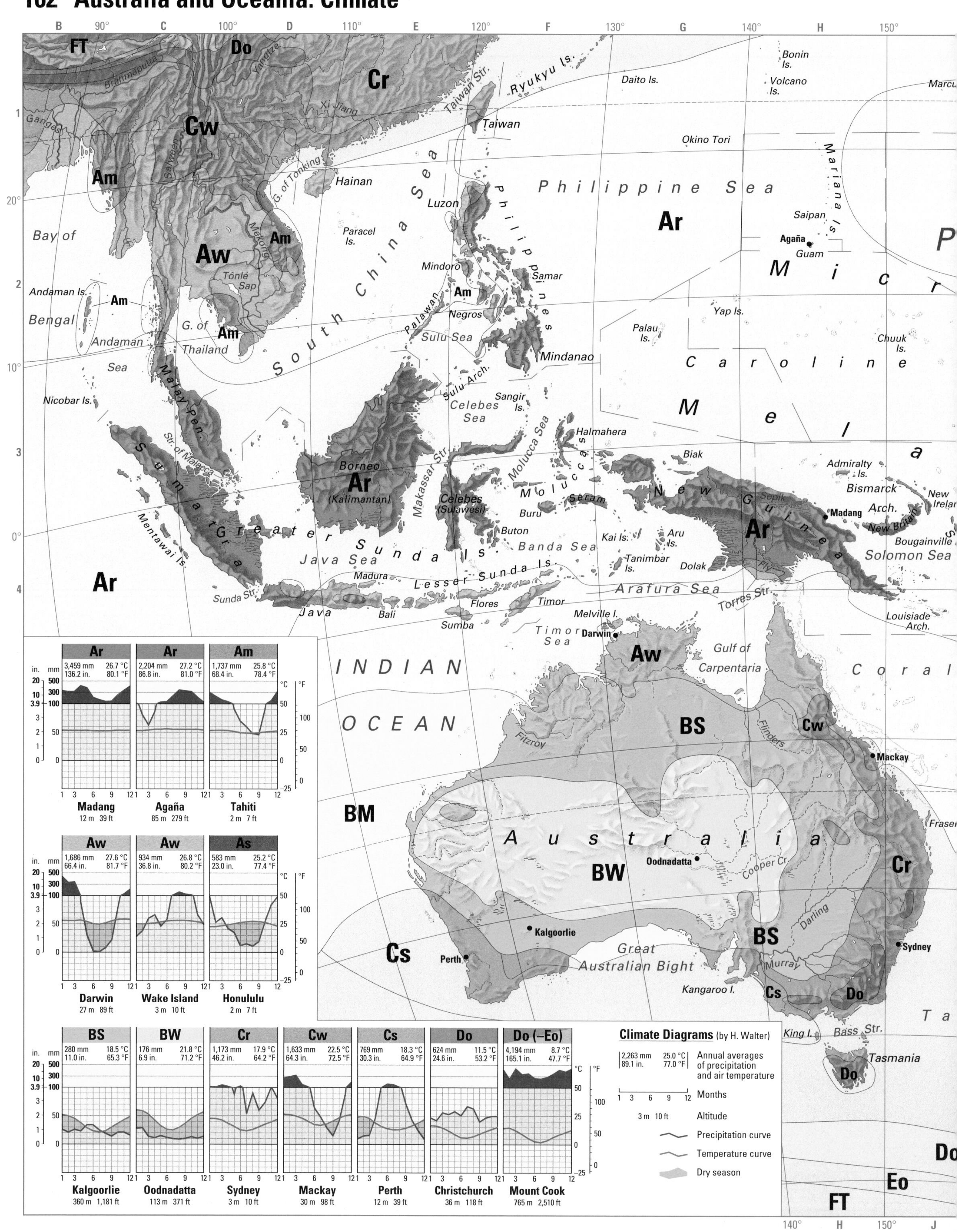

B 90° C 100° D 110° E 120° F 130° G 140° H 150°
1
20°
2
10°
3
0°
4
FT
Do
Cr
Cw
Am
Aw
Ar
BS
BW
BM
Cs
Eo
Brahmaputra
Yangtze
Ganges
Salween
Xi Jiang
Mekong
Tônle Sap
Ryukyu Is.
Taiwan Str.
Taiwan
Daito Is.
Bonin Is.
Volcano Is.
Okino Tori
Mariana Is.
Saipan
Agaña
Guam
Hainan
G. of Tonking
Paracel Is.
Luzon
Philippine Sea
Philippines
Mindoro
Samar
Negros
Palawan
Sulu Sea
Mindanao
Sulu Arch.
Bay of Bengal
Andaman Is.
Andaman Sea
G. of Thailand
Nicobar Is.
South China Sea
Malay Pen.
Str. of Malacca
Sumatra
Mentawai Is.
Borneo (Kalimantan)
Makassar Str.
Celebes Sea
Sangir Is.
Celebes (Sulawesi)
Molucca Sea
Moluccas
Halmahera
Buru
Seram
Buton
Banda Sea
Kai Is.
Aru Is.
Tanimbar Is.
Dolak
Greater Sunda Is.
Java Sea
Madura
Lesser Sunda Is.
Sunda Str.
Java
Bali
Flores
Timor
Sumba
Timor Sea
Arafura Sea
Torres Str.
Fly
Melville I.
Darwin
Micronesia
Melanesia
Yap Is.
Palau Is.
Caroline Is.
Chuuk Is.
Biak
Admiralty Is.
Bismarck Arch.
Madang
New Britain
New Ireland
Bougainville
Solomon Sea
New Guinea
Sepik
Louisiade Arch.
Marcus
INDIAN OCEAN
Gulf of Carpentaria
Coral Sea
Fitzroy
Flinders
Mackay
Fraser
Australia
Oodnadatta
Cooper Cr.
Darling
Kalgoorlie
Great Australian Bight
Perth
Sydney
Murray
Kangaroo I.
King I.
Bass Str.
Tasmania
Tasman

Madang | Ar | 3,459 mm 136.2 in. | 26.7 °C 80.1 °F | 12 m 39 ft
Agaña | Ar | 2,204 mm 86.8 in. | 27.2 °C 81.0 °F | 85 m 279 ft
Tahiti | Am | 1,737 mm 68.4 in. | 25.8 °C 78.4 °F | 2 m 7 ft
Darwin | Aw | 1,686 mm 66.4 in. | 27.6 °C 81.7 °F | 27 m 89 ft
Wake Island | Aw | 934 mm 36.8 in. | 26.8 °C 80.2 °F | 3 m 10 ft
Honolulu | As | 583 mm 23.0 in. | 25.2 °C 77.4 °F | 2 m 7 ft
Kalgoorlie | BS | 280 mm 11.0 in. | 18.5 °C 65.3 °F | 360 m 1,181 ft
Oodnadatta | BW | 176 mm 6.9 in. | 21.8 °C 71.2 °F | 113 m 371 ft
Sydney | Cr | 1,173 mm 46.2 in. | 17.9 °C 64.2 °F | 3 m 10 ft
Mackay | Cw | 1,633 mm 64.3 in. | 22.5 °C 72.5 °F | 30 m 98 ft
Perth | Cs | 769 mm 30.3 in. | 18.3 °C 64.9 °F | 12 m 39 ft
Christchurch | Do | 624 mm 24.6 in. | 11.5 °C 53.2 °F | 36 m 118 ft
Mount Cook | Do (–Eo) | 4,194 mm 165.1 in. | 8.7 °C 47.7 °F | 765 m 2,510 ft
in. mm 20 500 10 300 3.9 100 3 2 50 1 0 0
°C °F 50 100 25 50 0 0 -25
1 3 6 9 12

Climate Diagrams (by H. Walter)
2,263 mm 89.1 in. 25.0 °C 77.0 °F Annual averages of precipitation and air temperature
1 3 6 9 12 Months
3 m 10 ft Altitude
Precipitation curve
Temperature curve
Dry season
140° H 150° J

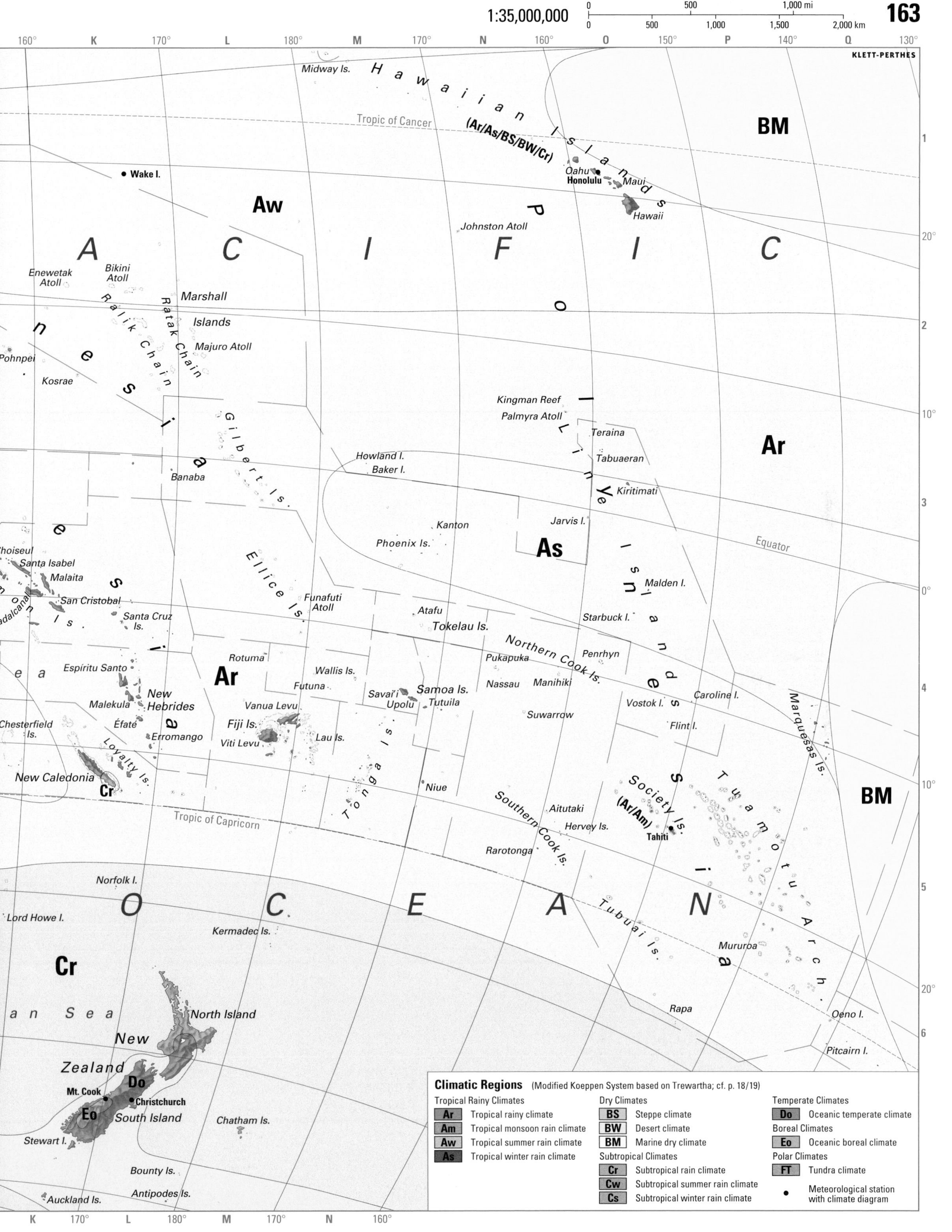
1:35,000,000
0 500 1,000 mi
0 500 1,000 1,500 2,000 km
KLETT-PERTHES
Midway Is.
Hawaiian Islands
(Ar/As/BS/BW/Cr)
Tropic of Cancer
BM
Wake I.
Oahu
Honolulu
Maui
Hawaii
Aw
Johnston Atoll
PACIFIC
OCEAN
Enewetak Atoll
Bikini Atoll
Marshall Islands
Ralik Chain
Ratak Chain
Majuro Atoll
Pohnpei
Kosrae
Micronesia
Polynesia
Melanesia
Gilbert Is.
Banaba
Kingman Reef
Palmyra Atoll
Line Is.
Teraina
Tabuaeran
Ar
Howland I.
Baker I.
Kiritimati
Kanton
Phoenix Is.
Jarvis I.
As
Equator
Choiseul
Santa Isabel
Malaita
Solomon Is.
San Cristobal
Ellice Is.
Funafuti Atoll
Malden I.
Atafu
Tokelau Is.
Starbuck I.
Santa Cruz Is.
Rotuma
Northern Cook Is.
Penrhyn
Pukapuka
Espíritu Santo
Ar
Wallis Is.
Futuna
Samoa Is.
Savai'i
Upolu
Tutuila
Nassau
Manihiki
Vostok I.
Caroline I.
New Hebrides
Malekula
Éfaté
Erromango
Vanua Levu
Fiji Is.
Viti Levu
Lau Is.
Suwarrow
Flint I.
Marquesas Is.
Chesterfield Is.
Loyalty Is.
New Caledonia
Cr
Tonga Is.
Niue
Society Is.
(Ar/Am)
Tahiti
Tuamotu Arch.
BM
Southern Cook Is.
Aitutaki
Hervey Is.
Rarotonga
Tropic of Capricorn
Norfolk I.
Lord Howe I.
Kermadec Is.
Tubuai Is.
Mururoa
Cr
Tasman Sea
North Island
New Zealand
Rapa
Oeno I.
Pitcairn I.
Do
Mt. Cook
Christchurch
Eo
South Island
Chatham Is.
Stewart I.
Bounty Is.
Antipodes Is.
Auckland Is.
Climatic Regions (Modified Koeppen System based on Trewartha; cf. p. 18/19)
Tropical Rainy Climates
Ar Tropical rainy climate
Am Tropical monsoon rain climate
Aw Tropical summer rain climate
As Tropical winter rain climate
Dry Climates
BS Steppe climate
BW Desert climate
BM Marine dry climate
Subtropical Climates
Cr Subtropical rain climate
Cw Subtropical summer rain climate
Cs Subtropical winter rain climate
Temperate Climates
Do Oceanic temperate climate
Boreal Climates
Eo Oceanic boreal climate
Polar Climates
FT Tundra climate
Meteorological station with climate diagram

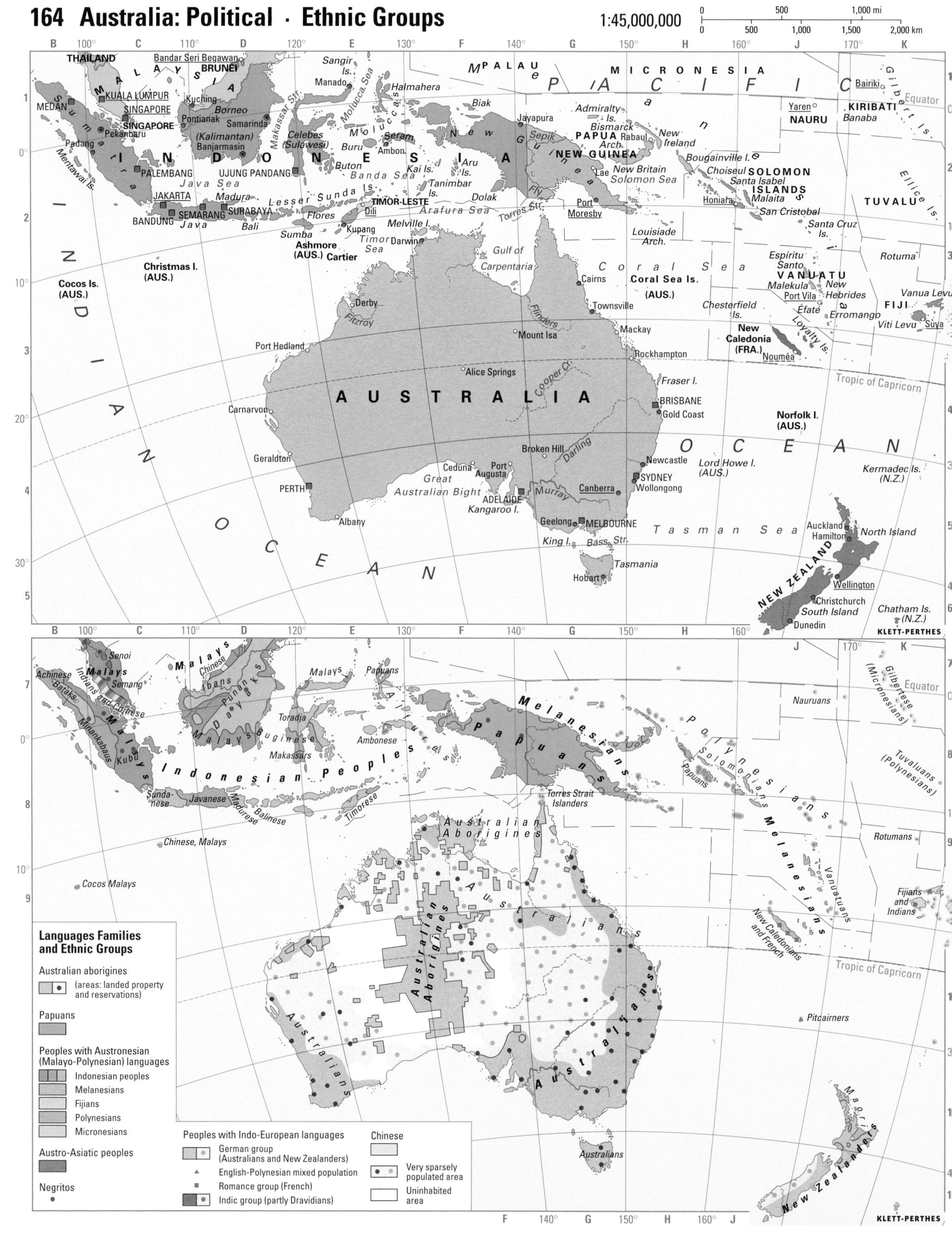

1:45,000,000
0 500 1,000 mi
0 500 1,000 1,500 2,000 km
THAILAND
Bandar Seri Begawan
BRUNEI
M A L A Y S I A
KUALA LUMPUR
SINGAPORE
MEDAN
Pekanbaru
Padang
Mentawai Is.
Sumatra
PALEMBANG
JAKARTA
BANDUNG
SEMARANG
SURABAYA
Java
Java Sea
Madura
Bali
Kuching
Pontianak
Borneo
(Kalimantan)
Banjarmasin
Samarinda
Makassar Str.
Celebes (Sulawesi)
UJUNG PANDANG
Sangir Is.
Manado
Molucca Sea
Halmahera
Moluccas
Buru
Seram
Ambon
Buton
Banda Sea
Kai Is.
Aru Is.
Tanimbar Is.
Lesser Sunda Is.
Flores
Sumba
Kupang
TIMOR-LESTE
Dili
Timor Sea
I N D O N E S I A
Biak
Jayapura
New Guinea
Sepik
Fly
Dolak
Arafura Sea
Torres Str.
PALAU
MICRONESIA
P A C I F I C
Admiralty Is.
Bismarck Arch.
Rabaul
New Ireland
PAPUA NEW GUINEA
Lae
New Britain
Solomon Sea
Port Moresby
Bougainville I.
Choiseul
Santa Isabel
SOLOMON ISLANDS
Malaita
Honiara
San Cristobal
Santa Cruz Is.
Louisiade Arch.
Bairiki
Gilbert Is.
Equator
Yaren
NAURU
KIRIBATI
Banaba
Ellice Is.
TUVALU
Rotuma
Espíritu Santo
VANUATU
Malekula
Port Vila
Éfaté
New Hebrides
Erromango
FIJI
Vanua Levu
Viti Levu
Suva
Loyalty Is.
New Caledonia (FRA.)
Nouméa
Chesterfield Is.
Coral Sea
Coral Sea Is. (AUS.)
Melville I.
Darwin
Ashmore (AUS.)
Cartier
Christmas I. (AUS.)
Cocos Is. (AUS.)
I N D I A N O C E A N
Gulf of Carpentaria
Cairns
Townsville
Flinders
Mackay
Mount Isa
Derby
Fitzroy
Port Hedland
Rockhampton
Alice Springs
Cooper Cr.
Fraser I.
A U S T R A L I A
BRISBANE
Gold Coast
Carnarvon
Norfolk I. (AUS.)
Tropic of Capricorn
Geraldton
Broken Hill
Darling
O C E A N
Lord Howe I. (AUS.)
Kermadec Is. (N.Z.)
Newcastle
SYDNEY
Wollongong
Canberra
Ceduna
Port Augusta
Great Australian Bight
ADELAIDE
Kangaroo I.
Murray
PERTH
Albany
Geelong
MELBOURNE
King I.
Bass Str.
Tasmania
Hobart
Tasman Sea
Auckland
Hamilton
North Island
NEW ZEALAND
Wellington
Christchurch
South Island
Dunedin
Chatham Is. (N.Z.)
KLETT-PERTHES
Senoi
Malays
Semang
Achinese
Bataks
Indians and Chinese
Minankabaus
Kubu
Chinese
Ibans
Punans
Dayaks
Toradja
Buginese
Makassars
Malays
Papuans
Alfures
Ambonese
Indonesian Peoples
Sunda-nese
Javanese
Madurese
Balinese
Timorese
Melanesians
Papuans
Polynesians
Solomon Papuans
Torres Strait Islanders
Australian Aborigines
Chinese, Malays
Cocos Malays
Australians
Nauruans
Gilbertese (Micronesians)
Tuvaluans (Polynesians)
Rotumans
Melanesians
Vanuatuans
Fijians and Indians
New Caledonians and French
Pitcairners
Maori
New Zealanders
Languages Families and Ethnic Groups
Australian aborigines
(areas: landed property and reservations)
Papuans
Peoples with Austronesian (Malayo-Polynesian) languages
Indonesian peoples
Melanesians
Fijians
Polynesians
Micronesians
Austro-Asiatic peoples
Negritos
Peoples with Indo-European languages
German group (Australians and New Zealanders)
English-Polynesian mixed population
Romance group (French)
Indic group (partly Dravidians)
Chinese
Very sparsely populated area
Uninhabited area
KLETT-PERTHES

Australia: Economy and Foreign Trade

1:45,000,000

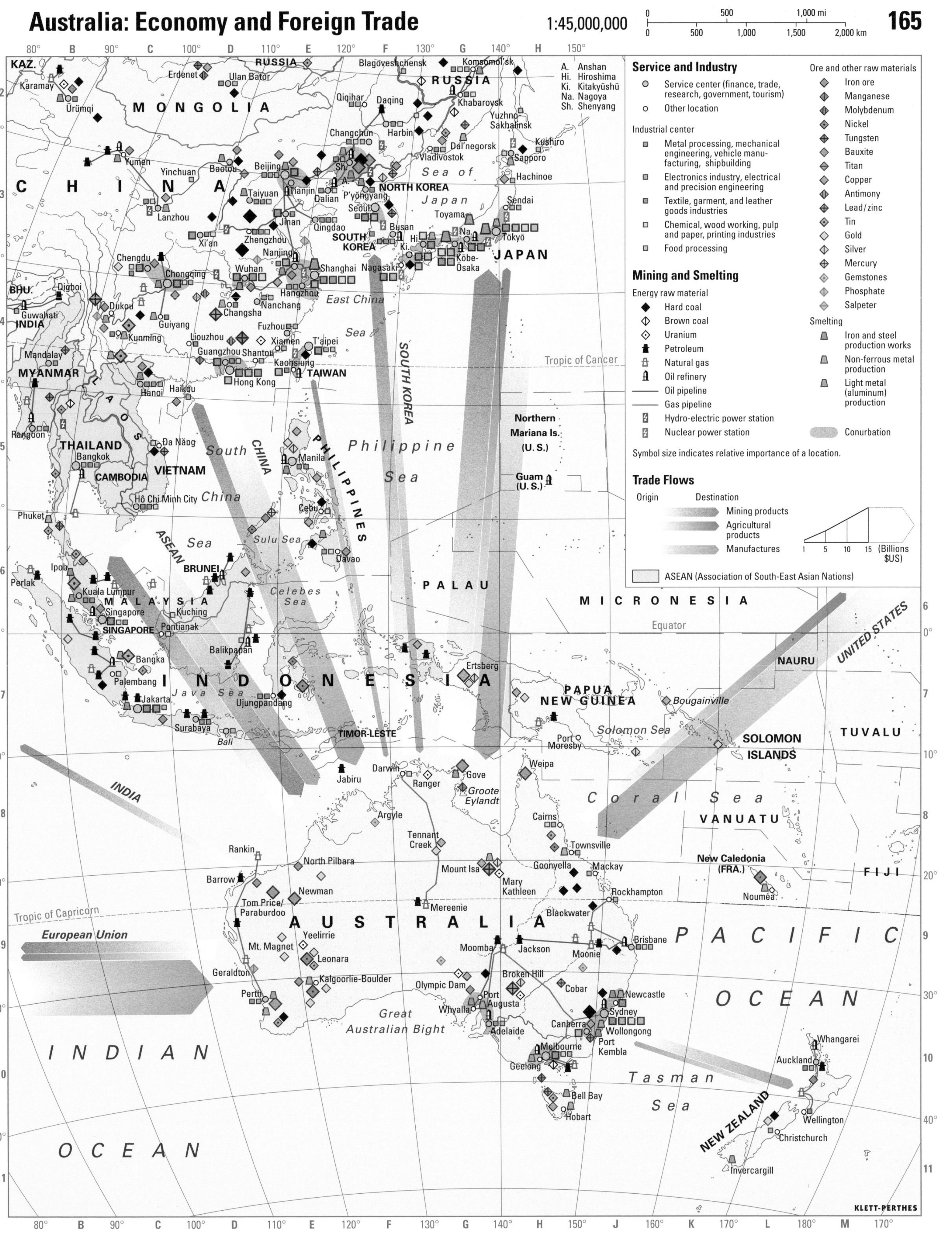

D 120° 156 E 125° F 130° G 135° H 140° J 145° 157 K 150° L

1 2 3 4 5 6 7 8 9 10

5° 10° 15° 20° 25° 30° 35° 40° 45°

Celebes (Sulawesi)
UJUNG PANDANG
Muna
Buton
Kabaena
Baubau
Banda Sea
Kai Is.
Kobroor
Aru Is.
Trangan
Damar Is.
INDONESIA
Kabia
Benteng
Sabalana Is.
Tanahjampea
Wetar
Babar
Yamdena
Tanimbar Is.
Saumlaki
Selaru
Dolak
Kangean Is.
Flores Sea
Lomblen
Alor
Huaki
Leti Is.
Dili
Bacau
Tutuala
TIMOR-LESTE
9,777 ft
2,980 m
Ramelau
Bali
12,225 ft
3,726 m
Bima
Labuhanbajo
7,874 ft
2,400 m
Maumere
Endeh
Flores
Mataram
Lombok
Denpasar
Sumbawa
Sumbawabesar
Waingapu
Savu Sea
Kefamenanu
Timor
4,019 ft
1,225 m
Kupang
Sumba
Sawu
Roti
Timor Sea
Ashmore
Ashmore Reef (AUS.)
and
Cartier Is.
Arafura Sea
Melville I.
Bathurst I.
Croker I.
Wessel Islands
Cape Wessel
Cape Arnhem
Darwin
1,201 ft
366 m
Jabiru
Arnhem Land
Pine Creek
Katherine
Gulf of Carpentaria
Groote Eylandt
Cape Londonderry
Joseph Bonaparte Gulf
Victoria
Wyndham
Larrimah
Daly Waters
Wellesley Islands
Kimberley
Mount Wells
3,183 ft
970 m
Cape Lévêque
Wave Hill
Derby
Broome
Fitzroy
Halls Creek
Northern Territory
Tanami Desert
Tanami
Tennant Creek
1,138 ft
347 m
Burketown
Camooweal
Great Sandy Desert
Yuendumu
Lake Mackay
Port Hedland
Marble Bar
Dampier
Roebourne
Barrow Is.
North West Cape
Onslow
Western Australia
Hamersley Range
4,111 ft
1,253 m
Ashburton
Newman
Gibson Desert
5,023 ft
1,531 m
Macdonnell Ranges
Alice Springs
Ayers Rock (Uluru)
2,845 ft
867 m
Kulgera Roadhouse
Simpson Desert
Musgrave Ra.
4,708 ft
1,435 m
AUSTRALIA
Gascoyne
Carnarvon
Lake Carnegie
2,169 ft
661 m
Wiluna
Meekatharra
Cape Inscription
Denham
Murchison
Great Victoria Desert
Mount Magnet
Leonara
Laverton
Lake Barlee
Mullewa
Geraldton
Dongara
Lake Moore
Menzies
Kalgoorlie-Boulder
Coolgardie
Rawlinna
Nullarbor Plain
Cook
Tarcoola
Moora
Meeredin
Norseman
PERTH
Northam
Mandurah
Collie
Narrogin
Katanning
3,642 ft
1,110 m
Bunbury
Esperance
Augusta
Cape Leeuwin
Cranbrook
Albany
Eucla
Fowlers Bay
Ceduna
Great Australian Bight
INDIAN OCEAN
Oodnadatta
Lake Eyre Basin
South Australia
Lake Eyre
-39 ft
-12 m
Coober Pedy
Marree
Lake Torrens
Leigh Creek
Kingoonya
Lake Gairdner
3,901 ft
1,189 m
Port Augusta
Whyalla
Streaky Bay
Kimba
Spencer Gulf
Port Pirie
Peterborough
Wallaroo
Mount Hope
Port Lincoln
ADELAIDE
Victor Harbour
Murray Bridge
Kangaroo Island
Kingscote
Innamincka
Cooper Creek
112 ft
34 m
Lake Frome
Broken Hill
Papua New Guinea
New Guinea
Digul
Fly
Merauke
Gulf of Papua
Daru
Kikori
Kundiawa
Goroka
Lae
Bulolo
Kerema
Mt. Victoria
13,363 ft 4,073 m
Port Moresby
Owen Stanley Ra.
Popondetta
Solomon Sea
Trobriand Is.
Kiriwina I.
Fergusson I.
D'Entrecasteaux
Normanby
Esa'ala
Alotau
Abau
Samarai
Louisiade Arch.
PAPUA NEW GUINEA
Torres Strait
Badu
Moa
Prince of Wales I.
Cape York
Bamaga
Cape York Pen.
Coen
Cooktown
Mossman
Cairns
Mareeba
Bartle Frere
5,322 ft
1,622 m
Innisfail
Ingham
Coral Sea
(AUS.)
Normanton
Croydon
Forsayth
Flinders
Townsville
Bowen
Charters Towers
Kajabbi
Cloncurry
Mount Isa
Richmond
Hughenden
4,131 ft
1,259 m
Mackay
Dajarra
Winton
Great Dividing Range
Georgina
Queensland
Diamantina
Clermont
Rockhampton
761 ft
232 m
Longreach
Barcaldine
Emerald
Blackall
Gladstone
Bundaberg
Monto
Great Artesian Basin
Yaraka
Windorah
Birdsville
Tambo
Theodore
Gayndah
Maryborough
Murgon
Injune
Charleville
Quilpie
Roma
Miles
Caloundra
3,750 ft
1,143 m
Dalby
Toowoomba
Warwick
Cunnamulla
Dirranbandi
Goondiwindi
Thargomindah
Gold Coast
272 ft
83 m
Lismore
Grafton
Milparinka
Warrego
Walgett
Moree
5,276 ft
1,608 m
Narrabri
Armidale
Bourke
Coffs Harbour
New South Wales
Coonamble
Tamworth
Cobar
Nyngan
Dubbo
Darling
Ivanhoe
Parkes
Orange
Cessnock
Lithgow
Newcastle
Katoomba
SYDNEY
4,600 ft
1,402 m
Wentworth
Renmark
Mildura
Balranald
Griffith
Wagga Wagga
Goulburn
Wollongong
Narrandera
Canberra
Nowra
Swan Hill
Murray
Albury
Wodonga
Mt. Kosciusko
7,310 ft
2,228 m
Australian Alps
Shepparton
Bendigo
Wangaratta
Bega
Bombala
Horsham
Victoria
Naracoorte
Hamilton
MELBOURNE
Orbost
Cape Howe
Ballarat
Bairnsdale
Mount Gambier
Geelong
Sale
Moe
Portland
Warrnambool
Wonthaggi
Bass Strait
King Island
Currie
Furneaux Is.
Cape Grim
Stanley
Burnie
Devonport
Launceston
Mt. Ossa
5,305 ft
1,617 m
Queenstown
Tasmania
Hobart
South East Cape

A 105° B 110° C 115° D 120° E 125° F 130° G 135° H 140° J 145° K 150° L

KLETT-PERTHES

1:20,000,000
SOLOMON ISLANDS
Solomon Islands
Choiseul
Santa Isabel
New Georgia
Malaita
4,702 ft
1,433 m
Honiara
8,028 ft
2,447 m
Guadalcanal
Mt. Makarakomburu
San Cristobal
Rennell
Santa Cruz Islands
Tikopia
VANUATU
New Hebrides
Espíritu Santo
Mt. Tabwemasana
6,165 ft
1,879 m
Port Vila
Efaté
Erromango
Tanna
Anatom
New Caledonia
(FRA.)
Mont Panié
5,341 ft 1,628 m
Nouméa
Loyalty Is.
Île des Pins
TUVALU
Ellice Islands
Funafuti
Rotuma
Wallis and Futuna
(FRA.)
FIJI
Vanua Levu
Viti Levu
Mt. Victoria
(Tomanivi)
4,337 ft
1,322 m
Suva
Lau Islands
KIRIBATI
Phoenix Islands
Tokelau
(N.Z.)
SAMOA
Samoa Islands
Apia
American Samoa
(U.S.)
Pago Pago
TONGA
Nuku'alofa
Tongatapu
Niue
Alofi
NIUE*
COOK ISLANDS*
Tropic of Capricorn
Norfolk Island
(AUS.)
Lord Howe I.
(AUS.)
PACIFIC OCEAN
Kermadec Is.
(N.Z.)
Tasman Sea
Three Kings
North Cape
Whangarei
Great Barrier Island
North Shore
Auckland
Manukau
Hamilton
Tauranga
Bay of Plenty
East Cape
North Island
Rotorua
Mt. Egmont
(Taranaki) 8,261 ft 2,518 m
Mt. Ruapehu
9,177 ft
2,797 m
Napier
Hawke Bay
Hastings
Palmerston North
Wellington
Lower Hutt
Nelson
Cook Strait
Southern Alps
Mount Cook
12,349 ft
3,764 m
Christchurch
South Island
Dunedin
Invercargill
Stewart I.
South West Cape
NEW ZEALAND
Chatham Is.
(N.Z.)
Bounty Is.
(N.Z.)
Antipodes Is.
(N.Z.)
Auckland Is.
(N.Z.)
* free association
with New Zealand

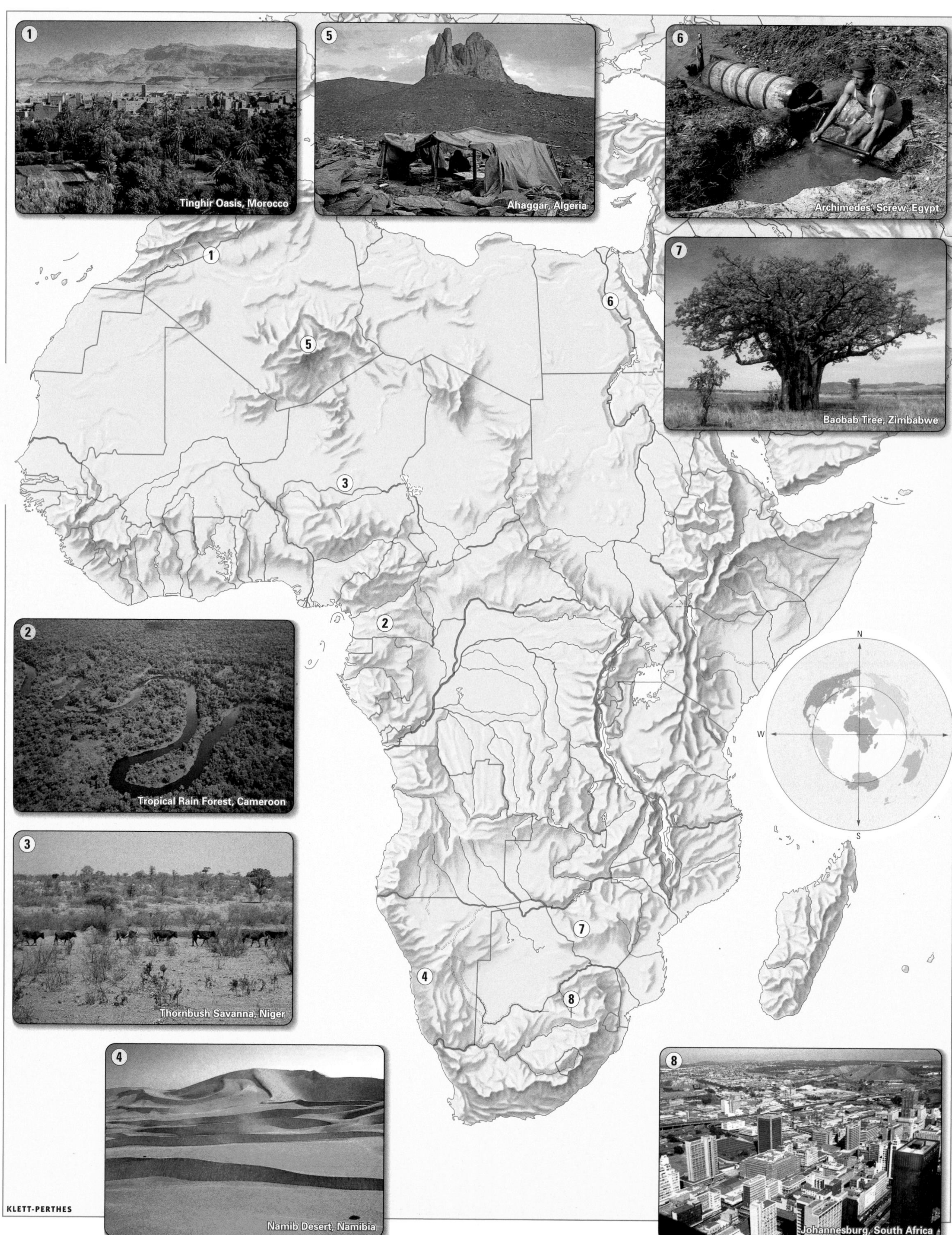
1
Tinghir Oasis, Morocco
5
Ahaggar, Algeria
6
Archimedes' Screw, Egypt
7
Baobab Tree, Zimbabwe
2
Tropical Rain Forest, Cameroon
3
Thornbush Savanna, Niger
4
Namib Desert, Namibia
8
Johannesburg, South Africa
N
W
E
S

Africa: Physical

1:40,000,000

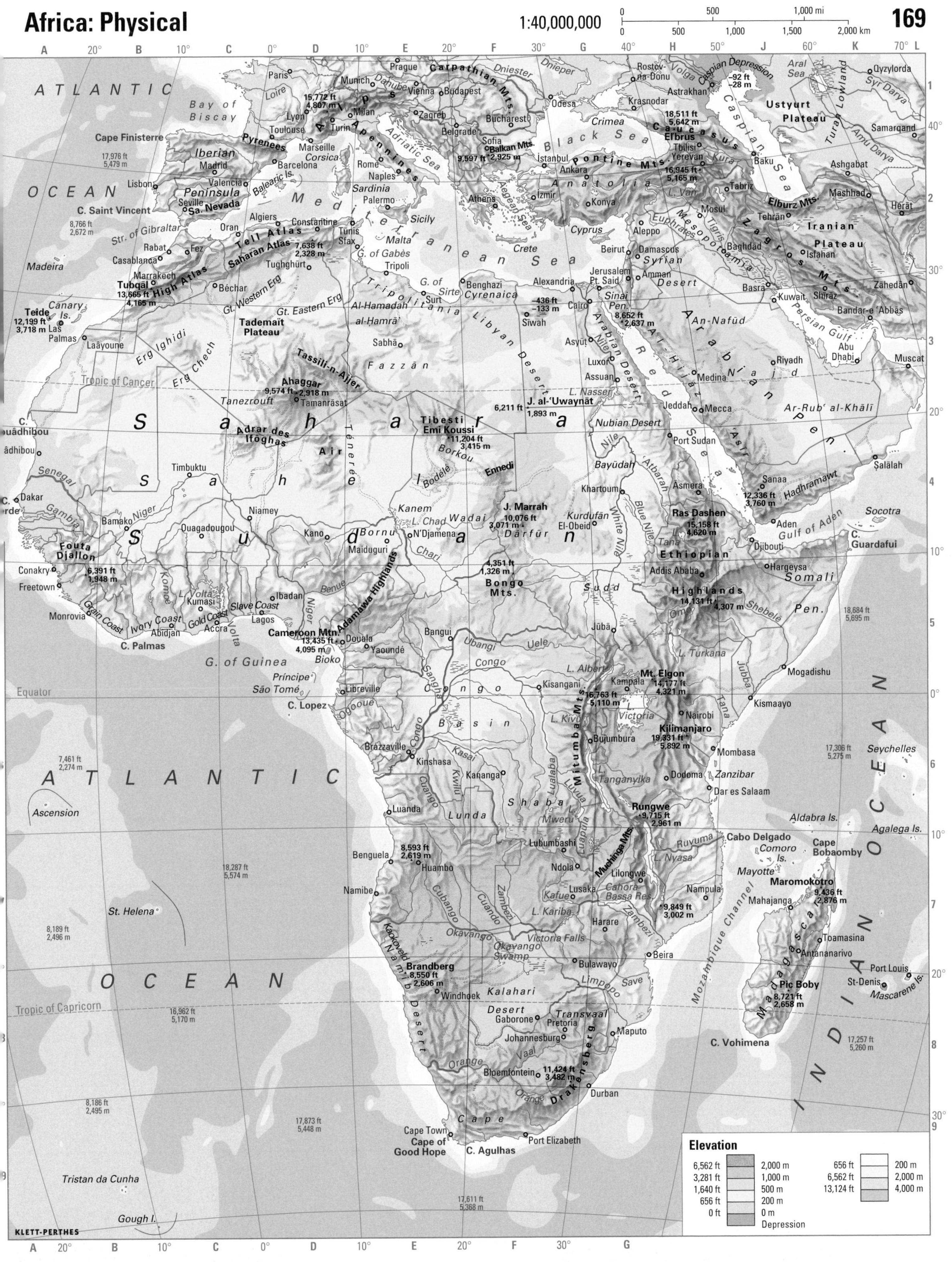

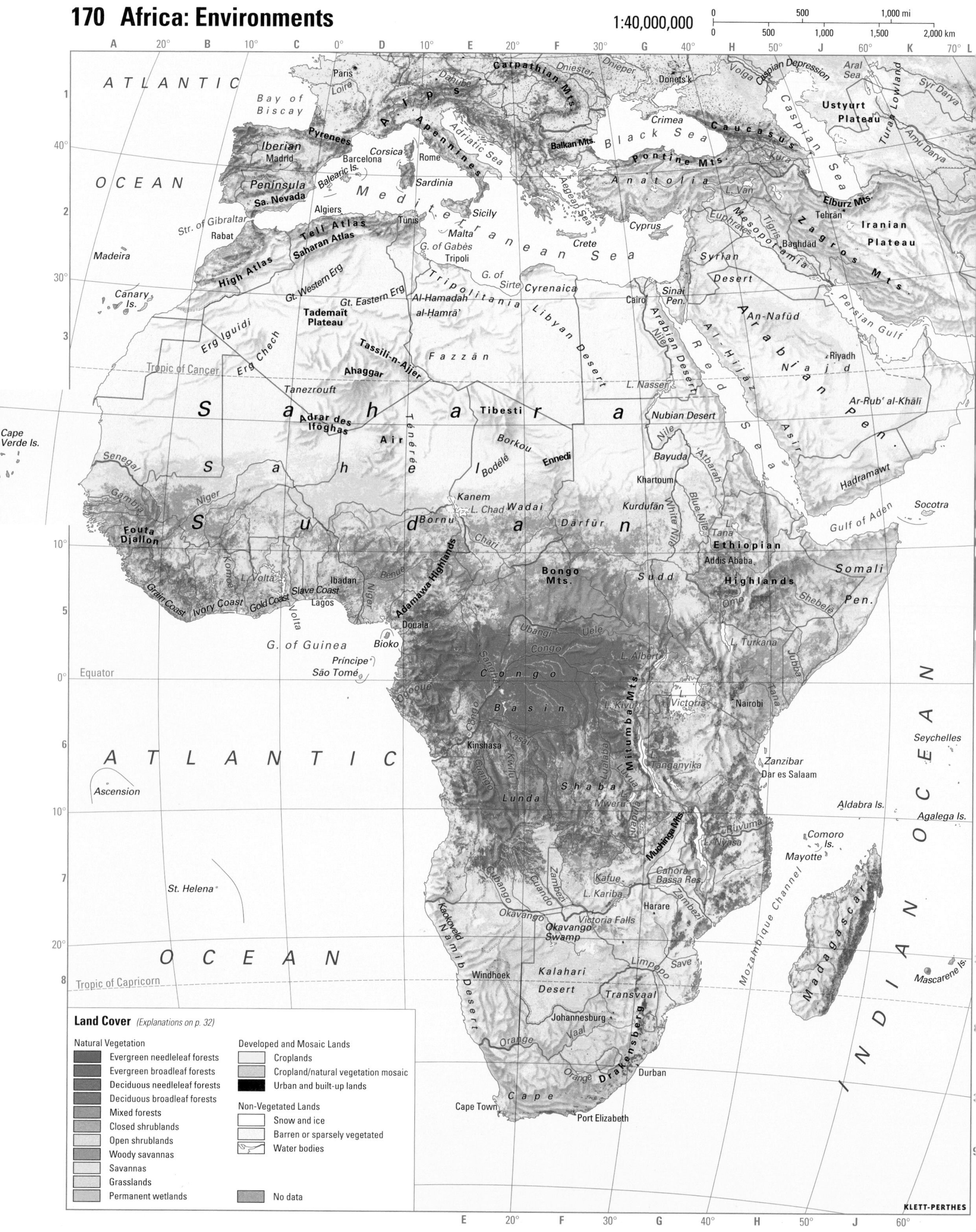
1:40,000,000
0 500 1,000 mi
0 500 1,000 1,500 2,000 km
ATLANTIC OCEAN
Bay of Biscay
Paris
Loire
Danube
Alps
Carpathian Mts.
Dniester
Dnieper
Donets'k
Volga
Caspian Depression
Aral Sea
Syr Darya
Ustyurt Plateau
Turan Lowland
Amu Darya
Caspian Sea
Crimea
Black Sea
Caucasus
Kura
Pyrenees
Iberian Peninsula
Madrid
Sa. Nevada
Barcelona
Balearic Is.
Corsica
Rome
Sardinia
Apennines
Adriatic Sea
Balkan Mts.
Pontine Mts.
Anatolia
Aegean Sea
L. Van
Elburz Mts.
Tehrān
Iranian Plateau
Zagros Mts.
Mediterranean Sea
Sicily
Malta
Crete
Cyprus
Euphrates
Tigris
Mesopotamia
Baghdād
Str. of Gibraltar
Rabat
Algiers
Tunis
Tell Atlas
Saharan Atlas
High Atlas
Madeira
Canary Is.
G. of Gabès
Tripoli
G. of Sirte
Cyrenaica
Tripolitania
Syrian Desert
Sinai Pen.
Cairo
Persian Gulf
Gt. Western Erg
Gt. Eastern Erg
Tademaït Plateau
Al-Hamadah al-Hamrā'
Libyan Desert
Arabian Desert
Nile
An-Nafūd
Erg Iguidi
Erg Chech
Tassili-n-Ajjer
Fazzān
Riyadh
Najd
Tropic of Cancer
Ahaggar
Tanezrouft
L. Nasser
Red Sea
Al-Hijaz
Arabian Pen.
Ar-Rub' al-Khālī
Sahara
Adrar des Ifôghas
Tibesti
Nubian Desert
Asir
Cape Verde Is.
Aïr
Ténéré
Borkou
Ennedi
Bodélé
Bayuda
'Atbarah
Senegal
Sahel
Khartoum
Hadramawt
Gambia
Niger
Kanem
L. Chad
Wadai
Kurdufān
White Nile
Blue Nile
Socotra
Gulf of Aden
Sudan
Fouta Djallon
Bornu
Dārfūr
L. Tana
Ethiopian Highlands
Addis Ababa
Somali Pen.
Chari
Bongo Mts.
Sudd
Komoe
L. Volta
Ibadan
Benue
Adamawa Highlands
Shebele
Omo
Grain Coast
Ivory Coast
Gold Coast
Slave Coast
Lagos
Volta
Douala
Ubangi
Uele
G. of Guinea
Bioko
L. Turkana
Príncipe
São Tomé
Congo
L. Albert
Jubba
Equator
Sangha
Congo Basin
Mitumba Mts.
L. Victoria
Nairobi
Ogooué
L. Kivu
Tana
Kinshasa
Kasai
Seychelles
ATLANTIC
Cuango
Kwilu
Lualaba
Tanganyika
Zanzibar
Dar es Salaam
Shaba
Luvua
Ascension
Lunda
Mweru
Luapula
Aldabra Is.
Agalega Is.
Muchinga Mts.
Ruvuma
L. Nyasa
Comoro Is.
Mayotte
INDIAN OCEAN
Cubango
Cuando
Zambezi
Kafue
Cahora Bassa Res.
St. Helena
L. Kariba
Harare
Mozambique Channel
Kaokoveld
Okavango
Victoria Falls
Okavango Swamp
Madagascar
Namib Desert
OCEAN
Limpopo
Save
Windhoek
Kalahari Desert
Mascarene Is.
Tropic of Capricorn
Transvaal
Johannesburg
Vaal
Orange
Drakensberg
Durban
Cape
Cape Town
Port Elizabeth
Land Cover (Explanations on p. 32)
Natural Vegetation
Evergreen needleleaf forests
Evergreen broadleaf forests
Deciduous needleleaf forests
Deciduous broadleaf forests
Mixed forests
Closed shrublands
Open shrublands
Woody savannas
Savannas
Grasslands
Permanent wetlands
Developed and Mosaic Lands
Croplands
Cropland/natural vegetation mosaic
Urban and built-up lands
Non-Vegetated Lands
Snow and ice
Barren or sparsely vegetated
Water bodies
No data
KLETT-PERTHES

1:40,000,000
0 500 1,000 mi
0 500 1,000 1,500 2,000 km
ATLANTIC OCEAN
ATLANTIC OCEAN
INDIAN OCEAN
Mediterranean Sea
Black Sea
Caspian Sea
Red Sea
Persian Gulf
G. of Guinea
Tropic of Cancer
Equator
Tropic of Capricorn
FRANCE
SPAIN
PORTUGAL
SWI.
AUT.
GER.
CZ.R.
POL.
SVK.
HUN.
SVN.
CRO.
B. & H.
SERB.
M.
ALB.
MAC.
GREECE
BUL.
ROM.
MOL.
UKRAINE
RUSSIA
KAZAKHSTAN
UZBEKISTAN
TURKMENISTAN
GEO.
ARM.
AZE.
TURKEY
CYPRUS
LEB.
SYR.
ISRAEL
JOR.
IRAQ
IRAN
AFG.
PAK.
KUW.
BHR.
QAT.
U.A.E.
SAUDI ARABIA
OMAN
YEMEN
ERITREA
DJI.
ETHIOPIA
SOMALIA
KENYA
UGANDA
RWA.
BDI.
TANZANIA
MALAWI
MOZ.
ZAMBIA
ZIM.
BOTSWANA
NAMIBIA
SOUTH AFRICA
SWA.
LES.
MADAGASCAR
MAURITIUS
Réunion (FRA.)
ANGOLA
DEM. REP. OF THE CONGO
CONGO
GABON
EQ.G.
SAO TOME AND PRINCIPE
CAMEROON
CENTRAL AFRICAN REPUBLIC
NIGERIA
NIGER
CHAD
SUDAN
EGYPT
LIBYA
TUN.
MALTA
ALGERIA
MOROCCO
Western Sahara
MAURITANIA
MALI
SENEGAL
GAM.
GUINEA-BISSAU
GUINEA
SI.L.
LIBERIA
CÔTE D'IVOIRE
BURKINA FASO
GHANA
TOGO
BENIN
Paris
Brest
Lyon
Toulouse
Marseille
Bilbao
Madrid
Barcelona
Valencia
Lisbon
Seville
Zürich
Milan
Turin
Tr.
Ri.
Vienna
Pr.
Br.
Budapest
Zagreb
Be.
Bucharest
Sofia
Thessaloniki
Athens
Rome
Naples
Cagliari
Palermo
Odesa
Kr.
Dn.
Donets'k
Si.
Kerch
Volgograd
Astrakhan
Atyraū
Mangghystaū
Tashkent
Gazli
Sa.
Türkmenabat
Ashgabat
Mashhad
Herāt
Groznyy
Tb.
Batumi
Baku
Yerevan
Tabrīz
Rasht
Tehrān
Isfahan
Saghand
Kermān
Shīrāz
Bandar-e Būshehr
Kangān
Istanbul
Ankara
Izmir
Antalya
Adana
Aleppo
Kirkūk
Baghdād
Baniyās
Beirut
Damascus
T.A.
Amman
Basra
Kuwait
Dubai
Doha
Abu Dhabi
Muscat
Riyadh
Yanbu'
Jeddah/ Mecca
Port Sudan
Āsmera
As-Ṣalīf
Aden
Dirē Dawa
Addis Ababa
Mogadishu
Khartoum
Al-Ubayyid
Alexandria
Cairo
Asyūt
Assuan
Tubruq
Marsā al-Buraygah
Awjilah
Sarīr
Ra's Lānūf
Tripoli
Tunis
Sfax
Sk.
'Annābah
Co.
Bijāyah
Algiers
Oran
Ḥāssī al-Raml
Ḥāssī Mas'ūd
Riqqān
'Ayn Ṣālaḥ
Rabat
Casablanca
Ṣāfī
Marrakech
Tenerife
Bū Krā'
Fdayrik
Taoudenni
Arlit
Bilma
Dakar
Bamako
Ouagadougou
Conakry
Freetown
Monrovia
Abidjan
Accra
Lagos
Ibadan
Kainji
Kaduna
Kano
Jos
Enugu
P.H.
Douala
Edéa
Doba
Ouadda
Bangui
Watsa
Kisangani
Kampala
Nairobi
Mombasa
Dar es Salaam
Libreville
Pt. Gentil
Moanda
Brazzaville
Kinshasa
Inga
Cabinda
Tshikapa
Mbuji-Mayi
Bukavu
Kalemie
Manono
Dundo
Luanda
Benguela
Lubumbashi
Ndola
Kabwe
Lusaka
Kariba
Cahora Bassa
Blantyre
Harare
Mutare
Gweru
Bulawayo
Beira
Tsumeb
Rössing
Walvis Bay
Windhoek
Orapa
Phalaborwa
Maputo
Johannesburg
Sishen
Postmasburg
Kimberley
Richards Bay
Durban
Okiep
Cape Town
Mosselbaai
Port Elizabeth
East London
Antananarivo
Service and Industry
Service center (finance, trade, research, government, tourism)
Other location
Industrial center
Metal processing, mechanical engineering, vehicle manufacturing, shipbuilding
Electronics industry, electrical and precision engineering
Textile, garment, and leather goods industries
Chemical, wood working, pulp and paper, printing industries
Food processing
Mining and Smelting
Energy raw material
Hard coal
Brown coal
Uranium
Petroleum
Natural gas
Oil refinery
Oil pipeline
Gas pipeline
Oil terminal embarkation
Hydro-electric power station
Nuclear power station
Symbol size indicates relative importance of a location.
Ore and other raw materials
Iron ore
Chromite
Cobalt
Manganese
Nickel
Vanadium
Tungsten
Bauxite
Copper
Lead/zinc
Tin
Gold
Silver
Platinum
Mercury
Gemstones
Asbestos
Sodium chloride
Phosphate
Salpeter
Smelting
Iron and steel production works
Non-ferrous metal production
Light metal (aluminum) production
Conurbation
Be. Belgrade
Br. Bratislava
Co. Constantine
Dn. Dnipropetrovs'k
Kr. Kryvyy Rih
M. Munich
P.H. Port Harcourt
Pr. Prague
Ri. Rijeka
Sa. Samarqand
Si. Simferopol'
Sk. Sakīkdah
T.A. Tel Aviv-Yafo
Tb. Tbilisi
KLETT-PERTHES

Africa: Political

1:40,000,000

0 500 1,000 mi
0 500 1,000 1,500 2,000 km
A B C D E F G H J K L
20° 10° 0° 10° 20° 30° 40° 50° 60° 70°
1 2 3 4 5 6 7 8 9
40° 30° 20° 10° 0° 10° 20° 30°
Tropic of Cancer
Equator
Tropic of Capricorn
Portuguese
Spaniards
Rifs
Kabyles
Arabs
Tamazight
Tachelhit
Berbers
Tuaregs
Tibbu
Moors (Arabs-Berbers)
Songhai
Nubians
Beja
Z.
Tukuler
Wolof
Serer
Soninke
Fulbe
Mandingo
Susu
Temne
Me.
W.
Kp.
Dan
Kru
Dyula
Senufo
Bambara
Dogon
Bobo
Lobi
Mosi
Gurma
Zarma
Baule
Akan
Gonja
Ewe
Bariba
Yoruba
Hausa
Kanuri
Kanem-bu
Daza
Zaghawa
Maba
For
Bagara (Arabs)
K.P.
Mubi
Bagirmi
Ma.
Ko.
Musgu
Runga
Plateau Peoples
Nupe
Tiv
Jukun
Mbum
Bini
Ibo
Ijo
Ib.
Tikar
Wute
Duala
Sara
Gbaya
Banda
Azande
Tigre
Ku.
Tigrai
Koma
Amhara
Danakil
Sh.
Berta
Oromo
Dinka
Nuer
Anuak
Kaffa
Si.
Somalis
Murle
Moru-Madi
Bari
Turkana
Karamojo
Acholi
Lendu
Mangbetu
Ngombe
Gbaya
Bangala
Baboa
Fang
Kota
Kele
Bobangi
Mongo-Kundu
Komu
Ganda
Kikuyu
Luo
Masai
Kamba
Rwanda
Rundi
Sukuma
Ki.
Sa.
Gogo
Mpongwe
Teke
Tetela
Kuba
Kongo
Luba
Nyam-wezi
Swahili
Lunda
Chokwe
Bambundu
Fipa
Hehe
Bena
Ngoni
Makonde
Bemba
Ovimbundu
Mbwela
Luchazi
Lunda
Lamba
Lala-Bisa
Yao
Nyanya
Makua
Lenje
Ila
Lozi
Tonga
Lomwe
Herero
Ambo
Kavango
Shona
Sena
Mata-bele
Ndau
Da-mara
Herero
Bushmen (San)
Venda
Tsonga
Sakalava
Malagasy
Pedi
Nd.
Swazi
Tswana
Nama (Khoin)
Zulu
Sotho
"Coloureds" and Afrikaners
Xhosa
Languages Families and Ethnic Groups
Afro-Asiatic (Hamito-Semitic) family
Semitic
Cushitic
Omotic
Berber
Chadic
Nilo-Saharian family
(dark-green: Nilotic)
Niger-Congo family
Mande
Kordofanian
Atlantic/Fulbe
Kru
Gur or Voltaic
Adamawa-Ubangi
Kwa
Benue-Congo (light-blue: Bantu)
Khoisan family
Austronesian family
Indo-European family
Afrikaans
Minorities
Pygmies (without own languages)
Europeans
Asiatic
Masai People, Ethnic group
Very sparsely populated area
Uninhabited area
Ib. Ibibio
K.P. Kordofanian Peoples
Ki. Kindiga
Ko. Kotoko
Kp. Kpelle
Ku. Kunama
Ma. Mandara
Me. Mende
Nd. Ndebele
Sa. Sandawe
Sh. Shilluk
Si. Sidamo
W. Wai
Z. Zenaga
KLETT-PERTHES

1:40,000,000

0 500 1,000 mi
0 500 1,000 1,500 2,000 km

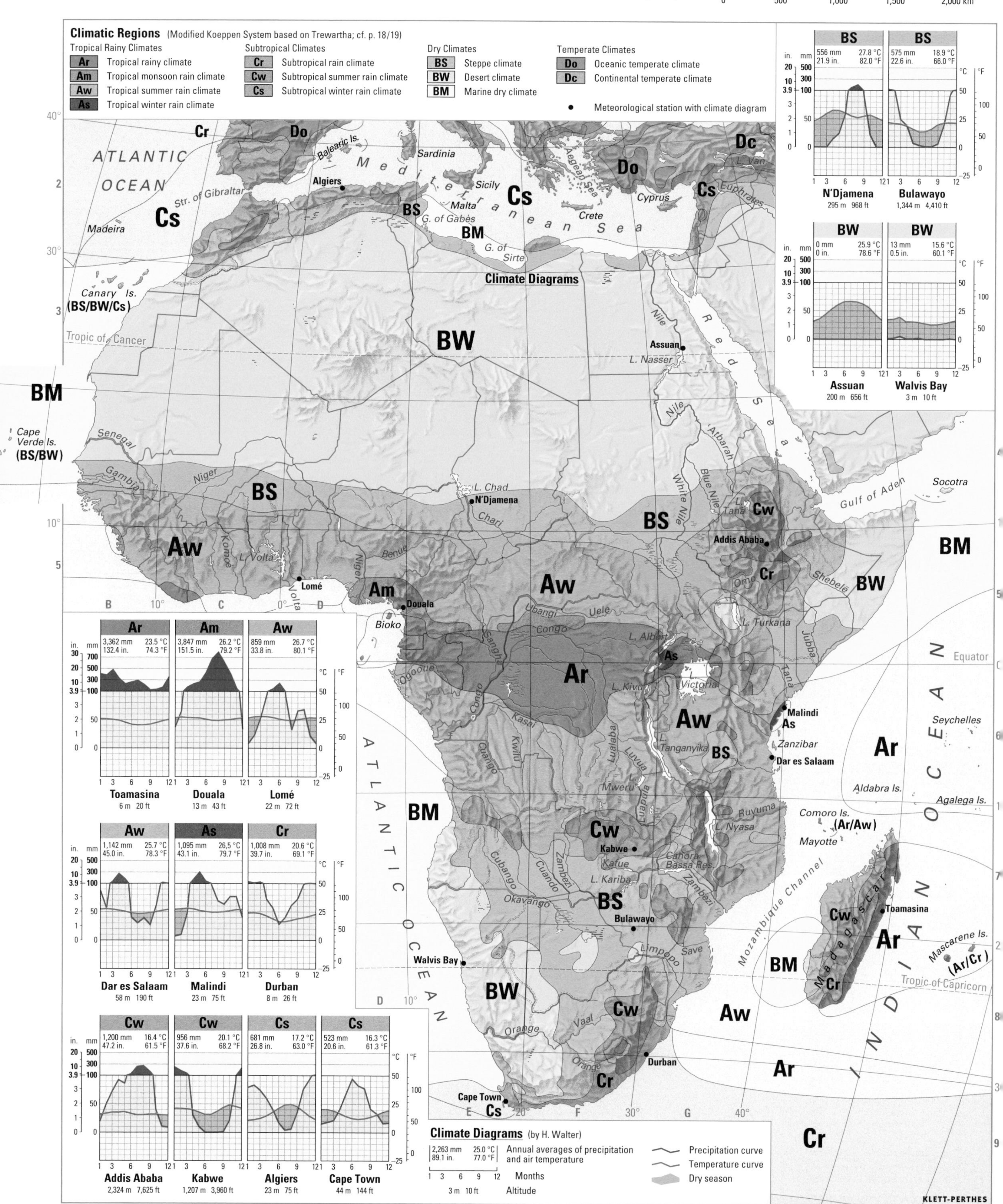

Vegetation Profiles

Tenerife

SW NE

Teide 12,199 ft 3,718 m

Mountain desert
Cushion dwarf & xeromorphic shrubland
Xeromorphic pine forest
Laurel forest
Semi-desert
Xeromorphic shrubland
Trade Winds

Tubqāl 13,665 ft 4,165 m

Alpine mat patches
Alpine cushion scrubland
Coniferous forest
Sclerophyllous forest
Xeromorphic shrubland

Assekrem 8,950 ft 2,728 m

Scarcely vegetated rocky slopes with isolated sclerophyllous shrubs
Semi desert with sclerophyllous & Acacia woodlands

Jabal Marrah 10,075 ft 3,071 m

Sclerophyllous woodlands
Upper drought-deciduous forest
Lower
Xeromorphic shrublands

Cameroon Mountain 13,435 ft 4,095 m

Edaphic desert
Afro-alpine scrub- & grassland
Shrubland
Upper montane forest
Lower
Montane tropicalrain forest
Lowland

Kilimanjaro 19,330 ft 5,892 m

SW NE

Cold desert
Afro-alpine dwarf shrub and grassland
Afro-alpine shrub and dwarf-shrub formations
Afro-alpine savanna
Montane forest (cloud forest)
Tropical rain forest
Drought-deciduous forest
Savanna

19,686 ft 6,000 m
16,405 ft 5,000 m
13,124 ft 4,000 m
9,843 ft 3,000 m
6,562 ft 2,000 m
3,281 ft 1,000 m
Sea level

Ecoregions

- Tropical rain forest (broadleaf evergreen)
- Coastal Forest and Mangrove
- Deciduous forest – woodland savanna
  - Guinea deciduous forest and woodland savanna
  - Zambezian Miombo woodland and humid savanna
  - Malagasy monsoonal savanna woodland
- Dry mixed woodland savanna
  - Sudan dry savanna and bushland
  - Zambezian woodland savanna
  - Malagasy mixed woodland savanna
- Thornbush savanna
  - Sahelian thornbush savanna
  - East African highland open savanna
  - Kalahari thornbush savanna
  - Malagasy bushland
- Semidesert
  - Sahelian semidesert
  - Nama-Karoo semidesert and succulent steppe
  - Somali semidesert shrubland
  - Turkana semidesert shrubland
  - Atlantic steppe
- Desert
- Subtropical hard-leaf scrublands
  - Mediterranean evergreen forest and hard-leaf scrub
  - Fynbos (Capensis)
- Temperate grassland (veld) and mountain grassland
- Montane forest and afroalpine savanna
  - Montane and cloud forest
  - Afromontane shrubby woodland
  - Ethiopian highland forest
  - Atlantic montane forest
- Azonal wetland savanna and swamps

Tell Atlas
Saharan Atlas
Tubqāl
High Atlas
Mediterranean Sea
G. of Sirte
Cyrenaica
Tripolitania
Teide
Canary Is.
Gt. Western Erg
Gt. Eastern Erg
Al-Hamadah al-Hamrā'
Tademaït Plateau
Libyan Desert
Arabian Desert
Nile
Red Sea
Erg Iguidi
Erg Chech
Tassili-n-Ajjer
Fazzān
Ahaggar
Assekrem
Tanezrouft
L. Nasser
Tropic of Cancer
Sahara
Adrar des Ifôghas
Tibesti
Nubian Desert
Aïr
Ténéré
Borkou
Bodélé
Ennedi
Bayuda
Atbarah
Sahel
Senegal
Gambia
Niger
Kanem
L. Chad
Wadai
J. Marrah
Dārfūr
Kurdufān
White Nile
Blue Nile
Tana
Gulf of Aden
Sudan
Fouta Djallon
Bornu
Chari
Ethiopian Highlands
Komoé
L. Volta
Benue
Adamawa Highlands
Bongo Mts.
Sudd
Somali Pen.
Shebele
Omo
Grain Coast
Ivory Coast
Gold Coast
Slave Coast
Volta
Cameroon Mtn.
Bioko
G. of Guinea
Ubangi
Uele
Congo
L. Turkana
L. Albert
Jubba
Congo Basin
Ogooué
Mitumba Mts.
L. Victoria
L. Kivu
Kilimanjaro
Tana
Equator
Kasai
Lualaba
Zanzibar
Tanganyika
Kwilu
Cuango
Lunda
Shaba
L. Mweru
Luvua
Luapula
Muchinga Mts.
Ruvuma
L. Nyasa
Comoro Is.
Mayotte
Mozambique Channel
Cubango
Cuando
Zambezi
Kafue
Cahora Bassa Res.
L. Kariba
Kaokoveld
Okavango
Okavango Swamp
Victoria Falls
Etosha Pan
Namib Desert
Kalahari Desert
Limpopo
Save
Transvaal
Madagascar
Tropic of Capricorn
Vaal
Orange
Drakensberg
Cape
Atlantic Ocean
Indian Ocean

B 10° C 0° D 10° E 20° F 30° G 40° H 50° J 60°
30° 20° 10° 0° 10° 20° 30°
3 4 5 6 7 8

KLETT-PERTHES

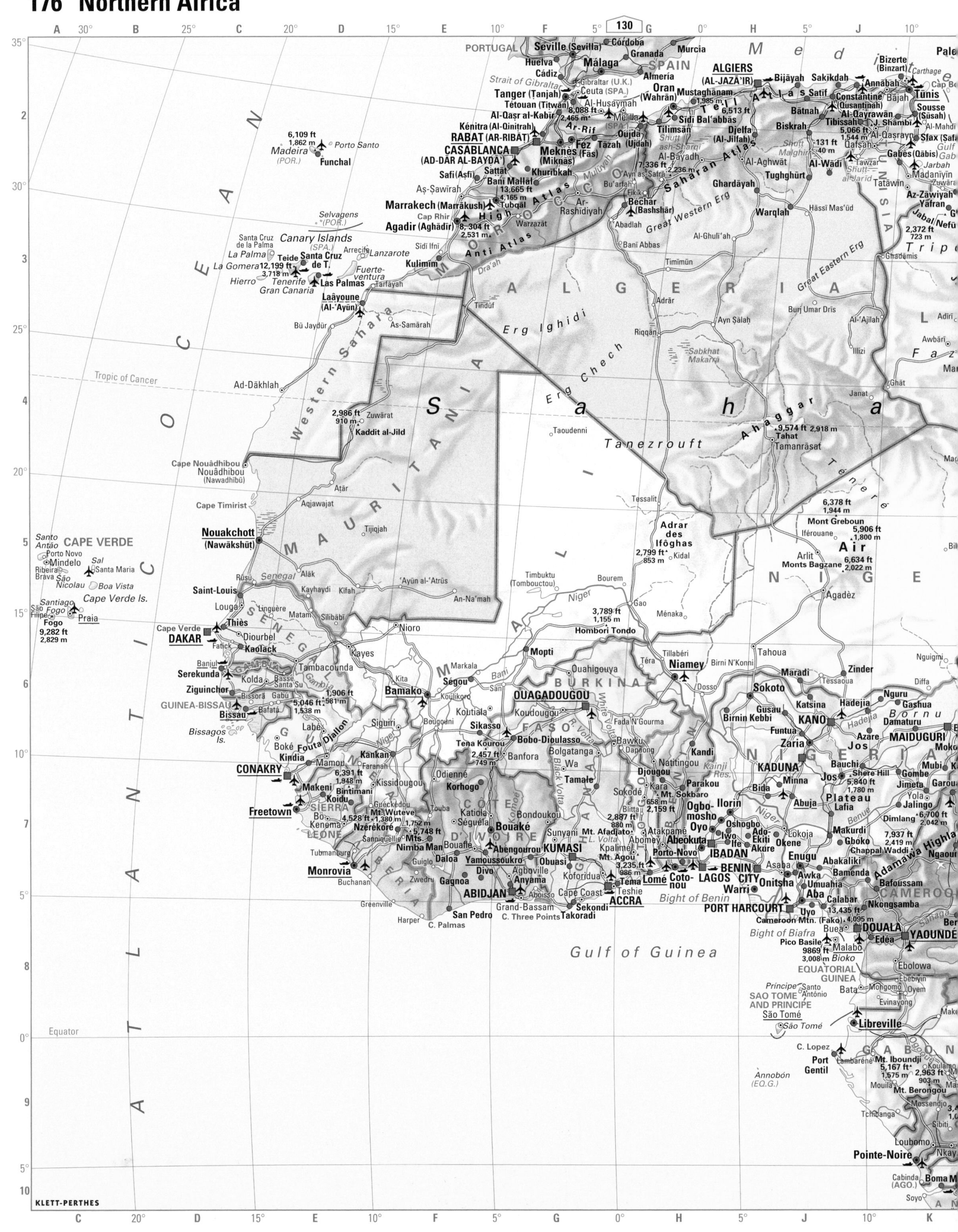
130
PORTUGAL
Seville (Sevilla)
Córdoba
Granada
Murcia
Huelva
Málaga
SPAIN
Cádiz
Almería
Strait of Gibraltar
Gibraltar (U.K.)
Ceuta (SPA.)
Tanger (Tanjah)
Tétouan (Titwān)
Al-Ḥusaymah
Melilla
Al-Qaṣr al-Kabīr
Oran (Wahrān)
Mustaghānam
ALGIERS (AL-JAZĀ'IR)
Bijāyah
Sakīkdah
Annābah
Constantine (Qusantīnah)
Bizerte (Binzart)
Carthage
Tūnis
Bājah
Sousse (Sūsah)
Al-Qayrawān
Sfax (Ṣafāqis)
Gabès (Qābis)
Jarbah
Madanīyīn
Taṭāwīn
Az-Zāwiyah
Yafran
Jabal Nefūsa
Ghadāmis
Tell Atlas
Saṭīf
Bātnah
Biskrah
Tibissah
J. Shāmbī
Al-Qaṣrayn
Qafṣah
Shaṭṭ Malghir
Tawzar
Shaṭṭ al-Jarīd
Al-Wādī
Sīdī Bal'abbās
Tilimsān
Shaṭṭ ash-Sharqī
Djelfa (Al-Jilfah)
Al-Aghwāṭ
Al-Bayaḍh
Saharan Atlas
Ghardāyah
Tughghūrt
Warqlah
Ḥāssī Mas'ūd
Kénitra (Al-Qinitrah)
RABAT (AR-RIBĀṬ)
CASABLANCA (AD-DĀR AL-BAYḌĀ')
Meknès (Miknās)
Fez (Fās)
Tāzah
Oujda (Ujdah)
Ar-Rif
Khurībkah
Safi (Asfi)
Saṭṭāt
Banī Mallāl
Aṣ-Ṣawīrah
Marrakech (Marrākush)
Tubqāl
High Atlas
MOROCCO
Ar-Rashīdiyah
Bu'arfah
Fikīk
Béchar (Bashshār)
Warzāzāt
Agadir (Aghādīr)
Cap Rhir
Anti Atlas
Sīdī Ifnī
Kulimīm
Dra'ah
Great Western Erg
Abadlah
Banī Abbas
Al-Ghulī'ah
Tīmīmūn
Great Eastern Erg
ALGERIA
Adrār
Tindūf
Ayn Ṣalaḥ
Burj Umar Drīs
Al-'Ajīlah
Riqqān
Erg Ighidi
Erg Chech
Sabkhat Makarrā
Illizi
Awbārī
Fazzān
Ghāt
Janat
Ahaggar
Tahat
Tamanrāsat
Tanezrouft
Sahara
Taoudenni
Ténéré
Tessalit
Adrar des Ifôghas
Kidal
Mont Greboun
Iférouane
Aïr
Arlit
Monts Bagzane
NIGER
Agadèz
Madeira (POR.)
Porto Santo
Funchal
Selvagens (POR.)
Canary Islands (SPA.)
Santa Cruz de la Palma
La Palma
La Gomera
Hierro
Teide
Tenerife
Santa Cruz de T.
Gran Canaria
Las Palmas
Arrecife
Lanzarote
Fuerteventura
Tarfāyah
Laâyoune (Al-'Ayūn)
Bū Jaydūr
As-Samārah
Western Sahara
Tropic of Cancer
Ad-Dākhlah
Zuwārat
Kaddit al-Jild
MAURITANIA
Cape Nouâdhibou
Nouâdhibou (Nawadhibū)
Aṭār
Cape Timirist
Aqjawajat
Tījiqjah
Nouakchott (Nawākshūt)
Alāk
Rūṣū
Kayhaydi
Kīfah
'Ayūn al-'Atrūs
An-Na'mah
Senegal
MALI
Timbuktu (Tombouctou)
Bourem
Gao
Ménaka
Niger
Hombori Tondo
Mopti
Nioro
Kayes
CAPE VERDE
Santo Antão
Porto Novo
Mindelo
Sal
Santa Maria
Ribeira Brava
São Nicolau
Boa Vista
Cape Verde Is.
Santiago
São Filipe
Fogo
Praia
Saint-Louis
Louga
Linguère
Matam
Silibābī
SENEGAL
Cape Verde
DAKAR
Thiès
Diourbel
Fatick
Kaolack
Banjul
GAMBIA
Serekunda
Tambacounda
Kolda
Basse Santa Su
Ziguinchor
Bissorã
Gabú
GUINEA-BISSAU
Bissau
Bafatá
Bissagos Is.
Kita
Markala
Ségou
Bamako
Koulikoro
Bani
San
Koutiala
Sikasso
Bougouni
Siguiri
GUINEA
Labé
Fouta Djallon
Boké
Kindia
Mamou
Faranah
Kankan
CONAKRY
Kissidougou
Guéckédou
Makeni
Bintimani
Koidu
SIERRA LEONE
Freetown
Bo
Kenema
Mt. Wuteve
Nzérékoré
Sanniquellie
Nimba Mts.
LIBERIA
Tubmanburg
Monrovia
Buchanan
Greenville
Harper
C. Palmas
Odienné
Korhogo
Touba
Katiola
Séguéla
CÔTE D'IVOIRE
Bouaké
Bondoukou
Man
Bouaflé
Abengourou
Yamoussoukro
Daloa
Guiglo
Zwedru
Divo
Agboville
Gagnoa
Anyama
ABIDJAN
Aboisso
Grand-Bassam
San Pedro
C. Three Points
Takoradi
Sekondi
Cape Coast
ACCRA
Tema
Teshie
Koforidua
Obuasi
KUMASI
Sunyani
GHANA
Mt. Afadjato
L. Volta
Kpalimé
Mt. Agou
Lomé
TOGO
Tamale
Black Volta
White Volta
Bolgatanga
Wa
Dapaong
Sokodé
Kara
Mt. Sokbaro
BENIN
Natitingou
Djougou
Parakou
Kandi
Bawku
Fada N'Gourma
Koudougou
OUAGADOUGOU
BURKINA FASO
Ouahigouya
Bobo-Dioulasso
Tena Kourou
Banfora
Téra
Tillabéri
Niamey
Birni N'Konni
Dosso
Tahoua
Maradi
Tessaoua
Zinder
Nguigmi
Diffa
Sokoto
Gusau
Birnin Kebbi
Katsina
Hadejia
Nguru
Gashua
Bornu
Damaturu
MAIDUGURI
KANO
Funtua
Zaria
Azare
Jos
Jos Plateau
Bauchi
Shere Hill
Gombe
Mubi
KADUNA
NIGERIA
Kainji Res.
Bida
Minna
Abuja
Lafia
Jimeta
Yola
Jalingo
Dimlang
Benue
Niger
Ilorin
Ogbomosho
Oshogbo
Oyo
Ado-Ekiti
Iwo
Ife
Akure
Okene
Lokoja
Makurdi
Gboko
Chappal Waddi
Abeokuta
Atakpamé
Abomey
Porto-Novo
Cotonou
IBADAN
LAGOS
BENIN CITY
Warri
Asaba
Onitsha
Enugu
Abakaliki
Awka
Umuahia
Aba
PORT HARCOURT
Bight of Benin
Calabar
Uyo
Bamenda
Bafoussam
Nkongsamba
Adamawa Highlands
Ngaoundéré
CAMEROON
Cameroon Mtn. (Fako)
Buea
DOUALA
Edéa
YAOUNDÉ
Sanaga
Bight of Biafra
Pico Basile
Malabo
Bioko
Ebolowa
EQUATORIAL GUINEA
Ebebiyin
Mongomo
Bata
Oyem
Evinayong
Gulf of Guinea
Príncipe
Santo António
SAO TOME AND PRINCIPE
São Tomé
Libreville
Equator
C. Lopez
Port Gentil
Lambaréné
Ogooué
GABON
Mt. Iboundji
Koulamoutou
Mouila
Mt. Berongou
Mossendjo
Tchibanga
Sibiti
Annobón (EQ.G.)
Loubomo
Nkayi
Pointe-Noire
Cabinda (AGO.)
Boma
Soyo
Mediterranean
Tripoli
ATLANTIC OCEAN
KLETT-PERTHES

1:20,000,000

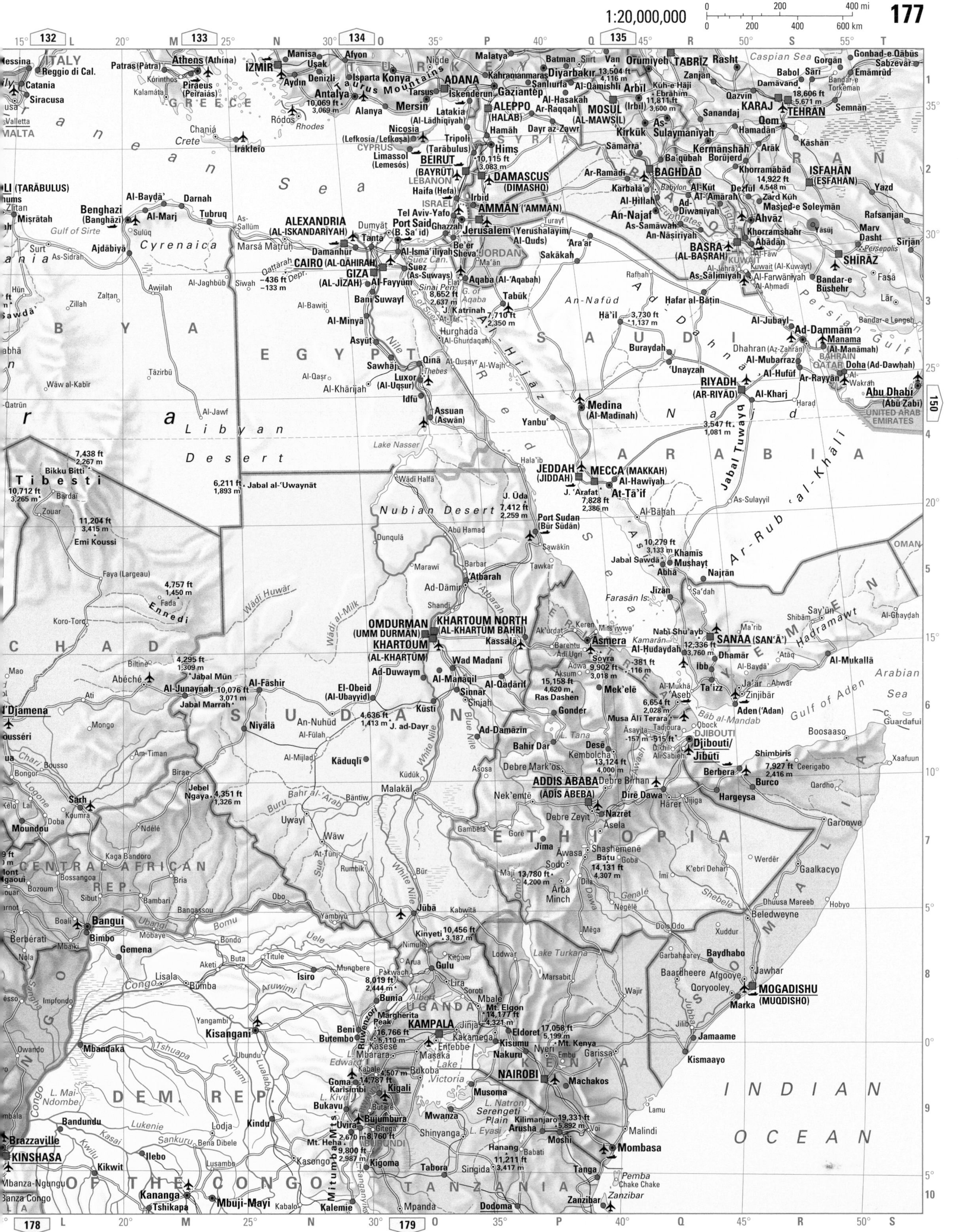
0 200 400 mi
0 200 400 600 km
132
133
134
135
150
178
179
Messina
ITALY
Reggio di Cal.
Catania
Siracusa
Valletta
MALTA
Patras (Pátra)
Athens (Athína)
Kórinthos
Piraeus (Peiraiás)
Kalamáta
GREECE
Chaniá
Crete
Iráklelo
Ródos
Rhodes
IZMIR
Manisa
Uşak
Aydın
Denizli
Afyon
Isparta
Konya
Antalya
10,069 ft
3,069 m
Alanya
Taurus Mountains
Niğde
ADANA
Tarsus
Mersin
Iskenderun
Malatya
Kahramanmaraş
Gaziantep
Şanlıurfa
Batman
Siirt
Van
Diyarbakır
13,504 ft
4,116 m
Al-Qāmishlī
Al-Ḥasakah
Orūmīyeh
TABRĪZ
Rasht
Caspian Sea
Gorgān
Gonbad-e Qābūs
Sabzevār
Zanjān
Babol
Sārī
Emāmrūd
Arbīl
Kūh-e Hājī Ebrāhīm
11,811 ft
3,600 m
Damāvand
18,606 ft
5,671 m
Bandar-e Torkeman
Qazvīn
KARAJ
TEHRĀN
Semnān
Sanandaj
Qom
Hamadān
Kāshān
Latakia (Al-Lādhiqīyah)
ALEPPO (HALAB)
Ar-Raqqah
MOSUL (AL-MAWṢIL)
(Irbil)
As-Sulaymānīyah
Kirkūk
Nicosia
(Lefkosia/Lefkoşa)
CYPRUS
Limassol (Lemesós)
Tripoli (Tarābulus)
Ḥamāh
Dayr az-Zawr
SYRIA
Ḥimṣ
10,115 ft
3,083 m
Sāmarrā'
Kermānshāh
Arāk
Ba'qūbah
Borūjerd
IRAN
BEIRUT (BAYRŪT)
LEBANON
DAMASCUS (DIMASHQ)
Ar-Ramādī
BAGHDĀD
Khorramābād
14,922 ft
4,548 m
ISFAHĀN (ESFAHĀN)
Yazd
Haifa (Ḥefa)
Karbalā'
Babylon
Al-Kūt
Dezfūl
Zard Kūh
Irbid
ISRAEL
AMMĀN ('AMMĀN)
Al-Ḥillah
Ad-Dīwānīyah
Al-'Amārah
Masjed-e Soleymān
Tel Aviv-Yafo
Jerusalem (Yerushalayim/Al-Quds)
Turayf
An-Najaf
As-Samāwah
An-Nāṣirīyah
Ahvāz
Rafsanjān
Yāsūj
Marv Dasht
Khorramshahr
Ābādān
Sīrjān
Persepolis
LI (ṬARĀBULUS)
Benghazi (Banghāzī)
Al-Bayḍā'
Darnah
Al-Marj
Ṭubruq
As-Sallūm
Miṣrātah
Zlitan
Gulf of Sirte
Sulūq
Cyrenaica
Ajdābiyā
Surt
As-Sidrah
ALEXANDRIA (AL-ISKANDARĪYAH)
Dumyāṭ
Port Said (B. Sa'īd)
Ṭanṭā
Ghazzah
Marsā Maṭrūḥ
Damanhūr
Al-Ismā'īlīyah
Suez Can.
Be'er Sheva
JORDAN
'Ar'ar
Sakākah
BASRA (AL-BAṢRAH)
Al-Fāw
KUWAIT
Kuwait (Al-Kuwayt)
Al-Jahrā'
As-Sālimīyah
Al-Farwānīyah
Al-Aḥmadī
SHĪRĀZ
Bandar-e Būshehr
Fasā
Qaṭṭārah Depr.
-436 ft
-133 m
CAIRO (AL-QĀHIRAH)
GIZA (AL-JĪZAH)
Suez (As-Suways)
Ma'ān
Aqaba (Al-'Aqabah)
Sinai Pen.
Elat
G. of Aqaba
Sīwah
Al-Jaghbūb
Awjilah
Zalṭan
Zillah
Al-Fayyūm
Banī Suwayf
8,652 ft
2,637 m
J. Katrīnah
Tabūk
Rafḥah
An-Nafūd
Ḥafar al-Bāṭin
Lār
Persian Gulf
Al-Bawītī
Al-Minyā
At-Tūr
G. of Suez
7,710 ft
2,350 m
Ḥā'il
3,730 ft
1,137 m
Ad-Dahnā
Al-Jubayl
Ad-Dammām
Bandar-e Lengeh
LIBYA
Asyūṭ
Hurghada (Al-Ghurdaqah)
SAUDI
Buraydah
Dhahran (Az-Zahrān)
Manama (Al-Manāmah)
BAHRAIN
QATAR
EGYPT
Nile
Sawhāj
Qinā
Thebes
Al-Quṣayr
Al-Wajh
Al-Ḥijāz
'Unayzah
Al-Mubarraz
Doha (Ad-Dawḥah)
Tāzirbū
Al-Qaṣr
Al-Khārijah
Luxor (Al-Uqṣur)
Idfū
Red Sea
RIYADH (AR-RIYĀḌ)
Al-Hufūf
Ar-Rayyān
Al-Wakrah
Abu Dhabi (Abū Ẓabī)
Wāw al-Kabīr
Qatrūn
Al-Jawf
Libyan Desert
Sahara
Assuan (Aswān)
Medina (Al-Madīnah)
Yanbu'
Najd
Al-Kharj
Ḥaraḍ
UNITED ARAB EMIRATES
3,547 ft
1,081 m
Jabal Ṭuwayq
Lake Nasser
ARABIA
Ar-Rub' al-Khālī
7,438 ft
2,267 m
Bikku Bitti
Tibesti
10,712 ft
3,265 m
Bardaï
Zouar
11,204 ft
3,415 m
Emi Koussi
6,211 ft
1,893 m
Jabal al-'Uwaynāt
Ḥala'ib
Wādī Ḥalfā
JEDDAH (JIDDAH)
MECCA (MAKKAH)
Al-Ḥawīyah
J. 'Arafat
7,828 ft
2,386 m
At-Tā'if
As-Sulayyil
Nubian Desert
J. Ūda
7,412 ft
2,259 m
Port Sudan (Būr Sūdān)
Al-Bāḥah
'Asīr
Dunqulā
Abū Ḥamad
Sawākin
10,279 ft
3,133 m
Khamīs Mushayṭ
Jabal Sawdā'
Abhā
Najrān
OMAN
Marawī
Barbar
'Aṭbarah
Tawkar
Faya (Largeau)
4,757 ft
1,450 m
Fada
Ennedi
Wādī Huwār
Wādī al-Milk
Ad-Dāmir
Shandī
Jīzān
Ṣa'dah
Farasān Is.
Koro-Toro
OMDURMAN (UMM DURMĀN)
KHARTOUM NORTH (AL-KHARṬŪM BAḤRĪ)
KHARTOUM (AL-KHARṬŪM)
Kassalā
Ak'ordat
Keren
Mits'iwa
Asmera
Nabī Shu'ayb
SANAA (ṢAN'Ā')
Ma'rib
Say'ūn
Shibām
Ḥaḍramawt
Al-Ghayḍah
Kamarān
Al-Ḥudaydah
12,336 ft
3,760 m
Dhamār
CHAD
Biltine
4,295 ft
1,309 m
Jabal Mūn
Abéché
Mao
Al-Fāshir
Al-Junaynah
10,076 ft
3,071 m
Jabal Marrah
Wad Madanī
Ad-Duwaym
Al-Manāqil
Al-Qaḍārif
Barentu
Adi Ugri
Ādwa
Āksum
Soyra
9,902 ft
3,018 m
-381 ft
-116 m
Ibb
Al-Bayḍā'
'Ataq
Al-Mukallā
Arabian Sea
El-Obeid (Al-Ubayyid)
Sinnār
Sinjah
15,158 ft
4,620 m
Ras Dashen
Mek'elē
Al-Mukhā
Aseb
Ta'izz
Ja'ār
Aḥwar
Zinjibār
Aden ('Adan)
Gulf of Aden
Ati
Mongo
N'Djamena
SUDAN
Niyālā
An-Nuhūd
4,636 ft
1,413 m
J. ad-Dayr
Kūstī
Blue Nile
Ad-Damāzīn
Gonder
6,654 ft
2,028 m
Musa Ālī Terara
Bāb al-Mandab
Asayita
-157 m
-515 ft
Tadjoura
Obock
DJIBOUTI
Djibouti/Jībūtī
Dikhil
Ali Sabieh
C. Guardafui
Boosaaso
Kousséri
Al-Fūlah
Am-Timan
Al-Mijlad
Kāduqlī
White Nile
Bahir Dar
L. Tana
Desē
Kembolcha
Awash
13,124 ft
4,000 m
Shimbiris
7,927 ft
2,416 m
Ceerigabo
Xaafuun
Chari
Bousso
Bongor
Birao
Jebel Ngaya
4,351 ft
1,326 m
Kūdūk
Malakāl
Asosa
Debre Mark'os
ADDIS ABABA (ĀDĪS ĀBEBA)
Debre Birhan
Dirē Dawa
Harer
Jijiga
Berbera
Burco
Hargeysa
Qardho
Logone
Sarh
Koumra
Kélo
Laï
Doba
Moundou
Bahr al-'Arab
Buru
Bāntiw
Uwayl
Nek'emtē
Nazrēt
Āsela
Debre Zeyit
Gambēla
Ndélé
Wāw
Gorē
ETHIOPIA
Jīma
Āwasa
Shashemenē
Batu
Goba
14,131 ft
4,307 m
Garoowe
CENTRAL AFRICAN REP.
Kaga Bandoro
Bossangoa
Bozoum
Bria
At-Tūnj
Sue
Rumbik
Būr
Sodo
Maji
13,780 ft
4,200 m
Ārba Minch
Omo
Dila
Dawa
Genalē
K'ebrī Dehar
Werdēr
Īmī
Shebelē
Gaalkacyo
SOMALIA
Sibut
Bambari
Obo
Bangassou
Jūbā
Kabwītā
Negēlē
Dhuusa Mareeb
Hobyo
Boali
Bangui
Bimbo
Berbérati
Ubangi
Bomu
Yambiyū
Kinyeti
10,456 ft
3,187 m
Nimule
Mēga
Dolo Odo
Beledweyne
Xuddur
Mobaye
Bondo
Uele
Gemena
Nola
Mbaki
Buta
Aketi
Titule
Isiro
Mungbere
Arua
Kitgum
Gulu
Lodwar
Lake Turkana
Garbahaarey
Baydhabo
Sangha
Lisala
Congo
Bumba
Aruwimi
Pakwach
8,019 ft
2,444 m
Albert
Lira
Soroti
Marsabit
Baardheere
Afgooye
Jawhar
Qoryooley
MOGADISHU (MUQDISHO)
Marka
Wajir
Impfondo
Bunia
UGANDA
Mbale
Mt. Elgon
14,177 ft
4,321 m
Yangambi
Kisangani
Margherita Peak
16,766 ft
5,110 m
Ruwenzori
Beni
Butembo
KAMPALA
Jinja
Kakamega
Eldoret
17,058 ft
5,199 m
Mt. Kenya
Jilib
Jubba
Jamaame
Owando
Mbandaka
Tshuapa
Lomami
Ubundu
Lualaba
Kasese
Mbarara
Masaka
Entebbe
Kisumu
Nakuru
Nyeri
Embu
Garissa
KENYA
Kismaayo
Edward
Goma
4,507 m
14,787 ft
Karisimbi
Kigali
Bukoba
Lake Victoria
NAIROBI
Machakos
L. Mai-Ndombe
DEM. REP. OF THE CONGO
L. Kivu
Bukavu
Butare
Musoma
L. Natron
Serengeti Plain
INDIAN OCEAN
Lamu
Bandundu
Lukenie
Lodja
Kindu
Bujumbura
Uvira
Gitega
BURUNDI
Mitumba Mts.
2,670 m
8,760 ft
Mt. Heha
9,800 ft
2,987 m
Mwanza
Shinyanga
L. Eyasi
Kilimanjaro
19,331 ft
5,892 m
Arusha
Moshi
Voi
Malindi
Mombasa
Brazzaville
KINSHASA
Kwilu
Kasai
Sankuru
Bena Dibele
Ilebo
Kasongo
Hanang
11,211 ft
3,417 m
Babati
Kikwit
Lusambo
Kigoma
Tabora
Singida
Tanga
Pemba
Chake Chake
Mbanza-Ngungu
Banza Congo
Kananga
Tshikapa
Mbuji-Mayi
Kabalo
Kalemie
L. Tanganyika
Mpanda
TANZANIA
Dodoma
Zanzibar
15°
20°
25°
30°
35°
40°
45°
50°
55°
35°
30°
25°
20°
15°
10°
5°
0°
5°
L
M
N
O
P
Q
R
S
T
1
2
3
4
5
6
7
8
9
10

176
Gulf of Guinea
Bight of Benin
Bight of Biafra
Equator
Tropic of Capricorn
A T L A N T I C
O C E A N
Ascension
St. Helena
(U.K.)
Tristan da Cunha
Monrovia
Tubmanburg
Buchanan
Greenville
Harper
C. Palmas
Guiglo
Daloa
Yamoussoukro
Zwedru
Gagnoa
Divo
Agboville
Anyama
ABIDJAN
San Pedro
Grand-Bassam
Aboisso
CÔTE D'IVOIRE
C. Three Points
Takoradi
Sekondi
Cape Coast
KUMASI
Obuasi
Koforidua
GHANA
ACCRA
Tema
Teshie
Kpalimé
Mt. Agou
3,235 ft
986 m
Lomé
Porto-Novo
Coto-nou
LAGOS
BENIN CITY
Warri
NIGERIA
Enugu
Asaba
Awka
Onitsha
Abakaliki
Umuahia
Aba
Uyo
PORT HARCOURT
Calabar
Bamenda
Bafoussam
Nkongsamba
CAMEROON
Cameroon Mtn. (Fako)
13,435 ft
4,095 m
Buea
DOUALA
Edéa
YAOUNDÉ
Pico Basile
9869 ft
3,008 m
Malabo
Bioko
EQUATORIAL GUINEA
Bata
Mongomo
Ebebiyin
Oyem
Ebolowa
Evinayong
Príncipe
Santo António
SAO TOME AND PRINCIPE
São Tomé
Annobón
(EQ.G.)
Libreville
Makokou
C. Lopez
Port Gentil
Lambaréné
GABON
Mt. Iboundji
5,167 ft
1,575 m
Koulamoutou
Moanda
2,963 ft
903 m
Masuku
Mouila
Mt. Berongou
Mossendjo
3,412 ft
1,040 m
Tchibanga
Sibiti
Djambala
Loubomo
Brazzaville
Pointe-Noire
Nkayi
Madingou
KINSHASA
CONGO
Ouésso
Impfondo
Owando
Ewo
Sangha
Congo
Ubangi
4,659 ft
1,420 m
Mont Ngaoui
Bossangoa
Bouar
Bozoum
Carnot
Sibut
Bambari
Boali
Bangui
Bimbo
Berbérati
Mbaiki
Nola
Bertoua
Gemena
Mobaye
Kaga Bandoro
Bria
Bangassou
Lisala
Mbandaka
Tshuapa
L. Mai-Ndombe
Bandundu
Lukenie
Kasai
Sankuru
Kwilu
Ilebo
Kikwit
DEM. REP. OF THE
Kananga
Tshikapa
Mbuji-Mayi
Mwene-
Lusambo
Cabinda
(AGO.)
Boma
Matadi
Mbanza-Ngungu
M'Banza Congo
Soyo
N'Zeto
Uíge
Cuango
LUANDA
Caxito
N'Dalatando
Malanje
Lunda
Lucapa
Saurimo
Dondo
Cuanza
Porto Amboim
Sumbe
ANGOLA
Lobito
Benguela
Môco
8,593 ft
2,619 m
Huambo
Bailundo
Kuito
Luena
Dilolo
Zambezi
Menongue
Cuando
Cunene
Cubango
Namibe
7,563 ft
2,305 m
Lubango
Cape Albina
Serra da Chela
Chiange
6,805 ft
2,074 m
Baynes Mts.
N'Giva
Cuangar
Rundu
Okavango
Oshakati
Oshikango
Ondangwa
Opuwo
Etosha Pan
Tsumeb
Outjo
Otavi
Grootfontein
Tsodilo Hills
4,885 ft
1,489 m
NAMIBIA
Namib Desert
Otjiwarongo
Brandberg
(Königstein)
8,550 ft
2,606 m
Karibib
Okahandja
Swakopmund
Walvis Bay
Windhoek
8,133 ft
2,479 m
Auasberge
Rehoboth
Gobabis
Ghanzi
BOTS
Kalah
Dese
Nossob
Mariental
Tsabong
Keetmanshoop
Lüderitz
Seeheim
Karasburg
Upington
Alexander Bay
Port Nolloth
Springbok
Orange
Prieska
Upper Karoo
Bitterfontein
Calvinia
Victoria West
Beaufort West
St. Helena Bay
Saldanha
CAPE TOWN
Table Mtn.
1,087 m 3,566 ft
Bellville
Worcester
Cape of Good Hope
7,631 ft
2,326 m
Gt. Karoo
L. Karoo
Oudtshoorn
Mossel Bay
George
Cape Agulhas
KLETT-PERTHES

1:20,000,000
0 200 400 mi
0 200 400 600 km
177
SUDAN
ETHIOPIA
SOMALIA
UGANDA
KENYA
RWANDA
BURUNDI
TANZANIA
ZAMBIA
MALAWI
MOZAMBIQUE
ZIMBABWE
SWAZILAND
LESOTHO
MADAGASCAR
COMOROS
MAURITIUS
SEYCHELLES
INDIAN
OCEAN
Mozambique Channel
Madagascar
Jūbā
Kinyeti 10,456 ft 3,187 m
Gulu
Lira
Mbale
KAMPALA
Jinja
Entebbe
Mt. Elgon 14,177 ft 4,321 m
Margherita Peak 16,766 ft 5,110 m
Kisangani
Isiro
Bunia
Beni
Butembo
Kasese
Mbarara
Masaka
Bukoba
Kigali
Goma
Karisimbi 14,787 ft 4,507 m
Bukavu
Uvira
Bujumbura
Gitega
Kindu
Kasongo
Mt. Heha 9,800 ft 2,987 m
Kigoma
Tabora
Singida
Shinyanga
Mwanza
Musoma
Kisumu
Eldoret
Kakamega
Nakuru
Nyeri
Mt. Kenya 17,058 ft 5,199 m
Embu
NAIROBI
Machakos
Garissa
Lamu
Malindi
Mombasa
Kilimanjaro 19,331 ft 5,892 m
Arusha
Moshi
Voi
Hanang 11,211 ft 3,417 m
Babati
Tanga
Pemba
Chake Chake
Zanzibar
DAR ES SALAAM
Morogoro
Dodoma
Iringa
Mafia
Kilwa Kivinje
Lindi
Mtwara
C. Delgado
Mocímboa da Praia
Mbeya
Rungwe 9,715 ft 2,961 m
Sumbawanga
Mpanda
Kalemie
Kabalo
Manono
Pweto
Kamina
Kasama
Mbala
Mzuzu
Songea
Lichinga
Lilongwe
Chipata
Mangochi
Zomba
Blantyre
Sapitwa 9,849 ft 3,002 m
Cuamba
Nampula
Nacala
Moçambique
Angoche
Mocuba
Quelimane
Tete
Garue
Caia
Marromeu
Chinde
Beira
Dondo
Chimoio
Mutare
Inyangani 8,504 ft 2,592 m
Monte Binga 7,992 ft 2,436 m
Likasi
LUBUMBASHI
Chililabombwe
Solwezi
Chingola
Mufulira
Ndola
Kitwe
Luanshya
Mansa
Mpika
Kabwe
LUSAKA
Kafue
Mazabuka
Choma
Livingstone
Hwange
HARARE
Chitungwiza
Kadoma
Kwekwe
Gweru
BULAWAYO
Masvingo
Great Zimbabwe
Francistown
Selebi-Phikwe
Serowe
Gaborone
Mochudi
Mafikeng
Polokwane
Phalaborwa
PRETORIA
Soshanguve
JOHANNESBURG
SOWETO
Benoni
Vereeniging
Sasolburg
Klerksdorp
Welkom
Newcastle
Bethlehem
Ladysmith
Maseru
Thabana-Ntlenyana 11,424 ft 3,482 m
Pietermaritzburg
DURBAN
Richards Bay
Kokstad
Umtata
Queenstown
Bhisho
Mdantsane
East London
Port Alfred
Port Elizabeth
Cape Recife
Nelspruit
Matola
MAPUTO
Mbabane
Manzini
Xai-Xai
Chibuto
Maxixe
Inhambane
Inharrime
Ponta da Barra
Vilanculos
Nova Mambone
Chokwe
MOGADISHU (MUQDISHO)
Marka
Afgooye
Jawhar
Baydhabo
Beledweyne
Gaalkacyo
Hobyo
Dhuusa Mareeb
Jamaame
Kismaayo
Jilib
Baardheere
Qoryooley
Garbahaarey
Doolo Odo
Xuddur
Wajir
Marsabit
Lodwar
Lake Turkana
Lake Victoria
L. Natron
Serengeti Plain
L. Eyasi
L. Rukwa
L. Mweru
L. Bangweulu
L. Kivu
L. Albert
L. Edward
L. Kariba
Cahora Bassa Res.
Lake Nyasa
Lake Tanganyika
Muchinga Mts.
Mitumba Mts.
Drakensberg
Ruwenzori
Batu 14,131 ft 4,307 m
13,780 ft 4,200 m
Sodo
Awasa
Goba
Arba Minch
Negele
Mēga
Imī
K'ebrī Dehar
Werdēr
Moroni
Kartala 7,746 ft 2,361 m
Ngazidja
Mutsamudu
Nzwani
Mwali
Mamoudzou
Mayotte (FRA.)
Îles Glorieuses (Fr.S.&A.L.)
Juan de Nova (Fr.S.&A.L.)
Bassas da India (Fr.S.&A.L.)
Europa (Fr.S.&A.L.)
Aldabra Is.
Cosmoledo Is.
Farquhar Is.
Cerf
Agalega Is. (MRS.)
Amirante Is.
Morne Seychellois 2,969 ft 905 m
Victoria
Mahé
Coëtivy
C. Bobaomby
Antsirañana
Nosy Be
Maromokotro 9,436 ft 2,876 m
Antalaha
Mahajanga
Marovoay
Mananara Avaratra
Nosy Sainte Marie
Maintirano
Amparafaravola
Ambatondrazaka
Toamasina
ANTANANARIVO
Antsirabe
Antanifotsy
Morondava
Mananjary
Fianarantsoa
Pic Boby 8,721 ft 2,658 m
Manakara
Farafangana
Morombe
Toliara
Ambovombe
Tôlañaro
Cape Vohimena
Tromelin (Fr.S.&A.L.)
Cargados Carajos Is. (MRS.)
Réunion (FRA.)
St-Denis
Piton des Neiges 10,069 ft 3,069 m
Port Louis
Mt. Piton 2,717 ft 828 m
Rodrigues I. (MRS.)
Fr.S.&A.L. French Southern and Antarctic Lands

1:40,000,000
0 500 1,000 mi
0 500 1,000 1,500 2,000 km
1 2 3 4 5 6 7 8 9 10 11 12
140° 130° 120° 110° 100° 90° 80° 70° 60° 50° 40°
I
Sakhalin
Sea of Okhotsk
Okhotsk
Kamchatka
Petropavlovsk-Kamchatskiy
15,584 ft 4,750 m
Klyuchevskaya Sopka
Palana
Commander Is.
Magadan
Verkhoyansk Range
Cherskiy Range
10,325 ft 3,147 m
7,838 ft 2,389 m
Verkhoyansk
Yakutsk
Aldan
Lena
Kolyma Ra.
6,437 ft 1,962 m
Koryak Ra.
8,405 ft 2,562 m
Kolyma
Indigirka
Cherskiy
Pevek
Anadyr'
6,047 ft 1,843 m
Chukot Ra.
C. Navarin
Bering Sea
Provideniya
Chukot Pen.
Chukchi Sea
C. Dezhnëv
St. Lawrence I.
Bering Strait
C. Pr. of Wales
Nome
Norton Sd.
Unalaska
Unimak I.
Fox Is.
Alaska Pen.
Yukon
Alaska
Brooks Range
9,058 ft 2,761 m
6,716 ft 2,047 m
Katmai
Mt. McKinley
20,321 ft 6,194 m
Fairbanks
Alaska Ra.
Kodiak I.
Anchorage
Valdez
PACIFIC OCEAN
G. of Alaska
Dawson
19,550 ft 5,959 m
Mt. Trudeau
Mackenzie Mts.
9,751 ft 2,972 m
Whitehorse
Mackenzie
KLETT-PERTHES
Tiksi
Laptev Sea
East Siberian Sea
New Siberian Islands
Wrangel I.
Putoran Mts.
Noril'sk
Yenisey
Khatanga
Taymyr Pen.
Dikson
C. Chelyuskin
Severnaya Zemlya
Kara Sea
Cape Karlsen
Gulf of Ob
Ob
Salekhard
Narodnaya
6,217 ft 1,895 m
Vorkuta
Novaya Zemlya I.
Kolguyev
C. Kanin Nos
Barents Sea
Franz Josef Land
ARCTIC OCEAN
North Pole
14,075 ft 4,290 m
17,877 ft 5,449 m
C. Morris Jesup
N. Magnetic Pole 2005
Point Barrow
Barrow
Beaufort Sea
Queen Elizabeth Is.
Sverdrup Is.
Parry Is.
McClure Str.
Amundsen Gulf
Banks I.
Inuvik
Great Bear Lake
Victoria I.
Resolute
Pr. of Wales I.
Lancaster Sd.
Boothia Pen.
G. of Boothia
Kugluktuk
Ikaluktutiak
Melville Pen.
Devon I.
Ellesmere I.
Qaanaaq
Upernavik
Baffin Bay
Qeqertarsuaq
Baffin Island
8,501 ft 2,591 m
Davis Strait
Nuuk
Peary Ld.
Greenland
9,882 ft 3,012 m
Gunnbjørn Fjeld
12,139 ft 3,700 m
Arctic Circle
Tasiilaq
C. Farewell
Denmark Strait
ATLANTIC OCEAN
Nordostrundingen
Greenland Sea
Jan Mayen
Iceland
Vatnajökull
6,952 ft 2,119 m
Reykjavík
Spitsbergen
Longyearbyen
Bear I.
Norwegian Sea
12,864 ft 3,921 m
Prime Meridian
North C.
Tromsø
Bodø
Trondheim
Galdhøpiggen
8,101 ft 2,469 m
Bergen
Scandinavia
Oslo
Göteborg
Stockholm
Baltic Sea
Helsinki
Tallinn
Riga
Vilnius
Minsk
Warsaw
Berlin
Copenhagen
Hamburg
Kiev
Moscow
Vologda
Syktyvkar
Volga
Dnieper
Arkhangelsk
Petrozavodsk
L. Onega
St. Petersburg
L. Ladoga
White Sea
Kola Pen.
Murmansk
North Sea
Great Britain
Shetland Is.
Faroe Is.
Glasgow
Elevation
6,562 ft 2,000 m
3,281 ft 1,000 m
1,640 ft 500 m
656 ft 200 m
0 ft 0 m
656 ft 200 m
6,562 ft 2,000 m
13,124 ft 4,000 m
19,686 ft 6,000 m
Inland ice, glaciers
Pack ice
Cold current
Warm current
Limit of drift ice
II
RUSSIA
UNITED STATES
Alaska
CANADA
Greenland (DEN.)
ICELAND
Svalbard (NOR.)
Bear I. (NOR.)
Jan Mayen (NOR.)
Faroe Is. (DEN.)
NORWAY
SWEDEN
FINLAND
EST.
LATVIA
LIT.
BELARUS
UKRAINE
POLAND
(Russia)
GER.
DEN.
NLD.
UNITED KINGDOM
IRELAND
British Is.
MOSCOW
KIEV
MINSK
WARSAW
BERLIN
COPENHAGEN
DEN. DENMARK
EST. ESTONIA
GER. GERMANY
LIT. LITHUANIA
NLD. NETHERLANDS
30 29 28 27 26 25 24 23 22 21 20 19

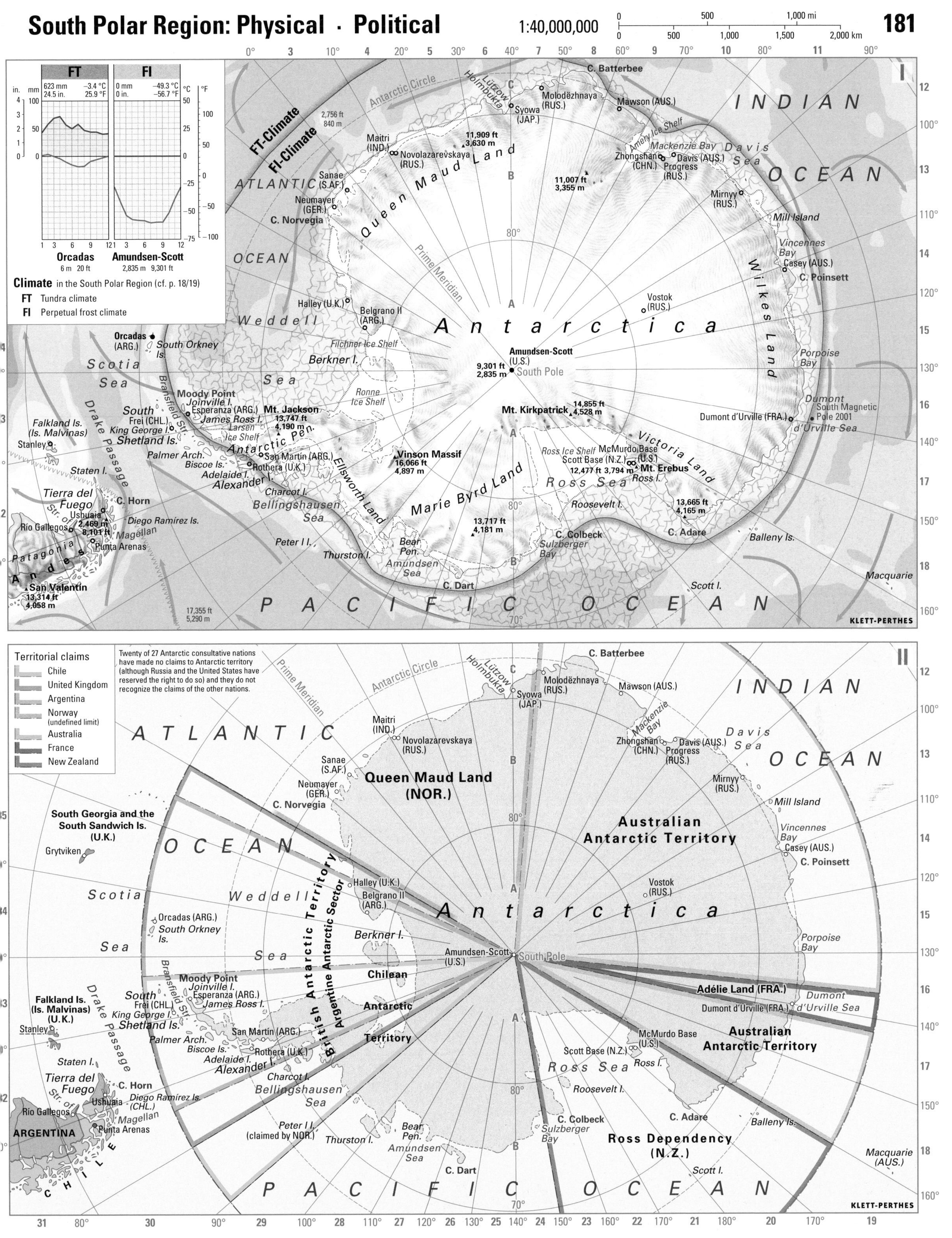
0 500 1,000 mi
0 500 1,000 1,500 2,000 km
FT
FI
623 mm 24.5 in. −3.4 °C 25.9 °F
0 mm 0 in. −49.3 °C −56.7 °F
Orcadas
6 m 20 ft
Amundsen-Scott
2,835 m 9,301 ft
Climate in the South Polar Region (cf. p. 18/19)
FT Tundra climate
FI Perpetual frost climate
FT-Climate
FI-Climate
INDIAN OCEAN
ATLANTIC OCEAN
PACIFIC OCEAN
Antarctica
Queen Maud Land
Wilkes Land
Marie Byrd Land
Victoria Land
Ellsworth Land
Weddell Sea
Scotia Sea
Ross Sea
Amundsen Sea
Bellingshausen Sea
Davis Sea
d'Urville Sea
Drake Passage
Amundsen-Scott (U.S.)
South Pole
Vostok (RUS.)
Mt. Kirkpatrick 14,855 ft 4,528 m
Vinson Massif 16,066 ft 4,897 m
Mt. Erebus 12,477 ft 3,794 m
McMurdo Base (U.S.)
Scott Base (N.Z.)
Mawson (AUS.)
Davis (AUS.)
Casey (AUS.)
Mirnyy (RUS.)
Progress (RUS.)
Zhongshan (CHN.)
Molodëzhnaya (RUS.)
Syowa (JAP.)
Maitri (IND.)
Novolazarevskaya (RUS.)
Sanae (S.AF.)
Neumayer (GER.)
Halley (U.K.)
Belgrano II (ARG.)
Orcadas (ARG.)
Esperanza (ARG.)
San Martín (ARG.)
Rothera (U.K.)
Dumont d'Urville (FRA.)
South Magnetic Pole 2001
Falkland Is. (Is. Malvinas)
South Shetland Is.
South Orkney Is.
Tierra del Fuego
C. Horn
Punta Arenas
Ushuaia
Río Gallegos
Stanley
Territorial claims
Chile
United Kingdom
Argentina
Norway (undefined limit)
Australia
France
New Zealand
Twenty of 27 Antarctic consultative nations have made no claims to Antarctic territory (although Russia and the United States have reserved the right to do so) and they do not recognize the claims of the other nations.
Queen Maud Land (NOR.)
Australian Antarctic Territory
Adélie Land (FRA.)
Ross Dependency (N.Z.)
British Antarctic Territory
Argentine Antarctic Sector
Chilean Antarctic Territory
South Georgia and the South Sandwich Is. (U.K.)
Grytviken
Peter I I. (claimed by NOR.)
Macquarie (AUS.)
ARGENTINA
CHILE
KLETT-PERTHES

Tables and Indexes

Greenland
(part of the Kingdom of Denmark)

Area: 2,166,086 km²
Population: 57,000 (2005)
Capital: Nuuk (Godthåb) (15,000)
Administration: 3 districts (landsdele)
Languages: Greenlandic (East Inuit), Danish, English
Religions: Lutheran 98%
Currency: Danish krone
Major cities:
Sisimiut (6,000), Ilulissat (5,000), Qaqortoq (3,000)

Guatemala
Republic of Guatemala
República de Guatemala

Area: 108,889 km²
Population: 12,559,000 (2005)
Capital: Guatemala Ciudad/Cd. de Guatemala (942,000)
Administration: 22 departments
Languages: Spanish, Mayan languages
Religions: Roman Catholic 60%, Protestant 30%
Currency: 1 quetzal = 100 centavos
Major cities:
Mixco (384,000), Villa Nueva (302,000), Quezaltenango (120,000), Cobán (52,000)

Guyana
Co-operative Republic of Guyana

Area: 214,969 km²
Population: 751,000 (2005)
Capital: Georgetown (249,000)
Administration: 10 regions
Languages: English, Hindi, Urdu, Indian languages
Religions: Protestant 34%, Hindu 33%, Roman Catholic 20%
Currency: 1 Guyana dollar = 100 cents
Major cities:
Linden (45,000), New Amsterdam (36,000)

Grenada
State of Grenada

Area: 344 km²
Population: 103,000 (2005)
Capital: Saint George's (4,000)
Administration: 6 councils, 1 dependency
Languages: English, English Creole, French Creole
Religions: Roman Catholic 58%, Protestant 38%
Currency: 1 East Caribbean dollar = 100 cents
Major cities:
Gouyave (3,000), Grenville (2,000)

Guernsey
(British crown dependency)
Bailiwick of Guernsey

Area: 78 km²
Population: 65,228 (2005)
Capital: Saint Peter Port (17,000)
Administration: none (British crown dependency)
Languages: English, French
Religions: Anglican, Roman Catholic, Presbyterian, Baptist
Currency: British pound and Guernsey pound
Major islands:
Vale (9,600), Castle (9,000), Saint Simpson (8,700)

Haiti
Republic of Haiti
Republique d'Haïti/
Repiblik Dayti

Area: 27,750 km²
Population: 8,528,000 (2005)
Capital: Port-au-Prince (991,000)
Administration: 9 departments
Languages: French/Creole
Religions: Roman Catholic 70%, Protestant 15%
Currency: 1 gourde = 100 centimes
Major cities:
Carrefour (336,000), Delmas (284,000), Cap-Haïtien (114,000), Gonaïves (64,000)

Guadeloupe
(overseas department of France)
Department of Guadeloupe
Département de la Guadeloupe

Area: 1,703 km²
Population: 448,000 (2005)
Capital: Basse-Terre (12,000)
Administration: none (overseas department of France)
Languages: French, Creole patois
Religions: Roman Catholic 84%
Currency: 1 euro = 100 cent
Major cities:
Les Abymes (63,000), Baie-Mahault (31,000), Le Gosier (29,000), Petit-Bourg (25,000)

Guinea
Republic of Guinea
République de Guinée

Area: 245,857 km²
Population: 9,402,000 (2005)
Capital: Conakry (1,091,000)
Administration: 33 prefectures and 1 special zone (Conakry)
Languages: French, Fulani, Malinke
Religions: Muslim 85%, Christian 8%
Currency: Guinea franc
Major cities:
Kindia (288,000), Nzérékoré (283,000), Kankan (261,000), Labé (89,000)

Honduras
Republic of Honduras
República de Honduras

Area: 112,492 km²
Population: 7,205,000 (2005)
Capital: Tegucigalpa (769,000)
Administration: 18 departments
Languages: Spanish, Indian languages, English
Religions: Roman Catholic 90%
Currency: 1 lempira = 100 centavos
Major cities:
San Pedro Sula (439,000), La Ceiba (111,000), Choloma (108,000), El Progreso (90,000), Choluteca (76,000), Comayagua (55,000)

Guam
(territory of the U.S.)
Territory of Guam

Area: 549 km²
Population: 170,000 (2005)
Capital: Agaña/Hagåtña (1,000)
Administration: none (territory of the U.S.)
Languages: English, Chamorro, Philippine languages
Religions: Roman Catholic 90%
Currency: US dollar
Major cities:
Tamuning (11,000), Mangilao (9,000), Yigo (8,000), Astumbo (6,000)

Guinea-Bissau
Republic of Guinea-Bissau
República da Guiné-Bissau

Area: 36,125 km²
Population: 1,586,000 (2005)
Capital: Bissau (292,000)
Administration: 8 regions and the capital
Languages: Portuguese, Crioulo
Religions: traditional beliefs 54%, Muslim 38%, Christian 8%
Currency: 1 CFA franc = 100 centimes
Major cities:
Bafatá (18,000), Gabú (9,600)

Hungary
Republic of Hungary
Magyar Köztársaság

Area: 93,029 km²
Population: 10,098,000 (2005)
Capital: Budapest (1,740,000)
Administration: 19 counties and the capital
Languages: Hungarian, German, Slovak, Croatian
Religions: Roman Catholic 63%, Protestant 26%
Currency: 1 forint = 100 filler
Major cities:
Debrecen (207,000), Miskolc (182,000), Szeged (164,000), Pécs (160,000), Győr (129,000)

This section provides 40 pages of data on 198 countries and their dependent political territories and exclaves. Countries are arranged in alphabetical order by the English short form of their name. Entries also include the English full-length name and the full name in official local languages. For countries with a federal structure, names of administrative units are listed in the customary English form (e.g. North Ossetia-Alania). The same form for these administrative units is used in the maps of the atlas.

Dependent territories and exclaves are listed after their respective nation, and inhabited external territories are listed both after their respective nation and under their own name, to make them easier to find.

Area and population figures for territorial units are based on the statistical yearbook of the Federal Republic of Germany (Statistisches Jahrbuch der Bundesrepublik Deutschland). Figures for federal administrative units are primarily from the Fischer Weltalmanach, an authoritative global statistical survey. Due to differences in the way inland waters are treated in area calculations, some area figures may differ from those of other statistical surveys.

Cities and their associated urban realms are depicted as accurately as possible in reference maps of the atlas. Thus, scale permitting, city symbols have been supplemented by representations of the area of the entire urban agglomeration (cf. Los Angeles). Correspondingly, the statistical gazetteer lists the population of the city proper and the population of a city's agglomeration (A) in relevant cases (cf. Athens). For cities in the U.S.A., the gazetteer lists Metropolitan Statistical Areas (MSAs) as defined by the U.S. Census Bureau.

Population figures are primarily taken from the Fischer Weltalmanach and from publications by national statistical bureaus. These publications also served as the principal source for information on language, religion and currency. Special care has been taken to include the most recent population figures available.

Under languages, the gazetteer mainly lists official languages, but also includes important non-official languages. Official languages are separated by slashes; other languages are separated by commas.

The gazetteer includes national flags for all countries and inhabited dependent territories. There are three special cases for flags of inhabited dependencies:

1) The following dependencies do not have a flag of their own, or have a territorial flag that has not been officially recognized. In these cases the flag of the mother country is depicted as the official flag. These dependencies include: Akrotiri Souvereign Base Area, Christmas Island, Cocos Islands, Dhekelia Souvereign Base Area, Johnston Atoll, Mayotte, Midway Islands, New Caledonia, Saint-Barthélémy, Saint-Martin, Saint Pierre and Miquelon, Tokelau, Wake Island, Wallis and Futuna.

2) The following dependencies have a flag of their own, but it should be noted that the flag may only be hoisted in second position together with the flag of their mother country. This rule applies to: American Samoa, Anguilla, Aruba, Bermuda, British Virgin Islands, Cayman Islands, Falkland Islands, Faroe Islands, French Polynesia, Gibraltar, Greenland, Guam, Montserrat, Netherlands Antilles, Norfolk Island, Pitcairn Islands, Puerto Rico, Saint Helena, Turks and Caicos Islands, Virgin Islands, U.S.

3) The following dependencies have a flag of their own and such a high level of autonomy that they either do not display the flag of their mother country at all or do not have to do so: Guernsey, Jersey, Man, Isle of, Northern Mariana Islands, Niue.

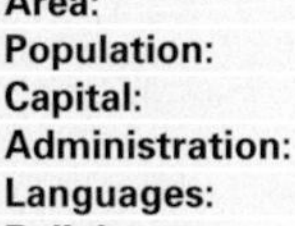

Afghanistan

Islamic Republic of Afghanistan
De Afghānistān Islāmī Jumhūrīyat/ Jomhūrī-ye Afghānestān

Area: 652,090 km²
Population: 27,145,000 (2007)
Capital: Kābul (2,956,000)
Administration: 34 provinces
Languages: Pashto/Dari
Religions: Muslim 99%
Currency: 1 afghani = 100 puls
Major cities:
Kandahār/Qandahār (226,000), Herāt (177,000), Jalālābād (168,000), Mazār-e Sharif (128,000), Baghlān (125,000), Kondūz (122,000), Meymaneh (76,000)

Akrotiri

Akrotiri Sovereign Base Area

Area: 123 km²
Population: 15,700 (total of Akrotiri and Dhekelia residents - including 7,700 Cypriots, 3,600 Service and UK-based contract personnel, and 4,400 dependents)
Capital: Episkopi Cantonment (base administrative center for Akrotiri and Dhekelia)
Languages: English, Greek
Currency: 1 euro = 100 cent

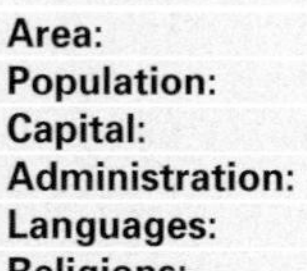

Albania

Republic of Albania
Republika e Shqipërisë

Area: 28,748 km²
Population: 3,190,000 (2007)
Capital: Tirana/Tiranë (343,000)
Administration: 12 counties
Languages: Albanian
Religions: Muslim 70%, Albanian Orthodox 20%, Roman Catholic 10%
Currency: 1 lek = 100 qindars
Major cities:
Durrës (100,000), Elbasan (88,000), Shkodër (83,000), Vlorë (78,000), Korçë (55,000)

Algeria

People's Democratic Republic of Algeria
Al-Jumhūrīyah al-Jazā'irīyah ad-Dīmuqrātīyah ash-Sha'bīyah

Area: 2,381,741 km²
Population: 33,858,000 (2007)
Capital: Algiers/Al-Jazā'ir (2,956,000)
Administration: 48 provinces (wilayat)
Languages: Arabic, Berber
Religions: Muslim 99,9%
Currency: 1 Alger. dinar = 100 centimes
Major cities:
Oran/Wahrān (656,000), Constantine/Qusantinah (462,000), 'Annābah (349,000), Bātnah (243,000), Saṭīf (212,000), Sīdī Bal'abbās (180,000), Biskrah (171,000), Djelfa/Al-Jilfah (154,000)

American Samoa

(territory of the U.S.)
Territory of American Samoa

Area: 199 km²
Population: 67,000 (2007)
Capital: Pago Pago on Tutuila (4,000)
Administration: none (territory of the U.S.)
Languages: Samoan/English/Tongan
Religions: Christ. Congregationalist 50%, Roman Catholic 20%
Currency: 1 dollar = 100 cents
Major cities:
Tafuna (11,000), Nu'uuli (5,000), Leone (4,000)

Andorra

Principality of Andorra
Principat d'Andorra

Area: 468 km²
Population: 75,000 (2007)
Capital: Andorra la Vella (21,000)
Administration: 7 parishes
Languages: Catalan, Spanish, French
Religions: Roman Catholic 92%
Currency: 1 euro = 100 cent
Major cities:
Escaldes-Engordany (15,500), Encamp (10,700), St. Juliá de Lòrio (7,800), La Massana (6,600)

Angola

Republic of Angola
República de Angola

Area: 1,246,700 km²
Population: 17,024,000 (2007)
Capital: Luanda (2,623,000)
Administration: 18 provinces
Languages: Portuguese, Bantu languages
Religions: Christian 89%, traditional beliefs
Currency: 1 readjusted kwanza = 100 lwei
Major cities:
Huambo (173,000), Lobito (137,000), Benguela (134,000), Kuito (89,000), Lubango (76,000)

Anguilla

(overseas territory of the U.K.)
Crown Colony of Anguilla

Area: 91 km²
Population: 13,000 (2007)
Capital: The Valley (1,400)
Administration: none (overseas territory of the U.K.)
Languages: English
Religions: Anglican 29%, Methodist 24%, other Protestant 30%
Currency: East Caribbean dollar
Major cities:
South Hill (1,500), North Side (1,200)

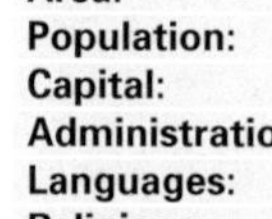

Antigua and Barbuda

Area: 457 km²
Population: 85,000 (2007)
Capital: Saint John's (24,000)
Administration: 6 parishes, 2 dependencies
Languages: English, Creole
Religions: Anglican 80%, Roman Catholic 20%
Currency: 1 Eastern Caribbean dollar = 100 cents
Major cities:
Codrington (1,200)

Argentina

Argentine Republic
República Argentina

Area: 2,780,400 km²
Population: 39,531,000 (2007)
Capital: Buenos Aires (2,776,000, A: 12,047,000)
Administration: 23 provinces, 1 federal district
Languages: Spanish, Indian languages
Religions: Roman Catholic 91%, Protestant 2%
Currency: 1 peso = 100 centavos
Major cities:
Córdoba (1,268,000), San Justo (1,254,000), Rosario (906,000), Lomas de Zamora (591,000), La Plata (553,000), Mar del Plata (542,000), San Miguel de Tucumán (526,000), Quilmes (519,000), Almirante Brown (514,000), Merlo (469,000), Salta (463,000), Lanús (453,000), General San Martín (405,000), Moreno (380,000)

External Territory:

Argentine Antarctic Sector

Sector Antártico Argentino
Claimed by Argentina

Area: 1,231,000 km²
Research stations

Armenia

Republic of Armenia
Hayastani Hanrapetut'yun

Area: 29,743 km²
Population: 3,002,000 (2007)
Capital: Yerevan (1,246,000)
Administration: 11 provinces
Languages: Armenian, Russian
Religions: Armenian Apostolic Church
Currency: 1 dram = 100 lumas
Major cities:
Gyumri (150,000), Vanadzor (106,000), Vagharshapat (56,000), Hrazdan (53,000), K'ap'an (46,000), Abovyan (45,000)

Aruba

(part of the Kingdom of the Netherlands)

Area: 193 km^2
Population: 104,000 (2007)
Capital: Oranjestad (30,000)
Administration: none (part of the Kingdom of the Netherlands)
Languages: Dutch, Papiamento, Spanish
Religions: Roman Catholic 82%, Protestant 8%
Currency: Aruban guilder/florin
Major cities:
Sint Nicolaas (17,000)

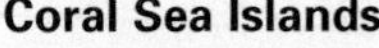

Coral Sea Islands

Territory of Coral Sea Islands

Reefs and islands scattered over a sea area of about 1 million km^2 (uninhabited)

Heard and the McDonald Islands

Territory of Heard and the McDonald Islands

Area: 412 km^2/uninhabited

Norfolk Island

Territory of Norfolk Island

Area: 35 km^2
Population: 2,000 (2007)
Capital: Kingston (880)

Bahrain

Kingdom of Bahrain
Mamlakat al-Baḥrayn

Area: 694 km^2
Population: 753,000 (2007)
Capital: Manama/Al-Manāmah (154,000)
Administration: 12 regions
Languages: Arabic, English
Religions: Muslim 80%
Currency: 1 Bahrain dinar = 1,000 fils
Major cities:
Al-Muḥarraq (92,000), Ar Rifā' (80,000), Hammād (53,000)

Australia

Commonwealth of Australia

Area: 7,692,024 km^2
Population: 20,743,000 (2007)
Capital: Canberra (340,000)
Administration: 6 states, 2 territories
Languages: English, Australian languages
Religions: Roman Catholic 27%, Anglican 21%, other Christian 21%
Currency: 1 Austral. dollar = 100 cents
Major cities:
Sydney (3,602,000; A: 4,232,000), Melbourne (3,489,000), Brisbane (1,653,000), Perth (1,397,000), Adelaide (1,111,000), Newcastle (494,000), Gold Coast (426,000)

	Area km^2	Population 2004	Capital
States			
New South Wales	800,640	6,731,000	Sydney
Queensland	1,730,650	3,882,000	Brisbane
South Australia	983,480	1,534,000	Adelaide
Tasmania	68,400	482,000	Hobart
Victoria	227,420	4,973,000	Melbourne
Western Australia	2,529,880	1,982,000	Perth
Territories			
Australian Capital Territory	2,360	312,000	Canberra
Northern Territory	1,349,130	200,000	Darwin

External Territories:

Ashmore and Cartier Islands

Territory of Ashmore and Cartier Islands

Area: 2 km^2/uninhabited

Australian Antarctic Territory

Claimed by Australia

Area: c. 6,120,000 km^2
Research stations

Christmas Island

Territory of Christmas Island

Area: 135 km^2
Population: 1,500 (2002)

Cocos (Keeling) Islands

Territory of Cocos Islands

Area: 14 km^2
Population: 630 (2004)

Austria

Republic of Austria
Republik Österreich

Area: 83,859 km^2
Population: 8,361,000 (2007)
Capital: Vienna/Wien (1,584,000)
Administration: 9 federal states
Languages: German/Slovene/Croatian/Hungarian (regionally)
Religions: Roman Catholic 73%, Protestant 5%
Currency: 1 euro = 100 cent
Major cities:
Graz (226,000), Linz (184,000), Salzburg (143,000), Innsbruck (113,000), Klagenfurt (90,000)

Azerbaijan

Azerbaijani Republic
Azərbaycan Respublikası

Area: 86,600 km^2
Population: 8,467,000 (2007)
Capital: Baku/Bakı (1,840,000)
Administration: 78 rayons
Languages: Azerbaijani, Russian
Religions: Muslim 90%
Currency: 1 manat =100 gopik
Major cities:
Gəncə (293,000), Sumqayıt (249,000)

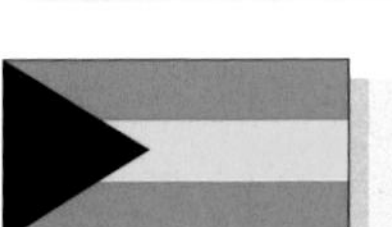

Bahamas, The

Commonwealth of The Bahamas

Area: 13,878 km^2
Population: 331,000 (2007)
Capital: Nassau (211,000)
Administration: 19 districts
Languages: English, Creole
Religions: Baptist 31%, Roman Catholic 16%, Anglican 16%
Currency: 1 Bahamian dollar = 100 cents
Major cities:
Freeport (27,000), Coopers Town (8,000), Marsh Habour (5,000), High Rock (4,000)

Bangladesh

People's Republic of Bangladesh
Gaṇprajātantrī Bānlādesh

Area: 147,570 km^2
Population: 158,665,000 (2007)
Capital: Dhaka (9,913,000)
Administration: 6 provinces
Languages: Bengali, English
Religions: Muslim 87% (mainly Sunni), Hindu 12%
Currency: 1 taka = 100 paisa
Major cities:
Chittagong (3,202,000), Khulna (811,000), Rajshahi (403,000), Sylhet (299,000), Tongi (296,000), Rangpur (264,000), Mymensingh (237,000)

Barbados

Area: 430 km^2
Population: 294,000 (2007)
Capital: Bridgetown (98,000)
Administration: 11 parishes
Languages: English, Bajan
Religions: Anglican 40%, other Protestants 30%, non-denominational 20%
Currency: 1 Barbados dollar = 100 cents
Major cities:
Speightstown (3,500), Bathsheba (1,800)

Belarus

Republic of Belarus
Respublika Belarus'

Area: 207,600 km^2
Population: 9,689,000 (2007)
Capital: Minsk (1,699,000)
Administration: 6 provinces, capital
Languages: Belarusian/Russian
Religions: Russian Orthodox 60%, Roman Catholic 8%
Currency: 1 Belarusian rouble = 100 kopeks
Major cities:
Homyel' (480,000), Mahilyow (361,000), Vitsyebsk (342,000), Hrodna (207,000), Brest (291,000)

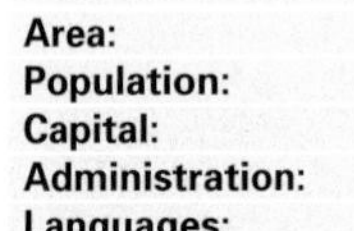

1 km^2 = 0.3861 square mile

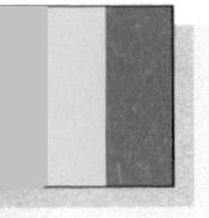

Belgium

Kingdom of Belgium
Royaume de Belgique/
Koninkrijk België/
Königreich Belgien

Area: 30,518 km²
Population: 10,457,000 (2007)
Capital: Brussels/Brussel/Bruxelles (143,000; A: 999,000)
Administration: 3 regions: Flanders, Wallonia, Brussels-Capital
Languages: French/Dutch/German
Religions: Roman Catholic 81%
Currency: 1 euro = 100 cent
Major cities:
Antwerp/Antwerpen (449,000), Ghent/Gent (226,000), Charleroi (200,000), Luik/Liège (185,000)

Belize

Area: 22,966 km²
Population: 288,000 (2007)
Capital: Belmopan (8,100)
Administration: 6 districts
Languages: English, English Creole, Spanish
Religions: Roman Catholic 58 %, Protestant 28%
Currency: 1 Belize dollar = 100 cents
Major cities:
Belize City (49,000), Orange Walk (13,000), San Ignacio (13,000)

Benin

Republic of Benin
Bénin
République du Bénin

Area: 112,622 km²
Population: 9,033,000 (2007)
Capital: Porto-Novo (210,000) (seat of government: Cotonou)
Administration: 12 regions
Languages: French, 50 tribal languages
Religions: traditional beliefs 60%, Christian 25%
Currency: 1 CFA franc = 100 centimes
Major cities:
Cotonou (800,000), Parakou (175,000), Djougou (132,000), Abomey (82,000)

Bermuda

(overseas territory of the U.K.)

Area: 53 km²
Population: 65,000 (2007)
Capital: Hamilton (890)
Administration: 9 parishes and 2 municipalities
Languages: English, Portuguese
Religions: Anglican 23%, Roman Catholic 15%
Currency: Bermudian dollar
Major cities:
Saint George (1,800)

Bhutan

Kingdom of Bhutan
Druk-Yul
Druk-Gyal Khab

Area: 46,500 km²
Population: 658,000 (2007)
Capital: Thimphu (74,000)
Administration: 20 districts
Languages: Dzongkha, various Tibetan and various Nepalese dialects
Religions: Buddhist 72%, Hindu 24%
Currency: 1 ngultrum = 100 chetrum
Major cities:
Phuntsholing (21,000)

Bolivia

Republic of Bolivia
República de Bolivia

Area: 1,098,591 km²
Population: 9,525,000 (2007)
Capital: Sucre (judicial, 216,000), La Paz (administrative)
Administration: 9 departments
Languages: Spanish/Quechua/Aymara
Religions: Roman Catholic 85%
Currency: 1 boliviano = 100 centavos
Major cities:
Santa Cruz (1,136,000), La Paz (793,000), El Alto (650,000), Cochabamba (517,000), Oruro (216,000

Bosnia and Herzegovina

Bosna i Hercegovina/
Bosna i Hercegovina/
Bosna i Hercegovina

Area: 51,197 km²
Population: 3,935,000 (2007)
Capital: Sarajevo (552,000)
Administration: Federation of B. and H., Serb Rep., and Brčko district
Languages: Bosnian/Croatian/Serbian
Religions: Muslim 40%, Orthodox Cath. 31%, Roman Cath. 15%
Currency: 1 convertible mark
Major cities:
Tuzla (230,000), Zenica (146,000), Banja Luka (143,000), Mostar (94,000), Bihać (65,000)

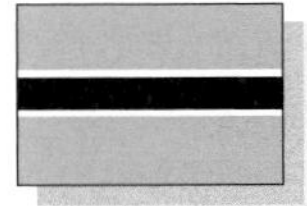

Botswana

Republic of Botswana
Lefatshe la Botswana

Area: 582,000 km²
Population: 1,882,000 (2007)
Capital: Gaborone (186,000)
Administration: 10 districts
Languages: English, Setswana
Religions: predominantly traditional beliefs, Christian 30%
Currency: 1 pula = 100 thebe
Major cities:
Francistown (82,000), Molepolole (55,000), Selebi-Pikwe (50,000), Maun (44,000), Serowe (42,000), Kanye (41,000)

Brazil

Federative Republic of Brazil
República Federativa do Brasil

Area: 8,547,404 km²
Population: 191,791,000 (2007)
Capital: Brasília (2,231,000)
Administration: 26 states, 1 federal district
Languages: Portuguese
Religions: Roman Catholic 75%
Currency: 1 real = 100 centavos
Major cities:
São Paulo (10,278,000; A: 19,037,000), Rio de Janeiro (6,094,000; A: 11,570,000), Salvador (2,673,000), Belo Horizonte (2,376,000), Fortaleza (2,375,000), Curitiba (1,758,000)

States	Area km²	Population 2007	Capital
Acre	153,150	655,000	Rio Branco
Alagoas	27,933	3,037,000	Maceió
Amapá	143,454	607,000	Macapá
Amazonas	1,577,820	3,305,000	Manaus
Bahia	567,295	13,904,000	Salvador
Ceará	146,348	8,169,000	Fortaleza
Espírito Santo	46,194	3,442,000	Vitória
Goiás	341,289	5,686,000	Goiânia
Maranhão	333,366	6,152,000	São Luís
Mato Grosso	906,807	2,835,000	Cuiabá
Mato Grosso do Sul	358,159	2,285,000	Campo Grande
Minas Gerais	588,384	19,382,000	Belo Horizonte
Pará	1,253,165	7,054,000	Belém
Paraíba	56,585	3,612,000	João Pessoa
Paraná	199,709	10,337,000	Curitiba
Pernambuco	98,938	8,467,000	Recife
Piauí	252,378	3,025,000	Teresina
Rio de Janeiro	43,910	15,490,000	Rio de Janeiro
Rio Grande do Norte	53,307	3,027,000	Natal
Rio Grande do Sul	282,062	10,916,000	Porto Alegre
Rondônia	238,513	1,551,000	Porto Velho
Roraima	225,116	399,000	Boa Vista
Santa Catarina	95,443	5,921,000	Florianópolis
São Paulo	248,809	40,809,000	São Paulo
Sergipe	22,050	1,988,000	Aracaju
Tocantins	278,421	1,322,000	Palmas
Federal district			
Distrito Federal	5,822	2,363,000	Brasília

British Virgin Islands

(overseas territory of the U.K.)

Area: 153 km²
Population: 23,000 (2007)
Capital: Road Town on Tortola (8,000)
Administration: none (overseas territory of the U.K.)
Languages: English
Religions: Protestant 86%, Roman Catholic 10%
Currency: 1 dollar = 100 cents
Major islands:
Tortola (17,000), Virgin Gorda (3,000)

Brunei

State of Brunei Darussalam
Negara Brunei Darussalam

Area: 5,765 km²
Population: 390,000 (2007)
Capital: Bandar Seri Begawan (67,000)
Administration: 4 districts
Languages: Malay, English
Religions: Muslim 67%, Buddhist 15%, Christian 10%
Currency: 1 Brunei dollar = 100 cents
Major cities:
Kuala Belait (21,000), Seria (21,000)

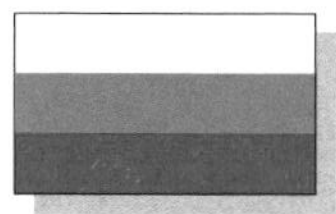

Bulgaria

Republic of Bulgaria
Republika Bŭlgariya

Area: 110,910 km²
Population: 7,639,000 (2007)
Capital: Sofia/Sofiya (1,096,000)
Administration: 28 provinces
Languages: Bulgarian, Turkish
Religions: Bulgarian Orthodox 86%, Muslim 13%
Currency: 1 lev = 100 stotinki
Major cities:
Plovdiv (341,000), Varna (315,000), Burgas (193,000), Ruse (162,000), Stara Zagora (144,000), Pleven (122,000), Sliven (101,000)

Burkina Faso

République Démocratique du Burkina Faso

Area: 274,200 km²
Population: 14,784,000 (2007)
Capital: Ouagadougou (710,000)
Administration: 45 provinces
Languages: French, Arabic
Religions: traditional beliefs 50%, Muslim 40%
Currency: 1 CFA franc = 100 centimes
Major cities:
Bobo-Dioulasso (310,000), Koudougou (72,000), Ouahigouya (52,000), Banfora (50,000)

Burundi

Republic of Burundi
Republika y'Uburundi/
République du Burundi

Area: 27,834 km²
Population: 8,508,000 (2007)
Capital: Bujumbura (319,000)
Administration: 15 provinces
Languages: Kirundi/French
Religions: Christian 68%, traditional beliefs
Currency: 1 Burundi franc = 100 centimes
Major cities:
Gitega (47,000), Muyinga (45,000), Ngozi (40,000), Ruyigi (37,000), Kayanza (26,000), Bururi (23,000)

Cambodia

Kingdom of Cambodia
Preăh Réachéanachâkr Kâmpŭchéa

Area: 181,035 km²
Population: 14,444,000 (2007)
Capital: Phnum Pénh (1,099,000)
Administration: 24 provinces
Languages: Khmer, French, Chinese
Religions: Buddhist 88%, Muslim 2%
Currency: 1 riel = 100 sen
Major cities:
Preah Seihânŭ (156,000), Bătdâmbâng (140,000), Siĕmréab (120,000)

Cameroon

Republic of Cameroon
République du Cameroun/
Republic of Cameroon

Area: 466,050 km²
Population: 18,549,000 (2007)
Capital: Yaoundé (1,249,000)
Administration: 10 provinces
Languages: French/English
Religions: Christian 53%, traditional beliefs 40%
Currency: 1 CFA franc = 100 centimes
Major cities:
Douala (1,495,000), Garoua (357,000), Bamenda (316,000), Maroua (272,000), Bafoussam (242,000)

Canada

Area: 9,984,670 km² (755,180 km² freshwater)
Population: 32,876,000 (2007)
Capital: Ottawa (828,000; A: 1,146,000)
Administration: 10 provinces, 3 territories
Languages: English/French
Religions: Roman Catholic 45%, Protestant 36%
Currency: 1 Canadian dollar = 100 cents
Major cities:
Toronto (4,367,000), Montréal (3,216,000), Calgary (951,000), Edmonton (938,000), Vancouver (546,000), Québec (491,000),

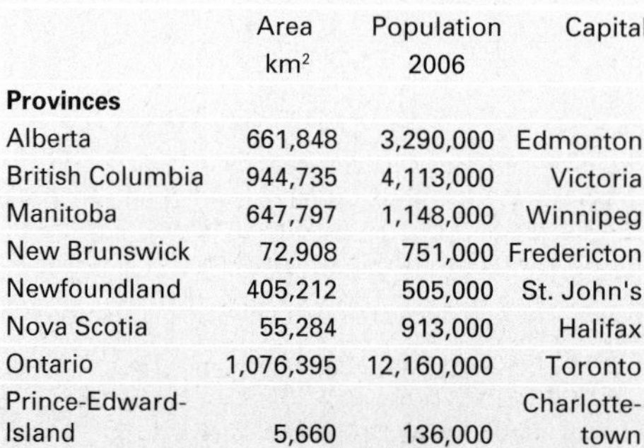

	Area km²	Population 2006	Capital
Provinces			
Alberta	661,848	3,290,000	Edmonton
British Columbia	944,735	4,113,000	Victoria
Manitoba	647,797	1,148,000	Winnipeg
New Brunswick	72,908	751,000	Fredericton
Newfoundland	405,212	505,000	St. John's
Nova Scotia	55,284	913,000	Halifax
Ontario	1,076,395	12,160,000	Toronto
Prince-Edward-Island	5,660	136,000	Charlotte-town
Québec	1,542,056	7,546,000	Québec
Saskatchewan	651,036	968,000	Regina
Territories			
Northwest Territories	1,346,106	41,000	Yellow-knife
Nunavut	2,093,190	29,000	Iqaluit
Yukon Territory	482,443	30,000	White-horse

Cape Verde

Republic of Cape Verde
República de Cabo Verde

Area: 4,033 km²
Population: 530,000 (2007)
Capital: Praia (95,000)
Administration: 17 municipalities
Languages: Portuguese
Religions: Roman Catholic 96%
Currency: 1 Cape Verde escudo = 100 centavos
Major cities:
Mindelo (63,000)

Cayman Islands

(overseas territory of the U.K.)

Area: 264 km²
Population: 47,000 (2007)
Capital: George Town on Grand Cayman (21,000)
Administration: 8 districts
Languages: English
Religions: Protestant
Currency: Caymanian dollar
Major islands:
Grand Cayman (40,000), Cayman Brac (1,800), Little Cayman (100)

Central African Republic

Ködrö tî Bê-Afrîka/
République centrafricaine

Area: 622,436 km²
Population: 4,343,000 (2007)
Capital: Bangui (636,000)
Administration: 16 prefectures and the capital
Languages: Sango/French
Religions: traditional beliefs 57%, Christian 30%, Muslim 15%
Currency: 1 CFA franc = 100 centimes
Major cities:
Bimbo (124,000), Berbérati (61,000), Bouar (40,000), Carnot (58,000), Bambari (52,000)

1 km² = 0.3861 square mile

Chad

Republic of Chad
République du Tchad/
Jumhūrīyat Tshād

Area: 1,284,000 km²
Population: 10,781,000 (2007)
Capital: N´Djamena (530,000)
Administration: 18 prefectures
Languages: French/Arabic
Religions: Muslim 50%, Christian 30%
Currency: 1 CFA franc = 100 centimes
Major cities:
Moundou (281,000), Sarh (100,000), Abéché (73,000), Kélo (42,000), Koumra (35,000), Pala (35,000), Am-Timan (28,000), Bongor (27,000)

Chile

Republic of Chile
República de Chile

Area: 756,626 km²
Population: 16,635,000 (2007)
Capital: Santiago (4,656,000)
Administration: 13 regions
Languages: Spanish, Indian languages
Religions: Roman Catholic 77%, Protestant 13%
Currency: 1 Chilean peso = 100 centavos
Major cities:
Puente Alto (493,000), Maipú (464,000), Viña del Mar (299,000), Antofagasta (298,000), Valparaíso (270,000), Talcahuano (247,000), San Bernardo (238,000), Temuco (253,000), Rancagua (207,000)

External Territories:

Islands in the Pacific Ocean:

Desventurados Islands/Islas Desventurados
Diego Ramírez Island/Islas Diego Ramírez
Easter Island/Isla de Pascua (Rapa Nui)
Juan Fernández Island/Islas Juan Fernández
Sala-y-Gómez

Chilean Antarctic Territory

Territorio Antártico Chileno
Claimed by Chile
Area: 1,250,000 km²
Research stations

China

People's Republic of China
Zhonghua Renmin Gongheguo

Area: 9,596,961 km²
Population: 1,344,004,000 (2007)
Capital: Beijing (10,839,000)
Administration: 23 provinces (China considers Taiwan its 23rd province), 5 autonomous regions, 4 municipalities, 2 special administrative regions
Languages: Chinese, minority languages
Religions: Non-religious 52%, Confucianist 20%, Atheist 12%
Currency: 1 Renminbi (yuan) = 10 jiao
Major cities:
Shanghai (12,887,000), Tianjin (9,156,000), Hong Kong/Xianggang (6,708,000), Wuhan (5,169,000), Chongqing (4,900,000), Harbin (4,266,000), Shenyang (4,828,000), Guangzhou (3,893,000), Chengdu (3,294,000), Xi´an (3,123,000), Changchun (3,093,000), Nanjing (2,740,000), Dalian (2,628,000), Qingdao (2,543,000), Jinan (2,568,000), Hangzhou (2,105,000), Zhengzhou (2,035,000), Shijiazhuang (1,983,000), Taiyuan (1,937,000), Changsha (1,737,000), Kunming (1,685,000), Nanjiang (1,650,000), Fuzhou (1,546,000), Lanzhou (1538000)

Christmas Island

(territory of Australia)
Territory of Christmas Island

Area: 135 km²
Population: 1,500 (2002)
Capital: The Settlement
Administration: none (territory of Australia)
Languages: English, Chinese, Malay
Religions: Buddhist 36%, Muslim 25%, Christian 18%
Currency: Australian dollar

Cocos (Keeling) Islands

(territory of Australia)
Territory of Cocos (Keeling) Islands

Area: 14 km²
Population: 630 (2004)
Capital: West Island
Administration: none (territory of Australia)
Languages: Malay (Cocos dialect), English
Religions: Sunni Muslim 80%, Christian
Currency: Australian dollar

Colombia

Republic of Colombia
República de Colombia

Area: 1,138,914 km²
Population: 46,156,000 (2007)
Capital: Bogotá (6,850,000)
Administration: 32 departments, capital
Languages: Spanish, Indian languages
Religions: Roman Catholic 95%
Currency: 1 Colombian peso = 100 centavos
Major cities:
Cali (2,288,000), Medellín (1,965,000), Barranquilla (1,330,000), Cartagena (903,000), Cúcuta (683,000), Bucaramanga (553,000), Pereira (420,000)

Comoros

Union of the Comoros
Udzima wa Komori
Ittiḥād al-Qumur
Union des Comores

Area: 1,861 km²
Population: 839,000 (2007)
Capital: Moroni (60,000)
Administration: 3 districts
Languages: Comorian, Arabic, French
Religions: Muslim 99%, Roman Catholic 1%
Currency: 1 Comorian franc = 100 centimes
Major cities:
Mutsamudu (31,000), Mitsamiouli (21,000), Domoni (19,000), Fomboni (13,000)

Congo, Democratic Republic of the

République démocratique du Congo

Area: 2,344,858 km²
Population: 62,636,000 (2007)
Capital: Kinshasa (6,789,000)
Administration: 10 regions, capital
Languages: French
Religions: Roman Catholic 42%, Protestant 25%
Currency: 1 Congolese franc
Major cities:
Lubumbashi (1,138,000), Mbuji-Mayi (971,000), Kolwezi (862,000), Kananga (577,000), Kisangani (536,000), Likasi (397,000)

Congo, Republic of the

République du Congo

Area: 342,000 km²
Population: 3,768,000 (2007)
Capital: Brazzaville (950,000))
Administration: 10 regions and 1 commune
Languages: French, Lingala
Religions: Roman Catholic 54%, traditional beliefs
Currency: 1 CFA franc = 100 centimes
Major cities:
Pointe-Noire (561,000), Loubomo (93,000), Nkayi (89,000), Mossendjo (28,000)

Cook Islands

(Independant Territory in Free Association with New Zealand)

Area: 237 km²
Population: 13,000 (2007)
Capital: Avarua (9,000)
Administration: island councils and district councils
Languages: English, Cook Islands Maori
Religions: Protestant 90%, Roman Catholic 10%
Currency: New Zealand dollar
Major cities:
Mangaia (330), Amuri (280), Omoka (180)

Costa Rica

Republic of Costa Rica
República de Costa Rica

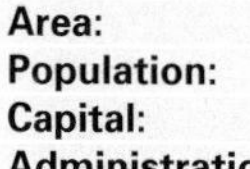

Area: 51,100 km²
Population: 4,468,000 (2007)
Capital: San José (337,000)
Administration: 7 provinces
Languages: Spanish, English, Creole
Religions: Roman Catholic 89%, Protestant 8%
Currency: 1 Costa Rican colon = 100 céntimos
Major cities:
Limón (61,000), Alajuela (48,000), San Francisco (45,000), Cinco Esquinas (40,000)

Côte d'Ivoire

Republic of Côte d'Ivoire
(Ivory Coast)
République de Côte d'Ivoire

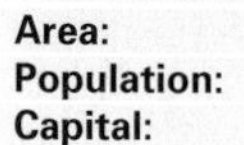

Area: 322,462 km²
Population: 19,262,000 (2007)
Capital: Yamoussoukro (299,000 (seat of government: Abidjan)
Administration: 19 regions
Languages: French, 60 native dialects
Religions: Muslim 40%, Christian 28%, traditional beliefs
Currency: 1 CFA franc = 100 centimes
Major cities:
Abidjan (3,548,0000), Bouaké (569,000), Daloa (213,000), Korhogo (175,000), Anyama (147,000)

Croatia

Republic of Croatia
Republika Hrvatska

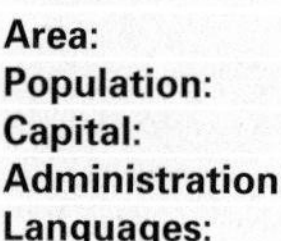

Area: 56,542 km²
Population: 4,555,000 (2007)
Capital: Zagreb (779,000)
Administration: 20 counties and 1 city
Languages: Croatian, Serbian, Hungarian, Italian
Religions: Roman Catholic 90%, Serbian Orthodox 4%
Currency: 1 kuna = 100 lipa
Major cities:
Split (189,000), Rijeka (144,000), Osijek (90,000), Zadar (73,000), Slavonski Brod (59,000)

Cuba

Republic of Cuba
República de Cuba

Area: 110,860 km²
Population: 11,268,000 (2007)
Capital: Havana/La Habana (2,185,000)
Administration: 14 provinces, 1 special municipality
Languages: Spanish
Religions: Non-denominational 56%, Roman Catholic 39%
Currency: 1 Cuban peso = 100 centavos
Major cities:
Santiago de Cuba (423,000), Camagüey (348,000), Holguín (319,000), Santa Clara (210,000)

Cyprus

Republic of Cyprus
Kypriakí Dimokratía/
Kıbrıs Cumhuriyeti

Area: 9,251 km²
Population: 855,000 (2007)
Capital: Nicosia/Lefkosía/Lefkoşa (201,000)
Administration: 6 districts
Languages: Greek/Turkish, English
Religions: Greek Orthodox 80%, Muslim (Sunni) 19%
Currency: 1 euro = 100 cent
Major cities:
Limassol/Lemesós (161,000), Lárnaka (71,000), Famagusta (23,000)

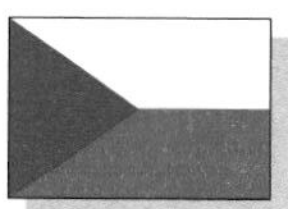

Czech Republic

Česká republika

Area: 78,860 km²
Population: 10,186,000 (2007)
Capital: Prague/Praha (1,179,000)
Administration: 14 districts
Languages: Czech, Slovak
Religions: Roman Catholic 39%, non-denominational 40%
Currency: 1 koruna = 100 halura
Major cities:
Brno (379,000), Ostrava (319,000), Plzeň (166,000), Olomouc (103,000), Liberec (99,800), České Budějovice (99,000), Hradec Králové (98,000)

Denmark

Kingdom of Denmark
Kongeriget Danmark

Area: 43,094 km²
Population: 5,442,000 (2007)
Capital: Copenhagen/København (1,086,000)
Administration: 5 regions
Languages: Danish, German
Religions: Protestant (Lutheran) 87%
Currency: 1 Danish krone = 100 øre
Major cities:
Århus (223,000), Odense (145,000), Ålborg (121,000), Esbjerg (73,000), Randers (56,000), Kolding (55,000), Vejle (50,000), Horsens (49,000)

Faroe Islands

Føroyar/Færøerne

Area: 1,396 km²
Population: 49,000 (2007)
Capital: Tórshavn (12,000)
Languages: Faroese/Danish
Religions: Protestant (Lutheran) 95%
Currency: 1 Faroese krona = 100 oyru

Greenland

Kalaallit Nunaat/Grønland

Area: 2,166,086 km²
Population: 58,000 (2007)
Capital: Nuuk (15,000)
Languages: Inuit/Danish
Religions: Protestant (Lutheran) 98%
Currency: 1 Danish krone = 100 øre

Dhekelia

Dhekelia Sovereign Base Area

Area: 131 km²
Population: 15,700 (total of Akrotiri and Dhekelia residents - including 7,700 Cypriots, 3,600 Service and UK-based contract personnel, and 4,400 dependents)
Capital: Episkopi Cantonment (base administrative center for Akrotiri and Dhekelia)
Languages: English, Greek
Currency: 1 euro = 100 cent

Djibouti

Republic of Djibouti
République de Djibouti/
Jūmhūrīyat Jībūtī

Area: 23,200 km²
Population: 833,000 (2007)
Capital: Djibouti/Jībūtī (547,000)
Administration: 6 districts
Languages: French/Arabic
Religions: Muslim 97%
Currency: 1 Djibouti franc = 100 centimes
Major cities:
Ali Sabieh (40,000), Tadjoura (22,000), Obock (18,000), Dikhil (12,000)

Dominica

Commonwealth of Dominica

Area: 751 km²
Population: 67,000 (2007)
Capital: Roseau (19,000)
Administration: 10 parishes
Languages: English, French Creole
Religions: Roman Catholic 80%, Protestant 13%
Currency: 1 East Caribbean dollar = 100 cents
Major cities:
Portsmouth (3,600), Marigot (2,900), Atkinson (2,500)

Dominican Republic

República Dominicana

Area: 48,442 km²
Population: 9,760,000 (2007)
Capital: Santo Domingo (2,667,000)
Administration: 31 provinces and 1 district
Languages: Spanish
Religions: Roman Catholic 90%
Currency: 1 Dominican peso = 100 centavos
Major cities:
Santiago (581,000), Concepción de la Vega (242,000), San Cristóbal (200,000)

1 km² = 0.3861 square mile

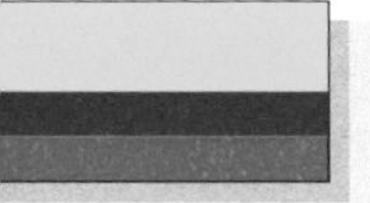

Ecuador

Republic of Ecuador
República del Ecuador

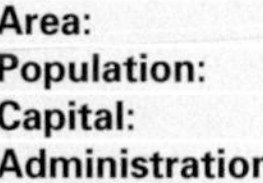

Area: 283,561 km^2
Population: 13,341,000 (2007)
Capital: Quito (1,399,000)
Administration: 22 provinces
Languages: Spanish, Indian languages
Religions: Roman Catholic 93%
Currency: 1 US-$ = 100 cents
Major cities:
Guayaquil (1,952,000), Cuenca (277,000), Santo Domingo de los Colorados (200,000), Machala (198,000), Manta (183,000), Portoviejo (170,000), Eloy Alfaro (168,000), Ambato (154,000)

Egypt

Arab Republic of Egypt
Jumhūrīyat Mişr al-'Arabīyah

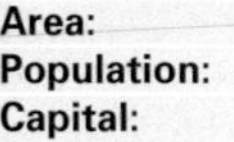

Area: 1,002,000 km^2
Population: 75,498,000 (2007)
Capital: Cairo/Al-Qāhirah (10,834,000)
Administration: 27 governorates
Languages: Arabic, French, English
Religions: Muslim 85%, Christian 10%
Currency: 1 Egypt. pound = 100 piastres
Major cities:
Alexandria/Al-Iskandarīyah (3,380,000), Giza/Al-Jīzah (2,566,000), Shubrā al-Khaymah (1,000,000), Port Said/Būr Sa'īd (528,000)

El Salvador

Republic of El Salvador
República de El Salvador

Area: 21,041 km^2
Population: 6,857,000 (2007)
Capital: San Salvador (526,000)
Administration: 14 departments
Languages: Spanish, Indian languages
Religions: Roman Catholic 80%
Currency: 1 colón = 100 centavos
Major cities:
Soyapango (330,000), Santa Ana (177,000), San Miguel (162,000), Mejicanos (160,000), Nueva San Salvador (125,000), Delgado (72,000)

Equatorial Guinea

Republic of Equatorial Guinea
República de Guinea Ecuatorial

Area: 28,051 km^2
Population: 507,000 (2007)
Capital: Malabo (60,000)
Administration: 7 provinces
Languages: Spanish, Fang, Bubi, Portuguese patois
Religions: Roman Catholic 90%
Currency: 1 CFA franc = 100 centimes
Major cities:
Bata (50,000), Luba (15,000)

Eritrea

State of Eritrea
Hagere Ērtra/Dawlat Irītrīyā

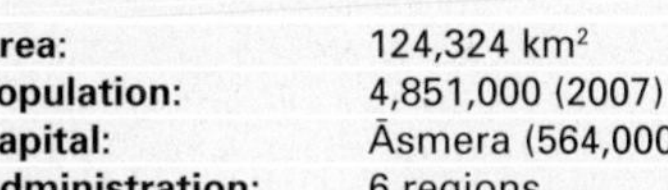

Area: 124,324 km^2
Population: 4,851,000 (2007)
Capital: Āsmera (564,000)
Administration: 6 regions
Languages: Tigrinya/Arabic, English
Religions: Eritrean Orthodox 50%, Muslim 50%
Currency: 1 nakfa = 100 cents
Major cities:
'Aseb (58,000), Keren (38,000), Ādī Ugrī (18,000)

Estonia

Republic of Estonia
Eesti Vabariik

Area: 43,432 km^2
Population: 1,335,000 (2007)
Capital: Tallinn (397,000)
Administration: 15 counties
Languages: Estonian, Russian
Religions: Protestant (Lutheran) 13%, Russian Orthodox 11%
Currency: 1 kroon = 100 sents
Major cities:
Tartu (101,000), Narva (68,000), Pärnu (51,000), Kohtla-Järve (47,000)

Ethiopia

Federal Democratic Republic of Ethiopia
Yltyop'iya Federalawi Demokrasiyawi Ripeblik

Area: 1,112,000 km^2
Population: 83,099,000 (2007)
Capital: Addis Ababa/Ādīs Ābeba (2,753,000)
Administration: 9 regions, 2 self governing-administrations
Languages: Amharic, English
Religions: Muslim (Sunni) 45%, Ethiopian Orthodox 40%
Currency: 1 birr = 100 cents
Major cities:
Dirē Dawa (255,000), Nazrēt (177,000)

Falkland Islands (Islas Malvinas)

(overseas territory of the U.K.; also claimed by Argentina)

Area: 12,173 km^2
Population: 3,000 (2007)
Capital: Stanley on East Falkland (2,000)
Administration: none (overseas territory of the U.K.)
Languages: English
Religions: primarily Anglican, Roman Catholic
Currency: Falkland Island pound
Major cities:
East Falkland (2,000), West Falkland (100)

Faroe Islands

(part of the Kingdom of Denmark)

Føroyar/Færøerne

Area: 1,396 km^2
Population: 49,000 (2007)
Capital: Tórshavn (12,000)
Administration: self-governing overseas administrative division of Denmark
Languages: Faroese, Danish
Religions: Evangelical Lutheran 95%
Currency: 1 Faroese krona = 100 oyru
Major cities:
Klaksvik (5,000), Hoyvik (3,000), Argir (2,000)

Fiji

Republic of the Fiji Islands
MatanituTu-Vaka-i-koya Ko Viti/
Republic of the Fiji Islands

Area: 18,333 km^2
Population: 839,000 (2007)
Capital: Suva (77,000)
Administration: 4 divisions
Languages: Fijian/English
Religions: Christian 53%, Hindu 38%, Muslim 8%
Currency: 1 Fiji dollar = 100 cents
Major cities:
Lautoka (36,000), Nadi (9,200), Labasa (6,500), Ba (6,300)

Finland

Republic of Finland
Suomen tasavalta/
Republiken Finland

Area: 304,530 km^2
Population: 5,277,000 (2007)
Capital: Helsinki/Helsingfors (559,000)
Administration: 5 provinces, autonomous province Åland
Languages: Finnish/Swedish
Religions: Protestant (Lutheran) 85%
Currency: 1 euro = 100 cent
Major cities:
Espoo (224,000), Tampere (201,000), Vantaa (184,000), Turku/Åbo (175,000), Oulu (126,000)

France

French Republic
République française

Area: 543,965 km^2
Population: 61,647,000 (2007)
Capital: Paris (2,143,000; A: 9,645,000)
Administration: 22 regions
Languages: French, regional languages
Religions: Roman Catholic 81%, Muslim 5%
Currency: 1 euro = 100 cent
Major cities:
Marseille (798,000; A: 1,350,000), Lyon (416,000; A: 1,349,000), Toulouse (391,000), Nice (341,000), Nantes (269,000), Strasbourg (264,000),

Monpellier (225,000), Bordeaux (215,000), Rennes (206,000), Le Havre (191,000), Reims (187,000), Lille (182,000), Saint-Étienne (180,000), Toulon (160,000), Grenoble (152,000), Angers (151,000)

Overseas Departments:

French Guiana
Department of Guiana
Département de la Guyane

Area: 83,534 km²
Population: 202,000 (2007)
Capital: Cayenne (66,000)

Guadeloupe
Department of Guadeloupe
Département de la Guadeloupe

Area: 1,628 km²
Population: 441,000 (2008)
Capital: Basse-Terre (10,000)

Martinique
Department of Martinique
Département de la Martinique

Area: 1,100 km²
Population: 399,000 (2007)
Capital: Fort-de-France (131,000)

Réunion
Department of Réunion
Département de la Réunion

Area: 2,504 km²
Population: 807,000 (2007)
Capital: Saint-Denis (159,000)

Overseas Collectivities:

Mayotte
Territorial Collectivity of Mayotte
Collectivité territoriale de Mayotte

Area: 374 km²
Population: 209,000 (2007)
Capital: Dzauodi (12,000)

Saint Pierre and Miquelon
Territorial Collectivity of Saint Pierre and Miquelon
Collectivité territoriale de Saint-Pierre-et-Miquelon

Area: 242 km²
Population: 6,000 (2007)
Capital: Saint-Pierre (5,700)

French Polynesia
Territory of French Polynesia
Territoire de la Polynésie française

Area: 4,000 km²
Population: 263,000 (2007)
Capital: Papeete (26,000)

French Southern and Antarctic Lands
Territoire des Terres australes et antarctiques françaises

The territories comprise:
Keguelen Islands (7,215 km²)
Crozet Islands (515 km²)
Amsterdam Island (54 km²)
Saint-Paul Island (7 km²)
Adélie Land/Terre Adélie, *claimed by France* (432,000 km²)

Wallis and Futuna
Territory of Wallis and Funtuna
Territoire de Wallis-et-Futuna

Area: 255 km² (Wallis 159 km², Futuna 64 km², Alofi 51 km²)
Population: 15,000 (2007)
Capital: Matâ-Utu (1,300)

Saint Barthélémy
Overseas Collectivity of Saint Barthélémy
Collectivité d'outre-mer de Saint-Barthélémy

Area: 21 km²
Population: 6,852 (1999)
Capital: Gustavia

Saint-Martin
Overseas Collectivity of Saint Martin
Collectivity d'outre mer de Saint-Martin

Area: 54.4 km²
Population: 33,000 (2004)
Capital: Marigot

Sui Generis Collectivity
Collectivité sui generis

New Caledonia
Territory of New Caledonia and Dependencies
Territoire de la Nouvelle-Calédonie et Depandances

Area: 19,060 km²
Population: 225,000 (2008)
Capital: Noumea

French Polynesia
(overseas lands of France)

Territory of French Polynesia
Territoire de la Polynésie française/
Polynesia farani

Area: 4,000 km²
Population: 263,000 (2007)
Capital: Papeete (26,000)
Administration: none (overseas lands of France)
Languages: French/Polynesian
Religions: Protestant 54%, Roman Catholic 30%
Currency: Comptoirs Francais du Pacifique franc
Major cities:
Faaa (29,000), Punaauia (26,000), Mahina (14,000)

Gabon
Gabonese Republic
République gabonaise

Area: 267,667 km²
Population: 1,331,000 (2007)
Capital: Libreville (573,000)
Administration: 9 provinces
Languages: French, Fang, Bantu languages
Religions: Roman Catholic 60%, traditional beliefs 30%
Currency: 1 CFA franc = 100 centimes
Major cities:
Port Gentil (109,000), Masuku (43,000), Oyem (31,000), Moanda (30,000), Mouila (22,000)

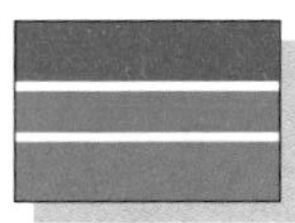

Gambia, The
Republic of The Gambia

Area: 11,295 km²
Population: 1,709,000 (2007)
Capital: Banjul (34,000, A: 271,000)
Administration: 5 divisions and 1 city
Languages: English, Mandinka, Fulani, Wolof, Arabic
Religions: Muslim 85%, Christian 10%
Currency: 1 dalasi = 100 bututs
Major cities:
Serekunda (219,000), Brikama (102,000), Bakau (48,000), Farafenni (37,000), Lamin (17,000), Basse Santa Su (16,000), Sukuta (15,000)

Georgia
Sakartvelo

Area: 69,700 km²
Population: 4,395,000 (2007)
Capital: Tbilisi (1,082,000)
Administration: 2 autonomous republics, 1 autonomous region, 9 districts
Languages: Georgian, Russian
Religions: Georgian Orthodox 84%
Currency: 1 lari = 100 tetri
Major cities:
Kutaisi (186,000), Batumi (122,000), Rustavi (116,000), Zugdidi (69,000), Gori (50,000)

Germany
Federal Republic of Germany
Bundesrepublik Deutschland

Area: 357,027 km²
Population: 82,599,000 (2007)
Capital: Berlin (3,338,000)
Administration: 16 federal states
Languages: German
Religions: Protestant 34%, Roman Catholic 33%
Currency: 1 euro = 100 cent
Major cities:
Hamburg (1,729,000), Munich/München (1,235,000), Cologne/Köln (969,000), Frankfurt a.M. (644,000), Dortmund (591,000), Stuttgart (588,000)

Ghana
Republic of Ghana

Area: 238,539 km²
Population: 23,478,000 (2007)
Capital: Accra (1,719,000)
Administration: 10 regions
Languages: English, more than 40 languages
Religions: Christian 60%, traditional beliefs 35%
Currency: 1 cedi = 100 pesewas
Major cities:
Kumasi (1,170,000), Tamale (290,000), Tema (263,000), Obuasi (132,000), Teshie (92,000)

Gibraltar
(overseas territory of the U.K.)

Area: 6 km²
Population: 29,000 (2007)
Capital: Gibraltar (26,000)
Administration: none (overseas territory of the U.K.)
Languages: English, Spanish, Italian, Portuguese
Religions: Roman Catholic 85%, Churchof England 7%
Currency: Gibraltar pound

Greece
Hellenic Republic
Ellinikí Dimokratía

Area: 131,626 km²
Population: 11,147,000 (2007)
Capital: Athens/Athína (746,000; A: 3,188,000)
Administration: 13 regions and the Monastic Republic of Mount Athos
Languages: Greek
Religions: Greek Orthodox 97%
Currency: 1 euro = 100 cent
Major cities:
Thessaloníki (364,000), Piraeus/Peiraiás (175,000), Patras/Pátra (161,000), Peristério (140,000)

Greenland
(part of the Kingdom of Denmark)
Kalaallit Nunaat Grønland

Area: 2,166,086 km²
Population: 58,000 (2007)
Capital: Nuuk (Godthab) (15,000)
Administration: 3 districts (landsdele)
Languages: Greenlandic (East Inuit), Danish, English
Religions: Lutheran 98%
Currency: Danish krone
Major cities:
Sisimiut (6,000), Ilulissat (5,000), Qaqortoq (3,000)

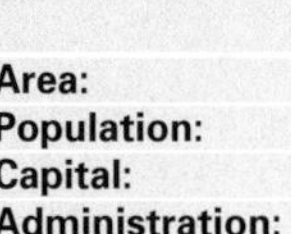

Grenada
State of Grenada

Area: 344 km²
Population: 106,000 (2007)
Capital: Saint George's (4,000)
Administration: 6 councils, 1 dependency
Languages: English, English Creole, French Creole
Religions: Roman Catholic 58%, Protestant 38%
Currency: 1 East Caribbean dollar = 100 cents
Major cities:
Gouyave (3,000), Grenville (2,000)

Guam
(territory of the U.S.)
Territory of Guam

Area: 549 km²
Population: 173,000 (2007)
Capital: Agaña/Hagåtña (1,000)
Administration: none (territory of the U.S.)
Languages: English, Chamorro, Philippine languages
Religions: Roman Catholic 90%
Currency: US dollar
Major cities:
Tamuning (11,000), Mangilao (9,000), Yigo (8,000), Astumbo (6,000)

Guatemala
Republic of Guatemala
República de Guatemala

Area: 108,889 km²
Population: 13,354,000 (2007)
Capital: Guatemala Ciudad/ Cd. de Guatemala (942,000)
Administration: 22 departments
Languages: Spanish, Mayan languages
Religions: Roman Catholic 60%, Protestant 30%
Currency: 1 quetzal = 100 centavos
Major cities:
Mixco (384,000), Villa Nueva (302,000), Quezaltenango (120,000), Cobán (52,000)

Guernsey
(British crown dependency)
Bailiwick of Guernsey

Area: 78 km²
Population: 66,000 (2007)
Capital: Saint Peter Port (17,000)
Administration: none (British crown dependency)
Languages: English, French
Religions: Anglican, Roman Catholic, Presbyterian, Baptist
Currency: British pound and Guernsey pound
Major islands:
Vale (9,600), Castle (9,000), Saint Simpson (8,700)

Guinea
Republic of Guinea
République de Guinée

Area: 245,857 km²
Population: 9,370,000 (2007)
Capital: Conakry (1,091,000)
Administration: 33 prefectures and 1 special zone (Conakry)
Languages: French, Fulani, Malinke
Religions: Muslim 85%, Christian 8%
Currency: Guinea franc
Major cities:
Kindia (288,000), Nzérékoré (283,000), Kankan (261,000), Labé (89,000)

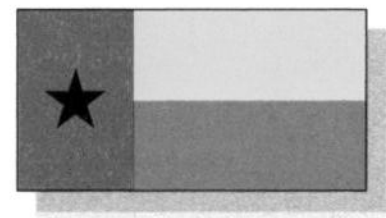

Guinea-Bissau
Republic of Guinea-Bissau
República da Guiné-Bissau

Area: 36,125 km²
Population: 1,695,000 (2007)
Capital: Bissau (292,000)
Administration: 8 regions and the capital
Languages: Portuguese, Crioulo
Religions: raditional beliefs 54%, Muslim 38%, Christian 8%
Currency: 1 CFA franc = 100 centimes
Major cities:
Bafatá (18,000), Gabú (9,500)

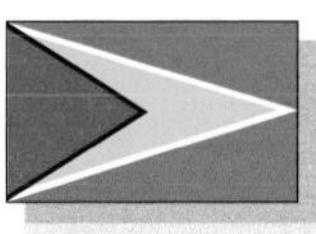

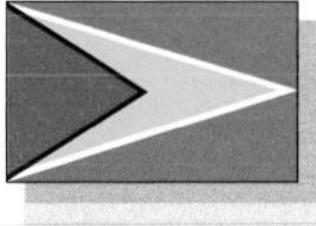

Guyana
Co-operative Republic of Guyana

Area: 214,969 km²
Population: 738,000 (2007)
Capital: Georgetown (249,000)
Administration: 10 regions
Languages: English, Hindi, Urdu, Indian languages
Religions: Protestant 34%, Hindu 33%, Roman Catholic 20%
Currency: 1 Guyana dollar = 100 cents
Major cities:
Linden (45,000), New Amsterdam (36,000)

Haiti
Republic of Haiti
République d'Haïti/
Repiblik Dayti

Area: 27,750 km²
Population: 9,598,000 (2007)
Capital: Port-au-Prince (991,000)
Administration: 10 departments
Languages: French/Creole
Religions: Roman Catholic 70%, Protestant 15%
Currency: 1 gourde = 100 centimes
Major cities:
Carrefour (336,000), Delmas (284,000), Cap-Haïtien (114,000), Gonaïves (64,000)

Honduras
Republic of Honduras
República de Honduras

Area: 112,492 km²
Population: 7,106,000 (2007)
Capital: Tegucigalpa (769,000)
Administration: 18 departments
Languages: Spanish, Indian languages, English
Religions: Roman Catholic 90%
Currency: 1 lempira = 100 centavos
Major cities:
San Pedro Sula (439,000), La Ceiba (111,000), Choloma (108,000), El Progreso (90,000), Choluteca (76,000), Comayagua (55,000)

Hungary

Republic of Hungary
Magyar Köztársaság

Area: 93,029 km²
Population: 10,030,000 (2007)
Capital: Budapest (1,740,000)
Administration: 19 counties and the capital
Languages: Hungarian, German, Slovak, Croatian
Religions: Roman Catholic 63%, Protestant 26%
Currency: 1 forint = 100 filler
Major cities:
Debrecen (207,000), Miskolc (182,000), Szeged (164,000), Pécs (160,000), Győr (129,000)

Iceland

Republic of Iceland
Lýðveldið Ísland

Area: 103,000 km²
Population: 301,000 (2007)
Capital: Reykjavík (113,000)
Administration: 8 regions
Languages: Icelandic
Religions: Protestant (Lutheran) 93%, Roman Catholic 1%
Currency: 1 króna = 100 aurar
Major cities:
Kópavogur (25,000), Hafnarfjörður (21,000), Akureyri (16,000)

India

Republic of India
Bhāratīya Gaṇarājya/
Republic of India

Area: 3,287,263 km²*
Population: 1,169,016,000 (2007)*
Capital: New Delhi (295,000)
Administration: 28 states, 7 union territories
Languages: Hindi/English/17 other official languages
Religions: Hindu 80%, Muslim 11%
Currency: 1 rupee = 100 paise
Major cities:
Mumbai/Bombay (11,914,000; A: 16,368,000), Delhi (9,817,000; A: 12,791,000), Kolkata/Calcutta (4,580,000; A: 13,217,000), Bangalore (4,292,000), Chennai/Madras (4,216,000), Ahmadabad (3,515,000), Hyderabad (3,450,000), Pune (2,540,000)

	Area km²	Population 2001	Capital
States			
Andhra Pradesh	275,045	75,728,000	Hyderābād
Arunāchal Pradesh	83,743	1,091,000	Itānagar
Assam	78,438	26,638,000	Dispur
Bihār	99,200	82,879,000	Patna
Chhattisgarh	146,361	20,796,000	Raipur
Goa	3,702	1,344,000	Panaji
Gujarāt	196,024	50,597,000	Gāndhīnagar
Haryāna	44,212	21,083,000	Chandīgarh
Himachal Pradesh	55,673	6,077,000	Shimla
Jammu and Kashmir*	100,569	10,070,000	Srīnagar
Jharkhand	74,677	26,909,000	Rānchi
Karnātaka	191,791	52,734,000	Bangalore
Kerala	38,863	31,839,000	Thiruvananthapuram
Madhya Pradesh	297,085	60,385,000	Bhopāl
Mahārāshtra	307,713	96,752,000	Mumbai
Manipur	22,327	2,389,000	Imphāl
Meghālaya	22,429	2,306,000	Shillong
Mizoram	21,081	891,000	Āīzawl
Nāgāland	16,579	1,989,000	Kohīma
Orissa	155,707	36,707,000	Bhubaneshwar
Punjab	50,362	24,289,000	Chandīgarh
Rājasthān	342,239	56,473,000	Jaipur
Sikkim	7,096	540,000	Gangtok
Tamil Nadu	130,058	62,111,000	Chennai
Tripura	10,486	3,191,000	Agartala
Uttarakhand	63,157	8,480,000	Dehra Dūn
Uttar Pradesh	231,254	166,053,000	Lucknow
West Bengal	88,752	80,221,000	Kolkata (Calcutta)
Union Territories			
Andaman and Nikobar Islands	8,249	356,000	Port Blair
Chandīgarh	114	901,000	Chandīgarh
Dādra and Nagar Haveli	491	220,000	Silvassa
Damān and Diu	112	158,000	Damān
Delhi	1,483	13,783,000	New Delhi
Lakshadweep	32	61,000	Kavaratti
Puducherry	492	974,000	Pondicherry

* Incl. results for the Indian part of Jammu and Kashmir, the political status of which is still uncertain

Indonesia

Republic of Indonesia
Republik Indonesia

Area: 1,922,570 km²
Population: 231,627,000 (2007)
Capital: Jakarta (9,341,000)
Administration: 33 provinces, incl. 2 special-regions and capital district
Languages: Bahasa Indonesia, 250 (est.) languages or dialects
Religions: Muslim 87%, Christian 10%
Currency: 1 rupiah = 100 sen
Major cities:
Surabaya (2,743,000), Bandung (2,429,000), Medan (1,942,000), Palembang (1,394,000)

Iran

Islamic Republic of Iran
Jomhūrī-ye Eslāmī-ye Īrān

Area: 1,629,807 km²
Population: 71,208,000 (2007)
Capital: Tehrān (6,759,000)
Administration: 28 provinces
Languages: Farsi (Persian), Kurdish, Turkic languages
Religions: Muslim 99%
Currency: 1 rial = 100 dinars
Major cities:
Masshad (1,887,000), Isfahan/Eṣfahān (1,266,000), Tabrīz (1,191,000), Shīrāz (1,053,000), Karaj (1,018,000), Ahvāz (805,000), Qom (778,000)

Iraq

Republic of Iraq
Al-Jumhūrīyah al-ʿIrāqīyah

Area: 438,317 km²
Population: 28,993,000 (2007)
Capital: Baghdād (5,772,000)
Administration: 18 governorates
Languages: Arabic, Kurdish, Turkish
Religions: Muslim 95%
Currency: 1 Iraqi dinar = 1000 fils
Major cities:
Mosul/Al-Mawṣil (1,740,000), Basra/Al-Baṣrah (1,300,000), Arbīl/Irbīl (891,000), Kirkūk (784,000), As-Sulaymānīyah (683,000)

Ireland

Éire
Ireland

Area: 70,273 km²
Population: 4,301,000 (2007)
Capital: Dublin (495,000)
Administration: 4 provinces (26 counties, 4 countyboroughs)
Languages: Irish/English
Religions: Roman Catholic 88%
Currency: 1 euro = 100 cent
Major cities:
Cork (123,000), Tallaght (63,000), Limerick (54,000), Blanchardstown (50,000), Waterford (45,000)

Israel

State of Israel
Medinat Yisraʾel/
Dawlat Isrāʾīl

Area: 22,145 km²
Population: 6,928,000 (2007)
Capital: Jerusalem/Yerushalayim/Al-Quds (692,000)
Administration: 6 districts
Languages: Hebrew/Arabic, Yiddish
Religions: Jewish 79%, Muslim 15%
Currency: 1 new sheqel = 100 agorot
Major cities:
Tel Aviv-Yafo (364,000), Haifa/Ḥefa (271,000), Rishon Le Ẕiyyon (215,000), Ashdod (192,000)

Palestinian-administered Territories:

Gaza Strip

Area: 364 km²
Population: 1,482,000 (2007)
Religions: Muslim 99%, Christian 0,7%, Jewish 0,3% (1992)
Major cities:
Gaza/Gazzah (362,000), Khān Yūnis (111,000)

West Bank

Area: 5,633 km²
Population: 2,536,000 (2004)
Religions: Muslim 80%, Jewish 12%, Christian 8% (1992)
Major cities:
Hebron/Al-Khalīl (147,000), Nābulus (121,000), Tulkarm (41,000)

Italy

Italian Republic
Repubblica Italiana/
République italienne/
Italienische Republik

Area: 301,336 km²
Population: 58,877,000 (2007)
Capital: Rome/Roma (2,541,000)
Administration: 20 regions
Languages: Italian/French (regionally)/ German (regionally)
Religions: Roman Catholic over 90%
Currency: 1 euro = 100 cent
Major cities:
Milan/Milano (1,247,000), Naples/Napoli (1,009,000), Turin/Torino (862,000), Palermo (683,000), Genoa/Genova (605,000), Bologna (373,000)

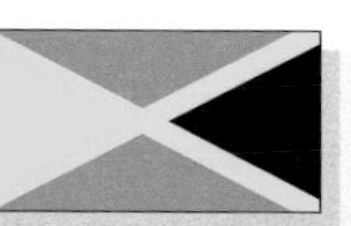

Jamaica

Area: 11,420 km²
Population: 2,714,000 (2007)
Capital: Kingston (577,000)
Administration: 14 parishes
Languages: English, Jamaican Creole
Religions: Protestant 56%, Roman Catholic 5%
Currency: 1 Jamaican dollar = 100 cents
Major cities:
Spanish Town (145,000), Portmore (103,000), Montego Bay (83,000), Mandeville (47,000)

Japan

Nihon-Koku

Area: 377,880 km²
Population: 127,967,000 (2007)
Capital: Tōkyō (8,483,000) (A: 12,445,000)
Administration: 47 prefectures
Languages: Japanese, Korean, Chinese
Religions: Shinto 87%, Buddhist 74%
Currency: 1 yen = 100 sen
Major cities:
Yokohama (3,433,000), Ōsaka (2,484,000), Nagoya (2,109,000), Sapporo (1,823,000), Kōbe (1,478,000), Kyōto (1,387,000), Fukuoka (1,302,000)

Jersey

(British crown dependency)

Bailiwick of Jersey

Area: 116 km²
Population: 91,000 (2007)
Capital: Saint Helier (29,000)
Administration: none
Languages: English, Portuguese
Religions: Anglican, Roman Catholic, Baptist
Currency: British pound and Jersey pound
Major cities:
Saint Saviour (12,000), Saint Brelade (11,000), Grouville (4,800)

Johnston Atoll

(territory of the U.S.)

Area: 2.6 km²
Population: No indigenous inhabitants; all US government personnel left the island in May 2005. In previous years, an average of 1,100 military and civilian contractor personnel were present on the island.
note: closed to the public

Jordan

Hashemite Kingdom of Jordan
Al-Mamlakah al-Urdunīyah al-Hāshimīyah

Area: 88,342 km²
Population: 5,924,000 (2007)
Capital: Amman/ʿAmmān (1,766,000)
Administration: 12 governorates
Languages: Arabic
Religions: Muslim 80%, Christian minority
Currency: 1 Jordan dinar = 1000 fils
Major cities:
Az-Zarqā' (477,000), Irbid (258,000), Ar-Ruṣṣayfah (228,000), Aqaba/Al-ʿAqabah (80,000), As-Salṭ (56,000), Mādabā (56,000)

Kazakhstan

Republic of Kazakhstan
Qazaqstan Respublīkasy/
Respublika Kazakhstan

Area: 2,724,900 km²
Population: 15,422,000 (2007)
Capital: Astana (313,000)
Administration: 14 regions and 2 cities
Languages: Kazakh, Russian
Religions: Muslim 50%, Christian 50%
Currency: 1 tenge = 100 tiyn
Major cities:
Almaty (1,129,000), Qaraghandy (437,000), Shymkent (360,000), Taraz (330,000), Öskemen (311,000), Pavlodar (301,000), Semey (270,000), Aqtöbe (253,000), Qostanay (221,000)

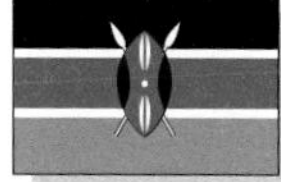

Kenya

Republic of Kenya
Jamhuri ya Kenya

Area: 582,000 km²
Population: 37,538,000 (2007)
Capital: Nairobi (2,143,000)
Administration: 7 provinces and the capital
Languages: Kiswahili, English
Religions: traditional beliefs 60%, Roman Catholic 26%
Currency: 1 Kenya shilling = 100 cents
Major cities:
Mombasa (665,000), Kisumu (323,000), Nakuru (219,000), Eldoret (167,000), Machakos (144,000), Meru (126,000), Nyeri (99,000), Thika (83,000)

Kiribati

Republic of Kiribati
Ribaberikin Kiribati/
Republic of Kiribati

Area: 717 km²
Population: 95,000 (2007)
Capital: Bairiki (2,200)
Administration: 3 units
Languages: Kiribati/English
Religions: Roman Catholic 53%, Protestant 39%
Currency: 1 Australian dollar = 100 cents
Island Groups:
Gilbert Islands, Phoenix Islands, Line Islands

Korea, North

Democratic People's Republic of Korea
Chosŏn Minjujuŭi In'min Konghwaguk

Area: 120,538 km²
Population: 23,790,000 (2007)
Capital: P'yŏngyang (2,741,000)
Administration: 9 provinces, 2 special cities
Languages: Korean, Russian, Chinese
Religions: Atheist 68%, traditional beliefs
Currency: 1 won = 100 chon
Major cities:
Namp'o (731,000), Hamhŭng (710,000), Ch'ŏngjin (582,000), Kaesŏng (334,000), Sinŭiju (326,000), Wŏnsan (300,000), Kanggye (211,000)

Korea, South

Republic of Korea
Taehan Min'guk

Area: 99,538 km²
Population: 48,224,000 (2007)
Capital: Seoul (10,231,000)
Administration: 9 provinces, 7 special cities
Languages: Korean, English, Japanese
Religions: Protestant 31%, Confucianist 22%, Buddhist 19%
Currency: 1 won = 100 chon
Major cities:
Busan (3,655,000), Daegu (2,474,000), Incheon (2,466,000), Taejŏn (1,366,000), Gwangju (1,351,000), Suwon (1,154,000), Ulsan (883,000)

Kosovo

Republic of Kosovo
Republika e Kosovës/
Republika Kosova

Area: 10,887 km²
Population: 2,126,000 (2007)
Capital: Prishtina/Prishtine (207,000)
Administration: 30 municipalities
Languages: Albanian/Serbian
Religions: Muslim, Serbian Orthodox, Roman Catholic
Currency: 1 euro = 100 cent
Major cities:
Prizren (127,000), Pejë (81,000), Gjakovë (77,000), Mitrovicë (75,000), Gjilan (71,000)

Kuwait

State of Kuwait
Dawlat al-Kuwayt

Area: 17,818 km²
Population: 2,851,000 (2007)
Capital: Kuwait/Al-Kuwayt (29,000)
Administration: 6 governorates
Languages: Arabic, English
Religions: Muslim 95%, Christian 2%
Currency: 1 Kuwait dinar = 1000 fils
Major cities:
As-Sālimīyah (130,000), Hawallī (107,000), Jalīb ash-Shuyūkh (102,000), Al-Fuḥayḥīl (51,000)

Lebanon

Lebanese Republik
Al-Jumhūrīyah al-Lubnānīyah

Area: 10,452 km²
Population: 4,099,000 (2007)
Capital: Beirut/Bayrūt (2,115,000)
Administration: 5 governorates and the capital
Languages: Arabic, Armenian, French, English
Religions: Muslim 60%, Christian 40%
Currency: 1 Leban. pound = 100 piastres
Major cities:
Tripoli/Ṭarābulus (200,000), Ṣaydā (140,000), Ṣūr (110,000), An-Nabatīyat at-Tahtā (98,000)

Liechtenstein

Principality of Liechtenstein
Fürstentum Liechtenstein

Area: 160 km²
Population: 35,000 (2007)
Capital: Vaduz (5,000)
Administration: 11 communes
Languages: German
Religions: Roman Catholic 83%, Protestant 7%
Currency: 1 Swiss franc = 100 centimes
Major cities:
Schaan (5,600), Triesen (5,000), Balzers (4,000)

Kyrgyzstan

Kyrgyz Republic
Kyrgyz Respublikasy/
Kyrgyzskaya Respublika

Area: 199,900 km²
Population: 5,317,000 (2007)
Capital: Bishkek (750,000)
Administration: 7 provinces and the capital
Languages: Kyrgyz/Russian
Religions: Muslim (Sunni) 75%, Russian Orthodox 20%
Currency: 1 som = 100 tyiyn
Major cities:
Osh (209,000), Džalal-Abad (70,000), Karaköl (64,000), Tokmak (59,000), Kara-Balta (55,000)

Lesotho

Kingdom of Lesotho
Mmuso wa Lesotho/
Kingdom of Lesotho

Area: 30,355 km²
Population: 2,008,000 (2007)
Capital: Maseru (271,000)
Administration: 10 districts
Languages: Sesotho/English
Religions: Roman Catholic 44%, Protestant 30%
Currency: 1 loti = 100 lisente
Major cities:
Teyateyaneng (14,000), Mafeteng (13,000), Hlotse (10,000)

Lithuania

Republic of Lithuania
Lietuvos Respublika

Area: 65,300 km²
Population: 3,390,000 (2007)
Capital: Vilnius (543,000)
Administration: 10 provinces
Languages: Lithuanian, Russian
Religions: Roman Catholic 80%, Russian Orthodox, Protestant
Currency: 1 litas = 100 centas
Major cities:
Kaunas (381,000), Klaipėda (194,000), Šiauliai (136,000), Panevėžys (122,000), Alytus (71,000), Marijampolė (48,000)

Laos

Lao People's Democratic Republic
Sathalanalat Paxathipatai Paxaxôn Lao

Area: 236,800 km²
Population: 5,859,000 (2007)
Capital: Viangchan (663,000)
Administration: 16 provinces, 1 municipality, 1 special zone
Languages: Lao, French, English
Religions: Buddhist 58%, Tribal religionist 34%
Currency: 1 kip = 100 at
Major cities:
Savannakhét (68,000), Louangphrabang (58,000)

Liberia

Republic of Liberia

Area: 111,369 km²
Population: 3,750,000 (2007)
Capital: Monrovia (550,000)
Administration: 14 counties
Languages: English, Gola, Kpelle
Religions: traditional beliefs 70%, Muslim 20%, Christian 10%
Currency: 1 Liberian dollar = 100 cents
Major cities:
Zwedru (37,000), Harper (33,000), Buchanan (28,000)

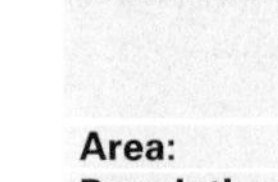

Luxembourg

Grand Duchy of Luxembourg
Groussherzogtum Lëtzebuerg/
Großherzogtum Luxemburg/
Grand-Duché de Luxembourg

Area: 2,586 km²
Population: 467,000 (2007)
Capital: Luxembourg (77,000)
Administration: 3 districts incl. 12 cantons
Languages: Letzeburgish/German/French
Religions: Roman Catholic 95%
Currency: 1 euro = 100 cent
Major cities:
Esch-sur-Alzette (27,000), Differdange (18,000), Dudelange (17,000)

Latvia

Republic of Latvia
Latvijas Republika

Area: 64,589 km²
Population: 2,277,000 (2007)
Capital: Rīga (764,000)
Administration: 26 districts, 7 special cities
Languages: Latvian, Russian
Religions: Lutheran 55%, Roman Catholic 24%
Currency: 1 lats = 100 santimi
Major cities:
Daugavpils (115,000), Liepāja (89,000), Jelgava (63,000), Jūrmala (56,000)

Libya

Socialist People's Libyan Arab Jamahiriya
Al-Jamāhīrīyah al-'Arabīyah al-Lībīyah ash-Sha'bīyah al-Ishtirākīyah

Area: 1,759,540 km²
Population: 6,160,000 (2007)
Capital: Tripoli/Ṭarābulus (1,776,000)
Administration: 13 regions (baladiyat)
Languages: Arabic, Tuareg
Religions: Muslim 97%
Currency: 1 Libyan dinar = 1000 dirhams
Major cities:
Benghazi/Banghāzī (655,000), Al-Khums (271,000), Miṣrātah (191,000), Az-Zāwiyah (140,000), Ṭubruq (137,000), Al-Baydā' (122,000), Darnah (113,000)

Macedonia, The Former Yugoslav Republic

porenešna jugoslovenska Repubika Makedonija

Area: 25,713 km²
Population: 2,038,000 (2007)
Capital: Skopje (467,000)
Administration: 123 communes
Languages: Macedonian, Albanian, Turkish
Religions: Macedonian Orthodox 67%, Muslim 30%
Currency: 1 denar = 100 deni
Major cities:
Kumanovo (103,000), Bitola (86,000), Prilep (73,000), Tetovo (71,000)

1 km² = 0.3861 square mile

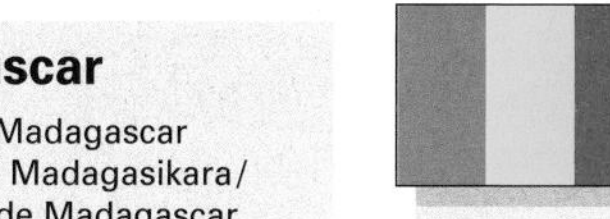

Madagascar

Republic of Madagascar
Repoblikan'i Madagasikara/
République de Madagascar

Area: 587,041 km²
Population: 19,683,000 (2007)
Capital: Antananarivo (1,111,000)
Administration: 6 provinces
Languages: Malagasy/French
Religions: traditional beliefs 52%, Roman Catholic 25%, Protestant 20%
Currency: 1 Madagascar ariary = 5 iraimbilanja
Major cities:
Fianarantsoa (130,000), Toamasina (127,000)

Malawi

Republic of Malawi
Mfuko la Malaŵi/
Republic of Malawi

Area: 118,484 km²
Population: 13,925,000 (2007)
Capital: Lilongwe (598,000)
Administration: 3 regions
Languages: Chichewa/English
Religions: Christian 75%, traditional beliefs 10%
Currency: 1 kwacha = 100 tambala
Major cities:
Blantyre (646,000), Mzuzu (102,000), Zomba (90,000), Nioro (67,000), Karonga (28,000), Kasungu (28,000)

Malaysia

Area: 330,242 km²
Population: 26,572,000 (2007)
Capital: Kuala Lumpur (1,298,000)
Administration: 13 states, 3 federal territories
Languages: Malay, Chinese, Tamil
Religions: Muslim 53%, Buddhist 17%
Currency: 1 ringgit = 100 sen
Major cities:
Ipoh (566,000), Kelang (563,000), Petaling Jaya (438,000), Johor Baharu (385,000), Shah Alam (320,000), Kuantan (238,000)

Maldives

Republic of Maldives
Divehi Raajjeyge Jumhooriyyaa

Area: 298 km²
Population: 306,000 (2007)
Capital: Malé (74,000)
Administration: 20 districts (administrative atolls) and the capital district
Languages: Maldivian (Divehi)
Religions: Sunni Muslim 99%
Currency: 1 rufiyaa = 100 laari

Mali

Republic of Mali
République du Mali

Area: 1,248,574 km²
Population: 12,337,000 (2007)
Capital: Bamako (954,000)
Administration: 8 regions and the capital
Languages: French, Bambara
Religions: Muslim 80%, traditional beliefs 18%
Currency: 1 CFA franc = 100 centimes
Major cities:
Sikasso (128,000), Mopti (116,000), Ségou (102,000), Kayes (83,000), Koutiala (95,000)

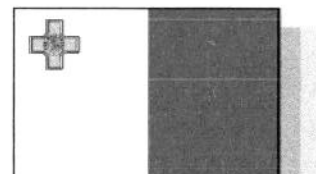

Malta

Republic of Malta
Repubblika ta' Malta/
Republic of Malta

Area: 316 km²
Population: 407,000 (2007)
Capital: Valletta (7,200)
Administration: 6 regions
Languages: Maltese/English
Religions: Roman Catholic 93%, Anglican
Currency: 1 euro = 100 cent
Major cities:
Birkirkara (22,000), Qormi (19,000), Mosta (18,000), Zabbar (15,000)

Man, Isle of

(British crown dependency)

Area: 572 km²
Population: 79,000 (2007)
Capital: Douglas (25,000)
Administration: 24 local authorities
Languages: English
Religions: Anglican, Roman Catholic
Currency: British pound and Manx pound
Major cities:
Onchan (9,000), Ramsey (8,000), Peel (4,000)

Marshall Islands

Republic of the Marshall Islands

Area: 181 km²
Population: 59,000 (2007)
Capital: Dalap-Uliga-Darrit (16,000)
Administration: 34 districts
Languages: English, Marshallese
Religions: Protestant 63%, Roman Catholic 7%
Currency: 1 U.S. dollar = 100 cents
Major cities:
Ebeye (9,300), Rairok (3,800)

Mauritania

Islamic Republic of Mauritania
Al-Jumhūrīyah al-Islāmīyah al-Mūrītānīyah

Area: 1,025,520 km²
Population: 3,124,000 (2007)
Capital: Nouakchott/Nawākshūṭ (415,000)
Administration: 13 regions
Languages: Arabic, French, Wolof
Religions: Muslim 99,6%
Currency: 1 ouguiya = 5 khoums
Major cities:
Nouâdhibou/Nawadhībū (73,000), Rūsū (49,000), Kayhaydi (34,000), Zuwārat (34,000), Kīfah (33,000)

Mauritius

République of Maurice

Area: 2,040 km²
Population: 1,262,000 (2007)
Capital: Port Louis (144,000)
Administration: 9 districts, 3 dependencies
Languages: English, French
Religions: Hindu 53%, Christian 30%
Currency: 1 Mauritius rupee = 100 cents
Major cities:
Beau Bassin-Rose Hill (104,000), Vacoas-Phoenix (100,000), Curepipe (79,000)

Mayotte

(territorial collectivity of France)

Territorial Collectivity of Mayotte
Collectivité territoriale de Mayotte

Area: 374 km²
Population: 209,000 (2007)
Capital: Dzaoudzi (12,000)
Administration: none
Languages: French
Religions: Muslim 98%, Roman Catholic
Currency: 1 euro = 100 cent
Major cities:
Mamoudzou (55,000), Koungou (18,000), Sada (9,000)

Mexico

United Mexican States
Estados Unidos Mexicanos

Area: 1,964,375 km²
Population: 106,535,000 (2007)
Capital: Mexico City/Cd. de México (8,605,000) (A: 17,309,000)
Administration: 31 states, 1 federal district
Languages: Spanish, Mayan dialects
Religions: Roman Catholic 90%
Currency: 1 Mexican peso = 100 centavos
Major cities:
Guadalajara (1,648,000), Ecatepec (1,619,000), Puebla (1,346,000), Nezahualcóyotel (1,225,000), Juárez (1,218,000), Tijuana (1,212,000)

Micronesia

Federated States of Micronesia

Area: 701 km²
Population: 111,000 (2007)
Capital: Palikir
Administration: 4 states
Languages: English, 9 indigenous languages
Religions: Roman Catholic 59 %, Protestant 39 %
Currency: 1 U.S. dollar = 100 cents
Major cities:
Weno (16,000), Nett (5,900), Kitti (5,100), Tol (4,800)

Midway Islands

(territory of the U.S.)

Area: 5 km²
Population: No indigenous inhabitants; approximately 40 people live on the atoll (staff of US Fish and Wildlife Service and service contractors)

Moldova

Republic of Moldova
Respublica Moldova

Area: 33,800 km²
Population: 3,794,000 (2007)
Capital: Chişinău (662,000)
Administration: 32 raions (including Gagauz Autonomous Region and Transdniestrian Republic)
Languages: Moldovian, Russian
Religions: predominantly Eastern Orthodox
Currency: 1 leu = 100 bani
Major cities:
Tiraspol (187,000), Bălţi (151,000)

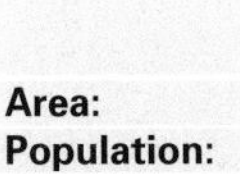

Monaco

Principaltiy of Monaco
Principauté de Monaco

Area: 1.95 km²
Population: 33,000 (2007)
Capital: Monaco (1,000)
Administration: 4 districts
Languages: French, Monegasque, Italian and English
Religions: Roman Catholic 90 %, Protestant 6 %
Currency: 1 euro = 100 cent
Major cities:
Monte Carlo (16,000), La Condamine (12,000)

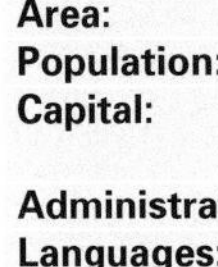

Mongolia

Mongol Uls

Area: 1,564,100 km²
Population: 2,629,000 (2007)
Capital: Ulan Bator/Ulaanbaatar (760,000)
Administration: 21 provinces, 1 municipality
Languages: Khalkha Mongol, Russian, Kazakh
Religions: Buddhist 90 %, trad. beliefs
Currency: 1 tugrik = 100 möngö
Major cities:
Darhan (73,000), Erdenet (66,000), Choybalsan (42,000), Ölgiy (30 000)

Montenegro

Republic of Montenegro
Republika Crna Gora

Area: 13,812 km²
Population: 598,000 (2007)
Capital: Podgorica (260,000)
Administration: 21 municipalities
Languages: Serbian, Bosnian, Albanian
Religions: Serbian Orthodox 75 %, Muslim 15 %, Roman Catholic 4 %
Currency: 1 euro = 100 cent
Major cities:
Nikšić (58,000), Pljevlja (22,000)

Montserrat

(overseas territory of the U.K.)

Area: 106 km²
Population: 6,000 (2007)
Capital: Plymouth (destroyed by the volcano in 1997); interim government: Brades
Administration: 3 parishes
Languages: English
Religions: Anglican
Currency: East Caribbean dollar

Morocco

Kingdom of Morocco
Al-Mamlakah al-Maghribīyah

Area: 458,730 km² (without Western Sahara)
Population: 31,224,000 (2007)
Capital: Rabat (1,623,000)
Administration: 16 regions
Languages: Arabic, Berber, French
Religions: Muslim 89 %
Currency: 1 dirham = 100 centimes
Major cities:
Ad-Dār al-Baydā (Casablanca) (2,934,000), Fās (947,000), Marrākuš (823,000), Aġādīr (679,000), Ṭanğah (Tanger) (670,000), Miknās (536,000)

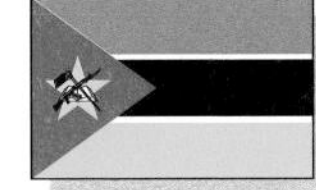

Mozambique

Republic of Mozambique
República de Moçambique

Area: 799,380 km²
Population: 21,397,000 (2007)
Capital: Maputo (1,114,000)
Administration: 10 provinces and the capital
Languages: Portuguese, Kiswahili
Religions: traditional beliefs 47 %, Christian 37 %, Muslim 18 %
Currency: 1 metical = 100 centavos
Major cities:
Matola (521,000), Beira (487,000), Nampula (372,000), Chimoio (210,000), Nacala (194,000)

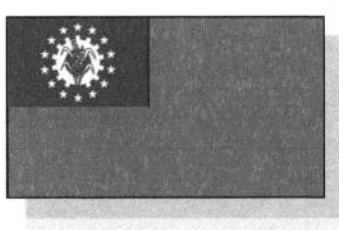

Myanmar

Union of Myanmar
Pyidaungzu Myanma Naingngandaw

Area: 676,578 km²
Population: 47,798,000 (2007)
Capital: Rangoon/Yangon (4,504,000) (seat of government: Naypyidaw)
Administration: 7 states, 7 divisions
Languages: Burmese, English
Religions: Buddhist 87 %, Christian 6 %
Currency: 1 kyat = 100 pyas
Major cities:
Mandalay (533,000), Mawlamyine (220,000), Pegu/Bago (151,000), Pathein (144,000)

Namibia

Republic of Namibia

Area: 824,269 km²
Population: 2,074,000 (2007)
Capital: Windhoek (234,000)
Administration: 13 regions
Languages: English, Afrikaans, German
Religions: Protestant 62 %, Roman Catholic 20 %
Currency: 1 Namibia dollar = 100 cents
Major cities:
Walvis Bay (50,000), Oshakati (37,000), Ondangwa (33,000), Rehoboth (21,000), Swakopmund (18,000), Rundu (18,000)

Nauru

Republic of Nauru

Area: 21 km²
Population: 10,000 (2007)
Capital: Yaren (4,000)
Administration: 14 districts
Languages: Nauruan/English
Religions: Protestant 60 %, Roman Catholic 30 %
Currency: 1 Australian dollar = 100 cents

1 km² = 0.3861 square mile

Nepal

Nepāl
Nepal Sanghiya Loktantrik Ganatantra

Area: 147,181 km^2
Population: 28,196,000 (2007)
Capital: Kathmandu (672,000)
Administration: 5 regions
Languages: Nepali, Maithili, Bhojpuri
Religions: Hindu 80%, Buddhist 10%
Currency: 1 Nepalese rupee = 100 paisa
Major cities:
Biratnagar (167,000), Lalitpur (163,000), Pokhara (156,000), Birganj (112,000)

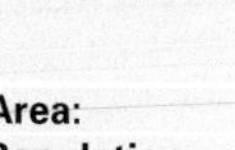

Netherlands, The

Kingdom of The Netherlands
Koninkrijk der Nederlanden

Area: 33,873 km^2
Population: 16,419,000 (2007)
Capital: Amsterdam (737,000) (seat of government: The Hague/'s-Gravenhage)
Administration: 12 provinces
Languages: Dutch/Frisian (regionally)
Religions: Roman Cath. 30%, Protestant 20%, Muslim 6%
Currency: 1 euro = 100 cent
Major cities:
Rotterdam (600,000), The Hague/'s-Gravenhage (458,000), Utrecht (265,000), Eindhoven (206,000), Tilburg (198,000), Groningen (177,000)

Overseas Territories:

Aruba

Area: 193 km^2
Population: 104,000 (2007)
Capital: Oranjestad (30,000)
Languages: Dutch, Papiamento, Spanish
Currency: Aruban guilder/florin

Netherlands Antilles

Nederlandse Antillen

Area: 800 km^2
Population: 192,000 (2007)
Capital: Willemstad (133,000)
Languages: Dutch, Papiamento, English
Currency: Netherlands Antillean guilder

Netherlands Antilles

(part of the Kingdom of the Netherlands)
Nederlandse Antillen

Area: 800 km^2
Population: 192,000 (2007)
Capital: Willemstad (133,000)
Administration: none (part of the Kingdom of the Netherlands)
Languages: Dutch, Papiamento, English
Religions: Roman Catholic 80%, Protestant 8%
Currency: Netherlands Antillean guilder
Major cities:
Princess Quarter (13,000), Cole Bay (7,000)

New Caledonia

(sui generis collectivity/ collectivité sui generis)
Territory of New Caledonia and Dependancies/Territoire de la Nouevelle-Calédonie et Dep.

Area: 19,058 km^2
Population: 225,000 (2008)
Capital: Nouméa (99,000)
Administration: none
Languages: French, Melanesian–Polynesian dialects
Religions: Roman Catholic 60% Protestant 30%
Currency: Comptoirs Francais du Pacifique francs
Major cities:
Mont-Dore (26,000), Dumbéa (22,000)

New Zealand

Aotearoa

Area: 270,500 km^2
Population: 4,179,000 (2007)
Capital: Wellington (166,000)
Administration: 16 regions
Languages: English/Maori
Religions: Christian 62%, Maori Churches
Currency: 1 New Zealand dollar = 100 cents
Major cities:
Auckland (337,000), Christchurch (322,000), Manukau (282,000), North Shore (184,000)

Independant Territory in Free Association with New Zealand

Niue

Republic of Niue

Area: 260 km^2
Population: 2,000 (2007)
Capital: Alofi (600)

Overseas Territories:

Ross Dependency

Claimed by New Zealand
Area: 750,310 km^2
Research stations

Tokelau

Area: 12 km^2
Population: 1,000 (2007)

Nicaragua

Republik of Nicaragua
República de Nicaragua

Area: 119,838 km^2
Population: 5,603,000 (2007)
Capital: Managua (909,000)
Administration: 15 departments, 2 autonomous regions
Languages: Spanish, Indian languages
Religions: Roman Catholic 89%, Protestant 5%
Currency: 1 córdoba = 100 centavos
Major cities:
León (150,000), Chinandega (96,000), Masaya (93,000), Granada (93,000)

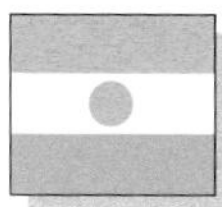

Niger

Republic of Niger
République du Niger

Area: 1,267,000 km^2
Population: 14,226,000 (2007)
Capital: Niamey (675,000)
Administration: 8 departments
Languages: French, Hausa, Djerma
Religions: Muslim 95%, traditional beliefs
Currency: 1 CFA franc = 100 centimes
Major cities:
Zinder (171,000), Maradi (147,000), Agadèz (77,000), Tahoua (72,000), Arlit (67,000), Dosso (43,000)

Nigeria

Federal Republic of Nigeria

Area: 923,768 km^2
Population: 148,093,000 (2007)
Capital: Abuja (403,000)
Administration: 36 states and the capital
Languages: English, French, Hausa
Religions: Muslim 45%, Protestant 26%, Roman Catholic 12%
Currency: 1 naira = 100 kobo
Major cities:
Lagos (9,954,000), Kano (3,413,000), Ibadan (3,202,000), Kaduna (1,563,000), Port Harcourt (1,133,000), Benin City (1,113,000)

Niue

(Independant Territory in Free Association with New Zealand)
Republic of Niue

Area: 260 km^2
Population: 2,000 (2007)
Capital: Alofi (600)
Administration: 14 villages
Languages: Niuean, English
Religions: Ekalesia Niue (Niuean Church) 75%, Latter-Day Saints 10%
Currency: New Zealand dollar
Major cities:
Hakupu (220), Tamakautoga (140), Tuapa (130)

Norfolk Island

(territory of Australia)
Territory of Norfolk Island

Area: 35 km^2
Population: 2,000 (2007)
Capital: Kingston (880)
Administration: none (territory of Australia)
Languages: English, Norfolk
Religions: Church of England 35%, Roman Catholic 12%, Uniting Church 11%
Currency: Australian dollar

Northern Mariana Islands

(commonwealth in political union with the U.S.)
Commonwealth of the Northern Mariana Islands

Area: 464 km²
Population: 84,000 (2007)
Capital: Garapan on Saipan (4,000)
Administration: none (commonwealth in political union with the U.S.)
Languages: English, Chamorro,
Religions: Roman Catholic
Currency: US dollar
Major cities:
San Antonio (6,000), San Vincente (5,000), Tanapag (4,000)

Norway

Kingdom of Norway
Kongeriket Norge

Area: 385,155 km²
Population: 4,698,000 (2007)
Capital: Oslo (523,000)
Administration: 19 counties
Languages: Norwegian, Sami
Religions: Protestant (Lutheran) 89%
Currency: 1 Norwegian krone = 100 øre
Major cities:
Bergen (237,000), Trondheim (154,000), Stavanger (112,000), Kristiansand (75,000)

Svalbard

Svalbard

Area/Population: 61,020 km²/2,600 inhabitants

Jan Mayen

Area: 377 km²/uninhabited

External Territories:

Bouvet Island

Bouvetøya

Area: 59 km²/uninhabited

Peter I Island

Peter I. Øy, *Claimed by Norway*

Area: c. 180 km²/uninhabited

Queen Maud Land

Dronning Maud Land, *Claimed by Norway*

Area: 2,500,000 km²/uninhabited

Oman

Sultanate of Oman
Salṭanat 'Umān

Area: 309,500 km²
Population: 2,595,000 (2007)
Capital: Muscat/Masqaṭ (A: 540,000)
Administration: 59 provinces
Languages: Arabic, Baluchi, English
Religions: Muslim 88%
Currency: 1 Omani rial = 1000 baiza
Major cities:
As-Sīb (248,000), Ṣalālah (186,000), Maṭraḥ (154,000), Ṣuḥār (135,000), Ruwī (117,000), Saḥam (85,000), Nazwá (69,000), Ar-Rustāq (81,000)

Pakistan

Islamic Republic of Pakistan
Jamhūryat Islāmī Pākistān

Area: 796,096 km² (excluding the disputed area of Kashmir)
Population: 163,902,000 (2007)
Capital: Islamabad (799,000)
Administration: 4 provinces, capital, Tribal Areas
Languages: Urdu, Panjabi, Sindhi
Religions: Muslim almost 100%
Currency: 1 Pakistan rupee = 100 paisa
Major cities:
Karachi (9,269,000), Lahore (5,063,000), Faisalabad (1,977,000), Rawalpindi (1,406,000)

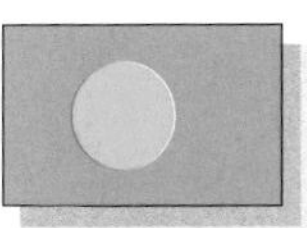

Palau

Republic of Palau
Belu'u er a Belau/
Republic of Palau

Area: 490 km²
Population: 20,000 (2007)
Capital: Melekeok (400)
Administration: 16 states
Languages: Palauan/English
Religions: Roman Catholic 41%, Protestant 25%, traditional beliefs 25%
Currency: 1 U.S. dollar = 100 cents
Major cities:
Koror, Ngetbong, Airai

Panama

Republic of Panama
República de Panamá

Area: 75,517 km²
Population: 3,343,000 (2007)
Capital: Panama City/Panamá (416,000)
Administration: 9 provinces, 5 autonomous territories
Languages: Spanish, Indian languages
Religions: Roman Catholic 86%,
Currency: 1 balboa = 100 centésimos
Major cities:
San Miguelito (294,000), David (77,000), Colón (71,000), Santiago (41,000)

Papua New Guinea

Independent State of Papua New Guinea
Papua-Niugini/
Gau Hedinarai ai Papua-Matamata Guinea

Area: 462,243 km²
Population: 6,331,000 (2007)
Capital: Port Moresby (254,000)
Administration: 19 provinces, National Capital District
Languages: English/Pidgin/Motu
Religions: Protestant 58%, Roman Catholic 33%
Currency: 1 kina = 100 toea
Major cities:
Lae (78,000), Arawa (36,000), Mount Hagen (28,000), Madang (27,000), Wewak (23,000)

Paraguay

Republic of Paraguay
República del Paraguay/
Tetâ Paraguay

Area: 406,752 km²
Population: 6,127,000 (2007)
Capital: Asunción (561,000)
Administration: 17 departments and the capital
Languages: Spanish/Guaraní
Religions: Roman Catholic 90%
Currency: 1 guaraní = 100 céntimos
Major cities:
Ciudad del Este (223,000), San Lorenzo (203,000), Luque (170,000), Capiatá (154,000), Lambaré (120,000), Fernando de la Mora (114,000)

Peru

Republic of Peru
República del Perú

Area: 1,285,216 km²
Population: 27,903,000 (2007)
Capital: Lima (7,912,000)
Administration: 25 departments
Languages: Spanish/Quechua/Aymara
Religions: Roman Catholic 89%, Protestant 3%
Currency: 1 nuevo sol = 100 céntimos
Major cities:
Arequipa (710,000), Trujillo (604,000), Callao (512,000), Chiclayo (583,000), Iquitos (334,000), Piura (308,000), Huancayo (305,000)

Philippines

Republic of the Philippines
Republika ng Pilipinas

Area: 300,000 km²
Population: 87,960,000 (2007)
Capital: Manila (1,581,000)
Administration: 81 provinces and 131 chartered cities
Languages: Pilipino, Tagalog, English
Religions: Roman Catholic 83%, Protestant 5%
Currency: 1 Philipp. peso = 100 centavos
Major cities:
Quezon City (2,174,000), Caloocan (1,178,000), Davao (1,147,000), Cebu (777,000)

Pitcairn Islands

(overseas territory of the U.K.)
Pitcairn, Henderson, Ducie, and Oeno Islands

Area: 35.5 km² (Pitcairn 4.6 km², Henderson 31 km², Oeno 5 km², Ducie 4 km²)
Population: 48 (2007)
Capital: Adamstown on Pitcairn (is the only settlement)
Administration: none (overseas territory of the U.K.)
Languages: English, Pitcairnese (a mixture of English and Tahitian)
Religions: Seventh-Day Adventist 100%
Currency: New Zealand dollar

1 km² = 0.3861 square mile

Poland

Republic of Poland
Rzeczpospolita Polska

Area: 312,685 km^2
Population: 38,082,000 (2007)
Capital: Warsaw/Warszawa (1,672,000)
Administration: 16 provinces (voivodships)
Languages: Polish, German, Ukrainian
Religions: Roman Catholic 91%
Currency: 1 złoty = 100 groszy
Major cities:
Łódź (789,000), Kraków (759,000), Wrocław (640,000), Poznań (579,000), Gdańsk (461,000), Szczecin (415,000), Bydgoszcz (374,000)

Portugal

Portuguese Republic
República Portuguesa

Area: 91,906 km^2
Population: 10,623,000 (2007)
Capital: Lisbon/Lisboa (557,000; A: 2,050,000)
Administration: 18 districts, 2 autonomous regions
Languages: Portuguese
Religions: Roman Catholic 92%, Protestant 2%
Currency: 1 euro = 100 cent
Major cities:
Porto (263,000), Amadora (175,000), Braga (112,000), Coimbra (104,000), Funchal (on Madeira) (104,000), Setúbal (97,000), Agualva-Cacém (82,000), Vila Nova de Gaia (70,000)

Autonomous Regions:

Azores

Autonomous Region of the Azores
Açores

Area: 2 352 km^2
Population: 242,000 (2005)
Capital: Ponta Delgada (20,000)

Madeira

Autonomous Region of Madeira

Area: 779 km^2
Population: 245,000 (2005)
Capital: Funchal (104,000)

Puerto Rico

(commonwealth associated with the U.S.)

Estado Libre Asociado de Puerto Rico/
Commonwealth of Puerto Rico

Area: 9,084 km^2
Population: 3,991,000 (2007)
Capital: San Juan (418,000)
Administration: none (commonwealth associated with the U.S.)
Languages: Spanish/English
Religions: Roman Catholic 72%, Protestant 5%
Currency: 1 dollar = 100 cents
Major cities:
Bayamón (204,000), Ponce (153,000), Carolina (170,000), Caguas (87,000)

Qatar

State of Qatar
Dawlat Qaṭar

Area: 11,437 km^2
Population: 841,000 (2007)
Capital: Doha/Ad-Dawḥah (339,000)
Administration: 9 municipalities
Languages: Arabic, Urdu, Farsi (Persian), English
Religions: Muslim (Sunni) 92%, Hindu
Currency: 1 Qatari riyal = 100 dirhams
Major cities:
Ar-Rayyān (273,000), Al-Wakrah (31,000)

Romania

România

Area: 238,391 km^2
Population: 21,438,000 (2007)
Capital: Bucharest/București (1,922,000)
Administration: 41 counties and the capital
Languages: Romanian, Hungarian, German
Religions: Romanian Orthodox 87%
Currency: 1 leu = 100 bani
Major cities:
Iași (322,000), Timișoara (318,000), Cluj-Napoca (318,000), Constanța (311,000), Craiova (303,000)

Russia

Russian Federation
Rossiyskaya Federatsiya

Area: 17,075,400 km^2
Population: 142,499,000 (2007)
Capital: Moscow/Moscwa (8,718,000; A: 12,410,000)
Administration: 21 republics, 1 autonomous oblast, 10 autonomous areas (avtonomnyy okrug), 6 territories (kray), 48 provinces (oblast), 2 cities of federal status: Moskva, Sankt Peterburg
Languages: Russian, languages of the minorities
Religions: Russian Orthodox 24%, Muslim 10–15%
Currency: 1 rouble = 100 kopeks
Major cities:
Saint Petersburg/Sankt Peterburg (4,628,000), Novosibirsk (1,393,000), Nižnij Novgorod (1,343,000), Ekaterinburg (1,257,000), Samara (1,146,000), Omsk (1,138,000), Kazan' (1,090,000), Ufa (1,088,000), Čeljabinsk (1,081,000), Perm' (1,005,000), Volgograd (1,011,000), Rostov-n.-D. (998,000), Voronež (902,000), Saratov (864,000), Krasnojarsk (759,000), Tol'jatti (724,000), Ul'janovsk (662,000), Iževsk (650,000), Krasnodar (635,000), Jaroslavl' (609,000), Chabarovsk (604,000), Vladivostok (597,000), Irkutsk (587,000), Barnaul (573,000), Novokuzneck (565,000), Penza (525,000), Rjazan' (524,000), Lipeck (519,000)

Republics	Area km^2	Population 2005	Capital
Adygea	7,600	444,000	Maykop
Altay	92,600	204,000	Gorno-Altaysk
Bashkortostan	143,600	4,079,000	Ufa
Buryatia	351,300	969,000	Ulan-Ude
Chechnya	15,700	1,141,000	Groznyy
Khakassia	61,900	541,000	Abakan
Chuvashia	18,300	1,299,000	Cheboksary
Dagestan	50,300	2,622,000	Makhachkala
Ingushetia	3,600	482,000	Nazran'
Kabardino-Balkaria	12,500	897,000	Nal'chik
Kalmykia/ Khalmg Tangch	76,100	290,000	Ėlista
Karachay-Cherkessia	14,100	435,000	Cherkessk
Karelia	172,400	703,000	Petrozavodsk
Komi	415,900	996,000	Syktyvkar
Mari El	23,200	717,000	Yoskar-Ola
Mordovia	26,200	867,000	Saransk
Sakha	3,103,200	951,000	Yakutsk
North Ossetia-Alania	8,000	704,000	Vladikavkaz
Tatarstan	67,836	3,769,000	Kazan'
Tuva	170,500	308,000	Kyzyl
Udmurtia	42,100	1,553,000	Izhevsk

Rwanda

Rwandese Republic
Republika y'u Rwanda/
République rwandaise/
Rwandese Republic

Area: 26,338 km^2
Population: 9,725,000 (2007)
Capital: Kigali (412,000)
Administration: 12 prefectures
Languages: Kinyarwanda/French/English
Religions: Christian c. 50%, traditional beliefs c. 50%
Currency: 1 Rwanda franc = 100 centimes
Major cities:
Butare (43,000), Ruhengeri (29,000)

Saint-Barthélémy

(overseas collectivity of France)

Overseas Collectivity of Saint Barthelemy/Collectivité d'outre mer de Saint-Barthélemy

Area: 21 km^2
Population: 7,000 (2008)
Capital: Gustavia
Administration: none
Languages: French, English
Religions: Roman Catholic, Protestant
Currency: 1 euro = 100 cent

Saint Helena
(overseas territory of the U.K.)

Crown Colony of Saint Helena and Dependencies

Area: 410 km^2 (St. Helena 122 km^2)
Population: 7,000 (2007)
Capital: Jamestown (640)
Administration: 1 administrative area and 2 dependencies
Languages: English
Religions: Anglican (majority)
Currency: Saint Helenian pound
Dependencies:
Ascension (88 km^2/1,100 inh.), Tristan da Cunha (98 km^2/300 inh.), Gough (90 km^2/uninh.), Inaccessible (10 km^2/uninh.), Nightingale (2 km^2/uninh.)

Saint Kitts and Nevis

Federation of St. Kitts and Nevis

Area: 261 km^2
Population: 50,000 (2007)
Capital: Basseterre (13,000)
Administration: 14 parishes
Languages: English, English Creole
Religions: Anglican 36%, Methodist 32%, Roman Catholic 11%
Currency: 1 Eastern Caribbean dollar = 100 cents
Major cities:
Charlestown (1,700)

Saint Lucia

Area: 616 km^2
Population: 165,000 (2007)
Capital: Castries (A: 64,000)
Administration: 10 districts
Languages: English, English Creole
Religions: Roman Catholic 77%, Protestant 19%
Currency: 1 Eastern Caribbean dollar = 100 cents
Major cities:
Vieux Fort (23,000), Micoud (15,000), Soufrière (14,000), Gros Islet (12,000)

Saint-Martin
(overseas collectivity of France)

Overseas Collectivity of Saint Martin
Collectivité d'outre mer de Saint-Martin

Area: 54.4 km^2
Population: 29,000 (2008)
Capital: Marigot
Administration: none
Languages: French
Religions: Roman Catholic
Currency: 1 euro = 100 cent

Saint Pierre and Miquelon
(territorial collectivity of France)

Territorial Collectivity of Saint Pierre and Miquelon/Collectivité territoriale de Saint-Pierre-et-Miquelon

Area: 242 km^2
Population: 6,000 (2007)
Capital: Saint-Pierre (5,700)
Administration: none
Languages: French
Religions: Roman Catholic 99%
Currency: 1 euro = 100 cent

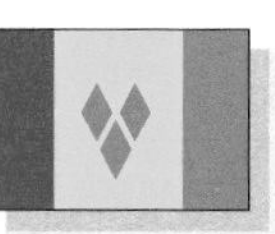

Saint Vincent and the Grenadines

Area: 388 km^2
Population: 120,000 (2007)
Capital: Kingstown (14,000)
Administration: 6 parishes
Languages: English, English Creole
Religions: Protestant 75%, Roman Catholic 9%
Currency: 1 Eastern Caribbean dollar = 100 cents
Major cities:
Georgetown (St. Vincent) (14,000)

Samoa

Independent State of Samoa
Malo Tutoatasi o Samoa/
Independent State of Samoa

Area: 2,935 km^2
Population: 187,000 (2007)
Capital: Apia (34,000)
Administration: 11 districts
Languages: Samoan/English
Religions: Protestant 71%, Roman Catholic 22%
Currency: 1 tala = 100 sene
Major cities:
Sataua, Salelologa

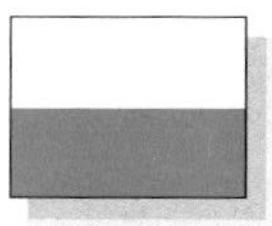

San Marino

Republic of San Marino
Repubblica di San Marino

Area: 61 km^2
Population: 31,000 (2007)
Capital: San Marino (4,400)
Administration: 9 districts (castelli)
Languages: Italian
Religions: Roman Catholic 93%
Currency: 1 euro = 100 cent
Major cities:
Serravalle (7,300)

Sao Tome and Principe

Democratic Republic of Sao Tome and Principe
República Democrática de São Tomé e Príncipe

Area: 1,001 km^2
Population: 158,000 (2007)
Capital: São Tomé (52,000)
Administration: 6 districts on São Tomé, self-government of Príncipe
Languages: Portuguese, Portuguese Creole
Religions: Roman Catholic 80%, Protestant 10%
Currency: 1 dobra = 100 cêntimos
Major cities:
Santo António (1,000)

Saudi Arabia

Kingdom of Saudi Arabia
Al-Mamlakah al-ʻArabīyah as-Saʻūdīyah

Area: 2,250,000 km^2
Population: 24,735,000 (2007)
Capital: Riyadh/Ar-Riyāḍ (4,087,000)
Administration: 13 regions
Languages: Arabic, English
Religions: Muslim 98%
Currency: 1 riyal = 100 halalas
Major cities:
Jeddah/Jiddah (3,192,000), Mecca/Makkah (1,355,000), Medina/Al-Madīnah (891,000), Ad-Dammām (764,000), Aṭ-Ṭā'if (658,000)

Senegal

Republic of Senegal
République du Sénégal

Area: 196,722 km^2
Population: 12,379,000 (2007)
Capital: Dakar (2,079,000)
Administration: 11 regions
Languages: French/Wolof
Religions: Muslim 94%, Christian 5%
Currency: 1 CFA franc = 100 centimes
Major cities:
Thiès (256,000), Kaolack (228,000), Ziguinchor (181,000), Saint-Louis (132,000)

Serbia

Republic of Serbia
Republika Srbija

Area: 77,474 km^2
Population: 8,032,000 (2007)
Capital: Belgrade/Beograd (1,281,000)
Administration: 161 municipalities (Serbia Proper, Vojvodina Autonmous Province)
Languages: Serbian, Hungarian
Religions: Serbian Orthodox 85%, Roman Catholic 5%
Currency: 1 Serbian dinar = 100 para
Major cities:
Novi Sad (198,000), Niš (173,000), Kragujevac (145,000)

1 km^2 = 0.3861 square mile

Seychelles

Republic of Seychelles
Repiblik Sesel/
Republic of Seychelles/
République des Seychelles

Area: 455 km²
Population: 87,000 (2007)
Capital: Victoria (60,000)
Administration: 23 districts
Languages: Creole/English/French
Religions: Roman Catholic 90%, Anglican 8%
Currency: 1 Seychelles rupee = 100 cents

Slovenia

Republic of Slovenia
Republika Slovenija

Area: 20,273 km²
Population: 2,002,000 (2007)
Capital: Ljubljana (264,000)
Administration: 182 municipalities, and 11 urban municipalities
Languages: Slovene, Croatian, Hungarian, Italian
Religions: Christian 74%, Muslim 2%
Currency: 1 euro = 100 cent
Major cities:
Maribor (94,000), Celje (38,000), Kranj (36,000), Velenje (27,000), Koper (24,000)

Currency: 1 rand = 100 cents
Major cities:
Cape Town (2,984,000), Durban (2,531,000), Johannesburg (1,976,000), Soweto (1,465,000), Port Elizabeth (776,000), Benoni (488,000), Vereeniging (463,000), Pietermaritzburg (458,000), East London (426,000), Tembisa (377,000), Bloemfontein (349,000), Boksburg (348,000), Vanderbjilpark (338,000), Newcastle (309,000), Krugersdorp (270,000)

External Territory:

Prince Edward and Marion Islands

Prince Edward Island: 41 km²/uninhabited
Marion Island: 388 km²/uninhabited

Sierra Leone

Republic of Sierra Leone

Area: 71,740 km²
Population: 5,866,000 (2007)
Capital: Freetown (837,000)
Administration: 4 provinces
Languages: English, Mende, Krio
Religions: Muslim 60% traditional beliefs 30%
Currency: 1 leone = 100 cents
Major cities:
Koidu (116,000), Makeni (116,000), Bo (84,000), Kenema (74,000)

Solomon Islands

Area: 28,446 km²
Population: 496,000 (2007)
Capital: Honiara (50,000)
Administration: 9 provinces, Capital Territory
Languages: English, Melanesian languages
Religions: Christian c. 95%
Currency: 1 Solomon Islands dollar = 100 cents
Major cities:
Gizo (7,000), Auki (5,000), Kirakira (3,000), Buala (2,000)

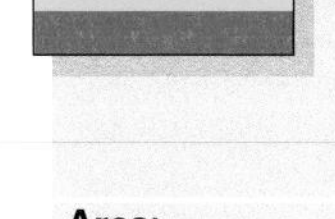

Spain

Kingdom of Spain
Reino de España/
Regne d'Espanya/
Reino de España/
Espainiako Erresuma

Area: 504,790 km²
Population: 44,279,000 (2007)
Capital: Madrid (3,017,000)
Administration: 17 autonomous communities
Languages: Castilian Spanish/Catalan (reg.)/Galician (reg.)/Basque (reg.)
Religions: Roman Catholic 96%
Currency: 1 euro = 100 cent
Major cities:
Barcelona (1,527,000), Valencia (792,000), Seville/Sevilla (704,000), Zaragoza (620,000), Málaga (536,000), Murcia (378,000), Las Palmas (371,000), Palma de Mallorca (358,000), Bilbao (354,000), Valladolid (319,00), Córdoba (315,000), Alicante (294,000), Vigo (288,000), Gijón (270,000)

Singapore

Republic of Singapore
Republik Singapura/
Republic of Singapore/
Xinjiapo Gongheguo/
Singapur Kutiyarasu

Area: 682 km²
Population: 4,436,000 (2007)
Capital: Singapura (3,263,000)
Administration: 5 divisions
Languages: Malay/English/Chinese/Tamil
Religions: Buddhist 32%, Taoist 22%, Muslim 15%, Christian 13%
Currency: 1 Singapore dollar = 100 cents

Somalia

Somali Republic
Jamhuuriyadda Soomaaliya

Area: 637,657 km²
Population: 8,699,000 (2007)
Capital: Mogadishu/Muqdisho (1,212,000)
Administration: 18 regions
Languages: Somali, Arabic, Italian
Religions: Muslim (Sunni) almost 100%
Currency: 1 Somali shilling = 100 cents
Major cities:
Hargeysa (328,000), Berbera (233,000), Marka (230,000), Kismaayo (183,000)

Places under Spanish Sovereignty in North Africa:

Ceuta

Place of Ceuta

Area: 19 km²
Population: 72,000 (2006)

Melilla

Place of Mellia

Area: 13 km²
Population: 67,000 (2006)

Slovakia

Slovak Republic
Slovenská republika

Area: 49,035 km²
Population: 5,390,000 (2007)
Capital: Bratislava (428,000)
Administration: 8 regions
Languages: Slovak/Hungarian
Religions: Roman Cath. 69%, Protestant 8%
Currency: 1 Slovak koruna = 100 haliers
Major cities:
Košice (236,000), Prešov (93,000), Nitra (87,000), Žilina (85,000), Banská Bystrica (83,000)

South Africa

Republic of South Africa/
iRiphabliki yaseMtzantsi Afrika/
iRiphabliki yaseNingizimu Afrika/
Republiek van Suid-Afrika/
Rephaboliki ya Afrika-Borwa

Area: 1,219,090 km²
Population: 48,577,000 (2007)
Capital: Pretoria (1,474,000) legislative centre: Cape Town judical centre: Bloemfontein
Administration: 9 provinces
Languages: English/Xhosa/Zulu/Afrikaans/Pedi/Tswana/Sotho/Tsonga/Swazi/Venda/Ndebele
Religions: Christian 78%, traditional beliefs 10%, Hindu 2%

Sri Lanka

Dem. Socialist. Rep. of Sri Lanka
Shrī Laṅkā Prajātāntrika Samājavādī Janarajaya/
Ilankai Jananāyaka Choşhalichak Kuṭiyarachu

Area: 65,610 km²
Population: 19,299,000 (2007)
Capital: Colombo (642,000) (legislative capital: Sri Jayawardenepura)
Administration: 9 provinces
Languages: Sinhala/Tamil, English
Religions: Buddhist 69%, Hindu 16%, Muslim 8%
Currency: 1 Sri Lankan rupee = 100 cents
Major cities:
Moratuwa (177,000), Yāpanaya (Jaffna) (146,000), Negombo (122,000), Sri Jayawardenepura (116,000)

Sudan, The

Republic of the Sudan
Jumhūrīyat as-Sūdān

Area: 2,505,810 km²
Population: 38,560,000 (2007)
Capital: Khartoum/Al-Kharṭūm (2,731,000)
Administration: 26 states
Languages: Arabic, English
Religions: Muslim 70%, traditional beliefs 20%
Currency: 1 Sudan. dinar = 100 piastres
Major cities:
Omdurman/Umm Durmān (1,271,000), Khartou North/Al-Kharṭūm Baḥrī (1,256,000)

Suriname

Republic of Suriname
Republiek Suriname

Area: 163,820 km²
Population: 458,000 (2007)
Capital: Paramaribo (205,000)
Administration: 9 districts, capital district
Languages: Dutch, English, Hindi
Religions: Hindu 27%, Roman Catholic 23%, Muslim 20%, Protestant 19%
Currency: 1 Suriname guilder = 100 cents
Major cities:
Lelydorp (16,000), Nieuw Nickerie (11,000)

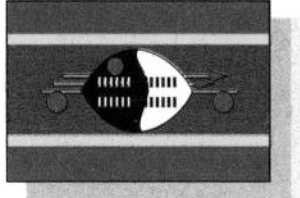

Swaziland

Kingdom of Swaziland
Umbuso waka'Ngwane

Area: 17,364 km²
Population: 1,141,000 (2007)
Capital: Mbabane (80,000)
Administration: 4 districts
Languages: Swazi, English
Religions: Christian 78%, traditional beliefs 21%
Currency: 1 lilangeni = 100 cents
Major cities:
Manzini (78,000)

Sweden

Kingdom of Sweden
Konungariket Sverige

Area: 410,934 km²
Population: 9,119,000 (2007)
Capital: Stockholm (762,000)
Administration: 21 counties (län)
Languages: Swedish, Finnish, Sami
Religions: Protestant (Lutheran) 89%, Roman Catholic 2%
Currency: 1 krona = 100 öre
Major cities:
Göteborg (474,000), Malmö (267,000), Uppsala (181,000), Linköping (136,000), Västerås (130,000), Örebro (126,000)

Switzerland

Swiss Confederation
Schweiz. Eidgenossenschaft/Confédération suisse/Confederazione Svizzera/Confederaziun Svizr

Area: 41,285 km²
Population: 7,484,000 (2007)
Capital: Berne/Bern (123,000)
Administration: 20 cantons, 6 demi-cantons
Languages: German/French/Italian/Romansch
Religions: Roman Catholic 42%, Protestant 35%
Currency: 1 Swiss franc = 100 centimes
Major cities:
Zürich (343,000), Geneva/Genève (178,000), Basel (165,000), Lausanne (116,000)

Syria

Syrian Arab Republic
Al-Jumhūrīyah al-ʿArabīyah as-Sūrīyah

Area: 185,180 km², including the Golan Heights (1,154 km²)
Population: 19,929,000 (2007)
Capital: Damascus/Dimashq (2,195,000)
Administration: 13 provinces, capital district
Languages: Arabic, Kurdish, Armenian
Religions: Muslim 90%, Christian 9%
Currency: 1 Syrian pound = 100 piastres
Major cities:
Aleppo/Halab (2,229,000), Ḥimṣ (811,000), Latakia/Al-Lādhiqīyah (312,000), Hamāh (264,000)

Taiwan

Republic of China
Ta Chung-Hwa Min-Kwo

Area: 36,006 km²
Population: 22,689,000 (2004)
Capital: T'aipei (2,640,000)
Administration: 5 municipalities, 16 counties, 2 special municipalities
Languages: Mandarin Chinese
Religions: Buddhist 43%, Taoist 34%
Currency: 1 New Taiwan dollar = 100 cents
Major cities:
Kaohsiung (1,494,000), T'aichung (1,006,000), T'ainan (741,000), Panch'iao (533,000)

Tajikistan

Republic of Tajikistan
Jumhurii Tojikiston
Respublika Tadzhikistan

Area: 143,100 km²
Population: 6,736,000 (2007)
Capital: Dushanbe (576,000)
Administration: 2 provinces and the Badakhshan Autonomous Republic and the capital
Languages: Tajik, Russian, Uzbek
Religions: Muslim (mainly Sunni) 80%
Currency: 1 Somoni = 100 Diram
Major cities:
Khujand (147,000), Kŭlob (80,000)

Tanzania

United Republic of Tanzania
Jamhuri ya Muungano wa Tanzania/
United Republic of Tanzania

Area: 883,749 km²
Population: 40,454,000 (2007)
Capital: Dodoma (204,000) (seat of government: Dar es Salaam)
Administration: 26 regions
Languages: Swahili/English
Religions: Muslim 35%, Roman Catholic 33%, Protestant 13%
Currency: 1 Tanzania shilling = 100 cents
Major cities:
Dar es Salaam (1,436,000), Mwanza (223,000), Tanga (188,000), Zanzibar (158,000)

Thailand

Kingdom of Thailand
Ratcha Anachak Thai

Area: 513,115 km²
Population: 63,884,000 (2007)
Capital: Bangkok/Krung Thep (6,320,000)
Administration: 76 provinces
Languages: Thai, Chinese, Malay, English
Religions: Buddhist 94%, Muslim 4%
Currency: 1 baht = 100 stangs
Major cities:
Nonthaburi (291,000), Udon Thani (220,000), Nakhon Ratchasima (204,000), Hat Yai (186,000)

Timor-Leste

The Democratic Republic of Timor-Leste
República Democrátika Timor Loro Sa'e/República Democrática de Timor-Leste

Area: 18,889 km²
Population: 1,155,000 (2007)
Capital: Dili (56,000)
Administration: 13 administrative districts
Languages: Tetum, Portuguese, Bahasa Indonesia
Religions: Catholic 91%
Currency: 1 U.S. dollar = 100 cent
Major cities:
Dare (19,000), Baucau (14,000), Maliana (12,000), Ermera (12,000)

Togo

Togolese Republic
République togolaise

Area: 56,785 km²
Population: 6,585,000 (2007)
Capital: Lomé (375,000 A: 1,194,000)
Administration: 5 regions
Languages: French/Ewe/Kabye
Religions: traditional beliefs 50%, Christian 35%, Muslim (Sunni) 15%
Currency: 1 CFA franc = 100 centimes
Major cities:
Sokodé (99,000), Kpalimé (79,000), Atakpamé (67,000), Kara (51,000), Tsévié (38,000)

1 km² = 0.3861 square mile

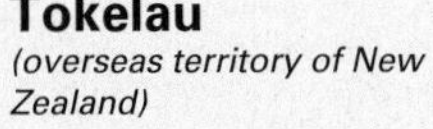

Tokelau

(overseas territory of New Zealand)

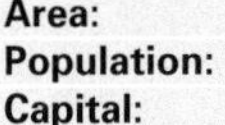

Area: 12 km²
Population: 1,000 (2007)
Capital: none; each atoll has its own administrative center
Administration: none (overseas territory of New Zealand)
Languages: Tokelauan, English
Religions: Protestant 70%, Roman Catholic 28%
Currency: New Zealand dollar

Tonga

Kingdom of Tonga
Pule'anga Tonga

Area: 649 km²
Population: 100,000 (2007)
Capital: Nuku'alofa (22,000)
Administration: 5 divisions
Languages: Tongan, English
Religions: Protestant 44%, Roman Catholic 16%
Currency: 1 pa'anga = 100 seniti
Islands (Pop.):
Tongatapu (67,000), Vava'u (16,000), Ha'apai (8,100), Eua (4,900)

Trinidad and Tobago

Republic of Trinidad and Tobago

Area: 5,128 km²
Population: 1,333,000 (2007)
Capital: Port of Spain (49,000)
Administration: 10 counties
Languages: English, French, Spanish
Religions: Christian 40%, Hindu 24%
Currency: 1 Trinidad and Tobago dollar = 100 cents
Major cities:
San Fernando (55,000), Arima (30,000)

Tunisia

Republic of Tunisia
Al-Jumhūrīyah at-Tūnisīyah

Area: 162,155 km²
Population: 10,327,000 (2007)
Capital: Tūnis (691,000)
Administration: 24 Governorates
Languages: Arabic, French
Religions: Muslim (mainly Sunni) 99%
Currency: 1 Tunisian dinar = 1000 millimes
Major cities:
Sfax/Şafāqis (263,000), Aryānah (206,000), Sousse/Sūsah (149,000), Al-Qayrawān (115,000), Gabes/Qābis (109,000)

Turkey

Republic of Turkey
Türkiye Cumhuriyeti

Area: 779,452 km²
Population: 74,877,000 (2007)
Capital: Ankara (3,203,000)
Administration: 81 provinces
Languages: Turkish, Kurdish, Arabic
Religions: Muslim 99%
Currency: 1 Turkish lira = 100 kurush
Major cities:
İstanbul (8,832,000), İzmir (2,250,000), Bursa (1,184,000), Adana (1,133,000), Gaziantep (862,000), Konya (761,000), Antalya (606,000)

Turkmenistan

Turkmenistan

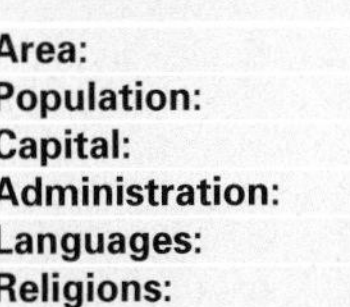

Area: 488,100 km²
Population: 4,965,000 (2007)
Capital: Ashgabat/Aşgabat (605,000)
Administration: 5 regions, capital district
Languages: Turkmen, Russian, Uzbek
Religions: Muslim (mainly Sunni) 90%
Currency: 1 manat = 100 tenesi
Major cities:
Türkmenabat (203,000), Daşhowuz (165,000), Mary (123,000), Balkanabat (119,000), Türkmenbaşi (70,000)

Turks and Caicos Islands

(overseas territory of the U.K.)

Area: 430 km²
Population: 27,000 (2007)
Capital: Cockburn Town on Grand Turk (100)
Administration: none (overseas territory of the U.K.)
Languages: English
Religions: Baptist 40%; Anglican 18%, Methodist 16%
Currency: US dollar
Major islands:
Providenciales (13,000), Grand Turk (4,000)

Tuvalu

Area: 27 km²
Population: 11,000 (2007)
Capital: Funafuti (4,000, on island) (seat of government: Vaiaku)
Administration: 9 atolls
Languages: Tuvaluan/English
Religions: Protestant 98%
Currency: 1 Australian dollar = 100 cents

Uganda

Republic of Uganda
Jamhuri ya Uganda/
Republic of Uganda

Area: 242,554 km²
Population: 30,884,000 (2007)
Capital: Kampala (1,209,000)
Administration: 91 districts
Languages: Kiswahili/English, Bantu languages
Religions: Roman Catholic 40%, Protestant 26%, Muslim 5%
Currency: 1 Uganda shilling = 100 cents
Major cities:
Gulu (113,000), Lira (90,000), Jinja (87,000)

Ukraine

Ukrayina
Ukraina

Area: 603,700 km²
Population: 46,205,000 (2007)
Capital: Kiev/Kyyiv (2,611,000)
Administration: 24 provinces, 2 municipalities, Aut. Republic of Crimea
Languages: Ukrainian, Russian
Religions: Orthodox, Roman Cath. 11%
Currency: 1 hryvna = 100 kopiykas
Major cities:
Karkiv (1,470,000), Dnipropetrovs'k (1,065,000), Odesa (1,029,000), Donets'k (1,016,000), Zaporizhzhya (815,000)

United Arab Emirates

Al-Imārāt al-ʻArabīyah al-Muttaḥidah

Area: 83,600 km²
Population: 4,380,000 (2007)
Capital: Abū Ẓabī (552,000)
Administration: 7 emirates
Languages: Arabic, Hindi, Urdu, Farsi, English
Religions: Muslim 96%
Currency: 1 dirham = 100 fils
Major cities:
Dubayy (941,000), Ash-Shāriqah (450,000), Al-ʻAyn (348,000), ʻAghmān (225,000), Ras al-Khaymah (102,000), Al-Fughayrah (54,000)

United Kingdom

United Kingdom of Great Britain and Northern Ireland

Area: 243,820 km²
Population: 60,769,000 (2007)
Capital: London (7,172,000; A: 7,375,000)
Administration: *England:* Greater London, 6 metropolitan counties, 34 nonmetropolitan counties, 46 unitary authorities
Wales: 22 unitary authorities
Scotland: 32 unitary authorities
Northern Ireland: 26 districts

Languages: English, Welsh, Scottish, Gaelic
Religions: Protestant 43%, Roman Catholic 11%
Currency: 1 pound sterling = 100 pence
Major cities:
Birmingham (971,000; A: 2,284,000), Glasgow (630,000; A: 1,168,000), Liverpool (469,000), Leeds (443,000; A: 1,499,000), Sheffield (440,000), Edinburgh (431,000), Bristol (421,000), Manchester (394,000; A: 2,245,000), Leicester (331,000), Coventry (303,000)

	Area km²	Population 2005	Capital
England	130,439	50,449,000	London
Wales	20,768	2,959,000	Cardiff
Scotland	78,783	5,095,000	Edinburgh
Northern Ireland	14,120	1,724,000	Belfast

Crown Dependencies:

Channel Islands: Guernsey, Jersey
Area: 194 km² (Jersey 116 km²; Guernsey and dependencies 78 km²)
Population: 149,000 (2007)
Major cities: St. Helier (29,000) on Jersey, St. Peter Port (17,000) on Guernsey

Isle of Man
Area: 572 km²
Population: 79,000 (2007)
Major cities: Douglas (25,000)

Dependent Territories:

Akrotiri
Akrotiri Sovereign Base Area
Area: 123 km²
Population: 15,700 (total of Akrotiri and Dhekelia residents)
Capital: Episkopi Cantonment (base administrative center for Akrotiri and Dhekelia)

Anguilla
Crown Colony of Anguilla
Area: 91 km²
Population: 13,000 (2007)
Capital: The Valley (1,400)

Bermuda
Area: 53 km²
Population: 65,000 (2007)
Capital: Hamilton (890)

British Antarctic Territory
Claimed by the United Kingdom, Argentina and partly by Chile
Area: c. 1,710,000 km²
(South Orkney Is., South Shetland Is., Antarctic Pen., Filchner and Ronne Ice Shelves, Coast Land)
Research stations

British Indian Ocean Territory
Claimed by Mauritius
Area: 60 km² (land area)
Population: No permanent population

British Virgin Islands
Area: 153 km²
Population: 23,000 (2007)
Capital: Road Town on Tortola (8,000)

Cayman Islands
Area: 264 km²
Population: 47,000 (2007)
Capital: George Town (21,000)

Dhekelia
Dhekelia Sovereign Base Area
Area: 130.8 km²
Population: 15,700 (total of Akrotiri and Dhekelia residents)
Capital: Episkopi Cantonment (base administrative center for Akrotiri and Dhekelia)

Falkland Islands (Islas Malvinas)
Claimed by Argentina
Area: 12,173 km²
Population: 3,000 (2007)
Capital: Stanley (2,000)

Gibraltar
Colony of Gibraltar
Area: 6 km²
Population: 29,000 (2007)

Montserrat
Area: 102 km²
Population: 6,000 (2007)
Capital: interim government: Brades

Pitcairn Islands
Pitcairn, Henderson, Ducie, and Oeno Islands
Area: 35.5 km²
Population: 48 inhabitants (2007)
Capital: Adamstown

Saint Helena
Crown Colony of Saint Helena and Dependencies
Area: 410 km² (St. Helena 122 km²)
Population: 7,000 (2007)
Capital: Jamestown (640)

South Georgia and the South Sandwich Islands
Claimed by Argentina
Area: 3,755 km² / 337 km²
Population:
South Georgia: no permanent population
South Sandwich Islands: uninhabited

Turks and Caicos Islands
Area: 430 km²
Population: 26,000 (2007)
Capital: Grand Turk (3,800)

United States / U.S.A.
United States of America

Area: 9,631,418 km²
Population: 305,826,000 (2007)
Capital: Washington D.C. (563,000; MSA: 5,090,000)
Administration: 50 states and the District of Columbia
Languages: English/regionally Spanish
Religions: Protestant 58%, Roman Catholic 21%, other Christian 6%, Jewish 2%, Muslim 2%
Currency: 1 dollar = 100 cents
Major cities:
New York (8,086,000; MSA: 18,641,000), Los Angeles (3,820,000; MSA: 12,829,000), Chicago (2,869,000; MSA: 9,334,000), Houston (2,010,000; MSA: 5,076,000), Philadelphia (1,479,000; MSA: 5,773,000), Phoenix (1,388,000; MSA: 3,593,000), San Diego (1,267,000; MSA: 2,931,000), San Antonio (1,215,000; MSA: 1,821,000), Dallas (1,208,000; MSA: 5,590,000), Detroit (911,000; MSA: 4,484,000), San Jose (898,000), Indianapolis (783,000), Jacksonville (774,000), San Francisco (752,000; MSA: 4,157,000), Columbus (728,000), Austin (672,000), Memphis (646,000), Baltimore (629,000; MSA: 2,616,000), Milwaukee (587,000), Forth Worth (585,000), El Paso (584,000), Boston (582,000; MSA: 4,440,000), Seattle (569,000; MSA: 3,142,000), Denver (557,000)

MSA Metropolitan Statistical Area

	Area* km²	Population 2006	Capital
States			
Alabama	135,775	4,599,000	Montgomery
Alaska	1,700,138	670,000	Juneau
Arizona	295,276	6,166,000	Phoenix
Arkansas	137,742	2,811,000	Little Rock
California	424,002	36,458,000	Sacramento
Colorado	269,618	4,753,000	Denver
Connecticut	14,358	3,505,000	Hartford
Delaware	6,448	853,000	Dover
District of Columbia	177	582,000	Washington
Florida	170,314	18,090,000	Tallahassee
Georgia	153,952	9,364,000	Atlanta
Hawaii	28,313	1,285,000	Honolulu
Idaho	216,456	1,467,000	Boise
Illinois	150,007	12,832,000	Springfield
Indiana	94,328	6,314,000	Indianapolis
Iowa	145,754	2,982,000	Des Moines
Kansas	213,111	2,764,000	Topeka
Kentucky	104,665	4,206,000	Frankfort
Louisiana	134,275	4,288,000	Baton Rouge
Maine	91,653	1,322,000	Augusta
Maryland	32,134	5,616,000	Annapolis
Massachusetts	27,337	6,437,000	Boston
Michigan	250,465	10,096,000	Lansing
Minnesota	225,182	5,167,000	Saint Paul
Mississippi	125,443	2,911,000	Jackson
Missouri	180,546	5,843,000	Jefferson City
Montana	380,850	945,000	Helena
Nebraska	200,358	1,768,000	Lincoln
Nevada	286,367	2,496,000	Carson City
New Hampshire	24,219	1,315,000	Concord

1 km² = 0.3861 square mile

New Jersey	22,590	8,725,000	Trenton
New Mexico	314,939	1,955,000	Santa Fe
New York	141,080	19,306,000	Albany
North Carolina	139,397	8,857,000	Raleigh
North Dakota	183,123	636,000	Bismarck
Ohio	116,103	11,478,000	Columbus
Oklahoma	181,048	3,579,000	Oklahoma City
Oregon	254,819	3,701,000	Salem
Pennsylvania	119,291	12,441,000	Harrisburg
Rhode Island	4,002	1,068,000	Providence
South Carolina	82,902	4,321,000	Columbia
South Dakota	199,744	782,000	Pierre
Tennessee	109,158	6,039,000	Nashville
Texas	695,676	23,508,000	Austin
Utah	219,902	2,550,000	Salt Lake City
Vermont	24,903	624,000	Montpelier
Virginia	110,792	7,643,000	Richmond
Washington	184,672	6,396,000	Olympia
West Virginia	62,759	1,818,000	Charleston
Wisconsin	169,643	5,557,000	Madison
Wyoming	253,349	515,000	Cheyenne

* including inland water

Outlying Territories in the Caribbean:

Navassa
claimed by Haiti
Navassa Island

Area/Population: 5 km²/uninhabited

Puerto Rico
Estado Libre Asociado de Puerto Rico/
Commonwealth of Puerto Rico

Area: 9,084 km²
Population: 3,991,000 (2007)
Capital: San Juan (418,000)
Languages: Spanish/English
Religions: Roman Catholic 72%, Protestant 5%
Currency: 1 dollar = 100 cents
Major cities:
Bayamón (204,000), Ponce (153,000), Carolina (170,000), Caguas (87,000)

Virgin Islands, U. S.
United States Virgin Islands

Area: 386 km²
Population: 111,000 (2007)
Capital: Charlotte Amalie (11,000)
Languages: English, Spanish, Creole

Outlying Territories in the Pacific Ocean:

American Samoa
Territory of American Samoa

Area: 199 km²
Population: 67,000 (2007)
Capital: Pago Pago on Tutuila (4,000)
Languages: Samoan/English/Tongan

Baker Island
Area: 2.3 km²/uninhabited

Guam
Territory of Guam

Area: 549 km²
Population: 173,000 (2007)
Capital: Agaña/Hagåtña (1,000)
Languages: English, Chamorro, Philippine languages

Howland Island
Area: 2.3 km²/uninhabited

Jarvis Island
Area: 7.7 km²/uninhabited

Johnston Island
Area: 2.6 km²
Population: No indigenous inh.; all US government personnel left the island. In prev. years, an average of 1,100 military and civilian contractor personnel was present on the island.

Kingman Reef
Area: 8 km²/uninhabited

Midway Islands
Area: 5 km²
Population: 40 (2005)

Northern Mariana Islands
Commonwealth of the Northern Mariana Islands

Area: 464 km²
Population: 84,000 (2007)
Capital: Garapan on Saipan (4,000)
Languages: English, Chamorro

Palmyra Island
Area: 6 km²/uninhabited

Wake Island
Area: 7.8 km²
Population: c. 75 (2007)

Uruguay
Oriental Republic of Uruguay
República Oriental del Uruguay

Area: 176,215 km²
Population: 3,340,000 (2007)
Capital: Montevideo (1,379,000)
Administration: 19 departments
Languages: Spanish
Religions: Roman Catholic 78%, Protestant 2%
Currency: 1 Uruguayan peso = 100 centésimos
Major cities:
Salto (105,000), Paysandú (84,000), Maldonado (67,000), Las Piedras (66,000), Rivera (63,000)

Uzbekistan
Republic of Uzbekistan
O'zbekiston Respublikasi
Respublika Uzbekistan

Area: 447,400 km²
Population: 27,372,000 (2007)
Capital: Tashkent/Toshkent (2,197,000)
Administration: 13 provinces, Karakalpak Autonomous Republic
Languages: Uzbek, Russian
Religions: Muslim (Sunni) 88%
Currency: 1 sum = 100 teen
Major cities:
Namangan (377,000), Samarqand (362,000), Andijon (324,000), Bukhara/Buxoro (238,000)

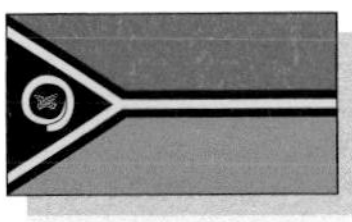

Vanuatu
Republic of Vanuatu
Ripablik blong Vanuatu/
Republic of Vanuatu/
République de Vanuatu

Area: 12,109 km²
Population: 226,000 (2007)
Capital: Port Vila (34,000)
Administration: 6 provinces
Languages: Bislama/English/French
Religions: Christian 80%, traditional beliefs
Currency: 1 vatu = 100 centimes
Major cities:
Luganville (10,000)

Vatican City
The Vatican City State
Status Civitatis Vaticanae/
Stato della Città del Vaticano

Area: 0,44 km²
Population: 532 (2004)
Languages: Latin/Italian
Religions: Roman Catholic 100%
Currency: 1 euro = 100 cent

Venezuela
Republic of Venezuela
República Bolivariana de Venezuela

Area: 912,050 km²
Population: 27,657,000 (2007)
Capital: Caracas (1,976,000)
Administration: 23 states and capital district
Languages: Spanish, Indian languages
Religions: Roman Catholic 86%, Protestant 5%
Currency: 1 bolívar = 100 céntimos
Major cities:
Maracaibo (1,764,000), Valencia (1,339,000), Barquisimeto (876,000), Ciudad Guayana (704,000), Petare (369,000), Maracay (394,000)

Vietnam

Socialist Republic of Vietnam
Công-hòa xã-hôi chu-nghia Viêt-Nam

Area: 331,690 km²
Population: 87,375,000 (2007)
Capital: Hanoi/Ha Nôi (2,842,000)
Administration: 8 regions
Languages: Vietnamese, Chinese, French
Religions: Buddhist 55%, Roman Catholic 5%
Currency: 1 dong = 100 xu
Major cities:
Chi Minh City/Thanh-Phô Hô Chi Minh (5,378,000), Hai Phong (591,000), Đa Năng (459,000), Buôn Ma Thuôt (384,000), Huê (277,000)

Western Sahara

Al-Jumhūrīyah al-ʻArabīyah aṣ-Ṣaḥrāwīyah ad-Dīmuqrāṭīyah

Area: 252,146 km²
Population: 480,000 (2007)
Capital: Laâyoune/Al-ʻAyūn (139,000)
Administration: 4 provinces
Languages: Arabic, Spanish
Religions: Muslim almost 100%
Currency: Moroccan dirham
Major cities:
Ad-Dākhla (58,000), As-Samārah (44,000), Bū Jaydūr (23,000)

Virgin Islands, U.S.

(territory of the U.S.)

United States Virgin Islands

Area: 386 km²
Population: 111,000 (2007)
Capital: Charlotte Amalie (11,000)
Administration: none (territory of the U.S.)
Languages: English, Spanish, Creole
Religions: Baptist 42%, Roman Catholic 34%
Currency: US dollar
Major cities:
Anna's Retreat (8,000), Charlotte Amelie West (5,000), Frederiksted Southeast (3,000)

Yemen

Republic of Yemen
Al-Jumhūrīyah al-Yamanīyah

Area: 527,968 km²
Population: 22,389,000 (2007)
Capital: Ṣanʻā' (1,590,000)
Administration: 21 governorates
Languages: Arabic
Religions: Muslim 99%
Currency: 1 Yemeni rial = 100 fils
Major cities:
ʻAdan (Aden) (608,000), Taʻizz (318,000), Al-Ḥudaydah (300,000), Al-Mukallā (122,000), Ibb (103,000)

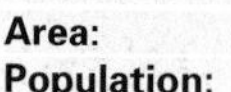

Wake Island

(territory of the U.S.)

Area: 7.8 km²
Population: no indigenous inhabitants U.S. military personnel have left the islands, but contractor personnel remain, 75 contractor personnel were present (2007)

Zambia

Republic of Zambia

Area: 752,614 km²
Population: 11,922,000 (2007)
Capital: Lusaka (1,718,000)
Administration: 9 provinces
Languages: English, Bantu languages
Religions: Christian 72%, traditional beliefs 27%
Currency: 1 kwacha = 100 ngwee
Major cities:
Ndola (375,000), Kitwe (364,000), Kabwe (177,000), Chingola (147,000), Mufulira (122,000), Luanshya (116,000), Livingstone (109,000)

Wallis and Futuna

(overseas territory of France)

Territory of the Wallis and Futuna Islands
Territoire des Wallis-et-Futuna

Area: 255 km²
Population: 15,000 (2007)
Capital: Matâ'utu (1,300)
Administration: none (overseas territory of France)
Languages: French, Polynesian languages
Religions: Roman Catholic 97%
Currency: Comptoirs Francais du Pacifique franc
Major cities:
Alele (900), Utufua (750), Ono (750)

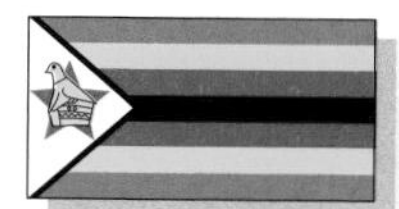

Zimbabwe

Republic of Zimbabwe

Area: 390,757 km²
Population: 13,349,000 (2007)
Capital: Harare (1,868,000)
Administration: 8 provinces and 2 cities
Languages: English, Shona, Sindebele Bantu languages
Religions: Christian 55%, tradit. beliefs
Currency: 1 Zimbabwe dollar = 100 cents
Major cities:
Bulawayo (1,004,000), Chitungwiza (424,000), Mutare (159,000), Gweru (158,000)

1 km² = 0.3861 square mile

Earth Dimensions

Radius at the equator	6378,160 km
Half axis	6356,775 km
Amount of flattening of the geoid at the poles	1/298,254
Circumference at the equator	40075,161 km
Circumference over the poles	40008,006 km
Length of a degree at the equator	111,320 km
Average length of a meridian degree	111,133 km
Total surface	510,068 million km^2
Land surface (c. 29%)	c. 148,1 million km^2
Ocean surface (c. 71%)	c. 362,0 million km^2
Mass	5,976 x 10^{24} kg
Volume	1,083 x 10^{12} km^3
Mean density	5,517 g/cm^3
Sideric time per rotation	23^h 56^m $4{,}09^s$
Mean distance Earth-Sun	149,598 million km
Distance Earth–Sun in aphelion (farthest from sun)	152,099 million km
Distance Earth–Sun in perihelion (nearest to sun)	147,096 million km
Length of the earth's orbit around the sun	939,886 million km
Tilt of the earth's axis in relation to its orbital plane (ecliptic), in 2000	23° 26' 21'', 4
Average orbital speed around the sun	29,783 km/s
Sidereal year	365^d 6^h 9^m 9^s
Tropical year	365^d 5^h 48^m 46^s
Average distance Earth–Moon	384,400 km
Distance Earth–Moon in apogee (farthest from earth)	406,740 km
Distance Earth–Moon in perigee (nearest to earth)	356,410 km
Sidereal month	27^d 7^h 43^m 12^s
Synodic month	29^d 12^h 44^m 3^s

The Continents

	Area in km^2	Population 2007
Europe	10,142,000	695,609,000
Asia	44,817,000	4,091,260,000
Australia and Oceania	8,515,000	34,267,000
Africa	30,260,000	965,136,000
North America	24,683,000	527,041,000
South America	17,650,000	383,999,000
Antarctica	12,400,000	–
World	148,467,000	6,697,312,000

210 Countries and their Areas

	km²
1. Russia	17,075,400
2. Canada	9,984,670
3. United States	9,631,418
4. China	9,596,961
5. Brazil	8,547,404
6. Australia	7,692,024
7. India	3,287,263
8. Argentina	2,780,400
9. Kazakhstan	2,724,900
10. Sudan, The	2,505,810
11. Algeria	2,381,741
12. Congo, Dem. Rep. of the	2,344,858
13. Saudi Arabia	2,250,000
14. Mexico	1,964,375
15. Indonesia	1,922,570
16. Libya	1,759,540
17. Iran	1,629,807
18. Mongolia	1,564,100
19. Peru	1,285,216
20. Chad	1,284,000
21. Niger	1,267,000
22. Mali	1,248,574
23. Angola	1,246,700
24. South Africa	1,219,090
25. Colombia	1,138,914
26. Ethiopia	1,112,000
27. Bolivia	1,098,591
28. Mauritania	1,025,520
29. Egypt	1,002,000
30. Nigeria	923,768
31. Venezuela	912,050
32. Tanzania	883,749
33. Namibia	824,269
34. Mozambique	799,380
35. Pakistan	796,096
36. Turkey	779,452
37. Chile	756,626
38. Zambia	752,614
39. Myanmar	676,578
40. Afghanistan	652,090
41. Somalia	637,657
42. Central African Republic	622,436
43. Ukraine	603,700
44. Madagascar	587,041
45. Botswana	582,000
46. Kenya	582,000
47. France	543,965
48. Yemen	527,968
49. Thailand	513,115
50. Spain	504,790
51. Turkmenistan	488,100
52. Cameroon	466,050
53. Papua New Guinea	462,243
54. Morocco	458,730
55. Uzbekistan	447,400
56. Iraq	438,317
57. Sweden	410,934
58. Paraguay	406,752
59. Zimbabwe	390,757
60. Norway	385,155
61. Japan	377,880
62. Germany	357,027
63. Congo, Republic of the	342,000
64. Vietnam	331,690
65. Malaysia	330,242
66. Côte d'Ivoire	322,462
67. Poland	312,685
68. Oman	309,500
69. Finland	304,530
70. Italy	301,336
71. Philippines	300,000
72. Ecuador	283,561
73. Burkina Faso	274,200
74. New Zealand	270,500
75. Gabon	267,667
76. Western Sahara	252,146
77. Guinea	245,857
78. United Kingdom	243,820
79. Uganda	242,554
80. Ghana	238,539
81. Romania	238,391
82. Laos	236,800
83. Guyana	214,969
84. Belarus	207,600
85. Kyrgyzstan	199,900
86. Senegal	196,722
87. Syria	185,180
88. Cambodia	181,035
89. Uruguay	176,215
90. Suriname	163,820
91. Tunisia	162,155
92. Bangladesh	147,570
93. Nepal	147,181
94. Tajikistan	143,100
95. Greece	131,626
96. Eritrea	124,324
97. Korea, North	120,538
98. Nicaragua	119,838
99. Malawi	118,484
100. Benin	112,622
101. Honduras	112,492
102. Liberia	111,369
103. Bulgaria	110,910
104. Cuba	110,860
105. Guatemala	108,889
106. Iceland	103,000
107. Korea, South	99,538
108. Hungary	93,029
109. Portugal	91,906
110. Jordan	89,342
111. Azerbaijan	86,600
112. Austria	83,859
113. United Arab Emirates	83,600
114. Czech Republic	78,860
115. Serbia	77,474
116. Panama	75,517
117. Sierra Leone	71,740
118. Ireland	70,273
119. Georgia	69,700
120. Sri Lanka	65,610
121. Lithuania	65,300
122. Latvia	64,589
123. Togo	56,785
124. Croatia	56,542
125. Bosnia and Herzegovina	51,197
126. Costa Rica	51,100
127. Slovakia	49,035
128. Dominican Republic	48,442
129. Bhutan	46,500
130. Estonia	43,432
131. Denmark	43,094
132. Switzerland	41,285
133. Guinea-Bissau	36,125
134. Taiwan	36,006
135. Netherlands, The	33,873
136. Moldova	33,800
137. Belgium	30,518
138. Lesotho	30,355
139. Armenia	29,743
140. Albania	28,748
141. Solomon Islands	28,446
142. Equatorial Guinea	28,051
143. Burundi	27,834
144. Haiti	27,750
145. Rwanda	26,338
146. Macedonia	25,713
147. Djibouti	23,200
148. Belize	22,966
149. Israel	22,145
150. El Salvador	21,041
151. Slovenia	20,273
152. Timor-Leste	18,889
153. Fiji	18,333
154. Kuwait	17,818
155. Swaziland	17,364
156. Bahamas, The	13,878
157. Montenegro	13,812
158. Vanuatu	12,109
159. Qatar	11,437
160. Jamaica	11,420
161. Gambia, The	11,295
162. Kosovo	10,887
163. Lebanon	10,452
164. Cyprus	9,251
165. Brunei	5,765
166. Trinidad and Tobago	5,128
167. Cape Verde	4,033
168. Samoa	2,935
169. Luxembourg	2,586
170. Mauritius	2,040
171. Comoros	1,861
172. Sao Tome and Principe	1,001
173. Dominica	751
174. Kiribati	717
175. Micronesia	701
176. Bahrain	694
177. Singapore	682
178. Tonga	649
179. Saint Lucia	616
180. Palau	490
181. Andorra	468
182. Antigua and Barbuda	457
183. Seychelles	455
184. Barbados	430
185. St. Vincent and the Grenadines	388
186. Grenada	344
187. Malta	316
188. Maldives	298
189. Saint Kitts and Nevis	261
190. Niue	260
191. Cook Islands	237
192. Marshall Islands	181
193. Liechtenstein	160
194. San Marino	61
195. Tuvalu	27
196. Nauru	21
197. Monaco	1.95
198. Vatican City	0.44

1 km² = 0.3861 square mile

	Inhabitants 2007
1. China	1,336,317,000
2. India	1,169,016,000
3. United States	305,826,000
4. Indonesia	231,627,000
5. Brazil	191,791,000
6. Pakistan	163,902,000
7. Bangladesh	158,665,000
8. Nigeria	148,093,000
9. Russia	142,499,000
10. Japan	127,967,000
11. Mexico	106,535,000
12. Philippines	87,960,000
13. Vietnam	87,375,000
14. Ethiopia	83,099,000
15. Germany	82,599,000
16. Egypt	75,498,000
17. Turkey	74,877,000
18. Iran	71,208,000
19. Thailand	63,884,000
20. Congo, Dem. Rep. of the	62,636,000
21. France	61,647,000
22. United Kingdom	60,769,000
23. Italy	58,877,000
24. Myanmar	48,798,000
25. South Africa	48,577,000
26. Korea, South	48,224,000
27. Ukraine	46,205,000
28. Colombia	46,156,000
29. Spain	44,279,000
30. Tanzania	40,454,000
31. Argentina	39,531,000
32. Sudan, The	38,560,000
33. Poland	38,082,000
34. Kenya	37,538,000
35. Algeria	33,858,000
36. Canada	32,876,000
37. Morocco	31,224,000
38. Uganda	30,884,000
39. Iraq	28,993,000
40. Nepal	28,196,000
41. Peru	27,903,000
42. Venezuela	27,657,000
43. Uzbekistan	27,372,000
44. Afghanistan	27,145,000
45. Malaysia	26,572,000
46. Saudi Arabia	24,735,000
47. Korea, North	23,790,000
48. Ghana	23,748,000
49. Taiwan (2004)	22,689,000
50. Yemen	22,389,000
51. Romania	21,438,000
52. Mozambique	21,397,000
53. Australia	20,743,000
54. Syria	19,929,000
55. Madagascar	19,683,000
56. Sri Lanka	19,299,000
57. Côte d'Ivoire	19,262,000
58. Cameroon	18,549,000
59. Angola	17,024,000
60. Chile	16,635,000
61. Netherlands, The	16,419,000
62. Kazakhstan	15,422,000
63. Burkina Faso	14,784,000
64. Cambodia	14,444,000
65. Niger	14,226,000
66. Malawi	13,925,000

	Inhabitants 2007
67. Guatemala	13,354,000
68. Zimbabwe	13,349,000
69. Ecuador	13,341,000
70. Mali	13,337,000
71. Senegal	12,379,000
72. Zambia	11,922,000
73. Cuba	11,268,000
74. Greece	11,147,000
75. Chad	10,781,000
76. Portugal	10,623,000
77. Belgium	10,457,000
78. Tunisia	10,327,000
79. Czech Republic	10,186,000
80. Hungary	10,030,000
81. Dominican Republic	9,760,000
82. Rwanda	9,725,000
83. Belarus	9,689,000
84. Haiti	9,598,000
85. Bolivia	9,525,000
86. Guinea	9,370,000
87. Sweden	9,119,000
88. Benin	9,033,000
89. Somalia	8,699,000
90. Burundi	8,508,000
91. Azerbaijan	8,467,000
92. Austria	8,361,000
93. Serbia	8,032,000
94. Bulgaria	7,639,000
95. Switzerland	7,484,000
96. Honduras	7,106,000
97. Israel	6,928,000
98. El Salvador	6,857,000
99. Tajikistan	6,736,000
100. Togo	6,585,000
101. Papua New Guinea	6,331,000
102. Libya	6,160,000
103. Paraguay	6,127,000
104. Jordan	5,924,000
105. Sierra Leone	5,866,000
106. Laos	5,859,000
107. Nicaragua	5,603,000
108. Denmark	5,442,000
109. Slovakia	5,390,000
110. Kyrgyzstan	5,317,000
111. Finland	5,277,000
112. Turkmenistan	4,965,000
113. Eritrea	4,851,000
114. Norway	4,698,000
115. Croatia	4,555,000
116. Costa Rica	4,468,000
117. Singapore	4,436,000
118. Georgia	4,395,000
119. United Arab Emirates	4,380,000
120. Central African Republic	4,343,000
121. Ireland	4,301,000
122. New Zealand	4,179,000
123. Lebanon	4,099,000
124. Bosnia and Herzegovina	3,935,000
125. Moldova	3,794,000
126. Congo, Republic of the	3,768,000
127. Liberia	3,750,000
128. Lithuania	3,390,000
129. Panama	3,343,000
130. Uruguay	3,340,000
131. Albania	3,190,000
132. Mauritania	3,124,000

	Inhabitants 2007
133. Armenia	3,002,000
134. Kuwait	2,851,000
135. Jamaica	2,714,000
136. Mongolia	2,629,000
137. Oman	2,595,000
138. Latvia	2,277,000
139. Kosovo	2,126,000
140. Namibia	2,074,000
141. Macedonia	2,038,000
142. Lesotho	2,008,000
143. Slovenia	2,002,000
144. Botswana	1,882,000
145. Gambia, The	1,709,000
146. Guinea-Bissau	1,695,000
147. Estonia	1,335,000
148. Trinidad and Tobago	1,333,000
149. Gabon	1,331,000
150. Mauritius	1,262,000
151. Timor-Leste	1,155,000
152. Swaziland	1,141,000
153. Cyprus	855,000
154. Qatar	841,000
155. Fiji	839,000
Comoros	839,000
157. Djibouti	833,000
158. Bahrain	753,000
159. Guyana	738,000
160. Bhutan	658,000
161. Montenegro	598,000
162. Cape Verde	530,000
163. Equatorial Guinea	507,000
164. Solomon Islands	496,000
165. Western Sahara	480,000
166. Luxembourg	467,000
167. Suriname	458,000
168. Malta	407,000
169. Brunei	390,000
170. Bahamas	331,000
171. Maldives	306,000
172. Iceland	301,000
173. Barbados	294,000
174. Belize	288,000
175. Vanuatu	226,000
176. Samoa	187,000
177. Saint Lucia	165,000
178. Sao Tome and Principe	158,000
179. St. Vincent and the Grenadines	120,000
180. Micronesia	111,000
181. Grenada	106,000
182. Tonga	100,000
183. Kiribati	95,000
184. Seychelles	87,000
185. Antigua and Barbuda	85,000
186. Andorra	75,000
187. Dominica	67,000
188. Marshall Islands	59,000
189. Saint Kitts and Nevis	50,000
190. Liechtenstein	35,000
191. Monaco	33,000
192. San Marino	31,000
193. Palau	20,000
194. Cook Islands	13,000
195. Tuvalu	11,000
196. Nauru	10,000
197. Niue	2,000
198. Vatican City (2004)	532

North America

Mount McKinley (Alaska Range)	6,194 m
Mount Logan (Saint Elias Mountains)	5,959 m
Pico de Orizaba (Mexico)	5,610 m
Popocatépetl (Mexico)	5,452 m
Nevado de Colima (Sierra Madre Occidental)	4,450 m
Mount Whitney (Sierra Nevada)	4,418 m
Mount Elbert (Rocky Mountains)	4,399 m
Mount Rainier (Cascade Range)	4,392 m
Tajumulco (Sierra Madre)	4,220 m
Mount Waddington (Coast Mountains)	4,016 m
Cerro Mohinora (Sierra Madre Occidental)	3,992 m
Mount Robson (Rocky Mountains)	3,954 m
Chirripó Grande (Cordillera de Talamanca)	3,820 m
Gunnbjørn Fjeld (Greenland)	3700 m
Cerro Peña Nevada (Sierra Madre Oriental)	3,664 m
Pico Duarte (Hispaniola)	3,175 m
Blue Mountain Peak (Jamaica)	2,256 m
Mount Mitchell (Appalachian Mountains)	2,037 m
Pico Turquino (Sierra Maestra)	1,974 m

South America

Aconcagua (Andes)	6,962 m
Pissis (Andes)	6,882 m
Ojos del Salado (Andes)	6,880 m
Huascarán (Andes)	6,768 m
Llullaillaco (Andes)	6,723 m
Sajama (Andes)	6,542 m
Illimani (Andes)	6,462 m
Chimborazo (Andes)	6,310 m
Cotopaxi (Andes)	5,897 m
Pico Cristóbal Colón (Sierra Nevada de Santa Marta)	5,775 m
Huila (Andes)	5,750 m
Pico Bolívar (Cordillera de Mérida)	5,007 m
San Valentín (Cordillera Patagónica)	4,058 m
Pico da Neblina (Guiana Highlands)	3,014 m
Pico da Bandeira (Brazilian Highlands)	2,890 m
Yogan (Tierra del Fuego)	2,469 m

Europe

Mont Blanc (Western Alps)	4,807 m
Dufourspitze, Monte Rosa (Pennine Alps)	4,634 m
Matterhorn (Pennine Alps)	4,478 m
Finsteraarhorn (Bernese Alps)	4,274 m
Jungfrau (Bernese Alps)	4,158 m
Pelvoux (Western Alps)	4,102 m
Gran Paradiso (Alpi Graie)	4,061 m
Bernina (Rhaetian Alps)	4,049 m
Ortles (Central Alps)	3,905 m
Monte Viso (Cottian Alps)	3,841 m
Grossglockner (Hohe Tauern)	3,798 m
Mulhacén (Sierra Nevada)	3,481 m
Aneto (Pyrenees)	3,404 m
Marmolada (Dolomites)	3,342 m
Etna (Sicily)	3,323 m
Zugspitze (Bavarian Alps)	2,962 m
Musala (Rila)	2,925 m
Ólympos (Piería)	2,917 m
Vihren (Pirin)	2,914 m
Gran Sasso d'Italia (Abruzzi)	2,912 m
Triglav (Julian Alps)	2,864 m
Monte Cinto (Corsica)	2,706 m
Jezerca (North Albanian Alps)	2,694 m
Gerlachovský Štít (High Tatra)	2,655 m
Picos de Europa (Cantabrian Mountains)	2,648 m
Almanzor (Sierra de Gredos)	2,592 m
Grintavec (Karawanken)	2,559 m
Moldoveanu (Transylvanien Alps)	2,544 m
Durmitor (Dinaric Alps)	2,522 m
Galdhøpiggen (Scandinavia)	2,469 m
Ídi (Crete)	2,456 m
Ágios Ilías (Taïgetos)	2,407 m
Botev (Balkan Maountains)	2,376 m
Pietrosu (Carpathian Mountains)	2,303 m
Golyam Pereli (Rhodope Mountains)	2,191 m
Öræfajökull (Iceland)	2,119 m
Kebnekaise (Scandinavia)	2,111 m
Ďumbier (Low Tatra)	2,043 m

Asia

Mt. Everest (Himalayas)	8,850 m
K2 (Karakoram Range)	8,611 m
Dhaulagiri (Himalayas)	8,167 m
Nanga Parbat (Himalayas)	8,125 m
Muztag Feng (Kunlun Shan)	7,723 m
Kongur Shan (Kunlun Shan)	7,719 m
Tirich Mir (Hindu Kush)	7,690 m
Gongga Shan (Daxue Shan)	7,556 m
Peak Somoni (Pamirs)	7,495 m
Jengish Chokusu/ Shengli Feng (Tien Shan)	7,439 m
Lenin Pik (Trans Alai)	7,134 m
Nyainqêntanglha (Nyainqêntanglha Shan)	7,111 m
Damāvand (Elburz Mountains)	5,671 m
El'brus (Caucasus)	5,642 m
Pik Piramidalnyy (Turkestan Range)	5,621 m
Chimtarga (Zeravshan Range)	5,489 m
Ararat (Armenian Highlands)	5,165 m
Klyuchevskaya Sopka (Kamchatka)	4,750 m
Zard Kūh (Zagros Mountains)	4,548 m
Belukha (Altay)	4,506 m
Uludoruk (Eastern Taurus Mount.)	4,135 m
Kinabalu (Borneo)	4,101 m
Ich Bogd (Govi Altayn Nuruu)	3,957 m
Kaçkar (Pontine Mountains)	3,932 m
Erciyeş (Anatolia)	3,917 m
Otgon Tenger (Khangai)	3,905 m
Kerinci (Sumatra)	3,800 m
Mount Fuji (Honshu)	3,776 m
Rinjani (Lombok)	3,726 m
Semeru (Java)	3,676 m
Nabī Shua'yb (Yemen)	3,760 m
Munku-Sardyk (Eastern Sayan)	3,491 m
Rantekombola (Celebes)	3,455 m
Pobeda (Cherskiy Range)	3,147 m
Phan Si Pang (Hoanglien Son)	3,143 m
Kyzyl Taiga (Western Sayan)	3,121 m
Qurnat as Sawdā' (Lebonan Mount.)	3,083 m
J. ash Shām (Oman Mountains)	2,980 m
Mount Apo (Mindanao)	2,954 m
Mount Pulog (Luzon)	2,929 m
Baitou Shan/Paekdu-san (China/North Korea)	2,744 m
Anai Mudi (Western Ghats)	2,695 m
J. Katrīna (Sinai Peninsula)	2,637 m
Pidurutalagala (Ceylon)	2,524 m
Tahan (Malay Peninsula)	2,187 m
Tardoki-Jani (Sikhote Alin Range)	2,077 m
Ólympus (Cyprus)	1,953 m

Australia an Oceania

Carstensz Pyramid/ Puncak Jayakesuma (Maoke Range)	4,884 m
Mount Wilhelm (Bismarck Range)	4,509 m
Mauna Kea (Hawaii)	4,205 m
Mount Victoria (Owen Stanley Range)	4,073 m
Mount Cook (Southern Alps)	3,754 m
Mount Ruapehu (North Island, New Zealand)	2,797 m
Mount Balbi (Bougainville Isl.)	2,685 m
Mount Popomanaseu (Guadalcanal)	2,331 m
Mont Orohena (Tahiti)	2,241 m
Mount Kosciusko (Australian Alps)	2,228 m
Mount Tabwemasana (Espiritu Santo)	1,879 m
Mont Panié (New Caledonia)	1,628 m
Mount Ossa (Tasmania)	1,617 m
Mount Victoria (Viti Levu)	1,322 m

Africa

Kilimanjaro (Tanzania)	5,892 m
Mount Kenya (Kenya)	5,199 m
Margherita Peak (Ruwenzori)	5,110 m
Ras Dashen (Ethiopian Highlands)	4,620 m
Tubqāl (High Atlas)	4,165 m
Cameroon Mountain (Cameroon)	4,095 m
Pico de Teide (Tenerife)	3,718 m
Thabana Ntlenyana (Drakensberg)	3,482 m
Emi Koussi (Tibesti)	3,415 m
Kinyeti (Lolibai)	3,187 m
Jebel Marrah (Darfur)	3,071 m
Piton des Neiges (Réunion)	3,069 m
Pico Basile (Bioko)	3,008 m
Sapitwa (Mlanje)	3,002 m
Tahat (Ahaggar)	2,918 m
Maromokotro (Madagascar)	2,876 m
Môco (Bié Plateau)	2,619 m
Brandberg (Namibia)	2,606 m
Kompasberg (Sneeuberg)	2,504 m
Shimbiris (Somalia)	2,416 m
Kartala (Ngazidja)	2,361 m
Bintimani (Loma Mountains)	1,948 m
Pico Ruivo (Madeira)	1,847 m
Shere Hill (Jos Plateau)	1,780 m
Tamgue (Fouta Djallon)	1,538 m
Table Mountain (South Africa)	1,087 m

Antarctica

Vinson Massif	4,897 m
Mount Kirkpatrick	4,528 m
Mount Jackson	4,190 m
Mount Erebus	3,794 m

1 m = 3,28095 ft

Major Rivers

North America

Mississippi/Missouri	6,420 km
Mackenzie/Peace River	4,241 km
Mississippi	3,778 km
Missouri	3,725 km
Yukon	3,185 km
Rio Grande/ Rîo Bravo del Norte	2,840 km
Nelson/Saskatchewan	2,575 km
Arkansas	2,348 km
Colorado	2,333 km
Ohio/Allegheny	2,101 km
Columbia	2,000 km
Snake	1,670 km
Churchill	1,609 km
Brazos	1,485 km
Tennessee/French Broad	1,421 km
Fraser	1,368 km
Saint Lawrence	1,287 km
Hudson	492 km

South America

Amazonas	6,437 km
Paraná/Rîo de la Plata	4,264 km
Madeira	3,240 km
Purus	3,211 km
São Francisco	3,199 km
Japurá/Caquetá	2,816 km
Tocantins	2,699 km
Orinoco	2,575 km
Paraguay	2,549 km
Rîo Negro	2,253 km
Tapajós/Juruena	2,200 km
Xingu	2,100 km
Uruguay	1,609 km
Magdalena	1,538 km

Europe

Volga	3,531 km
Danube	2,858 km
Ural	2,428 km
Dniepr	2,201 km
Kama	2,032 km
Don	1,870 km
Pechora	1,809 km
Oka	1,480 km
Belaya	1,430 km
Dniester	1,352 km
Rhine	1,320 km
Vyatka	1,314 km
Northern Dvina/Sukhona	1,302 km
Elbe	1,165 km
Desna	1,130 km
Vychegda	1,130 km
Donets	1,053 km
Vistula	1,047 km
Western Dvina	1,020 km
Loire	1,020 km
Tagus	1,007 km
Tisza	966 km
Prut	950 km
Meuse/Maas	933 km
Oder	912 km
Ebro	910 km
Rhône	812 km
Seine	776 km
Klarälven/Göta Älv	720 km
Po	652 km
Glomma	598 km
Maritsa	533 km
Kemijoki	483 km
Tevere	393 km
Shannon	361 km
Thames	346 km

Asia

Yangtze	5,526 km
Yellow River	5,464 km
Amur/Shilka/Onon	4,416 km
Ob/Katun	4,345 km
Lena	4,313 km
Irtysh	4,248 km
Mekong	4,184 km
Yenisey	4,102 km
Syr Darya/Naryn	3,012 km
Lower Tunguska	2,989 km
Indus	2,897 km
Brahmaputra	2,896 km
Tarim/Yarkant	2,750 km
Euphrates	2,736 km
Amu Darya/Panj/Vakhan	2,574 km
Kolyma	2,513 km
Ganges	2,511 km
Salween	2,414 km
Aldan	2,242 km
Xi Jiang	2,129 km
Irrawaddy	2,092 km
Sungari	1,927 km
Tigris	1,899 km

Australia and Oceania

Darling	2,740 km
Murray	2,570 km
Murrumbidgee	2,160 km
Lachlan	1,480 km
Sepik	1,127 km
Fly	1,120 km
Flinders	832 km
Waikato	425 km

Africa

Nile/Kagera	6,671 km
Congo	4,374 km
Niger	4,184 km
Zambezi	2,736 km
Ubangi/Uele	2,300 km
Kasai	2,153 km
Orange River	2,092 km
Cubango/Okavango	1,800 km
Juba	1,650 km
Limpopo	1,600 km
Volta	1,600 km
Lomami	1,450 km
Senegal	1,430 km
Chari	1,400 km
Vaal	1,251 km
Gambia	1,127 km

Major Islands (In some cases small adjacent islands are included.)

North America

Greenland	2,166,086 km²
Baffin Island	688,808 km²
Victoria Island	217,291 km²
Ellesmere Island	196,237 km²
Newfoundland	112,300 km²
Cuba	105,007 km²
Hispaniola	75,606 km²
Banks Island	70,028 km²
Devon Island	55,247 km²
Axel Heiberg Island	43,178 km²
Melville Island	42,150 km²
Southampton Island	41,215 km²
Prince of Wales Island	33,338 km²
Vancouver Island	31,285 km²
Somerset Island	24,786 km²
Bathurst Island	16,042 km²
Prince Patrick Island	15,848 km²
King William Island	13,111 km²
Ellef Ringnes Island	11,250 km²
Bylot Island	11,067 km²
Jamaica	10,962 km²
Cape Breton Island	10,311 km²
Puerto Rico	8,644 km²
Andros Island	5,957 km²
Long Island	4,463 km²
Guadeloupe	1,433 km²

South America

Tierra del Fuego	47,000 km²
Chiloé Island	8,395 km²
East Falkland	6,605 km²
Isabela Island	5,825 km²
Trinidad	4,820 km²
West Falkland	4,532 km²

Europe

Great Britain	219,081 km²
Iceland	103,000 km²
Ireland	84,420 km²
Novaya Zemlya (North Island)	48,904 km²
Spitsbergen	39,044 km²
Novaya Zemlya (South Island)	33,275 km²
Sicily	25,426 km²
Sardinia	23,813 km²
North East Land	14,530 km²
Corsica	8,682 km²
Crete	8,263 km²
Sjælland	7,016 km²
Kolguyev	5,250 km²
Euboea	3,655 km²
Mallorca	3,505 km²
Vaigach Island	3,383 km²
Gotland	3,001 km²
Fyn	2,977 km²
Saaremaa	2,714 km²
Hinnøy	2,198 km²
Lésvos	1,630 km²
Rhodes	1,398 km²
Öland	1,344 km²
Lolland	1,241 km²
Hiiumaa	965 km²
Rügen	926 km²
Menorca	683 km²
Corfu	592 km²
Bornholm	588 km²
Isle of Man	572 km²
Krk	410 km²
Malta	246 km²
Fehmarn	185 km²
Île d'Oléron	175 km²

Asia

Borneo (Kalimantan)	736,000 km²
Sumatera	425,000 km²
Honshu	227,414 km²
Celebes (Sulawesi)	180,000 km²
Java	126,650 km²
Luzon	104,700 km²
Mindanao	94,600 km²
Hokkaido	78,073 km²
Sachalin	76,400 km²
Ceylon	65,610 km²
Kyushu	36,554 km²
Taiwan	36,000 km²
Hainan	34,000 km²
Timor	33,850 km²
Shikoku	18,256 km²
Halmahera	17,800 km²
Seram	17,150 km²
Flores	14,250 km²
October Revolution Island	14,200 km²
Sumbawa	13,280 km²
Samar	13,080 km²
Negros	12,700 km²
Bangka	11,930 km²
Palawan	11,785 km²
Kotelnyy Island	11,665 km²
Panay	11,515 km²
Bolshevik Island	11,312 km²
Sumba	11,150 km²
Mindoro	9,735 km²
Buru	9,500 km²
Cyprus	9,251 km²
Komsomolets Island	9,200 km²
Wrangel Island	7,300 km²
New Siberia	6,200 km²

Australia and Oceania

New Guinea	771,600 km²
South Island (New Zealand)	151,971 km²
North Island (New Zealand)	114,489 km²
Tasmania	64,410 km²
New Britain	36,500 km²
New Caledonia	16,177 km²
Viti Levu	10,429 km²
Hawaii (Big Island)	10,414 km²
Bougainville Island	10,050 km²
New Ireland	8,600 km²
Guadalcanal	6,475 km²
Melville Island	5,800 km²
Vanua Levu	5,556 km²
Kangaroo Island	4,350 km²
Espíritu Santo	3,677 km²
Savai'i	1,715 km²
Tahiti	1,042 km²

Africa

Madagaskar	587,041 km²
Socotra	3,580 km²
Réunion	2,512 km²
Tenerife	2,057 km²
Bioko	2,017 km²
Mauritius	1,865 km²
Zanzibar	1,658 km²
Ngazidja	1,148 km²
Santiago	991 km²
Pemba	984 km²
Madeira	740 km²

Antarctic Region

Kerguelen Island	5,820 km²
South Georgia	3,755 km²
Ross Island	2,300 km²

1 km² = 0.3861 square mile

Major Lakes (* excluding islands)

North America	
Lake Superior	82,103 km²
Lake Huron	59,570 km²
Lake Michigan	57,757 km²
Great Bear Lake	31,328 km²
Great Slave Lake	28,568 km²
Lake Erie	25,667 km²
Lake Winnipeg	24,387 km²
Lake Ontario	19,011 km²
Lake Nicaragua	8,029 km²
Lake Athabasca	7,935 km²
Reindeer Lake	6,651 km²
Great Salt Lake	5,905 km²
Nettilling Lake	5,542 km²
Lake Winnipegosis	5,374 km²
Lake Manitoba	4,624 km²

Europe	
Lake Ladoga	18,135 km²
Lake Onega	9,720 km²
Vänern*	5,584 km²
Lake Peipus	3,550 km²
Vättern*	1,899 km²
Saimaa	1,460 km²
Lake Seg	1,200 km²
Mälaren*	1,140 km²
Beloye Ozero	1,125 km²
Inari Lake	1,085 km²
Päijänne*	1,054 km²
Lake Ilmen	982 km²
Oulu Lake	893 km²
Balaton	592 km²
Lake Geneva	580 km²
Lake Constanze	572 km²
Hjälmaren	484 km²
Lough Neagh	388 km²
Lake Garda	370 km²
Mjøsa	368 km²
Torne Lake	322 km²
Lake Neusiedl	320 km²
Lake Neuchâtel	218 km²
Lago Maggiore	212 km²
Müritz	110 km²
Chiemsee	80 km²
Loch Ness	65 km²

Australia and Oceania	
Lake Eyre	c. 9,300 km²
Lake Torrens	c. 5,700 km²
Lake Gairdner	c. 4,700 km²
Lake Taupo	606 km²

South America	
Lake de Maracaibo	13,512 km²
Lake Titicaca	8,288 km²
Lake Poopó	2,530 km²
Lago Argentino	1,415 km²
Lake Nahuel Huapi	550 km²

Asia	
Caspian Sea	367,000 km²
Baykal	31,499 km²
Lake Balkhash	18,428 km²
Aral Sea	c. 17,000 km²
Ysyk-Köl	6,099 km²
Koko Nor	5,000 km²
Lake Urmia	4,686 km²
Lake Tajmyr	4,560 km²
Lake Khanka	4,401 km²
Lake Van	3,713 km²
Lake Sevan	1,360 km²
Dead Sea	910 km²
Lake Biwa	672 km²

Africa	
Lake Victoria	69,484 km²
Lake Tanganyika	32,893 km²
Lake Nyassa	28,878 km²
Lake Chad	10,000–25,000 km²
Lake Turkana	6,405 km²
Lake Albert	5,374 km²
Lake Mweru	4,920 km²
Lake Tana	3,630 km²
Lac Kivu	2,650 km²
Lake Edward	2,200 km²

Additional Resources
Estimated resources based on general geologic conditions as well as proven resources that cannot be recovered under current economic conditions or with existing available technology.

Agricultural Trade
Trade in food (food and live animals, beverages and tobacco, animal and vegetable oils, fats and waxes, oilseeds and oleaginous fruit), raw materials (hides, skins and furskins, crude rubber, cork and wood, pulp and waste paper, textile fibres and their wastes, crude animal and vegetable materials).

Armed Conflict
An armed conflict is defined as a contested incompatibility that concerns government and/or territory where the use of armed force between two parties, of which at least one is the government of a state, results in at least 25 battle-related deaths (PRIO 2005).

Battle-Deaths
Deaths resulting directly from violence inflicted through the use of armed force by a party to an armed conflict during contested combat. Contested combat is use of armed force by a party to an armed conflict against any person or target during which the perpetrator faces the immediate threat of lethal force being used by another party to the conflict against him/her and/or allied fighters (Lacina & Gleditsch 2005).

Biodiversity
Number and variety of living organisms; includes genetic diversity, species diversity, and ecological diversity.

Biogeographical Realm
Continental-scale biogeographic regions defined by differences in geologic and climatic history which contain distinct assemblages of plants and animals, particularly at higher taxonomic levels.

Biome (formally known as Major Habitat Types or MHTs)
Broad kinds of ecoregions that:
a) experience comparable climatic regimes;
b) have similar vegetation structure;
c) display similar spatial patterns of biodiversity;
d) contain flora and fauna with similar guild structures and life histories;
e) have similar minimum requirements and thresholds for maintaining certain biodiversity features; and
f) have similar sensitivities to human disturbance.

Birth Rate
The annual number of births per 1,000 total population. This rate is often referred to as "crude birth rate" since it does not take a population's age structure into account.

Carbon Dioxide Emissions
The emissions data are in accordance with the source categories of the IPCC Guidelines for National Greenhouse Gas Inventories. The sources considered are: Fuel combustion, energy industries, transport, industrial processes, solvent and other product use, agriculture and waste. Not included are emissions resulting from fuel sold to ships or aircraft engaged in international transport and emissions from biomass burning or emissions or removals from the land-use change and forestry sector.

Climate Diagram (by H. Walter)
Climate diagrams summarize average climatic variables by month. In these diagrams by H. Walter, months are placed along the bottom horizontal axis. Average precipitation and temperature are indicated along the left and right axes, respectively. 20 mm of monthly precipitation (left axis) equals 10 °C average temperature (right axis). When the precipitation curve falls below the temperature curve, the gap between them emphasizes a dry season. When the precipitation curve exceeds the temperature curve, this denotes a moist season.

Coefficient of variation
The coefficient of variation is defined as the ratio of standard deviation to the average. It is a measure of relative variability. A high coefficient of variation means that the standard deviation is high compared to average. This means that precipitation in single years may differ considerably from the long term average.

Combined Gross Enrollment Ratio [for Primary, Secondary and Tertiary Schools]
The number of students enrolled in primary, secondary and tertiary levels of education, regardless of age, as a percentage of the population of official school age for the three levels.

Commodity Concentration of Exports
The related measure used by UNCTAD is the Hirschman index, which is calculated using the shares of products in a country's exports. The maximum value of the index is 1, and its minimum (theoretical) value is zero, for a country with no exports. The lower the index, the less concentrated are a country's exports.

Crisis
A crisis is a tense situation in which at least one of the parties uses violent force in sporadic incidents.

Current Forest
Land spanning more than 0.5 hectares with trees higher than 5 meters and a canopy cover of more than 10 percent, or trees able to reach these thresholds in situ. It does not include land that is predominantly under agricultural or urban land use.

Death Rate
The annual number of deaths per 1,000 total population. This rate is often referred to as "crude death rate" since it does not take a population's age structure into account.

Deforestation
A non-temporary change of land use from forest to other land use or depletion of forest crown cover to less than 10 percent. Clear cuts (even with stump removal) if shortly followed by reforestation for forestry purposes are not considered deforestation.

Desertification
Land degradation in arid, semi-arid and dry sub-humid areas resulting from various factors, including climate variations and human activities.

Digital Access Index (DAI)
The index combines eight variables, covering five areas, to provide an overall country score. The areas are availability of infrastructure (fixed telephone subscribers per 100 inhabitants, mobile cellular subscribers

per 100 inhabitants), affordability of access (Internet access price as percentage of GNI per capita), educational level (adult literacy, combined primary, secondary and tertiary school enrolment level), quality of ICT services (international Internet bandwidth [bits] per capita, broadband subscribers per 100 inhabitants), and Internet usage (Internet users per 100 inhabitants).

Ecoregion
An ecoregion is defined as a large area of land or water that contains a geographically distinct assemblage of natural communities that
a) share a large majority of their species and ecological dynamics;
b) share similar environmental conditions, and;
c) interact ecologically in ways that are critical for their long-term persistence.

Electoral Democracy
To qualify as an electoral democracy, a state must have satisfied the following criteria:
a) A competitive, multiparty political system.
b) Universal adult suffrage for all citizens (with exceptions for restrictions that states may legitimately place on citizens as sanctions for criminal offenses).
c) Regularly contested elections conducted in conditions of ballot secrecy, reasonable ballot security, and in the absence of massive voter fraud that yields results that are unrepresentative of the public will.
d) Significant public access of major political parties to the electorate through the media and through generally open political campaigning.

Employment in Agriculture, Industry and Services
The agriculture, industry and services sectors are defined by the International Standard Industrial Classification (ISIC) System:
a) The agricultural sector comprises activities in agriculture, hunting, forestry and fishing.
b) The industry sector comprises mining and quarrying, manufacturing, construction and public utilities (electricity, gas and water).
c) The services sector consists of wholesale and retail trade, restaurants and hotels, transport, storage and communications, finance, insurance, real estate and business services, and community, social and personal services.

Eurozone
European Union member states which have adopted the Euro (€) as their common currency.

Exploitable Resources
Proven resources that are recoverable under present economic conditions with existing available technology.

Female and Male Earned Income
Female and male earned income are crudely estimated on the basis of data on the ratio of the female non-agricultural wage to the male non-agricultural wage, the female and male shares of the economically active population, the total female and male population and GDP per capita (PPP US$).

Female Proportion of Labor Force
The share of the female population ages 15 and above who supply, or are available to supply, labour for the production of goods and services.

Foreign Aid
Foreign aid includes both official development assistance (ODA) and official aid (OA).

Foreign Direct Investment
Foreign direct investment is net inflow of investment to acquire a lasting management interest (10 percent or more of voting stock) in an enterprise operating in an economy other than that of the investor. It is the sum of equity capital, reinvestment of earnings, other long-term capital, and short-term capital as shown in the balance of payments.

Freedom Rating
Countries are evaluated based on a checklist of questions on political rights (electoral process, political pluralism and participation, functioning of government, discretionary political rights) and civil liberties (freedom of expression and belief, associational and organizational rights, rule of law, personal autonomy and individual rights) that are derived in large measure from the Universal Declaration of Human Rights (Freedom House 2005).

Full Schengen Member
The EU has set up a Schengen area – consisting of EU member states that have signed the Schengen agreements (1985 and 1990) on the free movement of persons and the harmonization of border controls in Europe. Member states are: Austria, Belgium, Denmark, Finland, France, Germany, Greece, Italy, Luxembourg, Netherlands, Portugal, Spain, and Sweden. In addition, non-EU states Iceland and Norway have been included in the Schengen area since 1996 (full members in 2001).

Gini Coefficient
The Gini Coefficient measures the extent to which the distribution of income (or consumption) among individuals or households within a country deviates from a perfectly equal distribution. A value of 0 represents perfect equality, and a value of 100 perfect inequality.

Government Expenditures
The sum of the final consumption expenditures of the general government, plus property income paid, plus subsidies paid, plus social benefits other than in-kind paid, plus other current transfers paid, plus net capital transfers paid, plus Gross capital formation and net acquisitions of non-produced non-financial assets, minus consumption of fixed capital.

Gross Domestic Product (GDP)
The sum of value added by all resident producers in the economy plus any product taxes (less subsidies) not included in the valuation of output. It is calculated without making deductions for depreciation of fabricated capital assets or for depletion and degradation of natural resources. Value added is the net output of an industry after adding up all outputs and subtracting intermediate inputs.

Gross National Income (GNI)
Gross national income (GNI) is the sum of value added by all resident producers plus any product taxes (less subsidies) not included in the valuation of output plus net receipts of primary income (compensation of employees and property income) from abroad.

HIPC Initiative
The HIPC (Heavily Indebted Poor Countries) Initiative currently identifies 38 countries, 32 of them in Sub-Saharan Africa, as potentially eligible to

receive debt relief. Through the HIPC Initiative, nominal debt service relief of more than US$ 56 billion has been approved for 28 countries, reducing their Net Present Value of external debt by approximately two-thirds. Of these countries, 19 have reached the completion point and have been granted unconditional debt service relief of over US$ 37 billion.

Human Development Index (HDI)
A composite index measuring average achievement in the three basic dimensions of human development – a long and healthy life (life expectancy at birth), knowledge (combined gross enrollment ratio for schools) and a decent standard of living (Gross Domestic Product per capita).

Indebtedness
Present value of debt is the sum of short-term external debt plus the discounted sum of total debt service payment due on public, public guaranteed, and private non-guaranteed long-term external debt over the life of existing loans. Countries with a present value of debt service greater than 220 % of exports or 80 % of Gross National Income (GNI) were classified as severely indebted, countries that were not severely indebted but whose present value of debt service exceeded 132 % of exports or 48 % of GNI were classified as moderately indebted, and countries that did not fall into either group were classified as less indebted.

Infant Mortality Rate
The annual number of deaths of infants under age 1 per 1,000 live births.

Internally Displaced Persons
A person who, owing to well-founded fear, or fact, of being persecuted for reasons of race, ethnicity, religion, nationality, membership of a particular social group or political opinion, has moved from her/his habitual place of residence within the country of his/her nationality and is unable or, owing to such fear, is unwilling to return to it.

Life Expectancy at Birth
The average number of years a newborn infant can expect to live under current mortality levels.

Manufactured Goods
Iron and steel, chemicals, other semi-manufactures, machinery and transport equipment (power-generating machinery, other non-electrical machinery, office machines and telecommunications equipment, electrical machinery and apparatus, automotive products, other transport equipment), textiles, clothing, and other consumer goods.

Military Expenditures
The figure is calculated by multiplying the estimated defense spending in percentage terms by the Gross Domestic Product (GDP) calculated on an exchange rate basis, not Purchasing Power Parity (PPP) terms. Dollar figures for military expenditures should be treated with caution because of different price patterns and accounting methods among nations, as well as wide variations in the strength of their currencies.

Mining Trade
Trade in ores and other minerals (crude fertilizers and crude minerals, metalliferous ores and metal scrap), fuels, and non-ferrous metals.

Natural Resources
Materials that occur in nature and are essential or useful to humans, such as water, air, land, forests, fish and wildlife, topsoil, and minerals.

Net Migration Rate
The number of immigrants minus the number of emigrants over a period, divided by the person-years lived by the population of the receiving country over that period. It is expressed as net number of migrants per 1,000 population.

Official Aid (OA)
Official aid loans must meet the same criteria as Official Development Assistance (ODA), but are made to countries and territories in transition.

Official Development Assistance (ODA)
Official development assistance comprises grants or loans to developing countries and territories on the OECD/DAC list of aid recipients that are undertaken by the official sector with promotion of economic development and welfare as the main objective and at concessional financial terms (if a loan, having a grant element of at least 25 %). Technical cooperation is included. Grants, loans and credits for military purposes are excluded.

Original Forest
The world's estimated original forest cover between the end of the last ice age and the expansion of the Europeans – c. 8,000 years ago.

Population under 15 and over 65
The total population in these ages is often considered the "dependent ages".

Projected Population
Projected population based upon reasonable assumptions on the future course of fertility, mortality and migration. Projections are based upon official country projections, series issued by the UN or the U.S. Census Bureau, or Population Reference Bureau projections.

Purchasing-power parity (PPP)
The number of currency units required to buy goods equivalent to what can be bought with one unit of the currency of the base country or with one unit of the common currency of a group of countries. Also referred to as Purchasing Power Standard. The PPP may be calculated over all of GDP, but also at levels of aggregation, like capital formation

Refugee
A person who, owing to well-founded fear, or fact, of being persecuted for reasons of race, ethnicity, religion, nationality, membership of a particular social group or political opinion, is outside the country of his/her nationality and is unable or, owing to such fear, is unwilling to avail him/herself of the protection of that country; or who, not having a nationality and being outside the country of former habitual residence as a result of such events, is unable or, owing to such fear, is unwilling to return to it.

Renewable Water Resources
Renewable water resources is the sum of internal and external renewable water resources. It corresponds to the maximum theoretical amount of water available for a country on an average year on a long reference period.

Seats in National Legislature Held by Women
Refers to seats in a lower or single house or an upper house or senate, where relevant.

Severe Crisis
A conflict is considered to be a severe crisis if violent force is repeatedly used in an organized way.

Sex Ratio
Number of males per 100 females in the population.

Soil Orders
Soil taxonomy at the highest hierarchical level identifies 12 soil orders. The names for the orders and taxonomic soil properties relate to Greek, Latin, or other root words that reveal something about the soil.

Total External Debt
Total external debt is debt owed to non-residents repayable in foreign currency, goods, or services. It is the sum of public, publicly guaranteed, and private non-guaranteed long-term debt, use of IMF credit, and short-term debt. Short-term debt includes all debt having an original maturity of one year or less and interest in arrears on long-term debt.

Under-Five Mortality
The probability that a newborn baby will die before reaching age five, if subject to current age-specific mortality rates.

Undernourished
In FAO's estimates, food consumption is expressed in terms of dietary energy, and people in households consuming less than a certain minimum energy requirement are considered to be undernourished. The minimum daily requirement, which takes into account the calories needed to maintain body weight while performing light activity, varies from country to country but is approximately 1,900 kcal per capita, depending on age, sex and average height.

Urban Population
Population living in urban areas as defined according to the national definition used in the most recent population census. Typically, the population living in towns of 2,000 or more or in national or provincial capitals is classified "urban".

Violent Conflict
A conflict is defined as the clashing of interests on national values of some duration and magnitude between at least two parties (organized groups, states, groups of states, organizations) that are determined to pursue their interests and win their cases. A violent conflict is a type of conflict in which violent force is used at least sporadically by at least one conflict party (HIIK 2004).

Vulnerability
Defines the extent to which climate change may damage or harm a system. It depends not only on a system's sensitivity but also on its ability to adapt to new climatic conditions.

War
A war is a type of violent conflict in which violent force is used with a certain continuity in an organized and systematic way. The conflict parties exercise extensive measures, depending on the situation. The extent of destruction is massive and of long duration.

Water Stress
Water stress is defined as a country's estimated volume of water used per annum expressed as a percentage of the estimated available water resource. Four levels of stress are identified:

1. Low water stress (water use of less than 10 % of the available water resource).
2. Moderate water stress (water use in the range 10 to 20 % of the available resource).
3. Medium to high water stress (water use in the range 20 to 40 % of the available resource).
4. High water stress (water use of more than 40 % of the available water resource).

Water Scarcity
When fresh water availability falls below 1,000 cubic meters per person per year, countries experience chronic water scarcity, in which the lack of water begins to hamper economic development and human health and well-being.

Water Use
Annual gross quantity of water produced and used for agricultural, industrial and domestic purposes. It does not include other in-situ uses: energy, mining, recreation, navigation, fisheries and the environment, which are typically non-consumptive uses of water. Water use = a) agricultural water use + b) domestic water use + c) industrial use.

a) Annual quantity of water used for agricultural purposes including irrigation and livestock watering. By default, livestock water use is accounted for in agricultural water use. However, some countries include it in domestic water withdrawal. Methods for computing agricultural water withdrawal vary from country to country.
b) Annual quantity of water use for domestic purposes. It is usually computed as the total amount of water supplied by public distribution networks, and usually includes the withdrawal by those industries connected to public networks.
c) Annual quantity of water use by self-supplied industries not connected to any distribution network.

Finding a name

- The index contains all names that appear in the maps of the atlas
- Names are arranged alphabetically
- Letters with diacritical marks are alphabetized like regular letters. The ligatures æ and œ are treated as "ae" and "oe", respectively. The special letter ð is regarded as dh, þ as th, ə as e, and the German ß as ss.
- Names that are abbreviated in the maps of the atlas are always spelled out in the index:

  Cheyenne [= Ch.]

- Additions (in parentheses) show local names. Local names are also listed separately and include a reference to the primary name.

  Venice (Venezia)
  Venezia → Venice

Finding the location of a name

- The numbers and letters after each place name indicate the page number of the map, the letter of the reference grid column, and the number of the reference grid row. The place is located at the intersection of the row and column on the page listed. However, on two-page map spreads, the index only lists the number of the left page, even if the place is located on the right page. If there is more than one map on a page, the page number is followed by a Roman numeral that refers to the specific map.

Center Hill Lake ⌣	**100**	B 1/2
Port of Spain	**115**	II B 3
Walburg, Saint	**84**	F 2

Additional information

- Thematic entries in the index are marked with special symbols. Explanations for these symbols are included at the bottom of the index pages. For example, a mountain peak is listed as follows:

  Adelunga ▲ **148** P 10

- Entries with identical names include additional geographic information in brackets:

  Aberdeen *[U.K.]*
  Aberdeen *[U.S., Maryland]*
  Aberdeen *[U.S., Mississippi]*
  Aberdeen *[U.S., South Dakota]*
  Aberdeen *[U.S., Washington]*

  Long Island *[Bahamas]*
  Long Island *[Canada]*
  Long Island *[Papua New Guinea]*
  Long Island *[U.S.]*

A

⛊ Independent country
⛉ Dependent territory
▽ Federal state, province, territory
👥 People, ethnic group, tribe
⧗ Indian reservation/reserve
⌂ National Park
Π Industrial region
∴ Historical site
⌓ Research station
⊕ Continent, realm
⋍ Region, peninsula
⛰ Mountain range, mountains
▲ Peak
)(Pass
✱ Ice shelf, glacier

River, canal
Waterfall
Lake, lakes, reservoir
Swamp
Salt flat
Sea
Strait
Bay, gulf
Cape
Island, islands
Ocean current
Ocean floor landforms
Tectonic feature
Atmospheric phenomena
Time zone
Geographical grid

Independent country
Dependent territory
Federal state, province, territory
People, ethnic group, tribe
Indian reservation/reserve
National Park
Industrial region
Historical site
Research station
Continent, realm
Region, peninsula
Mountain range, mountains
▲ Peak
)(Pass
∗ Ice shelf, glacier

River, canal
Waterfall
Lake, lakes, reservoir
Swamp
Salt flat
Sea
Strait
Bay, gulf
Cape
Island, islands
Ocean current
Ocean floor landforms
Tectonic feature
Atmospheric phenomena
Time zone
Geographical grid

⛊ Independent country
⛉ Dependent territory
▽ Federal state, province, territory
⚇ People, ethnic group, tribe
X Indian reservation/reserve
⇧ National Park
Ⲡ Industrial region
∴ Historical site
⌂ Research station
⊛ Continent, realm
⌒ Region, peninsula
▲▲ Mountain range, mountains
▲ Peak
)(Pass
✱ Ice shelf, glacier

River, canal
Waterfall
Lake, lakes, reservoir
Swamp
Salt flat
Sea
Strait
Bay, gulf
Cape
Island, islands
Ocean current
Ocean floor landforms
Tectonic feature
Atmospheric phenomena
Time zone
Geographical grid

Independent country
Dependent territory
Federal state, province, territory
People, ethnic group, tribe
Indian reservation/reserve
National Park
Industrial region
Historical site
Research station
Continent, realm
Region, peninsula
Mountain range, mountains
Peak
Pass
Ice shelf, glacier

River, canal
Waterfall
Lake, lakes, reservoir
Swamp
Salt flat
Sea
Strait
Bay, gulf
Cape
Island, islands
Ocean current
Ocean floor landforms
Tectonic feature
Atmospheric phenomena
Time zone
Geographical grid

⛊ Independent country
⛊ Dependent territory
⛉ Federal state, province, territory
⚇ People, ethnic group, tribe
⧗ Indian reservation/reserve
۩ National Park
⌶ Industrial region
∴ Historical site
⌂ Research station
⊕ Continent, realm
▱ Region, peninsula
▲▲ Mountain range, mountains
▲ Peak
)(Pass
✱ Ice shelf, glacier

River, canal
Waterfall
Lake, lakes, reservoir
Swamp
Salt flat
Sea
Strait
Bay, gulf
Cape
Island, islands
Ocean current
Ocean floor landforms
Tectonic feature
Atmospheric phenomena
Time zone
Geographical grid

Independent country
Dependent territory
Federal state, province, territory
People, ethnic group, tribe
Indian reservation/reserve
National Park
Industrial region
Historical site
Research station
Continent, realm
Region, peninsula
Mountain range, mountains
Peak
Pass
Ice shelf, glacier

River, canal
Waterfall
Lake, lakes, reservoir
Swamp
Salt flat
Sea
Strait
Bay, gulf
Cape
Island, islands
Ocean current
Ocean floor landforms
Tectonic feature
Atmospheric phenomena
Time zone
Geographical grid

Independent country
Dependent territory
Federal state, province, territory
People, ethnic group, tribe
Indian reservation/reserve
National Park
Industrial region
Historical site
Research station
Continent, realm
Region, peninsula
Mountain range, mountains
▲ Peak
)(Pass
Ice shelf, glacier

River, canal
Waterfall
Lake, lakes, reservoir
Swamp
Salt flat
Sea
Strait
Bay, gulf
Cape
Island, islands
Ocean current
Ocean floor landforms
Tectonic feature
Atmospheric phenomena
Time zone
Geographical grid

Independent country
Dependent territory
Federal state, province, territory
People, ethnic group, tribe
Indian reservation/reserve
National Park
Industrial region
Historical site
Research station
Continent, realm
Region, peninsula
Mountain range, mountains
▲ Peak
)(Pass
* Ice shelf, glacier

ᔕ River, canal
Waterfall
◡ Lake, lakes, reservoir
Swamp
Salt flat
≋ Sea
Strait
≋) Bay, gulf
)≋ Cape
⏖ Island, islands
Ocean current
⋀⋀ Ocean floor landforms
Tectonic feature
Atmospheric phenomena
◷ Time zone
Geographical grid

Independent country
Dependent territory
Federal state, province, territory
People, ethnic group, tribe
Indian reservation/reserve
National Park
Industrial region
Historical site
Research station
Continent, realm
Region, peninsula
Mountain range, mountains
▲ Peak
Pass
Ice shelf, glacier

River, canal
Waterfall
Lake, lakes, reservoir
Swamp
Salt flat
Sea
Strait
Bay, gulf
Cape
Island, islands
Ocean current
Ocean floor landforms
Tectonic feature
Atmospheric phenomena
Time zone
Geographical grid

⛊ Independent country
◑ Dependent territory
⛉ Federal state, province, territory
👥 People, ethnic group, tribe
⧗ Indian reservation/reserve
⌂ National Park
Д Industrial region
∴ Historical site
⌂ Research station
⊕ Continent, realm
⌓ Region, peninsula
⛰ Mountain range, mountains
▲ Peak
)(Pass
✱ Ice shelf, glacier

River, canal
Waterfall
Lake, lakes, reservoir
Swamp
Salt flat
Sea
Strait
Bay, gulf
Cape
Island, islands
Ocean current
Ocean floor landforms
Tectonic feature
Atmospheric phenomena
Time zone
Geographical grid

Independent country
Dependent territory
Federal state, province, territory
People, ethnic group, tribe
Indian reservation/reserve
National Park
Industrial region
Historical site
Research station
Continent, realm
Region, peninsula
Mountain range, mountains
▲ Peak
Pass
Ice shelf, glacier

River, canal
Waterfall
Lake, lakes, reservoir
Swamp
Salt flat
Sea
Strait
Bay, gulf
Cape
Island, islands
Ocean current
Ocean floor landforms
Tectonic feature
Atmospheric phenomena
Time zone
Geographical grid

E

■ Independent country
◨ Dependent territory
□ Federal state, province, territory
👥 People, ethnic group, tribe
Ⲭ Indian reservation/reserve
⌂ National Park
⊓ Industrial region
∴ Historical site
⊿ Research station
⊕ Continent, realm
⌓ Region, peninsula
⛰ Mountain range, mountains
▲ Peak
)(Pass
* Ice shelf, glacier

River, canal
Waterfall
Lake, lakes, reservoir
Swamp
Salt flat
Sea
Strait
Bay, gulf
Cape
Island, islands
Ocean current
Ocean floor landforms
Tectonic feature
Atmospheric phenomena
Time zone
Geographical grid

- Independent country
- Dependent territory
- Federal state, province, territory
- People, ethnic group, tribe
- Indian reservation/reserve
- National Park
- Industrial region
- ∴ Historical site
- Research station
- Continent, realm
- Region, peninsula
- Mountain range, mountains
- ▲ Peak
-)(Pass
- ✱ Ice shelf, glacier

F

River, canal · Waterfall · Lake, lakes, reservoir · Swamp · Salt flat · Sea · Strait · Bay, gulf · Cape · Island, islands · Ocean current · Ocean floor landforms · Tectonic feature · Atmospheric phenomena · Time zone · Geographical grid

Independent country
Dependent territory
Federal state, province, territory
People, ethnic group, tribe
Indian reservation/reserve
National Park
Industrial region
Historical site
Research station
Continent, realm
Region, peninsula
Mountain range, mountains
Peak
Pass
Ice shelf, glacier

River, canal
Waterfall
Lake, lakes, reservoir
Swamp
Salt flat
Sea
Strait
Bay, gulf
Cape
Island, islands
Ocean current
Ocean floor landforms
Tectonic feature
Atmospheric phenomena
Time zone
Geographical grid

⛊ Independent country
◧ Dependent territory
⛉ Federal state, province, territory
👥 People, ethnic group, tribe
⧗ Indian reservation/reserve
⇑ National Park
⛫ Industrial region
∴ Historical site
⛺ Research station
⊛ Continent, realm
⌓ Region, peninsula
⛰ Mountain range, mountains
▲ Peak
)(Pass
✱ Ice shelf, glacier

River, canal
Waterfall
Lake, lakes, reservoir
Swamp
Salt flat
Sea
Strait
Bay, gulf
Cape
Island, islands
Ocean current
Ocean floor landforms
Tectonic feature
Atmospheric phenomena
Time zone
Geographical grid

Independent country
Dependent territory
Federal state, province, territory
People, ethnic group, tribe
Indian reservation/reserve
National Park
Industrial region
Historical site
Research station
Continent, realm
Region, peninsula
Mountain range, mountains
Peak
Pass
Ice shelf, glacier

River, canal
Waterfall
Lake, lakes, reservoir
Swamp
Salt flat
Sea
Strait
Bay, gulf
Cape
Island, islands
Ocean current
Ocean floor landforms
Tectonic feature
Atmospheric phenomena
Time zone
Geographical grid

■ Independent country
◨ Dependent territory
□ Federal state, province, territory
👥 People, ethnic group, tribe
Ⅹ Indian reservation/reserve
⇧ National Park
Д Industrial region
∴ Historical site
⊿ Research station
⊙ Continent, realm
⊵ Region, peninsula
⛰ Mountain range, mountains
▲ Peak
)(Pass
✱ Ice shelf, glacier

River, canal
Waterfall
Lake, lakes, reservoir
Swamp
Salt flat
Sea
Strait
Bay, gulf
Cape
Island, islands
Ocean current
Ocean floor landforms
Tectonic feature
Atmospheric phenomena
Time zone
Geographical grid

Independent country
Dependent territory
Federal state, province, territory
People, ethnic group, tribe
Indian reservation/reserve
National Park
Industrial region
Historical site
Research station
Continent, realm
Region, peninsula
Mountain range, mountains
▲ Peak
Pass
Ice shelf, glacier

River, canal
Waterfall
Lake, lakes, reservoir
Swamp
Salt flat
Sea
Strait
Bay, gulf
Cape
Island, islands
Ocean current
Ocean floor landforms
Tectonic feature
Atmospheric phenomena
Time zone
Geographical grid

◼ Independent country
◨ Dependent territory
◻ Federal state, province, territory
👥 People, ethnic group, tribe
⅄ Indian reservation/reserve
⇧ National Park
⎍ Industrial region
∴ Historical site
⌂ Research station
◎ Continent, realm
⊵ Region, peninsula
▲▲ Mountain range, mountains
▲ Peak
)(Pass
∗ Ice shelf, glacier

River, canal
Waterfall
Lake, lakes, reservoir
Swamp
Salt flat
Sea
Strait
Bay, gulf
Cape
Island, islands
Ocean current
Ocean floor landforms
Tectonic feature
Atmospheric phenomena
Time zone
Geographical grid

Independent country
Dependent territory
Federal state, province, territory
People, ethnic group, tribe
Indian reservation/reserve
National Park
Industrial region
∴ Historical site
Research station
Continent, realm
Region, peninsula
Mountain range, mountains
▲ Peak
)(Pass
∗ Ice shelf, glacier

River, canal
Waterfall
Lake, lakes, reservoir
Swamp
Salt flat
Sea
Strait
Bay, gulf
Cape
Island, islands
Ocean current
Ocean floor landforms
Tectonic feature
Atmospheric phenomena
Time zone
Geographical grid

■ Independent country
Dependent territory
Federal state, province, territory
People, ethnic group, tribe
Indian reservation/reserve
National Park
Industrial region
∴ Historical site
Research station
Continent, realm
Region, peninsula
Mountain range, mountains
▲ Peak
)(Pass
∗ Ice shelf, glacier

River, canal
Waterfall
Lake, lakes, reservoir
Swamp
Salt flat
Sea
Strait
Bay, gulf
Cape
Island, islands
Ocean current
Ocean floor landforms
Tectonic feature
Atmospheric phenomena
Time zone
Geographical grid

L

Independent country
Dependent territory
Federal state, province, territory
People, ethnic group, tribe
Indian reservation/reserve
National Park
Industrial region
∴ Historical site
Research station
Continent, realm
Region, peninsula
Mountain range, mountains
▲ Peak
)(Pass
∗ Ice shelf, glacier

River, canal
Waterfall
Lake, lakes, reservoir
Swamp
Salt flat
Sea
Strait
Bay, gulf
Cape
Island, islands
Ocean current
Ocean floor landforms
Tectonic feature
Atmospheric phenomena
Time zone
Geographical grid

■ Independent country
◘ Dependent territory
▢ Federal state, province, territory
⚇ People, ethnic group, tribe
⧗ Indian reservation/reserve
⌂ National Park
⊓ Industrial region
∴ Historical site
⊿ Research station
⊕ Continent, realm
⌒ Region, peninsula
▲▲ Mountain range, mountains
▲ Peak
)(Pass
* Ice shelf, glacier

River, canal
Waterfall
Lake, lakes, reservoir
Swamp
Salt flat
Sea
Strait
Bay, gulf
Cape
Island, islands
Ocean current
Ocean floor landforms
Tectonic feature
Atmospheric phenomena
Time zone
Geographical grid

M

Independent country
Dependent territory
Federal state, province, territory
People, ethnic group, tribe
Indian reservation/reserve
National Park
Industrial region
Historical site
Research station
Continent, realm
Region, peninsula
Mountain range, mountains
▲ Peak
Pass
Ice shelf, glacier

River, canal
Waterfall
Lake, lakes, reservoir
Swamp
Salt flat
Sea
Strait
Bay, gulf
Cape
Island, islands
Ocean current
Ocean floor landforms
Tectonic feature
Atmospheric phenomena
Time zone
Geographical grid

Independent country
Dependent territory
Federal state, province, territory
People, ethnic group, tribe
Indian reservation/reserve
National Park
Industrial region
Historical site
Research station
Continent, realm
Region, peninsula
Mountain range, mountains
Peak
Pass
Ice shelf, glacier

River, canal
Waterfall
Lake, lakes, reservoir
Swamp
Salt flat
Sea
Strait
Bay, gulf
Cape
Island, islands
Ocean current
Ocean floor landforms
Tectonic feature
Atmospheric phenomena
Time zone
Geographical grid

Independent country
Dependent territory
Federal state, province, territory
People, ethnic group, tribe
Indian reservation/reserve
National Park
Industrial region
∴ Historical site
Research station
Continent, realm
Region, peninsula
Mountain range, mountains
▲ Peak
)(Pass
∗ Ice shelf, glacier

- River, canal
- Waterfall
- Lake, lakes, reservoir
- Swamp
- Salt flat
- Sea
- Strait
- Bay, gulf
- Cape
- Island, islands
- Ocean current
- Ocean floor landforms
- Tectonic feature
- Atmospheric phenomena
- Time zone
- Geographical grid

◼ Independent country
◪ Dependent territory
◻ Federal state, province, territory
⚇ People, ethnic group, tribe
X Indian reservation/reserve
⇧ National Park
Π Industrial region
∴ Historical site
◬ Research station
⊛ Continent, realm
⌁ Region, peninsula
⛰ Mountain range, mountains
▲ Peak
)(Pass
* Ice shelf, glacier

∽ River, canal
⌇ Waterfall
◡ Lake, lakes, reservoir
⩶ Swamp
⩡ Salt flat
≋ Sea
≍ Strait
≋) Bay, gulf
≫ Cape
≃ Island, islands
⇝ Ocean current
⩘ Ocean floor landforms
⌁ Tectonic feature
☁ Atmospheric phenomena
◷ Time zone
⊘ Geographical grid

Independent country
Dependent territory
Federal state, province, territory
People, ethnic group, tribe
Indian reservation/reserve
National Park
Industrial region
∴ Historical site
Research station
Continent, realm
Region, peninsula
Mountain range, mountains
▲ Peak
)(Pass
* Ice shelf, glacier

River, canal
Waterfall
Lake, lakes, reservoir
Swamp
Salt flat
Sea
Strait
Bay, gulf
Cape
Island, islands
Ocean current
Ocean floor landforms
Tectonic feature
Atmospheric phenomena
Time zone
Geographical grid

Independent country
Dependent territory
Federal state, province, territory
People, ethnic group, tribe
Indian reservation/reserve
National Park
Industrial region
∴ Historical site
Research station
Continent, realm
Region, peninsula
Mountain range, mountains
▲ Peak
Pass
✱ Ice shelf, glacier

O

River, canal
Waterfall
Lake, lakes, reservoir
Swamp
Salt flat
Sea
Strait
Bay, gulf
Cape
Island, islands
Ocean current
Ocean floor landforms
Tectonic feature
Atmospheric phenomena
Time zone
Geographical grid

Independent country
Dependent territory
Federal state, province, territory
People, ethnic group, tribe
Indian reservation/reserve
National Park
Industrial region
∴ Historical site
Research station
Continent, realm
Region, peninsula
▲▲ Mountain range, mountains
▲ Peak
Pass
Ice shelf, glacier

River, canal
Waterfall
Lake, lakes, reservoir
Swamp
Salt flat
Sea
Strait
Bay, gulf
Cape
Island, islands
Ocean current
Ocean floor landforms
Tectonic feature
Atmospheric phenomena
Time zone
Geographical grid

Independent country
Dependent territory
Federal state, province, territory
People, ethnic group, tribe
Indian reservation/reserve
National Park
Industrial region
∴ Historical site
Research station
Continent, realm
Region, peninsula
Mountain range, mountains
▲ Peak
)(Pass
✱ Ice shelf, glacier

∽ River, canal
≺ Waterfall
⌣ Lake, lakes, reservoir
⌣ Swamp
Salt flat
≈ Sea
≍ Strait
≈) Bay, gulf
⟩≈ Cape
⌓ Island, islands
Ocean current
Ocean floor landforms
Tectonic feature
Atmospheric phenomena
Time zone
Geographical grid

Independent country
Dependent territory
Federal state, province, territory
People, ethnic group, tribe
Indian reservation/reserve
National Park
Industrial region
Historical site
Research station
Continent, realm
Region, peninsula
Mountain range, mountains
Peak
Pass
Ice shelf, glacier

River, canal
Waterfall
Lake, lakes, reservoir
Swamp
Salt flat
Sea
Strait
Bay, gulf
Cape
Island, islands
Ocean current
Ocean floor landforms
Tectonic feature
Atmospheric phenomena
Time zone
Geographical grid

Independent country
Dependent territory
Federal state, province, territory
People, ethnic group, tribe
Indian reservation/reserve
National Park
Industrial region
Historical site
Research station
Continent, realm
Region, peninsula
Mountain range, mountains
Peak
Pass
Ice shelf, glacier

River, canal
Waterfall
Lake, lakes, reservoir
Swamp
Salt flat
Sea
Strait
Bay, gulf
Cape
Island, islands
Ocean current
Ocean floor landforms
Tectonic feature
Atmospheric phenomena
Time zone
Geographical grid

R

Independent country
Dependent territory
Federal state, province, territory
People, ethnic group, tribe
Indian reservation/reserve
National Park
Industrial region
Historical site
Research station
Continent, realm
Region, peninsula
Mountain range, mountains
▲ Peak
)(Pass
∗ Ice shelf, glacier

River, canal
Waterfall
Lake, lakes, reservoir
Swamp
Salt flat
Sea
Strait
Bay, gulf
Cape
Island, islands
Ocean current
Ocean floor landforms
Tectonic feature
Atmospheric phenomena
Time zone
Geographical grid

Independent country
Dependent territory
Federal state, province, territory
People, ethnic group, tribe
Indian reservation/reserve
National Park
Industrial region
Historical site
Research station
Continent, realm
Region, peninsula
Mountain range, mountains
▲ Peak
)(Pass
✱ Ice shelf, glacier

River, canal
Waterfall
Lake, lakes, reservoir
Swamp
Salt flat
Sea
Strait
Bay, gulf
Cape
Island, islands
Ocean current
Ocean floor landforms
Tectonic feature
Atmospheric phenomena
Time zone
Geographical grid

■ Independent country
Dependent territory
Federal state, province, territory
People, ethnic group, tribe
Indian reservation/reserve
National Park
Industrial region
Historical site
Research station
Continent, realm
Region, peninsula
Mountain range, mountains
▲ Peak
Pass
Ice shelf, glacier

River, canal
Waterfall
Lake, lakes, reservoir
Swamp
Salt flat
Sea
Strait
Bay, gulf
Cape
Island, islands
Ocean current
Ocean floor landforms
Tectonic feature
Atmospheric phenomena
Time zone
Geographical grid

⛊ Independent country
◐ Dependent territory
⛉ Federal state, province, territory

⚇ People, ethnic group, tribe
⧖ Indian reservation/reserve
⇧ National Park
⌂ Industrial region

∴ Historical site
◒ Research station
◍ Continent, realm
⛰ Region, peninsula

▲▲ Mountain range, mountains
▲ Peak
)(Pass
✱ Ice shelf, glacier

River, canal
Waterfall
Lake, lakes, reservoir
Swamp
Salt flat
Sea
Strait
Bay, gulf
Cape
Island, islands
Ocean current
Ocean floor landforms
Tectonic feature
Atmospheric phenomena
Time zone
Geographical grid

Independent country
Dependent territory
Federal state, province, territory
People, ethnic group, tribe
Indian reservation/reserve
National Park
Industrial region
Historical site
Research station
Continent, realm
Region, peninsula
Mountain range, mountains
▲ Peak
Pass
Ice shelf, glacier

River, canal
Waterfall
Lake, lakes, reservoir
Swamp
Salt flat
Sea
Strait
Bay, gulf
Cape
Island, islands
Ocean current
Ocean floor landforms
Tectonic feature
Atmospheric phenomena
Time zone
Geographical grid

⛊ Independent country
◧ Dependent territory
⛉ Federal state, province, territory
👥 People, ethnic group, tribe
Ⲭ Indian reservation/reserve
⇧ National Park
Ⲡ Industrial region
∴ Historical site
⌂ Research station
◎ Continent, realm
◣ Region, peninsula
▲▲ Mountain range, mountains
▲ Peak
)(Pass
✻ Ice shelf, glacier

River, canal
Waterfall
Lake, lakes, reservoir
Swamp
Salt flat
Sea
Strait
Bay, gulf
Cape
Island, islands
Ocean current
Ocean floor landforms
Tectonic feature
Atmospheric phenomena
Time zone
Geographical grid

⛊ Independent country
⛉ Dependent territory
⛉ Federal state, province, territory
⚇ People, ethnic group, tribe
Ⴟ Indian reservation/reserve
⌂ National Park
Ⴈ Industrial region
∴ Historical site
⌐ Research station
⊛ Continent, realm
⌙ Region, peninsula
▲▲ Mountain range, mountains
▲ Peak
)(Pass
✱ Ice shelf, glacier

T

River, canal
Waterfall
Lake, lakes, reservoir
Swamp
Salt flat
Sea
Strait
Bay, gulf
Cape
Island, islands
Ocean current
Ocean floor landforms
Tectonic feature
Atmospheric phenomena
Time zone
Geographical grid

Independent country
Dependent territory
Federal state, province, territory
People, ethnic group, tribe
Indian reservation/reserve
National Park
Industrial region
Historical site
Research station
Continent, realm
Region, peninsula
Mountain range, mountains
▲ Peak
Pass
Ice shelf, glacier

River, canal
Waterfall
Lake, lakes, reservoir
Swamp
Salt flat
Sea
Strait
Bay, gulf
Cape
Island, islands
Ocean current
Ocean floor landforms
Tectonic feature
Atmospheric phenomena
Time zone
Geographical grid

Independent country
Dependent territory
Federal state, province, territory
People, ethnic group, tribe
Indian reservation/reserve
National Park
Industrial region
Historical site
Research station
Continent, realm
Region, peninsula
Mountain range, mountains
▲ Peak
Pass
Ice shelf, glacier

River, canal
Waterfall
Lake, lakes, reservoir
Swamp
Salt flat
Sea
Strait
Bay, gulf
Cape
Island, islands
Ocean current
Ocean floor landforms
Tectonic feature
Atmospheric phenomena
Time zone
Geographical grid

■ Independent country
◘ Dependent territory
▽ Federal state, province, territory
⚇ People, ethnic group, tribe
Ⲭ Indian reservation/reserve
⇧ National Park
⊓ Industrial region
∴ Historical site
⌂ Research station
◉ Continent, realm
⩩ Region, peninsula
▲▲ Mountain range, mountains
▲ Peak
)(Pass
* Ice shelf, glacier

River, canal
Waterfall
Lake, lakes, reservoir
Swamp
Salt flat
Sea
Strait
Bay, gulf
Cape
Island, islands
Ocean current
Ocean floor landforms
Tectonic feature
Atmospheric phenomena
Time zone
Geographical grid

■ Independent country
◘ Dependent territory
◻ Federal state, province, territory
⚇ People, ethnic group, tribe
Ⅹ Indian reservation/reserve
⇧ National Park
⊓ Industrial region
∴ Historical site
◿ Research station
⊛ Continent, realm
⌊ Region, peninsula
▲▲ Mountain range, mountains
▲ Peak
)(Pass
✱ Ice shelf, glacier

River, canal
Waterfall
Lake, lakes, reservoir
Swamp
Salt flat
Sea
Strait
Bay, gulf
Cape
Island, islands
Ocean current
Ocean floor landforms
Tectonic feature
Atmospheric phenomena
Time zone
Geographical grid

Independent country
Dependent territory
Federal state, province, territory
People, ethnic group, tribe
Indian reservation/reserve
National Park
Industrial region
Historical site
Research station
Continent, realm
Region, peninsula
Mountain range, mountains
Peak
Pass
Ice shelf, glacier

River, canal
Waterfall
Lake, lakes, reservoir
Swamp
Salt flat
Sea
Strait
Bay, gulf
Cape
Island, islands
Ocean current
Ocean floor landforms
Tectonic feature
Atmospheric phenomena
Time zone
Geographical grid

Independent country
Dependent territory
Federal state, province, territory
People, ethnic group, tribe
Indian reservation/reserve
National Park
Industrial region
∴ Historical site
Research station
Continent, realm
Region, peninsula
Mountain range, mountains
▲ Peak
)(Pass
* Ice shelf, glacier

Z

River, canal
Waterfall
Lake, lakes, reservoir
Swamp
Salt flat
Sea
Strait
Bay, gulf
Cape
Island, islands
Ocean current
Ocean floor landforms
Tectonic feature
Atmospheric phenomena
Time zone
Geographical grid

◆ Independent country
◐ Dependent territory
◇ Federal state, province, territory
People, ethnic group, tribe
Ⲗ Indian reservation/reserve
⇧ National Park
Industrial region
∴ Historical site
Research station
Continent, realm
Region, peninsula
▲▲ Mountain range, mountains
▲ Peak
)(Pass
* Ice shelf, glacier

Alexander GlobalAtlas für Baden-Württemberg. Gotha, 2004.
Alexander KombiAtlas Erdkunde, Geschichte, Sozialkunde, Wirtschaft. Gotha 2003.
Auswärtiges Amt der Bundesrepublik Deutschland: Länder- und Reiseinformationen [auswaertiges-amt.de/www/de/laenderinfos/index_html].

Barthlott, W., Biedinger, N., Braun, G., Feig, F., Kier, G., & J. Mutke (1999): Global Biodiversity: Species numbers of vascular plants. Bonn [botanik.uni-bonn.de/system/phytodiv.htm].
BGR (2005): Reserven, Ressourcen und Verfügbarkeit von Energierohstoffen 2004 – Kurzstudie. Hannover.
Bundeszentrale für politische Bildung: Wissen, Lexika, Begriffe nachschlagen [bpb.de/wissen/H75VXG,0,0,Begriffe_nachschlagen.html].
Castles, St., & M. J. Miller (2003): The Age of Migration. Basingstoke.
CIA: The World Factbook 2005 [cia.gov/cia/publications/factbook/].
CIESIN, Columbia University, CIAT: Gridded Population of the World (GWP), Version 3 [sedac.ciesin.columbia.edu/gpw].
CRED: EM-DAT – The International Disaster Database [em-dat.net/].

Der Fischer Weltalmanach 2006. Frankfurt a.M., 2005.
Diercke Länderlexikon. Braunschweig, 2005.
Diercke Weltatlas. Braunschweig, 2005.
DWD: Global Precipitation Climatology Centre [orias.dwd.de/GPCC/GPCC_Visualizer].

Engelman, R., & P. LeRoy (1993): Sustaining Water – Population and the Future of Renewable Water Supplies [cnie.org/pop/pai/water-12.html].

FAO (2000): Definitions and Basic Principles of Sustainable Forest Managements in Relation to Criteria and Indictors [fao.org/documents/show_cdr.asp?url_file=/docrep/003/x6896e/x6896e0e.htm].
FAO (2002): Monitoring Food Deprivation and Related Indicators. Rome [adb.org/documents/events/2002/reta5917/monitoring.pdf].
FAO (2003): Review of World Water Resources by Country. Rome [fao.org/documents/show_cdr.asp?url_file=/DOCREP/005/Y4473E/Y4473E00.HTM].
FAO (2004): The State of Food Insecurity in the World 2004. Rome [fao.org/documents/show_cdr.asp?url_file=/docrep/007/y5650e/y5650e00.htm].
FAO (2004): Global Forest Resources. Assessment Update 2005. Terms and Definitions [fao.org/forestry/site/fra2005-terms/en].
FAO: FAOSTAT Data – Food Balance Sheets [faostat.fao.org/faostat/collections?version=ext&hasbulk=0&subset=nutrition].
FAO: FAOSTAT Data – Agricultural Production [faostat.fao.org/faostat/collections?version=ext&hasbulk=0&subset=agriculture].
FAO: Global Forest Resources Assessment [fao.org/forestry/site/32033/en].
Fitchard, K. (2003): Mapping the Global Internet [telephonyonline.com/mag/telecom_intelligence_broadband_economy_41/index.html].
Fiziko-geograficheskiy Atlas Mira. Moscow, 1964.
Freedom House: Freedom in the World 2005 [freedomhouse.org/template.cfm?page=35&year=2005].
Freedom House: Map of Freedom 2005 [freedomhouse.org/template.cfm?page=20&year=2005].

HIIK (2004): Conflict Barometer 2004. Heidelberg [hiik.de/en/index_e.htm].

ILO (2001): Key Indicators of the Labour Market. Geneva.
IPCC (1995): Scientific-Technical Analyses of Impacts, Adaptations and Mitigation of Climate Change. Cambridge [ipcc.ch/pub/sarsum2.htm].
ITU [2003]: ITU Digital Access Index: World's First Global ICT Ranking [itu.int/newsarchive/press_releases/2003/30.html].

Kyoto Protocol to the UNFCC [unfccc.int/resource/docs/convkp/kpeng.pdf].
Kyoto Protocol – Status of Ratification [unfccc.int/files/essential_background/kyoto_protocol/application/pdf/kpstats.pdf].

Lacina, B., & N. P. Gleditsch (2005). Monitoring Trends in Global Combat: A New Dataset of Battle Deaths. European Journal of Population, 21 (2/3): 145–166.

Meller, E., Middelschulte, A., Milojcic, G., Reichel, W., & G. Schöning (2004): Jahrbuch der europäischen Energie- und Rohstoffwirtschaft 2005. Essen.
Metcalf, Th. R. (2005): Tropical Storms, Worldwide [solar.ifa.hawaii.edu/Tropical/tropical.html].
MPI: Migration Information Source [migrationinformation.org/GlobalData/].
Münchener Rückversicherungs-Gesellschaft (1998): World Map of Natural Hazards. München.

OCHA: OCHA Natural and Environmental Disaster Reporting and Involvement in 2005 [reliefweb.int/rw/RWB.NSF/db900SID/AHAA-6LDW2W?OpenDocument].
OECD (2002): New Definition of General Government Total Expenditures. Paris [oecd.org/dataoecd/9/17/1949944.doc].
OECD: International Migration Data [oecd.org/document/36/0,2340,en_2825_494553_2515108_1_1_1_1,00.html].
OECD: Aid Statistics, Donor Aid Charts [oecd.org/countrylist/0,2578,en_2649_34447_1783495_1_1_1_1,00.html].
Olson, D. M., Dinerstein, E., et al. (2001): Terrestrial Ecoregions of the World: A New Map of Life on Earth. BioScience, 51 (11): 933 – 938 [worldwildlife.org/science/pubs/bioscience.pdf].

PRB (2004): 2004 World Population Data Sheet. Washington, D.C. [prb.org/pdf04/04WorldDataSheet_Eng.pdf].
PIK, Department of Climate System (2005): PIK data bank [Observation period: 1974–2003].
PriMetrica, Inc. (2003): Major Interregional Internet Routes [thispointer.com/images/gig2004fig15zoom.gif].
PRIO (2005): Armed Conflict Dataset Codebook. Oslo [prio.no/cscw/armedconflict].

Schroeder, F.-G. (1998): Lehrbuch der Pflanzengeographie. Wiesbaden.
Smithsonian Institution: Global Volcanism Program [volcano.si.edu/world/].
Snead, R. E. (1972): Atlas of World Physical Features. New York, London, Sydney, Toronto.
Stalker, P.: Stalker's Guide to International Migration [pstalker.com/migration/index.htm].
Statistisches Bundesamt Deutschland: Länderprofile [destatis.de/allg/d/veroe/l_profile/lprofil_ueb.htm].
Statistisches Jahrbuch 2005 für das Ausland. Wiesbaden, 2005.

The Statesman's Yearbook: The Politics, Cultures and Economies of the World. Basingstoke, 2004.
The Weather Underground: Hurricane Archive [wunderground.com/hurricane/at2005.asp].
The World Bank Group: World Development Indicators – Data Query [devdata.worldbank.org/data-query/].
The World Bank Group: World Development Indicators [devdata.worldbank.org/wdi2005/Section4.htm].
The World Bank Group: Development Education Program. Glossary [unesco.org/education/tlsf/theme_c/mod13/www.worldbank.org/depweb/english/modules/glossary.htm].
The World Bank Group: Millennium Development Goals [ddp-ext.world bank.org/ext/GMIS/gdmis.do?siteId=2&menuId=LNAV01HOME1]

Udvardy, M. D. F. (1975). A classification of the biogeographical provinces of the world. Morges. = IUCN Occasional Paper, 18.
UN: Peacekeeping operations [un.org/Depts/dpko/dpko/index.asp].
UNAIDS (2004): Report on the global AIDS epidemic 2004. Geneva [unaids.org/bangkok2004/report_pdf.html].
UNCTAD (2004): UNCTAD Handbook of Statistics 2004. New York, Geneva. [unctad.org/en/docs/tdstat29_enfr.pdf].
UNDP [2004]: Human Development Report 2004. New York [hdr.undp.org/reports/global/2004/pdf/hdr04_complete.pdf].
UNEP: The GEO Data Portal [geodata.grid.unep.ch].
UNEP, WCMC: Global Distribution of Original and Remaining Forests [unep-wcmc.org/index.html?].
UNESCO, AETFAT, UNSO: White's Vegetation Map of Africa [geodata.grid.unep.ch].
UNFCCC [2005]: GHG – Definitions [ghg.unfccc.int/definitions.html].
UNHCR (2005): Refugee Status Determination – Identifying who is a refugee. Geneva [unhcr.ch/cgi-bin/texis/vtx/home/opendoc.pdf?tbl=RSDLEGAL&id=43141f5d4].
UNHCR (2005): 2004 Global Refugee Trends. Geneva [unhcr.org/cgi-bin/texis/vtx/events/opendoc.pdf?tbl=STATISTICS&id=42b283744].
UNICEF (2004): The State of the World's Children 2005. New York [unicef.org/sowc05/english/sowc05.pdf].
United Nations Statistical Yearbook 2002–2004. New York, 2005.
UNPD (2004): World Urbanisation Prospects. The 2003 Revison. New York [un.org/esa/population/publications/wup2003/WUP2003 Report.pdf].
UNPD (2005): World Population Prospects: The 2004 Revision. New York [un.org/esa/population/publications/WPP2004/2004Highlights_finalrevised.pdf].
UNWTO: Facts and Figures, Tourism Indicators [world-tourism.org/facts/menu.html].
UNWTO (2004): Tourism Market Trends 2004 – World Overview & Tourism Topics. Madrid.
USDA, NRCS: Global Soil Regions Map [soils.usda.gov/use/worldsoils/mapindex/order.html].
USDA, NRCS: Global Desertification Vulnerability Map [soils.usda.gov/use/worldsoils/mapindex/desert.html].
USGS: World Petroleum Assessment 2000 – Description and Results [pubs.usgs.gov/dds/dds-060/].
USGS: Glossary [biology.usgs.gov/s+t/noframe/z999.htm].
USGS, EROS Data Center (2000): Global 1 km Land Cover – IGBP Legend (1993) [geodata.grid.unep.ch].
Weber, L., & G. Zsak (2003): World Mining Data. Vienna [wmc.org.pl/wmd2003.pdf]
WEC: Survey of Energy Resources [worldenergy.org/wec-geis/publications/reports/ser/overview.asp].
White, F. (1983): Vegetation of Africa – a descriptive memoir to accompany the Unesco / AETFAT / UNSO vegetation map of Africa. Paris. = Natural Resources Research Report, XX.
WHO (2005): World Health Statistics 2005. Geneva [who.int/healthinfo/statistics/whostat2005en1.pdf].
WMO, UNESCO (1997): The World Water – is there enough? [unesco.org/science/waterday2000/Brochure.htm].
WTO: International Trade Statistics 2004. [wto.org/english/res_e/statis_e/its2004_e/its2004_e.pdf].
WWF [2002]: WWF Ecoregions – Terrestrial Ecoregions Legend [geodata.grid.unep.ch].
WWF [2002]: WWF Ecoregions – Major Habitat Types (Biomes) Legend [geodata.grid.unep.ch].
WWF: Conservation Science – Terrestrial Ecoregions of the World [worldwildlife.org/science/data/attributes.cfm].

Picture Credits

Arco Digital Images, Lünen 26.3 (D. Meissner); Australische Botschaft, Berlin 159.2; Avenue Images, Hamburg Titelbild (imagesbroker/Arco/LaTerraMagica); Bähr, Kiel 104.1; Blickwinkel, Witten 27.12; Bricks, Erfurt 68.8; Corbis, Düsseldorf 159.5 (Amos Nachoum); Eckenfelder, Wenigenlupnitz 116.3; Ehlers, Bonn 168.6; Enkelmann, Filderstadt 68.4, 140.6; Gerster, Zumikon 68.2; getty images, Munich 68.6; Hahn, Stuttgart 68.7; Hess, Buckow 116.1; Hokenmaier, Wäschenbeuren 168.1; Itar Tass, Moscow 116.8, 140.1; Jürgens Ost + Europa Photo, Berlin 26.2; Kastner, Nürnberg 140.5; Klett Archiv 116.7; Kraus, Wäschenbeuren 68.5; Leicht, Mutlangen 68.3; Maresch, Rutesheim 159.3, 159.7; MEV, Augsburg 168.2; Mitsubishi, Rüsselsheim 140.7; Mühr, Karlsruhe 104.2; Müller, Würzburg 140.8; Newig, Flintbek 116.5, 116.9, 168.8; Pasca, Tübingen 104.7; Reckziegel, Schnepfenthal 26.4, 140.2; Ria „Nowosti", Berlin 116.6; Richter, Röttenbach 26.5, 26.8, 26.9, 27.10, 27.13, 116.4; Rother, Schwäbisch Gmünd 27.14, 68.1, 104.4, 104.5, 104.6, 104.8, 104.9, 116.2, 140.3, 140.4, 159.6, 159.8, 159.9, 159.10, 168.4, 168.5; Schmidtke, Melsdorf 168.7; Schulz, Schwäbisch Gmünd 168.3; Still Pictures, London 26.1 (Patrick Frischknecht), 26.7 (Ted Mead); Stock4B, Munich 26.6 (Peter von Felbert); Tierbildarchiv Angermayer, Holzkirchen 27.11; von der Ruhren, Aachen 104.3; Zauner, Ludwigsburg 159.1, 159.4.